LABOR
and the
ECONOMY
An Introduction to Analysis, Issues, and Institutions

Gary A. Moore
Associate Professor of Business and Economics
State University of New York
College of Geneseo

Randyl D. Elkin
Director of Industrial Relations Graduate Programs
Associate Professor of Economics
West Virginia University

Published by

H75 **SOUTH-WESTERN PUBLISHING CO.**

CINCINNATI   WEST CHICAGO, ILL.   DALLAS   PELHAM MANOR, N.Y.   PALO ALTO, CALIF.

ISBN: 0-538-08750-1

Library of Congress Catalog Card Number: 81-85863

2 3 4 5 6 7 8 D 9 8 7 6 5 4 3
Printed in the United States of America

Cover Photo:
    H. Armstrong Roberts
Photo Credits:
    page 1—**ibid,** inc.
    page 111—Webb/Magnum Photos, Inc.
    page 261—**ibid,** inc.

PREFACE

During the last few decades, the study of labor economics has branched into at least three interrelated directions. The interest in micro and macroeconomic theory, as applied to the labor factor of production, is an outgrowth of the earlier classical and neoclassical contributions in this area. This theoretical approach has gained renewed acceptability as more sophisticated models and methods of analysis have been developed. Refined statistical and econometric techniques have also been applied in a much more comprehensive fashion to test numerous labor market hypotheses. Second, systematic human resource development and planning have become notable parts of both public and private policy-making, and the focus of labor studies has expanded somewhat to include consideration of the many problems and policies related to the full utilization of human resources. Finally, the study of labor-management relations and the effects of unionism have continued to receive careful attention. Analyses of the collective bargaining process in particular and labor-management interaction in general, both in the private and public sectors, are integral parts of many undergraduate labor courses.

The focus and composition of undergraduate course offerings in labor have changed considerably in an attempt to include all or many of these developments. At institutions of sufficient size, labor offerings have been divided into separate upper-division "institutional" and "human resources" programs. At many of these universities, an introductory labor economics or labor problems course is the first course taken before students embark upon the more specialized upper-division courses. A large number of other institutions offer sophomore-junior-senior level labor economics courses which attempt to survey both the analytical and policy dimensions of the study of labor in a rigorous, yet issued-oriented manner. These courses typically require only the principles of economics sequence, at most, as a prerequisite for study, and they are often the first and last labor course that students take.

This text has been written with these curricular developments in mind. It is designed specifically for two types of courses mentioned above: (1) the undergraduate labor course which is a prerequisite for more specialized undergraduate or graduate study in human resources and/or labor relations; and (2) The one-semester or one-quarter survey course in labor economics or labor problems which is the only labor course taken by many undergraduate economics and business students.

There are, of course, a number of labor economics and labor problems textbooks currently on the market. As is the case with most writers of new texts, we have been forced to confront the question—why yet another? In our judgement, the existing texts fall roughly into three categories. Category one includes largely descriptive, institutional texts which are used primarily in labor problems and nontheoretical labor economics courses. We have attempted to write a book which is more balanced and somewhat more analytical than existing texts in this category. It is our belief that an understanding of the modern tools of economic analysis, presented at the appropriate level, is essential for the intelligent consideration of labor problems and policies.

Category two falls at the other extreme of the labor text continuum. This category includes the theoretically-oriented upper or graduate level texts which are designed to emphasize "the new analytical labor economics," although allegedly in an applied manner. We have often found books in this category to be well-written and extremely useful as reference volumes, but pedagogically inappropriate for use in the types of undergraduate courses for which this text is intended. In spite of claims to the contrary, in most cases these books are simply too theoretical for students with only a principles background, and they typically contain little or no treatment of policy or industrial relations. Although this text does not sacrifice analytical rigor where it is necessary for clear exposition, we do not hesitate to admit that instructors who emphasize theoretical sophistication may find this volume will require supplementary reading assignments.

Category three contains those books which attempt to include thorough coverage of the analytical, policy, *and* institutional aspects of modern labor markets. We believe that texts in this category tend to be overly long, and yet often inadequate in their treatment of one or more of these aspects. By paying close attention to a balanced, concise presentation of the subject matter, we feel we have overcome this problem. In short, our objective has been to develop a highly readable and pedagogically useful book which presents a balanced treatment of theoretical principles as applied to contemporary labor market problems, policies and institutions.

In pursuit of this objective, the reader will notice the following differentiating features in this text:

Readability and level of presentation. We have painstakingly attempted to write the book in a clear, conversational style which presents necessary theoretical concepts in a truly useful, enlightening manner for students with only a principles of economics background. Although reviewers have given us high marks in this effort, we recognize that most authors make similar claims. We are willing to place our fate in the hands of student users.

Breadth and policy orientation. The text objectively blends theory, policy, and labor relations topics, with strong emphasis on applying theory to important policy questions. Full chapters are devoted to unemployment and underemployment, wage-price-employment policies, human resource development policies, discrimination, poverty, labor law, labor dispute settlement, and the impact of unions on the economy.

Logical sequence. We believe that the sequence of topics is a logical one for maximum student understanding, although the chapters stand independently for those instructors who prefer a different topical organization. After an initial overview, the text presents micro labor market theory under competitive assumptions, followed by imperfectly competitive features of actual labor market operations; policy issues to which the theory is applied; and the economics of unions and labor-management relations.

Currentness. Within the constraints of publication lag, every effort has been made to incorporate the most current data, issues, and empirical and theoretical contributions into the text. Examples of such contemporary subjects include: (1) the search process; (2) segmented labor market theory; (3) the microeconomic foundations of macro models; (4) post-Keynesian views on labor markets; (5) supply-side theoretical and policy concerns; (6) the alternative work scheduling movement; (7) recent structuralist and frictionalist contributions; (8) human resource planning in the firm; (9) the comparable worth controversy; (10) social experimentation in labor markets; (11) participative management; (12) the union growth-union avoidance conflict; (13) labor legislation; (14) strike alternatives; and (15) unions and productivity.

Pedagogical aids. Perhaps more than any other objective, we have attempted to design a text which is a useful teaching device. Every chapter contains a chapter summary, review questions, additional references, and a list of key terms with a complete glossary at the end of the book. Every chapter also ends with a short reading entitled "The World of Work . . ." These readings include excerpts from an article, report, Congressional hearing or testimony which relates the chapter material to real world issues. Finally, a complete collective bargaining simulation exercise is included at the end of the text for those instructors who wish to expose their students first-hand to the nuances of labor-management conflict.

The completion of complicated projects is inevitably facilitated by the assistance of many people, and this work is certainly no exception. Campbell R. McConnell at the University of Nebraska-Lincoln lent his considerable expertise to the original conceptualization of the text. Various drafts of the manuscript have been used in our classes in recent years, and we have relied heavily on student opinions of these drafts and of other texts in formulating our final product. Useful comments were provided by our colleagues David A. Martin and Charles Davis at SUNY-Geneseo and Owen A. Tapper at West Virginia University. We are particularly indebted to those faculty members around the country who provided detailed reviews of the manuscript while it was being written and refined. These perceptive scholars and teachers are gratefully acknowledged:

Harold W. Davey	James Heisler
Iowa State University	Hope College
Frank W. Gery	David B. Lipsky
Saint Olaf College	Cornell University
Jack B. Goddard	Brian Rungeling
Northeastern Oklahoma State University	University of Central Florida

West Virginia University graduate students Paul Burdeaux, Robin Longo, and Lori J. Paletta provided both valuable support and critiques of the manuscript. Cynthia Woodruff, Jennie Rector, Lora Grinder, Joan Strobel, Viola Huffman, and Brenda Jones all provided invaluable deciphering and typing skills. Finally, we are grateful to our wives, JoAnn and Susan, for their more intangible but no less valuable support and patience while we struggled with this project.

We hope that the users of *Labor and the Economy* will ultimately also contribute to its improvement. To this end, we sincerely encourage readers to provide us with any comments or suggestions to enhance its quality and usefulness.

Gary A. Moore

Randyl D. Elkin

CONTENTS

PART 3
COLLECTIVE BARGAINING: PRACTICES & PERSPECTIVES

1 The Economic Analysis of Labor

The systematic study of human resources in an economy must involve a number of dimensions. In all economic systems, except those characterized by complete central planning, labor market forces in some way contribute to the determination of wage levels and wage differentials, the occupational allocation of labor, and the level of total employment. These labor market forces may be quite complex in the real world, but it is important to gain insight into the various economic principles which govern the operation of labor markets. Without this insight as a background for further study, it is virtually impossible to understand labor market conditions, problems, and institutions. Therefore, Part I of this text is designed to present the essentials of modern economic analysis as applied to labor.

Some fundamental principles of economics (and labor economics) are reviewed in Chapter 1, and labor market institutions and problems are also highlighted. Chapter 2 presents the basic supply and demand principles which are useful in studying labor markets, while Chapter 3 surveys actual labor market operations under competitive and imperfectly competitive conditions. In Chapter 4, the transition is made to a macro-economic view of labor, where the economic concepts of supply, demand, wages, prices, and employment are viewed from an economy-wide perspective.

Chapter 1

Labor and the Economy: An Overview

As citizens in an advanced industrial society we are all called upon to assume numerous, often interrelated roles, e.g., taxpayer, consumer, employer, manager, laborer, civil servant. In terms of time, effort, and necessity for livelihood, no role is more important in our present and future lives than the one we play as members of the labor force. It is inevitable that we will find ourselves constantly involved with the issues and concepts which constitute the study of labor and the economy, and this involvement can be made much more meaningful if we are informed players. In a nutshell, that is the purpose of this volume.

Since much of this book concerns labor economics, it is appropriate to begin by inquiring about the nature of this subject as a distinct area of study. What exactly is involved in the study of labor economics, and why is it a subject worthy of such individual attention? The presentation of summary answers to these questions is the objective of this introductory chapter. Labor economics is, first of all, a branch of the study of economics. Although it will be assumed that the reader has some prior understanding of basic economic principles, a short review at the beginning of this chapter may be in order. The chapter will then proceed to a discussion of those elements which make labor economics a distinct branch of the economics tree. Since much of economics is concerned with markets and market behavior, it follows that labor economics must involve the description and analysis of labor market behavior. An introduction to the concept of a labor market, and the forces which operate within it, is presented next in the chapter.

There is much more to the study of labor, however, than just an analysis of labor market forces, because there are critically important institutional forces which influence the operation of U.S. labor markets—institutions such as business firms, trade unions, and the government. An overview of these institutions is also presented in this chapter. Finally, one needs only to pick up a daily newspaper to be reminded that there are many crucial and unresolved issues which relate closely to the study of labor. Why is the unemployment rate consistently so high? Is it wise to increase the minimum wage? Do American trade unions have excessive power? Do affirmative action policies give preferential treatment to minorities, and if so, is this justifiable? Gaining familiarity with labor market forces and institutions will allow the reader to evaluate issues and alternative policies more intelligently. Some of these important issues are highlighted in the last section of this chapter.

THE STUDY OF ECONOMICS

The Economic Problem of Scarcity

Various definitions of the study of economics are abundant. We need not concern ourselves here with the subtle distinctions among these definitions. It is sufficient for our purposes to remember that economics deals with the problem of scarcity and with the various ways in which scarce goods and resources are allocated so as to satisfy human wants and desires. In any society human wants may be regarded as unlimited, although some societies come much closer to fulfilling these wants than do others. Some societies are blessed with abundant and plentiful resources while others make do with woefully insufficient supplies, but all are confronted with scarcity.

A society's resources consist of natural resources such as land, forests and air, as well as manufactured aids to production like machines and buildings. In addition, the mental and physical contributions of human beings are a crucial component of a society's stock of productive resources. The obvious importance of these human resources gives some clue to the reason for studying labor economics distinctly. Economists lump all these resources together under either the term *factors of production* or the term *economic inputs*, because they all may be used as inputs to produce goods and services which satisfy human wants. The process of making goods and services to satisfy these wants is called *production*, and the process of using them to achieve satisfaction is called *consumption*.

Efficient Choice

Given the inevitable scarcity of resources, all societies are confronted with the problems of deciding "what" and "how" to produce, and "how to divide" the resulting production among their members. In other words, all societies must make choices because of scarcity. There is a good deal of variation among societies with respect to how these choices are made, i.e., which individuals or institutions make them. For example, the economic systems of such countries as Great Britain, India, the Soviet Union, and the United States are unalike primarily because somewhat different groups or organizations tend to make the economic choices in these systems. The general problems, however, are the same and choice is inevitable. Moreover, every society is concerned with making these choices in a socially efficient manner so as to minimize the use of scarce resources for a given amount of production.

The Market System

One important mechanism for coordinating these complex choice decisions in a society is the market system. The concept of a market is somewhat nebulous because markets may differ significantly in their structure and organization, and many do not exist in any specific geographic location. But generally, a *market* may be said to be an interface between buyers and sellers where the exchange of commodities takes place. A market system, consisting of many individual markets, is one where the decisions of individual households and firms exert the major influence over the choice decisions which any society must make. In this system of markets, the negotiation process between buyers and sellers in markets establishes a price which serves to allocate commodities and resources among competing uses. This, of course, is only one possible type of system for dealing with the economic problem of scarcity.

Consider a simplified, capitalist market system in which all market production is done by business firms who seek to maximize their profits and all consumption is done by satisfaction-seeking households. All resources are privately owned or controlled by households in this system, since everyone is in a household of some type. Hence, households are both buyers of goods and services and sellers of productive resources. Similarly, firms are both buyers of resources and sellers of goods and services. To envision this, a distinction is often made between *product markets,* where firms sell goods and services to consuming households, and *input markets,* where households sell economic inputs which they control to firms. Figure 1-1 illustrates these two sets of markets through which the decisions of firms and households are coordinated. Looking first at product markets, households desire goods and services to satisfy human wants, and these goods and services are available from firms in return for money payments. Households do not have sufficient resources to satisfy all their wants, and so they must choose among the large number of available goods and services. In product markets, product prices act as a signal which affects household consumption patterns and firm production choices.

In the input market portion of the diagram, economic inputs have been lumped into three categories: *land* (which includes all natural resources), *labor*

Figure 1-1   The Circular Flow of Commodities, Economic Inputs, and Money Payments Between Firms and Households

(all human resources), and *capital* (all manufactured resources). Because of limited resources, firms attempt to choose the combination of economic inputs which most efficiently produces the desired output. Once again prices, in this case input prices in the forms of rent, wages, and profits, act as signals in input markets. These prices determine firms' choices of hiring economic inputs and the households' choices of supplying these inputs. In both sets of markets, the money payments constitute the incomes which households or firms use to purchase the needed commodities or inputs. In this way, decisions of firms and households, which are affected by market price signals, determine what is produced, how it is produced (using what inputs), and how to divide the resulting output (those who are willing and able to pay the market prices get the output).

In the market system represented by this oversimplified but informative diagram, it is noteworthy that resources and commodities tend to be allocated efficiently by market forces alone. Of course, these market forces do not result from natural law or divine providence. Rather, they are the product of the conscious decisions of independent consumers and producers, each motivated by economic incentives. In the more complex real world, it is often necessary for the government to take action in an attempt to maintain these forces, a subject to which we will return shortly. Note also that the study of labor economics can now be more specifically identified within this circular flow framework. As shown, one type of input market is the labor market. *Labor economics*, then, involves the study of the various principles and institutions which govern the operation of labor markets.

The Method of Economics

The study of economics involves first the observation of economic behavior and phenomena. For example, in this book we will observe that the labor force participation of women has increased significantly in recent years, that more educated people tend to have higher lifetime earnings, and that wages for unionized workers tend to be somewhat higher than for nonunionized workers. These observations are not surprising, but why have they happened? Economic analysis, a second part of the study of economics, tries to develop principles or theories to explain these kinds of phenomena. These principles or theories are useful in allowing us to arrange, interpret, and generalize upon our economic observations in a systematic way. They permit us not only to explain and understand past economic behavior but also to predict and gain some control over future events.

Theories are useful, however, only if they explain real world economic behavior accurately. This suggests that theories must be tested empirically against economic behavior to ensure that they have explanatory and predictive power. Throughout this book we will note numerous empirical studies which have attempted to test the accuracy of theoretical explanations. Finally, observing and explaining economic phenomena allows us to gain insight into ways of influencing economic behavior in socially desirable ways. Developing policies to eliminate or improve economic problems requires an understanding of the causes of these problems. This book is quite policy-oriented, but careful observation and analysis of economic problems must precede a consideration of policy alternatives.

This brief review does not begin to do justice to the many intricacies involved in the discipline of economics. It does, however, provide a sufficient background so that we may now begin to consider the distinctive elements of the study of labor. A necessary point of departure is with a concept already presented above—the labor market.

LABOR MARKETS

A market was defined previously as an interface between buyers and sellers where commodities are exchanged. With respect to labor markets, the buyers are firms, the sellers are households, and the commodity is labor services. Some students are uncomfortable with this terminology when applied to labor markets because it seems awkward and impersonal. The buyer and seller roles are usually thought of in reverse, and it is particularly difficult to think of labor services as just another commodity. Nevertheless, the similarity of labor market forces to other types of market forces makes these terms appropriate.

In a freely competitive labor market, i.e., one where large numbers of independent workers and employers compete in a world of adequate information and labor mobility, the independent decisions of workers and employers result from market forces. Employers are free to hire the desired quantity and quality of workers at market-determined wages, and workers freely offer their labor services in amounts determined by these prevailing wages. Each worker is paid according to the value of his or her contribution to production, and labor is allocated efficiently.

Over a longer period of time, shifts in labor demand and supply are likely to occur. In the twentieth century U.S. labor market these shifts have fundamentally altered labor market conditions, as the data in Table 1-1 suggest. On the demand side, certain occupations have become less needed as technological change and changing product market conditions have occurred. For example, as technological advances have occurred in agriculture, permitting greater output with less labor input, the demand for agricultural workers has declined substantially. During the same period, the demand for workers in various service occupations has expanded considerably, especially for governmental service workers. Substantial changes in labor supply have also occurred, some of them in response to change in demand and some of them distinct from such changes. In the post-World War II period an influx of younger workers into the labor market occurred as a result of the post-war baby boom. For various sociocultural and economic reasons, many more women are also now actively participating in labor markets. These changing supply and demand conditions create temporary imbalances (shortages and surpluses) in labor markets. However, given freely competitive labor markets, these imbalances are corrected as the market prices or wage rates for particular kinds of workers increase or decrease to create new market equilibria.

Without going into a detailed discussion of labor supply and demand factors, which will be presented in subsequent chapters, Figure 1-2 depicts the simplified essence of this process. In diagram (a) the initial supply and demand conditions for hypothetical agricultural workers are shown by demand curve D_1 and supply curve S. A wage rate of OW_1 clears the market in the sense that the number of workers willing to supply labor services at a wage of OW_1 just equals the number of workers demanded by agricultural firms at that wage (OQ_1). If the demand for farm workers declines, as is shown by demand curve D_2, an initial surplus of workers now exists at the wage OW_1. But given this surplus, wages will tend to be forced downward toward OW_2, where the market is again cleared with fewer workers being employed (OQ_2) at the lower wage.

In diagram (b), a hypothetical labor market for teachers (an occupation

Table 1–1   Employed Persons 16 Years and Over, by Class of Worker
Annual Averages for Selected Years

	Year	Agriculture				Nonagricultural Industries						
		Total Em-ployed	Total	Wage & Salary Workers	Self-em-ployed Workers	Unpaid Family Workers	Total	Wage and Salary Workers				Self-em-ployed Workers	Unpaid Family Workers
								Total	Private House-hold	Govern-ment	Other		
Number Employed (in thousands)	1950	58,920	7160	1630	4340	1190	51,758	45,354	1862	5,789	37,704	6018	383
	1955	62,171	6450	1601	3726	1123	55,722	49,359	2054	6,821	40,484	5851	511
	1960	65,778	5459	1762	2795	901	60,318	53,417	2183	7,935	43,299	6303	598
	1965	71,088	4361	1387	2297	678	66,728	60,031	2166	9,608	48,257	6097	600
	1970	78,627	3462	1153	1810	499	75,165	69,446	1754	12,424	55,268	5217	502
	1975	84,783	3380	1280	1715	386	81,403	75,298	1348	14,525	59,426	5626	478
	1980	97,270	3309	1384	1628	297	93,960	86,706	1166	15,624	69,916	6850	404
Percent Distribution	1950	100%	12.2%	2.8%	7.4%	2.0%	87.8%	77.0%	3.2%	9.8%	64.0%	10.2%	0.7%
	1955	100	10.4	2.6	6.0	1.8	89.6	79.4	3.3	11.0	65.1	9.4	.8
	1960	100	8.3	2.7	4.2	1.4	91.7	81.2	3.3	12.1	65.8	9.6	.9
	1965	100	6.1	2.0	3.2	1.0	93.9	84.4	3.0	13.5	67.9	8.6	.8
	1970	100	4.4	1.5	2.3	.6	95.6	88.3	2.2	15.8	70.3	6.6	.6
	1975	100	4.0	1.5	2.0	.5	96.0	88.8	1.6	17.1	70.1	6.6	.6
	1980	100	3.4	1.4	1.7	.3	96.6	89.1	1.2	16.1	71.9	7.0	.4

Source: *Employment and Training Report of the President,* various years; and *Monthly Labor Review* p. 73. (Washington: U.S. Government Printing Office, August, 1981).

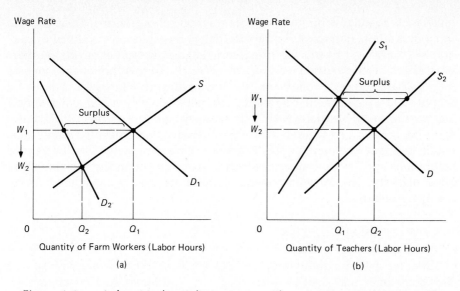

Figure 1-2   Labor Market Adjustments to Changing Demand and Supply
Conditions with Freely Competitive Markets

dominated historically by women) is shown to be at initial equilibrium, where
quantity supplied S_1 equals quantity demanded D. OQ_1 workers are hired at a
wage OW_1. As the supply of teachers increases to S_2 over time, a temporary
surplus again exists. Market forces tend to force the wage down toward OW_2,
once again clearing the market with more workers employed (OQ_2) at the lower
wage.

The type of market forces at work in these simple hypothetical situations
do, in fact, significantly influence relative wage rates and wage levels in the
U.S. economy. They also have a considerable effect upon how workers are
allocated among occupations in the economy. Nevertheless, this is a greatly
oversimplified and incomplete portrayal of actual labor market operations.
Unlike other markets, the employment of labor involves a personal relationship of some duration between employees and employers, and the conditions of work are an important part of that relationship. Furthermore, labor
services are not bought and sold in the sense that ownership changes hands;
rather they can be thought of as only being rented. Many such factors affect
labor market behavior, and it is largely these factors which necessitate the
study of labor separate from other branches of economics. The assumptions
underlying freely competitive labor markets are also generally not met in the
U.S. economy. Many employers are not small and independent, collusion
sometimes occurs among employers and workers, labor market information is
usually incomplete, and labor mobility is often restricted.

In addition, labor markets within labor markets frequently exist. Each
business firm may be said to constitute an *internal* labor market, although it is
interconnected with the *external* labor market outside the firm or plant. Because
of seniority provisions and internal hiring practices, many workers may move

much more readily within the plant or firm than between firms. There are also numerous labor submarkets in the external market, often determined by geographic proximity. Even within a given geographic market several authors have observed the existence of *dual labor markets*. In this framework, *primary markets* characterized by pleasant, remunerative work with good chances for security and advancement exist side by side with *secondary markets* consisting of low-paying, dead-end jobs with little permanence and chance for advancement. Disadvantaged workers who are undereducated, unskilled, and/or discriminated against tend to populate secondary labor markets.[1] Finally, various institutions and institutional rules have a great impact on the functioning of labor markets. The most important of these are briefly considered in the following section.

INSTITUTIONAL FORCES

Market determinations may be disliked by workers or employers, and they sometimes may lead to distressing social problems such as unemployment, poverty, and discrimination. Market forces may not lead to a fully employed economy and may generate income disparities among individual households which are socially unacceptable. If labor market participants do not act independently, the *economic exploitation* of certain individuals or groups may result. In response to these market weaknesses various labor market institutions and institutional rules have emerged to supplement, and in some cases to replace, market forces.

The most important institutions which intervene and compete for authority are business firms, trade unions, and the government. For example, the managers of many business firms may consider the determination of terms and conditions of employment to be a legitimate function of management alone. Trade unions emerged in the United States at least partially because this unilateral determination of employment terms tended adversely to affect worker welfare. The trade unionist feels that terms and conditions of employment should be determined by organized, bilateral labor-management negotiations culminating in a written agreement. This debate, and the resulting organized labor movement in the United States and elsewhere, has profoundly affected the functioning of labor markets.

To protect workers against management excesses and market weaknesses, and to protect certain management rights, the government (at all levels, but particularly the federal government) has increasingly intervened in the labor market. With the growth of strong national trade unions, a need for the regulation of labor-management relations emerged in the United States, and the federal and state governments have assumed this responsibility. To protect

---

1. See Peter Doeringer and Michael Piore, *Internal Labor Markets and Manpower Analysis* (Lexington, Mass.: D. C. Heath, 1971).

the welfare of workers, the government has also intervened frequently through legislation regulating such things as minimum wages and maximum hours, occupational safety and health, discriminatory employment practices, and education and training programs. As is the case with the collective bargaining process, governmental regulation significantly affects labor supply and demand, wage rates, and the allocation of labor in labor markets.

PROBLEMS AND POLICIES

It is not sufficient, nor particularly interesting, to study labor market forces and institutional factors in isolation from real world issues, problems, and policy alternatives which result from employment relations. An understanding of these forces and institutions is necessary in order to assess intelligently various issues and policies, but the study of labor becomes alive and exciting when background concepts are actually applied to real life situations. Fortunately (from the student's point of view), the study of labor involves no shortage of unresolved issues and problems.

Because of the dynamic nature of our economy, means must be devised to ensure that labor markets are efficient and flexible in adjusting to the changing conditions alluded to earlier. If there are advantages to maintaining competitive labor markets, then we need to make sure that these markets are, in fact, reasonably free and efficient. If one looks at the market for public school teachers in the late 1960s and 1970s, for example, where thousands of qualified applicants were competing for a very small number of available jobs, the conclusion must be drawn that some efficiency and flexibility were lacking in these markets. Accurate information on job and worker availability, sufficient labor mobility, adequate educational and training programs, and programs for exploited and disadvantaged groups must be provided.

In this regard, however, it is often argued that an affluent society such as ours has a responsibility to provide a minimally comfortable standard of living to all its members, especially given the vast differences in income and wealth that exist among families in our economic system. The disagreement over these matters centers largely around the best arrangement for achieving this responsibility, the level of responsibility, and the magnitude of public support which is feasible. More generally, many contemporary labor problems reflect the economic and psychological insecurity of workers in an industrialized society where the goal of productive efficiency may conflict with worker desires for job security and improved working conditions.

From a slightly different perspective, it is also argued that there is often a conflict between the workers who produce a product and the consumers who purchase and use it. Workers want high wages and fringe benefits, pleasant working conditions, sufficient leisure time, and a share in the decisions which affect them in the workplace. These desires, if met, may often raise the costs of production and conflict with the consumer's desire to purchase the best product at the lowest price. The problem is compounded, of course, because workers are also consumers. Just as it is important to devise effective methods of settling disputes between labor and management, it is equally necessary to reach some reasonable resolution of the conflict between worker and consumer groups.

In order to prevent the chronic problems of unemployment and inflation, an economic system must also discover effective programs for achieving an adequate total demand for labor while maintaining wage and price stability. The achievement of a fully employed economy has become a more or less official policy of the federal government in the United States, although disagreement persists concerning what constitutes full employment. Especially in the last 15 years, persistent problems of inflation have once again become matters of increased public attention. Determining adequate fiscal and monetary policies, wage-price guidelines or controls, and public service employment programs and the like are important unresolved issues.

CONCLUDING REMARKS

The preceding is certainly not an exhaustive list of labor problems and issues, but it does serve to highlight important and perplexing dilemmas which are related to the study of labor. The reader should now have a better understanding of the nature and importance of studying labor systematically. The remainder of this volume will lead students through the areas of study mentioned briefly in this chapter in a more detailed fashion. Chapters 2 to 4 in Part I of the text will present the elementary economic theory of labor market forces. As we have already discovered, the theory of purely competitive labor markets is decidedly oversimplified and incomplete. Nevertheless, we will begin by analyzing the operation of these theoretical labor markets, because it is important to gain a thorough feeling for the power of market forces in real labor markets. Later, many of the unrealistic assumptions will be dropped so as to achieve a more realistic picture of labor market behavior.

Part II of the book extends the analysis in Part I by considering several important labor market problems, as well as the policy alternatives available for dealing with these problems. As mentioned previously, labor market forces do not always generate socially desirable results. In some cases market forces are incapable of eliminating perplexing social problems such as poverty and unemployment. In others market pressures are circumvented so that problems such as discrimination may result. In other words, various degrees of market failure characterize U.S. labor markets, and the resulting problems have led to intervention by various institutions, particularly the federal government. Part II analyzes the most important of these problems and emphasizes the current and proposed public policies for dealing with them.

Part III completes the picture of U.S. labor markets by considering the institutionalized nature of labor-management relations. The evolution and ideology of U.S. trade unions will be examined, as will the government's attempts to regulate labor-management relations. The process of collective bargaining is carefully analyzed, and the section ends with an assessment of the overall impact of trade unionism on the U.S. economy.

The text should provide you with a thorough introduction to the tools of analysis and institutional dimensions which are useful in understanding labor market behavior. You will hopefully gain an appreciation of the importance and complexity of labor-related problems, and you should be able to assess more intelligently the various policy issues related to those problems as you move through the book. Good luck on the rest of your journey through the "world of labor."

CHAPTER SUMMARY

Economics involves the observation of economic behavior, the development and testing of theories to explain such behavior, and the consideration of policy issues related to economic problems. All branches of economics involve the problem of scarcity, i.e., the fact that every economic system has limited resources with which to satisfy the unlimited wants of it members. Choice is necessitated by this inevitable scarcity, and a market system (such as that which generally exists in the United States) tends to utilize the individual decisions of households and firms to make these necessary economic choices. Markets may be classified as either product markets or input markets, and one important type of input is labor. Labor economics is a branch of economics which deals with the labor factor of production.

In freely competitive labor markets, employer demand decisions and worker supply decisions are dictated by labor market prices, or wage rates. All workers receive a wage equal to the value of their production, and labor is allocated efficiently. Over time, wage rates in competitive markets fluctuate up and down to clear labor markets as supply and demand conditions change.

In addition to pure market forces, numerous other forces operate in real world labor markets. The assumptions of the competitive labor market model are typically unrealistic. Also, important institutions such as business firms, trade unions, and the government alter and sometimes supplant labor market forces. Familiarity with these market and institutional forces allows one to assess intelligently numerous critical problems and issues related to labor. Included among these problems are the maintenance of efficient labor markets, the resolution of conflicts between workers and consumers and between workers and management, the elimination of poverty and discrimination, and the achievement of full employment with price stability.

KEY TERMS

factors of production
economic inputs
production

consumption
economics
market

product markets
input markets
land
labor
capital
labor economics

internal labor markets
external labor markets
dual labor market theory
primary labor markets
secondary labor markets
economic exploitation

REVIEW QUESTIONS

1. What is the study of economics all a-bout? How does labor economics fit into this study?

2. The Clayton Antitrust Act of 1914 proclaimed that "labor is not a commodity." In what ways is labor different from commodities? Why is it important to study labor economics as a distinct branch of economics?

3. In what ways do economic market forces operate in labor markets? How are these market forces modified by institutional forces, and what are the major institutions which attempt these modifications?

4. Try to name three major economic issues which have no relationship to labor and labor markets. Is this possible?

5. Economic theories or principles are often abstract and seemingly oversimplified. Why is it necessary to consider carefully these theories before taking up problems and policies? (Why can't we skip Part I of this book and get on to the "good stuff"?)

ADDITIONAL REFERENCES

Doeringer, Peter, and Michael Piore. *Internal Labor Markets and Manpower Analysis*. Lexington, Mass.: D. C. Heath, 1971.

Freeman, Richard. *Labor Economics*, 2d ed., Englewood Cliffs, N.J.: Prentice-Hall, Inc., 1979, chap. 1.

Lekachman, Robert. *Economists at Bay*. New York: McGraw-Hill Book Co., 1976.

McConnell, Campbell R. *Economics*, 8th ed. New York: McGraw-Hill Book Co., 1981, Part I.

Rees, Albert. *The Economics of Trade Unions*. Chicago: University of Chicago Press, 1962.

Terkel, Studs. *Working*. New York: Pantheon Books, 1974.

THE WORLD
OF WORK . . .

The Aging of America's Labor Force: Problems and Prospects

One of the many labor-related problems which will require both market and institutional adjustments in the coming years is the aging of America's labor force. The short reading below is excerpted from a report appearing in the 1978 Employment and Training Report of the President, *an annual document prepared for the President by the Department of Labor for submission to Congress. This report discusses the problems of an aging labor force and the future prospects.*

Less than 20 years ago, a rough pyramid could be drawn to illustrate the age structure of the American population. A broad base of children and teenagers supported generally narrower population blocks, each representing a successively older age group. At the top of the pyramid, the smallest block (only about one-fourth as wide as the base block portraying children under 10 years old) represented the portion of the population aged 70 years and older. But that pyramidal picture is shifting rapidly. Less than 20 years from now, a sketch of the U.S. population by age segments will look much like an untidy rectangle. By 1990, over 39 million Americans will have reached or passed the age of 60, forming a cohort about equal in size to the number of Americans in their twenties or thirties. And the rectangle will bulge around its midsection. . . .

While the Nation is currently (and correctly) concerned with the special employment problems of its young people, it must be remembered that older workers also confront special problems. The 50-year-old worker is far more likely to be the primary family breadwinner than is the teenaged or young adult worker. Family and community ties, seniority protection, and pension plans may restrict an older worker's willingness to risk a job change or move to a new locale to take advantage of better employment opportunities. During periods of economic recovery, older workers are more likely than younger ones to reenter the active labor force at occupational and wage levels below those they held before becoming unemployed. Finally, training and retraining opportunities have generally been less accessible to older workers than to their younger colleagues.

. . . It is clear that early retirement is a two-sided issue: While it has been a blessing for some, it has seriously increased the risk of poverty in later years for many others. Thus, the retirement decision is not always entirely voluntary, even before age 65, and may lead to hardship.

The Federal Government is becoming more concerned about the implications of the Nation's aging work force and the employment-related problems of older workers. In the last quarter of 1977, Congress voted to bolster the social security fund by systematically increasing workers' contributions between 1978 and 1985; and legislation to prohibit mandatory retirement before age 70 for employees in most fields is being considered. . . . [Authors' note: Such legislation was enacted in 1979.] . . . The key question is the strength of the unwritten agreement between young and old embodied in the social security system: Will younger workers continue ungrudgingly to support an ever-larger group of nonworking older Americans, in the expectation that they in turn will be adequately supported during their predictably longer retirement years by the succeeding generation? The adjustments necessary to assure a positive response to this question are just beginning. . . .

Given the recent and projected demographic developments . . . the aging of America may seriously strain the Nation's resources. The problem of assuring adequate retirement income might not have become severe so long as the Nation had an expanding labor force and no sudden increase in the number of older retired workers and their dependents relative to the active labor force. But the growth of the retired population and its dependents (resulting, in part, from mortality reductions and the trend toward early retirement) has accelerated.

On the other hand, future generations of workers may be willing to contribute a greater proportion of their earnings to support the non-working older population, particularly if the reduced fertility rate results in a lowering of child rearing costs as the costs of supporting retirees increase. If, simultaneously, women enter the labor force at a rate greater than currently projected, a larger working population will share those increased retirement benefit costs.

Another possibility is that inflation and diminishing supplies of energy and other resources may mandate a greater reliance on labor-intensive economic processes, in which case there may be an increase in overall labor demand. This, along with other trends, such as the growing need for services for an expanding elderly population, could lead to increased employment of older persons, especially those in their sixties.

A more encouraging thrust, toward job creation geared to older workers, appears to be developing in both governmental and private sectors. . . .

A critical aspect of all these Government-sponsored projects is their demonstration that older men and women need not be restricted to a narrow range of occupations. For example, they work as deputy sheriffs, clerk-typists, instructors for the mentally retarded, fire wardens, and nutrition aides.

At the same time, private firms have increasingly begun to recognize the value of their otherwise retirable employees. For example, a major insurance company has begun the practice of retaining such persons as active members of local insurance agencies, primarily as informal trainers for new and younger agents. Retention of older workers, even on a reduced-hours, flexitime basis, may be a more cost-effective approach than hiring new full-time employees. Large corporations are also experimenting with full or partial educational leaves for their older employees, updating their skills for continued employment in the same organization.

. . . Beyond these promising efforts, major adjustments are in store for the American people and many of their institutions as a result of anticipated shifts in the age structure of the working population. . . .

_____

Source: Abridged from "The Aging of America's Labor Force: Problems and Prospects of Older Workers," in *Employment and Training Report of the President, 1978* (Washington: U.S. Government Printing Office, 1978), pp. 85–99.

Chapter 2

Labor Markets: Supply and Demand Forces

As indicated in Chapter 1, the supply decisions of individual workers and the labor demand decisions of employers are important forces in the operation of labor markets. Both institutional arrangements and these labor market supply and demand forces affect the allocation of labor and the determination of wages in our economy. Even though all these forces operate simultaneously, it is useful to consider carefully market forces in isolation before discussing institutional factors, and that is the major objective of this chapter. To keep the analysis simple and yet enlightening, it will be helpful to continue to assume that labor markets are perfectly competitive, while noting once again that this assumption is typically unrealistic and will be modified later.

To elaborate, perfectly competitive labor markets involve the following assumptions. On the supply side:

1. Workers have complete market knowledge, including information on wages and job opportunities.
2. Workers are rational and will respond to differences in wages and benefits.
3. Workers are freely mobile.
4. Workers act individually in making decisions and do not collude.

On the demand side of labor markets, perfect competition requires that:

1. Employers have perfect labor market knowledge.
2. Employers are rational and attempt to maximize profits.
3. Each employer acts as an individual and no employer has a large enough share of the total demand for labor to affect wages.

Within the context of this freely competitive labor market world, this chapter will first examine the basic components of the theory of labor supply, followed by a presentation of the essentials of labor demand theory. You will not be an accomplished theoretician when you finish this chapter, but that is not the objective. The chapter should provide you with the basic analytical tools for considering wage determination and labor allocation in Chapter 3, as well as contributing part of a framework for considering the numerous labor issues in Parts II and III.

SUPPLY FORCES

Labor supply questions deal with the amount of labor and the type of labor which workers will offer under various economic conditions. These questions are important because they relate to a number of issues and policies which will be taken up in later sections of this book: issues and policies such as unemployment and underemployment, changes in the labor force composition, training and retraining programs, poverty, and discrimination to name a few.

There are a number of dimensions to labor supply which will be considered in this section. During the short-run period of time when the population of working age is relatively constant, there are still both quantitative and qualitative aspects to the supply of labor. Both the number of workers available for work and the number of hours these workers choose to work per time period are relevant quantitative factors. In addition, the important qualitative considerations involve the level of training and skills which workers bring to their jobs. Both the quantitative and qualitative dimensions of labor supply have important implications for the problems of unemployment and underemployment.

Over a longer period of time, changes in the size of the working age population exert a major influence on labor supply. Also, changes in various other demographic and cultural factors over time have drastically altered the composition of the labor force. Both the short-run and long-run perspectives of labor supply will be analyzed in this section.

The Labor Force and Labor Force Participation

The *civilian labor force* is defined by the U.S. Bureau of the Census as "the number of civilian, noninstitutionalized persons 16 years of age and older who are either: (1) working full- or part-time for pay or profit; or (2) unemployed and actively seeking work." Some representative labor force data are provided in Table 2-1. Note that there are several important parts to this definition. Military personnel and those people in prisons, mental institutions, and the like are excluded, as are all people below 16 years of age. Both the part-time and full-time employed are included, with no distinction made between the two. More specifically, anyone working 1 hour or more for wages or salary during the reference week, and those who did 15 hours or more of unpaid work in a family business or farm are counted as employed. Any workers absent from work because of illness, vacation, or labor dispute are also considered to be employed. Finally, those without jobs who are actively looking for work, such as through employment agencies or local employers, are a part of the labor force. The number of people who are unemployed (out of work and actively seeking work) during any reference period is divided by the total number of people in the labor force to yield the unemployment rate.

Although this has basically been the means of measuring the size of the labor force in the United States since the 1930s, the method has received considerable criticism. For example, under this definition if a mother or father cares for their child full-time in the home, this person is not in the labor force because no compensation is involved; but if the same individual opens a commercial day care center, the service rendered now becomes worthy of inclusion in the labor force statistics. The person is now employed and in the labor force, whereas in the former case he or she was excluded. Numerous distortions may result from including part-time employees as members of the

Table 2-1   Employment Status of the Noninstitutionalized Population
16 Years and Over: Annual Averages for Selected Years
(number in thousands)

Year	Total Non-institu-tional Popu-lation	Total Labor Force, Including Armed Forces		Civilian Labor Force						
		Number	% Non-institu-tional Popu-lation	Total	Employed			Unemployed		
					Total	Agri-cul-ture	Non-agricul-tural Indus-tries	Number	% of Labor Force	Not in Labor Force
1950	106,645	63,858	59.9%	62,208	58,920	7160	51,752	3288	5.3%	42,787
1955	112,732	68,072	60.4	65,023	62,171	6449	55,718	2852	4.4	44,660
1960	119,759	72,142	60.2	69,628	65,778	5458	60,318	3852	5.5	47,617
1965	129,236	77,178	59.7	74,455	71,088	4361	66,726	3366	4.5	52,058
1970	140,182	85,903	61.3	82,715	78,627	3462	75,165	4088	4.9	54,280
1975	153,449	94,793	61.8	92,613	84,783	3380	81,403	7830	8.5	58,655
1980	166,246	106,821	64.3	104,719	97,270	3310	93,960	7448	7.1	59,425

Source: *Employment and Training Report of the President*, various years; and *Monthly Labor Review* (Washington: U.S. Government Printing Office, August, 1981), p. 71.

labor force (and as employed), particularly if many of these workers desire to work full-time but are unable to find full-time employment.

Also, the definition does not include those "discouraged workers" who have given up their job search because of inability to find work. These persons are no longer actively seeking work and are not counted in the labor force, and, therefore, not counted as unemployed. Because of this "discouraged worker" phenomenon many economists have criticized the Bureau of the Census definitions, arguing that the methods used may seriously understate the true jobless rate. On the other hand, there is evidence that some workers classified as unemployed may not be seeking work very actively, which would tend to overstate the magnitude of the unemployment problem. These types of concerns have led the government periodically to review its measurement of labor force statistics, the last two reviews having been completed in 1962 and 1979.[1] We will take up these measurement issues in more detail with our consideration of the full employment concept in Chapter 5.

Another concept for measuring quantitative labor supply characteristics is the *labor force participation rate* (LFPR), which is defined as the percentage of persons in a given population who are classified as in the labor force. LFPRs are often expressed in terms of various demographic categories of the population

1. See *Measuring Employment and Unemployment*, Report of the President's Committee to Appraise Employment and Unemployment Statistics (Washington: U.S. Government Printing Office, 1962), and Sar Levitan, "Labor Force Statistics to Measure Full Employment," *Society* (September-October, 1979), pp. 68-71.

such as age, sex, race, or marital status. Table 2-2, for example, presents LFPRs by age, sex, and race for selected years of the post-World War II period. As can be seen, significant variations in labor force participation exist among these groups. The participation rate is generally higher for men than for women, although the age patterns for men and women are dissimilar and the LFPR of women has increased substantially over the period. Also of significance is the larger decline in participation rates for nonwhite males. In order to explain some of these patterns, it is necessary to consider the basic theory of how individuals and households make decisions regarding their labor force participation.

Table 2-2   Civilian Labor Force Participation Rates for Persons
16 Years of Age and Over; By Race, Sex, and Age
Annual Averages, Selected Years

	Total	16-19 Years of Age	20 Years of Age and Over
Nonwhite			
Male			
1955	85.0%	60.8%	87.8%
1960	83.0	57.6	86.2
1970	76.5	47.3	81.4
1980	70.8	43.3	75.1
Female			
1955	46.1%	32.7%	47.5%
1960	48.2	32.9	49.9
1970	49.5	34.0	51.7
1980	53.4	35.9	55.8
White			
Male			
1955	85.4%	58.6%	87.5%
1960	83.4	55.9	86.0
1970	80.0	57.5	82.8
1980	78.3	63.8	79.9
Female			
1955	34.5%	40.7%	34.0%
1960	36.5	40.3	36.2
1970	42.6	45.6	42.2
1980	51.3	56.4	50.8

Source: *Economic Report of the President, 1981* (Washington: U.S. Government Printing Office, 1981), Table B-30.

The Individual's Supply of Labor

Individuals make decisions not only concerning whether or not to participate in the labor force but also concerning the extent of their participation, i.e., how many hours they wish to work per time period. The average hours of work per week has declined in the United States from around 55 at the turn of the century to slightly less than 40 today. Also, at any given point in time there is considerable variation in the hours worked per week by different people in the labor force. This can be seen by the percentage distributions of people working various hours per week shown in Table 2-3.

Table 2-3   Percentage Distribution of Hours of Work by Type of Industry
May, 1981

Hours per Week	All Industries	Agricultural	Nonagricultural
1-29	17.6%	22.4%	17.4%
30-34	6.5	6.3	6.5
35-39	7.3	4.5	7.4
40	43.8	17.2	44.7
41-48	9.8	7.5	9.9
49-59	8.4	13.7	8.2
60 and over	6.6	28.4	5.8

Source: U.S. Department of Labor, Bureau of Labor Statistics, *Employment and Earnings* (Washington: U.S. Government Printing Office, June, 1981), Table A-26.

Variations from the Standard Workweek. You may be saying to yourself: "Wait a minute! People don't really have any choice in the number of hours they work because the 40-hour workweek is standard." Although it is true that employer, legislative, and collective bargaining forces usually establish the normal workweek which wage-earners must accept, there is still much variation around the 40-hour norm. Many students and women, for example, may choose to work part-time because of commitments to school or home, and some workers may be forced into part-time employment by economic conditions. Workers may also choose to work more than the normal workweek by taking a second job. These multiple job holders, called *moonlighters*, may be young workers with low incomes and heavy family responsibilities, for example.[2] Of course, workers may choose or be required to work overtime, which has the effect of expanding the workweek for them. Also, many salaried professionals are not employed for a standard workweek, and in fact typically work more than 40 hours per week.

Labor Supply Curve. The theory of individual labor supply involves the number of hours workers will choose to work at various wage rates, and it is

2. On this subject, see R. Shisko and B. Rostker, "The Economics of Multiple Job Holding," *American Economic Review* (June, 1976), pp. 298-309.

based upon the assumption that workers seek to maximize their utility (satisfaction) in allocating their time between work and nonwork (leisure) activities. According to this theory, devoting time to leisure activities provides utility to individuals. Work time, which is the alternative to leisure time, provides utility indirectly because it generates income which can be used to purchase useful goods and services. The individual worker attempts to maximize his or her total utility by allocating the available time between work and leisure as efficiently as possible.

This theoretical framework has led to the development of the well-known backward bending individual labor supply curve presented in Figure 2-1. As curve S_L suggests, this hypothetical worker will not choose to work any hours below some wage level such as OW_1, normally called the *reservation wage*. As the wage increases above the reservation wage to OW_2, the worker chooses to work additional hours because of the inducement of the higher wage and the utility which can be derived from goods and services purchased with the additional income. Of course, in choosing to work more hours, the worker is giving up the utility which could have been gained from devoting that time to leisure. Up to OW_2, however, the utility gained from increased income is greater than that which is given up from foregone leisure, as this hypothetical worker assesses it.

Disregarding overtime premiums, however, as the wage continues to

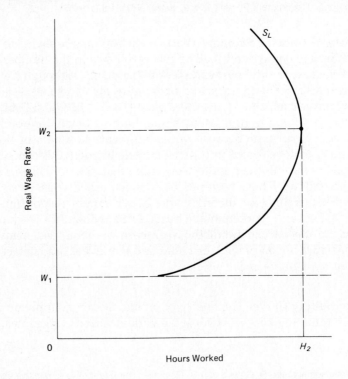

Figure 2-1   The Backward Bending Individual Labor Supply Curve

increase above OW_2, the additional utility to be gained is less than that which is given up in lost leisure time. Because of the law of diminishing marginal utility, the additional indirect utility derived from working more than OH_2 hours is small relative to the direct utility which could be gained from devoting additional hours to leisure activities. In short, additional leisure time provides a great deal of added satisfaction to us when we do not have very much of it.

Substitution and Income Effects. Put in a somewhat different way, this theory says that as wage rates increase while other economic variables (such as product prices and other income) remain constant, the price of leisure hours, expressed in terms of the wage given up, becomes higher. Workers will be motivated to substitute work hours for leisure hours, and this is appropriately called the *substitution effect*. However, it is also true that as the wage rate increases, individuals are "better off" than before because they have higher incomes. Economic analysis suggests that workers will therefore be motivated to buy more goods providing utility to them. Since leisure provides utility, this *income effect* will motivate the worker to desire more leisure, and therefore less work.

Clearly, in this model the ultimate decision of individuals regarding hours of work depends on whether the substitution or the income effect predominates.[3] The backward bending labor supply curve in Figure 2-1 suggests that when leisure hours are relatively plentiful and work hours are relatively small, the substitution effect is greater and more hours are worked as wage rates increase. But beyond some point such as OH_2, the income effect becomes greater as more leisure, which is now relatively scarce, is purchased with the increased income. As we shall see, the historical reduction in average hours worked per week in the United States can be explained partially in terms of workers choosing more leisure as real wages and incomes have increased over time.

Note also that wage rates in Figure 2-1 are expressed in real terms rather than in money terms. Real wages account for changes in the price level, or inflation, while money wages do not. For example, if the money wage rate increased by 10 percent from $5.00 to $5.50, and if the general level of prices also increased by 10 percent, real wages would be unchanged. Figure 2-1 simply says that workers respond to changes in real wages, or real purchasing power. We are not concerned with the macroeconomic issue of price level changes at this point, but this complication will be taken up in Chapter 4.

The Family Allocation of Labor

Although the analysis above concerning the individual's hours of work choice is an important quantitative labor supply dimension, most people live in

---

3. See the appendix to this chapter for a more complete theoretical explanation of income and substitution effects.

households or families rather than as single individuals. Because of this, it may be more enlightening to view the labor hours supplied decision as taking place within a family context, where the entire family collectively decides how to allocate the total available time between work and leisure. A problem arises here, however, with the traditional dichotomous classification of time as either work or leisure. Work time is that time devoted to activities for which the market pays compensation. By this definition housework-related activities which are necessary for the maintenance of the household must be leisure. Surely the majority of homemakers would disagree!

It is more appropriate to add a third category of time—nonmarket work—and consider the family as allocating its time among market work, nonmarket work, and leisure, all of which provide utility either directly or indirectly to members of the family. This theoretical framework suggests that the family will compare the productivity of each family member in the various time-use alternatives, and will allocate the greatest share of a member's time to those activities at which he or she is relatively more productive. To use an unfortunately stereotyped example, the family husband may be a great mechanic but a lousy cook. In this case he should specialize in mechanical market and/or nonmarket work, and some other member of the family should specialize in cooking.[4]

Permanent Wealth. The family allocation decision is also affected by the household's income from nonwork sources. Assume that there are two families which are alike in all relevant respects; the members of each family have the same relative productivities and the market activities of each family command the same market wages. Would we expect both families to allocate their time among market work, nonmarket work, and leisure in the same manner? The answer is "not necessarily," because one family may have a higher level of permanent wealth than does the other. For example, if family A had inherited common stock or other assets from some time in the past and family B had no such family resource, we would expect family A to offer fewer hours of market work than family B, because income from wealth is a substitute for market income.

Family Life Cycle. Over a longer period of time two other factors emerge which affect the household allocation of time. First, this theory suggests that over the family life cycle a given activity will be undertaken by a family member when it is relatively most advantageous to do so. Family members will tend to pursue schooling and education (nonmarket activities) when they are young, because the market wages foregone are relatively low for young people. The

---

4. Early significant contributions to household allocation of labor theory include Gary Becker, "A Theory of the Allocation of Time," *Economic Journal* (September, 1965), pp. 493-517; and W. G. Bowen and T. A. Finegan, *The Economics of Labor Force Participation* (Princeton, N.J.: Princeton University Press, 1969). See also the entire issue of the *Journal of Human Resources* (Spring, 1974).

wife may put off working and devote time to the home (nonmarket activity) while children are home full-time. The value of the wife's home activities may decline substantially after the children are in school, and she may then choose to specialize in market work as her home productivity declines. Secondly, over time the market wages available to some household members may increase (relative to other wages and prices), thus inducing more labor force participation from these members. Clearly, this has been one of the factors explaining the increased LFPR of married women in the postwar period.

Noneconomic Considerations. This theory for the family's allocation of labor does not imply that the decisions are governed totally by economic forces. It is still unusual in the United States to find the wife of a family assuming the major breadwinning responsibilities while the husband is the housekeeper. Is this solely because the husband is relatively more productive in the labor market and the wife more productive in the home? Probably not, as it is becoming increasingly likely that the wife's earning power equals or exceeds that of her husband in some families. But the economic specialization which would be necessary (in its simplest form, the wife working and the husband housekeeping) is still contrary to the social and cultural roles often assigned to each member.

Applications of Individual and Family Labor Allocation Theory

As indicated earlier, these theories of how individuals and families make their labor supply decisions have relevance for the changing LFPRs of various population subgroups. Referring back to Table 2-2, page 20, note once again that participation rates tend to be lower for nonwhite males than for white males. This observed effect corresponds to the higher market wages which generally prevail for whites. The higher wages, in turn, are related to discriminatory factors and the somewhat higher average education levels for whites. LFPRs are lower for younger people which is consistent with the family's decision to educate the young when alternative market wages for their services are relatively low. Similarly, the decline in the LFPR of older men can be explained by liberalized pension and social security retirement benefits which make market work alternatives less attractive. Participation rates are higher for men than for women, again consistent with the family specialization hypothesis.

LFPR of Married Women. However, the most significant trend in the post-World War II period has been the increased LFPR of married women. Economists have not reached complete agreement on the major causes of this extremely significant phenomenon, but the chief factors include the following: (1) growth in the average educational attainment of married women; (2) decline in fertility rates and average family size; (3) rise in real hourly earnings of married women; (4) development of labor-saving household devices; (5) changing sociocultural attitudes toward women and work; (6) expanding employment opportunities in service occupations; and (7) the decline in the average workweek and the increase in the number of part-time jobs.[5]

In terms of our household allocation theory, the above factors have clearly increased the value of the typical married woman's market work relative to her nonmarket work. Furthermore, as we noted, the three-category allocation of time is particularly significant for married women because they have historically borne the burden of most of the nonmarket work within the household. As family incomes have increased, the declining male participation rates may reflect a choice of more leisure, with the income effect predominating. Put differently, many males may now be on the backward bending portion of the individual labor supply curve. But for married females it has been possible to have more work time and more leisure as nonmarket work time has declined. This, coupled with the increased value of married women in the labor market, has led to a large increase in their LFPR. The substitution effect has clearly predominated for most married women, so that their labor supply curves are upward sloping.[6]

Cyclical Unemployment. It is also important to consider how the theories developed in the preceding paragraphs apply to cyclical changes in economic conditions. This topic was first analyzed systematically in the 1930s, and the analysis led to the development of the *added worker hypothesis.* This hypothesis argues that as unemployment increases and normal family breadwinners lose their jobs, additional family members enter the labor market in an attempt to maintain the family income. The implication of this argument is that LFPRs of some population groups will rise as the unemployment rate increases, and unemployment statistics may therefore somewhat overstate the problem.[7]

As mentioned earlier, there is an opposing view called the *discouraged worker hypothesis* which argues that displaced workers will become discouraged in looking for work when unemployment is severe and some will simply drop out of the labor force or choose not to enter when they otherwise would have. According to this view, participation rates (and the size of the labor force) will decline when unemployment is high, and unemployment statistics will understate the magnitude of the problem. These statistics will not include the hidden unemployed, who do not show up in the surveys as unemployed because they are no longer actively seeking work.

---

5. See Glen Cain, *Married Women in the Labor Force: An Economic Analysis* (Chicago: University of Chicago Press, 1966); and T. Aldrich Finegan, "Participation of Married Women in the Labor Force," in Cynthia B. Lloyd (ed.), *Sex Discrimination and the Division of Labor* (New York: Columbia University Press, 1975).

6. See Cain, *Married Women in the Labor Force,* chaps. 1, 2, 4.

7. See W. S. Woytinsky, *Employment and Earnings in the United States* (New York: Twentieth Century Fund, 1953).

Of course, these two effects undoubtedly exist simultaneously during recessionary periods. Since they suggest opposite results, the question of which effect predominates is an empirical one which can be answered by scientific observation and testing. Numerous studies have addressed the issue and they do indicate that both effects are present. Although there is evidence that wives enter the labor force seeking work when husbands are unemployed, supporting the added worker hypothesis, the majority of the studies conclude that the discouraged worker effect is greater when all households are considered. Hence, LFPRs tend to decline overall as economic conditions deteriorate and unemployment increases.[8]

The topics of unemployment and underemployment will be taken up again in further detail in Chapter 5. For our present purposes it is sufficient to note that the individual and family labor allocation theories which have been outlined are generally consistent with the actual levels of and fluctuations in LFPRs.

The Quality of the Labor Force

The former analysis treated the supply of labor as a "quantitative" phenomenon, dealing with supply in terms of numbers of workers or numbers of hours of work. Implicitly, this approach assumes that all workers possess similar skills and levels of training. But we know that this assumption is not a valid one for most labor markets. Workers display great variations in the skills, training, and education which are embodied in their labor services, and it is equally clear that differences in earnings are fundamentally related to these "qualitative" distinctions among workers. As we shall see in subsequent chapters, the increased educational level of the labor force and the growth in professional, technical, and skilled occupations reflect the importance of historical changes in the skill level.

Concern with the qualitative dimensions of the labor force is not new, but these concerns have become an integral part of conventional labor theory only in the last 25 years or so, during which time *human capital theory* has evolved.[9] The human capital approach recognizes that workers do display significant skill or productivity differences, and that the costs incurred by a worker in acquiring marketable skills can be considered an investment expected to yield increased earnings over the lifetime of the worker. In other words, the theory suggests that workers' earnings are dependent upon their productivity to the employer which in turn is related to workers' marketable skills. Some workers

---

8. See, for example, Bowen and Finegan, *The Economics of Labor Force Participation*, chap. 4; and S. D. Schweitzer and R. E. Smith, "The Persistence of the Discouraged Worker Effect," *Industrial and Labor Relations Review* (January, 1974), pp. 249-60.

9. See especially T. W. Schultz, "Investment in Human Capital," *American Economic Review* (March, 1961), pp. 1-17; and Gary S. Becker, *Human Capital: A Theoretical and Empirical Analysis, with Special Reference to Education* (New York: National Bureau of Economic Research, 1964).

have more relevant skills and are consequently more productive, and variations in workers' earnings are closely related to these productivity variations. Through education and training programs, for example, workers can acquire marketable skills which will enhance their earnings potential, and the cost of these programs may be considered an investment just like an investment in the stock market. The investment is expected to yield a lifetime return both to the individual and to society.

The analysis of investment in human capital is important for several reasons. First, it provides a partial explanation for wage differentials by race, sex, age, and occupation. Second, human capital analysis provides a framework for considering the public policy decision of how much society should invest in education and training programs, as compared with other expenditures programs. Third, it can assist in determining who should pay for investments in education and training—the student or trainee and his or her family, or society as a whole. Finally, human capital theory may help in explaining the varying participation rates of individuals in training programs and in postsecondary education. We will take up a number of these aspects of human capital analysis in subsequent chapters.

Labor Supply in the Long Run: Demographic Changes

The long-run supply of labor is affected by two major factors: (1) changes in the size and age distribution of the population and (2) changes in LFPRs of various groups within the population. We have already considered the latter factor; so we will focus our attention here upon the former. For most purposes, the supply of labor is now analyzed by economists and others from a relatively short-run perspective, ignoring long-run changes in population as they affect labor supply. Actually this short-run analysis is not all that short, in that we always know the number of people who can potentially enter the labor force for the next 16 years because they are already alive (of course, this ignores factors such as legal or illegal immigration). Nevertheless, population trends and forces affecting these trends have considerable significance for the long-run supply of labor. These issues have become particularly important in analyzing labor questions in less-developed countries where rapid population growth rates have often persisted. More recently, economists have begun to analyze family fertility as it relates to family income levels and labor market opportunities for family members.[10]

Labor Force Expansion. For the United States, the post-World War II baby boom has had a major economic impact. Postwar babies grew up to flood schools and colleges in the 1950s and 1960s, and they also entered the labor force in record numbers. Although the economy has become potentially more

---

10. See *Journal of Political Economy* (March, 1973), entire issue.

flexible as these young people have entered the labor force, considerable instability has also resulted as some of these people have not anticipated changing labor market conditions. To reiterate the example used in Chapter 1, until recently large numbers of college students continued to pursue degrees in elementary and secondary education, even though the market for most positions requiring this training was clearly saturated by the late 1960s. The problem was confounded by continued federal government loan programs which provided an incentive for students to pursue such degrees, rather than discouraging this pursuit.

As population growth rates have declined more recently in the United States, new issues have emerged. As the country has moved toward a situation of zero population growth (ZPG), the age distribution of the population has obviously changed. There is little growth in the number of people under 25 years of age; and the number between 25 and 65 (and eventually over 65) has increased substantially. It is estimated that the average age of the population will increase from about 32 at the present to over 40 by the year 2050. A little careful thought should suggest to you that there are some important implications of these inevitable changes. Because the 25-65 age group has expanded rapidly, and because these are the primary working years, the labor force has grown more rapidly than the population as a whole. Add to this the increased labor force participation of women generally, and a significant question emerges: Can the economy (and *should* the economy) grow rapidly enough to accommodate this labor force expansion? If the answer is "no," and it may be, then the painful implications are obvious. Fortunately, a recent report compiled by the Joint Economic Committee of the U.S. Congress concluded that this labor force expansion has already begun to stabilize; so the problem may not become much more severe than it is in the present.[11]

Changes in Consumer Demand. No matter when the peak expansion occurs, consumer demands will continue to change significantly, and production (and the kinds of workers demanded) must change in response. The diaper and toy industries, for example, will probably decline, and medical and leisure activity industries will continue to experience considerable expansion. Consumer demands are always changing, and these are no cause for great alarm. They do mean that the important flexibility in product and input markets mentioned earlier must be maintained.

Retirement Systems. Finally, an inevitable result of this changing age distribution of the population which has gained much recent attention is its

---

11. Joint Economic Committee Staff Study, *U.S. Long Term Economic Growth Prospects: Entering A New Era* (Washington: U.S. Government Printing Office, 1978). See also Paul O. Flaim and Howard N. Fullerton, Jr., "Labor Force Projections to 1990: Three Possible Paths," *Monthly Labor Review* (December, 1978), pp. 1-10.

impact upon the Social Security and private pension systems in the United States. An older population places a much greater burden on these retirement systems, and the proportionately smaller working-age population must finance this increased burden. The thought of a depleted private or public retirement fund is a frightening possibility for those currently in the early years of their labor force participation.[12] We will return to the Social Security issue in Chapter 9.

Labor Supply Curves

This section on labor supply forces can be concluded by briefly considering the pertinent labor supply curves which reflect our discussion above. We have already observed that the labor supply curves of many individuals may have both an upward sloping and a backward bending portion, as in Figure 2-1, page 22. A labor supply curve for the economy as a whole, plotting real wages on the vertical axis and the number of labor hours supplied on the horizontal axis, will probably have a similar shape for the United States during normal times. At the average real wage level, the curve probably is backward bending. What does this say for the developed American economy? It suggests that the primary overall tendency in our economy is for aggregate hours of work per time period to decline as real earnings increase (see Figure 2-2).[13]

Recall, however, that this overall tendency masks the labor supply behavior of various subgroups of the population. For men as a group, the clear tendency throughout most of the twentieth century has been to take more leisure time as real family incomes have increased. This has particularly taken the form of later entry into the labor force and earlier retirement from it, as well as a reduction in working hours during the working years. As noted, however, the female portion of the labor force has collectively supplied more labor services as family incomes have increased. In other words, the economy-wide female labor supply curve is in fact upward sloping to the right, but this factor is outweighed by the backward bending relationship for males as a group. This conclusion is consistent with the labor force participation data presented in Table 2-2, page 20.

What about the labor supply curve to a particular occupation or industry? If the quantity of labor hours offered per time period is measured against the pertinent average wage relative to other average wages, the curve will be upward sloping to the right. Let us consider this in more detail. In Figure 2-3

---

12. See, for example, Juanita M. Kreps, "Social Security in the Coming Decade: Questions for a Mature System," *Social Security Bulletin* (March, 1976); and John A. Brittain, "The Social Security System Is Not Perfect, But It's Not Bankrupt," *Challenge* (January-February, 1975), pp. 53-57.

13. See Paul Douglas, *The Theory of Wages* (New York: Macmillan Co., 1934), chap. 11; Clarence Long, *The Labor Force Under Changing Income and Employment* (Princeton, N.J.: Princeton University Press, 1958); and Belton M. Fleischer and Thomas J. Kniesner, *Labor Economics: Theory, Evidence, and Policy,* 2d ed. (Englewood Cliffs, N.J.: Prentice-Hall, Inc., 1980), chap. 4.

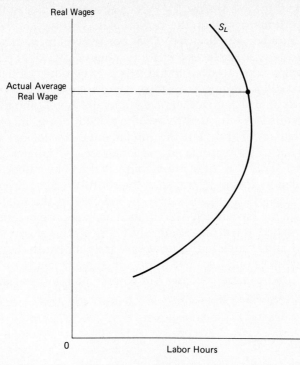

Figure 2-2   The Economy-Wide Labor Supply Curve

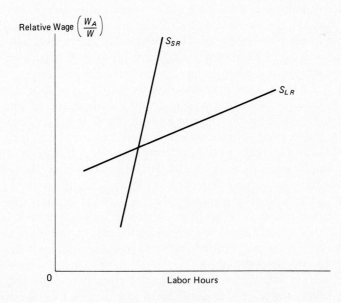

Figure 2-3   The Short-Run and Long-Run Supply of Labor
to an Occupation or Industry

the average wage in industry A (W_A) is measured relative to the average wage in all other industries W on the vertical axis. This type of measurement suggests that the labor supply curve will be positively sloped. Why? Because as the wage in industry A increases relative to other wages, labor (and consequently labor hours) will be attracted to industry A from other industries. Remember that we are still assuming that labor markets are competitive.

If we recognize that workers are not totally mobile and that workers must often be trained or educated to assume skilled jobs in many industries, the analysis changes slightly but the fundamental conclusion is not altered. In Figure 2-3 both a short-run (S_{SR}) and long-run (S_{LR}) labor supply curve for an industry are shown. If there are mobility restrictions and/or training requirements evident in this industry, then the short-run labor supply curve may be almost vertical. This suggests that an increase in the relative wage in the industry will not have much of an immediate response in terms of labor hours of work supplied. It will take some time for most workers to overcome mobility restrictions and complete the necessary training. In the long run, the time period is great enough so that these adjustments can occur, and the corresponding supply curve becomes more horizontal (more elastic) to reflect the greater supply response.

DEMAND FORCES

The central focus of our discussion on labor supply was the labor force participation decisions of individuals and households, for individuals and households are the suppliers. As we turn to a consideration of the demand side of labor markets, it is necessary to shift our focus to the demanders of labor—individual firms. The theory of labor demand is concerned with how much labor firms will desire to employ at various wage rates. Once the basic theory of both labor supply and labor demand is presented, it will be possible for us to consider in Chapter 3 the interaction of these supply and demand forces as they contribute to the setting of wages and the allocation of labor.

An understanding of labor market demand forces is important for a number of public policy questions which we will take up later. Is it possible, for example, that an increase in the governmentally established minimum wage will lead employers to hire fewer low-wage workers? If so, the governmental policy may have an unintended adverse effect. When the federal government attempts to stimulate the economy during a perod of high unemployment through expansionary fiscal and/or monetary policies, what will be the actual effect in terms of additional workers hired? Each of these important policy questions, as well as many others, relies for its answer at least partially on the nature of the demand for labor.

This section will develop the essential elements of the theory of labor demand, first at the level of the individual firm and then for the entire market and the economy as a whole. We will consider short-run demand forces first, including in our analysis the concept of the elasticity of labor demand. Finally, long-run adjustments will be added to complete the picture.

The Short-Run Demand for Labor: The Firm

In considering the demand for labor, we begin with the basic hiring, or demanding, unit: the firm. For our present purposes we will also be talking about a particular kind of simplified firm model in a particular time context. Let's assume that this hypothetical firm is operating with a given amount of technological expertise, that it uses only two economic inputs in production, labor and capital, that its operating objective is to maximize profits, and that it exists in competitive input and product markets. Finally, we will assume for now that the period of time in question is the short run, although this assumption will be modified later. In economics, the *short run* is a period of time during which at least one economic input is fixed in quantity. In our model the period of time is short enough so that our hypothetical firm cannot vary the quantities of capital inputs which it uses, and has discretion only over the amount of labor which it employs. A typical firm cannot modify the size of its plant and the quantities of its major capital inputs in a short period of time, but it can quickly expand or contract its work force. The actual period of time coinciding with the concept of the short run may be a few months or several years, depending upon the nature of the production process.

Two observations need to be made initially concerning the demand for labor as we explore the firm's demand decisions. First, the demand for labor is a *derived demand*, dependent upon the demand for the final goods and services which labor helps to produce. Obviously, if there is not much demand for the finished product, there will not be much demand for the labor which produces that product. Second, the demand for a given type of labor is related to how productive that labor is in producing the final goods or services. Some workers have higher productivity than others because of their greater education, training, innate skills, etc. Hence, the demand for labor has both an indirect product market dimension (labor market demand is derived from product market demand) and a direct labor market dimension (the productivity of workers in the labor market).

Law of Diminishing Returns. As mentioned, our hypothetical profit-maximizing firm is operating with a constant technology in purely competitive labor and product markets. The firm is attempting to maximize profits by choosing the optimal numbers of workers (or labor hours) to hire in combination with its fixed amount of capital. You should recall that a fundamental law of economics is relevant here: *the law of diminishing returns*. The law, depicted by the hypothetical data in Table 2-4, states that as more and more of a variable input (in this case labor) is added to a fixed input (capital), beyond some point the added units of the variable input will yield diminishing additional returns or product. In the simple example in Table 2-4, the firm has three machines and

Table 2-4   The Law of Diminishing Returns and the Demand for Labor
(Hypothetical Data)

(1) Units of Capital (Machines)	(2) Units of Labor (Workers)	(3) Total Product of Labor	(4) Marginal Product of Labor	(5) . Average Product of Labor	(6) Product Price	(7) Total Revenue	(8) Marginal Revenue Product
3	1	12	12	12.	$1	$12	$12
3	2	27	15	13.5	1	27	15
3	3	36	9	12.	1	36	9
3	4	42	6	10.5	1	42	6
3	5	45	3	9.	1	45	3
3	6	45	0	7.5	1	45	0
3	7	42	-3	6.	1	42	-3

cannot alter that number in the short run. As the firm experiments by employing more than 1 unit of labor to work with the machines, the resulting production (total product) first increases at an increasing rate, then at a decreasing rate, and finally it actually declines as the excessive workers apparently just get in each other's way. The rate of change in total product is measured by the marginal product of labor, which is defined as the additional output resulting from the hiring of one more unit of the variable input ($\Delta TP/\Delta L$). The average product of labor (TP/L) is the total output divided by the units of labor employed.

Relationships among Curves. The relationships among total product, average product, and marginal product may be clarified by diagramming the data in Table 2-4. In Figure 2-4, output or product is measured against the quantity of labor employed. The numbers in Table 2-4 have been translated into "smooth" curves in Figure 2-4 for simplicity, but this does not change the analysis or conclusions. Note first that all three curves rise, reach a maximum, and then begin to decline. This reflects the law of diminishing returns. Of particular importance for our purposes is the marginal product curve. Notice that it rises quickly, that it intersects the average product curve at the latter's maximum point, and that it intersects the horizontal axis ($MP = 0$) where the total product curve is at a maximum. These relationships are consistent with the data in Table 2-4, and they are not coincidental.

Mathematically, when any "average" value equals the "marginal" value, the average value is constant; it is neither increasing nor decreasing. Therefore, when the marginal product curve intersects the average product curve, at which point they are equal, the average product curve is neither rising nor falling. Similarly, from our definition of marginal product preceding, it follows that when marginal product is 0 (at 6 units of labor), total product is also constant; it is neither increasing nor decreasing.

Marginal Revenue Product. Within this theoretical framework, we can derive the firm's demand curve for this homogenous type of labor by translat-

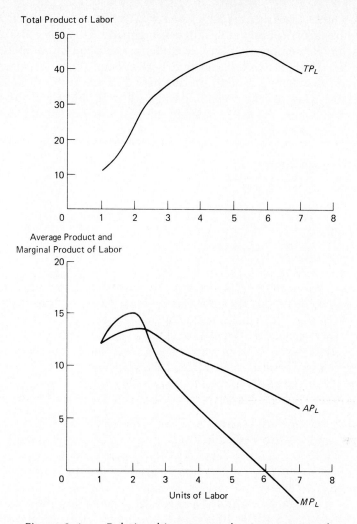

Figure 2-4   Relationships among the Average, Total
                and Marginal Products of Labor

ing the marginal product data into a dollar measure of each worker's contribution to output. Column 8 of Table 2-4, page 34, depicts the *marginal revenue
product (MRP)* of this labor, where *MRP* is defined as the additional revenue
forthcoming to the firm from selling the output of the last worker hired
($\Delta TR/\Delta L$ or MP_L × product price). Column 6 shows that the product market
where this output is sold is purely competitive because, as you should recall,
the firm sells all its output at a constant price, which equals marginal revenue,
under pure competition. For simplicity we have assumed a product price of $1,
although of course we could use other numbers.

   Think of the hiring process in terms of simple logic. The profit-maximizing
firm will continue to hire workers as long as the extra revenue which the last
worker's output generates *(MRP_L)* is greater than or equal to the extra cost of

that worker to the firm (the real wage rate W). Why? Because as long as $MRP_L \geqslant W$, an additional contribution to profit is being made. This process is depicted in Figure 2-5. Remember that by our earlier assumption of competition, no employer can affect the market wage rate. Let us assume that the real wage is $6 per hour and that all of our other productivity data are based upon 1 hour of work. The firm must pay the prevailing wage rate of $6, and it will hire workers up to the point where the MRP_L = $6. In this case the firm should stop hiring with the fourth worker.

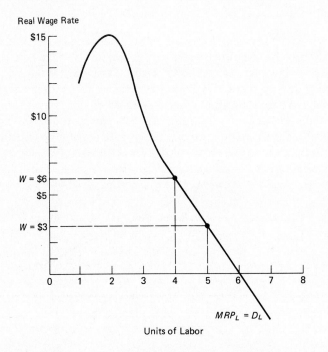

Figure 2-5   The Profit-Maximizing Hiring of Labor

The Firm's Demand for Labor Curve. An important observation can now be made. In the short run, the MRP_L curve is the labor demand curve for the firm. To make sure that this is clear, ask yourself what any demand curve depicts. The answer is that any demand curve shows the quantity demanded of, in this case, labor at various prices or wage rates. In Figure 2-5, we concluded that the profit-maximizing firm will choose to hire, or demand, four workers at a wage of $6. To hire fewer would mean sacrificing profits and to hire more would mean that the value of additional production is less than the extra cost. If we allow the market-determined wage rate to change to $3 as in Figure 2-5, we can see that the firm will hire an additional worker to conform to our hiring rule: $MRP_L \geqslant W$. In each case, the MRP_L curve shows the number of workers demanded by the firm at various wage rates. Hence, it is the labor demand curve.

Notice once again that the demand for labor curve has two conceptual components. Since we defined MRP_L as the MP_L times the product price, the labor demand curve reflects both the productivity of labor (MP_L) and the derived value of the output in the product market (product price). This suggests that labor demand could change over time because of a change in labor productivity and/or because of a change in the value of the output of labor in the product market.

Industry-wide or Economy-wide Labor Demand

The industry-wide or economy-wide labor demand curve is, in one sense, the aggregation of all the individual firms' labor demand curves; it also has a negative slope. However, some complications arise at the more aggregated level. Recall that when we developed the firm's labor demand curve, we assumed that the firm's product price remained constant as output and employment changed because we assumed that the product market is purely competitive. But the product price cannot remain constant as output changes for all firms in the industry (or economy) taken together. This is another way of saying that the product demand curve is horizontal for the purely competitive firm, but is downward sloping to the right for all firms in the industry taken together.

Assume that something causes the wage rate to decrease for all firms in our hypothetical industry. Our earlier analysis suggests that it will now be profitable for each firm to employ more labor per time period, and consequently to produce more output. But for the entire industry the product price must fall so that this additional output can be sold. Therefore the industry-wide labor demand curve cannot be the summation of all the firms' MRP curves, because these curves were developed on the assumption of a constant product price for each firm. As the employment and output are increased in response to the lower wage rate, product prices must fall, and the decrease in product price shifts the MRP curve toward the origin as in Figure 2-6 (recall that $MRP_L = MP_L \times$ product price). Thus, the labor demand curve for the industry or economy (D_I) cuts through a number of MRP curves, each of which corresponds to a different product price (see Figure 2-6.) Note also that the industry-wide demand curve is steeper in slope than the firms' MRP curves. This is an important implication which relates to the next labor demand concept which we take up: the elasticity of labor demand.

The Elasticity of Demand for Labor

Consider for a moment a union whose sole purpose is to increase the wages of its members, and let us introduce this union into our hypothetical industry above. We must, of course, depart from our purely competitive economy for a moment in order to introduce this union, but an important point will follow. The union officials know that a large increase in wages may force

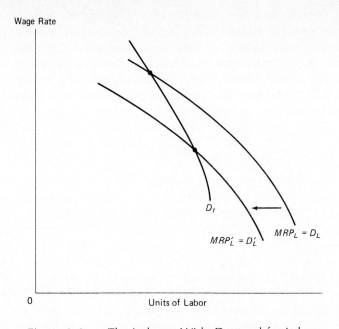

Figure 2-6   The Industry-Wide Demand for Labor

firms to employ fewer workers because they know that the labor demand curves are downward-sloping to the right. The shape of the demand curve will determine whether there will be a large or small loss of employment associated with the wage rate increase. Obviously the union would prefer a small adverse employment effect. The question is this: Would our union prefer to organize workers in only a few firms (where the labor demand is represented by the *MRP* curves in Figure 2-6), or would it attempt to organize the entire industry (so that the labor demand is depicted by D_I in Figure 2-6)? Clearly, the adverse employment effect would be less if the union could organize the entire industry and face demand curve D_I. This is consistent with a number of past real world instances where unions in the United States have lost significant numbers of members because they failed to organize the entire industry.

We are not considering the impact of unions in this chapter, but the example above illustrates an important demand concept. The effect of a wage change on employment depends upon the responsiveness, or *elasticity*, of the labor demand curve. Many readers will be familiar with this concept from introductory economics as it is applied to product demand curves. Conceptually, the term is the same when applied to labor markets. The elasticity of demand for labor e_L may be defined as follows:

$$e_L = \frac{\%\ \text{change in employment of labor}}{\%\ \text{change in wage rate}} = \frac{\dfrac{\Delta L}{L_o}}{\dfrac{\Delta W}{W_o}}$$

Note that the numerator and denominator in the definition above are inversely related in most instances, so the expression will usually be negative. The larger the magnitude of e_L (ignoring the negative sign), the greater the employment change resulting from a change in the wage rate.

Returning to our union example and to Figure 2-6 for visual reference, assume first that the union is able to organize workers in only one firm and that it successfully bargains for a wage increase from $6 per hour ($W_0$) to $7 per hour after unionizing all workers in this firm. Suppose further that employment in this firm decreases from 100 to 70 workers as a result of the wage increase. The elasticity of labor demand e_L is

$$e_L = \frac{\frac{-30}{100}}{\frac{1}{6}} = \frac{-30\%}{16.66\%} = -1.8$$

and a significant adverse employment effect has occurred. Furthermore, notice that the wage bill, i.e., the total wages paid by the firm, has declined from $600 ($6 × 100 workers) per hour to $490 ($7 × 70 workers).

Now assume that the union is successful in organizing every worker in every firm in the industry and that the wage increase from $6 to $7 leads to a decrease in industry employment from 1000 to 900. The elasticity of labor demand is now

$$e_L = \frac{\frac{-100}{1000}}{\frac{1}{6}} = \frac{-10\%}{16.66\%} = -.6$$

with a much smaller adverse employment impact in percentage terms.

The elasticity of demand for labor varies among different kinds of labor as well as between individual firms and the industry. In general, this elasticity depends upon the following propositions[14]:

1. *The larger the number of inputs which are close substitutes for labor, the greater will be the elasticity of demand for labor.* If firms can easily substitute other inputs for labor when the wage rate goes up, they will do so and the adverse employment effect will be relatively large. In our previous example concerning firm and industry labor demand curves, each individual firm had available a very close substitute when it alone was confronted with a wage rate increase—the labor of all the other firms.

---

14. These determinants of the elasticity of a derived demand were first developed by Alfred Marshall. See Marshall, *Principles of Economics*, 8th ed. (New York: Macmillan Co., 1920), pp.383-86.

2. *The greater the elasticity of product demand, the greater will be the elasticity of demand for labor.* Since the demand for labor is a derived demand, a small increase in the price of a product with an elastic demand will lead to a relatively large decrease in sales and output of that product, and hence in the amount of labor demanded. If the product is not essential, the labor which helps produce it will be less essential.

3. *The larger the labor cost–total cost ratio, the greater will be the elasticity of demand for labor.* If labor accounts for 90 percent of total costs, any wage increase will significantly increase total costs and product price. The resulting decrease in sales will cause a relatively large decrease in the amount of labor demanded. This effect will not be very great if labor costs are a small proportion of total costs, which has been referred to by labor groups as "the importance of being unimportant."

4. *The greater the supply responsiveness (or elasticity) of other inputs, the greater will be the elasticity of demand for labor.* In addition to the existence of substitutes (point 1), their easy obtainability for a slight increase in price is important. If for a slight price increase other inputs are easily obtainable, this is a responsive supply which will significantly decrease the amount of labor demanded. For example, if machines are easily obtainable as a substitute for labor without paying premium prices for them, then a wage increase will be more likely to have large adverse employment effects.

5. *The elasticity of demand for labor will be greater in the long run than in the short run.* Relating back to proposition 1, a greater time period allows greater adjustment and the development of substitutes.

The Long-Run Demand for Labor

So far we have limited our discussion to the short run where at least one input is fixed in quantity, although our analysis of elasticity recognized the longer run adjustment and the possibility of substituting other inputs for labor. By definition the long run is a period of time sufficiently long so that all inputs can be varied by the firm. In the short run the firm's only response to a wage rate change is to vary labor employment and output. When faced with a wage rate increase in the long run, however, the firm can substitute capital or other inputs for labor and maintain its output level. Thus the employment of labor may be reduced when wages increase either because output is contracted or because other inputs are substituted for labor to maintain the output level. This observation merely leads us back to proposition 5 above that the demand curve for labor will tend to be more elastic in the long run.

Once again this conclusion has important implications for the functioning of real world labor markets. To return again to our union example, this theoretical conclusion suggests that unions will be more successful in imposing above-equilibrium wage rates in the short run, while in the long run this influence may be largely negated by increased input flexibility. This conclusion is also consistent with numerous real world observations. In the long run firms may even choose to relocate their physical plants and facilities as a response to excessive increases in labor costs. Recent movements of several major corporate production operations to the South or abroad may be explained partially by this phenomenon.[15]

CONCLUDING REMARKS

You have been exposed to a number of theoretical labor market concepts in this chapter. Many of these concepts are simple extensions of basic economic principles, but you should not be lulled to sleep by their simplicity. Labor market supply and demand forces are extremely important influences upon the actual operation of labor markets in the United States. An understanding of the concepts presented in this chapter is not sufficient to enable you to comprehend and explain all labor market occurrences which you confront, but it is necessary to provide a framework for further analysis and study. There are several more building blocks to be added before the process is complete.

It should also be noted that the labor demand theory reviewed here, sometimes called the *marginal productivity theory*, has been the subject of some criticism. Some economists have argued that real world businesses rarely make the kinds of marginal calculations implied in the theory. Others contend that many businesses are motivated by objectives other than pure profit maximization, especially in corporate settings where ownership and management of the enterprise are separate functions of different groups, i.e., stockholders and managers. Defenders of marginal productivity theory respond that marginal analysis of the type suggested in the theory is in fact typical of the economic calculations made by firms. They admit that other objectives such as growth, sales, or even prestige may be prevalent in many firms, but they argue that the goal of profit maximization is still a dominant business objective.[16]

We will accept the labor market theory presented in this chapter as a point of departure for subsequent elaboration. The next step is to take these supply and demand concepts, dropping some largely unrealistic assumptions as we go, and consider the questions of how wages are determined and how resources are allocated by market and nonmarket forces. These considerations are presented in Chapter 3.

---

15. On the subject of labor demand adjustments see, for example, Daniel S. Hamermesh, "Econometric Studies of Labor Demand and Their Application to Policy Analysis," *Journal of Human Resources* (Fall, 1976), pp. 507-25.

16. See, for example, Richard Lester, "Shortcomings of Marginal Analysis for Wage-Employment Problems," *American Economic Review* (March, 1946), pp. 63-82; and Fritz Machlup, "Marginal Analysis and Empirical Research," *American Economic Review* (September, 1946), pp. 519-54.

CHAPTER SUMMARY

Labor market supply and demand forces have an important impact upon the allocation of resources and the determination of wages in our economy. This chapter has presented the basic components of labor supply and demand theory, given the assumption of purely competitive labor markets.

The most basic measurements of labor supply are the concepts of the labor force and the labor force participation rate. Theoretically the analysis of labor supply begins with the individual worker who is motivated to work by income but who is also motivated to not work by the utility of leisure. The individual attempts to maximize total utility in allocating hours to work and leisure. Leisure (or income) becomes particularly valuable when it is scarce; the rational individual may first increase work time as wages increase but will eventually increase leisure time resulting in the backward-bending labor supply curve. The theoretical analysis becomes more complicated when the family, rather than the individual, is defined as the relevant decision-making unit. Here a third category of time allocation, nonmarket work, must be added to account for the valuable but uncompensated household efforts of family members. The family labor supply decision is affected also by permanent wealth, foregone alternatives over the family life cycle, and noneconomic considerations.

In addition to quantitative labor supply factors, the quality of the labor force may be considered abstractly through human capital theory. This approach views the acquisition of marketable, productivity-enhancing skills as investments intended to yield increased lifetime earnings. The education and training decisions of many workers can be analyzed from this perspective.

Over a longer period of time, it is also important to consider changing population and age distribution patterns as they affect the labor force and consumer demands. All these considerations yield expected relationships between wages and the quantity of labor supplied which can be expressed by short-run and long-run labor supply curves.

Labor demand is a derived demand, dependent upon labor productivity but also derived from the demand for the final product. A profit-maximizing firm in the short run will hire labor as long as the expected additional revenue from the last worker hired *(MRP)* is greater than or equal to the additional cost *(WR)*. Geometrically, the firm's marginal revenue product for labor curve is equivalent to the labor demand curve in the short run. For the entire industry or economy, the labor demand curve is derived from a number of possible MRP_L curves, each of which corresponds to a different product price.

A very important theoretical and practical labor demand concept is the elasticity of labor demand, which measures the responsiveness of labor demand to a wage change. In the long run, for example, the demand curve for labor will tend to be more elastic as firms may substitute additional capital inputs for production if labor costs (wages) increase.

KEY TERMS

civilian labor force
labor force participation rate
moonlighting

reservation wage
substitution effect
income effect

added worker hypothesis
discouraged worker hypothesis
human capital theory
law of diminishing returns
total product of labor

average product of labor
marginal product of labor
marginal revenue product
elasticity of demand for labor

REVIEW QUESTIONS

1. What have been the major trends in the labor force and labor force participation rate statistics in the United States in the twentieth century? How would you explain the significant increase in the LFPR for women?

2. How would you explain the backward bending range of the individual labor supply curve? Would you say that most medical doctors engaged in private practice are on the forward sloping or backward bending portion of their labor supply curves? Why?

3. Recently, the mandatory retirement requirement at age 65 has been raised or eliminated for most workers. What impacts would you expect this to have on labor supply over time? Think this through carefully and defend your answers.

4. Theoretically, under what conditions would a profit-maximizing firm be "underhiring" labor? If the product which a certain type of labor produces suddenly becomes in high demand, what would you predict would happen to the demand for this labor? Why?

5. As a union leader interested in increasing workers' wages would you prefer to organize a skilled craft or an unskilled group of workers? Explain your answer with reference to the determinants of the elasticity of demand for labor.

6. To what extent have you considered labor market demand and supply conditions in making your educational and career choices? Based upon what you learned in this chapter, what can you conclude about the expected labor market for your preferred line of work 10 years from now?

ADDITIONAL REFERENCES

Becker, Gary S. *Human Capital: A Theoretical and Empirical Analysis.* New York: National Bureau of Economic Research, 1964.

Bowen, William G., and A. T. Finegan. *The Economics of Labor Force Participation.* Princeton, N.J.: Princeton University Press, 1969.

Cain, Glen G. *Married Women in the Labor Force.* Chicago: University of Chicago Press, 1966.

Fleisher, Belton M., and Thomas J. Kniesner, *Labor Economics: Theory, Evidence, and Policy.* 2d ed., Englewood Cliffs, N.J.: Prentice-Hall, Inc., 1980, chaps. 3 and 4.

Kreps, Juanita, and Robert Clark. *Sex, Age, and Work: The Changing Composition of the Labor Force.* Baltimore and London: Johns Hopkins University Press, 1975.

Owen, John O. *Working Hours,* Lexington, Mass.: D. C. Heath, 1979.

Rothschild, K. W. *The Theory of Wages.* New York: Augustus M. Kelley, 1967, chaps. II and III.

Schultz, T. W., ed. *Economics of the Family.* Chicago: University of Chicago Press, 1974.

THE WORLD
OF WORK . . .

More Wives in the Labor Force Have Husbands
with "Above-Average" Incomes

Not only has the labor force participation rate of married women increased significantly in the post-war period, but certain patterns of participation by family income level have emerged. In the excerpt below the results of a study dealing with this subject are summarized, and the income distribution implications are noted.

Did the wives who entered the labor force in great numbers during the 1960s and 1970s come from lower income families, middle income families, or upper income families?

Data collected in the Current Population Survey show that 60 percent of the total net increase in the number of working wives occurred among wives who had husbands with incomes in the upper middle and upper ranges. Moreover, among these women, the older wives (those age 35 and over) with school-age children experienced significant increases in their rates of labor force activity relative to their counterparts in the lower and lower middle income ranges. Nevertheless, wives whose husbands had below-average (lower and lower middle) incomes continued to have higher rates of labor force participation, regardless of their age and fertility status.

Between 1960 and 1977, the number of married women in the labor force rose from 10.9 million to 19.6 million, an increase of 8.7 million working wives. About 2.7 million of them were from families in which husbands' incomes were in the upper middle range of the income distribution, and 2.4 million had husbands with incomes in the upper range. Therefore, women from the top half of the income distribution accounted for 58.5 percent of the total increase.

The relationship between the labor force participation rate of married women and the income of their husbands has been observed to be negative. Moreover, when regression analysis was used to control for age, the presence of small children, the educational level of wives, and other factors, the relationship remained negative. In recent years, a number of economists have found that the basic participation-income relationship has be-come *less* negative. In fact, when the various factors related to the participation of married women and their husbands' income are controlled, the results suggest that the labor force rate has been rising more for wives whose husbands' incomes are in the top half of the income distribution than it has for those whose husbands' incomes were in the lower half. . . .

Childbearing and childrearing usually have at least a temporary impact on labor force activity, although their deterrent effect is much less pronounced today than in the past. Married women under age 35 and married women age 35 and over were divided into three fertility groups: wives with no children under 18, wives with children age 6 to 17 only, and wives with children under age 6. Among the younger married women, absolute changes in participation rates of wives with children under age 6 and those with no children under age 18 were about the same, regardless of the husband's income. For wives with children age 6 to 17 only, participation rates increased by a greater amount in the upper half of the distribution than in the lower half. However, this fertility group was small (in 1977, it accounted for only 18 percent of the younger wives), so its change did not have much impact on participation rates for all married women under age 35.

Among older married women (age 35 and over) with children age 6 to 17 only, participation rates were much greater if their husbands had above-average incomes. Furthermore, there was a slight indication of the same pattern for those with no children under 18. In 1977, these two fertility groups accounted for over 90 percent of all the married women age 35 and over, and, consequently, they had a substantial impact on the total rates when all the fertility groups are combined. For older women with children under 6, a very small group, changes in participation rates were generally uniform across the distribution of husbands' income.

Some economists have pondered the effect of this uneven increase in the number of working wives on the overall national distribution of income. If wives of upper middle and upper income husbands are entering the labor force in relatively greater numbers, it is probable that when their earnings are added to the incomes of their husbands, the gap between above-average income families and below-average income families will widen. . . .

_____

Source: Abridged from Paul Ryscavage, "More Wives in the Labor Force Have Husbands with 'Above-Average' Incomes," *Monthly Labor Review* (June, 1979), pp. 40-42.

APPENDIX
The Theory of Choice
Between Work and Leisure[1]

The individual worker's allocation of time between hours of work and hours of leisure is often analyzed with the tools of consumer demand theory. The theory assumes that individuals derive satisfaction, or utility, from both income (obtained from market work) and leisure. Any satisfaction gained from working, per se, is ignored and only the income resulting from work is presumed to provide utility. The worker will therefore maximize his or her utility by choosing the optimal allocation of time between income-generating activities (work) and leisure.

This theoretical framework is presented in Figure 2-A1. The diagram portrays the preference map for a hypothetical worker confronted with the allocation decision mentioned above. This individual's preferences with respect to income and leisure are depicted by a series of indifference curves (U_1, U_2, and U_3), each of which shows different combinations of income and leisure which generate equivalent total utility to the worker. These indifference curves have the same characteristics as the indifference curves utilized in consumer demand theory—they are negatively sloped and convex from the origin, they cannot cross, and curves further from the origin represent higher levels of satisfaction.[2] The convexity is depicted also by the concept of the *marginal rate of substitution (MRS)*. The MRS between income and leisure shows the relative ease by which leisure can be substituted for income, and it is measured by the expression $\Delta I/\Delta L$. ΔI represents the amount of income that the worker is subjectively willing to give up in order to gain a given increment of leisure ΔL, without changing the total level of satisfaction (i.e., while staying on the same indifference curve).

Note that Figure 2-A1 shows a diminishing marginal rate of substitution as leisure is substituted for income ($\Delta I_1/\Delta L_1 > \Delta I_2/\Delta L_2$). This merely says that if the worker's income is high and hours of work long, he or she will be willing to give up a substantial chunk of that income in order to acquire a relatively small increase in leisure. Conversely, when income is low and leisure hours large, the worker will give up a considerable amount of leisure to gain a relatively small increase in income. Remember also that indifference curves are a conceptual device used to portray a worker's subjective preferences.

Figure 2-A1 alone can tell us nothing about the actual optimal allocation of time for this worker. To derive the optimal number of hours worked, we must know the wage rate for the worker's occupation (note that Figure 2-A1 assumes that there are 100 nonsleeping hours per week available for work and leisure combined, so that leisure hours are measured from left to right and work hours from right to left on the horizontal axis). Assume that this wage rate is $5

---

1. This appendix presumes some knowledge of the concepts of intermediate price theory.
2. Consult any intermediate price theory text for the reasons for these characteristics.

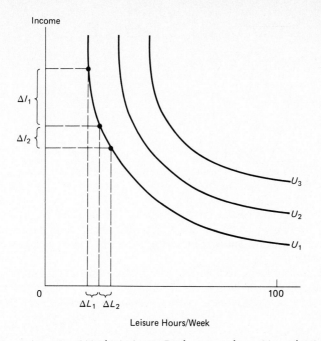

Income

ΔI_1

ΔI_2

U_3

U_2

U_1

0   ΔL_1 ΔL_2 100

Leisure Hours/Week

Figure 2-A1   Income (Work)-Leisure Preferences for a Hypothetical Worker

per hour, and ignore overtime increments. If our worker worked all 100 hours, he or she would earn $500 (point *a* in Figure 2-A2). If he or she did not work at all, the income would of course be $0 (point *b* in Figure 2-A2). Theoretically any option between these two extremes is possible. The line *ab* is the *budget constraint* associated with a wage rate of $5, and it is an objective, measurable constraint as opposed to the subjective indifference curves.

The point in the indifference map actually chosen will be the one which maximizes total utility. In other words, the optimal allocation will be on the furthest out attainable indifference curve. In Figure 2-A2 the optimal point is point *O′,* which corresponds on the vertical axis to 40 hours of leisure, 60 hours (100 – 40) of work, and $300 of weekly income. No other allocation will yield as much satisfaction. Geometrically, point *O′* is the point of tangency of the budget constraint and indifference curve U_2, and the slopes of the two curves are of course equal at that point. The variable slope of an indifference curve is $-\Delta I/\Delta L$, or -1 times the *MRS* defined earlier. The constant slope of the budget constraint *ab* is also $-\Delta I/\Delta L$ notationally. If you hypothetically allow *L* to decrease by 1 hour (and hours worked to increase by 1 hour), the positive increment in income ΔI is the hourly wage rate. Hence, the slope of the budget constraint is -1 times the wage rate, and the optimal allocation of time between work and leisure can be expressed algebraically as

$$-MRS = -WR$$

To put it differently, the optimum occurs where the worker's subjective willingness to substitute between income and leisure *(MRS)* equals the worker's objective ability to substitute *(WR).*

The remaining question of importance concerns the response of the worker when the wage rate changes. In Figure 2-A3 we assume that the wage rate has gone from $5 to $7, so that our worker can now earn $700 per week in the unlikely event that he or she works 100 hours (budget constraint *cb*). This enables the worker to attain a higher level of total

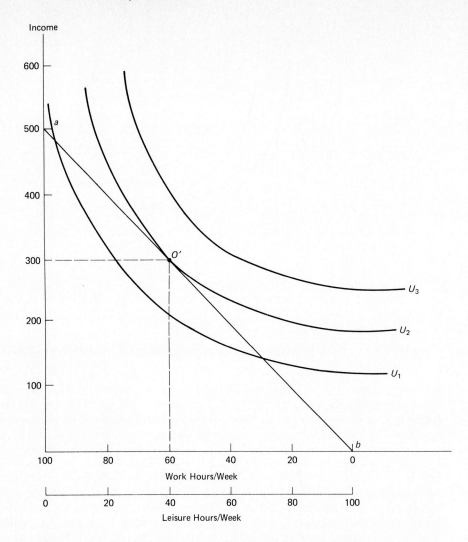

Figure 2-A2   Optimal Allocation of Time Between Work (Income) and Leisure

satisfaction on indifference curve U_3. The optimal allocation is now shown at point O'', with 54 hours of work and 46 hours of leisure. In this instance the worker is working fewer hours than previously.

It does not necessarily follow that a worker will work fewer hours as the wage rate increases. As we observed in the main text of Chapter 2, the backward bending labor supply curve suggests that hours worked may increase or decrease as the wage increases. In terms of the theoretical analysis presented here, the uncertainty of the effect may be explained by observing that the wage increase actually has two effects which work in opposite directions: the *income effect* and the *substitution effect*.

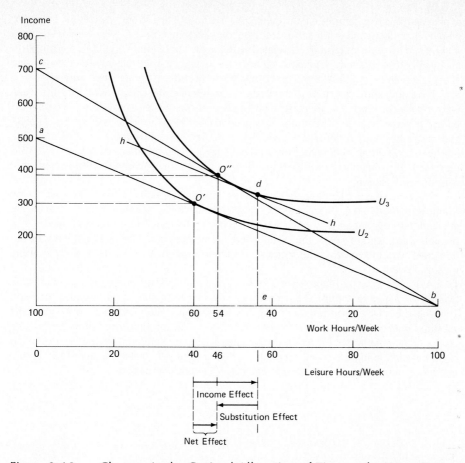

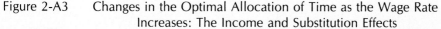

Figure 2-A3   Changes in the Optimal Allocation of Time as the Wage Rate
Increases: The Income and Substitution Effects

First, the wage increase means that at every combination of work and leisure the worker
is now better off (has more income and is on a higher indifference curve) than under the old
wage rate. It follows that the worker can afford to buy more of all goods which provide utility,
including leisure. This is the income effect, and it suggests that the worker will tend to desire
more leisure, and therefore less work, as affluence increases.

On the other hand, as the wage rate increases it becomes more costly to take additional
hours of leisure. The price of leisure, the hourly wage that must be foregone in order to take
an additional hour of leisure, has gone up. Since we normally desire less of a commodity
when its relative price has gone up, it would be expected that the worker will take less leisure
while substituting more hours of work. This is the substitution effect.

The effects are isolated geometrically in Figure 2-A3. In order to visualize the two
effects separately, it is necessary to assume that they occur one at a time, although they are
actually simultaneous. Let's assume that the income effect of the wage rate increase occurs,
but the substitution effect does not. We must geometrically allow the worker to become
better off (i.e., attain the satisfaction associated with indifference curve U_3), but not allow the
relative price of leisure, the wage rate, to increase (i.e., not allow the slope of budget line *ab*

to change). This is accomplished in Figure 2-A3 by constructing hypothetical budget line *hh,* which is parallel to budget line *ab* but tangent to indifference curve U_3. The movement from 40 hours to *0e* hours of leisure, associated with the movement from equilibrium point *0'* to the hypothetical tangency point *d,* is the income effect. For a wage rate increase, the income effect taken alone will lead the worker to work fewer hours, as described above.

If we now allow the slope of the budget line to reflect the actual increase in the wage rate, and the corresponding increase in the price of leisure, we must move from hypothetical point *d* to actual point *0''*. The slope of budget line *cb* reflects the actual new wage rate of $7 and the higher price of leisure. As we argued earlier, the substitution effect of the wage increase, taken alone, should lead the worker to devote less time to leisure since its price has increased. The movement from *0e* hours of leisure to 46 hours in Figure 2-A3 is consistent with our expectation.

The two effects taken together work in opposite directions, as we observed. In the example of Figure 2-A3, the income effect is greater than the substitution effect so that the net effect of the wage increase is that the worker chooses to work fewer hours. However, it is possible that a worker's work (income)-leisure preferences could be such that the substitution effect would outweigh the income effect, resulting in more hours worked as wage increases occur.

As was noted in the main text of Chapter 2, as wages have increased in the United States over time the general trend has been for hours worked to decline in the twentieth century. This suggests that for the population as a whole the income effect has outweighed the substitution effect. However, remember that this conclusion does not follow for all subgroups of the population. Evidence clearly suggests that for married women the substitution effect has predominated. This is consistent with our observation that the labor force participation of women has increased dramatically in the postwar period.

Chapter 3

Labor Market Operations:
Wage Determination and
Resource Allocation

At the center of any consideration of labor market operations are the questions of how wage levels are determined and how labor is allocated to the production of various goods and services. As we shall see in subsequent chapters, many serious economic problems which confront our society are related to the efficiency (or inefficiency) of these labor market operations. We begin in this chapter by combining the supply and demand concepts developed in Chapter 2 so that we may analyze the processes of wage determination and resource allocation under conditions of pure competition.

However, most labor markets do not meet the requirements of perfect competition. The assumption that neither workers nor employers have any power over labor markets is often unrealistic, and we will drop that assumption later to consider various imperfectly competitive labor market models and situations. The impact of the government in areas such as occupational licensing and minimum wage legislation will also be considered. The assumptions of labor mobility and perfect information noted in Chapter 2 are also seldom met. In this chapter we consider restrictions on labor mobility such as segmented labor markets, as well as the implications of a heterogeneous labor force resulting from the differing human capital endowments of individuals. In addition, we will analyze employer and worker job search behavior under imperfect labor market information. Finally, we consider the actual compensation decisions of firms which have discretion over such decisions. By the end of this chapter, you should have a reasonably good feel for the complexity of labor market operations. This will make it much easier and more meaningful to tackle the perplexing problems of wage differentials, inflation, and unemployment presented in Chapter 4.

WAGE AND RESOURCE ALLOCATION
UNDER PURE COMPETITION

You will recall that the assumptions required for perfectly competitive labor markets were outlined at the beginning of Chapter 2. Given these conditions, labor supply and demand forces interact to determine the number of workers employed in each occupation and the wage that will be paid. If we combine an industry-wide labor demand curve such as the one portrayed in Figure 2-6, page 38, with a labor supply curve to an occupation (see Figure 2-3, page 31) a labor market equilibrium results such as the one shown in Figure 3-1a. For this occupation, a total of OL_1 workers (labor hours) will be hired and each employer must pay the market wage OW_1. Since, by our assumptions, each employing firm is too small to influence the market wage rate and all workers in an occupation are equally skilled, the individual firm can hire as many workers as it wishes at the market wage. This means that the supply of labor in this occupation to each firm is perfectly elastic at the market wage, as shown in Figure 3-1b. The individual firm will choose to hire OL_2 workers (labor hours) by the process described in Chapter 2. We could construct similar supply and demand situations for each occupation in the economy, and for each there would be a stable equilibrium wage and employment level. This is assured because each firm hires the profit-maximizing quantity of labor.

It is important to note that labor is allocated efficiently by competitive market forces. *Allocative efficiency* requires that each worker be working where he or she is most productive. This situation maximizes total production in the economy. Assume for a moment that worker A is most productive in occupation 1 but is currently employed in occupation 2. Since each firm pays a market wage rate which reflects worker productivity (recall that $MRP_L = WR$ was the hiring rule derived in Chapter 2), worker A will be induced by the higher wage rate to shift to occupation 1. Thus, the maximizing decisions of individual firms and workers ensure an efficient allocation of labor.

Competitive labor markets also reallocate labor efficiently over time as supply and demand conditions change. This fact was already noted in Figure 1-2, page 9. Changing supply and/or demand conditions are frequent in most

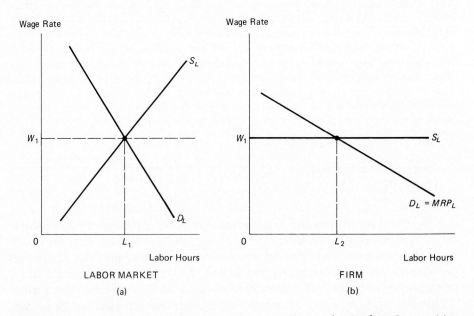

Figure 3-1   Wage and Employment Determination under Perfect Competition

market economies, and the resulting changes in market wage rates act as signals to maximizing firms and workers. The responses of workers and firms to these new market signals ensure that labor is reallocated efficiently over time, as observed in Chapter 1.

The perfectly competitive labor market model is an oversimplified abstraction of reality, but this does not mean that the model is irrelevant for the study of labor market operations. Many of the tools of analysis which we have used in developing the competitive model, such as supply and demand functions, market equilibrium, elasticity, short run and long run, are best learned using the competitive model. These concepts are equally useful, however, in analyzing real world, imperfect labor markets. Furthermore, the competitive model may be used as a standard by which to judge the efficiency and possible social costs of real world labor markets, and we can assess more intelligently the social trade-offs involved in deviations from pure competition. Finally, as we shall see, the competitive model still provides considerable explanatory and predictive power in analyzing labor market behavior. This is the ultimate test of a model.

WAGES AND RESOURCE ALLOCATION: IMPERFECTLY COMPETITIVE LABOR MARKETS

Because of the simplicity of the perfectly competitive labor market model, we must consider a number of more realistic modifications. In this section, we drop the assumption that neither workers nor employers have any control over labor markets. We will also consider a couple of examples of governmental influence on labor market operations. Of course, each of our examples will represent a departure from perfect competition, and a corresponding departure from optimal efficiency in resource allocation.

Monopsony

Although somewhat unusual, there are situations in our economy where one firm is the dominant employer of a particular kind of labor in a given geographic area. These dominant employers are not small and powerless relative to the relevant labor market; rather they exert a significant amount of control over the labor market. The extreme case is that of a *monopsony labor market*, where there is only one buyer of labor. A strict monopsony situation is unlikely to exist, but the results of the monopsony model can be generalized to the "dominant employer" case.

The monopsonistic firm cannot assume that an unlimited number of workers will be available at the prevailing market wage rate. The firm will probably have to raise the wage rate to attract additional workers from other companies or occupations in other geographic areas, since it is the only firm hiring in a given geographic labor market. As the only firm in this labor market it has the power to establish the necessary wage rate, rather than just accepting the wage established by the market. Graphically, this firm faces an upward-sloping labor supply curve such as S_L in Figure 3-2. This supply curve S_L indicates the wage rate, or *average labor cost* (*ALC*), that is necessary to attract the desired number of workers. If more workers are needed, the wage must increase to draw them into the firm.

Marginal Labor Cost. An interesting point emerges here, however. Since, by assumption, these workers are all equally qualified, how can the firm pay different wage rates to equally productive workers who are simply hired at different times? The answer is: It can't. When our monopsony firm pays a higher wage to attract an additional worker, it must also increase the wage of all existing employees to that level. Therefore, the additional cost to the firm per hour of hiring one more worker is not only the wage rate of the added worker, but also the increases in the wage rates of the existing workers. Put differently, the *marginal labor cost* per hour (*MLC*) is greater than the *ALC*, or the wage rate. Notice that Figure 3-2 portrays this situation. The *MLC* curve lies above and diverges from the *ALC*, or labor supply, curve. To reiterate, the *MLC* curve depicts both the added labor cost of additional workers hired and the wage increments paid to existing workers. As we observed earlier, the firm's labor demand curve is equivalent to the MRP_L curve.

How will our monopsony firm behave in this situation? To maximize its profits, it should hire workers as long as the extra revenue from the production

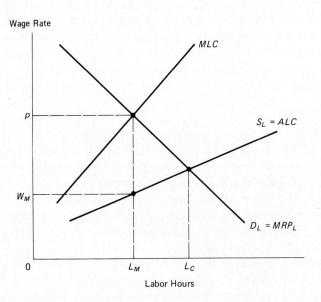

Figure 3-2   Wage and Employment Determination under Monopsony

of additional workers is greater than or equal to the extra cost of hiring additional workers. The additional revenue is once again measured by the MRP_L, but now the additional cost is not just the wage rate, but the total MLC. The firm should hire up to the point where $MRP_L = MLC$ to maximize profits. This corresponds to OL_M labor hours in Figure 3-2.

Wage Rates and Resource Allocation. The one remaining question is a tricky one. What wage rate will be paid to these OL_M workers? The answer becomes somewhat more apparent if we rephrase the question. What wage rate will be necessary to get OL_M workers to supply their services to our monopsonistic firm? Worded in this way, it should be clear that the answer comes from the labor supply curve. The wage rate associated with the supply of OL_M workers is OW_M.

As we projected earlier, monopsony forces in labor markets alter the wage determination and resource allocation processes. Note in Figure 3-2 that the equilibrium wage rate OW_M is less than the marginal revenue product of labor, OP, whereas under perfect competition, $MRP_L = WR$. This has been referred to as the "monopsonistic exploitation of labor." Remember also that with perfect competition the equilibrium employment level was where the MRP_L equaled the supply price of labor, WR. With monopsony, the equilibrium employment is at a lower level (OL_M rather than OL_C). Hence, the theory suggests that monopsony leads to lower wages and less employment than would be the case under perfectly competitive conditions. These wage and employment restrictions of the monopsony firm, dictated by its desire to maximize profits, tend to distort the efficiency of the allocative mechanism which we previously observed in competitive labor markets.

Although there are few examples of pure monopsony in today's labor markets, there is evidence that some workers confront conditions that approximate monopsony. Several studies have demonstrated the existence of monopsony power in professional sports, because player contracts limit the mobility of professional athletes once they have signed with a particular team.[1] This monopsony power of sports employers was lessened in the 1970s as professional athletes gained the opportunity for free agent status under some conditions. Nevertheless, the baseball strike of 1981 was fought primarily over the issue of compensation to teams losing free agents to the highest bidder. Monopsony employer power has also been found to be present in some markets for nurses and school teachers.[2]

---

1. See Simon Rottenburg, "The Baseball Player's Labor Market," *Journal of Political Economy* (June, 1956), pp. 242-58; and Roger G. Noll (ed.), *Government and the Sports Business* (Washington: The Brookings Institution, 1974).

2. See C. R. Link and John H. Landon, "Monopsony and Union Power in the Market for Nurses," *Southern Economic Journal* (April, 1975), pp. 649-59; and Landon and Robert N. Baird, "Monopsony in the Market for Public School Teachers," *American Economic Review* (December, 1971), pp. 966-71.

Labor Supply Restrictions

In the real world of labor markets there are a number of possible restrictions on the entry of workers into a particular occupation. These restrictions were not considered in our earlier perfectly competitive assumptions. Entry into occupations requiring specific skills and training is limited by the capacity of training institutions and programs. To practice medicine, one must be accepted into and graduate from a medical school; and to practice carpentry on certain jobs, one may have to enter and complete a union-sponsored apprenticeship program.

Most states require licenses to engage in certain occupations such as hairdressing or real estate sales, and the licensing standards are often established by those already in the occupation. Licensing which restricts entry into occupations is typically the result of laws enacted to protect consumers and ensure high-quality goods and services. However, several studies have concluded that licensing laws are abused, that the benefits to consumers are often questionable, and that they permit the establishment of artificially high wages and discriminatory practices in the restricted occupation.[3]

The theoretical results of these restrictions are shown in Figure 3-3. Given unrestricted competitive conditions, OL_1 workers (labor hours) would be hired at an equilibrium wage of OW_1 and resources would be allocated efficiently in this market. Assume, however, that a supply restriction of the type mentioned above is imposed so that only OL_R workers can actually enter the occupation. Given this imposed shortage of workers, the demand curve indicates that employers are willing to pay a wage of OW_R, considerably higher than the competitive wage. This higher wage would be advantageous, of course, to those fortunate enough to be in the restricted occupation.

It makes no difference if the restriction is created by a union, by a training institution, or by government; nor does it matter if there is justification for the restriction, which there often is. The result is that the allocative mechanism is always distorted. Note in Figure 3-3 that the effective labor supply curve becomes abc rather than $absS_L$ with the restriction. Although additional workers would like to supply their services as the wage increases above OW_b, they are precluded from doing so by the restriction. Hence, above point b on the effective supply curve abc changes in the wage rate do not lead to any changes in employment. Therefore, labor cannot be reallocated as changes in market conditions are reflected in wage rate changes. Furthermore, the workers who are excluded by the entry restriction are forced into nonrestricted occupations, increasing the labor supply and decreasing the market wage there. Once again, labor markets are not allowed to perform their optimal resource allocation

3. See Benjamin Shimberg, et al., *Occupational Licensing: Practices and Policies* (Washington: Public Affairs Press, 1973); and B. Peter Pashigian, "Occupational Licensing and the Interstate Mobility of Professionals," *Journal of Law and Economics* (April, 1979), pp. 1-26.

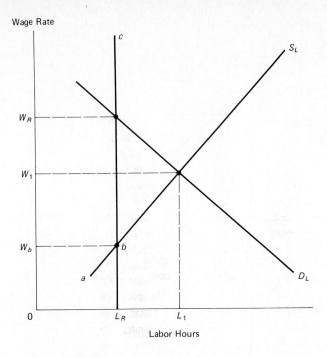

Figure 3-3   Supply Restriction

function. Labor is underallocated to the restricted occupation and overallo-cated to the unrestricted ones.

Wage Imposition

The misallocation effects discussed above occurred because of external restrictions on labor market entry, or supply. Let's now consider a somewhat different kind of restriction, one on wage levels. Using Figure 3-4 as a point of reference, assume the initial competitive conditions exist with a resulting wage of OW_1 and employment of OL_1. Now assume that some outside influence demands that a wage of OW_R be paid, rather than OW_1. What would be the effect of this wage imposition? At a wage of OW_R employers are willing to hire (demand) only OL_R rather than OL_1 labor hours. Employment again declines, but now because of the imposition of an artificially high wage rate rather than because of entry restriction. Note also that an even larger number of workers, OL_2, are willing to work at the higher wage rate, but the services of many of them ($OL_2 - OL_R$) are not demanded. Once again some workers are forced out of this occupation and must spill over into others, depressing wages in the occupations into which they are driven. The wage structure is distorted and labor is again misallocated.

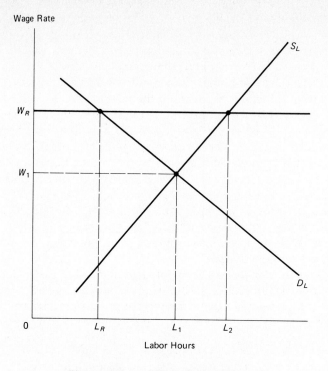

Figure 3-4   Wage Imposition

Unions. What outside influence might have the power and desire to impose the artificially high wage rate? Certainly a trade union is one possibility. A union which is successful in organizing all or almost all workers in an industry or occupation may have the power to impose such a wage level. However, where trade unions exist, wage levels are usually determined by collective bargaining, and employers are likely to resist strongly such a union objective. Furthermore, since there is an excess supply of workers who are willing to work at the higher wage but who cannot find employment (once again, $OL_2 - OL_R$), these excess workers may face a strong incentive to accept work from a nonunion employer at a somewhat lower wage. In other words, in some cases unions may desire to impose a high wage but may be unable to do so successfully.

Minimum Wage Laws. Another important example of an outside influence establishing a wage above the competitive level is the federal government and our minimum wage law.[4] The present hourly minimum of $3.35 which

---

4. The source of the federal minimum wage law is the Fair Labor Standards Act of 1938, the most recent amendment to which became effective January 1, 1979. Many states also have their own minimum wage statutes.

became effective in 1981 applies to most, but not all, workers in the United States, with employees of small trade and service firms, farms, and domestic households the main exclusions. Although the federal minimum wage is typically no more than 50 percent of average hourly earnings in manufacturing industries, it still may be higher than the competitive market wage for some unskilled, low-productivity workers. If the market for such low-skilled workers can be portrayed by a diagram similar to that in Figure 3-4 with OW_1 as the market wage and OW_R as the legislated minimum wage, an important and ironic possibility emerges. The diagram suggests that the imposition of wage rate OW_R on this market will decrease employment from OL_1 to OL_R. Furthermore, workers wish to work more hours (and/or more workers wish to work) in this labor market at the higher wage OW_R. Thus, it is possible that a government program designed to provide some income protection to low-wage workers may actually be detrimental to some of them. It may force employers to lay off or cut back the hours of some low-wage workers; thus their income would actually decline.

Actually, the ultimate employment impact of an increased statutory minimum wage depends upon the elasticity of demand (and supply) of the affected occupations. If you visually superimpose a highly inelastic (near vertical) labor demand curve in Figure 3-4, you can see that the lost employment resulting from the imposition of minimum wage OW_R is much less than that resulting with demand curve D_L. This brings us back to the question of what determines the elasticity of labor demand, a question which we answered in Chapter 2. Low-productivity, unskilled workers are not likely to be producing essential goods or offering essential services, and the availability of substitutes for their efforts is likely to be great. These theoretical observations lead us to conclude that the demand for the type of labor most affected by the minimum wage is probably rather elastic, and the potential adverse employment effect correspondingly large.

A large body of research exists on this subject. Although results differ, the majority of studies seem to support the theoretical conclusion that the imposition of the minimum wage does have an adverse effect on employment in some industries.[5] Furthermore, recent studies increasingly suggest that the minimum wage is particularly harmful to certain low-wage subgroups of the population such as teenagers, perhaps contributing significantly to the severe teenage unemployment problem.[6] In every Congressional debate over increasing the minimum wage since 1973, some form of teenage exemption to the

---

5. See Robert S. Goldfarb, "The Policy Content of Quantitative Minimum Wage Research," *Proceedings of the Industrial Relations Research Association,* 1974, pp. 261-68; and Finis Welch, "Minimum Wage Legislation in the United States," *Western Economic Journal* (September, 1974), pp. 285-319.

6. See, for example, Douglas Adie, "Teenage Unemployment and Real Federal Minimum Wages," *Journal of Political Economy* (March-April, 1973), pp. 435-41; James F. Ragan, Jr., "The Failure of the Minimum Wage Law," *Challenge* (May-June, 1978), pp. 61-65; and Belton M. Fleisher, *Minimum Wage Regulation in Retail Trade* (Washington: American Enterprise Institute, 1981).

standard has been proposed. To date, however, no such special treatment has been adopted.

ADDITIONAL ASPECTS OF IMPERFECTLY COMPETITIVE LABOR MARKETS

Four remaining, interrelated assumptions of competitive labor markets will be modified or dropped in this section to gain a more realistic picture of actual labor market operation. Specifically, we have implicitly or explicitly assumed that labor is homogeneous, that labor market information is complete or perfect, that labor is perfectly mobile, and that employers have no wage-setting discretion. In the remainder of this chapter we drop these assumptions one by one and consider the expected results. We will analyze the search process engaged in by workers and employers to cope with inperfect information. We will also consider the concept of segmented labor markets as an alternative explanation of labor market imperfections. Finally, the compensation discretion of firms will be discussed.

Worker Heterogeneity: Human Capital Revisited

As long as we assume that all workers have equivalent skills and abilities, it is consistent to think in terms of one wage rate and one employment level. However, what makes labor economics more important and more interesting, as well as more frustrating, is that the labor force is highly differentiated. To be acceptable, our analysis must be useful in explaining the wage and employment outcomes of these differences. Although there is disagreement on the most appropriate explanations of these differences, many economists believe that a primary characteristic which differentiates workers is their skill level. Furthermore, they believe that an explanation of how the demand and supply of these skills is determined requires a simple modification of competitive labor market theory, rather than a rejection of the theory.

The modification assumes that acquiring marketable skills involves costs and lifetime earnings benefits. The acquisition process can therefore be treated as an investment, and the modified theory involves the previously mentioned principles of investment in human capital. Some important policy implications of this theory are taken up in Chapter 7, and some criticisms are presented later in this chapter. Here we will merely outline rudiments of the theory as they apply to individual workers.[7]

---

7. As cited originally in Chapter 2, the primary original sources of the modern development of human capital theory are T. W. Schultz, "Investment in Human Capital," *American Economic Review* (March, 1961), pp. 1-16; and Gary S. Becker, *Human Capital* (New York: National Bureau of Economic Research, 1964). More recently, see Mark Blaug, "The Empirical Status of Human Capital Theory: A Slightly Jaundiced Survey," *Journal of Economic Literature* (September, 1976), pp. 827-55.

Costs and Benefits. Human capital theory is based upon a simple set of relationships: education and training enhance a worker's productivity or skill level, which in turn enhances the worker's lifetime earnings. You should not be deceived by the simple logic of these relationships, however. A number of complex issues lie beneath the surface. Keep in mind, for example, that this theory emphasizes solely the monetary costs and benefits of an investment in education or training, while ignoring any nonmonetary considerations. There may be a considerable psychological cost involved in taking a course in differential equations. Similarly, there is probably an important lifetime enjoyment, or consumption, benefit resulting from completing a course in music appreciation. However, neither of these nonmonetary effects is considered in human capital analysis.

What are the relevant monetary costs and benefits to be included? The relevant benefits of a human capital investment are the lifetime additions to earnings attributable to that investment. Thus, the relevant benefits of an investment in a college education are the lifetime earnings above those which the individual could have earned without the college education. The relevant costs are, first, all out-of-pocket costs which would not have been incurred had the individual not made the investment. For a college education these would include tuition, fees, books, and other incidental expenses. Excluded would be room and board since these costs would be incurred anyway. The second and more important type of cost is the opportunity cost of the individual's time: the amount of income that the person gives up during the investment period by not engaging in full-time market work.

Present Value. There is one additional complication which must be clarified before the investment decision process can be completed. Human capital investment decisions are made in the present, but the benefits (and occasionally the costs) are derived in the future. Assume, for example, that an individual can expect an additional $5000 per year in earnings for 40 years as a result of an investment in a college education. Are the total benefits merely $5000 × 40 years, or $200,000? Unfortunately no, because these $5000 increments are future earnings to be received from 1 to 40 years from now, and individuals value a sum of money more today than the same sum of money in the future.

Consider it this way. If the market rate of interest is 8 percent and you put about $92 in the bank today, you will receive about $100 a year from today. The *present value* of $100 to be received in 1 year is not $100, but only about $92 today. In general the present value of future earnings is derived by discounting those earnings by the market interest rate. Furthermore, earnings to be received in the more distant future must be discounted more heavily. Specifically, the present value of $100 to be received 1 year from now, given an 8 percent interest rate, is $100/1.08 = $92.59. The present value of $100 to be received 2 years from now is $100/(1.08)^2 = $100/1.17 = $85.47, and so on. Make sure that you understand the idea of discounting future earnings to their present value before continuing.

We now have a grasp of the relevant costs, benefits, and discounting procedure utilized in human capital analysis. Using our numerical example from above, let us assume that the relevant costs of the college education are $50,000. The present value of the earnings stream is summarized as follows:

$$\text{Present value} = \frac{\$5000}{(1 + .08)} + \frac{\$5000}{(1 + .08)^2} + \frac{\$5000}{(1 + .08)^3} + \ldots + \frac{\$5000}{(1 + .08)^{40}}$$

$$= \sum_{i=1}^{40} \frac{\$5000}{(1 + .08)^i} = \$59,623$$

These hypothetical calculations can be explained as follows. We assume that an individual can expect an additional $5000 per year in earnings resulting from a college education, beginning at age 23 and ending at age 62 (40 years). The summation notation, $\sum_{i=1}^{40}$, merely expresses in summary form the addition of the discounted $5000 for each of 40 years into the future at an 8 percent discount rate. The result, which can be looked up in any discounting table, suggests that the value today of that expected additional earnings stream is $59,623. If the cost, including foregone earnings, of the college education is $50,000, we can conclude that the investment pays off in the sense that the discounted expected benefits exceed the costs.

Private Rate of Return. Alternatively, we can approach this human capital question by calculating the private rate of return from this investment. With this method, we ask the question: What rate of return is our hypothetical individual earning on his or her college investment of $50,000? After all, if it is only the monetary return that matters, should not this investment yield at least a rate of return equivalent to alternative investment opportunities? The *private rate of return* on any investment is the rate of interest at which the present value of the individual earnings attributable to that investment is equal to the private cost of the investment. In our example, the unknown rate of return *r* must be substituted for the known interest rate, 8 percent, to satisfy the following:

$$\text{Total cost (\$50,000)} = \text{present value} = \sum_{i=1}^{40} \frac{\$5000}{(1 + r)^i}$$

Using a present value table to solve for *r* in our example, we discover that the rate of return on the human capital investment is between 9 and 10 percent per year. If this rate of return exceeds the rate for alternative investments, then the human capital investment should be made.

On-the-Job Training. It is also possible for human capital investment to occur outside of a school or training institution setting, such as in the case of on-the-job training. In this case the cost of the investment may be incurred by the trainee, by the training firm, or by both. To understand this, it is necessary to distinguish between two types of on-the-job training. *General training* is training which is equally useful in all firms and industries, such as training in the ability to read. *Specific training* is training that is useful only in the firm that provides the training, such as tank repair training in the military. Although most training involves elements of both, the distinction is nevertheless important. It will generally not be advantageous for a firm to invest in general training for its employees, because the firm has no way of capturing the returns from this investment. If it attempts to pay a wage below the market wage after the training in order to capture the return, the employee will probably accept the higher market wage with another firm. However, firms may very well finance the investment in specific training because they can realize a return in the form of the difference between the worker's posttraining value to the firm and the posttraining wage rate.

Skill and Earnings Differentials. There are a number of complications to human capital analysis, but for now we are concerned with the application of this theory to explain skill and earnings differentials in labor markets. Whether the investment is in a college education, a training program, or some other form of human capital improvement, different individuals will expect different rates of return from the same type of investment. Individuals differ in their ability to transform a human capital investment into increased skills and potential earnings. Another explanation of observed skill and earnings differentials is that individuals also differ with respect to the amount of funds which are available to them for investment and/or the opportunity to shift the costs to someone else. In supply and demand terms, individuals have different demands for human capital based on their interests and abilities, and they face different supplies of training opportunities. These differences in trainability and opportunities are viewed as a major explanation of skill and earning differences among workers.

To envision this analysis, consider Figure 3-5.[8] The horizontal axis shows differing dollar amounts that might be invested by individuals in training and education. The vertical axis measures the additional future earnings that result from an additional dollar invested. Each D curve in Figure 3-5 is a demand curve for training for one individual. These curves slope downward to the right as do other demand curves, and this means that dollar returns gradually decline as more and more money is invested in training. Notice also that the training demand curve for individual 1 (D_1) is lower than that of individual 2 (D_2). This simply says that the same amount of money invested by both individuals will yield a greater return to individual 2, because that person has

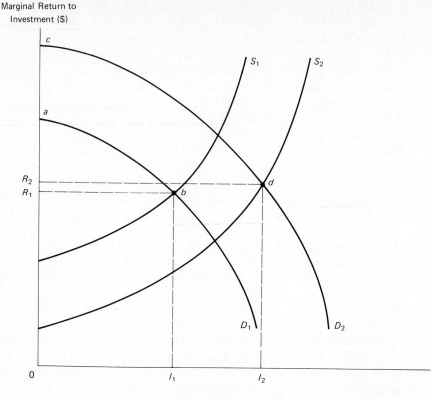

Figure 3-5   The Effect of Training, Ability, and Opportunity on Earnings

greater ability, i.e., trainability and potential productivity. Hence, these curves can be called *ability curves*.

The *S* curves are supply curves for training. Their upward-sloping shape suggests that as the expected return to training increases, the amount that will be invested also increases. Notice again that the supply curves for the two individuals differ. Individual 2 will invest more, for the same expected return, than will individual 1. This suggests that individual 2 has greater access to funds for investment from parents, savings, or financial institutions. Put differently, individual 2 has greater opportunity for investment in training, and the *S* curves can therefore be called *opportunity curves*.

The amount that each individual invests in training, and the additional earnings that result from the investment, is determined by the intersection of his or her demand (ability) and supply (opportunity) curves. Individual 1 will invest I_1, while individual 2 will invest I_2. Furthermore, the vertical distances under the demand curves are the marginal returns from each level of investment. By adding up these marginal returns for each training investment level, we arrive at the total additional earnings resulting from the investment for each individual. For individual 1, the adding up of these marginal returns yields the area $Oabl_1$ under demand curve D_1. For individual 2, the total additional earnings from the training investment are area $Ocdl_2$ under demand curve D_2.

Individual 2 obviously will have greater lifetime earnings than individual 1, assuming that their earnings were equal prior to the training or education. Why is this so? Figure 3-5 suggests that part of the explanation lies in the greater ability of individual 2, and part results from the greater opportunities for training enjoyed by individual 2. The diagram is also useful for considering the case of equal opportunity. If everyone had completely equal opportunity for human capital investment, then everyone would have the same supply curve. Earnings differentials would still exist, but they would be smaller and would result only from ability differences. To generalize from Figure 3-5, the inequality in labor incomes in a society depends upon how the demand-supply intersection points of all individuals are distributed in the diagram. In other words, differences in labor incomes can be explained by individual differences in human capital investment opportunities, and by differing abilities to benefit from those investments.

Imperfect Information and the Search Process

If complete information on job vacancies and worker availability exists, and if labor is mobile, this will do much to ensure that labor markets are operating efficiently in the allocation and reallocation of labor. But these are big, unlikely "ifs." More typically, workers have limited information about jobs, and employers have limited information about available workers. Employers and workers must engage in a search process to increase their information and range of choice, and this process consumes time and money.

Workers' Search Process. Job seekers may be unemployed or presently employed. It is more difficult for employed workers to engage in active search because time spent at work is typically unavailable for search activities. The cost of search for the employed worker is primarily the leisure time or nonmarket activity which is sacrificed during nonworking hours.

Unemployed workers who are engaging in full-time search may have voluntarily quit their previous jobs, have been fired or laid off, or be just entering or reentering the labor force. Theoretically, the voluntarily unemployed worker will have quit his or her old job if the estimated value of the expected job is greater than the value of the old job plus the income and time loss of the search process. Quit rates in the United States generally increase during periods of economic prosperity, when wages are increasing and job vacancies are abundant. These quit rates also tend to be higher in occupations where relative wages are low, skill requirements are limited, and/or firm-specific training is minimal. Obviously, in such occupations workers place a relatively small present and future value on their existing job.

The unemployed job searcher incurs costs, primarily in the form of the earnings a worker gives up by leaving an old job or by refusing job offers. These costs can, of course, be reduced if unemployment compensation is available. The costs increase as the duration of search is prolonged, but the probability of finding better job openings also increases as the search is lengthened in time. The process is really another kind of investment, involving expected net benefits but also risk and uncertainty.

Since the worker usually encounters only one job vacancy at a time, he or she must have some decision rule to be used in accepting or rejecting job offers. This will take the form of a reservation, or minimally acceptable, wage plus other minimally acceptable job characteristics. As the duration of search continues, the costs of search increase and the decision rule will probably be lowered. Eventually the worker concludes that the probable benefits of continued search are less than the additional costs, and she or he will accept the best available offer.

The search process occurs through numerous methods and channels which vary with the skill requirements of the job, the reason for the unemployment, and the age of the job seeker.[9] Various kinds of informal channels are used primarily by semiskilled and unskilled workers. These include referrals from employees and friends, responses to a vacancy notice posted on the premises, and unsolicited walk-in applications. More formal channels are utilized predominantly by skilled and professional workers. Skilled crafts workers tend to seek employment through union hiring halls. Newspaper ads are another formal source, although one which is initiated primarily by employers. Public and private employment agencies are also commonly used formal channels, with private agencies being particularly important in white-collar urban labor markets.

Employer's Search Process. Turning now to the employer's search process, it has often been observed that wage costs are to some extent a substitute for search costs. What does this mean? A high-wage employer will probably incur lower search costs because the high wages will induce sufficient numbers of qualified job applicants. Conversely, low-wage employers must spend more on recruitment to offset the labor market disadvantage resulting from the low wages.

For most jobs the employer begins with a set of hiring qualifications which are used to screen candidates. Employers are usually confronted with a large number of potential or actual applicants for each job opening, and the use of a set of qualifications reduces the list of applicants to more manageable dimen-

---

9. See Carl Rosenfeld, "Jobseeking Methods Used by American Workers," *Monthly Labor Review* (August, 1975), pp. 39-42; and Donald E. Pursell and William D. Torrence, "Age and the Job-Hunting Methods of the Unemployed," *Monthly Labor Review* (January, 1979), pp. 68-69.

sions. In addition, these qualifications presumably reflect those characteristics most important for job performance. There is a thin line, however, which separates job-related qualifications from discriminatory qualifications, a topic to which we return in Chapter 8.

In a manner similar to the worker's search process, the employer may have to vary the qualifications and the duration of search as labor market conditions change. If no applicant initially meets the qualifications, the employer must compare the cost of lowering the standards with the cost of additional search at the present standards. If economic conditions are good, lowering the qualifications may be necessary because the pool of unemployed job searchers is small. When unemployment is sizable, the cost of securing additional applicants who meet the original qualifications will be less.

One other aspect of the employer search process deserves attention. In many large firms an extensive hierarchy of jobs exists, ranging from clerical and maintenance jobs to major executive positions. For many of these jobs the employer may be either unable or unwilling to find applicants outside of the firm, which creates the possibility of the *internal labor market* mentioned in Chapter 1.[10] There may be no qualified applicants for some highly specialized jobs, and personnel practices or the union contract may dictate that present employees be considered first for job vacancies. If such an internal labor market exists, workers tend to be hired at the bottom of their relevant skill ladder and are then advanced up the internal ladder as openings emerge. Only certain entry-level jobs are open to outside hiring, and the only connection between the internal and external labor markets is at these "ports of entry." Of course, most vacancies occurring in the firm will probably necessitate outside hiring, but that hiring will be at the bottom-level port of entry as other existing workers move up the job ladder to fill the actual vacancy. If external hiring occurs only at the ports of entry, it is important to note that the employer is really hiring trainability from the outside rather than any specific job skills.[11]

Internal labor markets present an important labor mobility implication. If such practices are widespread, it will be difficult for many workers to move horizontally or upwardly to another firm. They will confront openings only at the other firm's ports of entry, in addition to the possibility of losing accrued pension and seniority benefits. It should be expected, therefore, that they will have considerable attachment to their present job and will not be freely mobile in the competitive labor market sense.

---

10. The concepts of internal and external labor markets were first systematically developed in Clark Kerr, "Labor Markets: Their Character and Consequences," *American Economic Review* (May, 1950), pp. 278-91. More recently, see Peter Doeringer and Michael Piore, *Internal Labor Markets and Manpower Analysis* (Lexington, Mass.: D. C. Heath, 1971).

11. For an elaboration, see John T. Dunlop, "Job Vacancy Measures and Economic Analysis," in *The Measurement and Interpretation of Job Vacancies* (New York: National Bureau of Economic Research, 1966), pp. 27-48.

Segmented Labor Markets

There are several important policy implications of job search theory which involve efforts to improve labor market information and mobility. The theory also provides valuable implications for unemployment compensation policy, which we take up in Chapter 9. Before considering the mobility issue more thoroughly, we will briefly review an approach to labor market imperfection which has emerged as a partial challenge to conventional human capital types of analysis. It is actually an outgrowth of the internal labor market theories which emerged in the 1950s and is based upon the belief that labor markets are separated into segments which are largely distinct, unrelated, and insulated. We have already touched on several aspects of segmented labor market theory, and here we will bring the elements of this approach together.[12]

Job Competition Theory. Several economists in the 1960s and 1970s observed that the principles of human capital theory did not seem to apply in many labor markets, e.g., unskilled labor markets in urban ghettos.[13] Increased education and training do not seem to lead to higher earnings and less unemployment, as the theory would suggest. These economists argued that it is often the demand-oriented structural characteristics of labor markets rather than the personal characteristics of workers which explain wage and employment levels.

One variant of the segmented labor market approach is the *job competition theory*.[14] This theory argues that the number of job slots is determined primarily by the existing technology. Workers' skills and their reservation wages are largely irrelevant in determining the number of jobs that are filled. Wages are determined by social custom and institutional forces, according to the theory, and are usually inflexible. A queue of workers at a fixed wage constitutes the available labor supply, and employers use various screening devices to fill job vacancies. The theory emphasizes that most hiring, promotion, and training decisions are made in the kind of internal labor market which we have already discussed.

Dual Labor Market Theory. Job competition theory has been extended to form the *dual labor market theory* mentioned in Chapter 1. To review, it is argued here that there are two distinct types of labor markets—primary and second-

---

12. An extensive survey is contained in Glen G. Cain, "The Challenge of Segmented Labor Market Theories to Orthodox Theory: A Survey," *Journal of Economic Literature* (December, 1976), pp. 1215-57.

13. See David M. Gordon, *Theories of Poverty and Underemployment* (Lexington, Mass.: D. C. Heath, 1972); and Bennett Harrison, "Education and Underemployment in the Urban Ghetto," in Gordon (ed.), *Problems in Political Economy: an Urban Perspective* (Lexington, Mass.: D. C. Heath, 1971).

14. See, most recently, Lester Thurow, *Generating Inequality* (New York: Basic Books, 1975), chaps. 4 and 5.

ary—with little mobility between the two. *Primary labor markets* consist of jobs with larger firms, many of which are unionized, and which are characterized by relatively high wages, good promotion possibilities, stable employment, ample training opportunities, and good working conditions. *Secondary labor markets*, by contrast, contain jobs that are unstable, low-skill, low-paying, and dead-end with little chance for promotion and training. Workers in secondary labor markets are particularly susceptible to discrimination and unfair discipline, and they receive little positive reinforcement from their work experiences. Therefore, according to the theory, their low skill and motivation are not inherent personal characteristics, but rather result primarily from the secondary labor market environment in which they find themselves trapped.[15]

Policy Implications. It is noteworthy that there are important differences between the policy implications of human capital theory and those of segmented labor market theory. To improve the economic position of the disadvantaged and the functioning of labor markets, human capital theorists advocate public programs of education, training, and job search assistance, several of which we will review in Chapter 7. However, segmented labor market theorists deemphasize or reject this intervention to improve the supply in labor markets. Because they emphasize the prevalence of internal and dual labor market forces, they advocate intervention on the demand side of labor markets in the form of public sector employment, wage subsidies, and antidiscrimination policies. The debate continues over these conflicting views of labor market operation, and this continuing dialogue is quite important for the evaluation of our labor market policies.

Labor Mobility and Turnover

Labor must be mobile if the economy is to be able to reallocate labor resources efficiently in response to changing consumer demands for goods and services. Over long periods of time workers in the United States have moved in significant numbers out of declining occupations and into expanding ones. Yet, over shorter periods of time, our discussions of the search process and segmented labor markets suggested that substantial barriers to mobility exist. Employers want to avoid the costs of search and training, and workers also incur search costs and lost benefits when they change employment. What do we know about the extent of actual labor mobility in the United States?

Actually, there are different definitions of labor mobility. Several recent studies have attempted to determine the extent to which workers change occupational categories during a specific period of time.[16] These studies seem

---

15. Doeringer and Piore, *Internal Labor Markets and Manpower Analysis*, chap. 8.

16. See James J. Byrne, "Occupational Mobility of Workers," *Monthly Labor Review* (February, 1975), pp. 53-59; and Dixie Sommers and Alan Eck, "Occupational Mobility in the American Labor Force," *Monthly Labor Review* (January, 1977), pp. 3-19.

to indicate that, on the average, between 8 and 9 percent of the U.S. labor force changes occupations annually, including intrafirm changes. As would be expected, the likelihood of occupational change is significantly greater for younger workers than for older ones. The movement of blue-collar workers into other blue-collar occupations is much greater than their movement into white-collar occupations.[17]

Another dimension of labor mobility is geographic mobility. Roughly 1 out of 16 Americans moves across county lines each year, and the ratio is about 1 in 8 if intracounty moves are included.[18] These ratios have been quite consistent over most of the post-World War II period. But these figures are not totally appropriate for considering the frequency of labor mobility. People move for many reasons besides improved employment: health, better residence environment, etc. It has been estimated that no more than 60 percent of all moves were explained by purely economic decisions.[19] In addition, the rate of residence change is once again highest for younger people, many of whom are simply leaving school and entering the full-time labor market for the first time.

A final method of analyzing labor mobility is to look at labor turnover from the point of view of the firm. Labor turnover is the total movement of workers into and out of the firm, and typically emphasis is given to the voluntary separation component of this movement, the quit rate. We have already mentioned the quit rate in our discussion of the search process, and we observed then that quit rates increase during times of economic expansion and decrease during contractions. In the last 30 years, annual quit rates in the United States have generally constituted from 1 to 3 percent of the labor force, and the trend has been slightly downward. Although disagreement persists, most economists have accepted the conclusion reached by Parker and Burton that these statistics seem to suggest a recent decline in voluntary labor turnover in the United States.[20]

If they are correct, why has this decline occurred? Numerous economists have argued that the increasing seniority rights, pensions, and other fringe benefits associated with job retention have made it much more costly for employees to quit their jobs. We will discuss fringe benefits in more detail in the following section. Similarly, from the employer's point of view the costs of recruiting, screening, and training new employees create an incentive to retain existing skilled workers. These two factors taken together suggest that, in

17. Carl Rosenfeld, "Occupational Mobility during 1977," *Monthly Labor Review* (December, 1979), pp. 44-48.

18. U.S. Bureau of the Census, "Geographic Mobility: March, 1975 to March, 1979," *Current Population Reports,* Series 9-20, No. 353 (Washington: U.S. Government Printing Office, 1980).

19. *Manpower Report of the President, 1974* (Washington: U.S. Government Printing Office, 1974), pp. 83-89.

20. John E. Parker and John F. Burton, Jr., "Voluntary Labor Mobility in the U.S. Manufacturing Sector," in John F. Burton, Jr., Lee K. Benham, William M. Vaughn, and Robert J. Flanagan (eds.), *Readings in Labor Market Analysis* (New York: Holt, Rinehart and Winston, Inc., 1971), pp. 266-73.

practice, varying the employment of labor in the firm is not as easy and costless as competitive theory suggests.[21]

What can we conclude about labor mobility in the United States? In the long run labor markets continue to exhibit considerable flexibility, but it is apparent that most workers are not completely mobile over any relatively short duration of time. Furthermore, a significant proportion of the apparent flexibility of U.S. labor markets involves involuntary mobility, and the voluntary component seems to be declining. The existence of internal labor markets and increasingly structured employment relationships contribute to worker immobility. And while it is true, as we observed earlier, that there is frequent occupational movement within the secondary type of dual labor market, this is not the kind of movement that contributes to efficiency and flexibility in resource allocation. Those unskilled workers who maintain a loose attachment to the labor force are not moving up the occupational ladder in response to economic incentives and their own enhanced skills. They are merely shifting from one dead-end job to another.

Compensation Discretion at the Firm Level

We have already recognized the possibility, or probability, that firms have considerable discretion over the wages that they pay. Although market forces clearly influence most wage rates, there typically remains a range of choice for firms, even for a given skill level and locality. This follows from the imperfectly competitive, segmented nature of many labor markets. In this section we consider the so-called high-wage firm, the internal wage structure and wage policies of the firm, and the type of compensation which is becoming increasingly important as a discretionary element—fringe benefits.

The High-Wage Firm. Organized labor has historically claimed as a major bargaining objective the achievement of "equal pay for equal work." This objective is dramatically evident in the following description of the wage inequality problems of the preunion steel industry:

> . . . Loud speakers blared at the mill gates, "Who said a craneman is worth twenty cents more in Pittsburgh than in Chicago? . . . How about your mill? Is a millwright in the blooming mill worth eighteen cents more than a millwright in the electric furnace department? No! . . . Join the union and bring justice to all workers! . . ."[22]

---

21. See Walter Oi, "Labor as a Quasi-Fixed Factor," *Journal of Political Economy* (December, 1962), pp. 538-55.

22. Clinton S. Golden and Harold J. Ruttenburg, *The Dynamics of Industrial Democracy* (New York: Harper and Bros., 1942), pp. 169-70.

Since this objective remains a major priority today, it must follow that all firms still do not pay equivalent wages for the same skill in the same region. Ample evidence exists to suggest that this is true, as wages may vary by as much as 30 percent for a single occupation in a single city. Furthermore, these wage differences apparently cannot be explained fully by differences in the quality of workers in terms of education and training.[23]

Firms that pay relatively high wages tend to have certain characteristics which distinguish them from low-wage companies. Firms with larger plants tend to pay higher wages than small-plant firms. High-profit companies tend to be high-wage companies. As our analysis of labor demand elasticity in Chapter 2 would suggest, firms with low labor cost–total cost ratios tend to pay relatively high wages. Once again, it is important to be unimportant! Also the greater the extent of unionization and product market concentration, the greater the tendency for high wages. These characteristics of high-wage firms are not surprising, and they are also obviously interrelated.[24]

A firm does not always have a choice over some of these characteristics. Its influence over the degree of unionization and product market concentration, for example, may be limited. Nevertheless, there may actually be economic advantages in choosing to pay high wages, although they may not be obvious at first glance. The rate at which workers quit will probably be lower if relatively high wages are paid. Since it is costly to recruit new workers, this is an economic advantage. High wages may deter unionization in nonunion companies, and they will tend to minimize the losses of work stoppages in union companies. The high-wage company can probably demand higher job qualifications for hiring, and better job performance after hiring. As we have already observed, the firm will also incur lower search costs if it pays high wages.

In addition, the high-wage company can better withstand fluctuations in economic activity. During periods of increasing labor demand the high-wage firm has an obvious preferred status among job applicants. As the high-wage company expands employment, the low-wage firm will find it increasingly difficult to hire and retain workers. It will probably find it necessary to increase its wages even more rapidly than the high-wage firm in order to overcome this problem. During periods of economic contraction the reverse is true, and low-wage firms can resume their previous policies. This is why most area wage

23. See Albert Rees and George P. Schultz, *Workers and Wages in an Urban Labor Market* (Chicago: University of Chicago Press, 1970).

24. Early work on this subject may be found in Sumner H. Slichter, "Notes on the Structure of Wages," *Review of Economics and Statistics* (February, 1950), pp. 80-91. See more recently P. K. Sawhney and Irwin L. Herrnstadt, "Interindustry Wage Structure Variations in Manufacturing," *Industrial and Labor Relations Review* (April, 1971), pp. 407-19; and Arthur Butler and Kye Kim, "The Dynamics of Wage Structures," *Southern Economic Journal* (April, 1973), pp. 588-600.

structures contract during upswings in economic activity and expand during periods of considerable slack.[25]

The Firm's Wage Structure and Personnel Policies. The discussion above concentrated on comparisons of average wage levels by occupation among firms competing in the same labor market. Another important aspect of wage setting at the firm level is the array of wage rates paid for each individual job title within the firm. This array constitutes the internal wage structure of the firm.

Some types of labor are undoubtedly in demand throughout the local labor market, and the market will therefore play a major role in establishing rates of pay which tend to prevail throughout the area. However, in our earlier analysis of internal labor markets we observed that the outside market may predominate at only certain points in the firm's occupational hierarchy. Many jobs may involve specific kinds of skills which are much more useful and pertinent within a particular firm or industry, and these jobs are often filled from within. Collective bargaining, management discretion, and occasionally legislation determine the ranking of these jobs and the wage structure for them.

The determination of the firm's occupational hierarchy and wage structure is a part of what is normally called the personnel function of the firm. In its broadest sense, the personnel function involves the management and encouragement of all human efforts directed toward the achievement of the firm's objectives. Thus a wide range of concerns, including worker productivity, training, selection and placement, health and safety, compensation, and governmental compliance, fall within the domain of the personnel function.

Within the firm personnel is basically a staff function, which means that personnel functions are primarily advisory and supportive in nature. The personnel staff assists line managers in acquiring, training, compensating, and monitoring workers and advises managers on matters such as interpretation of labor agreements, governmental regulations, etc. In the smallest companies the personnel function is handled primarily by another staff officer, such as the controller. In most firms of sufficient size, however, there are separate personnel units or departments at the corporate, division, and/or plant levels.

With respect to the compensation aspects of the personnel function, a systematic wage structure within a firm is viewed as a means to attract, retain, develop and reward competent workers. Market forces may play a substantial role in compensation decisions for some types of jobs, but most firms also engage in systematic job design, analysis, and classification to define the internal wage relationships. In most instances, these efforts have resulted in one or more systems of *job evaluation* which define the relative worth of various

---

25. See Michael L. Wachter, "Cyclical Variation in the Interindustry Wage Structure," *American Economic Review* (March, 1970), pp. 75-84.

jobs within the firm. A hypothetical example of such a system is found in Table 3-1.

Table 3-1   A Hypothetical Job Evaluation Wage Schedule

Hourly Wage Rates

Labor Grade	Start	Step 1	Step 2	Step 3	Step 4
1	$4.50	$4.65	$4.80	$4.95	$5.10
2	5.05	5.20	5.35	5.50	5.65
3	5.60	5.75	5.90	6.05	6.20
4	6.15	6.30	6.45	6.60	6.75
5	6.70	6.85	7.00	7.15	7.30
6	7.25	7.40	7.55	7.70	7.85
7	7.80	7.95	8.10	8.25	8.40
8	8.35	8.50	8.65	8.80	8.95
9	8.90	9.05	9.20	9.35	9.50
10	9.45	9.60	9.75	9.90	10.05

After job rating criteria are established and weights are assigned to each criterion, the jobs are rated and grouped into a number of labor grades. Usually the highest and lowest wage rates are set next, and then the rate of increase for the intermediate grades is determined. As you might expect, in unionized plants management and union officials often disagree on the wage levels and wage differentials among different labor grades. Unions have generally been reluctant to accept rigid job evaluation schemes, arguing that they represent too much unilateral management wage-setting power.

Fringe Benefits. Throughout all our discussions of wages and wage determination we have implicitly assumed that employee compensation and money wages are equivalent. There is, however, an additional and increasingly important component of total compensation—*fringe benefits.* These nonwage fringes are types of compensation not paid currently in money to employees, but paid on behalf of employees for some employee benefit. The most common fringes are retirement pensions (including Social Security); life, health, disability, and dental insurance programs; and paid vacations and holidays. Actually the term "fringe" is misleading when analyzing modern compensation schemes, because fringe benefits are not the small supplements to wages which they were in the past. Recent estimates suggest that fringe benefits now average over 30 percent of payrolls in the United States, and they may constitute as much as 45 percent of payroll for some large companies.[26] Overall, the

26. U.S. Chamber of Commerce, *Employee Benefits, 1980* (Washington: U.S. Chamber of Commerce, 1980).

increasing importance of fringe benefits in employee compensation is portrayed in Table 3-2.

Table 3-2   Fringe Benefits as a Percentage of Total Compensation
Selected Years

Year	(1) Compensation of Employees (billions of $)	(2) Supplements to Wages and Salaries (billions of $)	Column 2 as a Percentage of Column 1
1960	$ 293.7	$ 22.4	7.6%
1965	392.9	34.5	8.8
1970	601.9	60.5	10.1
1975	928.8	122.1	13.1
1980	1596.5	252.9	15.9

Source: U.S. Department of Commerce, Bureau of Economic Analysis, *Survey of Current Business* (Washington: U.S. Government Printing Office, July, 1981 and preceding July issues), Table A.

Why has there been such rapid growth in compensation by nonwage fringes, particularly since World War II? There are important advantages to both employers and employees resulting from fringe benefit compensation which have led to this growth. Even if the employee must contribute, lower group insurance rates permit benefits to workers at much lower costs than the workers would have to pay individually. In addition, employer contributions to pensions or medical insurance programs are not taxable as employee wages. Although workers must pay income taxes on employer contributions to pensions when they receive the pension benefits, the tax rate will usually be lower because they are retired. Employee unions have also pushed for larger fringe benefit packages as an indicator of union strength.

Employers also derive certain benefits from the payment of fringes. Because the value of some benefits increases with length of service to the firm, they act to reduce labor turnover and subsequent recruiting and training costs. For example, the length of the paid vacation period is usually related to the duration of service to the firm, and pension benefits may not become fully vested with the individual worker until some period of service has been surpassed. Increased wages carry with them certain other mandatory cost increases such as Social Security taxes, overtime costs, and pension contributions. An equivalent increase in nonwage benefits avoids these mandated cost side effects. For these reasons, and because our society is increasingly placing a premium on health, leisure, and the quality of life, the importance of fringe benefit compensation is expected to continue to grow in the foreseeable future.

CONCLUDING REMARKS

At the beginning of this chapter we observed that you should have a good feel for how labor markets actually function after completing the chapter. One thing should now be clear: Labor markets operate with considerable complexity! The market forces developed in Chapter 2 and brought together in this chapter exert a substantial influence on labor markets. If you are not convinced, ask any nuclear or chemical engineer who has benefited from the recent upsurge of concern over energy problems, or any public school teacher who has suffered from the demographic declines affecting that profession. Furthermore, there are real social benefits from a system of labor markets which allocates labor with reasonable efficiency. We have also noted here, of course, that real world labor markets are characterized by many deviations from competition which complicate their operation. To complete the section on economic analysis of labor markets, we need to move from an analysis of individual labor market behavior to an economy-wide perspective. Many of you will recognize this as a move from microeconomics to macroeconomics, and this transition in Chapter 4 will permit our first look at the pressing issues of inflation, unemployment, and wage differentials.

CHAPTER SUMMARY

In purely competitive labor markets, market supply and demand conditions determine the equilibrium wage rate, and each individual firm will choose to hire the profit-maximizing number of workers by equating the market-determined wage rate with the MRP_L. Competitive labor markets allocate and reallocate labor efficiently because the private maximizing decisions of firms and workers ensure that labor will be employed where it is most productive.

A number of imperfections exist in most labor markets, however, all of which cause misallocation problems. In a monopsony, or single-employer, labor market the employer faces an upward-sloping labor supply curve and may choose the wage and employment level. The monopsony employer will pay a lower wage and employ fewer workers to achieve profit maximization.

There are also various forms of supply restriction existent in labor markets, such as occupational licensing and union apprenticeship programs. These entry restrictions create an underallocation of labor to the affected market. A similar result occurs when an artificially high wage rate is imposed on a market, for example, by a trade union or by the government through minimum wage laws. Once again, labor is underallocated to the affected market.

To gain a complete picture of labor market operation, it is also necessary to modify the competitive assumptions of worker homogeneity, perfect information, labor mobility, and market wage determination. Human capital theory has developed as a means of explaining labor force differentiation. Under this theory workers differ primarily by skill level, and skills are enhanced by education and training. The acquisition of additional education and training can be viewed as an investment yielding a rate of return, and individuals differ in trainability and the availability of training opportunities.

The existence of incomplete labor market information implies that employers and workers must engage in a search process to increase their information and range of choice. Since the process is costly and time consuming, they both must weigh the expected costs and benefits in determining the duration of search. In addition, employers may seek to fill many job openings from within the firm through the internal labor markets.

Several related theories of segmented labor markets have emerged recently which argue that it is the segmented structural characteristics of labor markets rather than the personal (human capital) characteristics of workers which determine wage and employment levels. It follows from this that public policy must emphasize intervention to stimulate the demand for disadvantaged workers. Finally, most firms have considerable discretion over the wages that they pay. Some can be characterized as high-wage firms and others as low-wage. Most firms have now also established internal job evaluation systems which define the relative worth of jobs, and they have increasingly resorted to fringe benefit compensation in addition to or as an alternative to wage compensation.

KEY TERMS

allocative efficiency
monopsony labor market
average labor cost
marginal labor cost
present value of future earnings
private rate of return on investment
general training

specific training
internal labor markets
the job competition model
dual labor market theory
primary labor markets
secondary labor markets
job evaluation system
fringe benefits

REVIEW QUESTIONS

1. What is meant by allocative efficiency, and how do competitive forces in labor markets achieve such efficiency? Would it be possible for some central planning authority to make all labor allocation decisions with equal efficiency? Defend your answer.

2. Would the monopsony model be useful in explaining wage and employment determination for a public school employer located in a sparsely populated area of western Nebraska, 50 miles from the nearest other public school? Think about this, and explain your reasoning.

3. As a labor expert, you are called upon to testify before Congress on the impact of the minimum wage and the types of changes which should be implemented. What would you recommend?

4. Milton Friedman has argued that all governmental licensing requirements for occupations should be eliminated, including those for medical occupations. Would you agree? Why or why not?

5. Some experts have argued that human capital analysis is inadequate in analyz-

ing the investment in college decision, because only monetary benefits and costs are included. Explain this line of reasoning and critically evaluate it.

6. By now you have some idea of the occupation which you wish to enter after completing your education. Does human capital theory or labor market segmentation theory more accurately describe the market for this occupation? What factors will influence the wage or salary which you expect to receive, and what job search channels do you expect to use?

ADDITIONAL REFERENCES

Blaug, Mark. "The Empirical Status of Human Capital Theory: A Slightly Jaundiced Survey," *Journal of Economic Literature* (September, 1976), pp. 827-55.

Bunting, Robert L. *Employer Concentration in Local Labor Markets.* Chapel Hill, N.C.: University of North Carolina Press, 1962.

Cain, Glen G. "The Challenge of Segmented Labor Market Theories to Orthodox Theory: A Survey," *Journal of Economic Literature* (December, 1976).

Fleisher, Belton M. *Minimum Wage Regulation in Retail Trade.* Washington: American Enterprise Institute, 1981.

Glueck, William F. *Foundations of Personnel.* Dallas, Tex.: Business Publications, Inc., 1979.

Rees, Albert, and George P. Schultz. *Workers and Wages in an Urban Labor Market.* Chicago, Ill.: University of Chicago Press, 1970.

Swanson, G. I., and J. Michaelson (eds.). *Manpower Research and Labor Economics.* Beverly Hills, Calif.: Sage Publications, 1980.

THE WORLD
OF WORK . . .

The Impact of the Minimum Wage

A recent report of the Federal Reserve Bank of Kansas City deals with the characteristics and causes of youth unemployment. A major focus of this report is on the impact of the minimum wage, and this excerpt summarizes two recent studies on that subject.

Analysis of the impact of minimum wage legislation on the labor market has been an extremely popular subject in the economic literature in recent years. The effect on youth unemployment has received particular attention for several reasons. First, young people are much more likely than adults to work in low-wage employment. Second, the youth unemployment rate, especially that for minority teenagers, has risen dramatically in recent years. Third, this tremendous unemployment increase has occurred just as a new minimum wage bill has been passed by Congress.

Among economists, the issue is not whether the minimum wage has good or bad effects. Economic theory and virtually all studies of the issue are in agreement that, at best, the minimum wage is a highly inefficient tool for redistributing income. At worst, it is also a major cause of economic dislocation, distortion, and unemployment. The question that the literature has generally addressed, then, is just how serious are the various effects on the economy. For a variety of reasons, however, this question has proven extremely difficult to answer.

A major factor in this difficulty is certainly the poor quality of the available data. Many of the major series needed for a thorough analysis simply do not exist. Other series are too recent to be useful in time-series analysis, while still other data are of such dubious quality that their use leads to very tenuous results. A second factor is the complexity of the real world, always a problem in research of this nature. Finally, even without these difficulties, there would probably remain among the model builders substantial disagreement as to the exact form of the "correct" model, and the proper variables to include.

Despite these complications, the great weight of evidence is on the side of those who stress the negative aspects of the minimum wage. Two recent studies, one by James F. Ragan, Jr., and one by Edward M. Gramlich, provide further support to this negative view. Using previously unexploited data and a new model specification, Ragan finds that the minimum wage has had a major disemployment effect on teenagers, especially on black youth. In addition, the participation rate of minority teenagers is reduced by the minimum wage, further worsening their economic predicament.

In a very complicated article, Gramlich examines a number of important issues involving not only teenagers, but adult males and adult females as well. Gramlich, too, finds a disemployment effect for teenagers, though of smaller magnitude than Ragan. He also finds such an effect for adult males, but not for females. Using these results and some guidelines derived from a series of complex theoretical models, Gramlich concludes that the low-wage sectors of these three groups may not be worse off, taken as a whole, because the disemployment effects do not outweigh the greater income received by those continuing to be employed at the higher minimum. However, because of the many assumptions involved in Gramlich's methodology, other economists have questioned the validity of this conclusion.

Other results, however, are striking. Gramlich finds, for example, that despite what he characterizes as "slight displacement" for teenagers as a whole, large numbers of previously full-time teenage workers have been pushed into involuntary part-time employment by the minimum wage. The income and training losses due to this displacement are probably quite severe. Gramlich also calculates a significant inflationary effect of the minimum wage, principally through its impact on the total wage bill. Finally, Gramlich shows clearly that the goal of redistributing income through the minimum wage, or lifting low-income families out of poverty by raising the minimum, is illusory. Especially for teenagers, but for adults as well, the relationship between low individual wages and low family income is so slight that the minimum wage is very unlikely to have the hypothesized strong redistributive effects.

Source: An excerpt from *The Growth of Youth Unemployment: Characteristics and Causes*, Federal Reserve Bank of Kansas City (June, 1979), pp. 20-21.

Chapter 4

Wages and Employment
in the Economy

It is virtually impossible to pick up a daily newspaper without being confronted with some news event related to wage-price levels and/or employment and unemployment in the U.S. economy. Major union-management contract negotiations and settlements are frequent news items. Changes in employment and unemployment statistics are reported monthly, and the significance of these changes is interpreted. On several occasions in the last 20 years, the federal government's attempt to establish counter-inflationary guidelines for wage and price increases has become newsworthy. It is sometimes frustrating (perhaps mind-boggling is a better word!) to try to understand our wage-price-employment problems and the policies that are utilized to combat them. Nevertheless it is extremely important to have some basis for evaluating these problems and policies, and this chapter will be useful in that regard.

As mentioned previously, in this chapter we will move away from the analysis of wages and employment in a single market and toward an economy-wide perspective. We begin by considering the wage structure and wage differentials in the economy, because this provides a convenient transition from the micro to the macro analysis. Next, a simple model of the macro economy is presented which will provide a context for our subsequent discussion of macroeconomic variables and problems. We will be particularly concerned with the general levels of money wages and real wages, and the relationship of each of these to prices, employment, labor productivity, and labor's share of the national output and income. An understanding of these macroeconomic variables will be important for our consideration of labor problems and policies in Part II of the text.

THE WAGE STRUCTURE AND WAGE DIFFERENTIALS

We have now analyzed a number of market and nonmarket forces which affect wage determination. The actual *wage structure* in the United States consists of the entire array of wages for all occupations and all individuals which result from the forces we have observed. It is important to observe this wage structure for at least two reasons. First, wage differentials are supposed to reflect differences in labor demand and labor productivity, as we have already noted. Therefore, wage differentials provide an important clue in assessing the efficiency of U.S. labor markets. Second, wage differentials are obviously related to the total income distribution in the economy, and we can gain some understanding of the poverty problem in the United States by observing the wage structure.

Perhaps the most noteworthy observation is that the U.S. wage structure exhibits large differences in earnings among individuals and various groups of individuals. There are many ways to group individuals for purposes of analyzing wage differentials, e.g., by employing firm, by occupation, by race, by sex, and by union status, to name a few. In addition, individual differences in earnings within these groups are significant. We have already discussed interfirm and intrafirm wage differentials in Chapter 3. In this section we concentrate on occupational and individual wage differentials, and in subsequent chapters we will consider the impact of race, sex, and union status on the wage structure.

Occupational Wage Differentials

Table 4-1 provides some summary data on wage differentials for various occupational groups. The data probably reveal the general kind of occupational differentials that you would expect. It is important to remember, however, that

Table 4-1   Median Annual Earnings of Full-Time Male Workers by Major Occupational Group, Selected Years

Occupational Group	1939 Earnings	1939 Index (Laborers = 100)	1955 Earnings	1955 Index (Laborers = 100)	1979 Earnings	1979 Index (Laborers = 100)
Professional and Technical	$2100	212	$5382	174	$17,432	163
Managers and Proprietors	2254	227	5584	180	18,148	169
Clerical	1564	157	4162	134	10,145	95
Sales	1451	146	4937	160	13,208	123
Crafts	1562	157	4712	152	15,756	147
Operatives	1268	128	4046	131	10,972	103
Services, except Private Households	1019	103	3565	115	9,528	89
Farm Laborers and Supervisors	365	37	—	—	8,164	76
Laborers, except Farm	991	100	3105	100	10,712	100

Sources: Herman P. Miller, *Income Distribution in the United States* (Washington: U.S. Government Printing Office, 1966); and U.S. Department of Commerce, *Statistical Abstract of the United States, 1980* (Washington: U.S. Government Printing Office, 1981).

there is a wide range of earnings for particular occupations within each occupational group. Thus, with a finer breakdown of occupations we would discover considerable overlap of earnings among these occupational groups. To use an extreme example, the clergy (a "professional" occupation) earn considerably less on the average than airline pilots (skilled "crafts people").

One other observation is important with respect to Table 4-1. If we express the changes in occupational group wages relative to changes in non-farm laborers' wages, which is done with index numbers in the table, it would appear that the wages of most skilled occupational groups have declined relative to the wages of unskilled laborers. For example, in 1939 the average wages of crafts people were 157 percent of unskilled laborers' average wages. By 1979, this ratio had declined to 147 percent.

What explanations exist for the differentials and patterns portrayed in Table 4-1? Under competitive labor market conditions, for example, we can draw certain conclusions. Occupations differ in a number of respects, such as employment security, length of training and training costs required, and general pleasantness of the job. Given the assumptions of competitive labor markets, including flexible wages, labor mobility, and perfect labor market information, wage differences would exist to offset differences in occupational characteristics that do not change over time. Put differently, wage differentials serve to equalize the net advantage of each occupation, with higher wages established by supply and demand for occupations which are otherwise least advantageous.[1]

It is tempting to conclude, however, that this explanation is inconsistent with much of reality. Many well-paid occupations seem to have excellent job security, fringe benefits, prestige, and working conditions. We should not be too harsh on competitive theory, however. Actually, the theory does a reasonably good job in helping to explain wage differentials among lower occupational levels, and it is also useful in explaining the declining differential over time between skilled and unskilled jobs which we observe in Table 4-1. The movement of unskilled agricultural labor into the non-farm labor force has declined in the post-World War II period because the farm population has been declining. Rapidly expanding education and training opportunities have further limited the size of the unskilled labor pool. In simple supply-demand terms, these factors suggest a sharp decline in the supply of unskilled labor. Although the demand for unskilled labor has also declined, it appears that the supply has fallen even more rapidly, leading to a relative increase in unskilled labor earnings.[2]

Competitive theory is less appropriate, however, when we look at the

---

1. For a recent source on this subject which finds only limited evidence of such compensating wage differentials, see Robert S. Smith, "Compensating Wage Differentials and Public Policy: A Review," *Industrial and Labor Relations Review* (April, 1979), pp. 339-52.

2. See Melvin Reder, "Wage Differentials: Theory and Measurement," in *Aspects of Labor Economics* (Princeton, N.J.: Princeton University Press, 1962), pp. 257-311.

upper occupational levels. Many of these jobs seem to contain the best of all possible worlds—job security, pleasant work conditions, excellent nonwage benefits, and high-earnings levels. Certainly the educational investment necessary to enter most of these occupations may explain part of the high-wage levels. In addition, we have already observed that all individuals do not have equal access to educational opportunities. Able students from lower-income families are sometimes still deterred from pursuing a college education by limited access to funds for financing the education. They are even more likely to be prevented from pursuing the graduate or professional degrees necessary to enter many of the professions. This situation is probably worsened because there are not enough professional school places, even for those who are willing and able to pay the costs. Thus, for example, many capable students are denied admission to medical, law, and business schools every year because these professional schools do not have the capacity to accommodate all qualified students. In short, the continued economic and social stratification of the population, as well as ability differences, contribute significantly to professional-nonprofessional wage differentials.[3]

Individual Wage Differentials

As human capital theory has developed systematically in the last 20 years, several economists have approached the question of wage differentials from within this theoretical framework. As would be expected, this type of analysis attempts to explain wage differences on the basis of differences in individual workers, rather than differences in jobs or social stratification. Let us assume that we have a list of, say, 10,000 workers and the annual wages for each, but we do not know the actual job which each worker holds. Assume also that we have access to a considerable amount of personal information on each worker. Could we develop a model which would explain the differences in wages among these workers with this personal information and, if so, what personal variables would be important in the explanation? This is the type of question posed by human capital theorists, and it has led to a number of useful and interesting research studies.[4] Basically, the studies have isolated three major categories of important personal variables—training, ability, and parents' socioeconomic status—plus a fourth miscellaneous category. We may summarize such models in the following way:

3. A classic study which reaches this conclusion is Milton Friedman and Simon Kuznets, *Income from Independent Professional Practice* (New York: National Bureau of Economic Research, 1945).

4. Recent examples of such studies include John C. Hause, "Ability and Schooling as Determinants of Lifetime Earnings, or If You're So Smart, Why Aren't You Rich," in F. Thomas Juster (ed.), *Education, Income and Human Behavior* (New York: McGraw-Hill Book Co., 1975); Paul Taubman, "Earnings, Education, Genetics and Environment," *Journal of Human Resources* (Fall, 1976), pp. 447-61; and Zvi Griliches, "Estimating the Return to Schooling: Some Econometric Problems," *Econometrica* (January, 1977), pp. 1-22.

$$(1) \; E = f \, (T, A, S, O)$$

where

E = individual earnings

T = measures of the quantity and quality of training

A = individual ability

S = measures of the parents' socioeconomic background

O = other explanatory variables

Training Variables. We have already noted that the amount of formal schooling and on-the-job training which a worker acquires should have a major effect on his or her lifetime earnings. The studies clearly lend support to this argument. There is a definite positive relationship between years of formal schooling and subsequent earnings. Several studies have also attempted to measure the quality of formal schooling as an explanatory variable.[5] Although difficult to measure, studies which have used measures of school quality (school expenditures per student, class size, etc.) have often found them to be significantly related to earnings. Similar problems exist in measuring the quantity and quality of on-the-job training, but several studies have also found this variable to be an important factor in enhancing earnings.

Why does additional education lead to additional lifetime earnings? The answer may seem obvious, but actually there is considerable disagreement. Hopefully, of course, additional education enhances potential productivity on the job. It may also lead to greater labor force participation and hours worked, which would increase earnings. It is also possible, however, that employers may use education as a device to screen job applicants, even if that education is not actually necessary to perform the job adequately. This is an important issue which will be taken up again in Chapter 7.

Ability. Ability is, of course, a very vague term. A person's ability consists of many factors, and the importance of these various factors varies from job to job. Conceptually, ability may mean something similar to "trainability," since most firms must in some way train all employees. For research purposes measurement is once again an obvious problem, and most studies have relied on ability indicators such as aptitude test scores, IQ scores, or class rank in high school or college. Using such measures, ability differences have been shown to be an important variable in explaining wage differentials.[6]

One problem with such conclusions, however, is that it is difficult to sort out the independent effects of ability and education on subsequent earnings. People with greater measurable abilities tend to complete more years of school-

---

5. For example, see George E. Johnson and Frank P. Stafford, "Social Returns to Quantity and Quality of Schooling," *Journal of Human Resources* (Spring, 1973), pp. 139-55.

6. See Hause, op. cit.; and Taubman, op. cit.

ing. Does the additional schooling, by itself, lead to increased earnings, or were the people with additional schooling more able to begin with? In the latter case it might be their innate abilities and not their schooling which enhanced their lifetime earnings. This is an important question, but one which does not lend itself to easy statistical measurement.

Parental Socioeconomic Status. Several studies have used measures such as family income level, father's and/or mother's educational attainment, and father's occupational level as indicators of socioeconomic status. Although the measure varies, almost all studies have found family socioeconomic status to be an important influence on lifetime earnings of children.[7] Obviously higher income families can more likely afford additional education for their children, but there may also be more subtle factors operating. Educated parents are likely to emphasize the importance of schooling to their children. They are also more likely to provide the early home environment conducive to motivating learning and school achievement, which in turn makes it more likely that the children will be successful in entering and completing higher levels of schooling. We do not know the precise importance of these subtle factors, but they appear to be operating in a significant way.[8]

As indicated, numerous studies have now been undertaken with samples of individuals similar to our hypothetical 10,000 workers, and utilizing models similar in form to equation (1). The other personal variables have included such things as union membership, race, sex, age, and geographic location. The studies are plagued by numerous conceptual and measurement difficulties, many of which we have noted. Nevertheless this relatively new approach to wage differentials, which emphasizes differences in the supply of personal characteristics rather than differences in labor market demand factors, has shown considerable promise as a method to improve our knowledge of the causes of earnings differences.

A SIMPLE MACRO MODEL

To complete our transition from micro- to macroeconomic analysis, we develop in this section a basic macroeconomic model to provide an analytical framework for subsequent inquiry. The model is based for the most part upon the pathbreaking work of John Maynard Keynes, whose important book, *The*

---

7. See, for example, Jere Behrman and Paul Taubman, "Intergenerational Transmission of Income and Wealth," *American Economic Review* (May, 1976), pp. 436-40.

8. The sociological literature in particular places great emphasis upon these socioeconomic factors. See, for example, Christopher Jencks, et al., *Inequality: A Reassessment of the Effect of Family and Schooling in America* (New York: Basic Books, 1972).

General Theory of Employment, Interest and Money, published in 1936, revolutionized the discipline of economics.[9] Keynes' primary focus was upon the determinants of the level of employment in the economy, and his timely work appeared during the Great Depression. His central thesis was that industrialized capitalist economies are susceptible to unemployment which is not automatically eliminated by self-correcting market forces.

Microeconomic Foundations

In Chapter 2 we analyzed the supply and demand operations in individual labor markets. We concluded there that workers' labor supply decisions are responsive to changes in real wages rather than money wages. Similarly, we noted that employment decisions by the firm are also responsive to real wage changes, because firms were assumed to be profit maximizers. For example, if money wages increase by 10 percent but prices also increase by 10 percent, it does not follow that firms will reduce the employment of labor. Since real wages are unchanged in this example, it should still be profitable to employ, or demand, the same quantity of labor as before. We may express these relationships formally as follows:

(2) $W = \dfrac{w}{P}$

(3) $D_L = f(W)$

(4) $S_L = f(W)$

where

w = money wages
P = the price level, or average prices in the economy
W = real wages
D_L = labor market demand
S_L = labor market supply

Although there is not universal agreement among economists that the real wage is the variable to which workers and employers respond, we shall accept this premise as a basis for further analysis.[10]

---

9. John Maynard Keynes, *The General Theory of Employment, Interest and Money* (New York: Harcourt, Brace and Company, Inc., 1936).

10. For other views on this subject, see Ronald Bodkin, "Real Wages and Cyclical Variations in Employment: A Reexamination of the Evidence," *Canadian Journal of Economics* 2, 3 (August, 1969), pp. 353-74; and James Tobin, "Inflation and Unemployment," *American Economic Review* (March, 1972), pp. 1-18.

It follows that a reduction in money wages will not stimulate more employment if the price level is also declining by a similar magnitude. If, for example, money wages decline by 10 percent but prices also decline by 10 percent, real wages and employment are unchanged. This was a fundamental argument of Keynes, who rejected the traditional view that unemployment could be reduced during a depressed economic period by a cut in money wages. Although money wages are established by the types of labor market and institutional forces which we have previously discussed, real wages depend upon the economy's overall level of output and employment. This overall level is in turn determined by the relationship between aggregate supply and aggregate demand.

The aggregate supply schedule for an economy clearly must reflect the product supply decisions of individual firms. For an individual firm, the supply price for a given quantity of goods is the price which will generate enough revenue to induce the firm to supply that quantity. In the short run where labor is the only variable input, this supply price is the firm's marginal cost of production. In other words, the supply price must be sufficient to cover the firm's additional costs of production if an additional unit of output is to be supplied. And since labor is the only variable input, the marginal cost of production is equal to the money wage rate divided by the marginal product of labor:

$$(5)\ MC = \frac{w}{MP_L}$$

where
w = money wage rate
MC = marginal cost of production
MP_L = marginal product of labor

Think of it this way: If the money wage is $5 per hour and the output of an additional worker (MP_L) is 5 units per hour, all other costs constant, the cost of producing an additional unit (MC) is $1. Since we noted in Chapter 2 that the marginal product of labor declines due to diminishing returns, equation (5) suggests that the MC or supply price must increase as supply increases. This results in the traditional upward-sloping supply curve depicted in Figure 4-1a for the firm. By merely summing the supply or marginal cost curves for all firms in an industry, the industry supply curve of Figure 4-1b is derived. This curve shows the industry-wide quantities of output that will be supplied at various prices.

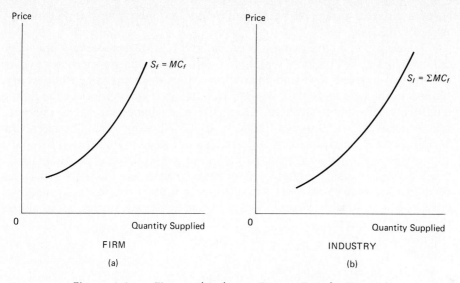

Figure 4-1   Firm and Industry Output Supply Curves

Aggregate Supply[11]

The industry supply curves of all industries taken together provide the information required to generate the *aggregate supply* curve for the economy. To follow the Keynesian approach, the aggregate supply curve shows the relationship between various employment levels in the economy and the aggregate annual revenues, or gross national product (GNP), required to justify that employment. Consider Table 4-2. These hypothetical data for an economy

Table 4-2   A Hypothetical Aggregate Supply Schedule

Employment N (millions of workers)	Wage Bill wN, where $w = \$10,000$ (billions of dollars)	Fixed Cost F (billions of dollars)	Gross Revenues (GNP) or Aggregate Supply Required (ZZ) (billions of dollars)	Gross Profits ($ZZ - wN - F$) (billions of dollars)
0	$ 0	$100	$ 0	–$100
40	400	100	550	50
50	500	100	725	125
60	600	100	950	250
70	700	100	1225	425
80	800	100	1550	650

11. For a more extensive treatment of this model, see Sidney Weintraub, "A Macroeconomic Approach to the Theory of Wages," *American Economic Review* (December, 1956), pp. 835-56; and Wallace C. Peterson, *Income, Employment, and Economic Growth*, 4th ed. (New York: W. W. Norton & Company, 1978), chaps. 4 and 5.

assume a fixed amount of capital equipment and an average annual money wage of $10,000.

For example, if employment is provided for 70 million workers, the wage bill wN will be $700 billion (70 million × $10,000). Adding a markup to cover $100 billion in fixed costs and $425 billion in gross profits suggests that employers in the aggregate will require $1225 billion in gross revenues to justify employing 70 million workers. Using the same logic, the gross revenues required to employ 80 million workers are $1550 billion, etc. The aggregate supply curve ZZ associated with these data is shown in Figure 4-2. Its shape suggests that the level of gross revenues, or gross national product (GNP), must increase to justify higher levels of employment. As a matter of fact, gross revenues must increase more rapidly than employment, because marginal costs rise as output increases. Therefore, the aggregate supply curve slopes upward at an increasing rate.

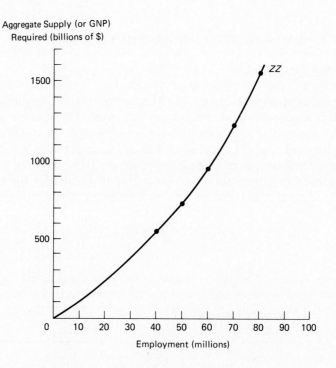

Figure 4-2   The Aggregate Supply Curve

Aggregate Demand

The actual level of employment that occurs in an economy results from the interaction of aggregate supply and *aggregate demand*. Keynes emphasized that aggregate demand was the crucial factor in determining the aggregate level of income and employment, although as we shall see aggregate supply forces have received more recent attention. In an economy with no foreign trade, the aggregate demand function relates employment levels to the gross current dollar revenues that firms expect to receive from the sale of their output to households, businesses, or the government.[12] This may be expressed as follows:

(6) $DD = C + I + G$

where

DD = aggregate demand
C = consumption expenditures of households
I = investment expenditures of businesses
G = government expenditures

This merely says that the gross revenues which businesses expect to receive for their collective output are equal to the sum of household consumption expenditures, business investment expenditures, and government expenditures. Keynes viewed the rate of investment I as particularly important in determining aggregate demand because of its volatility.

The aggregate demand curve DD is presented in Figure 4-3 along with the aggregate supply function developed earlier. The positive slope of the curve suggests that firms will employ more labor as total consumption, investment, and/or government expenditures increase. Notice that the actual employment level ON is determined by the intersection of aggregate supply and aggregate demand. Only at this level of employment do aggregate expenditures in the economy correspond to aggregate output.

A fundamental conclusion which Keynes drew from this type of analysis was that the actual employment ON was not necessarily a full employment level. For instance, in Figure 4-3 employment level ON_f may represent that level necessary to employ all individuals looking for work. Aggregate demand, however, is not high enough to create that many employment opportunities, and some workers (ON_f–ON) are involuntarily unemployed. And, as noted previously, even a reduction in money wages will not eliminate this unemployment because employment only responds favorably to real wage reductions.

Real wages, as Keynes argued, are determined along with the employment level by the level of aggregate demand. Where aggregate demand is

---

12. This description of the aggregate demand function focuses upon employment and departs from the conventional presentation for that reason. For another use of this approach, see Ingrid H. Rima, *Labor Markets, Wages, and Employment* (New York: W. W. Norton and Company, 1981), pp. 262-68.

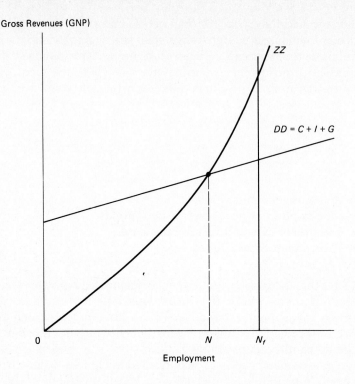

Figure 4-3   Aggregate Demand, Aggregate Supply, and Employment

insufficient to promote full employment, this suggests that real wages are too high. But since money wages tend to be inflexible downward, another key Keynesian observation, aggregate demand must increase sufficiently to raise the general price level if employment is to be stimulated. Why is this so? Referring back to equations (2) and (3), remember that the real wage W is equal to the money wage divided by the price level (w/P), and that the demand for labor is responsive to real wage changes [$D_L = f(W)$]. Real wages must decline if employment is to be stimulated, and if money wages don't go down then the price level must go up to reduce real wages. If this doesn't happen then involuntary unemployment persists, and if it does happen the result is inflation, a subject to which we shall soon return.

MONEY WAGES, PRICES, AND EMPLOYMENT

In this section we concentrate more explicitly on the general level of money wages, the economy-wide average of all individual firms' current wage decisions. Of particular importance is the relationship over time between rates of change in money wages and changes in two other key economic variables:

the unemployment rate and the price level. An understanding of different views on the nature of these elusive relationships is crucial as background for considering the full employment and price stability policy issues of the following chapters.

The General Level of Money Wages

Changes in the general level of money wages for the United States in the twentieth century are summarized in column 1 of Table 4-3. Of course, the trend in money wages has been consistently upward during this period, but there are substantial differences in the rates of increase for different periods. It should be apparent from Table 4-3, for example, that money wages have tended to increase rapidly during war periods and to increase slowly during periods of strong economic contraction. In every year since 1933, however, the general level of money wages has increased. To understand more clearly the fluctuations in the rate of increase in money wage levels, we must consider the crucial wage-price and wage-employment relationships mentioned earlier.

Table 4-3   Percentage Changes in Money Wages, Consumer Prices, and Real Wages in U.S. Manufacturing, 1900-1980

Years	Money Hourly Wages	Consumer Prices	Real Hourly Wages
1900-1910	+ 29%	+16%	+14%
1910-1920	+130%	+70%	+35%
1920-1930	+ 16%	+ 1%	+16%
1930-1940	+ 26%	−16%	+50%
1940-1950	+131%	+72%	+34%
1950-1960	+ 57%	+23%	+28%
1960-1970	+ 49%	+31%	+13%
1970-1980	+ 98%	+85%	+ 8%

Sources: Calculated from data in W. S. Woytinsky, et al., *Employment and Wages in the United States* (New York: Twentieth Century Fund, 1953); Albert Rees, *New Measures of Wage Earner Compensation in Manufacturing, 1914-57* (New York: National Bureau of Economic Research, 1960); and statistics from the *Monthly Labor Review* (August, 1981), pp. 89 and 104.

Wage-Price Relationships

Prior to the 1950s increases in the price level, or inflation, were thought to be caused exclusively by excessive aggregate demand in the economy. This excessive aggregate demand meant that prices increase, if monetary growth permits, because the productive capacity of the economy cannot meet the demand for goods and services at existing prices. With this *demand-pull theory of inflation,* money wages eventually increase but only in an attempt to keep up with the increasing prices.

In the 1950s an alternative theory was proposed which was based upon the observation that unions and firms exercise a considerable amount of discretion, or market power, over wage and price setting. We have already noted the existence of this discretionary market power, but in this context it suggests that inflation may occur even without excessive aggregate demand if unions demand excessive wage settlements and/or if firms increase prices without an increase in market demand. According to this *cost-push theory of inflation,* inflation may occur simply because excessive wage (or profit) costs are passed on by the firm in the form of higher prices independent of demand forces. Although these higher prices might initially result in a loss of sales, output, and employment, recent studies have argued that the increase in unemployment is prevented by an expansionary monetary policy. In other words, the money supply is allowed to grow to accommodate the rise in prices so that increased unemployment is avoided. Of course, this merely sustains or intensifies the inflation and gives it more of a demand-pull flavor. Therefore, in practice it is often difficult to separate demand-pull from cost-push forces.[13]

The debate over these competing theories has continued since the 1950s, and we will explore some of the resulting policy implications in greater detail in Chapter 6. For now, however, we should note that the cost-push theory does highlight a set of economic variables which are extremely important in understanding the nature of the wage-price relationship. One variable which we must introduce is the concept of *labor productivity,* or output per labor hour Q/LH. As the name suggests, this is a measure of the average output Q for every labor hour of labor input (LH). Labor productivity typically rises from one year to the next in the U.S. economy, although the movement is somewhat erratic as Table 4-4 indicates.

Another important variable of concern for our present purposes is the concept of *unit labor costs (ULC),* or the average labor costs to the firm for each unit of production. This would of course be calculated by dividing total labor costs to the firm *(TLC)* by the total units of production Q. Hence,

$$(7) \quad ULC = \frac{TLC}{Q}$$

But let's consider equation (7) in more detail. Total labor costs to the firm can also be expressed as the average money wage rate w times the total labor hours of labor input *(LH)*. Therefore, equation (7) can be rewritten as:

---

13. See for example, F. D. Holzman, "Inflation: Cost-Push and Demand-Pull," *American Economic Review* (March, 1970), pp. 24-42.

Table 4-4   Labor Productivity Index and Annual Percentage Changes in Labor Productivity, U.S. Private Business Sector, 1950-1980

Year	Labor Productivity Index (1977 = 100)	Annual % Change in Labor Productivity
1950	50.3	
1955	58.2	
1960	65.1	
1965	78.2	
1970	86.1	
1973	94.8	2.7%
1974	92.7	−2.3%
1975	94.8	2.3%
1976	97.9	3.3%
1977	100.0	2.1%
1978	99.8	−0.2%
1979	99.4	−0.4%
1980	99.1	0.3%

Source: *Monthly Labor Review* (August, 1981), Table 31.

$$(8) \quad ULC = \frac{w(LH)}{Q} \quad \text{or} \quad ULC = w\left(\frac{LH}{Q}\right) \quad \text{or} \quad ULC = \frac{w}{(Q/LH)}$$

Bear with this algebraic manipulation, because we will soon reach an important conclusion. Note in particular the last method of expressing equation (8). The expression in parentheses (Q/LH) is the labor productivity variable which we defined earlier, and the entire equation suggests that there are definite relationships among money wages, labor productivity, and unit labor costs. Equation (8) is also conceptually the same as equation (5), which we used in developing the basic macro model. To make sure that you understand these relationships, consider the following example. If output per labor hour (Q/LH) is 10 units of production and the average money wage w is $4 per hour, then unit labor costs *(ULC)* are $4/10 = $.40. Now let's allow labor productivity to increase by 10 percent $(Q/LH = 11/1)$, and the average wage to increase by the same 10 percent ($w = 4.40). What has happened to the unit labor costs? If you are following the analysis, you should conclude that unit labor costs are unchanged $(ULC = $4.40/11 = $.40)$.

What have we observed? We can conclude from our example that as long as money wage increases correspond to labor productivity increases, unit labor costs do not change. The significance of this conclusion should become more apparent by looking at Figure 4-4, which depicts the very close historical relationship between unit labor costs and the price level. This close relationship provides some support to the cost-push theorists' contention that cost factors play an important role in price setting. Our example also suggests one very important reason why unit labor costs, and subsequently prices, may increase. If wages increase more rapidly than labor productivity, equation (8) clearly indicates that unit labor costs will rise. Thus there is an important relationship between money wage increases and price increases, if wage increases exceed labor productivity advancements and if the resulting increases in unit labor costs are passed on by the firm in the form of higher prices.

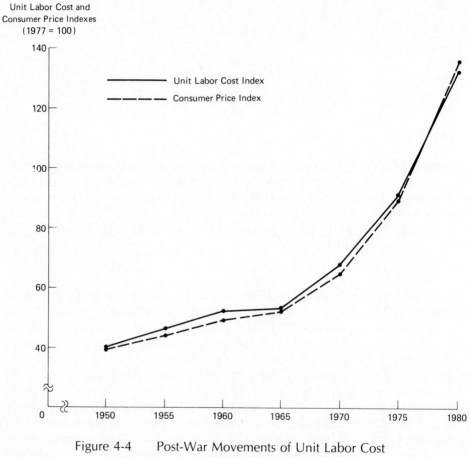

Figure 4-4   Post-War Movements of Unit Labor Cost
and Consumer Price Indexes

There are a number of policy implications resulting from this relationship which we will take up in Chapter 6. For now, remember that what we observe in Figure 4-4 is not a direct relationship between money wages and prices, but rather a relationship between unit labor costs and prices. Unit labor costs are related to money wages through the crucial labor productivity variable [see equation (8) again]. Remember also that it may not really matter whether an initial increase in the price level is caused by excessive aggregate demand or by cost-push pressures. As soon as people begin to expect continued inflation, labor will demand compensating wage increases (which are probably in excess of the labor productivity increase) and employers will probably grant the increases. Prices will then be adjusted accordingly, with perhaps an additional price increase to achieve additional profits. This scenario typifies the familiar *wage-price spiral* which has plagued the U.S. economy for much of the last 15 years.

Wage-Employment Relationships

One of the important observations that economists have made for some time is the one alluded to earlier—money wages tend to increase slowly during recessionary periods. In other words, when labor markets are characterized by high unemployment, money wages advance at slow rates. The nature of this wage-employment relationship has been the subject of much study in the post-World War II period.

The Phillips Curve. As you may remember from previous coursework in economics, the relationship between rates of change in money wages and rates of unemployment was first analyzed systematically by Professor A. W. Phillips.[14] He noted for Great Britain a strong inverse relationship between these two economic variables, and this negative relationship was formalized into a *Phillips curve* of the type depicted in Figure 4-5. A similar relationship has

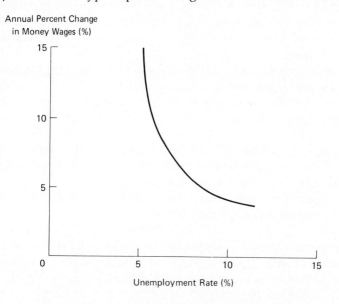

Figure 4-5   A Hypothetical Phillips Curve

---

14. A. W. Phillips, "The Relation Between Unemployment and the Rate of Change of Money Wage Rates in the United Kingdom, 1861-1957," *Economica* (November, 1958), pp. 283-99.

been derived for the United States in numerous studies, although the experience of the 1970s discussed later has caused a reappraisal by some economists.

The rationale lying behind the Phillips curve relationship goes something like this. First, it has been observed by Keynes and others that money wages tend to be inflexible downward, and the data in Table 4-3, page 93, confirm this. To put it differently, money wages will increase during tight labor market conditions (low unemployment), where excess demand may exist for many types of labor. But money wages will not decrease when a loose labor market and excess labor supply exist. With reference to Figure 4-5, even with substantial overall unemployment, such as 7 or 8 percent, some labor markets will be tight in the sense that the number of job vacancies exceeds the number of unemployed. In these tight markets money wages will obviously be pulled up. But in the majority of labor markets where an excess supply of unemployed labor exists, there will be no corresponding decrease in money wages because of downward wage inflexibility.

Hence, even with substantial unemployment there will be some upward pressure on money wages, and as unemployment decreases with an increase in aggregate demand, the upward pressure on money wages increases. This upward pressure on money wages as labor markets tighten may be intensified further if unions become more aggressive in their wage demands and if employers are more willing to grant such demands. Recall from our earlier discussion that the increases in money wages as labor markets tighten may be greater than increases in labor productivity, and therefore may be inflationary. Our macroeconomic model also suggested that aggregate demand and prices must increase in this situation if the level of employment is to increase toward full employment.

The implications of the Phillips curve analysis are straightforward, and the policy alternatives perplexing. If such a stable Phillips curve relationship exists in the United States, it suggests that our economy confronts a trade-off between unemployment on the one hand and inflationary money wage rate increases on the other. In other words, we must accept either considerable unemployment, substantial inflation, or some slightly lesser combination of the two. This either-or dilemma became the "worst of all possible worlds" in the 1970s, moreover, because we experienced simultaneously increasing, unacceptable levels of inflation and unemployment beginning in the 1973-1975 period. How was this stagflation possible?

The Accelerationist Theory. One view which emerged is that the Phillips curve trade-off simply does not exist as a stable, long-run relationship. This view, associated initially with the work of Nobel-laureate Milton Friedman,[15] can be summarized by reference to Figure 4-6. For convenience, Figure 4-6 replaces "the rate of change in money wages" on the vertical axis with "the rate

---

15. Milton Friedman, "The Role of Monetary Policy," *American Economic Review* (March, 1968), pp. 1-17.

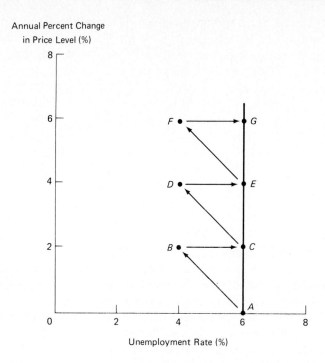

Figure 4-6   The Accelerationist Long-Run Phillips Curve

of change in the price level." This allows us to view inflation directly on the vertical axis; remember that we can make this transition because any increases in money wages which exceed labor productivity increases are inflationary. Put simply, if we subtract the average annual increase in labor productivity from the vertical axis of Figure 4-5, we have essentially the vertical axis of Figure 4-6.

Assume that the economy is experiencing price stability (no inflation), but with unemployment at 6 percent. This corresponds to point A in Figure 4-6. Now assume that aggregate demand in the economy increases as the result of money supply growth. This increase pulls up prices and, since money wages remain constant initially, business profits increase and real wages decline. Firms will respond by increasing production and hiring more workers, so that unemployment decreases and the economy moves to point B in Figure 4-6. So far this is a conventional Phillips curve type of reaction which shows a trade-off between (higher) inflation and (less) unemployment.

According to the accelerationist economists who accept this theory, however, point B is not a stable, long-run point. Workers will soon realize that, since the price level has increased and their money wages have remained unchanged, their real wages have decreased. Therefore, workers will demand and receive money wage increases to restore their lost real wages. But this, in turn, will decrease business profits back toward their previous level, and firms will respond by cutting back production and laying off recently hired workers. The economy moves back to the original 6 percent unemployment rate, but now at a higher rate of inflation because the increased aggregate demand still exists (point C). The movement from point A to point B was merely a temporary adjustment, and after money wages caught up with price increases the economy settled back into a 6 percent unemployment rate with higher prices. If additional demand stimuli occur the process may be repeated, but each time the economy will return to what accelerationists call the *natural rate of unemployment* (points A, C, E, and G in Figure 4-6). Hence the long-run Phillips curve may be essentially vertical, and any policy which attempts to stimulate the economy to diminish unemployment will only fuel the fires of inflation, with no lasting improvement in the unemployment problem. It is also possible, according to the accelerationists, that the natural rate of unemployment has increased in recent years. If this is so, the accelerationist theory provides a plausible explanation for the stagflation dilemma of the last decade.

The Post-Keynesian View. Economists in the tradition of John Maynard Keynes have not accepted the accelerationist view, in part because the view suggests that Keynesian-type demand management will be futile and inflationary. More recently, a school of post-Keynesian economists has synthesized Keynesian views of aggregate demand with various theories of institutional barriers in the economy. As with Keynes, post-Keynesians view the rate of investment as a key determinant of aggregate demand and economic growth. They also emphasize the dynamic, growing nature of our economy and the important role played by major institutions such as banks, multinational corporations, and trade unions.[16]

Post-Keynesians divide product markets into two categories: competitive markets in which prices are determined by demand and supply forces and "fixprice" markets where prices are set by large corporations to cover production costs plus a profit markup to finance investment expenditures. These latter markets are much more prevalent in industrialized economies, according to post-Keynesians, and prices in "fixprice" markets are not responsive to changes in demand. When demand changes, the volume of output produced by firms will change, but prices will remain largely unaffected.[17]

Post-Keynesians also contend that wages are often administered by trade unions and government regulations rather than being set by labor market supply and demand forces. They view wage determination and unemployment as two distinct processes, with the volume of employment determined by

---

16. See, for example, Alfred S. Eichner (ed.), *A Guide to Post-Keynesian Economics* (New York: M. E. Sharpe, Inc., 1979).

17. On this topic, see Howard M. Wachtel and Peter D. Adelsheim, "How Recession Feeds Inflation: Price Markups in a Concentrated Economy," *Challenge* (September-October, 1977), pp. 6-13.

Keynesian aggregate demand forces.[18] The Phillips curve then, either in its traditional downward-sloping or accelerationist vertical form, is largely irrelevant because it attempts to portray a close connection between wages, prices and unemployment which does not exist.

Post-Keynesian theory provides a somewhat different explanation for our recent stagflation experience. During a recessionary period when sales are declining, large oligopolistic firms will reduce output and employment but will seek to maintain their profits at prerecession levels. Even though slackening demand by itself might dictate a price moderation strategy to these firms, in fact they will probably increase their prices in an attempt to maintain profit levels for investment. If this market power is extensive enough in our economy, it suggests that inflation can sometimes be expected even when unemployment is high and increasing. Here again, if these pricing strategies have been used with more frequency in recent years, it provides a possible explanation for stagflation.

We have observed some of the views on wage-price and wage-employment relationships in this section. These relationships provide us with some explanations for the pattern of increases in money wages which was shown in Table 4-3, page 93. Unfortunately, however, it is clear that economists as social scientists do not always agree on the nature of these relationships. Hopefully you are already thinking about the important policy implications of these various explanations, and the next several chapters will satisfy your desire to pursue this topic further. In this chapter, we turn finally to a related topic already mentioned but not fully explained—the general level of real wages.

THE REAL WAGE LEVEL

Although the causes of fluctuations in money wages over time are noteworthy for numerous policy considerations, over longer periods of time the movement of real wages is of particular importance. Since real wages reflect true purchasing power, it is this concept which tells the individual if she or he is economically better off over time. Economy-wide real wage increases also imply that the society is becoming more affluent in terms of the average standard of living which it can offer its citizens. Columns 2 and 3 of Table 4-3, page 93, adjust the money wage levels in the United States over time for price level changes, so that real wage movements are shown in column 3. Notice that although fluctuations in real wages are evident, the trend is again consistently upward. It is particularly important to observe that money wages and real wages do not seem to move together in any consistent pattern. They both have moved up over time, but certainly not at the same rates nor at the same times.

---

18. See Eileen Appelbaum, "Post-Keynesian Theory: The Labor Market," *Challenge* (January-February, 1979), pp. 39-47.

Real Wages and Labor Productivity

We have already noted in our basic macro model the belief that labor demand and supply are related to real wages, not money wages, and that real wages are related to the level of aggregate output in the economy. Let's explore this issue further by considering the following logic. In a macroeconomic sense the dollar value of the annual national output (*GNP*), after adjustments for depreciation and some business taxes, is equivalent to the annual national income. Put differently, a year's production of goods and services generates a total income for workers, property owners, etc. which is equal to the value of that production after adjustments. Labor collectively does not receive all of the national income in a given year, however. A portion of the national income is received by property, or capital, owners in return for the productive use of their property. These relationships may be formalized in the following set of simple equations:

$$(9) \ NI = NO$$

$$(10) \ LS(NI) = LS(NO)$$

$$(11) \ \frac{LS(NI)}{LH} = \frac{LS(NO)}{LH}$$

where

NI = annual national income, in constant dollars of purchasing power
NO = annual national output, in constant dollars, after adjustments
LS = labor's share of the national income, in percentage form
LH = total hours of labor input

Equations (9) and (10) merely restate what was said above: National income equals national output, and labor's share of national income is equivalent to its share of national output. If we divide both sides of equation (10) by total labor hours, the equality remains. Of course, over time national income, national output, and labor hours will change. But if we assume that labor's percentage share of national income *(LS)* is constant over time, then an important conclusion emerges from equation (11): Any changes in *LS(NI)/LH* over time must equal the changes in *NO/LH* over the same time. Now think carefully about what *LS(NI)/LH* and *NO/LH* really represent. If the total national income earned by labor in our economy is divided by total labor hours for the same period, wouldn't this yield the economy-wide average hourly wage rate (actually the real wage rate because of the way we defined national income)? Since *NO/LH* defines aggregate labor productivity (output per labor hour) in dollar terms, we can conclude that changes in the economy's real wage level over time are closely related to changes in labor productivity, as follows: If *LS* is constant

$$\frac{LS(NI)}{LH} = \text{real wage level, and} \quad \frac{NO}{LH} = \text{labor productivity,}$$

then equation (11) says that

$$\Delta \text{ real wage level} = \Delta \text{ labor productivity}$$

This is an important conclusion, because it suggests that any permanent increase in purchasing power and economic affluence in our economy is tied closely to increases in labor productivity and the growth of aggregate output.

Labor Productivity in the United States. On the average, national output per labor hour (NO/LH) in the United States has been rising at around the rate of 3 percent per year for much of the twentieth century, and real wages have exhibited a very similar average rate of increase. However, the rate of increase in labor productivity has slowed somewhat in the 1970s and 1980s as Table 4-4, page 94, indicates. If this downturn in productivity growth continues, the implications for the future are disturbing. Since real wage levels are tied closely to productivity growth, slower productivity growth implies slower growth in real wages. Put differently, the expectation that most people have of steadily improving their standard of living over time may be unattainable. Furthermore, we noted previously that productivity growth is necessary to keep money wage increases from fueling inflation.

Explanations for Productivity Slowdown. What explanation do we have for this productivity slowdown, and what are the prospects for the future? Over time, labor productivity growth results primarily from three sources: (1) an increase in the amount of capital per worker, (2) research and development impacts, and (3) improvements in the quality of the labor force. The major source of increased productivity in the past has clearly been the increased quantity and efficiency of capital (machinery) with which labor works. The agricultural sector provides a prime example of rapid increases in labor productivity resulting from more and better machines. In the last 10 years, however, the rate of capital investment has declined as profit margins declined and interest rates and the price of capital equipment escalated.[19] It has also been

---

19. U.S. Department of Labor, *Economic Report of the President, 1979* (Washington: U.S. Government Printing Office, 1979), p. 68.

argued by many authorities that the expansion in government regulations applying to businesses has forced them to divert funds from capital investment to regulatory compliance, thus hindering productivity growth.

Research and development expenditures have also tapered off in recent years and have declined as a percentage of GNP. The economic uncertainty which has pervaded our economy has tended to discourage long-range research and development by firms, as they have preferred to seek out short-term, minimal risk alternatives. Similarly, we have already noted the recent vast influx into the labor market of persons with little or no training—youth, minorities, and women disproportionately. In spite of the rapid improvement in the overall educational attainment of the labor force, this influx has had a further dampening effect on productivity growth.[20]

Fortunately, most experts project somewhat improved productivity growth in the next decade, although not on a level with the 1960s. The decline in the birthrate over the last 20 years means that fewer persons will be entering the labor force in the 1980s and 1990s. The labor force will therefore become increasingly dominated by older, more skilled workers. Capital investment is also expected to increase, but this will depend in large part upon the creation of a more favorable economic and regulatory climate.

Labor's Income Share

The above discussion of real wages assumed that labor's share of national income *(LS)* has been constant over time. It was long believed that, as long as statistically consistent data were analyzed, labor's share would in fact be relatively constant. Many studies and theories emerged to document and explain this presumed constancy.[21] However, more recent studies seem to indicate that labor's share has experienced a small increase in the past few decades, as shown in Table 4-5. There are numerous measurement problems involved in such estimates, but a pattern of slight increases in labor's share seems to be emerging for the United States as well as for other developed economies.[22]

What factors might explain this increase? In most developed countries the ratio of capital to labor used in production *(K/L)* has increased in the twentieth century. To once again use American agriculture as an extreme case in point, it should be obvious that many more machines K and many fewer laborers L are now being used in agricultural production. Simple supply-demand analysis would suggest that if capital supply is generally increasing relative to labor

---

20. Ibid.

21. See, for example, Paul H. Douglas, "Are There Laws of Production?" *American Economic Review* (March, 1948), pp. 7-41.

22. See K. Heidensohn, "Labor's Share in National Income—A Constant?" *Manchester School of Economic and Social Studies* (December, 1969), pp. 295-321; and William Nordhaus, "The Falling Share of Profits," *Brookings Papers on Economic Activity*, No. 1 (1974), pp. 169-208.

Table 4-5   Employee Compensation as a Share of National Income
Selected Years (billions of dollars)

Year	(1) National Income	(2) Employee Compensation	Column 2 ÷ Column 1
1940	$ 79.7	$ 52.1	65.4%
1945	180.6	123.1	68.2
1950	236.2	154.8	65.5
1955	328.0	224.9	68.6
1960	412.0	294.9	71.6
1965	566.0	396.5	70.0
1970	798.4	609.2	76.3
1975	1215.0	931.1	76.6
1980	2120.5	1595.4	75.2

Source: *Economic Report of the President, 1981*, Tables B-17 and B-19, and previous issues.

supply, the price or rate of return to capital will fall relative to the price of labor. Depending upon the relevant elasticities, this may contribute to a decrease in the capital share and an increase in the labor share. Also, returns to increasing rates of investment in human capital discussed earlier may have been a factor in the increase in labor's share. We can conclude that the pattern of increases in real wage levels in the United States, shown in Table 4-3, page 93, is closely related to both changes in labor productivity and changes in labor's share of the total national income. Changes in labor productivity have been by far the most important explanatory factor, but increases in labor's share have probably also made some small independent contribution.

CONCLUDING REMARKS

In this chapter we have attempted to complete our economic analysis of labor by moving to a macro view of labor in the American economy. The emphasis has been on developing a macroeconomic framework and exploring important relationships among critical macroeconomic variables which affect, and are affected by, labor. Thus we have discovered that there are certain systematic explanations for the wage differentials that persist over time, and for the movement of money and real wages. We do not have all the answers, and some of the explanations may even conflict with others, but hopefully the picture is clearer than it was when we began.

Throughout our discussion in these introductory chapters, the importance of economic forces and their constant interrelationships have been emphasized. The message should now be clear. These systematic forces and relationships are operating in our economy, and an understanding of their importance aids us in explaining the observed behavior in labor markets. Unfortunately we are not finished, because we have largely ignored a number of serious economic problems which result because of undesirable or inadequate labor market forces. We also chose to overlook temporarily the institutional forces of government and trade unions in labor markets. We now must turn in Part II to the economic problems resulting from labor market deficiencies and to the government's role in overcoming these deficiencies. Do not lose sight of the economic relationships which we have identified. As we shall see, they remain an important part of larger, more complex explanations of labor market behavior.

CHAPTER SUMMARY

An overview of the U.S. economy reveals certain systematic relationships among labor-related economic variables and certain explanations of their movement over time. In terms of the entire array of wages for all occupations and individuals, i.e., the wage structure, this chapter analyzes both occupational and personal wage differentials. The occupational wage structure exhibits predictable patterns, although with considerable variation within occupational categories. Competitive labor market theory provides a partial explanation for lower-level occupational wage differences and for the decline in the skill differential over time. Human capital theory, with its emphasis on personal variables such as training, ability, and socioeconomic status, has been used with some effectiveness to explain personal wage differentials.

A Keynesian-type macroeconomic model was also developed in this chapter to provide a framework for analyzing macroeconomic relationships. Its key feature is the derivation of aggregate supply and aggregate demand functions, which in turn interact to determine the levels of employment and real wages.

In looking at the economy-wide general level of wages over time, both price levels and unemployment rates seem to have some relationship to money wage levels. Price level increases provide a justification to labor for demanding money wage increases, and this process may result in a wage-price spiral. Phillips curve analysis suggests an inverse relationship between money wages and unemployment rates, although accelerationists and post-Keynesians disagree on the importance of this relationship in the long run. Real wage levels, on the other hand, are directly related to changes in labor productivity and in labor's share of the national income.

KEY TERMS

the wage structure
aggregate supply
aggregate demand
the general level of money wages
demand-pull theory of inflation
cost-push theory of inflation

labor productivity
unit labor costs
wage-price spiral
the Phillips curve
natural rate of unemployment
the general level of real wages

REVIEW QUESTIONS

1. Why is competitive labor market theory useful in explaining lower-level occupational wage differentials, but not so useful in explaining professional occupational wage differences?

2. Discuss the numerous measurement problems associated with the human capital approach to explaining personal wage differentials. Given these problems, does it make sense to continue the use of this method? What would you recommend?

3. In the basic macroeconomic model introduced in this chapter, why won't a decrease in money wages stimulate more employment? What is necessary to stimulate employment?

4. There are important relationships among the economic concepts of the price level, the level of money wages, the rate of increase in labor productivity, and unit labor costs. Carefully explain these relationships.

5. In terms of Phillips curve analysis, how would the accelerationists and the post-Keynesians explain the stagflation of the 1970s? Why do they disagree?

6. Explain the following statement. "In the economy as a whole, real wage levels may increase over time only if either: (1) labor productivity increases and/or (2) labor's share of the national income increases."

ADDITIONAL REFERENCES

Eichner, Alfred S. (ed.). *A Guide to Post-Keynesian Economics.* New York: M. E. Sharpe, Inc., 1979.

Keynes, John Maynard. *The General Theory of Employment, Interest and Money.* New York: Harcourt, Brace and Company, Inc., 1936, chaps. 1-3.

Mincer, Jacob. *Schooling, Experience and Earnings.* New York: National Bureau of Economic Research, 1974.

Perlman, Richard (ed.). *Wage Determination: Market or Power Forces?* Lexington, Mass.: D. C. Heath, 1964.

Perry, George L. *Unemployment, Money Wage Rates and Inflation.* Cambridge, Mass.: M.I.T. Press, 1966.

Peterson, Wallace C. *Income, Employment and Economic Growth,* 4th ed. New York: W. W. Norton and Company, 1978, chaps. 4 and 5.

Rima, Ingrid H. *Labor Markets, Wages and Employment.* New York: W. W. Norton and Company, 1981, chaps. 13 and 14.

THE WORLD
OF WORK . . .

Is There a General Theory of Stagflation?

Otto Eckstein, a Harvard University Professor and member of President Johnson's Council of Economic Advisors, recently testified before the Joint Economic Committee of Congress on stagflation. In the excerpts from his prepared statement below, he incorporates a number of the concepts which were discussed in this chapter.

Is it possible to identify a general theory of stagflation? The historical account makes clear that each episode contained various "chancy" elements.

. . . Thus, in a sense, the theory of stagflation cannot stand alone, but is simply the application of a general view of the economy as it operates in some particular circumstances which happen to produce the stagflation result. The question is not so much why there is stagflation, but why the economy has a permanent inflationary bias.

A broad range of economists would agree on the list of factors which imparts the inflation pressure into our economic performance, though they would surely disagree on the relative emphasis. First, in the short-run, the inflation rate does respond to the level of aggregate demand, and does so in a quite nonlinear fashion. In particular, when excess demand develops, even if it is only for some sectors of the economy, inflation gets much worse. . . .

Second, it is impossible to run the economy in the excess demand territory in the long-run. The public's inflation expectations gradually adjust to the correct levels. It therefore takes accelerating inflation to maintain a constant level of real activity. Since neither the financial system nor the public can live with accelerating prices, a recession is the inevitable outcome. I think this is the true and correct meaning of the common assertion that there is no Phillips curve in the long-run, that the unemployment-inflation tradeoffs are temporary.

Third, inflation expectations are formed rather gradually. The public partially discounts a temporary extreme condition in its consumer buying actions or in its willingness to buy fixed-income securities. But over a period of several years, inflation expectations are adjusted fully to reflect the true reality.

As a result, expectations are a major component of the core inflation rate. If expectations can be changed only very slowly, then wage and unit labor cost trends can change only very slowly. . . .

Fourth, shocks vary the inflation rate in the short-run, and are, in part, converted into long-term inflation as well. Whether a disturbance originates in a run-up of food prices which may be reversed later on, in higher minimum wages and payroll taxes, or in OPEC prices, long-term inflation expectations are affected, and a portion of the temporary inflation enters into wages, unit labor costs, capital costs and therefore the "core" inflation rate.

Fifth, the government is a major source of inflation shocks. There is a bias in a pluralistic democracy toward inflation-creating actions. The political process finds it very difficult to limit cost increases, as can be seen in the current troubles over the hospital containment program and truck deregulation, but finds it very easy to extend additional protection to various producer groups both on the business and labor sides. Special pleas are always very reasonable, and the lobbyists know their profession.

Sixth, there are major elements of monopoly in both product and labor markets which slow down the conversion of demand weakness into lower prices. Business prefers price discipline and the resultant shared quantity variations to competitive price cutting which would let recession produce a higher anti-inflation benefit.

Seventh, in a world which contains OPEC and the strong industrial economies of West Germany and Japan, any domestic inflationary bias is ultimately converted into a weakening exchange rate which fans the domestic inflation further.

These general ideas can be converted into a theory of stagflation. The actual inflation rate in any period has three components: (1) the core inflation rate based on unit labor and capital cost trends, (2) the shock inflation rate based on nonsystematic actions of the government and the outside world, (3) and the demand inflation rate, based on the aggregate level and composition of demand. . . .

_____

Source: Abridged from a prepared statement of Otto Eckstein in *Stagflation.* Hearings before the Special Study on Economic Change of the Joint Economic Committee—Congress of the United States. 96th Congress, 1st Session, April 30, 1979, pp. 24-25.

2 Labor Market Problems and Policies

We have surveyed a number of economic theories, concepts, and relationships which are important in determining the operation of labor markets and the macroeconomic levels of wages, prices, and employment. An understanding of these theories and concepts is also useful as a framework for considering the causes and consequences of a number of significant economic problems which affect human resources. In addition, assessing the policy alternatives available to combat these problems can be done more intelligently with this analytical background.

It is clear that the problems of unemployment, underemployment, inflation, discrimination, and poverty still plague the United States and most other developed economies. Part II of this text is devoted to a careful consideration of the extent, causes, and consequences of these problems, and to the policies which have been utilized and proposed to contend with them. Chapter 5 considers systematically the problems of unemployment and underemployment, as well as the goal of full employment. In Chapter 6, numerous employment policies are reviewed within the context of acceptable wage and price behavior. Chapter 7 encompasses a number of policies which have been developed in order to utilize human resources more fully and effectively in the present and the future. In Chapter 8, the perplexing problem of labor market discrimination is analyzed, and the controversial policy alternatives available to us are assessed. Finally, Part II concludes with Chapter 9 and the subject of poverty—its extent, causes, effects, and remedial programs.

Chapter 5

Unemployment, Underemployment and Full Employment

We have already touched on the issue of unemployment in several sections of this text. As a part of our discussion of labor supply in Chapter 2, we noted that those without jobs who are actively seeking work are a part of the labor force and are officially classified as unemployed. Chapter 3 discussed the unemployed worker who is engaged in the job search process, and Chapter 4 surveyed employment theory and macroeconomic wage-employment relationships. Unsurprisingly, we will also discover in Chapters 8 and 9 that unemployment affects the victims of discrimination disproportionately, and that it is a major cause of poverty.

We have not, however, considered systematically the measurement, costs, causes, and effects of unemployment, and that is a major purpose of this chapter. Here we attempt to gain a thorough understanding of this complicated and socially costly problem, so that the employment policy issues of the next two chapters can be taken up with the proper insight. This chapter also touches on the related issues of underemployment and the quality of work life which have gained recent attention. Finally, in the last section of the chapter, we seek an answer to the perplexing question: What is full employment?

THE NATURE AND MEASUREMENT OF UNEMPLOYMENT

In Chapter 3 we noted that competitive market forces will tend to create equilibrium in labor markets by establishing a wage rate which equates the quantities of labor supplied and demanded. But we have also observed repeatedly that most labor markets are not sufficiently competitive to achieve this result. We know that money wages tend to be inflexible downward, so that wage rates may not actually serve to clear markets as supply and demand conditions change. Furthermore, we have learned that there are time lag problems in this market adjustment process as workers and employers engage in the search process. Since labor demand is a derived demand, there must also be sufficient aggregate demand for goods and services in the economy if labor is to be fully employed at existing wage rates.

It follows from these observations that a general definition for *unemployment* would be the difference between the amount of labor supplied at existing wages and the amount of labor hired at those wages. An alternative approach would be to say that unemployment exists when individuals are willing and able to work at existing wages but cannot find employment without considerable delay. These are acceptable definitions for some purposes, but they leave many specific questions unanswered. How do we actually determine an individual's ability to do certain types of work, or his or her willingness to work? What about special cases such as homemakers, students, retired persons, etc.? Are they to be counted as unemployed? Is the number of employed persons or the number of unemployed persons the best measure of economic performance? Both of these numbers can increase simultaneously if the labor force is expanding. As we shall see, the best definition and measure of unemployment really depends on the intended use of that measure.

The official government unemployment statistics are compiled by the Bureau of the Census for the Bureau of Labor Statistics. Monthly surveys of a representative cross section of about 56,000 households, called the Current Population Survey, are the source of these data. Every individual surveyed is classified as either not in the labor force, employed, or unemployed, as noted in Chapter 2. *Unemployed persons* are those who did not have a job during the survey week, were available for and actively seeking work, or were waiting to be called back to a job from which they were laid off. The survey results are used to estimate economy-wide employment statistics such as the ones found in Table 5-1.[1]

Table 5-1   Employment Status of the Civilian Noninstitutionalized Population 16 Years of Age and Over, Selected Years
(numbers in thousands)

Year	Civilian Labor Force	Number Employed	Number Unemployed	Unemployment Rate	Number Not in Labor Force
1950	62,208	58,918	3288	5.3%	42,787
1955	65,023	62,170	2852	4.4	44,660
1960	69,628	65,778	3852	5.5	47,617
1965	74,455	71,088	3366	4.5	52,058
1970	82,715	78,627	4088	4.9	54,280
1975	92,613	84,783	7830	8.5	58,655
1980	104,719	97,270	7448	7.1	59,425

Source: *Monthly Labor Review* (Washington: U.S. Government Printing Office, August, 1981), p. 71.

1. See also Table 2-1, page 19.

As Table 5-1 indicates, there has been considerable variation in the overall unemployment rate over time, and some occupations or industries are often hit harder than others. Ordinarily, the housing industry and those industries producing nonessential goods are the first to suffer as the business cycle turns downward. The purchase of many consumer durable goods, such as automobiles, are most easily postponed as overall consumer spending begins to decline, and workers in these industries endure highly volatile unemployment rates. Similarly, certain geographic areas may be particularly hard hit if a depressed industry is concentrated in those regions. The economic downturn beginning in 1979, for example, was felt in the Detroit area more quickly and more severely than in much of the rest of the country.

The household surveys conducted by the Census Bureau also collect many other types of employment-related information: race, sex, and age of the respondents; full- and part-time employment status; reasons for and duration of unemployment; and job search methods of the unemployed. These collection efforts are an attempt to provide the most comprehensive set of employment statistics possible. Still there have been growing concerns about the validity and uses of these statistics.[2]

Fundamentally, the controversy over employment statistics centers around disagreement over the proper breadth of the definition of unemployment for policy purposes. One group of experts contends that the current definition is too narrow, in that it excludes discouraged workers, those who are involuntarily employed part-time, and the underemployed. In recessionary periods, all three of these groups tend to increase, and the reverse is true during economic expansions. Therefore it is argued that our present official definition of unemployment tends to understate the problem of unemployment in bad times and overstate it in good times.

Another school of thought favors limiting the unemployment definition to those persons with a strong labor force attachment who suffer significant economic hardship from their unemployment. In effect, this school argues that the current definition is too broad because it no longer is an accurate index of economic hardship. The impact upon the household of unemployment today is often lessened because more than one household member is in the labor force. Expanded unemployment compensation and, in some cases, employer-provided supplementary unemployment benefits further weaken the current official definition as a precise measure of hardship.

It has been noted for some time now that the employed-unemployed

2. See, for example, Geoffrey H. Moore, "A Measuring Stick of Employment," *The Wall Street Journal,* May 9, 1975; Irwin L. Kellner, "Counting the Employed, not the Unemployed," *The New York Times,* October 26, 1976; Sar A. Levitan and Robert Taggart, *Employment and Earnings Inadequacy: A New Social Indicator* (Baltimore: Johns Hopkins Press, 1974); and Sar A. Levitan, "Labor Force Statistics to Measure Full Employment," *Society* (September-October, 1979), pp. 68-71.

dichotomy is a poor index of economic hardship.[3] Although some families which suffer unemployment still live with reasonable comfort, many families with no one unemployed are still poor. The debate over definitions simply illustrates that no single employment statistic can satisfy all measurement requirements. Julius Shiskin, former Commissioner of the Bureau of Labor Statistics, has observed that different persons use the statistics for different purposes. The official unemployment statistic, for example, is a good measure of business cycle behavior. It is not, however, the best measure of the economic welfare of the labor force.[4]

These concerns prompted Congress in 1976 to establish the National Commission on Employment and Unemployment Statistics, chaired by Professor Sar A. Levitan, to examine various alternatives to existing methods of data collection and presentation.[5] In late 1979 the Commission issued its recommendations to the Secretary of Labor. Among the most noteworthy proposals of the Commission were the following:

1. Interview a larger number of households each month to obtain more reliable disaggregated data.
2. Publish statistics linking individuals' employment status with their earnings and family income status.
3. Include the armed forces stationed in the United States in the national count of employed workers.
4. Identify discouraged workers more objectively, but continue to exclude them from the count of the labor force.
5. Compile data pertaining to movements into and out of the labor force.
6. Give greater prominence to an array of alternative unemployment measures in addition to the official unemployment rate.[6]

You can see that the Commission's recommendations address most of the major concerns mentioned above. The recommendation concerning discouraged workers is particularly significant. The Commission recommended that the definition of discouraged workers be amended to include only those not currently in the labor force who are available for and desire to work, and who have actively sought work in the previous 6 months. The Commission was expressing a desire that the definition place more emphasis upon availability for work and labor force attachment. Interestingly, a minority of four members

---

3. Levitan and Taggart, ibid.; and Sar A. Levitan, Garth L. Mangum, and Ray Marshall, *Human Resources and Labor Markets*, 3d ed. (New York: Harper & Row, 1981), chap. 18.
4. Julius Shiskin, "Employment and Unemployment: The Doughnut or the Hole," *Monthly Labor Review* (February, 1976), pp. 3-10.
5. See Joint Economic Committee, *Public Hearings before the National Commission on Employment and Unemployment Statistics*, Vols. 1-3 (Washington: U.S. Government Printing Office, 1978-1979).
6. Levitan, "Labor Force Statistics to Measure Full Employment"; and Robert L. Stein, "National Commission Recommends Changes in Labor Force Statistics," *Monthly Labor Review* (April, 1980), pp. 11-21.

dissented and argued that those persons falling within the Commission's amended definition should be counted as officially unemployed.[7]

Although there may be disagreement about the best method of measuring unemployment statistically, most would agree that unemployment imposes significant psychological and economic costs on many individuals, families, communities, and society as a whole. Unemployed individuals lose self-respect and suffer rejection from their peers. Psychologically, unemployment may threaten the stability of the family. As breadwinners lose their jobs, economic frustrations within the family intensify and family relationships suffer. These individual effects have a social impact, as research studies have shown a clear relationship between increased unemployment and higher incidences of crime, physical and mental illness, and juvenile delinquency.[8]

The more readily measurable economic costs are also staggering. Since wages are the only source of income for most families, lost employment imposes severe economic hardship on many families. In early 1982, for example, almost 10 million workers were unemployed, and this figure does not include discouraged workers or those who were employed part-time because full-time work was not available. Also, during recessionary periods the duration of unemployment increases, as we have previously noted. Whereas in 1980 roughly 20 percent of the unemployed had been without work for 15 weeks or more, this figure was well over 30 percent by early 1982.[9] The unemployment compensation program clearly lessens the economic burden of unemployment, but coverage is incomplete and benefit levels are generally geared toward only about a 50 percent replacement of gross wages.

The economic costs to society are somewhat more elusive to individual citizens, but they are enormous nonetheless. An uninformed person might argue that the individual pays for unemployment only if he or she becomes unemployed, but this argument has little validity. The costs of all social assistance programs rise with increased unemployment, as do the social costs of crime prevention, health care, and the like. Individual citizens ultimately incur these added costs in the form of higher taxes and prices, and/or lower quality goods and services provided.

Furthermore, unemployment represents idle human resources from the economy's point of view. These resources could have contributed to the economy's production of goods and services, but their contributions are lost. Our society thus sacrifices a large and measurable amount of output annually due to unemployment, and we all suffer a loss of economic welfare because of this.

---

7. National Commission on Employment and Unemployment Statistics, *Counting the Labor Force: Readings in Labor Force Statistics* (Washington: U.S. Government Printing Office, December, 1979).

8. See M. Harvey Brenner, *Estimating the Social Costs of National Economic Policy: Implication for Mental and Physical Health and Criminal Aggression,* a study prepared for the Joint Economic Committee (Washington: U.S. Government Printing Office, 1976).

9. For a summary of recent studies in this area, see Community Council of Greater New York, *Research Utilization Update,* No. 8, June, 1980.

Economists usually refer to this lost output as the *GNP gap*, the difference between actual GNP and the potential GNP which would have resulted if the economy were fully employed. Table 5-2 depicts estimates of the dollar value of the GNP gap for recent years and their relationship to the annual unemployment rates. As can be clearly seen, we have suffered large dollar amounts of lost output in recent years which are directly related to the unemployment rate. In the recession of 1975, our lost output amounted to over $1000 per member of the civilian labor force. There is no doubt that we all suffer significant economic losses from unemployment.

Table 5-2   Actual and Potential GNP, the GNP Gap,
and Unemployment Rates, 1974-1980
(billions of 1972 dollars)

Year	Potential GNP	Actual GNP	GNP Gap	Unemployment Rate
1974	$1264.2	$1217.8	$46.4	5.6%
1975	1302.1	1202.3	99.8	8.5
1976	1341.1	1271.0	70.1	7.7
1977	1381.1	1332.7	48.7	7.0
1978	1422.9	1385.1	37.8	6.0
1979	1504.6	1483.0	21.6	5.8
1980	1548.5	1480.7	67.8	7.1

Source: *Economic Report of the President, 1981*, Table 27, and previous issues.

CHARACTERISTICS OF THE UNEMPLOYED

Even though we all pay the costs of unemployment in some way, we do not pay equally. Those who actually become unemployed obviously incur the most severe costs, and those who are unemployed tend to have certain characteristics. Put differently, unemployment has different direct impacts on various subgroups of the population. We have already noted that workers in durable goods industries tend to suffer disproportionately, and production workers generally experience more unemployment than do workers in service industries. In this section we summarize the personal characteristics which tend to identify the unemployed, and the reasons for these dominant characteristics.

Race, Sex, and Marital Status

Discrimination in labor markets, a subject which we will address systematically in Chapter 8, may be manifested in higher unemployment rates for females and nonwhites. The data in Table 5-3 examine this possibility. These data reveal that the overall nonwhite-white unemployment ratio has consistently been almost 2:1 since World War II, for example. Table 5-3 also indicates that nonwhite males are at a somewhat greater disadvantage (relative to white males) than are nonwhite females (relative to white females). Although not presented in Table 5-3, the racial differential is particularly pronounced among teenagers. In 1980, for example, the nonwhite unemployment rate for teenagers was over 40 percent, while the white teen unemployment rate had improved to around 15 percent.

Table 5-3   Annual Unemployment Rates by Sex and Race, Selected Years

Year	Total	White			Nonwhite		
		Total	Male	Female	Total	Male	Female
1955	4.4%	3.9%	3.7%	4.3%	8.7%	8.3%	8.5%
1960	5.5	4.9	4.8	5.3	10.2	10.7	9.4
1965	4.5	4.1	3.6	5.0	8.1	7.4	9.2
1970	4.9	4.5	4.0	5.4	8.2	7.3	9.3
1975	8.5	7.8	7.2	8.6	13.9	13.7	14.0
1980	7.1	6.3	6.1	6.5	13.2	13.3	13.1

Source: *Economic Report of the President, 1981*, Table B-31.

The data in Table 5-3 also clearly indicate that females experience more unemployment as a group than do men. In addition, marital status enters into the picture. Married men and women both experience less unemployment than their single counterparts, and a particularly acute problem arises in female-headed households. Over 85 percent of these female heads are either widowed, divorced, or separated, and their unemployment rate tends to hover in the 8-10 percent range no matter what the general economic conditions. Given their generally significant family responsibilities and low earnings potential, female household heads often suffer extreme disadvantages from unemployment.

Age

As mentioned above, unemployment has become an especially acute problem for young workers. As Table 5-4 indicates, double-digit unemployment has been a consistent characteristic of the under-age-20 component of the labor force for some time. Teenage joblessness has become the most critical single component of the unemployment problem. In recent years, almost half of the total number of unemployed workers has been under the age of 25, and the problem has been worsening, as Table 5-4 suggests.

Some differential unemployment impact also falls on older workers. The labor force participation rate for those 65 years of age and older is low due to retirement. Those in the labor force are usually part-time workers attempting

Table 5-4   Annual Unemployment Rates by Age, Selected Years

Age Group	1950	1955	1960	1965	1970	1975	1980
Total, 16 Years and Older	5.3%	4.4%	5.5%	4.5%	4.9%	8.5%	7.1%
16-17	13.6	12.3	15.5	16.5	17.1	21.4	20.0
18-19	11.2	10.0	14.1	13.5	13.8	18.9	16.1
20-24	7.7	7.0	8.7	6.7	8.2	13.6	11.5
25-34	4.8	3.8	5.2	3.7	4.2	7.8	6.9
35-44	3.8	3.4	4.1	3.2	3.1	5.6	4.6
45-54	4.2	3.4	4.1	2.8	2.8	5.2	4.0
55-64	4.8	4.2	4.2	3.1	2.7	4.6	3.3
65 and Older	4.5	3.6	3.8	3.3	3.2	5.3	3.1

Source: *Employment and Training Report of the President, 1981,* Table A-30.

to supplement Social Security and private pension benefits. Nevertheless, unemployment rates for this age group are often somewhat higher than for the 55-64 age group. Older workers usually have accumulated the greatest seniority benefits, but if they become unemployed they have greater difficulty finding new jobs. Hence, the duration of unemployment is greatest for these workers, even though the rate of unemployment is not excessive.

The prospects for the next decade appear somewhat mixed concerning the age-unemployment relationship. On the one hand, the significantly lower birthrates of the 1960s and 1970s indicate that there simply will be fewer young workers in the labor force in the next decade. This should help in alleviating the severe youth unemployment problem. However, recent studies have shown that many older workers are increasingly resisting retirement at the traditional age of 65. The extension of the mandatory retirement age, increases in service-oriented jobs, improved health and education levels, high inflation rates, and increased numbers of women in the labor force are all factors which may cause workers to postpone retirement. This phenomenon may worsen the unemployment problem for elderly workers, or it may cause some of these workers to displace younger workers in employment settings.[10]

Reasons for the Differential Impact

Young people, women, and nonwhite workers tend to be disproportionately unemployed, and the unemployment picture for these groups has worsened somewhat in the last 20-30 years, particularly for teenage workers.

---

10. U.S. Department of Labor, *Employment and Earnings* (Washington: U.S. Government Printing Office, September, 1978), Table A-17.

Why is this the case? Certainly discriminatory forces, which will be discussed in Chapter 8, provide part of the explanation. These groups are simply not provided with equal employment opportunities, particularly in the more pleasant and secure primary labor markets.

It is also revealing to consider the duration of unemployment and reasons for unemployment for these groups of workers. Most evidence for young and nonwhite workers suggests that these disadvantaged groups do not suffer significantly longer durations of unemployment than do prime age white males.[11] What they do experience are significantly more spells of unemployment in a given year. For young workers, the post-war baby boom led to a flood of new labor market entrants in the 1960s and 1970s. Those with few skills were forced more and more into the intermittent employment situations of the secondary labor market, where nonwhites already predominated. Young workers particularly are in and out of the labor market more frequently as they shop around for jobs, and women as a group tend to move in and out of the market more often for personal and family reasons. Overall, however, women do not have significantly more spells of unemployment than men.

These tendencies are revealed in the data of Table 5-5. For teenagers during 1980, the vast majority of the unemployment was related to reentry and

Table 5-5   Unemployment Rates by Age, Sex, Race and Reason for Unemployment, 1980

Reason for Unemploy-ment		Unemployment Rate				
	Total	Both Sexes, 16-19 years	Male, 20 years and over	Female, 20 years and over	White	Nonwhite
Lost Last Job	3.7%	4.1%	4.2%	2.8%	3.3%	6.4%
Left Last Job	.8	1.7	.6	.9	.8	1.2
Reentered Labor Force	1.8	5.1	.9	2.2	1.5	3.6
Never Worked Before	.8	6.8	.2	.3	.6	2.0
	7.1%	17.7%	5.9%	6.3%	6.3%	13.2%

Source: *Employment and Training Report of the President, 1981,* Table A-36.

11. See George L. Perry, "Unemployment Flows in the U.S. Labor Market," *Brookings Papers on Economic Activity,* No. 2 (1972), pp. 245-78.

initial entry into the labor market. Discouragement, inability to find work, completion of school, and return to school account for these high entry and reentry figures for young workers. The difference between the nonteen female and nonteen male unemployment rates is largely related to female reentry. Nonwhites, on the other hand, display greater tendencies for job loss, job quit, initial entry, and reentry than do their white counterparts.

In summary, unemployment tends to impact disproportionately on the young, females, and nonwhites. This differential impact has not improved in the last 20 years and has actually worsened significantly for teenage workers. These differentially affected groups have developed a somewhat more marginal attachment to the world of work, and this may have serious implications for future labor market activity.

In addition, since women, young people, and nonwhites now comprise a much larger percentage of the labor force than in previous times, the overall unemployment rate has tended to increase in recent years independent of cyclical forces. For example, the prime age (25-54) white male unemployment rate was about 3.8 percent in both 1960 and 1980. Yet the overall unemployment rate was 5.5 percent in 1960 and 7.1 percent in 1980. The difference? The increased percentage of relatively high unemployment nonwhites, women, and young workers in the 1980 labor force. This fundamental change in labor force composition has created serious problems for the battle against the inflation-unemployment dilemma, as we shall see in the next chapter.

CAUSES OF UNEMPLOYMENT

In the previous section we discussed the reasons for the differential impact of unemployment on various groups. Now we need to step back from our analysis of individual characteristics and impacts, and consider the general causes of unemployment on a macro, or economy-wide, level. The fundamental causes of unemployment are usually related to either insufficient aggregate demand in the economy as a whole, or to frictions and maladjustments in the labor market. This approach suggests the classification of unemployment into three basic types: frictional, cyclical, and structural. Although these categories are not mutually exclusive, they do provide a convenient framework for our discussion.

Frictional Unemployment

We observed in Chapter 3 that if labor market information is perfectly available to employers and workers, and if labor is perfectly mobile, labor market efficiency is greatly enhanced. There would be no reason to expect any delays in the movement of workers between jobs under these conditions. Unfortunately, we also noted that these conditions do not often prevail in our labor markets, and frictional unemployment is the likely result. *Frictional unemployment* is that which results from short-term fluctuations in labor markets and from imperfect information and labor immobility.

Seasonal Unemployment. Some frictional unemployment arises from periodic or seasonal fluctuations in the demand for labor. In some industries the number of workers needed varies on a day-to-day or week-to-week basis due to seasonal fluctuations related to weather conditions, buying habits, or recurring holidays. Agriculture and construction are industries whose activity is affected by changing weather conditions. The Christmas season impacts significantly on retailing and many other industries. In each case the resulting short-term variations in the demand for labor leave some workers frictionally unemployed. Such seasonal unemployment may also result from the supply side of labor markets; for example, when the labor force expands at the end of the school year.

Labor Immobility and Job Search. Even without these short-term variations, some frictional unemployment can always be expected because of imperfect information and worker immobility. Some workers are always going to be between jobs because of the time involved in overcoming information and mobility barriers. We referred to this time period in our earlier discussion of the search process. We have also observed that workers' and employers' willingness to engage in prolonged search depends upon general economic conditions, i.e., the relative number of job vacancies and unemployed workers. Although improved efficiency in labor markets can eliminate some of this frictional unemployment, a certain amount is inevitable. As we shall see, this is a primary reason why various definitions of full employment are always at greater than 0 percent unemployment.

Cyclical Unemployment

The various sets of unemployment data which we have analyzed clearly indicate that unemployment fluctuates with the general level of economic activity over time. Our economy often experiences levels of aggregate demand which are inadequate to generate employment for all workers who wish to work at existing wage levels. This is the essence of *cyclical unemployment,* which results from the derived nature of labor demand. Cyclical fluctuations in economic activity have consistently characterized our economy, and inadequate demand conditions prevail particularly during recessionary downswings. Reduced hours and some layoffs appear even in mild recessions, and more typically 2-4 million workers are temporarily or permanently displaced at the bottom of a business cycle.

In many ways cyclical unemployment is the most glaringly serious type which we face. Many people become discouraged about finding work during recessions and drop out of the labor force. Hence, the actual severity of the problem may be greater than our statistics reveal. Although we often read about the laid-off worker who receives 90-95 percent of previous after-tax wages through unemployment compensation and special "supplementary unemployment benefits" from the employer, this is a very atypical case. Most workers laid off during recessionary periods suffer significant economic hardship. The problem becomes even more tragic, as we shall see in the following chapter, because some recessionary forces are created by policy makers in an attempt to curb excessive inflation.

Structural Unemployment

At peaks in the business cycle, unemployment rates have recently still averaged around 5.0-6.0 percent. Many individuals remain persistently out of work at the same time that want ads in every daily newspaper contain literally hundreds of unfilled job vacancies. Presumably, aggregate demand for goods and services is sufficient during these periods of high economic activity to generate adequate numbers of jobs. And short-term frictional imperfections cannot account for anywhere near that amount of unemployment. The reason for much of this persistent unemployment, even when the total number of job vacancies is sufficient to accommodate the number of unemployed persons, is that the vacant job requirements do not match the skills and abilities of the unemployed. This is the essence of structural unemployment.

Structural unemployment is characterized by long-term, persistent mismatches between the supply of and demand for labor by skills and/or areas. Our economy is composed of large numbers of specific labor submarkets, and we have noted numerous barriers to the efficient movement of workers among those submarkets. As our earlier Phillips Curve analysis suggested, it is possible for some labor markets to be fully employed while an excess of workers over job vacancies exists simultaneously in other markets. The excess of unemployed workers cannot simply spill over into those markets where excess job vacancies exist.

Numerous factors may cause these structural imbalances to persist over time. Shifts in consumer tastes cause growth in some industries and decline in others, as well as geographic shifts in industry location. Technological change in production methods renders some employee skills obsolete. On the supply side, changes in the composition of the labor force, such as the recent influx of marginally skilled young workers, also contribute to structural imbalances when jobs requiring their skills do not exist in sufficient numbers.

The severity of structural unemployment depends largely upon the efficiency of labor market institutions in training and retraining workers, adopting production methods with flexible employment requirements, and eliminating excessive hiring requirements. Once again, labor mobility and labor market information barriers are a partial cause of structural unemployment, as was the case with frictional unemployment. But with structural imbalances the problem is not short run and transitional. In the absence of significant labor market adjustments, structural unemployment does not respond readily to changes in aggregate demand. Even at very high levels of aggregate demand, finding jobs for the structurally unemployed is often likened to attempting to "drive a square peg into a round hole." Even though the driving force (high aggregate demand) may be strong, they still do not fit. The macroeconomic result of increasing structural unemployment is to raise the rate of unemployment associated with a given rate of inflation.

UNDEREMPLOYMENT AND THE QUALITY OF WORK LIFE

As we now know, unemployment causes our society to produce below its potential. The economy is not efficiently utilizing its available resources and significant social costs result. Underutilization of human resources does not have to take the form of unemployment, however. The worker who is employed part-time because he or she cannot find full-time employment is being underutilized, although these workers do not show up in the unemployment statistics. The discouraged worker who wants and needs work but has dropped out of the labor force is obviously underemployed, although not technically unemployed. Similarly, the Ph.D. historian who drives a cab full time is underutilized and unnoticed in our employment statistics. Finally, the skilled production worker who is frequently absent from work because of job dissatisfaction is underemployed. *Underemployment* occurs when employed individuals are less productive than their skills and abilities would dictate, and it imposes the same kind of social costs on our economy as does unemployment.

In 1975 almost 4 million workers worked part-time involuntarily, and this figure remained at 3.5 million in 1980. This figure includes workers employed part-time because of slack work, material shortages, inability to find full-time work, etc. Remember that these people do not show up in the unemployment statistics, but they are clearly being underutilized by our society.

In 1980 roughly 6 million individuals not in the labor force reported that they wanted a job, but were not presently looking for a variety of reasons, including family responsibilities, ill health, and school attendance. Although these reasons are largely either voluntary or beyond the scope of public policy, some 1 million individuals wanting employment were not looking simply because they felt their search would be unsuccessful. Measurement of the discouraged worker phenomenon is admittedly imprecise, but discouragement is another type of socially costly underemployment.

We have no accurate statistics on the frequency of the historian-turned-cab driver type of underemployment, but we all know of such examples. According to a recent study by the University of Michigan's Survey Research Center, as much as 27 percent of the nation's labor force may have been working in jobs below their qualifications during the 1974-1975 recession. Furthermore, the increased educational attainment of the labor force suggests that this underemployment problem may not be limited to recessionary periods. Over the last 20 years estimates suggest that the proportion of college-educated men who accepted nonprofessional, nonmanagerial jobs increased threefold, and the proportion for women went up fourfold.[12]

---

12. *Wall Street Journal*, January 16, 1976, p. 1.

The issue of job dissatisfaction and the accompanying underutilization of human resources has also received much recent attention. The Institute for Social Research at the University of Michigan recently published the results of an 8-year survey project on the quality of work life.[13] The project surveyed employee job attitudes, expectations, and experiences in 1969, 1973, and 1977 in an attempt to measure job satisfaction in terms of comfort, challenge, financial rewards, relations with co-workers, resource adequacy, and promotions. Although a majority of workers remained satisfied with their jobs over this period, the survey results indicated a significant decline in specific job satisfaction between 1969 and 1977, particularly pronounced after 1973. The most frequent concerns were exposure to health or safety problems, unacceptable hours and working conditions, inadequate wages and benefits, and insufficient job options.

We noted in Chapter 4 that the apparent decline in labor productivity advances in the last decade creates major problems for macroeconomic stability. Unhappy workers tend to be underproductive and therefore underutilized. High turnover, absenteeism, and grievance rates are all examples of this dissatisfaction and underutilization. Most workers want challenging jobs, opportunity for professional and personal growth, and decision-making authority, but the world of work has become increasingly characterized by overspecialization, impersonal work settings, and narrowly concentrated decision making. In short, the rapidly changing nature of employment is creating increasing demands for improvement in the quality of work life.

Much current research is being undertaken to contend with this problem, and several related policies are discussed in Chapter 7. In general, recommendations have been of two types: redesign of work and increased flexibility in employment. Examples of the former are decentralized decision making, use of work teams, more attractive workplace surroundings, improved health and safety conditions, and basic changes in production processes. Increased flexibility suggestions include flexible working hours, improved part-time employment opportunities, and career development programs. This problem is likely to remain particularly acute in the last two decades of the twentieth century, and it will increasingly occupy the attention of employment planners and personnel managers.[14]

WHAT IS FULL EMPLOYMENT?

Given the enormous social costs involved with unemployment and underemployment, most industrialized economies have placed considerable em-

---

13. See Robert P. Quinn and Graham L. Staines, *The 1977 Quality of Employment Survey* (Ann Arbor, Mich.: Institute for Social Research, 1978); and Staines and Quinn, "American Workers Evaluate the Quality of Their Jobs," *Monthly Labor Review* (March, 1980), pp. 29-31.

14. See Jerome M. Rosow (ed.), *The Worker and the Job: Coping with Change* (Englewood Cliffs, N.J.: Prentice-Hall, 1974); and *Employment and Training Report of the President, 1978*, pp. 9-10.

phasis upon achieving a fully employed labor force in the twentieth century. But exactly what is full employment, and how do we know when it has been achieved? These are the questions addressed in this section. To provide background for our policy considerations in Chapter 6, this section reviews the evolution of employment policy and the full employment concept in the United States.

The Evolution of Employment Policy

Neoclassical labor market theory to which we have alluded earlier generated what now seems to be a quite naive conclusion: There could be no persistent involuntary unemployment, although temporary frictional imbalances in labor markets were possible. If the demand for labor declined, this theory argued that money wages and employment would fall. But those who were no longer working were voluntarily unemployed in the sense that they were not willing to work at the lower wage. Alternatively, if they were willing to work at lower wage rates, their competition would drive down wages further and eventually more workers could be hired. Furthermore, since product prices would also fall in this scenario because production costs declined, the process would automatically restore full employment as more goods and services were demanded at those lower prices.

The prevailing belief that any persistent unemployment must be voluntary became completely untenable during the Great Depression of the 1930s, when as much as 25 percent of the labor force was unemployed. It was painfully obvious that these people were not voluntarily unemployed, and that they were quite willing to accept jobs at lower wages if only such jobs existed. Yet many economists and policy makers continued to argue in the early 1930s that the economic system was capable of restoring full employment by itself, and that governmental intervention would only be counterproductive. However, the Great Depression eventually had such a devastating impact upon the entire industrialized world that the neoclassical analysis of unemployment was largely rejected. Public sentiment in the 1930s shifted drastically toward the belief that direct government actions were necessary to ensure employment opportunities for those individuals wishing to work. This sentiment was reflected in many New Deal policies initiated during the Roosevelt administration.

During the Depression and World War II period, other forces were also contributing to the growing sentiment favoring governmental employment policies. In 1936 John Maynard Keynes published *The General Theory*. As we noted in Chapter 4, Keynes concluded that unemployment could easily persist whenever the equilibrium level of aggregate expenditures in an economy was insufficient to employ the entire labor force. Full employment and price stability, therefore, were largely accidental rather than automatic consequences of the operations of a capitalist economy. It followed from the Keynesian theoretical framework that governmental initiatives such as tax cuts or direct government spending would typically be necessary to move the economy toward a full-employment equilibrium. Keynesian analysis provided an academic rationale for the types of employment policies that were already being implemented in the 1930s, and it legitimized a continuing government role thereafter.

A final force resulted from our involvement in World War II. In the 1943-1945 period our unemployment rate hovered around 1 percent! The economy was clearly capable of quick mobilization for maximum wartime production, given the proper amount of government impetus and planning. A logical conclusion seemed to be that peacetime prosperity was also attainable with governmental assistance. At the very least, it was believed that strong post-war governmental employment policies were necessary to avoid a return to pre-war miseries.

Full Employment Act. Although public sentiment strongly favored some continuing role for government in providing employment opportunities, there was much disagreement on the appropriate limits of governmental action in the immediate post-war period. In the debate over the enactment of the *Employment Act of 1946*, some contended that full-blown economic planning to achieve full employment would require a degree of centralized governmental control totally inconsistent with a free-enterprise capitalist system. Such centralized control was accepted as a necessary component of effective war-time mobilization, but many argued that its continuation into peacetime would threaten the economic freedom and personal liberties upon which our system is based. Proponents of comprehensive governmental policies, on the other hand, argued that there is no true economic freedom in a society where millions of able-bodied workers cannot find employment. To the advocates of employment planning, limiting economic freedom by governmental employment policy was no more threatening than the limits that we place upon our basic political freedoms—religion, speech, the press, etc. All these freedoms are qualified by a necessary concern for the rights of others.[15] This fundamental debate over the role of government in a democratic, capitalist society continues today, as we shall observe in Chapter 6.

The final Employment Act reflected a compromise of the opposing positions summarized above. For example, the original version of the act was entitled the Full Employment Act, but the title and contents were modified to commit the federal government "to promote *maximum* employment . . . in a manner calculated to foster and promote free competitive enterprise" (italics added). Nevertheless, the act is extremely significant because it represented a

---

15. See, for example, William Beveridge, *Full Employment in Free Society* (New York: W. W. Norton, 1945); Friederich Hayek, *Road to Serfdom* (Chicago: University of Chicago Press, 1944); Herman Finer, *Road to Reaction* (Boston: Little, Brown and Co., 1945); John Maurice Clark, *Alternative to Serfdom* (New York: Alfred Knopf Publishing, 1948); and Barbara Wootton, *Freedom Under Planning* (Chapel Hill, N.C.: University of North Carolina Press, 1945).

governmental pledge to engage in active employment policy making, a pledge which would have been politically and economically unthinkable 15 years previously. Every administration, both liberal and conservative, since 1946 has committed itself in some manner to the pursuit of full employment.

Humphrey-Hawkins Act. These same issues resurfaced once again during the 1974-1975 recession. At that time, Senators Javits and Humphrey introduced into Congress a bill establishing as national policy "the right of all Americans able, willing, and seeking to work to full opportunities for useful paid employment at fair rates of compensation." Entitled the Balanced Growth and Economic Planning Act of 1976, the bill proposed comprehensive national economic planning to achieve, among other things, a 3 percent rate of unemployment.

The bill subsequently generated heated debate between those advocating economic planning and those supporting maintenance of free enterprise. As a result the modified *Humphrey-Hawkins Act* soon appeared, in which all reference to economic planning was dropped. After further modification, this bill was enacted into law as the Full Employment and Balanced Growth Act of 1978. The act set goals for the reduction of unemployment to 4 percent and of inflation to 3 percent by 1983, the latter provision being added because of fears that an unemployment goal alone would have inflationary consequences. Although the act requires that the President and the Federal Reserve Board present annual plans for the attainment of the goals, no new programs or expenditures to create jobs or fight inflation were authorized. Furthermore, the President is allowed to modify the timetable for the unemployment goal when it is deemed desirable to do so.

In its final form, therefore, the act did not mandate nor provide funds for any additional employment or inflation programs, although it did reaffirm our commitment to full employment and price stability in specific terms. In a sense, the nation turned full circle in the late 1970s back to the events surrounding passage of the Employment Act of 1946. As noted, the earlier versions of that act called for an explicit commitment to full employment. Congress, however, was concerned about our ability to achieve that goal without conflicting with economic freedom and price stability, and the final Employment Act did not define a full employment target to be achieved above all other policy objectives. Similarly, some 30 years later these same concerns were ultimately reflected in the watered-down Humphrey-Hawkins bill which was enacted.

The Experience with Defining Full Employment

The task remains of defining full employment and considering the costs involved in achieving it. We can shed some light on this problem by reviewing our earlier definitions. We presented a general definition of unemployment as "the difference between the amount of labor supplied at existing wages and the amount hired at those wages." This is an acceptable theoretical definition of unemployment, but it is more useful for analyzing the operation of particular labor markets than for considering an economy-wide phenomenon for policy purposes. It would follow from this definition that full employment exists when the labor supplied at existing wages equals the amount hired at those wages. But that definition of full employment would require the absence of all frictional and structural unemployment, and we have observed that some unemployment of these types is almost always present. For our present purposes, this only suggests that full employment is not 0 percent unemployment.

One of the earliest international proponents of government action to ensure full employment was Sir William Beveridge, who defined full employment as "an excess of job vacancies as compared to unemployed persons."[16] In terms of our previous discussion, the Beveridge definition basically means that there would be no cyclical unemployment, although frictional and structural unemployment might persist. With respect to the accelerationist theory described earlier, the unemployment rate which would persist under the Beveridge definition is essentially the natural rate of unemployment. This definition also suggests a dilemma which we encountered previously. Recall our discussion of the Phillips curve, where we noted that as full employment is approached, inflation tends to result as wage increases in tight labor markets exceed labor productivity increases. A Beveridge-type full employment situation, therefore, is consistent with some structural and frictional unemployment, on the one hand, and it is in all likelihood inflationary in addition.

Much of our post-war experience in this country with defining full employment for policy purposes has focused upon these implications of the Beveridge-type full employment concept. Put bluntly, our definition of full employment has become a contingency definition, dependent upon the amounts of structural and frictional unemployment and the level of inflation that we are willing to consider inevitable or acceptable.

With respect to the inevitable amounts of structural and frictional unemployment, many economists and policy makers have argued that this component of total unemployment has increased in the last 20 years. In the 1960s, it was commonly believed that the unavoidable amount of frictional and structural unemployment was between 3 and 4 percent of the labor force. Today, many economists would contend that this full employment unemployment rate is in the 5-6 percent range[17] because certain groups with historically high unemployment rates, particularly young workers and women, have become larger components of the labor force. This trend tends to worsen the structural unemployment problem. We have also observed previously that the expansion of unemployment compensation coverage and benefits permits unemployed workers to prolong the job search process, contributing to higher levels of frictional unemployment.

---

16. Beveridge, ibid., p. 199.
17. See, for example, Geoffrey Moore, "Some Secular Changes in Business Cycles," *American Economic Review* (May, 1974), p. 133-37.

In terms of defining full employment with reference to an associated acceptable rate of inflation, consider Table 5-6. Soon after the enactment of the Employment Act, inflation displaced unemployment as public economic enemy 1. Immense amounts of forced savings which accumulated during World War II were unleashed upon the economy after the war, pushing up

Table 5-6   Annual Rates of Inflation and Unemployment, 1947-1980

Year	Consumer Price Index (1967=100)	Rate of Inflation (% change in CPI)	Rate of Unemployment
1947	66.9	14.4%	3.9%
1948	72.1	7.8	3.8
1949	71.4	−1.0	5.9
1950	72.1	1.0	5.3
1951	77.8	7.9	3.3
1952	79.5	2.2	3.0
1953	80.1	0.8	2.9
1954	80.5	0.5	5.5
1955	80.2	−0.4	4.4
1956	81.4	1.5	4.1
1957	84.3	3.6	4.3
1958	86.6	2.7	6.8
1959	87.3	0.8	5.5
1960	88.7	1.6	5.5
1961	89.6	1.0	6.7
1962	90.6	1.1	5.5
1963	91.7	1.2	5.7
1964	92.9	1.3	5.2
1965	94.5	1.7	4.5
1966	97.2	2.9	3.8
1967	100.0	2.9	3.8
1968	104.2	4.2	3.6
1969	109.8	5.4	3.5
1970	116.3	5.9	4.9
1971	121.3	4.3	5.9
1972	125.3	3.3	5.6
1973	133.1	6.2	4.9
1974	147.7	11.0	5.6
1975	161.2	9.1	8.5
1976	170.5	5.8	7.7
1977	181.5	6.5	7.0
1978	195.4	7.6	6.0
1979	217.4	11.3	5.8
1980	247.0	13.5	7.1

Source: *Monthly Labor Review*, August, 1981, Table 22; and *Economic Report of the President, 1981*, Tables B-31 and B-50.

the demand for goods and services and their prices. The next 10 years, however, were evidenced by rather remarkable price stability by today's standards. But notice also that the unemployment rate jumped to 5.5 percent in 1954 and remained at that level, on the average, for the next decade. Although these rates of unemployment generated considerable concern, as reflected in John F. Kennedy's politically successful 1960 pledge to "get the economy moving again," there was an equivalent fear that public policy directed toward a lower unemployment rate would rekindle inflationary pressures. Such pressures did reemerge, but not until we attempted to finance the Great Society social programs and the Vietnam War simultaneously during the Johnson administration of the late 1960s. During this administration, however, the average unemployment rate dropped by more than 1 percent from its average level of the previous decade.

The 1970s, of course, presented a much more dismal picture on both the inflation and unemployment fronts. In 1973 the Organization of Petroleum Exporting Countries (OPEC) first exerted its power to quadruple the price of oil, generating considerable inflationary pressure in the United States. Paradoxically, however, we also suffered a severe recession in the mid-1970s with brief periods of near-double digit unemployment. Some progress on employment was made in the late 1970s, but the unemployment record over the entire decade was still the worst of the post-Depression era. Nevertheless, by 1979 inflation was once again our major domestic problem, as we subsequently experienced almost 3 years of double-digit percentage increases in the price level.

For that matter, the rate of inflation throughout the 1970s was, on the average, at least 4 percentage points higher than during the previous 15 years. Furthermore, the inflation rate began to subside in 1981 only as near record rates of post-Depression unemployment were emerging.

We have already observed that our definition of full employment has crept upward due to increasing structural and frictional imperfections in labor markets. The data in Table 5-6, and a recognition of our continuing concern with inflation, lead us to a related conclusion. Not only must full employment be defined to account for some increased structural and frictional unemployment, but it also must be defined at a level consistent with a nonaccelerating rate of inflation. Once again, most consensus estimates of this full employment unemployment rate now fall in the 6 percent range, plus or minus a few tenths of a point.[18]

To summarize this search for a full employment definition, consider Figure 5-1, which depicts what evidence suggests is the relationship between

---

18. See U.S. Department of Labor, *Employment and Training Report of the President*, 1979, p. XIX; and George E. Johnson and Arthur Blakemore, "The Potential Impact of Employment Policy on the Unemployment Rate Consistent with Nonaccelerating Inflation," *American Economic Review* (May, 1979), pp. 119-23.

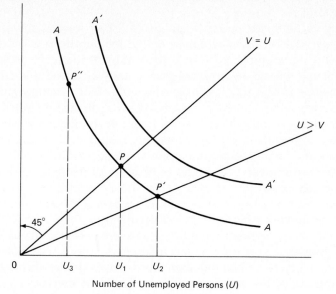

Figure 5-1   The Relationship Between Job Vacancies and Unemployment

job vacancies and unemployment.[19] Notice first that the number of job vacancies, or unfilled job openings, is measured on the vertical axis, and the amount of unemployment is measured on the horizontal axis. Curve AA shows a negative relationship between vacancies and unemployment; when unemployment is high, job vacancies will tend to be low, and vice versa. Note also, however, that the curve AA is convex from the origin. This means that even when labor markets are very tight, i.e., there are large numbers of job vacancies, some unemployment will persist (OU_3) because a large number of vacancies encourages workers to quit their jobs to search for better opportunities. Conversely, there will still be some unfilled vacancies even when unemployment is very high. These jobs might either require very unusual qualifications, or simply be extremely unattractive.

If labor markets were perfectly efficient and fully employed, as in the purely competitive model of Chapter 3, the economy would be at the origin in Figure 5-1. Where frictional and structural labor market imperfections exist, the economy will be located at some point on a curve such as AA. Note also that the 45° line in Figure 5-1 depicts geometrically all the points in the diagram where the number of job vacancies equals the number of unemployed, $V = U$. Any point on the 45° line, therefore, represents full employment according to the

19. See J. C. R. Down and L. A. Dicks-Mireaux, "The Excess Demand for Labour: A Study of Conditions in Great Britain, 1946-56," *Oxford Economic Papers* (February, 1958), pp. 1-33.

Beveridge definition mentioned earlier, although frictional and structural unemployment remain.

If the economy is currently on curve AA at point P, there is no cyclical unemployment because there are enough job vacancies to accommodate all those who are unemployed. The unemployment that persists (OU_1) must be frictional and structural. And since we already observed that OU_3 amount of unemployment is purely frictional, the amount of structural unemployment can be approximated by the distance $OU_1 - OU_3$ on the horizontal axis. Finally, if the economy is not fully employed in the Beveridge sense (such as at point P'), the number of unemployed persons is greater than the number of job vacancies and some cyclical unemployment exists ($OU_2 - OU_1$).

Two further observations are in order with reference to Figure 5-1. We have already concluded in discussing the Phillips Curve relationship that inflation will begin to set in as point P, where $V = U$, is approached. Any attempt to move further up curve AA (such as toward point P'') to diminish structural unemployment would create severe excess demand and demand-pull inflationary pressures. The second point therefore, which follows from the first, is that if cyclical unemployment has been eliminated through appropriate policy measures, the remaining structural and frictional unemployment can only be attacked at the probable cost of severe inflation, if the economy remains on curve AA. Of course, just as with the Phillips curve, structural and frictional imperfections may be improved by shifting the AA curve inward, i.e., by improving labor market efficiency. As noted earlier, however, we have not had great success in achieving such an inward shift. In fact, our recent experience suggests that increasing labor market imperfections may have caused an outward shift, such as to $A'A'$ in Figure 5-1.

The above discussion is not meant to suggest that all economists believe we must accept 6 percent unemployment inevitably, but it does imply that policies to lower the unemployment rate below this level must be carefully defined and targeted at structural and frictional imperfections, so as not to exacerbate inflationary pressures. We will discuss such policies in Chapter 6. For now we can conclude that the concept of full employment is not a stationary target, but rather a dynamic policy objective which must unfortunately be defined in relationship to a changing labor force and a socially acceptable rate of inflation.

UNRESOLVED ISSUES

There are, of course, numerous unresolved unemployment issues which persist in the United States today, and these will be taken up in the next chapter. The policy controversies are typically based upon disagreements over the predominant causes of unemployment. In the last 20 years or so, the Keynesian view that deficient aggregate demand is the primary explanation for high unemployment has been challenged on several fronts. Since the causes of unemployment are a subject of this chapter, we conclude by summarizing these important causal controversies.

The Structuralist Controversy

The structuralists have argued that a mismatch exists between the skills of the unemployed and the needs of employers due to the changing composition of demand, technological advancement, and geographic shifts in economic activity. Charles Killingsworth, a leading proponent of the structuralist theory, has argued that the increasing skill requirements of a technologically advanced society place an additional unemployment burden on the unskilled.[20] This "labor market twist," as Killingsworth called it, occurs even during peaks in cyclical economic activity and, therefore, is not the result of inadequate aggregate demand. According to this view, when structural imbalances increase, the result can be portrayed as an outward shift in the Phillips curve or in the AA curve of Figure 5-1. The rate of unemployment associated with a given level of inflation increases.

As a result of this view, structuralists such as Killingsworth conclude that a Keynesian-type policy of simply stimulating demand to lessen unemployment will lead to large price increases with only small reductions in unemployment. This will occur because the structurally unemployed, whose skills do not match the employment needs, will remain largely unemployed as demand increases. The demand stimulation will therefore result primarily in higher prices for existing goods rather than in greater output. Structuralists contend that the low unemployment of the mid- and late-1960s has been incorrectly attributed to the stimulative 1964 tax cut. In fact, so they argue, a good deal of the decline in unemployment during this period occurred simply because the government changed its official unemployment definition to exclude 14- and 15-year-olds and those in government training programs. Some additional decline in unemployment also resulted from our involvement in the Vietnam War.

Keynesian theorists respond to these criticisms by arguing that adequate aggregate demand would eliminate most labor market imbalances, given sufficient time. They contend, in effect, that "square pegs can be rounded" by high levels of economic activity which create private incentives for labor mobility, retraining, etc. They argue further that there is little evidence of the kind of industry-or-occupation-specific unemployment concentration which structuralists envision.[21] Of course, they also point to the 1964 tax cut as evidence of the success of stimulative demand management. They contend that reductions in unemployment were occurring as the result of the tax cut impetus before the unemployment redefinition and any significant involvement in Vietnam. We

---

20. See Charles Killingsworth, "Automation, Jobs, and Manpower," in *Nation's Manpower Revolution*, Part 5, Hearings Before the Subcommittee on Employment and Manpower of the U.S. Senate Committee on Labor and Public Welfare, 88th Congress, First Session (Washington: U.S. Government Printing Office, 1963); Killingsworth, "Policies to Achieve Full Employment," in *National Commission for Manpower Policy, Report 14* (Washington: U.S. Government Printing Office, 1976); and Killingsworth, "Structural Unemployment Without Quotation Marks," *Monthly Labor Review* (June, 1979), pp. 29-34.

21. *Economic Report of the President, 1963*, chap. 2.

will discuss several important policy implications of this controversy in the following chapter, so keep the arguments in mind.

The Frictionalist Controversy

As inflationary concerns have become more prominent in the last 15 years, several other criticisms of the Keynesian emphasis upon cyclical unemployment policy have emerged. One source of this criticism is the accelerationist theory outlined in Chapter 4, which emphasizes the futility of stimulating demand at the natural rate of unemployment. Another group of economists have stressed the increasing frictional nature of unemployment, particularly that which results from high labor turnover rates in certain labor markets. They have warned that expansionary governmental policy attempting to increase aggregate demand and employment is inflationary and ineffective in coping with frictional unemployment forces. Relying upon unemployment statistics such as those in Table 5-5, frictionalists argue that unemployment has become increasingly concentrated among certain groups which experience frequent spells of relatively short-term unemployment.[22]

We have already noted some support for this argument in our discussion of the reasons for the differential impact of unemployment. Frictionalists contend that these frequent spells of short-term unemployment concentrated in secondary labor markets have resulted primarily from demographic changes in the composition of the labor force. They view the increasing presence of young workers and women in the labor force, with their higher than average rates of labor turnover, as the major source of increases in the overall unemployment rate. R. J. Flanagan, for example, has demonstrated that a major reason for the U.S. Phillips Curve lying to the right of those of some other industrialized countries is the higher job turnover rate in the United States.[23]

Frictionalists also rely upon the recent advances in job search theory which we summarized in Chapter 3.[24] They contend that various institutional forces in labor markets such as unemployment compensation, minimum wages, and union-imposed wage rigidities have prolonged the job search process. Wages are not allowed to provide the proper signals to job searchers, and the existence of expanding unemployment compensation benefits lessens the private costs of extended search. Therefore, more turnover and spells of unemployment result in a higher overall unemployment rate, and once again expansionary governmental policies fuel inflation while not attacking the proper cause of unemployment.

---

22. See *Economic Report of the President, 1975*, p. 97.

23. See Robert M. Solow, "What Happened to Full Employment?" *Quarterly Review of Economics and Business* (Summer, 1973), pp. 7-19; and R. J. Flanagan, "The U.S. Phillips Curve and International Unemployment Differentials," *American Economic Review* (March, 1973), pp. 114-31.

24. See Edmund S. Phelps (ed.), *Microeconomic Foundations of Employment and Inflation Theory* (New York: W. W. Norton and Company, 1970), Part 1.

Referring again to Figure 5-1, page 133, the recent frictionalist literature suggests that when labor markets are tight ($V = U$ or $V > U$), money wages and searcher wage expectations rise. Quit rates increase as job search intensifies, and the duration of job search may also increase. Hence, inflationary wage increases may occur in tight labor markets without any reduction in the rate of unemployment because quit rates and search duration increase. This conclusion is quite consistent with the accelerationists' contention that higher inflation will not achieve a permanent reduction in unemployment below the natural rate.

CONCLUDING REMARKS

Economists and politicians are often accused of being unable to agree on crucial social issues. The conclusion we have drawn here is one which we will be forced to confront again, namely, that policy controversies usually result from disagreements over the causes of social problems. Nowhere is this more true than with the subject of unemployment. We have reached a basic agreement, due in large part to the tragic experience of the 1930s, that unemployment and underemployment are socially costly phenomena inflicted disproportionately on certain groups. But we still seek a consensus on the major cause of the problem.

Since labor market operations are constantly evolving and shifting as market and institutional forces change, the search for dominant causes and appropriate policies becomes more difficult. And as we shall see more clearly in the next chapter, policy makers are keenly aware of the inflationary potential of employment policy decisions. The distressing stagflation of the 1970s has forced a reappraisal of existing unemployment theories and policy prescriptions, and the pursuit of alternative or revised explanations continues.

CHAPTER SUMMARY

Unemployment exists by definition when the amount of labor supplied at existing wages exceeds the amount hired. Official government statistics count all those individuals not working and either seeking work or waiting to be called back from layoff as unemployed. While the government collects many types of employment and unemployment statistics, the reliability and uses of these statistics have been criticized. Much of this criticism results from the numerous purposes of compiling and analyzing employment data.

Unemployment imposes severe psychological and economic costs upon individuals and society as a whole. The costs to those who become unemployed are most obvious, but all of society suffers in terms of increased social outlays to the unemployed and lost output. Young, female, and nonwhite workers tend to be disproportionately unemployed, primarily because of more frequent spells of unemployment. These groups' unemployment status has tended to remain constant or to worsen in recent years, and since they constitute an increasing proportion of the labor force, the overall unemployment rate has crept upward secularly.

Unemployment can be categorized for discussion into frictional, cyclical, and structural types, although they are not independent. Frictional unemployment results from short-term fluctuations in labor markets and from information and mobility barriers. Cyclical unemployment is caused by inadequate levels of aggregate demand during downturns in the business cycle. Structural unemployment is characterized by long-run mismatches between labor supply and demand by skill and/or area. Much controversy over the dominant cause, and the related policy prescription, has emerged in the last two decades.

The economy also loses potential output and affluence when workers are underutilized, even when employed. Involuntary part-time employment, discouraged nonparticipating workers, menial tasks performed by the highly skilled and educated, and job dissatisfaction are all examples of underemployment. Alleviating underemployment and improving the quality of work life will be major topics on the policy agenda of the next quarter century.

Although nineteenth century neoclassical economists argued that there could be no persistent involuntary unemployment in a free market economy, this view has not been accepted since the disastrous Great Depression of the 1930s. Beginning with the path-breaking work of John Maynard Keynes in 1936, public sentiment has shifted to favor some government role in promoting employment opportunities. With respect to defining full employment, the current prevailing view is that it must be defined relative to the amounts of structural and frictional unemployment and the level of inflation which are considered acceptable or inevitable. The controversy over the dominant cause of our unemployment program continues, with different schools of thought contending that both the structural and frictional components have been increasing.

KEY TERMS

unemployment
GNP gap
frictional unemployment
cyclical unemployment
structural unemployment
underemployment

full employment (Beveridge definition)
full employment (current consensus definition)
The Employment Act (1946)
The Humphrey-Hawkins Act (1978)

REVIEW QUESTIONS

1. By early 1982, the unemployment rate exceeded 9 percent. Provide two reasons why this statistic presents an incomplete picture of the severity of the unemployment problem at that time.

2. Assume that the unemployment rate is hovering around 8 percent. How would you explain to a full-time employed friend who has just received a 10 percent wage increase that he or she is suffering significantly from the unemployment situation?

3. Why is the changing composition of the labor force such a crucial factor in assessing the unemployment problem?

4. Carefully distinguish among the causes of frictional, cyclical, and structural unemployment. Why is it difficult to determine precisely which type is dominant?

5. Some have argued that recent concerns about the quality of work life have resulted from a "spoiled" work force in the United States. Do you agree? Why or why not?

6. In order to assess and combat an economic problem, we must first be able to measure its magnitude. Why is this a particularly important and difficult problem with underemployment?

7. In his recent book *The Zero-Sum Society* (New York: Penguin Books, 1981, p. 61), Lester Thurow observes that "Unemployment is high, but it is concentrated among the young. If we are patient, many believe demography will sharply reduce the number of young people and the unemployment problem may cure itself." Critically evaluate this statement.

ADDITIONAL REFERENCES

Beveridge, William. *Full Employment in a Free Society.* New York: W. W. Norton, 1945.

Heilbroner, Robert. *Beyond Boom and Crash.* New York: W. W. Norton, 1978.

Levitan, Sar A., and Robert Taggart. *Employment and Earnings Inadequacy: A New Social Indicator.* Baltimore: Johns Hopkins Press, 1974.

Levitan, Sar A., Garth L. Mangum, and Ray Marshall, *Human Resources and Labor Markets,* 3d ed. New York: Harper & Row, 1981, Part I.

National Commission on Employment and Unemployment Statistics, *Counting the Labor Force Statistics,* Washington: U.S. Government Printing Office, December, 1979.

Shiskin, Julius. "Employment and Unemployment: The Doughnut or the Hole," *Monthly Labor Review* (February, 1976), pp. 3-10.

Walsh, Ruth M., and Stanley J. Birkin (eds.). *Job Satisfaction and Motivation: An Annotated Bibliography.* Westport, Conn.: Greenwood Press, 1979.

THE WORLD
OF WORK . . .

Job Search Activities of Discouraged Workers

The National Commission on Employment and Unemployment Statistics, established in 1976 and chaired by Professor Sar A. Levitan, faced the immensely difficult task of reviewing and making recommendations concerning the entire array of our labor force statistics. One major issue addressed by the Commission, as we noted earlier, concerned the inclusion of discouraged workers in the unemployment count. The reading below briefly discusses a study which was conducted to assist the Commission in its deliberations on this issue.

Among the many issues relating to the labor force definitions currently under consideration by the National Commission on Employment and Unemployment Statistics are two concerning "discouraged workers"—persons outside the labor force who want a job but who are not looking for work because they believe no jobs are available: (1) Can the current definition of discouraged workers be improved? and (2) Should discouraged workers be included in the unemployment count rather than classified as "outside the labor force" because they are not looking for work?

These issues have long been the subject of much controversy among various interest groups in our society (business, labor, minority groups) and among academic labor market analysts. Much of the controversy centers on the significance of current job search among those out of work, because job search activity is central to the Government's present definition of unemployment and is implied in the term "discouraged worker." A popular image of a discouraged worker is a person who has lost his last job and, after a long and unsuccessful search, has given up looking for work. The present definition of discouraged workers, however, is based mainly on the workers' perception of the labor market, not whether they have actually tested it in the recent past.

Although official Government statistics on discouraged workers based on the Current Population Survey (CPS) have been collected, analyzed, and published quarterly for the past decade, no information on the prior search activity of the discouraged and other persons outside the labor force has been available until the present time. A recent supplementary inquiry into such activity was conducted through the CPS in September and Octo-

ber of 1978. The special supplement was funded by the National Commission to help it evaluate the definition of discouragement and the inclusion of some or all of the discouraged in the definition of unemployment. The added questions provided information on the prior search activity of nonparticipants during the previous 12-month period on the premise that any job search conducted in an earlier period would not reflect current labor-market commitment or attachment.

The main finding from the special inquiry was that 44 percent (or 265,000) of the discouraged workers identified in September and October 1978 had looked for work during the previous 12-month period. The incidence of job search activity was about the same for men as for women; women make up about two-thirds of the discouraged worker total. . . .

The incidence of job search among discouraged workers appeared to be related to whether they also had some work experience during the prior year. Those who had no work experience were somewhat more likely to have looked for work during the past year than those with some work experience to have looked since they had lost or left their job.

Considering either recent work or search experience, 62 percent of the discouraged workers had some form of labor-market attachments during the prior 12-month period. . . .

In summary, according to present definitions and procedures used in the CPS, the majority of discouraged workers had not entered that state as a result of a recent period of fruitless search. However, more than 3 of 5 had either some work or search experience during the prior 12-month period.

According to the September-October survey

results, if those discouraged for job-market reasons who had sought work during the prior 6 months were added to the definition of unemployment, the jobless total for that period would have increased about 200,000, and the official jobless rate would have climbed 0.2 percentage point. However, this comparison should not be interpreted as a precise measure of such change in definition, because (1) the entire question pattern for measuring discouraged workers would have to be changed and (2) the questions would have to be asked of all sample respondents, not just of those in the outgoing rotation groups as is done presently. Further testing of these changes will be necessary to obtain a more definitive evaluation of the effect of changes in definitions, survey questions, and survey procedures on the unemployment rate.

———

Source: Abridged from Harvey R. Hamel, "Two-Fifths of Discouraged Sought Work During Prior 6-Month Period," *Monthly Labor Review* (March, 1979), pp. 58-60.

Chapter 6

Wage-Price-Employment Policies

As we observed in Chapter 5, a social and political consensus has emerged in most industrialized countries in the twentieth century which condemns unemployment as an immensely costly economic phenomenon, and which firmly establishes some governmental responsibility for maintaining high levels of employment. Many countries have supported the pledge to pursue full employment policies as a part of their membership obligations in the United Nations, for example. In this country recognition of governmental responsibility to eliminate unemployment was first formalized with the passage of the Employment Act of 1946, which states in Section 2:

> The Congress hereby declares that it is the continuing policy and responsi- bility of the Federal Government to use all practicable means . . . for the purpose of creating and maintaining, in a manner calculated to foster and promote free competitive enterprise and the general welfare, conditions under which there will be afforded useful employment opportunities, including self employment, for those able, willing, and seeking to work, and to promote maximum employ- ment, production, and purchasing power.

We noted in Chapter 5, however, that there is no similar consensus with respect to the causes of unemployment and the corresponding optimal policy or policy mix. Much of the policy dilemma can be summarized by a careful analysis of the statement from the Employ- ment Act quoted above. It is clear that this policy statement commits the federal government to promote "employment opportunities" and "maximum employment." The statement is also a pledge, however, that federal policy will "foster and promote free competitive enterprise" and will promote "maximum purchasing power." As we will observe repeatedly when addressing labor policy issues, multiple policy objectives may not be mutually attainable. There may be an inconsistency between a strong federal government role in seeking full employment, on the one hand, and "free competitive enterprise" on the other. Similarly, the experience of the 1970s and our discussion in Chapters 4 and 5 strongly suggest that policies to achieve full employment may be counterproductive in promoting "maximum purchasing power," i.e., price stability. Unfortunately, consideration of appropriate employment policies cannot occur in isolation from the debate over govern- ment's role in promoting free competition and in combating the extreme inflation of recent years.

The policy issues of this chapter are therefore quite complex, but they are ones for which public awareness and knowledge are essential. We begin to sort through this policy maze by briefly reviewing and extending what we learned in Chapters 4 and 5 about the economic relationships among money wages, prices, and employment. Next, a number of wage-price-employment policies will be outlined and related to the inflation and unemployment theories.

WAGE-PRICE-EMPLOYMENT RELATIONSHIPS REVISITED

The exact nature of the crucial relationships among wages, prices, and employment is one of many unsettled questions in economics, as we have noted. To provide background for the consideration of appropriate public policies, this section briefly reviews our earlier discussion of this question and adds some recent contributions to the debate.

A Conceptual Review

We developed a basic Keynesian-type macroeconomic model in Chapter 4 which identified aggregate demand in the economy as the major determinant of the levels of employment and real wages. We then considered two basic theories of inflation: demand-pull and cost-push. In the case of demand-pull inflation, prices increase because aggregate demand continues to increase when the economy's resources, including labor, are already fully employed. This is the classic case of "too much money chasing too few goods," and there is little doubt that the increased inflation which we experienced beginning in the late 1960s was initially of this variety (see Table 6-1).

Cost-push inflation, on the other hand, results from excessive production cost increases. Although usually associated with the exercise by firms or unions of market power in price and wage setting, cost-push pressures may also materialize from external shocks such as the previously mentioned OPEC price hikes or periodic poor agricultural harvests. With this theory, inflation occurs if excessive wage, profit, or other cost increases are passed on in the form of higher prices, even without excessive aggregate demand. We also demonstrated that money wage increases tend to be excessive, or cost-inflationary, only when such increases exceed increases in labor productivity. Within the framework of our macro model, cost-push inflation focuses the cause of inflation more on the aggregate supply side. Of course, we should also reiterate that inflation which begins as the result of demand-pull forces may be perpetuated as cost-push pressures emerge, so that ultimately the two separate forces cannot be isolated.

In addition, we reviewed in Chapter 4 the traditional Phillips Curve relationship between inflation and unemployment. This relationship specifies a fundamental trade-off between inflation and unemployment such that inflation sets in even before the economy reaches full employment. This premature inflation may result because of cost-push pressures or because of structural problems in labor market adjustment. Nevertheless, the Phillips Curve theory suggests that traditional government spending, taxation, and money supply policies of the type recommended by Keynes can be used to stimulate or contract aggregate demand and "pick an acceptable point" on the curve.

Table 6-1   Annual Rates of Inflation and Unemployment, 1960-1980

Year	Rate of Inflation (% change in CPI)	Rate of Unemployment
1960	1.6%	5.5%
1961	1.0	6.7
1962	1.1	5.5
1963	1.2	5.7
1964	1.3	5.2
1965	1.7	4.5
1966	2.9	3.8
1967	2.9	3.8
1968	4.2	3.6
1969	5.4	3.5
1970	5.9	4.9
1971	4.3	5.9
1972	3.3	5.6
1973	6.2	4.9
1974	11.0	5.6
1975	9.1	8.5
1976	5.8	7.7
1977	6.5	7.0
1978	7.6	6.0
1979	11.3	5.8
1980	13.5	7.1

Source: *Monthly Labor Review*, August, 1981, Table 22; and *Economic Report of the President, 1981*, Tables B-31 and B-50.

The accelerationist school led by Milton Friedman challenged the Phillips Curve analysis and its implications beginning in the late 1960s. Their analysis concludes that with inflation workers will demand money wage increases to restore their lost purchasing power. As real wages are restored, unemployment returns to its old level resulting in an essentially vertical long-run Phillips Curve. We also noted that post-Keynesian theorists reject the accelerationist theory, arguing that the market power of firms and unions permits the establishment of wages and prices independent of demand and employment decisions.

Finally, in Chapter 5 we summarized the basic theories pertaining to the causes of unemployment. We distinguished between cyclical and structural unemployment, and we observed that Keynesian theorists and structuralists have long disagreed on which type of unemployment predominates. In addition, frictional unemployment was defined, and the rise in the frictional component was noted. In considering the definition of full employment, we were careful to point out that experience has forced policy makers to redefine the term to reflect changing frictional and structural labor market imperfections as well as a concern for nonaccelerating inflation.

Some Recent Supply-Oriented Explanations

The macroeconomic concepts and theories which we have reviewed almost universally suggest that wage, price, and employment levels must simultaneously be considered in devising policies to combat the lingering stagflation of recent years. The theories differ, however, in explaining the nature of the interrelationships among these variables. With the exception of cost-push theory and the more recent contributions of the post-Keynesians, however, these theories rather consistently focus upon market and aggregate demand in attempting to explain the problems of unemployment and inflation. With their emphasis upon economic and psychological forces operating on the demand side of labor and product markets, these theories do not seem to recognize labor and product market structural imperfections and labor productivity sluggishness as major factors in explaining simultaneous inflation and unemployment. Yet we have noted repeatedly the importance of these factors. To incorporate them, we need to summarize several recently developed arguments which place more emphasis upon the supply, or cost, side of labor and product markets.

Post-Keynesian Arguments. Writers in the post-Keynesian tradition have tended to place great emphasis upon an original Keynesian argument that the price level is determined by the relationship between aggregate money wages and labor's average productivity.[1] We explored such a relationship in our discussion of wage-price relationships in Chapter 4, pages 92-97. We observed a close relationship among money wage increases, labor productivity increases, unit labor costs, and inflation. Several writers have argued, as we noted, that money wage increases have significantly surpassed the rate of growth of labor productivity, particularly in the growing service industries.[2] This, along with cost-plus pricing practices, generates permanent cost-push inflationary pressures by increasing unit labor costs, even when the aggregate demand for goods and services is not excessive.

An extension of this argument is even more explicitly post-Keynesian. Sidney Weintraub has formulated a Keynesian-type model to explain simultaneous increases in inflation and unemployment.[3] In this model Weintraub

1. On this relationship see, for example: Sidney Weintraub, *Classical Keynesianism, Monetary Theory and the Price Level* (Philadelphia: Chilton Company, 1961).

2. See, for example, Paul Streeton, "Wages, Prices and Productivity," *Kyklos,* Issue 15, 1962, pp. 723-33; and William J. Baumol, "Macroeconomics of Unbalanced Growth; The Anatomy of Urban Crisis," *American Economic Review* (June, 1967), pp. 415-26.

3. Sidney Weintraub, *Capitalism's Inflation and Unemployment Crisis* (Reading, Pa.: Addison-Wesley Publishing Co., 1978). See also Wallace C. Peterson, *Our Overloaded Economy: Inflation, Unemployment and the Crisis in American Capitalism* (New York: M. E. Sharpe, Inc., 1981).

also identifies wage increases in excess of labor productivity increases as the key cause of inflation, but he pursues both the demand- and supply-side implications of this argument. An economy-wide increase in money wages exceeding productivity increases, along with a constant markup over costs to determine the price level, results first in an increase in aggregate supply because unit labor costs have increased. Increases in money wages also increase consumer spending which results in increased aggregate demand. But since prices have increased (because unit labor costs have risen), the additional money incomes of wage earners may actually buy fewer goods and services than before. If fewer goods and services are purchased, fewer workers are needed and unemployment will increase. In this scenario prices and unemployment may increase simultaneously, and Weintraub contends that this theory in fact explains much of the stagflation of the 1970s.

Arthur Okun has developed a related, although more comprehensive, view of our contemporary economy which incorporates what he calls *the theory of implicit contracts*, along with a number of inflationary adaptations.[4] To Okun, our inflation has its roots in a wage-price system which has increasingly become insulated from market supply and demand forces. Most prices are set by sellers who are concerned primarily in maintaining customers and market shares over the long run. As with the Weintraub model, these prices are set to exceed costs by a percentage markup which varies infrequently. For example, beginning in mid-1981 the world economy experienced a surplus of oil supplies as oil-producing countries chose not to reduce production as rapidly as consumption was declining. Yet oil companies in the United States and elsewhere continued to purchase crude oil at inflated prices from many oil-producing countries, and the price of gasoline and other refined products did not decline significantly. Why? The answer lies partially in U.S. oil companies' desire to maintain stable long-run relationships with their suppliers. Given the political possibilities of another major disruption in crude oil supplies such as that which occurred during the Iranian revolution, U.S. oil companies chose to pay inflated prices in the hope that these countries would maintain supplies to the United States in the future.

Similarly, both union and nonunion wages are set primarily on the basis of common long-run interests of employers and skilled workers in maintaining their job relationships. Wage and other personnel policies are geared to long-run equitable treatment, which means that wages are not lowered by employers during economic downturns and they are normally increased to stay in line with those of other similar workers. Furthermore, these wage increases show little correspondence to productivity increases in many industries.

According to Okun, this cost-oriented price and equity-oriented wage

---

4. Arthur Okun, "The Invisible Handshake and the Inflationary Process," *Challenge* (January-February, 1980), pp. 5-12; and Okun, *Prices and Quantities: A Macroeconomic Analysis* (Washington: Brookings Institution, 1981).

system desensitizes the process from market forces and introduces a natural momentum in the rate of wage and prices increases. He feels this system is not the result of evil monopolies or overly powerful unions. Rather it is a set of " . . . rather efficient arrangements for a complex interdependent economy in which customers and suppliers, workers and employers benefit greatly from lasting relationships."[5] This extensive set of implicit contracts does, however, create the previously mentioned wage and price increase momentum which tends to continue even when the economy slows down.

Complicating this problem is an extensive array of inflationary adaptations which emerge as inflation comes to be expected. Not only do workers bargain to maintain their real wages through mechanisms such as cost-of-living escalator adjustments, but businesses also adapt. They adjust prices to reflect the anticipated replacement cost of plant and equipment, shorten the intervals at which they raise prices, and stop guaranteeing prices of goods delivered in the future. These adaptations, along with the wage-price system described by Okun, merely speed up the wage-price spiral even when unemployment levels are substantial.

Supply-Side Economics. A final set of supply-oriented factors, which has come to be loosely termed *supply-side economics,* became the focal point of the Reagan administration's economic program. Although the new supply-side economists share certain concerns with the post-Keynesians, their emphasis and policy recommendations are distinctly non-Keynesian.[6] The supply-side economics adopted by the Reagan administration focuses upon the expanded role of government in the economy as a major inflationary factor.

Supply-side economists note first that the tax bill collected by all levels of government has increased substantially, both absolutely and as a percentage of national income. Although Keynesians contend that higher taxes are anti-inflationary because private purchasing power declines, supply-side economists such as Arthur Laffer disagree. They argue that most business taxes are treated as business costs and are passed on to consumers through higher prices. In the 1970s state and local sales and excise taxes and the federal payroll tax showed particularly substantial increases. These increases have led to a kind of tax-push inflation, as supply-siders see it.

In addition, supply-side theory provides a different perspective on the sluggish productivity issue which we have addressed previously. The argument is that the growth of our tax and transfer payment system has negatively affected our incentives to work, save, invest, and innovate. High marginal rates of personal taxation provide lessened incentives for workers to work

5. Arthur Okun, "An Efficient Strategy to Combat Inflation," *The Brookings Bulletin* (Spring, 1979), p.2.

6. For a range of views on supply-side economics, see Senate Budget Committee, *Leading Economists' Views of Kemp-Roth* (Washington: U.S. Government Printing Office, 1978); and Arthur Laffer and Jan P. Seymour, *The Economics of the Tax Revolt: A Reader* (New York: Harcourt, Brace, Jovanovich, 1979).

longer hours or become more productive, as well as stifling the motivation and ability of workers to save. Transfer payments discourage some able-bodied individuals from seeking employment. Furthermore, excessive business taxes discourage risk taking, innovation, research and development, and investment in improved equipment and production processes. In combination, supply-side economists contend that these results of increased taxation have played a major role in slowing down employment and productivity growth and, consequently, in fueling inflation.

Finally, supply-side economics condemns much government regulation of the economy for its adverse impact upon productivity and costs. The former chairman of President Reagan's Council of Economic Advisors, Murray Wiedenbaum, has estimated that the total business costs of complying with government regulations in the United States may be as high as $100 billion annually.[7] Particularly in the last 15 years or so, government regulation of business has expanded to address problems of pollution, discrimination, worker safety and health, product safety, etc. Supply-side economists do not favor the abolition of all such programs, but they argue that the costs of such regulations often far exceed the benefits to society. These costs are also passed on to consumers, and they represent spending by firms which otherwise could be used to invest in productivity-enhancing machinery, equipment, and research.

WAGE-PRICE-EMPLOYMENT POLICIES

We have now reviewed a number of inflation and unemployment theories which are pertinent to our consideration of wage-price-employment policies. Several observations should be made or reiterated at this point. First, since there is no clear consensus on the causes of our current inflation and unemployment problems, we can expect a similar lack of consensus on the preferred policy prescriptions. Second, it should now be clearly evident that we cannot consider full employment policy in isolation from the inflationary implications of such policy. As a matter of fact, as we have observed, employment policy is now typically expressed in terms of achieving an unemployment rate consistent with a nonaccelerating rate of inflation.

Finally, it is useful to distinguish between general policies which are directed toward the current inflation-unemployment dilemma and more specific, long-run policies which are intended to improve labor market efficiency. The latter category would include employment and training programs for disadvantaged workers, improved labor market information services, alternative work schedules, and labor market discrimination policies. These employment policies which focus upon frictional and structural imperfections in labor markets will be discussed in detail in the next two chapters. In this section we

---

7. Murray Wiedenbaum, "The High Cost of Government Regulation," *Challenge* (November-December, 1979), pp. 32-39.

concentrate on the major stabilization policy alternatives which attempt to achieve a nonaccelerating inflation rate of unemployment.

Demand Management Policies

John Maynard Keynes challenged the neoclassical contention that flexible wages and prices in a free market economy would guarantee full employment. His theoretical demonstration that a capitalist economy could reach equilibrium with substantial unemployment due to inadequate aggregate demand has been the cornerstone of post-war employment policy.

Fiscal policy. Where such unemployment exists, Keynes argued that the federal government should rely upon *fiscal policy*, i.e., tax and expenditures policies, to stimulate aggregate demand and employment. When the government increases spending, aggregate demand and employment increase in the same way that they do when businesses or consumers increase their spending. Alternatively, or in conjunction with spending increases, tax cuts will also stimulate aggregate demand and employment, according to Keynes, because business and consumer spending will expand as disposable income increases. Of course it is now well understood that such discretionary fiscal policy will usually preclude the balancing of the federal budget, at least on an annual basis. Nevertheless, Keynes viewed federal budget deficits as a necessary component of stabilization policy when the economy is at a less-than-full employment equilibrium.

The fundamental purpose of discretionary fiscal policy in combating unemployment is to eliminate the GNP gap (shown in Table 5-2, page 118) so that the potential, or full employment, GNP is achieved. The resulting federal budget deficit is financed in one of two ways. The federal government may borrow from the general public, by selling interest-bearing government bonds, or it may borrow from the Federal Reserve system, our nation's central banking system. Ideally, this debt will be retired when the business cycle moves into an excessively expansionary phase and the federal government runs a budget surplus (increases taxes and/or decreases government spending) to slow down the economy.

In practice, several complications arise in the application of discretionary fiscal policy to stimulate employment. Time lags exist between the initial recognition of a recession and fiscal policy implementation. Our democratic form of government responds slowly and cautiously to changing economic conditions, even if a political consensus in favor of expansionary fiscal policy exists (and such a consensus often does not exist). It has even been argued recently that something called the *political business cycle* often receives more political attention than the economic business cycle.[8] This argument contends

---

8. See Edward R. Tufte, *Political Control of the Economy* (Princeton, N.J.: Princeton University Press, 1978).

that politicians are likely to manipulate fiscal policy to create the most favorable economic conditions just prior to Congressional and Presidential elections, to enhance their reelection chances.

These politically motivated fiscal policy decisions may actually contribute to economic instability over the economic business cycle. For example, there is considerable evidence that the economic policies adopted by the Nixon administration in 1971 and 1972 reflected political business cycle considerations. The August 1971 wage-price freeze was coupled with expansionary fiscal and monetary policies, resulting in declines in both the inflation and unemployment rates in 1972 (see Table 6-1). Although these policy decisions may have been politically expedient, they were economically irrational. By 1973, after reelection and after the freeze was lifted, the earlier inflationary pressures had been intensified by the expansionary fiscal and monetary policies, unleashing even more excess-demand inflationary pressures.[9]

A second practical complication is that budget deficits are typically not retired, or eliminated, during expansionary phases. There is a certain political bias in favor of deficits. Tax cuts are much more politically popular than are tax increases, and the same bias has often existed in favor of government spending increases if the benefits are widespread and visible. This complication has contributed to the well-known expansion of the national debt. Although the direct inflationary implications of a large national debt are probably exaggerated, consistently large budget deficits do have a number of adverse economic consequences. For example, recent high interest rates and the corresponding economic sluggishness can be attributed to projected budget deficits under the Reagan administration.[10]

Also, there are some disagreements about the effectiveness of fiscal policy in alleviating unemployment. Critics belonging to the monetarist school of thought argue that if budget deficits are financed by borrowing from the public, the increased government spending which results will be counteracted by decreased consumer spending by those purchasers of government bonds whose disposable incomes have been reduced by the bond purchases. There may be an economic stimulus if deficits are funded by borrowing from the Federal Reserve system, these critics argue, but this stimulus results from an expanded money supply rather than from fiscal policy per se.[11]

Finally, there is the previously mentioned criticism that fiscal policy adopted to combat unemployment may have unacceptable inflationary side-effects. Even if the unemployment rate associated with nonaccelerating infla-

---

9. See George P. Schultz and Kenneth W. Dam, "Reflections on Wage and Price Controls," *Industrial and Labor Relations Review*, 30:1977, pp. 139-51; and Lester Thurow, *The Zero-Sum Society* (New York: Penguin Books, 1981), chap. 3.

10. For a summary of national debt issues, see Campbell R. McConnell, *Economics* (New York: McGraw-Hill Book Co., 1981), pp. 255-59.

11. See, for example, Alan Reynolds, "Full Employment Budget: How Good a Guide to Public Policy?" *Tax Review* (April, 1977), pp. 14-15.

tion has now become as high as 5 or 6 percent, as many economists argue, this contention has not been widely accepted in political circles. Continued fiscal stimulus when the unemployment rate reaches this range will be almost purely inflationary, according to the accelerationists. In short, if political lags and motives can be minimized, fiscal policy may be a useful tool in lessening cyclical unemployment. However, if fiscal stimulus continues after the cyclical unemployment is eliminated, serious inflation is likely without further reductions in unemployment.

The fiscal policy ideas of Keynes gained increasing acceptance between 1940 and 1970 in the United States and elsewhere. The 1964 U.S. tax cut was in fact a classic example of Keynesian economics in practice. As Table 6-1 indicates, our unemployment record was actually quite impressive in the 5-year period following the tax cut, and Keynesian economists attribute this success largely to the tax cut program. By 1971, even conservative President Richard Nixon was led to proclaim, "I am a Keynesian."

Monetary Policy. In the last 20 years or so, the Keynesian emphasis upon fiscal policy to attain full employment levels of aggregate demand has been challenged by proponents of *monetarism.* The monetarist school, which in terms of ideology is similar to the accelerationist school discussed earlier, is once again led by Milton Friedman.[12] Monetarists contend that there is a close and dependable link between the money supply and aggregate economic activity. They believe that economic stability is best achieved through control of the growth of the money supply by the Federal Reserve system. Although Keynesians do not deny the usefulness of monetary policy,[13] the monetarist view is that the fiscal policy emphasis of Keynesian economics leads to weak and uncertain effects.

Monetarists believe that the large federal government role which fiscal policy entails often results in counterproductive, wasteful programs. They view the private enterprise capitalist economy as largely self-stabilizing, with the proper money supply guidance. The fact that our economy has not been stable in recent years can be explained by excessive reliance upon fiscal fine-tuning and inconsistent discretionary monetary policy. Even the high level of employment achieved in the 1960s after the 1964 tax cut is attributed to monetary rather than fiscal policy success by monetarists. Specifically, they argue that rapid increases in the money supply in 1963 and 1964 stimulated employment levels.

---

12. See Milton Friedman and Walter Heller, *Monetary vs. Fiscal Policy* (New York: W. W. Norton & Co., 1969); Friedman, "The Role of Monetary Policy," *American Economic Review* (March, 1968) pp. 1-17; and Friedman, "Nobel Lecture: Inflation and Unemployment," *Journal of Political Economy* (June, 1977), pp. 451-72.

13. Recent work has noted that considerable monetarist elements exist in Keynes' work. See, for example, Thomas M. Humphrey, "Keynes on Inflation," *Federal Reserve Bank of Richmond 1980 Annual Report*, 1981, pp. 5-16.

As we observed, accelerationist-monetarist economists such as Friedman argue that pure inflationary pressures are generated by inflationary expectations when aggregate demand continues to increase after reaching the natural rate of unemployment. To avoid these inflationary pressures, aggregate demand must be stabilized at a level consistent with the natural rate of unemployment. Since monetarists view the money supply as the key determinant of aggregate demand, they argue that the monetary authorities in the Federal Reserve system should stabilize the growth of the money supply. They do not advocate the use of discretionary monetary policy to fine-tune the economy, however. Rather, they recommend the use of a *monetary rule* whereby the money supply is rigidly increased at the same rate as the increase in real aggregate output in the economy. In a nutshell, if the money supply is allowed to grow at a constant 2-4 percent annually, any downturn in economic activity will soon be counteracted by expanded aggregate demand resulting from the money supply growth. Similarly, any inflationary levels of aggregate demand which arise will be diminished by a money supply which is inadequate to fund those levels of demand.

However, assume that the economy has achieved the natural rate of unemployment, and that monetary authorities attempt to diminish unemployment further by implementing a discretionary increase in the money supply which exceeds the monetary rule. The previously mentioned inflationary expectations mechanism takes over, but the expanded money supply merely fuels price and wage increases without any permanent reduction in unemployment. Hence, the deviation from the monetary rule not only is unsuccessful in expanding employment but also creates severe inflationary pressures.

Note carefully the important employment policy issues inherent in the Keynesian-monetarist debate. Keynesians advocate a strong federal government role in achieving full employment, primarily through discretionary fiscal fine-tuning to expand aggregate demand. At the very least, according to Keynesians, such policies will allow the economy to achieve an employment level consistent with an acceptable level of inflation. Monetarist theory, on the other hand, condemns as futile and inflationary any discretionary policy (fiscal or monetary) which attempts to move the level of unemployment below the natural rate. The monetarist-accelerationist school, therefore, provides a very clear anti-inflation policy: stable growth of the money supply in accordance with the growth in real aggregate output. But it offers no short-run employment policy to lower unemployment below the natural rate. In the long run, many monetarists favor policies to improve labor market efficiency which will lower the natural rate of unemployment.

Over the long run, most economists agree that persistent inflation cannot continue without increases in the money supply. Similarly, most agree that a policy of rigidly stabilizing the money supply for a sufficiently long period of time would eliminate most inflationary pressures. But strong disagreement exists over two related issues: (1) How much additional unemployment will result during the transitional period while a monetary rule depletes the economy of inflationary pressures? (2) What will be the length of the transitional period? Critics of monetarism contend that inflationary pressures and expectations which have become firmly imbedded in our economy during the last 15 years cannot be eliminated quickly without creating unacceptable economic hardship for many people. Lester Thurow, for example, has recently argued:

> The monetary authorities are confronted with the choice between letting the money supply grow and confirming the rate of inflation or stopping the money supply from growing and producing unemployment to go along with the inflation. But they do not have the power to stop inflation . . . without producing a major recession or depression.[14]

Put somewhat differently, opponents of monetarism argue that a rigidly tight monetary policy will lead primarily to diminished output and employment in the short run, without much of an effect on the inflation rate. Okun, for example, has estimated that a 1 percentage point reduction in the rate of inflation may be accompanied by as much as a 10 percent reduction in the year's GNP.[15] More recently, Ray Fair of Yale University utilized a simulation model of the U.S. economy in studying the effects of the tight money policy implemented by the Federal Reserve Board in late 1979. He concludes that this policy " . . . reduced real growth without having much effect on the rate of inflation."[16] Finally, critics point to the early 1980s experience as confirmation that tight monetary policy which reduces inflationary pressures also generates unacceptably high levels of unemployment.

Unfortunately, there has been no resolution of the Keynesian-monetarist debate among economists or policy makers. Our economy clearly needs enough fiscal and/or monetary discipline to avoid excessive demand inflationary pressures. The exact preferred form of this policy discipline, and the compatibility of employment policy with it, remain unresolved policy issues.

Public Service Employment. Since attempting to stimulate aggregate demand and employment through expansionary fiscal and/or monetary policies may have unacceptable inflationary side-effects, the federal government has become more involved in direct job creation during the last 15 years. Governmental efforts to check inflation by fiscal and monetary restraint in 1969 and 1970, for example, were coincident with an increasing unemployment rate which reached 6.6 percent by January of 1971. In spite of initial resistance from President Nixon, Congress passed the Emergency Employment Act in 1971 to provide roughly $2.25 billion to state and local governments for the temporary employment of 150,000 unemployed individuals. In 1973 the *Comprehensive*

14. Thurow, *The Zero-Sum Society*, p. 61.

15. Arthur Okun, "Upward Mobility in a High-Pressure Economy," *Brookings Papers on Economic Activity*, 1:1973, pp. 207-52.

16. Ray C. Fair, "Estimated Effects of the October 1979 Change in Monetary Policy on the 1980 Economy," *American Economic Review* (May, 1981), pp. 164-65.

Employment and Training Act (CETA) was passed, and 1974 saw enactment of the Emergency Jobs and Unemployment Assistance Act. These two acts together provided additional funds for *public service employment* (PSE) under CETA to combat both cyclical (CETA Title VI) and structural (CETA Title II) unemployment. Under President Carter, CETA PSE was expanded to 750,000 positions in 1978, although by early 1980 the program was down to 500,000 jobs. In 1981 President Reagan called for the virtual elimination of CETA PSE programs as a part of his budget-cutting initiatives, and most CETA PSE jobs were in fact phased out by 1982.

PSE is envisioned as a specific, often targeted employment policy tool that may reduce the natural unemployment rate in the long run, while lessening the inflation-unemployment trade-off in the short run. We know that unemployment rates vary considerably for various demographic subgroups of the labor force. Many analysts have concluded from this that while some labor markets are in equilibrium, others are characterized simultaneously by an excess supply of workers. PSE is viewed as the type of program which can be aimed directly at labor markets which are imbalanced, while not interfering with the others.[17]

Where PSE programs are targeted toward secondary workers, for example, the demand for such workers increases and unemployment among them will diminish. In principle, however, there should be little accompanying inflationary pressure from employing secondary wage earners because most would be employed in relatively low-paying occupations where wage-push inflationary pressures are minimal. Hence, the short-run trade-off between unemployment and inflation could be lessened. In the long run, if PSE programs are directed at disadvantaged workers who confront various labor market barriers to employment, the result may be a reduction in the natural rate of unemployment. Barbara Bergman and Robert Bennett, for example, conducted a study for the 1973-1975 period which simulated the effects of a hypothetical PSE program. They demonstrated that a large-scale PSE program could have reduced unemployment by an average of 1.2 percentage points over this period without causing any additional inflation.[18]

There are a number of weaknesses in PSE programs, however. It has repeatedly been argued that state and local governments will be tempted to use PSE funds to pay employees who they already employ, or who they already would have employed without PSE funds. Where this *fiscal substitution effect* occurs, no new jobs are actually created. Several empirical studies have demonstrated that some fiscal substitution occurs, although most studies con-

17. See James E. Pearce, "The Use of Employment and Training Programs to Reduce Unemployment," *Voice of the Federal Reserve Bank of Dallas* (November, 1979), pp. 2-12.

18. Barbara Bergman and Robert L. Bennett, "Macroeconomic Effects of a Humphrey-Hawkins Type Program," *American Economic Review* (May, 1977), pp. 265-70.

clude that the majority of PSE jobs have gone to individuals who otherwise would not have been employed.[19]

Critics of PSE also contend that the programs do not reach a large enough share of truly disadvantaged workers. Employers receiving PSE funds, like any other employers, have an incentive to hire the most qualified people who are eligible for PSE. This often leads them to hire the "least disadvantaged" of those who qualify for PSE. There is evidence that as many as one-half of CETA PSE participants in the early years of the program were not economically disadvantaged.[20] It is also argued that PSE is not sufficiently successful in ultimately placing workers in unsubsidized, non-PSE jobs. In 1979, for example, 53.5 percent of CETA Title VI PSE participants dropped out of the program or left for reasons unrelated to unsubsidized employment.[21]

We will discuss CETA more comprehensively in Chapter 7. With respect to PSE in CETA and other programs, a mixed conclusion must be drawn. Proponents of PSE continue to view it as a promising employment policy tool, especially in its apparent ability to create jobs without fueling inflation. They argue that most of the inefficiencies in our PSE programs were eliminated by the late 1970s, and that even more could have been accomplished with more adequate funding. Nevertheless, PSE critics won out in the Reagan administration as our employment policy shifted to the supply-side remedies which will be mentioned shortly.

Wage Subsidies. Unlike the CETA emphasis on public sector employment, a series of federal programs have emerged in the last 15 years to stimulate employment of disadvantaged workers in the private sector. Rather than paying the wages of workers who take public sector jobs, these programs involve the payment of wage subsidies, or the provision of tax credits, to private employers who expand their employment. Like PSE, however, these programs are intended to combat both short-run cyclical and longer-run structural unemployment problems, while hopefully lowering the noninflationary, natural unemployment rate.

The first federal wage subsidy effort began in 1967 with the establishment of the Concentrated Employment Program. Under this program employers were reimbursed for job training costs to encourage them to hire unskilled workers. Also enacted in the late 1960s, the Job Opportunities in the Business

---

19. See George E. Johnson and James D. Tomala, "The Fiscal Substitution Effect of Alternative Approaches to Public Service Employment Policy," *Journal of Human Resources* (Winter, 1977), pp. 3-26; and Johnson and Arthur Blakemore, "The Potential Impact of Employment Policy on the Unemployment Rate Consistent with Nonaccelerating Inflation," *American Economic Review* (May, 1979), pp. 119-23.

20. See *Employment and Training Report of the President, 1978* (Washington: U.S. Government Printing Office, 1978), p. 42.

21. *Employment and Training Report of the President, 1980* (Washington: U.S. Government Printing Office, 1980), Table 2, p. 28.

Sector program provided for the payment of training costs to firms that located in or near economically depressed areas.

Several tax credit programs were enacted in the late 1970s at both the federal and state levels. In 1977 the New Jobs Tax Credit was one of four programs included in President Carter's economic stimulus package. The 2-year program was intended to affect the additional hiring decisions of firms by providing a tax credit of 50 percent of the first $4200 of wages paid to each additional employee, up to a maximum of $100,000 per firm. To be eligible for this tax credit, employers were required to expand their employment, and the largest credits were paid for hiring unskilled and part-time workers. The Revenue Act of 1978 also contained provisions for tax credits of as much as 50 percent of the wages paid to members of targeted, disadvantaged groups.

The evidence on the effectiveness of wage subsidy programs is somewhat mixed, as was the case with PSE. The early subsidy programs such as Job Opportunities in the Business Sector were weakened by high employer administrative costs, low employer knowledge of the programs, and the belief on the part of some employers that only low-productivity workers could be hired under the program.[22] Perloff and Wachter found low employer knowledge of the New Jobs Tax Credit also, but they concluded that employment growth had occurred in firms that knew of the program.[23] The most positive estimates came from a study by Bishop and Haveman on the first year of the New Jobs Tax Credit program. They found preliminary evidence that the program improved both the level and composition of employment, while it contributed to a probable lowering of the nonaccelerating inflation rate of unemployment.[24] Once again, however, such wage subsidy programs were not given high priority in the supply-side dominated economic policies of the Reagan administration.

"Reaganomics"

The supply-side economics which formed the foundation of President Reagan's economic program identifies growth in government as the major cause of the stagflation of the last decade. The growth in government has had its adverse impact on the cost, or supply, side of labor and product markets. According to supply-side economists, the results have been tax-push inflation, diminished incentives to work and innovate, and overregulation.

---

22. See Daniel Hamermesh, "Subsidies for Jobs in the Private Sector," in John Palmer (ed.), *Creating Jobs: Public Employment Programs and Wage Subsidies* (Washington: The Brookings Institution, 1978).

23. Jeffrey M. Perloff and Michael L. Wachter, "The New Jobs Tax Credit: An Evaluation of the 1977-78 Wage Subsidy Program," *American Economic Review* (May, 1979), pp. 173-79.

24. John Bishop and Robert Haveman, "Selective Employment Subsidies: Can Okun's Law Be Repealed?" *American Economic Review* (May, 1979), pp. 124-30; and Bishop, "Employment in Construction and Distribution Industries: The Impact of the New Jobs Tax Credit," *Institute for Research on Poverty Discussion Papers* DP No.#601-80, 1980.

The policy prescriptions which follow from this analysis are straightforward, although quite controversial. Since unnecessary tax growth is a primary cause of our stagflation, it follows that a major tax cut should be implemented. This was, in fact, the cornerstone of supply-side policy under the Reagan administration, although it first surfaced in the form of the Kemp-Roth bill during the Carter administration. This bill was debated without passage by Congress in the late 1970s, and President Reagan strongly proposed its enactment as a part of his economic program in early 1981. The final tax bill enacted in 1981 bore close resemblance to the original Kemp-Roth proposal. It provided for a 25 percent across-the-board reduction in personal income tax rates, phased in over 3 years, plus cuts in taxes on corporations and capital gains. These cuts were envisioned to reduce tax-push cost pressures and enhance incentives to work and invest.

Two other major components of the Reagan supply-side program are government expenditure cuts and deregulation. The Reagan spending program included major cuts in nondefense expenditures. These cuts were particularly severe for social programs such as food stamps, Medicaid, and the previously mentioned CETA PSE program, all of which discourage work effort according to supply-side theory. In addition, President Reagan proposed a major review and reduction in the regulatory burden on business. It is not coincidental that Murray Wiedenbaum, mentioned earlier as a major critic of excessive governmental regulation, was appointed by President Reagan as chairman of his Council of Economic Advisors.

Supply-side economists foresee major economic improvements resulting from the Reagan program over time. The tax cuts will reverse the cost-increasing forces imposed by government on businesses in the past. In addition these cuts, along with cuts in government transfer programs and regulatory burdens, are expected to unleash a new surge of improved productivity and economic growth. With this growth in output and productivity, inflation is expected to decline at the same time that employment expands.

Another controversial contention of supply-side economists is that the tax cut will actually enhance the federal government's efforts to balance the budget, which in turn will permit more private borrowing, investment, and employment. This argument is based upon a theory associated with economist Arthur Laffer. The basic notion is that government tax revenues decline beyond some point as higher tax rates discourage economic activity, because declining economic activity means a lower tax base (lower national output and income) from which tax revenues are generated. In terms of a simplified example, a 20 percent tax rate on $100 of economic activity will generate more tax revenue ($20) than a 30 percent rate on $50 ($15). Once again, the alleged economic disincentives of high tax rates play a crucial role in the analysis. This is exactly the result expected by supply-side economists from the Reagan tax cuts. As tax rates are reduced, the resulting economic growth and productivity improvement are expected to expand the tax base and increase tax revenues. These increased tax revenues, coupled with federal expenditure cuts, were originally predicted to bring the federal budget into balance by 1984. By 1982, however, this original expectation was clearly seen as unattainable.

Although this supply-side approach has been enthusiastically supported and adopted by the Reagan administration as the means to curb inflation and stimulate employment, it has also been the subject of much criticism. The most overriding concern is that supply-side theory is largely untested. Concerning the alleged expansionary effects of the tax cut and the Laffer theory, critics agree that there is some high level of tax rates where tax revenues will decline. But, they argue, there is no evidence that we now have such high rates. If we do not, a cut in taxes may actually generate significantly less tax revenue, and a balanced federal budget will be impossible in practice. Opponents also contend that work and investment incentives will not be enhanced enough by tax cuts to pay for themselves through increased output and employment.[25]

Critics are also concerned that the tax cut may stimulate more inflationary pressures, rather than retarding them. Traditional Keynesian analysis suggests that personal tax cuts will stimulate aggregate demand. As taxes are diminished, increased after-tax incomes stimulate demand as spending increases. If this analysis is correct, more demand-pull inflationary pressures will be the likely result. As Robert Lekachman has recently argued, " . . . tax cuts are sure to increase consumer spending and stimulate more inflation before, at best, the productivity gains from larger investment could conceivably be realized."[26]

"Reaganomics" is also based heavily on the belief that tax and expenditure cuts will have a positive psychological effect upon the economy. In addition to increasing incentives for work and investment, the program is expected to instill a new confidence in consumers, businesses, and the financial community that the economy's health is improving. Inflationary expectations will therefore lessen, and the confidence will become self-fulfilling. This positive psychological impact was extremely slow in materializing in the early 1980s, however, as a tight monetary policy by the Federal Reserve Board and budget deficits kept interest rates at record high levels.

Liberal economists express strong disagreement with the general supply-side premise that big government must be replaced with free enterprise through reduced social expenditures, tax cuts, and deregulation. In so arguing, they point to the experience of other successful industrialized economies. Consider, for example, the following statement by Lester Thurow which appears in his best-selling book *The Zero-Sum Society*:

> In thinking about this solution, it is well to remember that none of our competitors became successful by following this route. Government absorbs

---

25. See testimony of Otto Eckstein in Senate Budget Committee, *Leading Economists' Views of Kemp-Roth*, op. cit., p. 53; and Henry J. Aaron and Joseph A. Pechman (eds.), *How Taxes Affect Economic Behavior* (Washington: The Brookings Institution, 1981).

26. Robert Lekachman, "But For Many It May Provide Pie in the Sky," *Rochester Times-Union*, Op-Ed page, February 10, 1981.

slightly over 30% of the GNP in the United States, but over 50% of the GNP in West Germany. Fifteen other countries collect a larger fraction of their GNP in taxes.

Other governments are not only larger; they are more pervasive. . . . Sweden is famous for its comprehensive welfare state. Japan is marked by a degree of central investment planning and government control that would make any good capitalist cry. Other governments own or control major firms, such as Volkswagen or Renault. Ours is not the economy with the most rules and regulations; on the contrary, it is the one with the fewest rules and regulations.[27]

The 1980s will provide a thorough experimentation with supply-side policies. Even before President Reagan took office, the Joint Economic Committee of the Congress in 1980 had explicitly gone on record in favor of tax cuts to improve productivity. It is important to reemphasize that these policies represent a dramatic departure from the Keynesian policy emphasis of the 1960s and 1970s.

Incomes Policies

Several critics of the Reagan administration supply-side policies have predicted that, when the Reagan policies fail, we will be forced to resort to some type of federal incomes policy, as we have on various occasions during the last 20 years. *Incomes policies* encompass a wide variety of initiatives which involve direct government influence on wages, prices, and real incomes in the economy. Such policies recognize the considerable market power over wage and price setting which exists in our economy. Given that power as a fact of life, incomes policies attempt to moderate wage and price decisions so that they are more compatible with the goals of full employment and price stability. Such policies are also viewed by proponents as necessary to dampen inflationary expectations. Incomes policies seek to shift the Phillips curve to the left, or to lower the natural rate of unemployment.

The Historical Experience with Incomes Policies. Mandatory wage and price controls were imposed during World War II and briefly during the Korean War. The objectives of these wartime controls, however, were significantly different from those of peacetime incomes policies. The first such peacetime incomes policy was established between 1962 and 1966 during the Kennedy and Johnson administrations. These voluntary wage and price guidelines were developed to provide labor and management with standards by which to judge the acceptability of wage and price increases. It is important to note that the annual inflation rate from 1960 to 1962 averaged about 1.5 percent, an amazingly low figure by current standards. The Kennedy-Johnson wage-price guidelines, therefore, were clearly established to avoid the anticipated infla-

---

27. Thurow, *The Zero-Sum Society*, p. 7.

tionary pressures of an expanding economy rather than to reduce existing rates of inflation.

Under this program, the basic noninflationary wage guideline was that wage increases (including fringe benefits) in each industry should equal the trend rate of increase in overall labor productivity. Recall that we reviewed earlier in this chapter the close relationship among money wages, labor productivity, unit labor costs, and prices. The Kennedy-Johnson wage guideline was based specifically on the premise that if wage increases do not exceed productivity increases, no upward pressure will be exerted on unit labor costs and prices. This guideline also provided for granting exceptions in industries with exceptionally high or low wage rates, or significant labor market disequilibria.

The basic Kennedy-Johnson price guideline was that prices should change in accordance with changes in unit labor costs. Hence for an industry following the wage guideline, prices should increase to cover increased unit labor costs if industry productivity was below the national trend rate. For example if the national trend rate of productivity increase was 3 percent, and the productivity increase in industry A was 2 percent, following the 3 percent wage increase guideline would increase unit labor costs by roughly 1 percent. Industry A's prices could therefore increase by 1 percent and be within the price guideline.

These guidelines were voluntary in the sense that no specific statute mandated compliance with the standards. The Kennedy and Johnson administrations used moral suasion in appealing to labor and business leaders to display socially responsible wage and price behavior. In practice, an occasional threat of antitrust investigation or Internal Revenue Service scrutiny accompanied this moral suasion. By 1966, compliance with the guidelines was breaking down as demand-pull pressures from the Vietnam War buildup began to emerge.[28]

In contrast to this voluntary incomes policy, the controls of the Nixon administration were mandatory and authorized by statute.[29] The Economic Stabilization Act of 1970 gave the President wide authority to stabilize wages, prices, and rents. Despite prior adamant opposition to wage-price controls, on August 15, 1971, President Nixon announced a 90-day freeze on all wages, prices, and rents to be enforced by a new Cost of Living Council. The freeze was intended to demonstrate the administration's preelection concern for inflationary pressures that were persisting in spite of increasing unemployment.

After the 90-day freeze, a Phase II period of wage and price controls was administered by a seven-member Price Commission and a fifteen-member Pay Board. Basic wages during Phase II were permitted to rise by 5.5 percent annually, with some exceptions. This figure was derived by summing the

28. See 1962 through 1968 issues of the *Economic Report of the President* for the changing status of the incomes policy over this period.

29. For a review of the Nixon incomes policies, see John Kraft and Blaine Roberts (eds.), *Wage and Price Controls: The U.S. Experience* (New York: Praeger Publishing Co.), 1975.

assumed 3 percent annual productivity growth rate and the 2.5 percent inflation rate goal.

In January 1973, the mandatory program was essentially converted to a voluntary one under Phase III. The standards remained basically the same, but the coverage was restricted and the Pay Board and Price Commission were discontinued. As Table 6-1 reveals, inflation accelerated during 1973, and another temporary freeze was announced in mid-June. By August, a relaxed set of Phase IV controls went into effect. When Phase IV ended in April of 1974 as Congress failed to renew the legislation, relatively few industries remained subject to the controls. In addition, inflation was by then proceeding at a double-digit rate.

The rate of inflation subsided somewhat after the recession of 1974-1975, but by 1978 it was on the increase once again. In late 1978 President Carter announced a new inflation policy which included voluntary wage and price guidelines once again.[30] Wages and fringe benefits in 1979 were to rise by no more than 7 percent annually, and price increases were to be limited to one-half of a percentage point below each firm's average annual rate of price increase for the 1976-1977 period. The goal of the Carter guidelines was to reduce inflation to 5.75 percent. Once again, exceptions to the standards were permitted for significant productivity increases, low-wage workers, previously negotiated collective bargaining agreements, and the preserving of historical pay relationships. A new feature of the Carter guidelines was the proposal for *real wage insurance,* whereby tax refunds would be paid to workers who adhered to the 7 percent wage standard if the annual inflation rate exceeded 7 percent. Although many economists supported the real wage insurance concept, that part of the program was subsequently rejected by Congress.

The task of monitoring voluntary compliance with the Carter guidelines was assigned to the preexisting Council on Wage and Price Stability. The focus of the Council's efforts was on the wage and price behavior of some 400 large corporations and the terms of major collective bargaining agreements.

The Effectiveness of Incomes Policies. What has our experience with incomes policies revealed to us concerning their effectiveness? Once again, the answers are not clear. Many studies were conducted on the effects of the Kennedy-Johnson guidelines, with mixed conclusions. In separate analyses, George Perry and Robert Solow found that wages and prices had risen 1 percent and 0.7 percent less, respectively, than they would have without the guidelines.[31] On the other hand, Robert J. Gordon was able to find no inde-

---

30. See U.S. Council on Wage and Price Stability, *Fact Book: Wage and Price Standards,* (Washington: U.S. Government Printing Office, October 31, 1978).

31. George L. Perry, "Wages and the Guideposts," *American Economic Review,* 57:1967, pp. 897-904; and Robert M. Solow, "The Wage-Price Issue and the Guideposts," in Frederick H. Harbison and Joseph D. Mooney (eds.), *Critical Issues in Employment Policy* (Princeton, N.J.: Princeton University Industrial Relations Section, 1966), pp. 57-73.

pendent effect attributable to the guidelines.[32] The difficulty in such studies, as is the case with much econometric work, is that accurate estimates must be made of the impact of a variable (the incomes policy) as compared to a hypothetical world where the variable does not exist. Without the aid of controlled experimental settings, such as those available to natural scientists, these impacts are very difficult to estimate with accuracy.

With regard to the Nixon controls, most evidence pertains to the late 1971 to early 1973 Phase II period. The majority of the studies conclude that Phase II controls reduced the annual rate of inflation by between 1 and 2 percentage points, with some lesser impact upon wages.[33] Several other analysts have argued that the Phase I and Phase II controls created serious distortions in many labor and product markets which actually intensified the rate of inflation thereafter. One recent study by Frye and Gordon concluded that the Nixon controls held down the price level by about 1.3 percentage points between mid-1971 and late 1972, but then they caused a rebound in inflation of 1.6 percentage points in 1974 and 1975.[34]

Judged purely in terms of the absolute 1978-1980 inflation record, the Carter program cannot be given high marks. These questions are relative ones, however. The Council on Wage and Price Stability estimated that its guidelines had reduced the rate of pure inflation by as much as 1.5 percentage points between March 1978 and March 1980, as compared with what it would have been in the absence of the guidelines.[35] And the unemployment rate also declined through most of this period. Nevertheless, the Reagan administration remained adamantly opposed to any type of incomes policy, choosing instead to rely upon the supply-side policies mentioned earlier.

The experience of other countries with incomes policies is similarly uncertain. Although incomes policies in European countries have tended to be more comprehensive and of longer duration than ours, overwhelmingly positive results have not been documented. In analyzing the experience of Western European nations, for example, Ulman and Flanagan found no instance where such policies had contributed significantly to a full employment, noninflationary economy.[36] And this study encompassed the pre-1970 period when the inflation-unemployment trade-off was much less severe in most countries than it is today.

---

32. Robert J. Gordon, "The Recent Acceleration of Inflation and Its Lessons for the Future," *Brookings Papers on Economic Activity*, I (Washington: The Brookings Institution, 1970), pp. 8-41.

33. See, for example, Robert F. Lanzillotti and Blaine Roberts, "An Assessment of the U.S. Experience With an Incomes Policy," Tulane Conference on Incomes Policy, 1973; and Kraft and Roberts, *Wage and Price Controls: The U.S. Experiment*, op. cit.

34. See George P. Schultz and Kenneth W. Dam, "Reflections on Wage and Price Controls," *Industrial and Labor Relations Review* (January, 1977), pp. 139-51; and Jon Frye and Robert J. Gordon, "Government Intervention in the Inflation Process: The Econometrics of 'Self-Inflicted Wounds'," *American Economic Review* (May, 1981), pp. 288-94.

35. Council on Wage and Price Stability, *Interim Report* (Washington: U.S. Government Printing Office, May 6, 1980).

36. Lloyd Ulman and Robert J. Flanagan, *Wage Restraint: A Study of Incomes Policy in Western Europe* (Berkeley, Calif., University of California Press, 1971).

Because of the mixed evidence which has been compiled on incomes policy effectiveness, several observers have recommended against their future use. Criticisms of incomes policies can be summarized under four categories. (1) It is argued that such policies interfere with the market mechanism, distorting resource allocation and precluding the flexible movement of wages and prices which is necessary to avoid shortages and surpluses. (2) Critics contend that incomes policies restrict basic personal and economic freedoms, such as freedom of choice and freedom of contract. (3) These policies entail a considerable administrative burden in seeking compliance, because there are usually considerable economic incentives to evade controls. (4) Monetarist critics contend that incomes policies simply will not work, since they do not attack the root cause of inflation—excessive growth of the money supply.[37]

Tax-Based Incomes Policies. In response to these criticisms, a growing number of economists have advocated that fiscal and monetary policy be supplemented with a *tax-based incomes policy* (TIP) to contend with the dual problems of inflation and unemployment. Originally proposed by Henry Wallich and Sidney Weintraub, TIP proposals all involve a system of special tax penalties and/or rebates to provide incentives to business and labor for compliance with wage and price guidelines.[38] The basic premise for TIP is the previously mentioned concern that the use of monetary and/or fiscal policy alone as anti-inflation measures results in unacceptable reductions in output and employment. TIP used in conjunction with tight monetary and fiscal policy can halt the "wage growth inertia" which is imbedded in our economy, proponents argue, permitting a reduction in inflation with less unemployment.

Furthermore, a TIP program may offer several advantages over the conventional incomes policies used in the past. Abba Lerner has argued, for example, that the limited success of past voluntary policies can be attributed to their preoccupation with holding almost all wage increases to the average productivity increase. Too little emphasis was placed upon bringing about larger or smaller wage adjustments where supply and demand conditions justified such adjustments. According to Lerner:

> The regulation, instead of working as a (crude) substitute for the price mechanism, became a price control—an interference with the price mechanism. . . . When the resistance was finally overcome by a bureaucratic recognition of the necessity for an "exception" . . . , workers everywhere else demanded equal treatment. The regulation then broke down and incomes

---

37. See Thomas M. Humphrey, "The Economics of Incomes Policies," in Thomas M. Humphrey (ed.), *Essay on Inflation*, 2d ed. (Richmond: Federal Reserve Bank of Richmond, 1980), pp. 173-75.

38. Henry C. Wallich and Sidney Weintraub, "A Tax-Based Incomes Policy," *Journal of Economic Issues* (June, 1971), pp. 1-19.

policy was abandoned. . . . The rules inevitably became much too complicated for general use long before they become sophisticated enough to be able to deal with all the different conditions which are effectively handled, in a market system, by the decentralized decision-makers. . . . [39]

Proponents such as Lerner argue that a TIP program would integrate the incentives and initiatives of decision makers into the operations of the incomes policy, resulting in enhanced resource allocation and economic freedom with less bureaucracy.

The original Wallich-Weintraub proposal has been termed the "stick" approach because it proposes using the tax system in a punitive way to limit wage increases. Under this plan, a national wage guideline would be established covering all compensation (including executive compensation and fringe benefits), and a tax surcharge would be imposed on any large corporation which exceeded the guideline in granting wage increases to its employees. For example, if the guideline was 7 percent and corporation A granted an 8 percent average annual increase in compensation, its corporate tax rate would be increased by some amount related to the excess over the guideline. If the tax surcharge was 6 percent for every percentage point by which the guideline was exceeded, corporation A would face a 52 percent corporate tax rate (the current 46 percent rate for most corporations plus a 6 percent surcharge).

Numerous variations of the Wallich-Weintraub plan have been proposed in recent years. Arthur Okun has suggested a more positive "carrot" approach which would lower the corporate tax rate for large firms that grant wage increases below the guideline.[40] Laurence Seidman has proposed a variant that incorporates both a "carrot" and a "stick" for granting responsible wage increases.[41] In response to the concerns of labor that TIP proposals are inequitably limited to wage increases, Seidman has more recently suggested a program which would include tax incentives for price restraint.[42]

All the TIP variations include the same alleged advantages. All proponents agree that union demands, employer-employee implicit contracts, and wage growth inertia cause most firms to implement larger wage and price increases at each unemployment level than are justified by pure market forces. In doing so, firms contribute to the situation where the unemployment rate associated with nonaccelerating inflation is too high. A TIP program would raise the resistance of management to excessive wage increase pressures, whether these pressures result from unions or from equity concerns and wage inertia. The tax penalty or credit would be certain to the firm at the time of the

39. Abba P. Lerner, "Stagflation—Its Cause and Cure," *Challenge* (September-October, 1977), p. 16.

40. Arthur Okun, "The Great Stagflation Swamp," *Challenge* (November-December, 1977), pp. 6-13.

41. Laurence S. Seidman, "A New Approach to the Control of Inflation," *Challenge* (July-August, 1976), pp. 39-43.

42. Laurence S. Seidman, "Equity and Tradeoffs in a Tax-Based Incomes Policy," *American Economic Review* (May, 1981), pp. 295-300.

wage decision, whereas the effect of monetary and fiscal restraint alone are uncertain to the firm.

The system would also be much more flexible than traditional incomes policies, according to its supporters, because wage increases above the guideline are not prohibited and do not require bureaucratic authorization. Hence, more economic freedom would be preserved, and larger wage and price increases could occur where strong market pressures call for such increases. In addition, most advocates would limit the TIP to only the largest 2000 or so corporations, thus significantly limiting the administrative burden of compliance regulation.

TIP proposals have not gone without criticism. Albert Rees, for example, has expressed concern that large firms would merely add the tax surcharge onto product prices and continue to grant excessive wage increases, thereby increasing inflation.[43] Seidman has responded that the tax penalty could be made severe enough to guarantee a profit squeeze from noncompliance, no matter how much market power the firm has. Rees has also contended that TIP proposals would increase the frequency and duration of strikes as workers become frustrated with the wage guideline. Okun and others have countered that some form of real wage insurance, similar to that proposed by President Carter and mentioned earlier, could be incorporated into the TIP program to ensure work cooperation.[44]

Critics have also disputed the contention that less bureaucracy and administrative costs would be involved with a TIP program. Most proposals have suggested using the Internal Revenue Service as a major administrative agency. With either the "carrot" or the "stick" approach, the monitoring and auditing costs of the IRS would be increased significantly. It is also necessary to identify and measure fringe benefit increases if these are to be included under the general wage guideline. This has always been a practical problem with incomes policies, but it becomes more crucial with TIP because the calculation of the appropriate tax subsidy or surcharge requires accurate measurement of the change in total compensation (including fringes). Finally, if a more comprehensive TIP were adopted which included tax incentives for price as well as wage restraint, the administrative burden would increase immensely.[45]

CONCLUDING REMARKS

There is no reason to conclude with an "Unresolved Policy Issues" section for this chapter. The different policy perspectives should be clear to you by

43. Albert Rees, "New Policies to Fight Inflation: Sources of Skepticism," *Brookings Papers on Economic Activity*, II (1978), pp. 453-90.

44. Okun, "The Great Stagflation Swamp," op. cit.

45. On these issues see Larry L. Dildine and Emil M. Sunley, "Administrative Problems of Tax-Based Incomes Policies," *Brookings Papers on Economic Activity*, II (1978), pp. 363-400.

now, and in one sense all the issues are unresolved. As mentioned in Chapter 5, the Humphrey-Hawkins Act provides a useful contemporary framework for considering once again the trade-offs inherent in employment and price stabilization policy making. The recurring recessionary and inflationary periods of the 1970s and early 1980s have cast serious doubts on our nation's ability to achieve economic stability. Traditional Keynesian macroeconomic policies seem to be insufficient. This has led some experts, including most supporters of the Humphrey-Hawkins Act, to conclude that new, more coordinated governmental initiatives are needed to manage the economy successfully. Many of these people would advocate the expanded use of a variety of demand management policies to create jobs, along with reliance upon an effective incomes policy of some type to ensure responsible wage and price behavior. Proponents of this view argue that a strong federal government role continues to be essential for economic stabilization, but that this role should involve new policy initiatives in a more coordinated and planned policy context.

Others, however, see our recent policy failures as indicative of a need to lessen significantly the government's presence in our market-oriented economy. Monetarists, accelerationists, and supply-side economists generally share the view that many public policies enacted during the last 50 years have unduly restricted the free operation of our economic system without achieving their intended results. For these advocates, less government intervention and perhaps more reliance upon a monetary rule for stabilization would allow an essentially free market economy to achieve an employment equilibrium without accelerating inflation.

Is it possible to draw any consensus policy conclusions from this seemingly irreconcilable debate? In one sense it is not, at least with respect to the fundamental issue of the role of the federal government. But some general policy directions can be formulated with which most economists would agree. First, enough monetary and/or fiscal restraint to avoid excess demand inflationary pressures is clearly necessary. Disagreements persist on the superiority of monetary versus fiscal policy, on the use of fixed versus discretionary rules, and on the sufficiency of these policies by themselves. Most economists would also agree that some protectionist, regulatory and tax programs of the federal government should be curtailed in the interest of reducing costs in the private sector. There is, of course, inevitable disagreement on which programs to cut. A majority of experts favor some direct role for the federal government in reducing the nonaccelerating inflation rate of unemployment over the long run. Whether this role should entail PSE, wage subsidies, training programs, and/or other programs remains in dispute.

These are agreements only of general policy direction. In terms of specific policy implementation, however, it must be concluded that the disagreements outweigh the agreements. Western industrialized nations have struggled for some time now with the seemingly conflicting goals of full employment, price stability, and free enterprise capitalism. Ultimately, of course, the priority given to various goals involves a political consensus such as the one which emerged strongly during the 1980 presidential election. That political consensus unmistakably called for less government and a strong dose of free market supply-side therapy. As suggested earlier, the Reagan economic program departed drastically from the prevailing policy of the past 20 years in its attempt to unleash the productive capabilities of our private enterprise system. As in the past, our future priorities will clearly be determined by the successes and failures of this latest policy approach.

CHAPTER SUMMARY

This chapter has emphasized that employment policy cannot be considered in isolation from the debate over government's role in promoting free competition and in combating inflation. Several views on the wage-price-employment relationship are reviewed which focus upon the demand side of labor and product markets. The post-Keynesian views of Weintraub and Okun place more emphasis upon money wage–productivity relationships and "implicit contracts" theory in attempting to explain simultaneous inflation and unemployment problems. The supply-side economics adopted by the Reagan administration also focuses upon the supply side of labor and product markets, although not within a Keynesian context. Supply-side economists emphasize that government intervention into the economy in the forms of high taxes, large transfer payments, and excessive regulation has restricted incentives to work, save, invest, and innovate, thereby increasing both inflation and unemployment.

Several wage-price-employment policies attempt to modify the demand side of labor and product markets to lessen inflation and unemployment. Fiscal policy (tax and expenditures policy) is used to stimulate or contract aggregate demand to stabilize the economy. Various time lags, political complications, deficit spending tendencies, and inflationary side-effects may lessen the effectiveness of fiscal policy.

Monetary policy attempts to achieve economic stability through control of the growth of the money supply. Most monetarists advocate a fixed monetary rule which allows the money supply to grow only as fast as the growth in real output. Critics of monetarism contend that rigid monetary policy alone will not be successful in reducing inflation without creating an extended period of unacceptably high unemployment. Public service employment (PSE), or direct job creation by the government, and governmental wage subsidies are two additional policies which have been used to stimulate employment for groups of workers.

With respect to policies affecting the supply side of labor and product markets, several schools of thought exist. The supply-side policies of the Reagan administration include tax cuts, government expenditure cuts, and deregulation to stimulate private productivity, savings, and investment. Critics, however, fear that the largely untested tax and expenditure cut theories will contribute to additional inflation and/or unemployment without providing the necessary private sector incentives. Numerous economists have advocated various incomes policies as a necessary component of stabilization policy. Such policies, which involve direct government influence on wages, prices, and real incomes, were employed in various forms during the peacetime administrations of Presidents

Kennedy, Johnson, Nixon, Ford, and Carter. A more recent proposed variation calls for a tax-based incomes policy (TIP) which would provide for tax penalties and/or rebates as incentives for compliance with wage and price guidelines. Proponents of incomes policies argue that they are necessary to lessen the pressure of union demands, implicit contracts, and wage growth inertia on wage and price levels. Critics contend that such policies restrict economic freedom and market forces, and that the past record indicates limited effectiveness coupled with unnecessary bureaucracy.

KEY TERMS

implicit contracts theory
supply-side economics
fiscal policy
the political business cycle
monetary policy (monetarism)
monetary rule
public service employment

Comprehensive Employment and
    Training Act (1973)
fiscal substitution effect
wage subsidies
incomes policies
real wage insurance
tax-based incomes policies

REVIEW QUESTIONS

1. Assume that the policy goals of full employment, price stability, and economic freedom are not mutually attainable, suggesting that priorities among the three goals must be established. How would a Keynesian, a monetarist, and a supply-side economist rank these policy goals? What ranking seems most defensible to you? Justify your priorities.

2. It is clear that if money wage increases are kept in line with productivity increases, inflationary pressures will be reduced significantly. Is it more feasible and equitable to limit money wage increases (through incomes policies) or stimulate large productivity increases (through supply-side policies) to bring these two variables in line? Why?

3. As a (soon-to-be?) skilled worker, do you expect to have an "implicit contract" with your employer which provides for equitable wage increases independent of market and productivity forces?

4. Both post-Keynesian and supply-side theories focus considerable attention upon the supply side of labor and product markets in explaining stagflation, and yet their conclusions and policy prescriptions differ drastically. Explain the basis for these differing conclusions and policy recommendations.

5. Summarize the policy debate between Keynesians and monetarists. Which view do you find most persuasive? Why?

6. Many economists have argued that inflationary expectations on the part of workers and employers become a self-fulfilling prophecy. In what sense is this true?

7. In his book *The Public Use of Private Interest* (Washington: Brookings Institution, 1977, p. 6), Charles Schultz criticizes one of our public policies tendencies as follows: "Instead of creating incentives so that public goals become

private interests, private interests are left unchanged and obedience to the public goals is commanded." Based upon this comment, would Schultz be more likely to favor a TIP program or wage-price controls? Explain your answer by relating various incomes policies to the quote.

ADDITIONAL REFERENCES

Aaron, Henry J., and Joseph A. Pechman. *How Taxes Affect Economic Behavior*. Washington: The Brookings Institution, 1981.

Friedman, Milton, and Walter Heller. *Monetary vs. Fiscal Policy*. New York: W. W. Norton and Company, 1969.

Kraft, John, and Blaine Roberts (eds.). *Wage and Price Controls: The U.S. Experience*. New York: Praeger Publishing Co., 1975.

Laffer, Arthur, and Jan P. Seymour. *The Economics of the Tax Revolt: A Reader*. New York: Harcourt, Brace, Jovanovich, 1979.

Okun, Arthur. *Prices and Quantities: A Macroeconomic Analysis*. Washington: The Brookings Institution, 1981.

Peterson, Wallace C. *Our Overloaded Economy: Inflation, Unemployment and the Crisis in American Capitalism*. New York: M. E. Sharpe, Inc., 1981.

THE WORLD
OF WORK . . .

Stagflation: New Forces Require New Prescriptions

In testimony before the Joint Economic Committee of the U.S. Congress in 1979, Arthur Okun discussed the new inflationary persistence of the 1970s and the diversified policy approach which he recommends. Excerpts from his remarks are found below.

. . . Unlike all previous reported U.S. recessions, the 1970 recession did not stop inflation in its tracks. Even more remarkably, the prolonged 1973-75 recession left us with a basic inflation rate of 6 percent.

The transformation of our inflationary behavior is rooted in a system of pricemaking that, throughout modern times has departed farther and farther from the textbook model. Most of our economy is dominated by cost-oriented prices and equity-oriented wages. Most prices are set by sellers with principal focuses on maintaining customers and market share over the long run. The pricing policies designed to treat customers reasonably relies on some standard measure of costs and a percentage markup that displays very little variation over the business cycle.

Similarly, the key to wage decisions in both nonunion and union areas is a common long-run interest of skilled workers and employers in maintaining their job relationships. Employers make investments in a trained, reliable, and loyal work force. They know that if they curbed wages stringently in a slump, they would pay heavily for that strategy with swollen quit rates by their workers during the next period of prosperity, and so during recession and slack periods, nonunion firms with workers on layoff and queues of eager job applicants find it worthwhile to raise the wages of their workers, in order to protect their longer-term personnel relationships.

. . . As people recognize the persistence of inflation, they change behavior in ways that make inflation more rapid and more tenacious. Prior to the 1970s, the U.S. economy had a basically noninflationary environment—average inflation rates in peacetime rarely exceeded 2 percent for any sustained period.

In that environment, price and wage decisions relied heavily on the dollar as a yardstick, a scorekeeping device, and a basis for planning and budgeting.

During the 1970s, these institutions changed as Americans adjusted to the persistence of inflation. The notion of par-for-the-course on wage increases was revised upward. Escalator clauses spread through the major collective bargaining contracts and thus made wages respond promptly to inflation in the cost of living. Businessmen began to adjust their pricing to reflect the growing gap between high replacement costs and low actual historical costs. They shortened the intervals at which they raised prices, and many stopped taking fixed-price orders. These adaptations to chronic inflation speed up the spiral, transmitting higher wages and other costs into higher prices and higher prices into higher wages even more rapidly.

That takes me to the second point. If left untreated, the syndrome of chronic inflation is likely to become more severe and to impose even greater economic and social costs in the 1980s. This neglect of inflation is malign, not benign.

. . . For the long run, no American can plan effectively in a world where the dollar remains the yardstick, but shrinks in real value at an uncertain rate.

Moreover, the ratcheting-up of inflation has produced a serious credibility gap between the citizenry and its elected officials. Americans have been told again and again that inflation would be curbed. But, in fact, it has kept ratcheting-up right to the present.

Finally, inflation has exacerbated social divisiveness. It is not easy for families to know where they stand in the price-wage race. They feel threatened by it and regard it as unfair. Many undoubtedly feel that they are behind in the race, even when that may not be objectively the case. And so, they feel that they have the short end of the stick and are convinced that somebody else must have the long end. The principal new product of the American economy in the decade of the 1970s has been sticks with two short ends.

Finally, I want to stress that an efficient anti-inflationary program must be diversified. It needs three major elements. First, enough fiscal-monetary discipline to provide a safety margin against excess demand. Second, a coordinated Federal initiative to reduce private costs; and third, constructive measures to obtain price and wage restraint.

We should set our fiscal and monetary policies to accept some down-side risks on output and employment in the short run. . . .

On the other hand, we must recognize the ill effects of overdoses of fiscal and monetary restraint. Those effects are clear in the sad experience of 1974-75, when we crusaded against inflation relying solely on tight budgets and tight money. . . .

There is no doubt that there is a pure fiscal monetary cure taken by itself for inflation. Nobody questions that. Nobody should. The questions all lie in the consequences of such a strategy. All the evidence suggests that those consequences for production, employment, capital formation, and for our social fabric would be horrendous. Average citizens cannot reasonably be expected to recognize those consequences fully, and it is understandable when some of them grasp at the straw of budget balancing in the hope of a rescue from inflation. But our political leaders ought to know better; and if they don't, they ought to be willing to learn better.

Turning to Federal cost-reducing initiatives, I want to stress that Federal policies have pervasive impacts on costs and prices in many sectors of the economy. The Federal Government adds to the price level when it imposes cost-raising taxes, like excises on products or payroll taxes on employers. Its social regulation for safety, health, and environment is a source of higher costs and prices—necessary in part, but unnecessary to some degree.

. . . In my judgement, the most serious inflationary stimulus in recent years came from a series of such self-inflicted wounds incurred during 1977: A major increase in payroll taxes on em-

ployers, a large rise in the minimum wage, reinstituted acreage controls in farming, added regulatory burdens on business, and new barriers to imports. . . .

. . . Finally, the need for price and wage restraint. During recent years, the price-wage spiral has been the most fundamental source of rapid inflation in the United States. Any efficient cure for inflation must get directly at that source.

. . . Informal semivoluntary policies of price and wage restraint have helped significantly over some periods of time. But such programs have been brittle in the face of changes in economic conditions and in business and labor reactions. And so they get phased out and then reshaped and reinstituted. Keeping an incomes policy in the anti-inflationary arena is not easy. P. T. Barnum once noted that keeping a lamb in a cage with a lion requires a large reserve supply of lambs. Similarly, society may need a reserve supply of incomes policies, because we will need some program of price-wage restraint for years to come.

Along with a number of economists, I have been advocating the development of a tax-based income policy, either in a reward or penalty form. There is a tremendous social interest in wage and price restraint, and it can be pursued better by providing market-type incentives for such restraint through the tax system than by relying on voluntary appeals or rigid mandatory rules.

. . . I do want to stress that my proposals are realistic. The only thing that bothers me is when people call them imaginative. In fact, there are two popular doctrines that require imagination. One predicts inflation will simmer down naturally or become tolerable to the American people. And the other proclaims that fiscal and monetary restraint alone can cure inflation without deep and prolonged recession. Those are the imaginative strategies. They have been tried and proven false.

Source: Abridged from the statement of Arthur M. Okun in *Stagflation*. Hearings before the Special Study on Economic Change of the Joint Economic Committee—Congress of the United States. 96th Congress, 1st Session, April 30, 1979, pp. 3-7.

Chapter 7

Human Resource Development and Planning

Chapter 6 focused upon various stabilization policies which may be used to achieve maximum employment consistent with nonaccelerating inflation. We observed there, however, that such policies must be complemented with programs designed to improve the marketable skills and productivity of workers and the efficiency of labor market operations, if long-run improvement in the level of employment is to be achieved. In short, the employment potential of the nation's human resources must be developed and realized. We first noted in Chapter 3 that various barriers, or labor market imperfections, impede the attainment of this potential.

For at least the last 20 years it has been a policy recognition in the United States that many individuals are unable to respond sufficiently to labor market incentives because of these barriers. Therefore, the government became involved in the 1960s in *manpower planning programs* to enhance the nation's employment potential. This term has now been replaced by either *employment and training policy* or *human resource development policy*, and we will use the latter term in this chapter. By whatever name, human resource development policy represents a wide range of endeavors designed to improve the quality of the labor supply and more efficiently use its potential. If employment goals such as those contained in the Humphrey-Hawkins Act are to be realized, job creation policies aimed at the demand side of labor markets are necessary, but not sufficient. Workers also must have skills which are demanded by employers, they and the jobs for which they qualify must be matched up efficiently, and their productive capabilities must be fully realized after they become employed.

These latter necessities are the essence of human resource development planning and policy, the fundamentals of which we take up in this chapter. We begin by tracing the emergence of human resource policy making in the United States. Next, the role of education and education policy in human resource development will be systematically considered, followed by a survey of programs aimed at training the structurally unemployed. Policies directed at occupational safety and health, labor market information, and alternative work patterns will also be discussed. Finally, the increasingly important human resource planning activities of private firms are addressed.

172

THE EMERGENCE OF FEDERAL HUMAN RESOURCE POLICY[1]

Early federal efforts at what could be loosely construed as human resource policy may be traced back as far as the Morrill Act of 1862, which established the nation's land grant universities. Somewhat later in the nineteenth century the federal government provided some financial aid for vocational education and minimally monitored apprenticeship programs in the skilled trades. But it was not until the Great Depression of the 1930s that any significant human resource policy was adopted.

The 1930s Through the 1950s

By 1933 commercial banks began to close, and the unemployment rate was approaching 25 percent of the labor force. In response to this vast underutilization of human resources, the Civilian Conservations Corps (CCC) program was adopted in March of 1933 as the first federal work relief and training program. Some 1500 camps for young, unmarried men were created to work on conservation and construction projects. Also in 1933 the Wagner-Peysner Act created the federally funded public employment services to place the unemployed in jobs. In 1935 the CCC was complemented by the establishment of the Work Projects Administration (WPA), an agency charged with developing and administering public service work programs for the able-bodied unemployed. One of the significant achievements of the WPA was the creation of the first sample survey of the unemployed. The Social Security Act of 1935 also provided the mechanism for establishing the federal-state system of unemployment insurance.

Of course, our involvement in World War II did much to alleviate the economic pains of the Great Depression, and many of the Depression era programs were allowed to expire. In 1944 Congress enacted the Servicemen's Readjustment Act (the G.I. Bill) largely as an act of appreciation for those who had served their country during the war. The act subsequently became an immensely important early human resource development program in providing education as well as vocational, technical, and on-the-job training to millions of honorably discharged veterans who otherwise would never have had such opportunities. As noted in Chapter 6, immediately after the end of World War II there was widespread concern with the possibility of a return of massive unemployment. Although the anticipated post-war recession never occurred, the enactment of the Employment Act in 1946 and the establish-

---

1. For a more thorough review of this subject, see Ewan Clague and Leo Kramer, *Manpower Policies and Programs: A Review, 1935-75* (Kalamazoo, Mich.: W. E. Upjohn Institute for Employment Research, 1976).

ment of the Council of Economic Advisors were intended to provide guidance to the President and Congress in formulating policies to combat unemployment.

There was little active human resource policy during the 1950s, although the seeds of future activity were being planted. Recessions of varying degrees of severity occurred in 1953, 1958, and 1961. Furthermore, by the late 1950s the so called "automation scare" was in full force. There was deep concern about the loss of jobs to increasingly automated production processes and about the loss of skills as automated jobs required only mechanical, intermediate-level skills. The unemployment problem became a major campaign issue of the 1960 Presidential election. As indicated earlier, a major theme of the Kennedy campaign was to "get the economy moving again," and the public expressed enough apprehension over unemployment to elect Kennedy by a slim margin.

The 1960s

The federal government had compiled a record of only intermittent, piecemeal attempts at human resource policy until the Kennedy administration took office. But several long-run forces were surfacing which favored more comprehensive efforts, in addition to the 1960 campaign issues. The pace of technological change had been forced to quicken during World War II and the ensuing cold war period, and that pace was maintained into the 1960s. A much more educated and better trained work force came to be demanded in the post-war period due to the increased technological requirements of many jobs and the educational attainment stimulated by programs such as the GI Bill. The new technologies also required large single-floor, continuous-process factories which were located primarily in suburban areas where land was available and taxes were lower. The unemployed, however, were increasingly located in central cities where they had migrated from rural areas to seek affordable housing. These people did not live where the jobs were, and public transportation was often inadequate.

All these forces seemed to converge during the early 1960s to demonstrate the need for more comprehensive federal human resource policies, and more fuel was added to the flame during the next turbulent decade. The post-war baby boom created a youth unemployment problem beginning in the 1960s which still plagues us today. The debate over the magnitude of the structural unemployment component began in earnest in the 1960s. This debate brought much public attention to the alleged structural changes which had permanently worsened the unemployment picture. The early 1960s also marked the beginnings of the massive civil rights movement. Initially targeted at overt segregation of blacks in many Southern states, attention soon turned to the provision of equal economic opportunity for many disadvantaged groups through programs designed to improve access to employment opportunities.[2] Finally, by the late 1960s human resource policy was envisioned as a major tool for combating skill bottlenecks which, as we first noted in Chapter 4, contribute to the Phillips Curve–type inflation-unemployment dilemma.[3]

The policy response to all these forces began in 1961 with enactment of the Area Redevelopment Act, which provided job-oriented training for unemployed and underemployed persons in high-unemployment areas. The most comprehensive early program was contained in the *Manpower Development and Training Act* of 1962 (MDTA) and its subsequent broadening amendments. It provided for institutional and on-the-job training for the unemployed, older workers, and disadvantaged youth; experimental and demonstration projects; and a variety of support services. Another major effort was the Equal Opportunity Act of 1964, which created a number of antipoverty programs such as the Job Corps and Neighborhood Youth Corps. The year 1964 also saw the passage of the Civil Rights Act, Title VII of which specifically prohibited discrimination in employment. In 1967, amendments to the Social Security Act created the Work Incentive Program as a training and jobs program for welfare recipients.[4]

The 1970s and 1980s

By the late 1960s, at least 17 federal government–administered programs existed which were categorized or targeted toward specific disadvantaged groups and problems. With the election of Richard Nixon in 1968, efforts began to decentralize and decategorize some of these programs. As the unemployment situation worsened in 1971, however, the Emergency Employment Act was passed to provide federal funds to local governments for hiring unemployed persons in public service jobs (see Chapter 6).

The debate over the preferred degree of centralization and categorization finally culminated in 1973 with the enactment of the Comprehensive Employment and Training Act (CETA). The act merged most of the prior statutes and categorical programs into a single system wherein local prime sponsors would receive and administer federal funds to shape human resource programs toward local needs. The act clearly represented a shift toward the decentralization and decategorization of federal human resource policy, although it has undergone several modifications in emphasis since its enactment. Originally stressing training and work experience programs, a shift toward public service

2. On this point, see Vernon M. Briggs, Jr., "The Employment and Income Experience of Black Americans," in Steven Picou and Robert E. Campbell (eds.), *Career Behavior of Special Groups* (Columbus, Ohio: Charles E. Merrill Publishing Co., 1975), pp. 382-403.

3. See Charles C. Holt, Duncan McRae, Stuart O. Schweitzer, and Ralph E. Smith, *The Unemployment-Inflation Dilemma: A Manpower Solution* (Washington: Urban Institute, 1971).

4. For more detail on the human resource programs of the 1960s, see Charles R. Perry, et al., *The Impact of Government Manpower Programs in General, and on Minorities and Women* (Philadelphia: Industrial Research Unit, The Wharton School, University of Pennsylvania, 1975).

employment occurred during the mid-1970s recession. Under the Carter administration emphasis was also placed upon improved management, private sector involvement, and youth unemployment programs. As already noted, the Reagan administration deemphasized the public service employment components as a part of its budget-cutting initiatives.

Some of these programs are discussed in greater detail in a later section on training the structurally unemployed. In analyzing the evolution of federal human resource policy in general, it is important to note that the programs have emerged in response to the dynamic nature of labor market operations. Because of numerous market imperfections, these operations have not proven to be sufficiently flexible to achieve the full employment potential of our nation's labor force. Furthermore, much of our human resource policy has been experimental as we seek more effective ways to enhance the employability of our work force. Although the level and form of this effort may change, the experimentation will continue throughout the 1980s as an important component of our search for full employment.

EDUCATION AND HUMAN RESOURCE DEVELOPMENT

If we were to analyze carefully the characteristics of the long-term unemployed and working poor as compared with the steadily employed nonpoor, perhaps no single characteristic would differentiate these two groups more explicitly than their differing education levels. Education has also played a major role in our economy's growth and development over the last century, and this has been the case for most other industrialized and developing nations as well. For example, in two separate studies of 75 nations conducted by Frederick Harbison and several colleagues, an extremely high correlation was found between these countries' levels of human resource development (measured primarily by the education of the labor force) and their gross national products.[5]

We first noted in Chapters 2 and 3 that the human capital approach to labor market analysis stresses education and training as major determinants of worker productivity and lifetime earnings. This approach is a fairly recent one, however, its contemporary origin being the work of Gary Becker and Theodore Schultz beginning around 1960.[6] It is not totally coincidental that total U.S. nominal expenditures on education increased from around $25 billion in 1960 to almost $165 billion in 1980. Over this same period of time the average

---

5. Frederick Harbison and Charles A. Meyers, *Education, Manpower and Economic Growth* (New York: McGraw-Hill Book Co., 1964); and Harbison, Joan Maruknick, and Jane R. Resnick, *Quantitative Analysis of Modernization and Development*, Research Report Series 115 (Princeton, N.J.: Princeton University Press, 1970).

6. Theodore W. Schultz, "Investment in Human Capital," *American Economic Review* (March, 1961), pp. 1-17; and Gary S. Becker, *Human Capital: A Theoretical and Empirical Analysis, with Special Reference to Education* (New York: National Bureau of Economic Research, 1964).

number of years of schooling completed by the civilian labor force increased from 10.9 to 12.7, and the proportion with some college education increased from 16.2 to 33.5 percent. The evidence is now clear that educational attainment is associated with enhanced employability and earnings; it also provides cultural, intellectual, and psychic benefits which improve the overall quality of life.

Beginning in the 1970s, however, our society's unbridled obsession with education came to be challenged. The generally weak performance of our economy in the last decade meant that expenditures for education programs stabilized, and educational institutions began to carefully scrutinize and cut programs as some institutional enrollments also stabilized and began to fall.

Critics also began to question the emphasis upon education for other reasons. Recall that human capital theorists treat the decision to invest in education just like other investment decisions, its desirability being based upon the expected private rate of return relative to that of alternative investments. Numerous studies in the 1960s reported high rates of returns for investments in schooling,[7] but the evidence compiled in the 1970s, particularly for college-level education investments, was much less encouraging. Richard Freeman has studied this issue extensively during the last decade, and he has provided evidence that the private rate of return to an investment in a college degree declined from 11 percent in 1959 to 8.5 percent in 1974. This, he argues, is the result of a decline in the relative economic rewards (lifetime earnings) attributable to a college education, as compared with a high school education. He also finds evidence that college enrollment declines in the 1970s reflect the realization on the part of young people that college investments have a lower payoff.[8]

The presumption that schooling is the crucial link between productivity and enhanced earnings has also been criticized. Although we have noted that there is a clear relationship between education and earnings, the exact causal linkage in that relationship is not so clear. The recent sociological literature has contributed evidence which suggests that family income, parental education, number of siblings and other home environment variables may be much more important than schooling in determining an individual's economic success. Christopher Jencks has even concluded that luck and personality may be the most decisive variables in predicting earnings.[9]

---

7. See, for example, B. Wilkinson, "Present Values of Lifetime Earnings for Different Occupations," *Journal of Political Economy* (December, 1966), pp. 556-72; Giora Hanock, "An Analysis of Earnings and Schooling," *Journal of Human Resources* (Summer, 1967), pp. 310-22; W. Lee Hansen, "Total and Private Rates of Return to Investment in Schooling," *Journal of Political Economy* (April, 1963), pp. 128-40.

8. See Richard B. Freeman, "Overinvestment in College Training," *Journal of Human Resources* (Summer, 1975), pp. 287-311; Freeman, *The Overeducated American* (New York: Academic Press, 1976); and Freeman, "The Decline in Economic Rewards to College Education," *Review of Economics and Statistics* (February, 1977), pp. 18-29.

9. Two major contributions to this literature are James S. Coleman, et al., *Equality of Educational Opportunity* (Washington: U.S. Office of Education, 1966); and Christopher Jencks, et al., *Inequality: A Reassessment of the Effect of Family and Schooling in America* (New York: Basic Books, 1972).

Others have emphasized what they see as increasing *credentialism* in labor markets. To these observers, certificates, diplomas, and degrees are useful per se in the employee selection process. They contend that firms minimize search costs by using educational credentials as an indicator of desirable employee characteristics. Credentialism is thus used as a screening device to limit job applicants, and some have argued that it results in discrimination against those with less formal education who could perform the job equally well. Dual labor market theorists have extended this argument to conclude that such credentialism tends to segregate women and minorities disproportionately into the low-paying secondary labor market, perpetuating income inequities.[10]

In spite of these recent criticisms and controversies, our nation has maintained a commitment to the importance of education as a component of human resource policy. Several specific aspects of this commitment are briefly taken up in the following sections.

Higher Education

Higher education, defined as all postsecondary education in colleges and universities, has exhibited remarkable enrollment growth throughout the post-World War II period. Most certainly the GI Bill played a major role in initially generating this trend, as noted earlier. In spite of the pessimistic observations by Freeman and others, the expected overall decline in college enrollments has not yet materialized. Demographic and perhaps human capital investment–related forces have begun to reduce enrollment in the traditional college-age group (18-21 years of age), but this trend has been counteracted by increased college enrollments for other age groups. Although overall enrollment declines have not yet occurred, there have been significant shifts in the distribution of enrollment favoring 2-year institutions and professional degree programs in fields such as the health sciences, engineering, and business.

It is likely that some decline in overall college enrollments will occur in the 1980s. The number of 18-year-olds in the U.S. population peaked in 1979 at about 4.3 million and will decline to around 3.5 million by 1986. Full-time–equivalent college enrollments are therefore expected to drop from about 10 million in 1982 to 9 million in 1988. Similarly, the supply of college graduates should decline slightly during the decade, as Table 7-1 indicates.[11]

The College-Educated Labor Market. Several experts have noted the somewhat unique nature of the college-educated labor market, some of the features of which we have already observed. Freeman has demonstrated that

---

10. On these points, see Ivar Berg, *Education and Jobs: The Great Training Robbery* (Boston: Beacon Press, 1971); and Peter Doeringer and Michael J. Piore, *Internal Labor Markets and Manpower Analysis* (Lexington, Mass.: D. C. Heath, 1971).

11. National Center for Education Statistics, *The Condition of Education* (Washington: U.S. Government Printing Office, 1978).

Table 7-1   Earned College Degrees in the Post-War Period

Year	Bachelor's and First Professional Degrees	Master's Degrees	Ph.D. Degrees
1948	271,000	42,000	4,200
1958	363,000	65,000	8,900
1970	772,000	211,000	29,000
1975	928,000	302,000	45,600
1980	1,090,700	373,200	38,900
1985*	1,025,000	405,000	42,000

*Projected
Source: National Center for Education Statistics, Washington.

the decision to attend college is largely determined by perceived economic prospects, i.e., income and employment opportunities. He has also argued that the supply of educated labor is quite inelastic in the short run, which is to say that increased demand for a particular educated occupation will not immediately lead to a forthcoming greater supply of qualified workers. The educational pipeline for high-demand occupations such as engineering represents several years of study, so that short-run adjustments take the form of salary increases or the hiring of less qualified persons. Because of these time lags, Freeman concludes that there is a long-run "feedback" process in these labor markets which tends to generate alternating shortages and surpluses of college graduates every 4 or 5 years.[12]

Although the demand side of the college-educated labor market reflects the changing industrial composition of employment, it has also been observed that demand and supply are interrelated. In other words, the amount of college graduates supplied determines, in part, the degree of their utilization by employers. This is merely another way to express the credentialism hypothesis, and it makes the future prediction of demand very uncertain. Another complicating factor is that few labor markets requiring college educations are closed. Significant numbers of scientists, engineers, and medical doctors, for example, have migrated to the United States in the post-World War II period. Finally, the private market for educated labor will not adequately perform the essential functions of basic research, preservation of cultural values, and the general advancement of knowledge. Therefore, governmental and private, nonprofit support is essential.

Government Funding of Education. Governmental support of educational programs has been pervasive at all levels of government. The provision of universal elementary and secondary education, for example, involved the

---

12. Freeman, *The Overeducated American*, p. 60.

expenditure of more than $100 billion in 1980. As noted earlier, the 1862 Morrill Act establishing the land-grant colleges constituted the first federal support to higher education, and the GI Bill represented another monumentally successful effort in this regard. Since World War II state and local support for 2-year and 4-year educational institutions has also increased phenomenally. The total expenditures for higher education institutions in 1980 exceeded $55 billion, an eightfold increase over 1960, and all but about 15 percent of that total came from state and local government sources.

At the federal level, large sums of funds have been provided in the last 25 years to support academic programs, especially in the natural and physical sciences and engineering. Similarly, basic research conducted at the nation's colleges and universities has been generously supported through various federally funded research foundations. Aid to students in the form of low-interest, deferred payment loans and need-based grants has enabled millions of students to complete college degree requirements. Currently the two major student programs are called Pell grants (previously BEOG grants) and Guaranteed Student Loans. In fiscal year 1981 the government spent more than $4 billion on these two programs alone. Although the growth in federal support for higher education slowed somewhat in the 1970s, more than $8 billion in total federal grants was still provided to higher education institutions in 1980, a tenfold increase over 1960 levels of support.

The decade of the 1980s represents a more uncertain period for higher education policy. Significant cuts in real appropriations for the federal student loan and basic research programs were implemented beginning in 1981. The previously mentioned doubts about education as a panacea for social ills have found their way into federal higher education policy making, and the extent to which state and local governments will be willing or able to fill the federal gap in funding remains unclear.

The Transition from School to Work

We have noted repeatedly the problem of youth unemployment, and much recent attention has been devoted to the transition from school to work for young people. The Department of Labor, for example, has begun funding of the *National Longitudinal Surveys* (NLS), a series of studies to trace a broad array of labor market experiences of various fixed age cohort panels through time. For example, in 1979 the Department of Labor authorized a 5-year panel study of several thousand youth who were between the ages of 14 and 21 in that year. Although the NLS studies have been used for a wide variety of purposes, one of the most important is to provide information on the school-to-work transitions of young people. This information will hopefully assist policy makers in alleviating youth unemployment.[13]

---

13. See David L. Featherman, "Issues for Manpower Research on Youth in the Transition from School to Work," *Journal of Economics and Business*, Vol. 32 (1979-1980), pp. 118-25.

A report by the National Commission for Employment Policy summarizes a national conference which also focused on this issue.[14] This report observed that young workers in the United States, especially those confined to secondary labor markets, lack information about occupations, careers, job openings, and employment services. The report found the greatest labor market disadvantages among young females and nonwhites without high school degrees. The conference participants recommended better coordination of human resource policies aimed at young people and more localized projects to bring together the participants in the school-to-work transition. Examples of these kinds of local efforts might include local councils composed of employers, educators, union members, parents, members of community organizations, and students. The report suggests that these councils could coordinate projects such as employment counseling services, community work-study programs, and job matching services. The report also contained recommendations for improved career education in the schools, better linkage of classroom and job experiences, and improved counseling and guidance.

The National Commission for Employment Policy itself recommended the implementation of several pilot models of a Youth Employment Corporation under CETA to improve federal human resource services to youth.[15] In modified form, this proposal was adopted by Congress in 1977 when it authorized renewed emphasis on youth employment programs in CETA. This renewed emphasis included programs for youth employment and training, a youth conservation corps, and community improvement and incentive projects. Although the number of young people is now beginning to decline as the result of reduced birthrates in the 1960s, this human resource problem will most certainly remain on the policy agenda of the 1980s.

Vocational Education

Federal support for vocational, or job preparation, education first emerged during World War I on a limited scale, with its focus upon meeting the skill needs of a few occupational categories. The Vocational Education Act of 1963 shifted emphasis to preparing specific groups of people for employment. The act broadened the definition of vocational education to allow expenditures for guidance, counseling, teacher training, and instructional materials. Congressional dissatisfaction with the program resulted in the Vocational Education Amendments of 1968 and 1976. The amendments decentralized the monitoring of vocational education programs into state advisory councils with independent budgets and staffs, and more categorical assistance was provided for the disadvantaged and handicapped, cooperative work-study ventures, the

14. National Commission for Manpower Policy, *From School to Work: Improving the Transition* (Washington: U.S. Government Printing Office, 1976).

15. National Commission for Employment Policy, *An Employment Strategy for the United States: Next Steps* (Washington: U.S. Government Printing Office, 1976), p. 78.

homemaking needs of working wives and the poor, and programs beginning prior to the eleventh grade and in postsecondary institutions.

In spite of federal efforts in the area of vocational education, the vast majority of funding comes from state and local governments. A little over $6 billion in public funds was provided for vocational education programs in 1980, for example, but over 90 percent of those funds came from state and local government sources. In real terms federal allocations for vocational education have declined significantly in the last 10 years, while total enrollments have doubled.[16]

Available data suggest that vocational education enrollments, in specially designated agencies as well as elementary and secondary schools, increased from less than 4 million prior to the Vocational Education Act of 1963 to more than 17 million by 1980. In recent years three out of every four high school students were receiving some vocationally oriented education. Furthermore, placement rates for those completing many types of vocational training are consistently above 95 percent. More recently, postsecondary and adult vocational education enrollments have risen more rapidly than secondary enrollments, as would be expected given the changing demographic trends.

Although there is some evidence to suggest a rate of return on investment in vocational education as high as 15-20 percent, more recent studies have found only limited evidence of improved stability of employment and enhanced incomes for vocational graduates. Critics have contended that too much emphasis is still placed upon agricultural, home economics, and other skills for which demand is declining. Local expenditures are often made with little regard for labor market conditions in the area. A fundamental debate centers on whether programs should concentrate on skill-specific on-the-job training or on more general classroom-oriented career development. The trend currently appears to be toward the latter.[17]

Financing Education

There is a strong probability that an individual's lifetime earnings and employability will be enhanced by additional education, although we have observed that the exact nature of this relationship is obscure. Whatever may be the current private rate of return to different levels of education, a strong economic argument could be made that if the only benefits are those that accrue to the individuals receiving the education, then those individuals

16. Sar A. Levitan, Garth L. Mangum, and Ray Marshall, *Human Resources and Labor Markets*, 3d ed. (New York: Harper & Row, 1981), pp. 151-53.

17. See Leonard A. Lecht, *Evolutionary Vocational Education—Policies and Plans for the 1970's* (New York: Praeger Publishing Co., 1974); Ernst W. Stromsdorfer, *Review and Synthesis of Cost-Effectiveness Studies of Vocational-Technical Education* (Columbus, Ohio: Ohio State University, 1972); National Academy of Education, *Education for Employment* (Washington: Acropolis Books, 1979); and Gene Bottoms, "Executive Directions," *Vocational Education* (January, 1979), pp. 10-11.

should pay the full costs of that education. Yet we have noted that elementary and secondary education is funded almost entirely by the general public through taxes, and a significant share of the costs of higher education is also funded through state and federal programs. What justification is there for such high levels of public financing?

Private and Social Benefits of Education. Human capital theory distinguishes between the *private rate of return* to a human capital investment (the rate of return calculated from the individual's investment costs and expected benefits) and the *social rate of return* (that calculated on the basis of society's investment costs and expected benefits). With respect to education it has long been argued that education involves "spillover" benefits to society which provide a rationale for at least partial public financing. Such spillovers may include direct economic benefits such as increased aggregate national output and income, as well as many indirect benefits such as improved democratic decision making and lower crime rates. In addition, equity considerations suggest that educational opportunities should be provided equally to all qualified persons, without regard to ability-to-pay constraints. If a more equal distribution of earned incomes is a social goal, a more equal distribution of educational opportunities may contribute to that goal. Therefore it is argued that public subsidies to education may improve both social efficiency (improved resource allocation and increased output) and social equity, although this is not necessarily the case.[18]

Funding of Elementary and Secondary Education. At the elementary and secondary level, the underlying equity principle is that the public should provide every student with the resources for universal education through the compulsory years. It is not the compulsion that justifies public financing, but rather the social benefits of an educated population and the private returns which we have concluded should be enjoyed by everyone. Although many students do attend private elementary and secondary schools, it is important to note that the vast majority of the population receives publicly funded education regardless of family income levels. This method of financing elementary and secondary education relies heavily upon local property tax revenues, and it has been criticized for providing inferior education for poorer school districts.

The major change in public school finance in the last decade has been the increased reliance placed upon state aid, which is financed primarily from state income and sales taxes. This shift has taken the form of attempts to equalize per pupil resources among school districts in the hope of equalizing educational

---

18. On these issues, see Richard Perlman, *The Economics of Education* (New York: McGraw-Hill Book Co., 1973), Part I; and Lester C. Thurow, "Measuring the Economic Benefits of Education," in Margaret S. Gordon (ed.)., *Higher Education and the Labor Market* (New York: McGraw-Hill Book Co., 1974), pp. 373-418.

opportunities. Another interesting but untried idea, called the *voucher plan,* was first proposed by Milton Friedman in the 1960s.[19] Under the simplest plan, each parent would receive a voucher per child equal to the average cost of educating a pupil in the public school system. The parent could then use the voucher to pay for public school education for the child, or could apply the voucher toward the cost of private school tuition. The result, according to Friedman, would be greater consumer (parent and student) choice in selecting quality schools, and better schools as they compete for students. Critics have argued successfully that such a program would lead to a proliferation of schools and a weakening of the current public school system.

Public Funding of Higher Education. The financing of higher education has become even more controversial in recent years. Here the social, as opposed to the private, benefits are more uncertain. We have noted that state and local governments provide the bulk of funding for public higher education, primarily through subsidized tuition which results in essentially equal out-of-pocket tuition for each resident student in each state. In addition to the elusive spillover benefits which society receives from higher education, the argument of equal educational opportunity is once again used to justify public subsidies.

These arguments were turned somewhat upside down in 1969 with the publication of an influential study by W. Lee Hansen and Burton A. Weisbrod.[20] Hansen and Weisbrod analyzed the income class distribution of costs and benefits for the California system of public higher education and concluded that the financing significantly redistributed income from poorer to richer income classes. This was, of course, a startling conclusion since it was assumed that public subsidies expanded educational opportunities for lower-income students. Their study did not deny this assumption, but it found that higher-income students were receiving a disproportionate share of the state subsidies. Although subsequent studies have criticized the Hansen-Weisbrod method and contradicted their findings,[21] recent higher education financing reforms have generally taken the form of more need-based student assistance and less across-the-board tuition subsidies to public institutions. The federal Pell Grants and numerous state need-based grants are such examples.

---

19. Milton Friedman, *Capitalism and Freedom* (Chicago: University of Chicago Press, 1962), chap. 6.

20. W. Lee Hansen and Burton A. Weisbrod, "The Distribution of Costs and Direct Benefits of Public Higher Education: The Case of California," *Journal of Human Resources* (Spring, 1969), pp. 176-91.

21. See, for example, E. Cohn, A. Gifford, and I. Sharkansky, "Benefits and Costs of Higher Education and Income Distribution: Three Comments," *Journal of Human Resources* (Spring, 1970), pp. 222-36; Joseph A. Pechman, "The Distributional Effects of Public Higher Education in California," *Journal of Human Resources* (Summer, 1970), pp. 361-70; Joseph W. McGuire, "The Distribution of Subsidy to Students in California Public Higher Education," *Journal of Human Resources* (Summer, 1976), pp. 343-53; and Gary A. Moore, "Equity Effects of Higher Education Finance and Tuition Grants in New York State," *Journal of Human Resources* (Fall, 1978), pp. 481-501.

In general, the trend in higher education finance has followed a set of recommendations put forth by the Carnegie Commission on Higher Education in 1973.[22] Among their recommendations were the following:

1. Future funding patterns should make the distribution of public support more selective with regard to financial need.
2. Public tuition should rise gradually to cover about one-third of educational costs.
3. A gradual narrowing of the tuition differential between public and private institutions should be sought through public tuition adjustments, state student aid programs, and private institutional aid.
4. State governments should develop comprehensive student assistance programs to enable low-income students to attend public or private institutions.

TRAINING THE STRUCTURALLY UNEMPLOYED

We have previously addressed the problem of structural unemployment in several contexts. We defined the problem in Chapter 5, and we also viewed evidence of its existence in discussing the uneven impact of unemployment (see Tables 5-3 and 5-4). In Chapter 6, we noted the likely inflationary consequences of attempting to reduce structural and frictional unemployment through conventional fiscal and monetary policies. It is now a commonly accepted fact that special employment and training programs are needed to assist the structurally unemployed, so that their employability is enhanced without exacerbating inflationary pressures. We have already discussed the major employment programs directed at the structurally unemployed—CETA Public Service Employment and employment tax credits—in Chapter 6. Here our emphasis is upon the training component of human resource development.

In the broadest sense the structural barriers in labor markets which create unemployment are quite pervasive, and include social-psychological handicaps and inadequate support services as well as deficient job skills and education. A recent report of the Joint Economic Committee of the Congress concluded:

> The structurally unemployed are Americans who cannot find work in bad or in good times. They are forgotten Americans. They do not want welfare, they want only the opportunity to become full participants in our economic life. We can't afford to waste the energy, the intelligence and the ingenuity of these people.[23]

---

22. Carnegie Commission on Higher Education, *Higher Education: Who Pays? Who Benefits? Who Should Pay?* (New York: McGraw-Hill Book Co., 1973).

23. Joint Economic Committee of the Congress of the United States, *The Effects of Structural Employment and Training Programs on Inflation and Unemployment* (Washington: U.S. Government Printing Office, 1979), p. v.

Viewed in this broad sense, almost all federal human resource development programs are aimed at least partially at the structurally unemployed.

Pre-CETA Programs

The evolution of the categorical programs enacted prior to CETA was summarized earlier in this chapter. Many of these categorical programs were maintained by local prime sponsors after the passage of CETA, although only the Job Corps and Work Incentive Programs remained as federal categorical programs under CETA. These programs have been classified into four major groups based upon the services offered and their expected short-term impact:[24]

1. Skill training programs
    a. MDTA institutional training
    b. MDTA on-the-job training
2. Job development programs
    a. Job Opportunities in the Business Sector (JOBS)
    b. Public Service Careers (PSC)
    c. Apprenticeship Outreach Program (AOP)
    d. Public Employment Program (PEP)
3. Employability development programs
    a. Opportunities Industrialization Centers (OIC)
    b. Concentrated Employment Program (CEP)
    c. Work Incentive Program (WIN)
    d. Job Corps
4. Work experience programs
    a. Neighborhood Youth Corps (NYC)
    b. Operation Mainstream

All these programs involve job training, although some also include direct employment, support services, etc. The most important categorical programs may be briefly described as follows:

MDTA institutional training. Classroom occupational training and support services for unemployed and underemployed persons who suffer skill deficiencies. Training relevant to the local labor market is provided at skills centers or at public or private vocational schools.

MDTA on-the-job training. Occupational training for the unemployed and underemployed provided generally through private industry at the work site. Training firms are reimbursed by the federal government for the training costs, and trainees are on the employer payrolls.

Job Opportunities in the Business Sector (JOBS). Training and employment for disadvantaged persons administered by the Department of Labor in

24. Perry, et al., *The Impact of Government Manpower Programs in General, and on Minorities and Women,* pp. 7-8.

conjunction with the National Alliance of Businessmen. In most cases, private employers contract with the Department of Labor to employ and train disadvantaged workers, and they are reimbursed by the federal government for extraordinary hiring and training costs.

Work Incentive Program (WIN). Training and support services for recipients of welfare payments under the Aid to Families With Dependent Children (AFDC) program, designed to move them to economic self-sufficiency. Work-eligible AFDC recipients are now required to register for the WIN program while receiving public assistance.

Job Corps. Training and support services for young men and women 14-21 years of age. Training is provided in skill training centers in or near the trainees' home communities. These centers are run by state and federal agencies, private industry, or private nonprofit agencies with federal funds.

Neighborhood Youth Corps (NYC). Training and work experience to students from low-income families while they are in school, or for school drop-outs.

Operation Mainstream. Training, employment, and support services for chronically unemployed needy adults who are ineligible for various reasons for assistance under other programs. Participants must be 22 years of age or older and at least 40 percent must be 55 or older.

Table 7-2 summarizes the enrollment and federal expenditures for the categorical programs over the period 1963-1974, prior to reorganization under CETA.

Table 7-2   Enrollment and Expenditures, Federal Manpower Programs 1963-1974 Fiscal Year Inclusive (Pre-CETA)

Program	Total Enrollment (thousands of persons)	Total Expenditures (thousands of dollars)
MDTA	2,519.1	$ 3,567,775
NYC	5,762.2	3,721,401
Operation Mainstream	180.1	490,436
Public Service Careers	160.1	339,946
Concentrated Employment Program	650.4	1,096,812
Work Incentive Program	997.7	886,427
JOBS	394.1	848,034
Job Corps	230.4	874,505
Public Employment Program	672.9	2,201,022
Totals	11,572.3	$14,085,480

Source: *Manpower Report of the President, 1975* (Washington: U.S. Government Printing Office, 1975), p. 317.

In terms of evaluating the effectiveness of the categorical programs, several cost-benefit studies in the 1960s drew favorable conclusions.[25] More recent studies have yielded less encouraging results, however. Levitan and Taggart found evidence that the JOBS program was not effective during periods of declining employment opportunities. Similarly, their initial evaluations of the WIN program concluded that relatively few enrollees in the program had been able to achieve economic self-sufficiency as a result of their enrollment.[26] Charles Perry and his colleagues surveyed many studies in drawing the conclusion that the posttraining earnings of program participants was clearly higher on the average than pretraining earnings. They also determined that program enrollees experienced overall increases in both employment rates and employment stability. In terms of moving the disadvantaged into the mainstream of employment, however, they found only minimal evidence of success.[27]

CETA

The 1973 Comprehensive Employment and Training Act was intended to accomplish three major goals. First, the planning and operation of CETA programs was transferred from federal control to state and local officials designated as *prime sponsors*. The basis for this change was the belief that local officials could develop services best suited to the needs of their areas. Second, the funding under CETA was decategorized so that local programs could be created without complying with specific federal categories of expenditures. Finally, funding was consolidated and coordinated through the local prime sponsors, rather than through the previous diverse network of local sponsoring agencies.

Prime sponsors under CETA are generally either states, cities, communities with populations of at least 100,000, or consortia of governmental units. Other than targeted programs (youth, special programs), CETA is typically directed toward an eligible population of economically disadvantaged, unemployed or underemployed individuals. An economically disadvantaged person is defined as a member of a family which receives cash welfare payments or whose annual income, adjusted for family size, does not exceed the poverty level. CETA also now requires the establishment of planning councils to include members from labor, business, clients, and community-based organizations. These councils are to act as advisory bodies to the prime sponsors.

---

25. For a survey of early studies, see Garth L. Mangum, *Contributions and Costs of Manpower Development and Training*, Policy Paper No. 5, Institute of Labor and Industrial Relations, University of Michigan and Wayne State University (December, 1967).

26. Sar Levitan and Robert Taggart, *Social Experimentation and Manpower Policy* (Baltimore: Johns Hopkins Press, 1971), pp. 47-55.

27. Perry et al., *The Impact of Government Manpower Programs in General, and on Minorities and Women.*

Table 7-3 summarizes the basic provisions of CETA after the most recent authorization amendments of 1978. Notice several components of CETA to which we have made reference previously. Titles II and VI contain the PSE programs for structural and cyclical unemployment, respectively. Title VII represents the efforts to increase private sector involvement in human resource programs which have been gaining emphasis in the last decade. Titles IV and VIII focus upon the youth unemployment problem which we have repeatedly addressed, including the school-to-work transition.

Table 7-3   Comprehensive Employment and Training Act
               as Amended in 1978 (Public Law 95-524)

Title I	*Administrative Provisions.* Organizational, planning, reporting, auditing, and other administrative provisions; general authorizations for fiscal years 1979-1982.
Title II	*Comprehensive Employment and Training Services.* Institutional and on-the-job training, work experience, job search assistance, and support services; counterstructural public service employment for long-term unemployed and welfare recipients.
Title III	*Special Programs.* Target group programs for native Americans, migrant and seasonal workers, ex-offenders, older workers, displaced homemakers, women, and the handicapped. Welfare reform demonstration projects.
Title IV	*Youth Programs.* Job Corps, summer program for disadvantaged youth, other youth programs.
Title V	*National Commission for Employment Policy.* Authorization of an advisory commission with both public and private members to be appointed by the President.
Title VI	*Public Service Employment.* PSE program authorizations related to the national unemployment rate for the low-income unemployed.
Title VII	*Private Sector Initiative Program.* Two-year demonstration of approaches to gain greater private sector involvement in training and employing the disadvantaged; established private industry councils to work with prime sponsors in improving access of CETA participants to private sector jobs.
Title VIII	*Young Adult Conservation Corps.* Conservation work in national parks, forests, and other public lands for youth 16-23 years of age.

Source: U.S. Department of Labor, *Employment and Training Report of the President, 1980* (Washington: U.S. Government Printing Office, 1980), p. 21.

Prior to the 1978 amendments, CETA had become increasingly dominated by the public service employment components which we discussed in Chapter 6. But these programs became the source of much controversy, as Garth Mangum and his colleagues have noted:

With three-quarters of a million persons employed under Titles II and VI, it required no great investigative reporter to find enough scandals to make a good story. Any relative of a public official in a public service employment slot, any rationing of available slots among political supporters, any previously laid-off local government employee picked up under CETA funds, any apparent frivolity in the design of activities were subject to adverse and often inflated publicity.[28]

To some extent, the 1978 amendments represented a return to the categorical programs and centralization of the pre-CETA era. More targeting of programs to those who were both unemployed and economically disadvantaged was required. New emphasis upon serving the handicapped, single parents, ex-offenders, and displaced homemakers, as well as youth, was included, as prime sponsor autonomy was curtailed.

Although the controversial PSE programs still received slightly over one-half of the total CETA outlays in 1980, training programs were being expanded, particularly the Title II and VII efforts. A new program of upgrading and retraining employed persons in dead-end, low-paying jobs was introduced in Title II. PSE was linked more closely with training, followed by the transition to unsubsidized jobs. Institutional and on-the-job training under Titles I and II, and the Job Corps for youth in Title IV, were given a higher priority between 1978 and 1980.[29] Of course, as already noted, major cuts in CETA appropriations were implemented by President Reagan in 1981, particularly in the PSE programs.

The 1978 amendments and the 1981 cuts in CETA appropriations were responses to numerous abuses and weaknesses in the programs. As mentioned previously, financially hard-pressed state and local prime sponsor governmental units sometimes laid off employees so that they could be rehired with CETA funds. This led Congress to place more stringent limitations on the duration of PSE, and the Department of Labor to promulgate rules prohibiting the substitution of CETA trainees for regular workers. CETA projects tended to become extensions of ordinary local and state government services rather than projects specifically designed to provide meaningful work and training for the disadvantaged. The lack of centralized fiscal controls of the decentralized programs also led to considerable fraud and mismanagement.[30]

Overall, about 60 percent of Title I, II, and VI enrollees in the 1978-1980 period were "positively terminated," which means they were either placed in unsubsidized employment, found jobs on their own, or were engaging in other activities that increased their employability. During this period, the Job Corps program of Title VI consistently had placement rates in the 90-95 percent

28. Garth Mangum, James Morlock, Marion W. Pines, and David Snedeker, *Job Market Futurity: Planning and Managing Local Manpower Programs* (Salt Lake City, Utah: Olympus Publishing Co., 1979), p. 47.

29. See U.S. Department of Labor, *Employment and Training Report of the President, 1980* (Washington: U.S. Government Printing Office, 1980), pp. 20-29.

30. See William Mirengoff, et al., *CETA: Assessment of Public Service Employment Programs* (Washington: National Academy of Sciences, 1980).

range.[31] More recently, the Employment and Training Administration has developed the *Continuous Longitudinal Manpower Survey* (CLMS) to track the employment and earnings experience of a sample of participants for 3 years after their enrollment in CETA programs. Preliminary results suggest that participants, particularly in on-the-job training programs, had significantly greater earnings than their nonparticipant counterparts. It also appears that the more disadvantaged participant groups measured the largest earnings increase.[32]

Although these data may suggest positive conclusions, the evaluation of CETA must in fact be much more qualified. Comprehensive data with which to evaluate CETA has been difficult to obtain. Although the government has put much time and money into evaluative studies, the lack of control groups until recently has made it difficult to draw definitive conclusions. Without a doubt the turnover in CETA programs has been high, the misuses of funds have been numerous, and the training for specific unsubsidized jobs has been inadequate.

Proponents of CETA and CETA-type efforts agree that the performance of these programs has been mixed. They argue, however, that we have never as a nation become fully committed to comprehensive human resource planning on the scale of the more successful European efforts. CETA supporters contend that the potential for abuse was greatly diminished by the 1978 amendments and Department of Labor regulations, and that most enrollees left the programs better off in employability or earnings potential than when they entered. They point to encouraging evidence that the private sector initiatives programs are meeting with success.

Critics have clearly won out for the foreseeable future, however. Public sentiment toward CETA has become decidedly negative as a result of publicity regarding the 1970s abuses. The Reagan expenditures cuts decimated the PSE programs, and federal human resource programs for the structurally unemployed have become at least temporarily a lower priority in the 1980s.

OCCUPATIONAL SAFETY AND HEALTH

Although occupational safety and health programs are often not included in discussions of human resource policy, they certainly fall within our earlier definition of such policies, i.e., they clearly seek to use the nation's labor force more efficiently. For many years work hazards were considered to be an inevitable part of work, and it was assumed that employees accepted the risk of injury as a part of the job. Occupational safety was not considered to be a matter of government concern until large-scale catastrophes occurred.

---

31. U.S. Department of Labor, *Employment and Training Report of the President, 1980* (Washington: U.S. Government Printing Office, 1980), pp. 28-38.
32. Ibid., p. 172.

The federal government was involved in a few piecemeal attempts at safety regulation prior to 1970, but for the most part such efforts were viewed as under the states' jurisdictional authority. Of course, this all changed with the enactment of the *Occupational Safety and Health Act of 1970* (OSHA). In the late 1960s, several factors contributed to a consensus favoring federal legislation. These factors include (1) a leveling off in the reduction of occupational injury frequency; (2) an increased awareness of occupational health problems associated with air contaminants, chemical agents, etc., such as the black lung problems in coal mining; (3) the spillover of the consumer movement into occupational safety and health issues; (4) increased emphasis on safety issues by organized labor; (5) the 1968 Mannington coal mine disaster.[33]

OSHA established three new federal agencies with authority over health and safety issues: the Occupational Safety and Health Administration in the Department of Labor; the National Institute of Occupational Safety and Health (NIOSH) in what was then the Department of Health, Education, and Welfare; and the independent Occupational Safety and Health Review Commission (OSHRC). The first two agencies were authorized to conduct workplace inspections and investigations, while OSHRC handles employer appeals of federal decisions. The law originally applied to every employer whose activities affected commerce, except state and federal government employers.

The act provided for interim safety and health standards until 1973, and then permanent and emergency temporary standards thereafter. Enforcement is based upon inspection by OSHA personnel, and until 1978 these inspections were often unannounced. In a 1978 U.S. Supreme Court decision, however, the court ruled that inspections without prior court-issued warrants are unconstitutional.[34] If an inspection reveals alleged violations, a citation is issued which the employer may contest. If contested, a hearing is held before OSHRC, and orders of the review commission are further reviewable by federal courts of appeal. Penalties for violations may be criminal or more typically civil, and may involve fines of $1,000 to $10,000 per violation.

It is well known that the enforcement of OSHA standards has been the subject of much criticism since the inception of the act. The standards soon proliferated to such an extent that the shape of toilet seats and the precise height of fire extinguishers were mandated. Criticism seems to come from all sides of the dispute. Employers claim that the compliance costs are an immense burden and that standards are often irrelevant to safety in particular work settings. Organized labor occasionally condemns OSHA officials for laxity in enforcing the standards and in imposing miniscule fines. As a result of these criticisms, by 1978 more than 1100 provisions that were seen as having no direct effect on worker safety and health were revoked. More emphasis was

33. Leo Teplow, "Comprehensive Safety and Health Measures in the Workplace," in Joseph Goldberg, et al. (eds.), *Federal Policies and Worker Status Since the Thirties* (Madison, Wis.: Industrial Relations Research Association, 1976), p. 222.

34. *Marshall v. Barlow's, Inc.*, 436 U.S. 307 (1978).

placed upon the "general duty of the employer" to provide a safe workplace, while the enforcement agency concentrated only upon the most serious hazards.[35]

Precise evidence on the impact of OSHA is hard to come by, primarily because of the difficulty of relating worker health and safety to industrial conditions. Because of these measurement problems, few studies have been able to isolate significant reductions in occupational injury, death, and illness attributable to OSHA. It has been estimated that even full compliance with existing standards would prevent at most 20-25 percent of occupational injuries, because of numerous other contributing factors not included in the standards. In cost-benefit terms, Northrup, Rowan, and Perry have estimated that the costs of compliance with the OSHA vinyl chloride standard alone would amount to over $200 million, or about $30,000 per endangered employee.[36] Although precise estimates of positive effects are rarely found, most experts agree that the regulations have greatly increased the attention given to health and safety issues in the workplace.

Beginning in 1974 President Ford ordered all agencies to include an inflation impact statement in proposed regulations, and more recently Presidents Carter and Reagan ordered cost-benefit analysis of such regulations with OSHA prominently in mind. In a potentially important U.S. Supreme Court decision in 1981, however, the court ruled that OSHA regulators do not have to satisfy a cost-benefit test before imposing rigid limits on worker exposure to toxic materials.[37]

The costs of OSHA compliance are measurable, and studies clearly suggest that they are considerable. The difficulty in utilizing cost-benefit analysis, however, lies on the benefit side of the balance sheet. As noted, it is extremely difficult to isolate reductions in worker injury and death directly attributable to OSHA. This is not to say that such reductions have not occurred, but only that their measurement is elusive. Even if such reductions in injury and death could be documented, the problem remains of putting a dollar value on them for cost-benefit analysis purposes. Supporters of OSHA contend that the costs of providing a safe workplace are legitimate costs of doing business which should be borne by employers. They argue that in the absence of standards businesses would shift the risks or costs to employees, or to society as a whole. Critics respond that regulatory costs for programs such as OSHA must be compared

---

35. On the evolution of OSHA standards, see Jack Finnegan, "A Redirection of Priorities," *Job Safety and Health* (February, 1978), p. 31; and the collection of papers in "An Assessment of Three Years of OSHA," *Proceedings of the Twenty-Seventh Annual Winter Meeting of the Industrial Relations Research Association, 1974* (Madison, Wis.: Industrial Relations Research Association, 1975), pp. 31-51.

36. Herbert R. Northrup, Richard L. Rowan, and Charles R. Perry, *The Impact of OSHA* (Philadelphia: Industrial Research Unit, The Wharton School, University of Pennsylvania, 1978), Part IV.

37. *American Textile Manufacturers' Institute v. Donovan*, 1981.

to the social benefits of the programs, if we are to minimize the previously mentioned inflationary impact of the regulations.

LABOR MARKET INFORMATION AND MATCHING

Although perfect labor market information was one of the simplifying assumptions which we made for analytical purposes in Chapter 2, we have often noted thereafter that imperfect information is one of the major barriers to labor market efficiency. In reality, workers available for work are often not aware of all labor market opportunities for which they may be qualified, and employers constantly are forced to make hiring decisions based upon limited information of the qualified labor pool available. In spite of these frictional problems, however, the federally funded, state-operated *Job Service* (formerly called the Employment Service) is the only nationally available local human resource agency in our country. It remains the most pervasive source of human resource services in most communities, despite what appears to be its inability to measurably improve labor market information problems.

As mentioned previously, the Wagner-Peyser Act of 1933 provided federal funds to states as an incentive to encourage them to establish their own employment services. In 1935 the Social Security Act created the unemployment compensation trust fund for those who were unemployed, although able and willing to work. Monitoring ability and willingness to work was assigned to the employment services, and federal funds to support these activities were provided out of the unemployment insurance payroll tax. Hence, after 1935 strong financial incentives existed for states to establish employment services, and all states quickly complied.

During the 1930s, the activities of the employment services centered on screening applicants for welfare, work relief projects, and unemployment compensation. When the nation entered World War II, the state employment services were placed under the jurisdiction of the federal War Manpower Commission, whose main function was the allocation of scarce labor resources for the war effort. After the war the service was defederalized and became heavily involved in demobilization and the transition to a peacetime economy. You will recall that there was much fear of the return of massive unemployment at this time, and the employment service developed programs of placement, job counseling, and labor market information for veterans and others to lessen adjustment problems. Similar efforts occurred before and after the Korean War in the early 1950s.[38]

During the 1950s, however, the employment service was generally inactive except for efforts in processing unemployment insurance claims. This focus proved to be extremely damaging to the image of the service in later

---

38. Levitan, Mangum, and Marshall, *Human Resources and Labor Markets*, pp. 473-74.

years. As a result, President Kennedy instituted a major reorganization and expansion of the employment service in 1962 which envisioned the agency as the primary local human resource center tied to a nationwide network of offices. The new thrust required the service to expand involvement with employers, schools, unions, and community development agencies to promote more efficient local labor market operations. The service became integrally involved in the employment and training programs of MDTA and the categorical programs in the 1960s. It also received a new mandate to concentrate on services for the disadvantaged after 1965.[39]

In the 1970s, internal reorganization of the Department of Labor led to the renaming of the service—first to Employment Service and subsequently to Job Service. Efforts were made to automate many aspects of the Job Service through computerized job banks, job matching, and reporting systems, and to renew its labor exchange function through increased contacts with local employers.[40]

Most experts agree that the Job Service has never reached its potential as a human resource development agency. Its existence as a voluntary public employment agency in a competitive decentralized economy has limited its effectiveness, as have the fluctuations in its mandated purpose from monitoring unemployment compensation eligibility to serving the disadvantaged to operating as a labor market exchange agency. The local Job Service offices are totally dependent upon the willingness of employers to use their services and hire referred individuals, and they are viewed as competing unsuccessfully with private employment agencies. Yet a consensus has rarely been reached on whether the Job Service exists primarily to serve employers or the unemployed.

Furthermore, disagreement exists over whether the disadvantaged should be the primary target group of agency activity. Evidence suggests that disadvantaged groups continue to represent a large proportion of placements made, but critics contend that services should be available to all who need them on an equal basis. Administering services and unemployment compensation predominantly to the disadvantaged has created serious image problems which hinder employer acceptability of the Job Service, according to some observers.

Today the Job Service continues to perform an amazingly wide variety of local human resource functions, and perhaps this fact more than any other precludes the total success of any single initiative. In addition to its labor exchange function, the service in 1980 was involved in the administration of 25 other laws, 17 Executive Orders, and 16 agreements with other federal agen-

39. See Stanley H. Ruttenberg and Jocelyn Gutchess, *The Federal-State Employment Service: A Critique* (Baltimore: Johns Hopkins Press, 1970), chap. 1.

40. For an elaboration of 1970s developments in the Job Service, see U.S. Department of Labor, *The Employment Service: An Institutional Analysis, Research and Development Monograph No. 51* (Washington: U.S. Government Printing Office, 1977).

cies. One of the latest additions to the list was the Targeted Jobs Tax Credit program mentioned in Chapter 6.[41] Ultimately, agreement on a limited number of streamlined job-matching functions will probably be necessary in order for the Job Service to realize its unfulfilled potential as the cornerstone of local human resource policy.

ALTERNATIVE WORK PATTERNS

The average workweek declined from an average of around 60 hours per week in 1900 to a little more than 40 hours by World War II. Since then a more stable workweek has existed, although there has been a further slight decline of approximately 10 percent in the last 30 years. The pre-war decline is attributed primarily to rising real wages over this period of time, which allows workers to enjoy higher standards of living and more leisure simultaneously. The Fair Labor Standards Act of 1938 also defined a standard workweek which soon came to be set at 40 hours. The leveling off in weekly hours in the post-war period has resulted from the increased family costs of living and the desire of employers to recoup their recruiting and training costs by maintaining hours of existing employees, even where overtime payments are necessary. Of course, in the post-war period the average work year has continued to decline as workers have benefited from longer vacations, sick leave, and holiday policies.

Recently, pressures have been emerging which favor some further redefinition of the workweek and work year. Parents of young children, students, older workers, and handicapped persons increasingly have expressed a need or preference for more flexible work schedules. Many employers have become convinced that revised work schedules improve the morale, retention, and recruiting of employees, as well as providing more time flexibility in the provision of services. Although the government has not enacted any comprehensive legislation dealing with alternative work schedules, it has become more interested in flexible work schedule proposals which alleviate peak-hour traffic congestion and electrical demands. The federal and some state governments are also closely investigating changes in work schedules as a means of creating more jobs or of lessening cyclical unemployment.[42]

Although production requirements may sometimes prohibit the use of alternative work schedules, several new patterns of work time have recently been proposed and implemented in various work settings. They include:

---

41. U.S. Department of Labor, *Employment and Training Report of the President, 1980,* p. 57.

42. For interesting discussions of alternative work pattern issues, see U.S. Department of Labor, *Employment and Training Report of the President, 1979,* pp. 77-92; National Commission for Manpower Policy, *Work Time and Employment,* Special Report No. 28, (Washington: U.S. Government Printing Office, 1978); Fred Best, "Preferences on Worklife Scheduling and Work-Leisure Tradeoffs," *Monthly Labor Review* (June, 1978), pp. 31-37; and William McGaughey Jr., *A Shorter Workweek in the 1980's* (White Bear Lake, Minn.: Thistlerose Publications, 1981).

The compressed workweek. Includes 4-day, 40-hour and 3-day, 36-hour schedules. Provides extended periods of weekly leisure time, but creates potential problems of increased work stress and fatigue and conflicts with overtime pay requirements beyond 8 hours per day.

Flexitime. Various schemes which provide employees some choice in devising their own daily or weekly work schedules, subject to weekly or monthly total hours requirements and core hours when all employees must be present. For example, an employee might be permitted to generate his/her own weekly schedule, as long as 40 total hours and the 10:00 a.m. to 2:00 p.m. period are worked. Improved morale and productivity are cited as advantages, while the potential conflicts with overtime pay requirements still exist as a disadvantage.

Job sharing. A given job is divided between two people. May reduce unemployment, create jobs for more workers who choose to work part-time, or serve to retain a valued employee whose services are no longer available full-time. Logistics and scheduling problems prevent widespread use.

Part-time employment. Around 12 million workers are now voluntarily employed part-time (less than 35 hours per week). Often preferable for students, parents of young children, older workers, moonlighters, and for employers in many service industries. Complicates wage and benefit determination, production scheduling, and recoupment of recruitment and training costs.

Work Sharing. Efforts to spread the available work among more workers by shortening the workday or workweek. Variations have included voluntary, "cafeteria-type" plans where workers are allowed to choose various reductions in weekly hours and pay, and "shared work compensation," where workers become eligible for partial unemployment compensation in return for workweek reductions. Reduces cyclical unemployment and spreads the hardships of recession more equally. May conflict with the seniority principle for layoff determination.[43]

In addition to these somewhat innovative plans, the more traditional shift work and overtime are also work schedules which deviate from the norm.

The federal government has recently passed two laws to create more alternative work schedule opportunities for federal employees. The Federal Employees Flexible and Compressed Work Schedules Act and the Federal Employees Part-Time Career Employment Act, both passed in 1978, require federal agencies to seek to establish part-time employment and flexible work schedules. In addition, the 1978 amendments to CETA require special consideration for alternative working arrangements under CETA programs. At the

---

43. U.S. Department of Labor, *Employment and Training Report of the President, 1979,* pp. 80-92.

state level, a few states have integrated shared work compensation programs into their unemployment insurance laws, with generally favorable results.

A few experts have even proposed consideration of rescheduling work lives, as well as workdays and workweeks. There is some evidence that many workers would prefer to interrupt their work lives periodically or at midlife for increased leisure and/or education, rather than to concentrate education and leisure at the beginning and end of the typical life cycle. Alternative work scheduling promises to be one of the most fascinating elements of human resource policy in the next 20 years, as policy makers increasingly confront the worker dissatisfaction and unemployment ramifications of traditional scheduling patterns.

HUMAN RESOURCE PLANNING IN THE FIRM

Until fairly recently the private sector has had little involvement in the planning or implementation of federal human resource policies. There has been a long-standing tendency for private firms in this country to view governmental efforts, be they human resource or other programs, as disruptive intrusions into the private economy. We have already noted instances of employer distrust and underutilization of several federal human resource programs. The JOBS program of the 1960s is a notable exception to this generalization.

This attitude has been changing with respect to human resource policy, however. Many businesses have realized that improving the employability of the nation's labor force is in both the private and the public interest, and this view is exemplified in the early successes of the CETA-Private Sector Initiatives program. Further evidence of a shift in private attitudes is found in a 1978 policy statement by the Committee for Economic Development (CED), an organization composed of many U.S. corporate leaders. This statement called for a new partnership between business and government in human resource policy making, particularly with respect to the hard-to-employ. The CED statement advocates private training, employment, skill development, and placement programs for disadvantaged workers and the structurally unemployed.[44]

Much of this new awareness concerning the importance of federal human resource policy has resulted from the rapidly increasing tendency toward human resource planning at the firm level. The traditional personnel department with its short-run approach to fill job vacancies and solve personnel problems as they occur is being replaced by "human resource planning"

---

44. Committee for Economic Development, *Jobs for the Hard-to-Employ: New Directions for a Public-Private Partnership* (New York: Committee for Economic Development, 1978).

departments which stress long-run designs and policies to meet organizational needs and objectives. Included in these planning efforts are systematic forecasts of future human resource needs, inventories of existing employee utilization and potential, identification of expected skill shortages, and comprehensive planning to avoid such shortages. This type of personnel planning, which includes the development of appropriate recruitment, training, and compensation plans, is becoming integrally coordinated with other long-run corporate planning.

The necessity for such efforts has been intensified by recent labor market and public policy developments. For example, in the past firms locating in large cities counted upon the existence and trainability of an ample labor supply in big city neighborhoods. The composition of these neighborhood populations changed drastically in the last 20 years, however, as more educated offspring moved to suburban areas. Inner city labor supplies became increasingly young, underprivileged, and untrained. Companies that did not relocate were confronted with entirely new kinds of training and job development problems which required new planning initiatives. In general, the overall changing composition of the labor force has pointed to the necessity of more comprehensive planning.

The rapidly changing technology in recent years has also increased the need for human resource planning at the firm level. A more rapid pace of technological advancement makes long-run planning more difficult, but also more necessary. In an environment where the quick adoption of new technologies is essential for success in many industries, planning for the acquisition of the related skills and knowledge is equally essential. Specialists must be located, recruited, and intensively trained in short periods of time in order for the firm to compete effectively.

Finally, since the mid-1960s firms have increasingly been required to compile accurate information on minority labor force availability, qualifications, trainability, and utilization for compliance with government Equal Employment Opportunity (EEO) legislation. They must carefully coordinate this information with their expected employment needs and attempt to eliminate the underutilization of target groups. In spite of criticisms of these governmental efforts from some sources, including businesses, many companies have improved their overall human resource planning immensely as a result. This has been a largely unintended, but nevertheless extremely beneficial, side effect of EEO policies.

Human resource planning in many firms is still somewhat underdeveloped and unscientific. Accurate planning is extremely difficult because so many uncontrollable and unpredictable variables are involved, e.g., major changes in public policy, the general state of the economy, further technological change, and the nature of the available labor supply. But the trend is clearly toward more planning efforts, as the systematic concern for human resource utilization becomes a matter of both private and public policy.

UNRESOLVED POLICY ISSUES

We have already discussed most of the unresolved policy issues in various sections of this chapter, and so a brief recapitulation with an eye to future needs should be sufficient here. With regard to education policy, for example, the fundamental issues center on the question of the most appropriate role for government in the financing of education, and at which level of government this financing should occur. The Reagan administration, for example, took the position in the early 1980s that the federal government has only a limited responsibility as a provider of support to higher education. This view certainly represents a departure from the prevailing view of the last 30 years. The success of vocational education programs will probably justify continued governmental support, and school-to-work transition efforts are expected to remain a priority as long as the youth unemployment problem remains severe.

The training programs under CETA have, until recently, concentrated on skill development and employment in the public sector, whereas most of the job vacancies are in the private sector. It is imperative that recent efforts to involve the local private sector in CETA planning and program implementation be expanded and refined. For CETA to justify its cost, more effective ways must be found to coordinate training programs with local labor needs of private firms. The same can be said for the Job Service, which must reassume its job exchange function by aggressively involving local employers in its activities and placement efforts. Furthermore, the complementary local activities of CETA and Job Service offices will require greater coordination.

The future for OSHA is highly dependent upon the emergence of more reliable estimates of its program benefits. Some economists have argued that imposing some form of injury rate tax on firms would be preferable to endless, detailed regulations in creating incentives for a safe workplace. This approach may become a more widely accepted policy alternative in the future. The fascinating possibilities for implementing alternative work schedules to meet employee, employer, and social needs will most certainly also become a higher priority in the years ahead.

The resolution of several more general policy questions lies at the heart of future human resource policy making. First, should human resource policies continue to focus their efforts predominantly upon disadvantaged individuals? As noted, the Job Service, CETA, and to some extent education programs have had such a focus, and this certainly is consistent with our earlier discussions of the differential impacts of unemployment. Such an emphasis, however, may have increased the expectations of both program participants and society as a whole beyond the programs' abilities to fulfill them.

Related to this issue is an even more fundamental question: In alleviating underutilization, is it preferable to concentrate on the demand side of labor markets (general expansion of the economy, job creation, alternative work patterns, antidiscrimination laws, occupational safety), or the supply side (education, training, and retraining programs)? To some extent the answer is obviously "both," but as we have already observed in Chapters 5 and 6, effective policy making is dependent upon the difficult task of determining the primary sources or causes of problems.

Another hotly contested issue will continue to be the debate over the use of cost-benefit analysis in human resource policy evaluation. This has been a high priority of recent administrations, but the Supreme Court in the previously mentioned Textile Manufacturers case has indicated that current legislation (OSHA, for example) may not require such analysis. Few economists would quarrel with the use of cost-benefit techniques where costs and particularly benefits are reasonably measurable, but serious measurement problems arise in determining the total private and social benefits of improved occupational safety or worker employability.

Finally, there is the most pervasive question of all, a question which we already raised in the last chapter: Can a more vigorous system of private enterprise alleviate human resource underutilization with reduced government involvement? Belief in an affirmative answer to this question is the underlying premise of the Reagan administration approach to human resource policy. If this view is correct, the other issues may become moot. If it is incorrect, we as a nation will continue to search for effective policies of human resource development in the coming years.

CONCLUDING REMARKS

Most economists agree that finding policies to achieve the full utilization of our nation's human resources is essential if we are to lower the unemployment rate associated with nonaccelerating inflation in the long run. Traditional stabilization policies alone have clearly proven to be inadequate in the last 20 years in leading our economy toward Humphrey-Hawkins–type full employment goals. We have reviewed in this chapter the major human resource policies which have been utilized in an attempt to achieve greater labor utilization, and we have assessed the effectiveness of these programs. As Levitan, Mangum, and Marshall have observed, the success or failure of such programs depends largely upon the expectations and social philosophy of the observer. Although most program enrollees have left these programs better off in some way, this may not be the kind of definitive success which society requires from such large expenditures.[45] Private sector initiatives appear to be the current priority, and the jury is still out on their success. To complete the picture, we turn in the next two chapters to subjects which are integrally related to human resource development, or the lack thereof—discrimination and poverty.

---

45. Levitan, Mangum, and Marshall, *Human Resources and Labor Markets*, pp. 460-62.

CHAPTER SUMMARY

Human resource development policies are those designed to improve the quality of the labor supply and more efficiently use its potential. Although numerous such programs were implemented during the Great Depression of the 1930s, the most noteworthy contemporary efforts have been the Manpower Development and Training Act of 1962 (MDTA) and the Comprehensive Employment and Training Act of 1973 (CETA).

Higher education policy has taken the form of large-scale federal grant and loan programs to students, and state funding of institutions. Elementary and secondary schools, on the other hand, have long been publicly funded, primarily by local property tax dollars. Policy makers continue to seek ways to support educational programs in an efficient and equitable manner, amidst some controversy over the appropriate role of government. Continuing policy efforts also support vocational education programs and assistance for the school-to-work transition.

Many of the federal training programs for the structurally unemployed are still within the CETA mandate, although numerous categorical programs were developed in the 1960s prior to CETA. The 1978 amendments to CETA attempted to eliminate abuses and provide more centralized direction, and they placed some additional emphasis upon training. CETA PSE funds were severely cut in 1981 in response to President Reagan's budget-cutting initiatives.

Other attempts to better utilize human resources include efforts to improve occupational health and safety, primarily through the Occupational Safety and Health Act of 1970 (OSHA). The act established federal agencies to develop workplace safety and health standards and to monitor compliance by worksite inspections. An excessive proliferation of standards resulted, although in the past few years the number of such standards has been reduced substantially. Another area of federal involvement has dealt with labor market information and matching through what is now the federal-state Job Service. The service has been assigned many potentially conflicting roles since its inception in the 1930s. The result has been lack of consistent direction and a generally distorted image. Finally, a number of alternatives to the conventional work week and work year have been proposed and/or implemented recently in the hope of achieving more work scheduling flexibility for workers and less unemployment. Such alternative work patterns are expected to become even more prevalent in the years ahead.

Human resource planning is also becoming much more important in the private sector, as firms are forced to confront the changing composition of the labor force, rapid technological change, and governmental mandates for the provision of equal employment opportunity. Numerous problems still exist in both public and private sector human resource development, and their resolution promises to be an important challenge for the years ahead.

KEY TERMS

human resource development policy
Manpower Development and Training Act (1962)

Equal Opportunity Act of 1964
credentialism
national longitudinal surveys
vocational education

private rate of return to human capital investment
social rate of return to human capital investment
voucher plan
CETA prime sponsors
continuous longitudinal manpower survey

Occupational Safety and Health Act of 1970
Job Service
flexitime
job sharing
work sharing

REVIEW QUESTIONS

1. Why were the early 1960s such a ripe period for the emergence of federal human resource policies? What were the important political, social, and economic forces at work during this period?

2. Give two economic reasons justifying the significant funding of higher education by state taxes. If individual students are the primary beneficiaries of higher education, why shouldn't they (you?) pay the costs?

3. Presumably you expect your education and training to enhance your lifetime earnings. Why? There are many factors involved in a careful consideration of this question; think it through thoroughly.

4. As we noted in Chapter 5, the nation's unemployment rate during the middle of World War II was less than 1 percent. Isn't this proof that, given enough economic expansion, the structurally unemployed can find jobs without massive federal training programs? Why or why not?

5. Assuming that you were an elected federal official in charge of human resource policy, wouldn't you have an obligation to compare the cost and benefits of various policies before implementation? To rephrase the same basic question considerably, doesn't an affluent society such as ours have a social obligation to pay whatever cost is involved in fully utilizing our human resources?

6. What social and economic pressures would exist to create safe and healthy workplaces if OSHA were eliminated? In your opinion, would these pressures be sufficient? Why or why not?

7. The average full-time worker today works approximately 2000 hours per year for around 45 consecutive years. Do you expect this to be your work life pattern? If you had complete flexibility in scheduling these 90,000 hours over your work life, how would you do so?

ADDITIONAL REFERENCES

Clague, Ewan, and Leo Kramer. *Manpower Policies and Programs: A Review, 1935-75.* Kalamazoo, Mich.: W. E. Upjohn Institute for Employment Research, 1976.

Committee for Economic Development. *Jobs for the Hard-to-Employ: New Directions for a Public-Private Partnership.* New York: Committee for Economic Development, 1978.

Freeman, Richard B. *The Overeducated American* New York: Academic Press, 1976.

Levitan, Sar A., Garth L. Mangum, and Ray Marshall. *Human Resources and Labor Markets*, 3d ed.. New York: Harper & Row, 1981.

Mangum, Garth, James Morlock, Marion W. Pines, and David Snedeker. *Job Market Futurity: Planning and Managing Local Manpower Programs.* Salt Lake City, Utah: Olympus Publishing Company, 1979.

Mendeloff, John. *Regulating Safety: An Economic and Political Analysis of Occupational Safety and Health Policy,* Cambridge, Mass.: M.I.T Press, 1979.

National Commission for Manpower Policy, *Work Time and Employment,* Special Report No. 28, Washington: U.S. Government Printing Office, 1978.

Perlman, Richard. *The Economics of Education.* New York: McGraw-Hill Book Co., 1973.

Ruttenberg, Stanley H., and Jocelyn Gutchess. *The Federal-State Employment Service: A Critique.* Baltimore: The Johns Hopkins Press, 1970.

THE WORLD
OF WORK . . .

Job Satisfaction and Occupational Safety and Health

One of the subjects of the "Quality of Employment Surveys" conducted by the Institute for Social Research at the University of Michigan (see Chapter 5) was job safety and health. The following excerpt describes some results of these surveys which relate to job satisfaction and perceived job safety.

In 1969, 1972, and most recently in 1977, the Institute for Social Research at the University of Michigan conducted opinion surveys of production workers, under U.S. Department of Labor sponsorship. These studies, known as the "Quality of Employment Surveys," gather data on numerous characteristics of the worker and his job, and perhaps most importantly, on the worker's subjective assessment of his worklife. . . .

Certain questions relate to job safety and health, or to workers' evaluation of safety as a job attribute. Under contract to the Department of Labor, the Center for Policy Alternatives at the Massachusetts Institute of Technology has examined data pertaining to a number of these safety- and health-related questions. . . .

Over the 8 years spanned by the Quality of Employment Surveys, work-injury rates reported by the Bureau of Labor Statistics have fallen. Similarly, results from the Quality of Employment Surveys also indicate that the number of injuries clearly related to job activities, such as fractures and cuts, has declined. It is surprising then, that when asked generally about "work-related" injuries, survey respondents note a slight increase between 1969 and 1977. A detailed breakdown of the types of injuries reported by the workers suggests the cause of this apparent paradox: health problems of various kinds are increasingly perceived as due to workplace exposures. Because of the difficulty in proving the work-relatedness of many of these health problems, such "injuries" are not reflected in government statistics.

It is likely that the increase in perceived injuries results from greater worker sensitivity to a variety of occupational hazards. In 1977, 78 percent of those surveyed noted one or more safety and health hazards in the workplace, compared

with only 38 percent in 1969. Respondents in the most recent study were asked to be more specific about the types of dangers they encountered on the job. Seventy-two percent of the men reported exposure to "fumes, dust, or other air pollution," as did 52 percent of the women. Similarly, 45 percent of the men and 21 percent of the women felt themselves exposed to "dangerous chemicals." . . .

Another trend evident in the data is the increase in work-related injuries reported by women. Female production workers averaged over twice as many injuries in 1977 as in either 1972 or 1969, perhaps because by making inroads into traditionally male occupations, women are sharing the greater risks of these jobs as well.

In the 1977 Quality of Employment Survey, workers were also asked questions about their level of job satisfaction. Workers who reported exposure to a greater number of hazards, or who felt these hazards were more severe than average, were significantly less satisfied with their jobs. . . .

In 1977, respondents were asked to decide whether they would prefer a 10-percent pay raise or various other job improvements. Among these other improvements was "a little safer or healthier working conditions." By this "revealed preference" method, it was determined that nearly a third of all production workers would be willing to trade the pay increase for more safety and health at work. . . .

Other studies have found a significant relationship between a worker's tenure and the probability that he will have an accident. The survey data illustrate this relationship dramatically: workers employed between 1 and 3 months report 3 times as many injuries as workers with 1 to 3 years on the job, and 8 times as many as those employed for more than 20 years.

. . . The Occupational Safety and Health

Administration (OSHA) collects data on inspection activity and fines as part of the Management Information System. By combining these data with those from the Quality of Employment Survey, it was possible to explore the relationship of worker-perceived hazards to the level of OSHA fines in any industry. Dollars of proposed penalty per hour of inspection time was chosen as a measure of the severity of safety violations noted by OSHA inspectors. This measure was assumed to be fairly independent of total industry employment.

OSHA's proposed penalty per hour of inspection time was higher in industries in which workers themselves noted the hazards of "noise," "dangerous work methods," "fire or shock," or "dangerous equipment." Worker perception of these dangers would thus seem to agree with the findings of OSHA inspectors.

. . . Information gathered in the Quality of Employment Surveys permits investigation of the relationship between various aspects of work, and worker satisfaction. The results of this study reveal that job safety and health are important concerns for most workers, and that such concerns are on the increase. While this conclusion should be encouraging to policymakers, certain problem areas in safety and health regulation were also identified.

The first of these involves the long recognized relationship between job tenure and injury probability. Stated simply, workers who are new on their jobs have several times the probability of injury of more experienced workers. At the same time, they are the least willing to report even severe perceived hazards to anyone, probably because hazard reports must usually be directed to management. Finally, union handling of safety-related grievances is often felt to be inadequate by union members, and, consequently, few reports of dangerous conditions are directed through union channels. Mechanisms are needed to encourage new workers to report what they feel are severe hazards, and to provide all workers with alternatives when appeals to management fail.

The results of this study have implications for employers as well. Unpleasant working conditions generally, and injury-causing hazards in particular seem to go hand in hand. It is likely that a concerned management acts to alleviate unpleasant working conditions, including hazards. On the other hand, it is possible that workers who report hazards tend to note unpleasant work conditions because of their general job dissatisfaction. Further investigations are needed to help pinpoint the relationship between inadequate job safety and health and individual firm management styles. Such studies could also clarify the role of hazard abatement in improving employee morale.

Source: Abridged from Richard L. Frenkel, W. Curtiss Priest, and Nicholas A. Ashford, "Occupational Safety and Health: A Report on Worker Perceptions," *Monthly Labor Review* (September, 1980), pp. 11-14.

Chapter 8

Labor Market Discrimination

In Chapter 3 we observed that if labor markets are purely competitive, each employer must pay the market-determined wage rate for a given occupation, and these wage rates reflect worker productivity. Surely there would appear to be nothing unfair or discriminatory about such labor market operations. Similarly, human capital theory is based on the assumption that earnings differences among workers can be explained primarily by differences in skill level, or productivity. Here wage differentials are acknowledged as common occurrences, but their explanation does not include the possibility that some individuals or groups of individuals are simply treated unfairly without economic justification.

However, we have already noted the potential for such unfair treatment in our discussion of wage differentials and segmented labor markets. More generally there is ample evidence that nonwhite and female workers, as groups, are still disadvantaged in labor markets relative to their white male counterparts. This disadvantage may be partially or totally the result of labor market discrimination.

We begin this chapter by asking the question: What is labor market discrimination? The answer is not nearly so obvious as you might expect. We then take a look at the actual patterns of employment and earnings categorized by race and sex over time in the United States. Next comes a consideration of various causes, explanations, or theories of labor market discrimination. In this section we will be concerned with whether or not discrimination can be explained by extending our earlier economic models. Finally, we review the most important laws and public policies designed to eliminate discrimination. As is almost always the case, our analysis will suggest that discrimination issues are complex, and that the remedial policies are imperfect and sometimes quite controversial.

WHAT IS LABOR MARKET DISCRIMINATION?

In its broadest sense, discrimination is simply the unfair or unjust treatment of an individual or group. This is a comprehensive and acceptable definition, and yet it leaves us with an important unanswered question: When does treatment become unfair or unjust? In other words, what rule or standard exists for determining injustice, and is it possible that you and I may disagree on what constitutes such unfair treatment? Perhaps we can develop a more refined definition.

Definitions

We could introduce a kind of standard by defining *social discrimination* as differential treatment based on something other than individual merit. This dictionary-type definition does give us a standard for acceptable differential treatment: individual merit. It also suggests that other standards such as appearance, religion, income, ethnic origin, race, or sex are discriminatory. The definition still leaves us with the problem of defining merit, and it also encompasses many possible forms of discrimination which go beyond the labor market. Social discrimination results from long-standing social tastes, attitudes, and customs, and it may be manifested in such nonmarket phenomena as unequal or segregated education, housing, public facilities, and the like.

Let us narrow our definition a bit further so as to define *labor market discrimination* as differential labor market treatment based upon something other than worker productivity. Now we are focusing on the labor market, and we have established a standard with which we are already familiar: labor productivity. This is the working definition which is used throughout this chapter, but you should keep in mind that the definition still lacks some precision and clarity. For example, we already know that there are many problems involved in defining and measuring productivity. In addition we have observed that labor productivity is partially dependent upon factors, such as the quantity and quality of capital, which are unrelated to a worker's innate skills and abilities.

Furthermore, where two people are treated differently in the labor market because of differing productivities, is it not possible that the differing productivities themselves resulted from previous social discrimination? Consider the obvious example of a black person from the inner city who has been subjected to an inferior education and who now enters the labor market upon graduating from high school. He or she is immediately less productive than a white graduate from a better school system, and therefore may be denied a job while the otherwise similar white is chosen. Is this discrimination? Most certainly the unequal schooling is an example of social discrimination, but the unequal treatment in the labor market resulted from differing productivities and therefore was not discriminatory by our definition. We encounter numerous other definitional problems of this type as we move through the chapter. But remember that ultimately we will consider policies to eliminate discrimination, and so it is essential that we first attempt to identify those types of labor market discrimination that are socially harmful.

Given our definition of labor market discrimination, it is possible to categorize various forms of unequal labor market treatment. *Wage discrimination* is the payment of different wages to different individuals or groups based upon some standard other than productivity. The slogan "equal pay for equal work" suggests the attempt to eliminate wage discrimination. *Employment discrimination* involves the use of different hiring, firing, or promotion standards not related to worker productivity. *Occupational discrimination* results because of the tendency for certain groups of workers to be segregated into certain kinds of jobs, where the segregation does not reflect productivity differences. We touched on this possibility in our discussion of segmented labor markets, and it has also been argued that much of the difference between male and female earnings is attributable to occupational discrimination, as we shall see later.

Costs of Labor Market Discrimination

There are, of course, significant noneconomic costs involved in labor market discrimination. The personal feelings of humility, self-worthlessness, frustration, and anger generated by labor market discrimination are serious enough by themselves to warrant remedial policies, even if there were no economic costs. These noneconomic costs are difficult to measure, but they are painfully real to the victims of discrimination.

The economic costs of discrimination are imposed both on individuals and on society as a whole. Those individuals discriminated against suffer reduced living standards in the form of lower wages and higher unemployment. They also tend to have fewer employment opportunities and to be segregated into low-paying occupations. Those who discriminate may benefit or they may lose from discrimination. The employer who hires a female at a lower wage than an equally qualified male may gain, for example, but if that employer refuses to hire females, an artificially high wage may have to be paid to hire an equally qualified male. Alternatively, the employer who refuses to hire females may be forced to hire less productive males as a result. This will mean less productivity and output for the employer, and therefore higher costs.

Society as a whole also suffers significant costs associated with discrimination. Our nation's total output of goods and services is reduced below the level that would exist without discrimination. If discrimination exists, it deprives society of the full contributions of qualified workers. If productive workers are unemployed or forced into lower paying, dead-end jobs by discrimination, these human resources are being underutilized by society. As noted previously, an underutilized labor force means that society's actual output is below its potential output, and all citizens are "poorer" than they otherwise would be. Even if most individuals do not discriminate, everyone pays this hidden price of discrimination. For example, in the late 1960s Lester Thurow estimated that the social loss of discrimination against blacks amounted to roughly $19 billion annually.[1] Remember, this was an estimate for blacks only and was derived some time ago. Obviously, the total social cost is now much greater.

---

1. Lester Thurow, *Poverty and Discrimination* (Washington: Brookings Institution, 1969), p. 158.

PATTERNS OF EMPLOYMENT AND EARNINGS BY RACE AND SEX

We now have a working definition of labor market discrimination and some understanding of its costs. But how extensive is this differential labor market treatment in today's society, and is discrimination the real explanation? After all, we all know that the United States has enacted major social programs in the last 20 years to combat discrimination, and we also have observed what would appear to be significant changes in social attitudes during our lifetime. In this section we examine the actual patterns of and trends in earnings and employment categorized by race and sex to see the magnitude and complexity of the problem.

Patterns by Race

Discrimination in the United States now seldom takes the form of paying equally qualified blacks and whites different wages for the same job in the same workplace, if for no other reason than because such practices are obviously illegal. In other words, wage discrimination as we have defined it is not common today. Nevertheless, the data in Table 8-1 reveal some disturbing facts about the economic well-being of nonwhite families relative to white families. One trend which clearly emerges is the significant relative income progress achieved by nonwhite families in the 1960s. Whereas the average nonwhite family earned 55 percent of what the average white family earned in 1960, that figure had improved to 64 percent by 1970. However, it appears that this improvement has not continued in any persistent form since 1970. The average nonwhite family was relatively no better off in 1980 than in 1970. One might add cynically that even the pattern of the 1960s, the decade of economic progress, still left nonwhite families earning less than two-thirds of their white counterparts on the average.

Table 8-1   White and Nonwhite Median Family Income
in Current Dollars, Selected Years

Year	Median White Family Income	Median Nonwhite Family Income	Nonwhite/White
1950	$ 3,445	$ 1,869	54.2%
1960	5,835	3,230	55.4
1970	10,236	6,516	63.7
1975	14,268	9,321	65.3
1980	21,904	13,843	63.2

Source: Bureau of the Census, *Current Population Reports: Consumer Income*, Series P-60, No. 127 (Washington: U.S. Government Printing Office, March, 1981), Table 3.

Social and Labor Market Discrimination. These are probably surprising and undoubtedly disappointing statistics to you. But are the data in Table 8-1 evidence of discrimination, and if so, of what type? We have already observed that pure wage discrimination is rare today, and so the existence of that type cannot be used to explain the patterns of Table 8-1. Also, since these data pertain to families rather than individuals, the differentials could simply be due to differences in the number of multiple-earner families between non-whites and whites, or to differences in hours worked. Alternatively, it is conceivable that the earnings gap could be explained by differences in productivity, schooling, and/or seniority. It is important to remember, however, that current differences in factors such as productivity, schooling, and seniority may actually be the result of past social and economic discrimination.

Recently there have been a number of careful statistical studies which have attempted to isolate the extent of past and present racial discrimination in earnings, after controlling for such factors as age, schooling, family characteristics, seniority, and hours worked.[2] Not surprisingly, all these factors do help to account for the earnings gap, but almost all studies have concluded that there remains a large portion of the gap, on the order of 25-50 percent, that cannot be explained by these other factors. Studies do suggest that the nonwhite-white annual earnings ratio for comparable new labor market entrants has improved to about 90 percent.[3] Nevertheless, there is little doubt that labor market discrimination is a major explanation for what remains of the white-nonwhite earnings differential.

Employment Discrimination. We need to look at two other factors which obviously contribute to the patterns observed in Table 8-1. As we noted earlier, employment discrimination occurs when different employment standards are used, in this case for whites and nonwhites, which are not related to productivity. Table 8-2 reveals one dimension of employment discrimination, differences in unemployment rates. Once again, a clear and fairly consistent pattern emerges. Nonwhite unemployment rates have averaged roughly double those of whites for the last 30 years, with no significant trend of improvement. If nonwhites are twice as likely as whites on the average to be unemployed, this fact is surely reflected in the earnings differentials of Table 8-1. Keep in mind again our earlier discussion of segmented labor markets where we observed that low-skilled, disadvantaged workers (particularly young minorities) tend to frequent the high turnover secondary labor markets.

---

2. See William Comanor, "Racial Discrimination in American Industry," *Economica* (November, 1973), pp. 363-78; Barry R. Chiswick, "Racial Discrimination in the Labor Market: A Test of Alternative Hypotheses," *Journal of Political Economy* (November-December, 1973), pp. 1330-52; Joan Gustafson Haworth, James Gwartney, and Charles Haworth, "Earnings, Productivity, and Changes in Employment Discrimination During the 1960s," *American Economic Review* (March, 1975), pp. 158-68; and James P. Smith and Finis Welch, *Race Differences in Earnings: A Survey and New Evidence* (Santa Monica, Calif.: Rand Corporation, 1978).

3. Finis Welch, "Black-White Differences in Returns to Schooling," *American Economic Review* (December, 1973), pp. 893-907.

Table 8-2   White and Nonwhite Civilian Unemployment Rates,
Selected Years

Year	White Unemployment Rate	Nonwhite Unemployment Rate	Nonwhite/White
1950	4.9%	9.0%	1.8
1955	3.9	8.7	2.2
1960	4.9	10.2	2.1
1965	4.1	8.1	2.0
1970	4.5	8.2	1.8
1975	7.8	13.9	1.8
1980	6.3	13.2	2.1

Source: *Economic Report of the President, 1981*, Table B-31.

Occupational Discrimination. Finally, and perhaps most importantly, even if all equally qualified whites and nonwhites received exactly the same compensation for the same job and had the same unemployment rates, there still would be earnings differences if they tended to work in different occupations. This would be an example of the occupational discrimination defined earlier, for which some evidence is provided in Table 8-3. The data in Table 8-3 should generate a mixed evaluation. On the one hand, from 1960 to 1980 the occupational distribution of nonwhites improved significantly, with substantial increases in the percentages of nonwhites employed in several white-collar

Table 8-3   Percentage Distribution of White and Nonwhite
Labor Force by Occupation, 1960 and 1980

Occupation	White		Nonwhite	
	1960	1980	1960	1980
Professional and Technical	12.2%	16.5%	4.8%	12.7%
Managers and Administrators	11.7	12.0	2.6	5.2
Sales Workers	7.0	6.8	1.5	2.9
Clerical Workers	15.7	18.6	7.3	18.4
Craft Workers	13.8	13.3	6.0	9.6
Operatives	17.9	13.5	20.4	19.4
Nonfarm Laborers	4.4	4.3	13.7	6.9
Service Workers	9.9	12.1	31.6	23.1
Farm Laborers	7.4	2.9	12.1	1.8
	100.0%	100.0%	100.0%	100.0%

Source: *Employment and Training Report of the President, 1981*, Table A-21.

occupations. On the other hand, however, the movement into positions of white-collar administrative authority was not very great. Relative to whites, nonwhite workers are still represented less frequently in the high-paying professional and managerial occupations.

There is little doubt from these data that nonwhites continue to suffer from significant labor market disadvantages relative to whites. Even more distressing is the fact that little improvement has been apparent since 1970, despite strong equal opportunity laws. It would appear that the economic expansion of the late 1960s did more to improve the economic plight of nonwhite Americans than did any laws or enlightened attitudes. Certainly there may be many explanations for these conditions; nevertheless, virtually every careful study of the labor market disadvantages of nonwhite Americans has concluded that some significant part of that continuing disadvantage is attributable to discrimination.

Patterns by Sex

We noted in Chapter 2 that the increased labor force participation of women in our society has been one of the most significant socioeconomic phenomena of the post-World War II period. As we also know, a movement demanding equal pay and equal employment opportunities for women has accompanied this phenomenon. Here again, pure wage discrimination against women may be rare today, but if we look at similar statistics to those which we observed earlier for whites and nonwhites, some alarmingly similar patterns become apparent.

Consider, for example, Table 8-4, which presents similar data to those found earlier in Table 8-1. These data are for full-time, employed individuals, not families, and thus the income differences cannot be explained by differences in the number of family wage earners, hours worked, or unemployment rates. Comparing full-time employed males and females since the mid-1950s, Table 8-4 reveals that the average female has never earned more than about 60

Table 8-4   Full-Time Year-Round Male and Female
Median Incomes, Selected Years

Year	Male Median Income	Female Median Income	Female-Male
1955	$ 4,241	$ 2,735	64.5%
1960	5,434	3,296	60.7
1965	6,598	3,816	57.8
1970	9,184	5,440	59.2
1975	12,934	7,719	59.7
1980	19,173	11,591	60.4

Source: Current Population Reports; Consumer Income, Series P-60, No. 127, Table 9.

percent of the average male's earnings for any sustained period since 1960. The economic upturns of the late 1960s and late 1970s benefited females to some extent, but once again the average working woman was relatively no better off in 1980 than in 1970 or 1960.

Occupational Discrimination. What explanations do we have for these disturbing statistics? There are many possible causes, some of which are discussed in the next section, but an extremely significant one can be seen by careful analysis of the data in Table 8-5. In a similar fashion to Table 8-3, this table presents the percentage occupational distribution of male and female workers for the years 1960 and 1980. These data reveal even more glaring inequities than did our earlier data for whites and nonwhites. Although female workers have progressed into white-collar occupations, particularly professional and technical ones, over this period, the occupational segregation remains clear in 1980. Over 50 percent of all female workers remain in clerical and service occupations, a percentage which is virtually unchanged since 1960. These occupations include relatively low-wage jobs as compared to supervisory positions, and as you can see only around 15 percent of men are employed in these occupations.

Table 8-5   Percentage Distribution of Male and Female
Labor Force by Occupation, 1960 and 1980

Occupation	Male		Female	
	1960	1980	1960	1980
Professional and Technical	10.9%	15.5%	12.4%	16.8%
Managers and Administrators	13.6	14.4	5.0	6.9
Sales Workers	5.8	6.0	7.7	6.8
Clerical Workers	7.2	6.4	30.4	35.1
Craft Workers	19.0	21.0	1.1	1.8
Operatives	19.6	16.8	15.2	10.7
Nonfarm Laborers	7.9	7.0	—	1.2
Service Workers	6.5	8.8	23.8	19.5
Farm Laborers	9.5	4.0	4.4	1.2
	100.0%	100.0%	100.0%	100.0%

Source: *Employment and Training Report of the President, 1981*, Table A-19.

Much research has been conducted by social scientists on this occupational segregation phenomenon as it pertains to "male jobs" and "female jobs," and several general observations should be mentioned.[4] The segregation is largely cultural and traditional in the United States, and not related to differences in ability. In several other countries women are prevalent in supervisory and professional occupations, as well as in many types of manual labor. In the United States, however, many women remain reluctant to pursue training for nontraditional occupations, and many employers still resist the hiring and promotion policies which would place women in positions of authority over men.

Also, the rapid growth of female labor force participation mentioned on several occasions previously has not been met by greatly increased demand for females in male-dominated occupations. With a few notable exceptions, female labor market entrants have been absorbed in those clerical and service occupations which they already dominated.

Employment Discrimination. As mentioned, the data in Table 8-4 are only for full-time, employed women. Since many women are part-time employees, either voluntary or involuntary, the relative earnings position of all employed women is actually worse than that shown in the table. Furthermore, the data do not account for differences in unemployment rates between men and women. Table 8-6 suggests that for the last 30 years or so women have experienced anywhere from 7 to 40 percent more unemployment than men.

Many statistical studies have dealt with the male-female earnings differential, and they generally have reached conclusions similar to the ones we have drawn from casually analyzing the data in Tables 8-4, 8-5, and 8-6. In plants or occupational settings where employees are predominantly or exclusively one sex, the wage levels in the male-dominated plants are usually 20-30 percent higher than in the female plants. In those careful studies where occupation, age, education, seniority, and total work experience differences are controlled for, the male-female earnings differences are still roughly 10-20 percent.[5] And several studies have concluded that the female relative earnings position gets worse with age, suggesting possible discrimination in promotion.[6] Once again

---

4. On this subject see Harriet Zellner, "Discrimination Against Women, Occupational Segregation, and the Relative Wage," *American Economic Review* (May, 1972), pp. 157-60; Mary H. Stevenson, "Relative Wages and Sex Segregation by Occupation," in Cynthia B. Lloyd (ed.), *Sex, Discrimination, and the Division of Labor* (New York: Columbia University Press, 1975); and Michelle Patterson and Laurie Engelberg, "Women in Male-Dominated Professions," in Ann H. Stromberg and Shirley Harkess (eds.), *Women Working* (Palo Alto, Calif.: Mayfield Publishing Company, 1978), pp. 266-92.

5. See, for example, Donald J. McNulty, "Differences in Pay Between Men and Women Workers," *Monthly Labor Review* (December, 1967), pp. 40-43; Albert Rees and George P. Schultz, *Workers and Wages in an Urban Labor Market* (Chicago: University of Chicago Press, 1970), chap. 11; and U.S. Department of Labor, *The Earnings Gap Between Women and Men* (Washington: U.S. Government Printing Office, 1979).

6. See Victor Fuchs, "Differences in Hourly Earnings Between Men and Women," *Monthly Labor Review* (May, 1971), pp. 9-15; and George E. Johnson and Frank P. Stafford, "The Earnings and Promotion of Women Faculty," *American Economic Review* (December, 1974), pp. 888-903.

we are left with the indisputable conclusions that labor market discrimination by sex exists, and that the economic status of women workers as a group relative to men has shown little improvement in the last 30 years. There are many individual exceptions to this conclusion, but the general pattern remains disappointing.

Table 8-6   Unemployment Rates for Those 20 Years of Age and Over, by Sex, Selected Years

Year	Male Unemployment Rate	Female Unemployment Rate	Female/Male
1950	4.7%	5.1%	1.09
1955	3.8	4.4	1.16
1960	4.7	5.1	1.09
1965	3.2	4.5	1.40
1970	3.5	4.8	1.37
1975	6.7	8.0	1.19
1980	5.9	6.3	1.07

Source: *Economic Report of the President, 1981*, Table B-31; and *Monthly Labor Review*, August, 1981, Table 2.

THEORIES OF LABOR MARKET DISCRIMINATION

It is very difficult to generalize concerning causes or theories of labor market discrimination. The explanations of sex discrimination may be different from those for racial discrimination, and there are complex social, psychological, and economic factors involved in any discrimination situation. Nevertheless, it is important for social scientists to analyze systematically this unfortunate labor market phenomenon, as a part of the search for a better understanding of human behavior. In this section we briefly review some of the more important contributions to our understanding of labor market discrimination, keeping in mind throughout that there is no single theory of this complex phenomenon. We are primarily concerned with economic theories of discrimination, but a very brief discussion of psychological and sociological theories is also presented. Ultimately, all the theories are considerably interrelated.

Psychological and Sociological Theories

Much of the psychological research on labor market discrimination focuses on the supply side of labor markets and emphasizes various presumed "personality deficits" which may hinder women and minorities. A female worker's desire for employment which will not inhibit her femininity would be an example of such a personality deficit. With these psychological theories, various personality conflicts are identified which restrict goal-related striving for women and minorities. Strong occupational aspirations and the accompanying behavior may be perceived by some women and minorities as deviant and inconsistent with their roles. Various motivation theories have also been employed under the assumption that whites and nonwhites, and men and women, differ in patterns of work motivation, work aspirations, reward incentives, and job expectations.[7] The research has been generally inconclusive in supporting these hypotheses as operational theories of labor market discrimination.

Several sociological theories have also contributed to our understanding. As a part of the general theory of *functionalism*, the family is viewed as an important subsystem in maintaining the whole social system. The family, as the "backbone of society," helps maintain a stable society by providing care for the young, comfort and relaxation for adults, and legitimate sexual outlets, among other things. As a possible explanation of sex discrimination in labor markets, this theory implies that it is functional from society's point of view to have women relatively uncommitted to careers.[8] One sociologist has gone so far as to suggest that men are essentially useless to society in any way other than the reproduction of the species, and in the absence of the equalizing and civilizing family unit they would become social parasites.[9]

The *exchange theory* of sociology has also been used in analyzing the supply side of labor market discrimination. In essence, the theory is similar to some economic theories in arguing that people compare rewards and costs in determining courses of action. For many women, for example, the world of work does not offer perceived rewards which justify the potential costs of fatigue and lost family security.[10]

Conflict theory hypothesizes constant power conflicts as the natural state of society. Society is seen as being stratified along a number of lines, including sex and race, with women and racial minorities as subordinates. In all but the most advanced technological societies, subordinates tend to perform menial or trivial tasks in the division of labor because they lack the power to confront the dominant white males.[11] Some conflict theorists have argued that in more advanced societies, conflicts between the sexes or races are used to divert attention away from the true oppressors: the ruling class elite.

---

7. See M. L. Katz, "Female Motive to Avoid Success: A Psychological Barrier or a Response to Deviancy?" (Princeton, N.J.: Educational Testing Service, 1973); and Patricia Gurin, "The Role of Worker Expectancies in the Study of Employment Discrimination," in Phyllis A. Wallace and Annette M. LaMond (eds.), *Women, Minorities, and Employment Discrimination* (Lexington, Mass: D. C. Heath and Company, 1977), pp. 13-37.

8. See Monica B. Morris, "Inequalities in the Labor Force: Three Sociological Explanations," in Stromberg and Harkess, *Women Working*.

9. George Gilder, *Sexual Suicide* (New York: Bantam Books, 1975).

10. This argument is presented in Kenneth Lassen, *The Workers* (New York: Bantam Books, 1971).

11. See, for example, Randall Collins, "A Conflict Theory of Sexual Stratification," *Social Problems* 17 (1971), pp. 3-21.

Neoclassical Economic Theories

The contributions to our understanding of discrimination by psychologists and sociologists have been considerable, but they are not within the main focus of this text. We devoted much of our attention in the first four chapters to conventional, or neoclassical, models of labor market behavior. With the exception of our discussions of segmented labor markets and post-Keynesian macroeconomic theory, all of our models have been in the neoclassical tradition. But until less than 20 years ago, neoclassical labor market models did not recognize or provide explanations for persistent discrimination.

The pioneering work in encompassing discrimination within conventional labor market models was conducted by Gary Becker.[12] Based on the conventional assumptions of utility-maximizing behavior and a competitive economy, Becker argued that certain employers, workers, and consumers have a *taste for discrimination*. These tastes become visible when these individuals demonstrate a willingness to pay something to be associated with some persons instead of others. For example, an employer who hires a male over a more productive female pays in the form of lost productivity to the firm. A white worker who accepts a lower salary to work in an all-white firm pays in the form of foregone income. Becker develops discrimination coefficients to measure these monetary payments. Market discrimination is defined by estimating the difference between the actual nonwhite-white (or female-male) wage ratio and the ratio which would exist if no one had a taste for discrimination.

In Becker's model, if an employer pays an average money wage rate of W, then $W(1 + d_i)$ defines a net wage rate where d_i is the discrimination coefficient. If the employer has a preference for a certain group of workers, d_i will be positive for that group; if the employer has a taste for discrimination against a certain group, d_i will be negative for that group. For example if $W = \$5.00$, the wage for white workers might be $6.00, and that for equally qualified nonwhite workers $4.00. In this case, $1.00 per hour measures the discrimination coefficient and market discrimination equals $-.33$ [the actual wage ratio ($4/$6) minus the nondiscriminatory wage ratio ($5/$5)].

This theory was a convenient extension of neoclassical economics, and it also had comforting implications. Because of competitive market forces, all individuals with tastes for discrimination, whether they be employers, consumers, or workers, would find themselves at a competitive disadvantage relative to nondiscriminators. To achieve economic survival, discriminators would be forced to cease discriminating, and market forces would ultimately eliminate discriminatory wage differentials. Any persistent labor market discrimination could only be the result of market imperfections or monopoly

---

12. Gary Becker, *The Economics of Discrimination* (Chicago: University of Chicago Press, 1957).

employer power, and these problems could be attacked by the enforcement of the antitrust laws.

On the supply side of labor markets, Becker and others have utilized human capital theory to explain race and sex earnings differences on the basis of productivity differences.[13] Women and nonwhites often have less investment in formal education and on-the-job training, and women particularly may rationally invest less because they do not expect to be in the labor market continuously. As you should recall, less human capital investment implies lower productivity which implies lower earnings. Once again, the human capital explanation is a consistent extension of other neoclassical labor market models.

In an alternative neoclassical model, Kenneth Arrow has suggested that employers may be motivated to discriminate because of their "perceptions of reality" rather than any inherent tastes for discrimination.[14] Arrow argued that a kind of *statistical discrimination* may occur when an employer lacks sufficient job-related information about a potential employee. Since, as we observed earlier, it is costly to acquire such information about an individual, employers may rely on their perceptions of the average characteristics of a group to which the individual belongs. Thus an employer may be reluctant to hire an individual female, for example, because he believes that females as a group are less productive or reliable than males. The belief may be valid or invalid, and the particular individual may be typical or atypical, but the result is the same.

The neoclassical monopsony model presented earlier has also been used to explain labor market discrimination. Janice Madden, for example, has argued that women and nonwhites are often less geographically mobile than their white male counterparts.[15] This may be due to family constraints, limited income, or restricted demand for their labor market services. Whatever the reasons, this relative immobility makes women and nonwhites more susceptible to any monopsony power which employers may have. You should recall from Chapter 3 that wages are set at artificially low levels under monopsony conditions.

Barbara Bergman has attempted to reconcile the predictions of the Becker model with the persistence of labor market discrimination.[16] Bergman's model

13. See Gary Becker, *Human Capital: A Theoretical and Empirical Analysis* (New York: National Bureau of Economic Research, 1964); and Jacob Mincer and Solomon Polachek, "Family Investments in Human Capital: Earnings of Women," *Journal of Political Economy* (March-April, 1974), pp. 76-111.

14. Kenneth Arrow, "Models of Job Discrimination," in Anthony Pascal (ed.), *Racial Discrimination in Economic Life* (Lexington, Mass.: D. C. Heath and Company, 1972), chap. 2.

15. See Janice Madden, *The Economics of Sex Discrimination* (Lexington, Mass.: D. C. Heath and Company, 1973).

16. Barbara Bergman, "The Effect on White Incomes of Discrimination in Employment," *Journal of Political Economy* (March-April, 1971), pp. 294-313; and Bergman, "Occupational Segregation, Wages and Profits when Employers Discriminate by Race or Sex," *Eastern Economic Journal* (April-July, 1974), pp. 103-10.

envisions two occupations requiring identical skills, but where one is prestigious and one menial. Nonwhites and women, even if as skilled as white males, are often restricted by demand factors to the low-status occupation. These types of occupations are characterized by a relatively large supply of workers due to restrictive employer tastes for discrimination. These occupations are overcrowded by nonwhites and females, and wages are consequently lower. The white male-dominated more prestigious occupations provide similarly higher wages.

Lester Thurow has also responded to the Becker model.[17] He contends that the Becker model is too narrow to describe fully the many kinds of discrimination that ultimately may become evident in the labor market. The wage discrimination envisioned by Becker will not disappear because it is complemented by occupational, human capital, financial, product market, and other types of more subtle discrimination, according to Thurow. He sees the persistence of these forces as resulting from the near-monopoly economic power of white males.

Institutional Economic Theories

Some economists have been generally dissatisfied with neoclassical explanations of labor market discrimination and have taken the view that discrimination has become institutionalized in our society in a way not accounted for in the neoclassical models. To some extent the contributions of Bergman and Thurow recognize institutionalized discrimination, but their emphasis is upon economic forces. Ray Marshall has recently argued that the neoclassical models, which concentrate on overt discrimination, fail to emphasize that:

> . . . inadequate education, segregated labor market institutions, and other forces which deny equal access to jobs, training and information greatly reduce the probability that those discriminated against will aspire to prepare for, or seek to enter the status occupations.[18]

For example, recall our discussion of internal labor markets where we observed that many high-level jobs in a firm are filled from within, with only lower entry level jobs being filled externally. If women or nonwhites are initially discriminated against in competing for these entry-level jobs, this discrimination will be compounded or institutionalized throughout the promotional ladder. Whether due to tastes or statistical perceptions, the initial discrimination results in less access, lower wages, and less on-the-job training for the affected groups.

---

17. Thurow, *Poverty and Discrimination*, chap. 7.
18. Ray Marshall, "The Economics of Racial Discrimination: A Survey," *Journal of Economic Literature* (September, 1974), p. 861.

The related dual labor market theory also leads to similar conclusions, as mentioned in previous chapters. If nonwhites or women are restricted disproportionately to the low-paying, dead-end secondary labor market, their economic disadvantage becomes similarly institutionalized. The Marxist contingent of dual labor market theorists goes even further to suggest an explanation similar to the sociologists' conflict theory. They argue that the ruling capitalist class uses the forces of racism and sexism to divide workers into primary and secondary labor markets, thereby preventing the development of a unifying working-class consciousness.[19]

Finally, some economists have noted the existence of another type of historically institutionalized labor market discrimination fostered by trade unions. In Chapter 3 we noted that institutions such as craft unions may effectively restrict the supply of workers into an occupation, thereby maintaining higher wages. But who are the workers who are restricted from entry, and how are they restricted? Clearly, if trade unions are successful in requiring union membership and/or the completion of a union-controlled apprenticeship program for entry into an occupation, union nonmembers are restricted from entry. Although considerable progress has been noted recently,[20] there is ample evidence that membership discrimination has been common in the past in many craft unions.[21]

GOVERNMENT POLICIES TO COMBAT DISCRIMINATION

It should now be clear that the continued existence of discrimination constitutes a serious weakness in the operation of labor markets. Historically, when weaknesses or flaws have appeared in our economic system, this has typically triggered intervention by the government in an attempt to correct the problem. Discrimination is certainly no exception. Now that we have some background in the various theories of labor market discrimination, we need to briefly review the major federal antidiscrimination laws before puzzling over the unresolved policy issues in the concluding section. Although not surveyed here, most states now have antidiscrimination laws similar to the federal ones mentioned below.

The *Equal Pay Act of 1963* was an amendment to the minimum wage provisions of the Fair Labor Standards Act of 1938. It prohibits wage discrimination based upon sex for equivalent jobs requiring substantially equal skill, effort, and responsibility, and performed under similar working conditions. Exceptions are granted for nondiscriminatory seniority, merit, and piecework

---

19. See Samuel Bowles and Herbert Gintis, "The Problem with Human Capital Theory—A Marxian Critique," *American Economic Review, Papers and Proceedings* (May, 1975), pp. 74-82.

20. See Orley Ashenfelter, "Racial Discrimination and Trade Unionism," *Journal of Political Economy* (May-June, 1972), pp. 435-64.

21. See, for example, Leonard Rapping, "Union-Induced Racial Entry Barriers," *Journal of Human Resources* (Fall, 1970), pp. 447-74.

compensation systems. The act is clearly limited in scope, pertaining only to wage discrimination based on sex, but it has contributed substantially to the elimination of such blatant discriminatory practices.

The major federal equal employment opportunity provisions are found in Title VII of the *Civil Rights Act of 1964,* as amended. These provisions prohibit discrimination in hiring, firing, promotion, training, fringe benefits, seniority, and retirement, on the basis of race, color, religion, sex, or national origin. The act prohibits such discrimination by employment agencies and labor organizations, as well as by employers, and it establishes the Equal Employment Opportunity Commission (EEOC) to administer the provisions of Title VII.

The EEOC is an independent five-member agency appointed by the President with the consent of the Senate. It is empowered to establish rules and regulations, subpoena records, process and seek conciliation of alleged violations of the law, conduct hearings and make findings, and bring civil actions requesting relief in the federal courts. The EEOC works through its regional offices and with various state agencies in carrying out the objectives of the federal law.

The 1972 amendments to the act extended coverage to all state and local government employers, while an earlier Presidential Executive Order (No. 11478 of 1969) guaranteed equal employment opportunity in federal agencies. The act as amended is the central component of the federal government's effort to eliminate discrimination in all aspects of employment. This effort has been supplemented more recently by the Age Discrimination in Employment Act of 1967, as amended, Title IX of the Educational Amendments of 1972, and Title V of the Rehabilitation Act of 1973. The former prohibits age discrimination against persons between the ages of 40 and 70; and Title IX prohibits sex discrimination in private and public educational programs receiving federal aid. Title V brings the disabled into the category of persons protected from employment discrimination.

Undoubtedly the most aggressive and controversial federal antidiscrimination effort pertains to employers operating under federal contracts or subcontracts. *Executive Order 11246 (1965),* as amended, prohibits discrimination in employment in such contracts or subcontracts on the basis of race, color, religion, national origin, sex, or disability. The amended order requires that each contractor agree not to discriminate in any aspect of employment, and it designates the Office of Federal Contract Compliance in the Department of Labor to enforce the provisions. Enforcement may take the form of cancelling, terminating, suspending, or delaying the contract if the contractor discriminates.

Most of the controversy surrounds the Department of Labor regulations established under the order. Almost all employers under federal government contracts or subcontracts must develop *affirmative action compliance programs.* The program must include a statistical analysis of the contractor's work force and of the available qualified labor pool. If this analysis shows a significant underutilization of affirmative action-targeted groups compared to their availability, the contractor is required to establish goals and timetables for increasing the employment of the underutilized group(s). The contractor must make "every good faith effort" to achieve the goals within the timetable, but is prohibited from setting rigid and inflexible quotas. A rigid quota is something arbitrarily imposed upon the work force, and no such quotas are required in affirmative action programs. A goal, on the other hand, is something sought in good faith. Contractors are not required necessarily to attain their affirmative action goals, but they must document their good faith efforts to do so.

UNRESOLVED POLICY ISSUES

The current antidiscrimination policies are a legitimate attempt by the federal government to eliminate an unacceptable and pervasive defect in labor market operations. Although there is little disagreement on the legitimacy or necessity of such intervention, much controversy surrounds the methods and effects of these policies.

Effectiveness of the EEOC

Critics of the EEOC point to evidence such as we looked at earlier in concluding that the agency has done little to improve the economic well-being of women and minorities. In fact, however, the data in Tables 8-3 and 8-6 which we discussed do show some improvement in the movement of women and minorities into professional, technical, and managerial occupations. Nevertheless, much of the earnings disparities remain. The EEOC has very limited enforcement powers without resorting to the courts, and it must rely primarily upon individual complaints. This requires a time-consuming process to review and process each complaint, resulting in a typical backlog of more than 100,000 cases. Critics also contend that the agency has exceeded its authority under the law by issuing rules challenging seniority systems and requiring preferential hiring in some instances.

Most experts would agree, however, that the EEOC has had a profound impact on hiring practices and employment patterns affecting minorities and women. In spite of its administrative problems and vocal opposition, it has won millions of dollars in court-ordered back pay for employees who were allegedly discriminated against by employers. It has successfully challenged many questionable employee selection, promotion, and training devices used by employers in a discriminatory manner. The continuation of earnings disparities and occupational segregation does not necessarily suggest a failure of EEOC policy. Rather, it indicates that historical patterns of discrimination, inadequate training and education, and frictional and structural labor market imbalances continue to hinder efforts aimed at achieving true equal employment opportunity. Many of these continuing problems are simply outside the scope of EEOC policy.

Supply Versus Demand Causes

A recognition of these problems has led to another debate which centers on the proper focus of antidiscrimination policy. Most of the governmental policies mentioned in this chapter are directed at the employer, or the demand side of the market. These policies implicitly presume that the kind of statistical or taste discrimination mentioned earlier actually pervades U.S. labor markets. Certainly much labor market discrimination does originate on the demand side, and present policies are essential in combating this.

But many employers and others have argued that a significant amount of the problem is on the supply side, and therefore demand-oriented policies often "bark up the wrong tree." To paraphrase, it is all well and good that the government requires active recruitment of qualified underutilized groups, but if qualified women and minorities are not available, of what good is the policy? Particularly in some scientific and technical occupations, the supply of qualified women and minorities is simply insufficient to meet the "good faith" demand. This implies that some of the psychological, sociological, and human capital theories mentioned earlier do have validity in explaining labor market discrimination. The problem actually originates on both sides of the market simultaneously, and we have already discussed several supply-oriented policies in Chapter 7.

Comparable Worth

During the 1970s federal government efforts to eliminate discriminatory earnings disparities focused upon both the desegregation of jobs and the enforcement of equality in pay within jobs. Through affirmative action programs, qualified women and minorities who were underrepresented in various jobs and training programs were sometimes permitted to fill job vacancy and training slots at preferential rates to lessen occupational segregation. "Equal pay for equal work" was then enforced through the Equal Pay Act and Title VII.

More recently the possibility of directly adjusting wage differentials among occupations has emerged under the objective of "equal pay for comparable worth."[22] Proponents of this approach argue that occupational desegregation and "equal pay for equal work" policies are too slow in eliminating earnings differentials between the sexes and races. Furthermore, particularly with respect to male-female disparities they contend that current policies overlook a major source of discrimination. Jobs dominated by women may pay less because they are "women's work" rather than because of any productivity-related factors of the work performed.[23]

---

22. See E. Robert Livernash (ed.), *Comparable Worth: Issues and Alternatives* (Washington: Equal Employment Advisory Council, 1980).

23. See George T. Milkovich, "Pay Inequalities and Comparable Worth," in *Proceedings of the 33rd Annual Meeting of the Industrial Relations Research Association* (Madison, Wisc.: IRRA, 1981), pp. 147-54.

The principal mechanism suggested for restructuring wage differentials is to set wages across various occupations based upon the notion of comparable worth or value. Comparable worth has been defined as "jobs that require comparable (not identical) skills, responsibility, and effort."[24] For example, if the female-dominated job of nursing was determined to have comparable worth to the male-dominated jobs in medical technology, this would call for an equalization of the respective wages for these jobs.

Critics of this approach argue that job worthiness is a subjective term which defies precise definition. Under current compensation practices, wage differentials are typically determined by a complex variety of factors including market forces, collective bargaining, economic conditions and technology, and employer policies. Although techniques of job analysis and evaluation are now commonly used, critics of comparable worth contend that there simply is no known technique by which intrinsic job worth can be measured. In addition, they argue that opening up all jobs for reclassification based upon a subjective theory would lead to tremendous labor dissatisfaction, as well as contribute to new skill shortages and surpluses as market forces are disrupted. In spite of these criticisms, as job evaluation techniques become more refined, the controversial doctrine of comparable worth is likely to remain a major issue in discrimination policy for the future.

Equal Opportunity Versus Equal Results

Perhaps the most perplexing of all unresolved discrimination policy issues relates to the timetable for eliminating market discrimination. To use the acronym of the National Organization of Women, disadvantaged groups want an end to discriminatory employment practices NOW. And certainly there is justification in this demand, given historical and continuing patterns of unequal treatment. But to rectify past patterns of discrimination completely and immediately requires more than just providing equal employment opportunities in the present and future. It is one thing to require "color-blind" and "sex-neutral" employment practices, and quite another to require employers to correct past patterns of discrimination through affirmative action and comparable worth procedures. The latter requirements are certainly more aggressive and more likely to yield immediate results, but at times they may also result in preferential treatment to the groups which were denied equal treatment in the past. As you undoubtedly know, there has been much intense debate concerning the social legitimacy of this method of combating discrimination.

To envision more clearly the essence of this problem, consider Figure 8-1. This diagram portrays the hypothetical economic progress (measured on the vertical axis) of two groups of people, groups A and B, over time (measured on the horizontal axis). Assume that these two groups of people are equal in all

---

24. Ibid., p. 151.

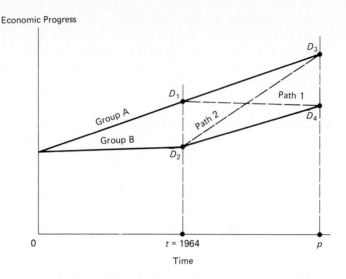

Figure 8-1   A Simple Model of Economic Progress and Discrimination

relevant respects when they begin to participate in the economic game. As the diagram indicates, group B immediately begins to fall behind group A in terms of economic progress, and by the time point t is reached group B is behind by the distance D_1D_2. Since we assumed that these two groups were equal at the start, the difference in economic progress can be attributed largely to the denial of equal opportunity to group B, i.e., to discrimination.

Point t is labeled as 1964 because that was the year in which the Civil Rights Act was passed. If we assume that this act was completely successful in eliminating discrimination after 1964, then we can expect that each group will progress equally thereafter. But notice that by the time point p (the present) is reached, the gap in economic progress, D_3D_4, is the same as it was in 1964! The provision of equal opportunity beginning in 1964 did not eliminate the effects of past discrimination; it merely kept the gap from getting wider. If the policy objective is that discriminatory effects should be eliminated, the mere provision of equal opportunity at some point in time does not achieve this goal.

Conceptually, there are two ways to ensure that both groups achieve equal economic results by the time point p is reached. One way would be to artificially slow down the progress of group A after 1964 until group B catches up. On the diagram, we could force group A to progress along path 1 until the two groups reach equality at point D_4. Alternatively, we could artificially speed up the progress of group B along path 2 until they reach equality at point D_3. Both of these alternatives involve the preferential treatment of group B for some period of time to eliminate the effects of past discrimination, and our society has been reluctant to accept such methods even though they have occasionally been upheld by the courts. Critics contend that this amounts to "reverse discrimination" and attempts to impose "equality of results" rather than "equality of opportunity." On the other hand, it may be little consolation to group B to know that they had equal opportunity after 1964, since without preferential programs their economic disadvantage relative to group A remains the same today as it was in 1964. The legitimacy and acceptability of affirmative action-type programs which attack past discriminatory effects will undoubtedly remain a hotly contested issue for some time.

This legitimacy is ultimately a legal question, and two recent Supreme Court cases have provided some clarification. In *Bakke v the California Board of Regents* (1978), the Supreme Court ruled on the constitutionality of a preferential admissions program at the University of California medical school at Davis which reserved 16 places per class for low-income minority students. The Court ruled that such a strict preferential quota, in the absence of past discriminatory patterns, was unconstitutional. It did add, however, that race could be a legitimate admissions criterion along with other factors to maintain cultural diversity.

In *United Steelworkers of America v Weber* (1979), the Court ruled on the legality of a private, voluntary training program which reserved half the training openings for blacks. The program, enacted jointly by the Kaiser Aluminum and Chemical Corporation and the United Steelworkers of America (AFL-CIO) in 1974, reserved one-half of the openings for blacks until the percentage of black skilled workers at Kaiser (roughly 2 percent prior to the enactment of the plan) approximates the percentage of blacks in the local labor force (roughly 40 percent). The legal issue was whether such a plan, with its potential for preferential treatment of blacks over whites, violated the nondiscrimination provisions of Title VII of the Civil Rights Act. The Supreme Court ruled that when such a plan is private, voluntary, temporary, and designed to eliminate racial imbalances, it is not in violation of the Act.

CONCLUDING REMARKS

The persistence of discrimination in U.S. labor markets is a striking example of a type of market failure which our society has found to be unacceptable. Our discussion in this chapter has concluded that some types of labor market discrimination still exist, and that the social costs of this discrimination are excessive. Various theories designed to explain this phenomenon have been surveyed, and they all shed some light on our understanding. In terms of our earlier analysis of labor market operations, however, one observation has become clear. In spite of the power of competitive labor market forces to operate in the absence of governmental intervention, serious weaknesses such as persistent discrimination require such intervention.

Given the need for public policy to remedy the market failure of continuing discrimination, the only remaining issue is the form which this public policy should take. We have concluded that discrimination is caused by a complex set of social, psychological, and economic factors operating on both the supply and demand sides of labor markets. It follows that public policy must be equally multifaceted. Some have argued that discrimination results from deeply imbedded social attitudes which cannot be painlessly legislated away overnight. There is certainly an element of truth to this argument, but those who suffer from discrimination are becoming increasingly reluctant to wait for social enlightenment in the uncertain future. Public policy makers will continue to seek methods of eliminating all traces of discrimination, while not losing sight of the legitimate rights of all citizens. It is a formidable task.

CHAPTER SUMMARY

Discrimination is a persistently serious problem in our society, and yet it is one which defies precise definition. Defining labor market discrimination as "differential labor market treatment based upon something other than labor productivity," we discover that it can take several different forms. Whether it be wage discrimination, employment discrimination, or occupational discrimination, the private and social costs are great. In addition to the psychological and monetary costs incurred by the victims of discrimination, all members of society pay in the form of lost output and foregone affluence. Our analysis of wage and employment patterns by race and sex clearly suggests the continued existence of discriminatory effects. Various psychological, sociological, and economic theories of discrimination have been developed which, when taken together, lead to the unsurprising conclusion that discrimination is a deeply embedded, pervasive social problem.

Discrimination is a classic example of the type of market failure which arises in a capitalist economy with some frequency (of course, it also may exist in other types of economic systems). Government intervention is usually required in cases of market failure to rectify or overcome the failure, and the government, particularly at the federal level, has become actively involved in antidiscrimination policy. The Civil Rights Act of 1964, and various other supplementary acts, prohibit a rather wide range of unequal employment opportunity situations. Among the most important and controversial supplemental policies are those enacted through Executive Order 11246, which prohibit employment discrimination by federal contractors and subcontractors. Regulations under these orders require the development of affirmative action compliance programs, whereby contractors must establish goals and timetables to increase the employment opportunities of underutilized groups. Affirmative action has generated considerable controversy because of the possibility that preferential treatment of previously underutilized groups may be necessary for compliance. Public policy makers are still seeking methods of quickly and equitably eliminating discrimination.

KEY TERMS

social discrimination
labor market discrimination
wage discrimination
employment discrimination
occupational discrimination

functionalism
exchange theory
conflict theory
taste for discrimination
statistical discrimination

Equal Pay Act (1963)
Civil Rights Act (1964)
affirmative action compliance programs

Bakke v the California Board of Regents (1978)
United Steelworkers of America v Weber (1979)

REVIEW QUESTIONS

1. Nobel Laureate Milton Friedman has stated, "It is a striking historical fact that the development of capitalism has been accompanied by a major reduction in the extent to which particular religious, racial, or social groups have . . . been discriminated against . . . there is an economic incentive in a free market to separate economic efficiency from other characteristics of the individual." [*Capitalism and Freedom* (Chicago: University of Chicago Press, 1962), pp. 108-9.] Critically evaluate this statement.

2. There appears to be a persistent pattern of occupational segregation between men and women. Is this pattern primarily a demand-side or supply-side market phenomenon? Defend your arguments.

3. How would you explain to a white male that he suffers "costs" from con-

tinued labor market discrimination against nonwhites and females?

4. Do you think it is possible to develop a single comprehensive theory of labor market discrimination? What would have to be included in such a theory?

5. A recent study at a college concluded that male professors earned, on the average, about $3000 more than female professors. What does this statistic alone tell you about the extent of discrimination at this college?

6. Do you think that legislation is helpful in eliminating attitudes of prejudice? If not, what alternatives are available to society?

7. It has been argued that the equal employment opportunity provisions of the Civil Rights Act require passive compliance, whereas affirmative action provisions require active compliance. Explain.

ADDITIONAL REFERENCES

Ashenfelter, Orley and Albert Rees (eds.). *Discrimination in Labor Markets.* Princeton, N.J.: Princeton University Press, 1973.

Becker, Gary. *The Economics of Discrimination.* Chicago: University of Chicago Press, 1957.

Hausman, Leonard J., Orley Ashenfelter, Bayard Rustin, Richard F. Schubert, and Donald Slainman (eds.). *Equal Rights and Industrial Relations.* Madison, Wis.: Industrial Relations Research Association, 1977.

Livernash, E. Robert (ed.). *Comparable Worth: Issues and Alternatives.* Washington: Equal Employment Advisory Council, 1980.

Marshall, Ray. "The Economics of Racial Discrimination: A Survey," *Journal of Economic Literature* (September, 1974), pp. 849-71.

Stromberg, Ann H., and Shirley Harkess (eds.). *Women Working.* Palo Alto, Calif.: Mayfield Publishing Company, 1978.

Wallace, Phyllis A., and Annette M. LaMond (eds.). *Women, Minorities, and Employment Discrimination.* Lexington, Mass.: D. C. Heath and Company, 1977.

THE WORLD OF WORK . . .

Differences in On-the-Job Training by Race and Sex

One possible explanation for the persistence of wage differentials by race and sex is that blacks and women receive less on-the-job training than do their white male counterparts. This possibility is examined in the recent study excerpted below.

Wages of blacks and women are still substantially lower than those for white men. The latest figures for the third quarter of 1980 showed that for full-time wage-and-salary workers, median weekly earnings for black men were about 75 percent of those for white men; the corresponding figures were 63 percent for white women and 58 percent for black women. Careful studies of differences in earnings by race and sex suggest that a sizable portion of the observed differences—perhaps half or more—are *unexplained* by underlying race/sex differences in the average level of apparent worker skills such as education and work experience. The indirect—and unproven—implication of this is that labor market discrimination is still prevalent. We also know that the jobs which women and blacks hold are worse in other ways as well—lower occupational status, less desirable working conditions, and greater vulnerability to cyclical unemployment.

But what about the skills and training that workers receive on the job? Are the jobs of women and blacks worse in that regard also? Do their jobs provide them with less opportunity for on-the-job training? A recent national survey suggests that the answer to this is yes, and that, for young black men especially, the amount of training provided on the job is quite limited.

Virtually all labor economists agree that on-the-job training is an important determinant of individual earnings and especially of the growth of earnings over the life cycle. It is commonplace now for economists to view a job as both a source of current income and as a place to learn new work skills or improve old ones—to acquire on-the-job training. Indeed, it appears that most of the skills actually used on the job are learned there, not in school. Those acquired skills lead to higher future earnings by increasing and enhancing an indi-

vidual's work skills and productivity. The continued acquisition of work skills on the job plays a central role in both the human capital model and even in labor market models which emphasize market segmentation, discrimination, and the role of institutional forces.

Information about the amount of skills and training provided on the job is also important for accurate race/sex wage comparisons. For example, if the jobs held by women and blacks offered fewer opportunities for skill acquisition and improvement, then current average wage differences by race and sex would understate the "true" differences. In that event, we might expect future race/sex earnings differences to grow as average skill levels diverged over the life cycle. Precisely the opposite interpretation would be appropriate if blacks, women, or both were receiving greater training opportunities.

. . . Some *direct* evidence on race/sex training differences is available in recent data provided by the Panel Study of Income Dynamics. This is a national longitudinal survey of the economic status of more than 5,000 families which has been conducted annually since 1968. In the study's 1976 interviews, questions relating to on-the-job training were included as part of an attempt to develop an extensive data base for the analysis of race and sex earnings differences.

. . . We can look at the question we originally asked: In addition to carrying lower wages and a higher probability of unemployment, do the jobs of blacks and women provide less on-the-job training? The answer, according to the Panel Study data, is yes. The average training period for white men is 2.25 years, while that for white women and for black men and black women is less than 1 year. And the same order of difference—more than 2 to 1—persists even when white men are compared with blacks and women within the same age group or educational category. Thus, the lower training periods are not explained by race/sex differences in age or educational attainment.

. . . While more than a quarter of white men were currently receiving training on their jobs (that is, their training period exceeded their job tenure), the corresponding figure was about 14 percent for white women and less than 9 percent for both black men and black women. Again, these race/sex differences remain even within age and educational groups. The differences between black and white men are especially large for workers between the ages of 18 and 35. Among white men, about 35 percent in this age group were receiving training compared with less than 10 percent for blacks.

Finally, the lower amounts of training for blacks and women do not appear to be because they hold low-wage jobs more often than white men. If we compare workers within the same hourly wage rate bracket, large differences in the percentages receiving training remain. Nearly a quarter of the white men in low-wage jobs (less than $4 per hour) were still receiving training, compared with 11 percent for white women and only about 5 to 6 percent for black men and women.

What do these findings tell us about the prospects for narrowing race/sex earnings differences? First, they suggest that current variations in earnings understate the true differences: blacks and women receive less training on their jobs than white men and a smaller percentage are currently receiving training. Assuming this training usually translates into higher future earnings, then we may expect the earnings gap to widen as these individuals become older. Second, there is some evidence that the low-wage jobs held by white men are very dissimilar from those of blacks and women. Many of these jobs for white men also provide training, so the low wage is probably only temporary; for the other groups, the proportion of low-wage workers receiving training is much less, suggesting a more permanent low-wage condition. Finally, the results imply that young black men continue to lag behind their white counterparts—the training differential was extremely large for this age group.

One thing this study does not tell us is *why* blacks and women tend to receive less training. We could, of course, use the training differential as yet another example of labor market discrimination, but that does not really provide much explanation or insight. Economists still know very little about the ways in which different people wind up in different jobs—some with high wages or extensive training, some with less of both—and even less about the reasons.

Source: Abridged from Saul D. Hoffman, "On-the-Job Training: Differences by Race and Sex," *Monthly Labor Review* (July, 1981), pp. 34-36.

Chapter 9

Poverty and Economic Insecurity

Perhaps the most perplexing paradox which has characterized the United States and many other industrialized economies over time has been the persistence of poverty amidst affluence. Ours is in some respects the richest country in the world, and yet millions of American families do not have enough income to provide minimally adequate food, clothing, and housing. Many other families, though able to provide for their most basic necessities, are unable to save or provide any economic security for themselves. Since various properties of a market-oriented capitalist economy tend to generate inadequate income or disruptions in the flow of income for some families and individuals, we once again have a significant economic problem which has justified government intervention. Since the major source of income for most Americans is labor income, most of this intervention is in the labor market. In the twentieth century, income maintenance and the redistribution of income have become legitimate functions of government in the United States and most other industrialized countries. Of course, the extent of the government's role in these areas remains a matter of considerable controversy.

We begin this chapter by briefly reviewing historical attitudes toward poverty and antipoverty programs in the United States. We then analyze carefully the actual patterns of income distribution over time. The central topic of this chapter, poverty or income inadequacy, is taken up next. We attempt first to clarify our understanding of the measurement, causes, and victims of poverty. This is no easy task, as we shall see, but it is necessary in order to evaluate intelligently present and proposed policy alternatives. We examine antipoverty policies closely in the latter part of the chapter, particularly in terms of the conflicting economic goals of equity and efficiency.

A BRIEF HISTORICAL PERSPECTIVE[1]

As is the case with any social problem, the public policy that is adopted to contend with poverty depends upon what society perceives as the cause of poverty. During the colonial period in the United States, for example, the prevailing Protestant work ethic viewed poverty as the just punishment for

---

1. See Bradley R. Schiller, *The Economics of Poverty and Discrimination*, 3d ed. (Englewood Cliffs, N.J.: Prentice-Hall, Inc., 1980), pp. 3-5. This is an excellent source on the subject of poverty.

wrongdoing or immorality. The appropriate antipoverty measures, therefore, were religious training and/or physical punishment to drive out sin. There was no need to alleviate the suffering of the poor, since this suffering was seen as a necessary by-product of immoral behavior. This view continued to predominate throughout much of the nineteenth century.

During the economic depressions of the 1890s and 1930s, however, a change in attitude became apparent. With 25 percent of the labor force unemployed by 1933, many reputable and responsible people were subjected to poverty for the first time. As one expert has noted, poverty gained a "middle-class constituency."[2] It was, of course, difficult for them to accept this condition as resulting from their immoral behavior, no matter how strongly they may have believed in that cause previously. The attitude emerged that poverty may be closely related to social and economic conditions largely outside the control of the individual.

Unfortunately, as we moved into a period of general prosperity after the Great Depression, we regressed somewhat back toward our earlier beliefs. With the passage of time, fewer and fewer people remembered (or chose to remember) the general deprivation of the 1930s. Although there was a social consensus that poverty could not be ignored, the belief persisted among many that the poor largely create their own destiny through inadequate ambition and motivation. Those who promoted this belief obviously concluded that we need not help those who will not help themselves. The following excerpt from an early 1960s editorial exemplifies the hostility toward the poor which has reemerged in this country, and which in large part remains with us today:

> Relief is gradually becoming an honorable career in America. It is a pretty fair life, if you have conscience nor pride. The politicians will weep for you. The state will give a mother a bonus for her illegitimate children, and if she neglects them sufficiently, she can save enough of her AFDC payments to keep herself and her boyfriend in wine and gin.[3]

There was to some extent a rediscovery of poverty in the 1960s. The publication of a book entitled *The Other America* by Michael Harrington in 1962 raised the consciousness of millions of Americans to the plight of the poor.[4] The New Frontier and Great Society programs of the Kennedy and Johnson administrations contributed further to this awareness. Nevertheless, the current social attitude toward poverty remains curiously ambivalent. It is probably fair to generalize that we as a society now recognize that social and economic forces may victimize the poor, but there remains a strong suspicion among many that the poor could support themselves adequately if we did not make public assistance so readily available. Since we do not agree on the causes of

---

2. Ibid., p. 4.
3. Quoted in Edgar May, *The Wasted Americans* (New York: Harper & Row, 1964), p. 7.
4. Michael Harrington, *The Other America*, rev. ed. (New York: The Macmillan Company, 1970).

poverty, we have found it very difficult as a society to agree on the most appropriate policy prescriptions. As noted, it is the major objective of this chapter to clarify some of these difficult causal and policy issues.

THE DISTRIBUTION OF INCOME IN THE UNITED STATES

Patterns

Let us begin with an examination of the pattern of income distribution in the United States. There are actually several ways of analyzing this issue, but the most common method generates the data in Table 9-1. For a number of selected years during the post-World War II period, Table 9-1 shows the percentage of U.S. families which earned incomes falling within various income classes. Note that the percentages are calculated in terms of constant 1980 dollars; so the impact of inflation during this period is negated. As observed earlier, we are an affluent society, and we have become more affluent over this period. The median family income in 1980 was over $21,000 as compared with $13,000 in 1950, after adjustment for inflation. This increased affluence is clearly depicted in Table 9-1, which shows that only 6.2 percent of all families earned less than $5000 in 1980, as compared with 17.4 percent in 1950. Similar improvement is seen in the other income classes over time. However, although improvement is evident, considerable income inequality still exists. The 6.2 percent figure for 1980 corresponds to almost 3 million families which attempted to survive on less than $5000 in annual income.

Table 9-1 shows that the entire income distribution has been moving up

Table 9-1   Percentage Distribution of Families by Total Income
in Constant 1980 Dollars, Selected Years

Real Income Class	Year				
	1950	1960	1970	1975	1980
Under $5000	17.4%	11.4%	6.1%	5.6%	6.2%
$5000-$9999	24.0	16.1	11.7	12.9	12.7
$10,000-$19,999		43.0	33.3	28.8	28.2
$20,000-$34,999			34.0	37.4	33.5
	58.6	29.5			
$35,000-$49,999			9.3	9.6	12.8
$50,000 and over			5.5	5.8	6.7
	100.0%	100.0%	100.0%	100.0%	100.0%

Source: *Current Population Reports; Consumer Income*, Series P-60, No. 127 (Washington: U.S. Government Printing Office, March, 1981), Table 4.

over time, in an absolute sense, as we have become more affluent as a society. Does this mean that poverty is less of a problem today? Let's consider some additional information before attempting to answer that question. Consider, for example, the data in Table 9-2. Here changes in the distribution of income are viewed from a relative perspective. All U.S. families are arrayed from richest to poorest and are then divided into five equal quintiles. In Table 9-2 the share of national income received by each of these quintiles is shown for the same selected years. Now a somewhat different conclusion emerges. The share of income going to each of the quintiles has been remarkably constant over this period. Put differently, the relative share of income accruing to each segment of the population has remained stable, and the share going to the lowest two quintiles has actually declined slightly (from 17.1 to 16.7 percent).

Table 9-2   Percentage Share of National Income Received by Each Fifth and the Top 5 Percent of Families, Selected Years

Income Quintiles	Year					
	1955	1960	1965	1970	1975	1980
Lowest Fifth	4.8%	4.8%	5.2%	5.4%	5.4%	5.1%
Second Fifth	12.3	12.2	12.2	12.2	11.8	11.6
Middle Fifth	17.8	17.8	17.8	17.6	17.6	17.5
Fourth Fifth	23.7	24.0	23.9	23.8	24.1	24.3
Highest Fifth	41.3	41.3	40.9	40.9	41.1	41.6
Top 5 Percent	16.4	15.9	15.5	15.6	15.5	15.3

Source: *Current Population Reports; Consumer Income*, Series P-60, No. 123, Table 13; and No. 127, Table 5.

It can be concluded from these data that most families have improved their economic status considerably in the last 25 years, but the relative income inequality has not lessened. Most low-income families are absolutely better off today than were low-income families in 1955, but they are receiving the same small share of the national income that they received then. In other words, the size of the economic "pie" has grown in the post-war period, but the percentage shares of that pie accruing to different income classes have remained about the same.

The Impact of Taxes and Transfer Payments

Two other factors must be addressed which may affect the income distribution. First, Tables 9-1 and 9-2 reflect before-tax family incomes. If the tax system takes more from the rich than from the poor, is it not likely that the after-tax income distribution is more equal than the before-tax distribution? Most evidence suggests that this is not the case, because the tax system (federal, state, and local taxes combined) tends to take about the same percentage of income from most families, regardless of income level.[5] The federal personal income tax provides for higher tax rates as family income increases, but the effective tax rates for most state and local taxes, including sales and property taxes, actually decline as income increases. The net result is a U.S. tax structure which is roughly proportional, leaving the before-tax and after-tax income distributions essentially equivalent.

Finally, some have criticized the Census Bureau data found in Tables 9-1 and 9-2 for the way in which transfer payments are treated. *Transfer payments* are government expenditures for which no goods or services are received by the government in return. Money transfers such as Social Security payments and unemployment compensation are included in the Census Bureau income calculations. Nonmonetary, or in-kind, transfers such as Medicare, housing subsidies, and food stamps, however, are not included. Since low-income people are the primary recipients of in-kind transfers, and since such transfers have expanded dramatically in the last two decades, critics argue that inclusion of these transfers would modify the income distribution calculations toward more equality. Even where such adjusted calculations have been made, however, the results suggest that the lowest income quintile has gained perhaps 3 percent in its income share at the expense of the highest income quintile.[6]

THE POVERTY PROBLEM: WHO AND WHY?

Our previous discussion has made clear the fact that there remains a wide disparity in incomes among families and individuals in the United States. We would probably all agree that some proportion of our population is poor, although we would undoubtedly disagree on the exact percentage. But to pursue the question of the extent of poverty is premature because we have not defined poverty yet. We need a working definition, one which will allow us to assess the magnitude of the problem.

Poverty Concepts and Measurement

The two general approaches to defining poverty are presented in Tables 9-1 and 9-2, although we did not emphasize poverty per se in our earlier discussions. The first general approach is the *absolute approach*, which defines poverty as a state wherein the individual or family cannot afford to purchase

---

5. See Joseph A. Pechman and Benjamin A. Okner, *Who Bears the Tax Burden?* (Washington: The Brookings Institution, 1974).

6. See Edgar K. Browning, "How Much More Equality Can We Afford?" *The Public Interest* (Spring, 1976), pp. 90-110.

some predetermined minimum amount of essential goods and services. With reference to Table 9-1, we might establish that any family with total income below $5000 has inadequate income to purchase the minimum essential goods and services. In 1980 this would lead to the conclusion that 6.7 percent of the U.S. families were poor.

But why the figure $5000? Why not $3000 or $8000? Presumably our poverty line must be related to the costs of meeting minimum nutritional requirements, and some form of clothing and housing allowances. These costs can be estimated without much difficulty, but what other essentials, if any, should be included? What about electricity, furniture, a car, a telephone, or life and health insurance? These items are clearly not essentials of life, but they have become virtual necessities in our relatively affluent society. Unfortunately, our society has not been able to reach agreement on what constitutes minimally essential goods and services, and this is the difficulty in the absolute approach.

Alternatively, we could take a *relative approach,* defining poverty as a state wherein the individual or family income is significantly below the average income. This approach can be exemplified by referring again to the format of Table 9-2. We could define poverty as some predetermined low end of the income distribution, such as the lowest fifth. This is a relative approach in the sense that poverty is defined relative to some summary income statistic such as average income. We would no longer have to debate what constitutes essential needs, but we have introduced a new problem. Since every income distribution will have a lowest fifth, no matter how high or low average incomes may be, poverty will always be perpetuated definitionally at some fixed percentage of the population.[7] This approach tells us nothing about the absolute standard of living of the poor.

For policy purposes, the absolute standard of poverty has generally been employed. Beginning in 1963, the absolute poverty line was established by the President's Council of Economic Advisors at $3000 for a family of four. This $3000 consisted of approximately $1000 for food and $2000 for nonfood items annually. Since then, various adjustments in the standard have been made for differences in family size, rural versus urban location, and cost-of-living increases. The average poverty level and poverty rates for several recent years are presented in Table 9-3. The poverty line has increased with inflation, and the poverty rate had declined substantially in the last 20 years. It is disturbing, however, to note once again the lack of progress during the economically troubled decade of the 1970s.

---

7. A variation of the relative approach intended to overcome this problem has been suggested by Victor Fuchs and others. By his definition, those families with incomes less than half of the median family income should be designated as poor. See Victor Fuchs, "Comment," in Lee Soltow (ed.), *Six Papers on the Size Distribution of Wealth and Income* (New York: Columbia University Press, 1969), pp. 198-202.

Table 9-3   The Official Poverty Level and Persons
Below the Poverty Level, Selected Years

Year	Average Poverty Level for Nonfarm Family of Four	Number of Persons Below Poverty Level	Poverty Rate
1960	$3023	39,851,000	22.2%
1965	3223	33,185,000	17.3
1970	3968	25,420,000	12.6
1975	5500	25,877,000	12.3
1980	8414	29,272,000	13.0

Source: *Current Population Reports; Consumer Income*, Series P-60, No. 124, Table A-1; and No. 127.

Who Are the Poor?

We accept as a working definition the absolute standard established by the Census Bureau, recognizing that there are limitations to this approach. In order to gain some preliminary insight into the causes of poverty, let's now look at some of the distinctive characteristics of the poor. Table 9-4 summarizes several important factors. Note that the table concentrates on the year 1980, when the overall percentage of persons below the poverty line was 13.0 percent. This summary figure conceals some important personal and demographic characteristics of the poor, however.

Table 9-4   Persons Below the Poverty Level by Family Status,
Sex of Head of Household, Race, and Age, 1980

Characteristic	Poverty Rate
All Persons	13.0%
65 Years and Older	15.7
White	10.2
Black	32.5
Spanish Origin	25.7
Persons in Families with Male Head	7.4%
White	6.4
Black	16.0
Spanish Origin	18.0
Persons in Families with Female Head	36.7%
White	28.0
Black	53.4
Spanish Origin	54.5

Source: *Current Population Reports; Consumer Income*, Series P-60, No. 127, Table 18.

First, observe that the poverty rate for those over 65 (15.7 percent) is higher than the overall rate. This suggests that poverty is a somewhat greater problem for the elderly, which is certainly true. However, with the substantial improvements in private pension and Social Security benefits in the last 15 years or so the severity of the problem for the elderly has actually diminished remarkably. For example, as recently as 1967 the poverty rate for those over 65 years of age was almost 30 percent. Nevertheless, some 3 million households headed by people over age 65 are poor today. Presumably they either fail to qualify for Social Security or other pension benefits, or the benefits are inadequate to lift them out of poverty.

Table 9-4 reveals that the most glaring characteristics of the poor relate to race and to sex of the household head. While roughly 10 percent of white individuals are poor, almost one-third of blacks and one-fourth of people of Spanish origin fall into the poverty category. These disparities remain on a somewhat smaller scale for individuals in a male-headed family. The most serious poverty rate problem clearly exists in female-headed families. While the overall poverty rate is roughly 7 percent for persons in male-headed families, it jumps to over 36 percent for those in families with a female head of household. For blacks and people of Spanish origin, their chances of being poor are greater than 50 percent if they are in a female-headed household. The data in Table 9-4 clearly suggest that poverty impacts disproportionately on nonwhite and female-headed households. In other words, one is more likely to be poor in such households. This does not indicate, however, that poverty is primarily a nonwhite phenomenon. In fact, an overwhelming majority of those individuals officially classified as poor are white.

One other characteristic of the poor deserves mention. As Harrington has noted, most of our poverty is hidden or invisible. Middle- and upper-class Americans simply do not confront the degradation of urban ghettos or the abject destitution found in some parts of rural America. We are insulated from their suffering and neglect and have therefore become somewhat desensitized to their plight.

Why Are the Poor Poor?

In general, the poverty problem is greater among the elderly, the non-white, and/or among those residing in a female-headed household, and the poor typically are hidden from our everyday lives. But these are merely descriptive characteristics of the poor, not the causes of their condition. The distinction is important because there is a tendency to confuse characteristics and causes. We have concluded that poverty is related to age, race, and sex of the household head, but we certainly have not concluded that these characteristics cause poverty. What, then, are the causes of poverty which tend to manifest themselves so strongly in elderly, nonwhite, and female-headed households?

Nonexistent Property Income. In seeking an answer to this important question, we can rely upon a number of concepts already developed in earlier chapters. Let us begin by referring back to the circular flow diagram presented in Figure 1-1, page 5. Here we noted that households receive income from selling land, labor, and capital which they own or control to firms. There are vast differences in the quantity of these resources that are controlled by different households. With respect to income received from property resources such as land and capital, the vast majority of such income is received by a very small percentage of the population. For example, the top 5 percent of income recipients in the United States receive over two-thirds of dividend payments and about one-half of all property income.[8] Therefore, one cause of poverty is the extremely uneven distribution of property income.

Nonparticipation in the Labor Market. Roughly 80 percent of all market-determined income is not property income, however, but labor income in the form of wages and salaries. If labor income is inadequate, poverty is a likely result. One obvious case in which labor income would be inadequate would be when no household members are in the labor force. Retirement, disability, and the discouraged worker phenomenon described earlier would all be reasons for nonparticipation in the labor force, resulting in the elimination of labor income.

Unemployment or Underemployment. It does not follow, however, that participation in the labor force ensures the elimination of poverty. First, you will recall from our earlier discussion that labor force participants are either employed part-time or full-time, or are unemployed and actively seeking work. Unemployment and involuntary part-time employment also result in inadequate labor income, and these are major sources of poverty.

Human Capital Deficiencies. To follow our line of reasoning further, even employment is not an automatic ticket out of poverty. In 1980, about 50 percent of all poor household heads worked during the year, and about 20 percent worked full-time throughout the year. One explanation for this working poor phenomenon might be what we could term human capital deficiencies. Some people do not possess the necessary skills and abilities to compete in the labor market, as we have observed earlier. These individuals will receive low wages for their low productivity, if they can find employment at all. It is also possible that individuals may possess training and education which are not demanded in the labor market. As we noted in Chapter 1, for example, many teachers

---

8. On this subject, see Lester C. Thurow, *Generating Inequality* (New York: Basic Books, Inc., 1975), chaps. 1 and 6.

trained in the 1970s possessed skills which were simply not demanded sufficiently to meet the supply. Training, retraining, and education programs of the types noted in Chapter 7 are necessary to enhance human capital and earnings for these structurally unemployed or underemployed people.

Discrimination. Finally, we observed in the last chapter that serious barriers to economic progress still exist in the United States in the form of discrimination. Whether it takes the form of wage, employment, or occupational discrimination in the labor market, labor income is diminished when such discrimination occurs. Unequal access to education and training programs caused by discriminatory barriers leaves its victims with institutionalized human capital deficiencies, again reducing their labor incomes. Women and minorities historically have had very little access to property ownership, the effect of which has been to foreclose them from opportunities to earn property income. It is not surprising, therefore, to observe the poverty characteristics exhibited in Table 9-4.

Perceived Causes of Poverty and Social Commitment. We have already discussed several public policies intended to combat these problems in earlier chapters. The rest of this chapter will highlight additional programs. One point must be reiterated before we consider these policy issues, however. The nature and extent of our social commitment to the "war on poverty" depends closely upon the perceived causes of poverty. Although we have summarized the causes above, the belief persists among many people that abundant opportunities for economic advancement exist for those who are motivated enough to seek them. According to this belief labor force nonparticipation, unemployment, and skill deficiencies are not really causes of poverty. Rather they are visible results of inherent weaknesses in individuals. Bradley Schiller has called this the flawed character argument,[9] and it is clearly related to earlier views that poverty status accrues necessarily to sinful people.

The alternative explanation, termed the restricted opportunity argument by Schiller, is different both in substance and in implication. Emerging as we have noted during economic depression, this view emphasized social, political, and economic forces outside the control of individuals as the roots of poverty. If the latter explanation is essentially correct, then as a humane society we have a strong obligation to eradicate those poverty-inducing forces. On the other hand, if the flawed character argument explains persistent poverty, then we need not alter the system significantly. Our social obligation can be on a much smaller scale because, as the saying goes, we should "help only those who are willing to help themselves."

---

9. Schiller, *The Economics of Poverty and Discrimination*, pp. 39-41.

GOVERNMENTAL ANTIPOVERTY PROGRAMS

As with other social problems, the ideal antipoverty policies would be ones which directly attack the root causes of poverty. Since we have seen that the causes are numerous and that strong differences of opinion exist, it is not surprising that there are a large number of government programs intended to deal with some aspect of poverty. Basically, poverty can be attacked by employment policy (job creation), policies to eliminate barriers between existing jobs and individuals, and/or income-maintenance policies.

Employment policy was the subject of Chapter 6. Policies to eliminate employment barriers are numerous and diverse, because there are many types of barriers. Human capital deficiency barriers and the related policies were the subject of Chapter 7. Another type of employment barrier, discrimination, was discussed in Chapter 8. In this section we concentrate primarily on the various income-maintenance programs designed to aid the needy.

Need-Based Programs

We can distinguish between two general categories of current income-maintenance programs on the basis of the benefit criterion which is used. *Need-based programs* determine the benefits on the basis of the need of the recipient, whereas the benefits of *work experience–based programs* are based upon previous work experience.

Minimum Wage Legislation. We mentioned minimum wage provisions briefly in Chapter 3. The minimal wage laws are a somewhat unique type of income-maintenance program because they do not entail transfer payment expenditures on the part of the federal government. The intent of the laws, however, is clearly to enhance the earnings of low-income workers. The Fair Labor Standards Act of 1938 was passed to regulate minimum wages and maximum hours in U.S. labor markets. The Act originally excluded from coverage agricultural workers, government employees, and administrative and professional workers. The original minimum wage for covered employment was established at 25 cents per hour.

Since 1938, numerous amendments to the Act have been passed, resulting in both higher minimum wages and extended employee coverage. The 1977 amendments established a new minimum at $2.65 per hour beginning in January of 1978, with provisions for annual increases up to $3.35 per hour beginning in 1981. Several amendments in the 1960s and 1970s considerably increased the coverage for nonsupervisory employees in the private sector. Now roughly 85 percent of such employees are covered by federal minimum wage provisions.

You will recall from our Chapter 3 discussion that the effectiveness of the minimum wage as an antipoverty device has been challenged. Several research studies have noted the unfavorable employment effects of the minimum wage, particularly on certain low-wage subgroups of the labor force which are particularly susceptible to poverty.[10] Persistently high teenage unemployment, for example, has been attributed partially to increases in the statutory minimum wage. There is evidence of numerous layoffs and labor hours reductions after the 1977 amendments were enacted, and this kind of effect results in lessened job opportunities and eventual promotion possibilities for the unskilled.

To contend with these problems for young, unskilled workers, a youth differential in the minimum wage has been repeatedly proposed. Such a differential was introduced in Congress both in 1974 and in 1977, but was defeated because of strong opposition from organized labor and other groups. In fact, the AFL-CIO favors further increases in the minimum wage as well as extensions in the coverage of the law.

It is also difficult to maintain the legislated minimum wage at a level which keeps up with inflation. The escalation provisions of the 1977 amendments were such an attempt, but a little calculation reveals that the legislated increases between 1978 and 1981 total 70 cents, or about 26 percent. Prices increased by well over 30 percent during this same period, however. Nevertheless, those who maintain their employment and labor hours after a minimum wage increase clearly benefit. There has been considerable improvement in the real minimum wage since 1938, and the resulting higher incomes have contributed to a lessening of poverty for many individuals and families. Unfortunately, those who lose their jobs or face a cutback in hours from a minimum wage increase are likely to drop deeper into poverty. To this latter group which is essentially priced out of the labor market by the minimum wage, society becomes obligated to provide other forms of public assistance, training, and rehabilitation.

Aid to Families with Dependent Children. Table 9-5 summarizes the major federal antipoverty programs which involve transfer payments. As noted previously, need-based transfer payments may be further divided into cash transfers and in-kind transfers, and the *Aid to Families with Dependent Children* program is the largest need-based cash transfer program. AFDC now serves primarily poor, female-headed families with small children, a logical emphasis given our earlier discussion of poverty characteristics. The program is currently supported by matching federal grants to states, but the states administer the programs and set benefit levels. Benefit levels vary greatly among states, and there is a requirement that healthy mothers whose youngest child is over 5 must register for training or employment.

In terms of benefit level variations, average monthly AFDC benefits recently ranged from a high of about $350 per family in California to less than $100 in Mississippi. These figures are presumably based upon the minimum

---

10. See footnotes 5 and 6 and the *World of Work* reading, Chapter 3.

Table 9-5   Expenditures for Major Federal Antipoverty Programs, 1980

	1980 Federal Expenditures (millions of dollars)
Need-Based	
AFDC	$ 7,308
Supplemental Security Income (SSI)	6,411
Food Stamps	9,117
Medicaid	14,028
Housing Assistance	5,514
Work Experience–Based	
Social Security (OASDHI)	$117,117
Unemployment Compensation	18,023
Medicare	35,034

Source: *The Budget of the United States Government, 1982*, pp. 235-52.

needs of AFDC families, but even in California the monthly benefit level is based upon a maximum rent of roughly $125 and no telephone allowance. Furthermore, to enter and remain on the AFDC rolls, families must typically possess no more than $1000 in personal property, plus additional allowances for auto and home ownership. Finally, even though AFDC is intended to provide assistance to needy families with children, it is estimated that only about 60 percent of poor families with children receive AFDC. This is because payments are often limited to fatherless homes, regardless of the need of poor male-headed families.[11]

In addition to these inadequacies and inequities, AFDC is often criticized for its work-disincentive effects. In most states, benefits are reduced by at least two-thirds of earnings after work-related expenses are deducted. This can be viewed as a very high tax on earned income. For example, consider a hypothetical welfare mother who currently receives $300 per month from AFDC for her family of four, and who earns $200 a month from part-time employment. Let us assume that she has the opportunity to acquire a full-time job which pays $400 per month. As a result of her extra $200 per month in earned income, her AFDC benefits would be reduced by roughly two-thirds of that extra earned income, or approximately $133. Thus, she would earn $400 per month and receive $167 from AFDC. Although her combined earned income and AFDC benefits would be greater than before ($567 per month, rather than $500), she is only $67 better off.

Because AFDC benefits were reduced, her extra earned income of $200 was in effect taxed at a rate of 66 percent, leaving only one-third, or $67. In

---

11. See Schiller, *The Economics of Poverty and Discrimination*, pp. 169-70.

terms of the work-leisure preference framework which was presented in Chapter 2, the choice to keep the part-time job and gain leisure costs only $67 per month. In all likelihood many of us would choose not to work additional hours if such a high tax were imposed upon our additional income.

Supplemental Security Income. Beginning in 1973, the federal government terminated grants to states for public assistance to the aged, blind, and disabled. As a replacement, the federally financed and administered *Supplemental Security Income* (SSI) program was created for these groups. Although roughly half the states continue to provide assistance to these groups, SSI establishes a nationwide minimum income floor for the aged, blind, and disabled who are unable to work.

Adopted under the Social Security system, more than 4 million individuals received average SSI benefits of about $140 per month in 1980. Approximately 2.5 million recipients were elderly persons who in most cases were ineligible for regular old age assistance under Social Security. As with AFDC, the benefit is reduced if the recipient has other earned or unearned income, and individual assets may not exceed certain limits.

Food Stamps. A major in-kind transfer program which has grown steadily in recent years is the food stamp program. The program is designed to provide all low-income people with a nutritionally adequate diet, and eligibility is based totally on family income and family size. Eligible families receive a monthly allotment of coupons which are redeemable for food. The larger the family size and the smaller the family income, the greater is the value of the stamp allotment. The grocer who receives the food stamps for food then cashes the stamps in at a local bank which in turn redeems them at face value from the government.

In effect, food stamps are a direct substitute for cash, although they must be used only for food purchases. The average food stamp allotment in 1980 was about $39 per month per person, or slightly less than $160 per month for a family of four. This corresponds to roughly 40 cents per person per meal. The value of food stamp allotments is adjusted annually to reflect higher food prices.

Medicaid. Medicaid is an in-kind benefit program providing medical services to eligible low-income families regardless of age and previous work experience. In 1981, the federal government paid at least half of the full cost of medical and hospital care, and the states paid the remainder. Most AFDC families and others classified as medically indigent are eligible for this program, which is financed by general tax revenues.

As Table 9-5 indicates, the Medicaid program entails even larger expenditures than does AFDC, reflecting the high costs of medical treatment. Those eligible for Medicaid because of low income essentially pass doctor or hospitalization costs on to the government, rather than paying the bills themselves or submitting them to private insurance companies. Although the amount of Medicaid benefits received obviously varies depending upon medical needs, the average value of the services received in 1980 exceeded $1000 for a family of four.

Housing Assistance. Housing assistance often takes the form of public housing projects, which may be owned and operated by the government. Rents are subsidized according to family income level, so that the tenants are in effect receiving an in-kind housing subsidy from the federal government. These subsidies averaged a little more than $1000 per family in 1980 for roughly 1 million low-income families. The government also sponsors housing assistance programs to low-income families who are renting or buying homes or apartments in the private market. Under these programs, rents or mortgage payments may be subsidized, or the government may guarantee and stand behind private mortgage loans. The Federal Housing Administration and the Farmers' Home Administration are primary agencies engaged in these housing assistance activities.

The need-based program benefits available to the poor and near poor are clearly substantial. A family of four eligible for the average benefits from food stamps, Medicaid, and housing assistance could have received an in-kind subsidy equivalent to more than $4000 in 1980. This would have been in addition to the average cash benefit of almost $4000 available from AFDC. The combination of both cash and in-kind assistance is therefore capable of lifting many families out of poverty. There are, however, numerous criticisms of these programs which we will soon consider in more detail.

Work Experience–Based Programs

In contrast to the need-based programs, a number of antipoverty programs provide benefits based on the prior work experience of the beneficiary. These programs differ significantly in philosophy from the need-based programs.

Social Security (OASDHI). The Old Age, Survivors, Disability, and Health Insurance system (OASDHI) is usually referred to as *Social Security*, because the program was established by the Social Security Act of 1935. As the name suggests, Social Security provides benefits to families who have lost income due to retirement, disability, or death of a breadwinner. The program is financed by equal payroll taxes levied on both the employer and employee, and benefits are paid directly from these payroll tax revenues. Although the original Social Security tax for employees was 1 percent of the first $3000 of income, both the tax rate and the wage base have increased rapidly in recent years. In 1982, the tax was 6.7 percent of the first $32,400 of annual income, and both the rate and wage base are scheduled to continue increasing as average wage levels rise. As Table 9-5 indicates, Social Security is by far the largest federal government antipoverty program, covering over 90 percent of currently employed individuals.

In one sense, however, Social Security is not an antipoverty program at all. As with all work experience–based programs, OASDHI benefit levels are determined primarily by the worker's previous employment earnings and OASDHI contributions, not strictly by family need. Thus a family headed by a high-salaried corporate executive who has made sizable payroll contributions into the program receives greater benefits than a low-income family upon retirement, disability, or death of the family head. For example, an individual retiring in 1981 at age 65 could have received a monthly OASDHI payment ranging from as little as roughly $170, to as much as almost $1200, depending upon the average monthly earnings of that insured worker. The primary purpose of Social Security, therefore, is to redistribute family income from higher earning years to lower earning years, rather than to redistribute income from high-income families to low-income families at a point in time. In this sense it is similar to an insurance or private pension plan.

Some current redistribution has increasingly been built into Social Security financing, however. Workers with low incomes do receive greater benefits for every dollar of taxes they pay than do high-income workers. Nevertheless, minimum retirement benefits for an elderly couple remain below the poverty level, so that such families must resort to the SSI program also to remain above the poverty line. For example, a worker retiring at age 65 with a spouse of the same age could have received as little as $3100 in annual OASDHI benefits in 1981.

Numerous problems have plagued the Social Security program in recent years. Since it is essentially a pay-as-you-go program, benefits paid this year are derived primarily from this year's payroll tax revenues. Recent legislation has tied benefit levels to the cost of living, resulting in rapidly increasing benefits. At the same time, however, high unemployment has slowed the growth of payroll tax payments so that inadequate funding has resulted. This financing problem is expected to intensify in the future as lower birthrates shrink the size of the labor force (payers) at the same time that the number of retirees (beneficiaries) increases. This has resulted in the recent legislation to increase the payroll tax liability of workers and employers, as well as a general reassessment of the purposes and limitations of the program.[12]

There are basically three interrelated questions being debated concerning Social Security.[13] First, should Social Security remain primarily an insurance

---

12. See Warren Shore, *Social Security: The Fraud in Your Future* (New York: The Macmillan Company, 1975); Alicia H. Munnell, *The Future of Social Security* (Washington, D.C.: The Brookings Institution, 1977); and Robert M. Ball, *Social Security, Today and Tomorrow* (New York: Columbia University Press, 1978).

13. On these issues, see Colin F. Campbell, *Financing Social Security* (Washington: American Enterprise Institute, 1979); and *Report of the Advisory Council on Social Security* (Washington: U.S. Government Printing Office, 1980).

program with benefits based upon previous earnings, or should it continue to move in the direction of a public assistance program with benefits based more upon need? Most experts favor the former, arguing that older persons have a right to spend their retirement years in dignity with an income based upon earned rights rather than need. These advocates argue that numerous other programs exist to assist the needy, whether they be elderly or not.

Second, as an income replacement program what proportion of real income should OASDHI replace? In the 1970s Congress increased benefit levels by 20 percent and indexed them to future levels of inflation which have been much higher than expected. There are strong arguments in favor of protecting OASDHI recipients from excessive income loss and inflation. Yet the legislated increases in benefits, coupled with shifts in the age distribution of the population, have created uncertainty regarding the working generation's ability and willingness to finance these benefit levels.

Both of these questions lead to the third: Should OASDHI be financed from general tax revenues rather than from the present "earmarked" payroll tax? Proponents of the shift to general tax revenue funding argue that it would result in greater equity and fiscal flexibility. Opponents of the shift contend that there are important restraints inherent in the current system wherein benefits are tied directly to a specific tax. They also feel that general revenue financing would contribute to a greater public assistance role for OASDHI, lessening the emphasis upon an individual's earned right to specific benefits.

Medicare. Medicare is a federal medical care program which provides largely prepaid medical care for old-age pensioners under the OASDHI system. The hospital insurance component of Medicare is financed by payroll taxes added to basic Social Security taxes. The medical insurance portion is funded by contributions from beneficiaries and from general tax revenues. Eligibility is basically the same as for the Social Security old-age retirement program. Medicare, unlike Medicaid, is therefore restricted to elderly individuals who have made payroll contributions into the OASDHI system during their work lives. The program was enacted in 1965 to protect eligible elderly persons from the rapidly escalating costs of medical care. As Table 9-5 on page 244 indicates, Medicare is currently the second most costly antipoverty program, and expenditures have far exceeded forecasts in recent years.

Unemployment Compensation. The unemployment insurance (UI) system in the United States is actually an aggregation of state programs which meet federal minimum standards. The federal government imposes a standard payroll tax liability on employers which currently is 3.4 percent of the first $6000 of annual wages paid to each covered employee. States are allowed to use about 80 percent of these tax revenues to fund their unemployment compensation programs, with the remainder retained by the federal government primarily for administrative expenses and maintaining state reserve accounts. Individual employers then are subject to varying UI tax rates, usually based upon an experience rating of their recent employment histories. The coverage of UI programs has been expanded and standardized over time so that about 90 percent of all employed individuals are now covered.

Eligibility conditions vary from state to state, but usually include the following:

1. There must be some waiting period during which the applicant is unemployed (usually 1 week).
2. The claimant must have worked some minimum time or earned some minimum amount in covered jobs (usually 15 weeks or $500).
3. The individual must register for work at an employment office.
4. Benefits may be refused to those who terminate their employment under specified conditions.

The general objective of these conditions is to restrict benefits to those who become unemployed through no fault of their own.

Weekly benefits also vary greatly from state to state. In general, the amount is based upon roughly 50 percent of previous earnings, subject to some maximum. These maximum weekly benefit amounts varied in 1981 from $74 in Indiana to $181 in the District of Columbia. Minimum weekly benefits varied from $5 in Hawaii to $38 in Virginia. In each state, the UI benefit for which an unemployed individual is eligible increases as the amount of previous earnings increases. Therefore the UI program, like OASDHI, is work experience–based rather than strictly need-based.[14]

Most state programs provide benefits for up to 26 weeks, but this duration has occasionally been inadequate in the last 10 years. Particularly during the 1974-1975 recession, unemployed workers were consistently running out of benefit eligibility and some states faced depleted funds. The federal government enacted several programs in the 1970s to extend the duration and subsidize state funds during periods of high unemployment.

There are numerous current issues and controversies related to the UI system, some of which we have noted previously. There has been a noticeable trend toward higher benefits and longer benefit periods, for justifiable reasons. At the same time, however, we have already observed the recent growth in part-time and secondary workers in the labor force. These people sometimes have only a marginal attachment to the labor force, and in these instances the temptation of increasing and usually tax-free UI benefits may actually encourage this marginal attachment. As noted earlier, several studies have found that increased UI benefits are associated with increased unemployment duration. The UI system must continue to search for effective methods to provide

---

14. U.S. Department of Labor, *Comparison of State Unemployment Insurance Laws* (Washington: U.S. Government Printing Office, 1981).

adequate benefits for the involuntary unemployed, without encouraging fraud and prolonged job search.[15]

Workers' Compensation. Workers' Compensation was the first type of social insurance to be developed in the United States, and it is the only one that is still exclusively state run. It is designed to provide benefits to employees for work-related injuries or diseases, and to pay benefits to dependents for work-related deaths. Coverage varies greatly from state to state. In some states employers may elect not to participate under the law if they prefer to risk suit for damages by injured employees. Various types of accidents and injuries are not covered in some states, and agricultural, domestic, and casual workers are often excluded.

Workers' compensation laws provide cash benefits, medical assistance, rehabilitation benefits, and vocational training according to four classes of disability: temporary total, permanent total, temporary partial, and permanent partial. Most state laws provide cash benefits based upon a percentage of the worker's wages, up to some maximum. Disability benefits, death benefits, and duration of payment also vary greatly among the state programs. For example, the maximum weekly payment for total disability ranges from $87.50 in Arkansas to $650.00 in Alaska.

A specific agency has been created in most states to administer the law. These agencies require that covered employers obtain insurance for their employees, either from private companies or state funds, or that they give proof of their ability to carry their own risk. There is no specific workers' compensation tax levied on either the employer or employee. Rather, an injured employee's compensation claim is against his or her employer, who is required to insure against such injuries.

CURRENT CRITICISMS AND WELFARE REFORM

There is little doubt that the array of governmental antipoverty programs has made an important contribution to the alleviation of poverty in the United States. As Table 9-3 indicates, the number of persons below the poverty level has declined significantly in the last 20 years. Yet the present "welfare system," as it is loosely termed, has been the subject of much criticism in recent years, some of which we have already noted. In this section we briefly summarize a number of these criticisms and the welfare reform proposals that have received recent attention.

---

15. For extended discussions of these issues, see Arnold Katz (ed.), "The Economics of Unemployment Insurance: A Symposium," *Industrial and Labor Relations Review* (July, 1977), pp. 431-528; and National Commission on Unemployment Compensation, *Unemployment Compensation: Studies and Research*, Vols. 1 and 2 (Washington: U.S. Government Printing Office, July, 1980).

Current Criticisms

Perhaps no area of public policy has received more criticism than the current welfare system. Many of these criticisms can be related back to our earlier observation that we have reached no social consensus on the causes of poverty. Current criticisms focus on the coverage, effects, and administration of present policy.

Unequal Coverage. It is not uncommon to find similarly situated families receiving greatly different amounts of support. Much of this results from variations in eligibility and benefit standards among states. On the one hand, assistance is occasionally made available to those who are not generally considered to be needy, such as college students and striking workers. Alternatively, many truly needy families somehow fail to receive any benefits at all. For example, a recent study of six low-income areas discovered that 40 percent of the households received no benefits.[16]

Incentives. It is commonly argued that several antipoverty programs create disincentives to work, as we noted earlier in our discussion of AFDC. Additional earned income also means that families will receive less in food stamp and housing assistance. Furthermore, since most states establish an income ceiling above which all benefits cease, there is a strong incentive to stay below that ceiling. It has been estimated that for a family receiving several types of assistance, the total tax on earned income may be as high as 80 percent. In other words, this family would actually get to keep only 20 cents out of every dollar earned.

Family Instability Effects. Particularly under the AFDC program, families with a husband present are often not eligible for benefits. This is a classic example of a shortsighted governmental endeavor which created unintended side-effects. It is obvious from the data in Table 9-4 that female-headed families are a major source of poverty. The AFDC program is targeted toward this source, but it also creates incentives for the creation of more female-headed families. If the husband lives separately, the family is eligible for benefits and the husband can earn an income, thereby increasing the family's total earnings. Although family income may be higher under this arrangement, it tends to be extremely disruptive to family stability and child care. This may ultimately affect children's schooling and training achievements in these families.

Inflationary Effects. Welfare system expenditures grew very rapidly during the 1960s and 1970s, even during times of economic stability and high employment. As we already observed for Social Security, rapid increases in

---

16. Irene Lurie (ed.), *Integrating Income Maintenance Programs* (New York: Academic Press, Inc., 1975), p. 11.

government spending for antipoverty programs have sometimes exceeded the growth in tax revenues, thereby contributing to budget deficits. These budget deficits have been one cause of inflation over this period. In recognition of these problems, the Reagan administration in 1981 proposed significant modifications in eligibility standards and benefit levels for several antipoverty programs, including food stamps and AFDC.

Administrative Problems. Many observers have argued that the piecemeal growth of our welfare system has created a costly and inefficient bureaucratic nightmare of overlapping programs and administrative red tape. Large staffs are required to administer the various programs, and welfare fraud has sometimes occurred. Rapid cost increases have been particularly prevalent in the in-kind transfer programs. Medicare, Medicaid, and housing assistance programs tend to increase the prices of medical care and housing, but these programs often do not allow the government to monitor the quality of service provision.

Welfare Reform

Given the criticisms and problems noted above, it is not surprising that various welfare reform proposals have emerged in the last 20 years. Presidents Nixon, Ford, Carter, and Reagan have all proposed major reforms of existing welfare programs, and Congress developed its own set of proposals in 1974. However, none of these programs has been enacted in its entirety.

The various proposals have contained several common objectives which might be summarized as follows: (1) the need to reduce inequities by establishing a national income floor; (2) the need to make more male-headed needy families eligible for AFDC benefits; (3) the need to improve equity by cashing out (giving poor families the cash equivalent to spend as they choose) as many in-kind programs as possible; and (4) the need to improve work incentives by lowering the tax (loss of welfare benefits) on earned income.

The Negative Income Tax. In terms of the mechanics of the recent proposals, they all resemble the negative income tax (NIT) plans which have been proposed by economists for many years.[17] A negative income tax is a tax system allowing families automatically to receive cash transfers (negative tax payments) if their income falls below an established level. There are two basic components to any NIT plan: (1) a basic allowance, or the guaranteed minimum income floor which would be paid to a family with no earned income, and (2) a marginal tax rate applied to earned income, which generates an offsetting tax payment against the basic allowance.

17. See Milton Friedman, *Capitalism and Freedom* (Chicago: The University of Chicago Press, 1963); or James A. Tobin, Joseph A. Pechman, and Peter M. Mieszkowski, "Is a Negative Income Tax Practical?" *Yale Law Journal* (December, 1967), pp. 1-27.

Consider Table 9-6, for example. Since every family would be guaranteed a $6000 income floor in this example, a family with no earned income pays no offsetting tax and receives a negative tax or subsidy of $6000 from the government. If a family has earned income for the year of $1500, they would receive $5250 from the government under our assumption of a 50 percent marginal tax rate, and their total income increases to $6750. In effect, their earned income is taxed at a rate of 50 percent and that $750 offsets the $6000 basic allowance to yield a net subsidy of $5250. In this hypothetical scheme the process would continue as earned income increases up to $12,000, whereupon the net subsidy becomes zero.

Table 9-6   The Mechanics of a Negative Income Tax Plan

(1) Basic Allowance	(2) Earned Income	(3) Tax Payment (50% rate)	(4) Net Subsidy	(5) Disposable Income
$6000	$ 0	$ 0	$6000	$ 6,000
6000	1,500	750	5250	6,750
6000	3,000	1500	4500	7,500
6000	4,500	2250	3750	8,250
6000	6,000	3000	3000	9,000
6000	7,500	3750	2250	9,750
6000	9,000	4500	1500	10,500
6000	10,500	5250	750	11,250
6000	12,000	6000	0	12,000

A number of variations can be developed by modifying the basic allowance and/or the marginal tax rate, but the mechanics remain the same. Adjustments could also be made for family size, geographic residence, etc. Such plans have been proposed as a partial or total replacement for the multitude of existing antipoverty programs, to be administered by the Internal Revenue Service and to provide benefits to everyone on the same basis. Although such plans have been advocated by both conservatives and liberals, they still involve a fundamental conflict of goals which hinders the enactment of any major welfare reform. This conflict is discussed in the following section.

Welfare Reform Evaluation. As a practical matter, the criticisms noted earlier suggest that any welfare reform program should be evaluated on the basis of at least three criteria. First, the program should actually guarantee an adequate income floor for all people, i.e., it should eliminate poverty. We may call this the income-maintenance criterion. Second, a reform program should be cost efficient. This cost-efficiency criterion suggests that the program should achieve its goal at a minimum cost. In particular, it should not subsidize those who are not needy. Finally, a new program should preserve incentives to work, the work-incentive criterion. If a program could be developed to meet these criteria simultaneously, it would surely be a significant improvement over the current system. As noted, our current welfare system does not score highly with respect to any of these criteria.

How do NIT plans fare with respect to the criteria? The answer depends upon the exact plan, but let's briefly evaluate the hypothetical plan of Table 9-6. Assuming that $6000 is the income floor deemed necessary to eliminate poverty, the NIT plan in Table 9-6 fulfills the income-maintenance criterion. Every family would have disposable income of at least $6000.

The cost-efficiency criterion creates certain problems, however. In order to assure the $6000 income floor for everyone while maintaining the 50 percent marginal tax rate, it is necessary to subsidize all families with earned incomes of up to $12,000. Some would argue that families with incomes of $10,000 or $11,000 are not truly needy. Therefore, the cost-efficiency criterion is not met. We could, of course, improve cost efficiency by increasing the marginal tax rate on earned income. For example, if we increase the marginal tax rate to 80 percent, we would only be obligated to subsidize families with earned incomes of up to $7500. You should verify this result with your own calculations.

But a marginal tax rate of 80 percent creates the same kind of work-incentive problems which we have noted under existing programs. Few people would be strongly motivated to work if they knew that they would gain only 20 cents in disposable income for each dollar earned by working. Hence an 80 percent marginal tax rate would not meet the work-incentive criterion. A 50 percent rate probably would maintain work incentives, because families are always much better off by working than by not working.

The purpose of this hypothetical evaluation is to demonstrate that it is virtually impossible to devise an antipoverty plan which simultaneously fulfills all of our criteria. The NIT plan of Table 9-6 fares well on income-maintenance and work-incentive grounds. It is not particularly cost efficient, however. By changing the marginal tax rate to 80 percent, we could construct a more cost-efficient program which still meets the income-maintenance criterion, but it does not preserve incentives to work. If you continue to adjust the basic allowance and tax rates of Table 9-6, you will discover the policy dilemma inherent in most welfare programs. NIT plans are no exception, but they would provide much greater uniformity and simplicity than the present system, and they would make possible the fulfillment of at least some of the criteria.

Social Experimentation. As we have noted earlier, concern about poverty was somewhat reborn in the 1960s. The political and social environment was conducive to the serious consideration of welfare reform proposals such as the NIT. Unfortunately, however, policy makers had little information on the likely social costs and benefits of such drastic reform. They were forced to rely upon academic arguments similar to the ones presented above and were therefore reluctant to embark on major reform. Of particular concern were the possible work disincentive, work behavior, family stability, and welfare cost effects of a minimum income guarantee.

In an effort to overcome this information problem, the largest social experimentation in U.S. history was undertaken in the late 1960s and 1970s under the sponsorship of the federal government. The primary purpose of the experiments was to provide reliable nationwide estimates of the labor supply and other effects and the costs of alternative NIT programs. The first experiments took place in New Jersey and Pennsylvania during 1968-1972. Subsequent experiments were conducted in rural Iowa and North Carolina (1969-1972); Gary, Indiana (1971-1974); and Seattle and Denver (late 1970s).

Low-income families were given income guarantees at several levels, and various marginal tax rates were imposed upon their earned incomes. Over several years, these families' responses were compared with control families who did not receive the income guarantees. At this time the results suggest that income guarantees have only a very small effect on the labor force participation and hours worked of husbands in male-headed families. Wives in white male-headed families reduced their labor force participation significantly, but wives in black male-headed families did not. Females in female-headed families showed some tendency to reduce participation with income guarantees. Overall, the results do not indicate severe work disincentives associated with NIT plans for male-headed families, although the conclusions for females seem to be quite sensitive to changes in the support level and tax rate. In addition, there is some disturbing preliminary evidence that income guarantees may actually induce family breakup rather than contribute to family stability.[18]

UNRESOLVED POLICY ISSUES

Once again, virtually every policy issue summarized in this chapter is an unresolved one. We do not have a coherent income-maintenance policy in the United States, nor have we exhibited a consistent direction in the pursuit of policy. As we have repeatedly noted, our society is torn between concern for the poor, on the one hand, and a belief that much of their suffering is self-inflicted, on the other. We must first resolve the issue of whether poverty is primarily self-determined or externally determined.

Even assuming for a moment that we can agree that poverty is generated primarily by economic and social forces external to individuals, other policy dilemmas remain. We concluded that there are fundamental goal conflicts in

18. See Joseph Pechman and P. Michael Timpane (eds.), *Work Incentives and Income Guarantees: The New Jersey Negative Income Tax Experiment* (Washington: The Brookings Institution, 1975); John L. Palmer and Joseph Pechman (eds.), *Welfare in Rural Areas: The North Carolina-Iowa Income Maintenance Experiments* (Washington: The Brookings Institution, 1978); and Sheldon Danziger, Robert Haveman, and Robert Plotnick, "How Income Transfers Affect Work, Savings, and the Income Distribution," *The Journal of Economic Literature* (September, 1981), pp. 975-1028.

the pursuit of effective antipoverty policy. Cost efficiencies and work incentives are key components in the efficient operation of a capitalist economy, but they often conflict with our desire to provide equitable income maintenance for those in need of assistance.

What policy makers really confront in seeking to alleviate poverty is what Arthur Okun has termed "the big trade-off."[19] In principle, our political and social institutions are based upon the premise of equal rights for all. Our market-oriented economic system, however, generates unequal incomes (economic rights) as a part of the necessary incentive structure for efficiency.

This fundamental conflict between the equality principles of democracy and the efficiency principles of capitalism is the source of the ultimate unresolved policy issue with respect to poverty. Policy makers must develop programs which alleviate poverty through income redistribution while minimizing the adverse effects upon economic incentives and efficiency.

CONCLUDING REMARKS

We have discovered that poverty is a somewhat elusive concept, but one that continues to plague our society in unacceptable proportions. Poverty is caused by a complex set of interrelated forces which tend to perpetuate themselves over time. Our antipoverty efforts have yielded some significant results, but we still suffer from disagreement over the specific causes of poverty which we should attack. The result is a multitude of somewhat overlapping, inefficient programs, with significant geographic variations in benefit levels. Various negative income tax reform proposals would eliminate some deficiencies in existing programs. However, any new programs still must contend with the goal conflicts which we have noted.

Ultimately, however, even an efficient and equitable income-maintenance program would not solve the poverty problem. Income-maintenance programs are transitional policies to meet the needs of individuals with income deficiencies. They do not eliminate the causes of those deficiencies. An effective antipoverty policy must also include programs which lead poor people in the direction of economic self-sufficiency. These programs must provide education, training, and jobs for economically disadvantaged individuals, and they must eliminate other barriers between these individuals and existing jobs.

CHAPTER SUMMARY

The personal distribution of income in the United States reveals significant income inequality. Most families have improved their absolute economic status considerably in the last 30 years, but relative income inequality has not lessened. Furthermore,

---

19. See Arthur M. Okun, *Equality and Efficiency: The Big Tradeoff* (Washington: The Brookings Institution, 1975).

taxes and transfer payments have not diminished income inequality on any large scale.

Poverty may be defined either absolutely or relatively, and the absolute standard is employed by the government. The poverty rate has declined significantly in the last 30 years, but severe problems still exist for racial minorities and female-headed households. In general, poverty is caused by one or more of the following: (1) nonexistent property income, (2) nonparticipation in the labor market, (3) unemployment, (4) human capital deficiencies, and (5) discrimination.

Poverty can be attacked by (1) employment policy, (2) policies to eliminate barriers between existing jobs and workers, and (3) income-maintenance programs. The latter may be subdivided into need-based programs (minimum wage legislation, AFDC, SSI, food stamps, Medicaid, and housing assistance) and work experience–based programs (OASDHI, Medi-care, Workers' Compensation, and unemployment compensation). The entire system of income-maintenance policies has been frequently criticized for its unequal coverage, work disincentives, administrative problems, and family instability and inflationary effects.

Welfare reform proposals have typically taken the form of some variant of the negative income tax (NIT) idea. These programs all include a guaranteed minimum income and a marginal tax rate on earned income. Any reform proposal confronts the conflicting policy goals of equity (adequate income maintenance for all) and efficiency (cost efficiency and preservation of incentives). The social experiments conducted during the last decade suggest that the work-disincentive effects of NIT programs are somewhat mixed. Ultimately, however, our society must develop effective programs to ensure economic self-sufficiency as well as transitional income maintenance.

KEY TERMS

transfer payments
absolute approach to defining poverty
relative approach to defining poverty
need-based poverty programs

work experience–based poverty programs
negative income tax
income-maintenance criterion
cost-efficiency criterion
work-incentive criterion

REVIEW QUESTIONS

1. Are there differences between equity and equality in the distribution of income? Can an unequal distribution of income be equitable? Why or why not?

2. Do you feel that an absolute or a relative standard of poverty makes more sense? Many poor families in the United States would not be classified as poor if they lived in a less-developed country such as India. Does this fact make them less poor?

3. How do the flawed character and restricted opportunities arguments proposed by Schiller lead to fundamentally different policy implications?

4. Okun has argued that capitalism and democracy are a "most improbable

mixture." In what sense is this true, and how does this create policy dilemmas with respect to poverty alleviation?

5. Many have argued that the efficiency of our present welfare system would be improved if we were to cash out many in-kind transfer programs, giving poor families the cash equivalent to spend as they choose. Evaluate the advantages and disadvantages of this argument.

6. Summarize the major strengths and weaknesses of our existing need-based income-maintenance programs.

7. Using the circular flow diagram depicted in Figure 1-1, page 5 as a reference point, explain the major causes of income inadequacy.

ADDITIONAL REFERENCES

Ball, Robert M. *Social Security, Today and Tomorrow*. New York: Columbia University Press, 1978.

Harrington, Michael. *The Other America: Poverty in the United States*, rev. ed. New York: The Macmillan Company, 1970.

Lurie, Irene (ed.). *Integrating Income Maintenance Programs*. New York: Academic Press, Inc., 1975.

Okun, Arthur. *Equality and Efficiency: The Big Tradeoff*. Washington: The Brookings Institution, 1975.

Schiller, Bradley R. *The Economics of Poverty and Discrimination*, 3d ed. Englewood Cliffs, N.J.: Prentice-Hall, Inc., 1980.

Thurow, Lester C. *Generating Inequality*. New York: Basic Books, Inc., 1975.

THE WORLD
OF WORK . . .

The Need for Welfare Reform

As an example of the concern of all recent administrations with reforming our welfare system, the following are excerpts from a statement submitted by Joseph A. Califano, Jr. to the Subcommittee on Public Assistance of the U.S. Senate in 1977. Mr. Califano was then the Secretary of Health, Education, and Welfare.

Mr. Chairman and Members of the Subcommittee, President Carter has made a pledge to the American people to undertake a major reform of our welfare system. In accordance with that pledge, he asked me to complete a comprehensive study of welfare reform by May 1. Today I am presenting to your Subcommittee what we learned and what we believe are the next steps to achieve reform.

. . . Past debates about welfare have too often focused on myths about the poor in America.

The most widespread myth is that people are poor because they don't work and don't want to work. The facts are that the majority of household heads in poverty are working; that nearly a third work full-time and still remain poor. The poor are poor, not because they won't work and don't work, but because when they do work they do not earn enough money to lift them out of poverty.

A second myth is that most of the poor are poor for life. The fact is that the poverty population is extremely fluid. Each year about 7.5 to 10 million people move above the poverty line and a like number become poor. This means that 30 to 40 percent of those who were poor in any given year are not poor the next year.

A third myth is that the poor are mostly nonwhite. The fact is that 69 percent of the American poor are white.

A fourth myth is that the poor don't know how to spend their money. The evidence we have shows that low-income people spend about 88 percent of their income on food, clothing, housing, medical care, and transportation—a somewhat greater proportion than do people with higher income.

A fifth myth is that most welfare families receive payments that are far too high. The fact is that in 24 states the combined benefits of AFDC and food stamps total less than three-fourths of the official poverty income level.

We cannot and must not develop and legislate a welfare reform program based upon myth. We must center the welfare debate around blunt talk about real facts.

What are some of these facts?

First, we must recognize that our array of assistance programs have been enacted piecemeal over a period of many years, each perhaps making sense in isolation, but no clear and consistent rationale underlies the system as a whole.

We know that in many states the welfare system provides inadequate assistance. . . . No system should ignore the plight of those in need.

We know that the present welfare system is unfair, treating people with equivalent needs differently. Take the case of Kansas City, Missouri and Kansas City, Kansas: Both have the same cost of living. A family of four residing in Kansas City, Missouri is eligible for $2,040 per year in AFDC benefits. If the family moves across the river to Kansas City, Kansas, its benefits will rise to $3,540 per year. If the family is also eligible for food stamps, the comparison is $3,468 versus $4,536. Nationally, benefits vary from just over $700 for a family of four to almost $6,000.

No system should treat people with equivalent needs so differently.

We know that the present welfare system is antiwork. Take the case of a man in Ohio with a wife and two children. If he works 20 hours per week at $2.30 per hour, his annual income including assistance is $5,184. . . . Now assume that the man doubles his earnings by working 40 hours per week rather than 20 hours. His income will be $5,256. . . . By increasing weekly work from 20 hours to 40 hours each week, the man can increase his net annual income by $72, but his family loses eligibility for Medicaid worth several hundred dollars per year on the average!

No system should make it financially more rewarding to be on welfare than in a job.

We know that the present system is antifamily. In 26 states, for example, cash assistance is provided only to single-parent families. Too often under the present system, it make financial sense for the man to leave the house so that the family will become eligible for benefits. No system should provide financial incentives for a family to split up.

We know that our present welfare system is an administrative nightmare. Administration and policy control for existing programs fall within the jurisdiction of nine federal executive departments, 21 Congressional Committees, 54 state welfare agencies, and more than 3,000 local welfare offices.

The complexity of the rules and regulations is legendary. The forms used by the Los Angeles welfare department, for example, measure 70 feet long when laid end to end—the manuals stack six feet high. . . . No system should be so complicated.

We know the myths and facts. We understand the problems.

Devising a new program, however, won't be easy. There are no simple solutions. The tradeoffs in designing welfare reform are excruciatingly tough.

How do we set benefits at adequate assistance levels and introduce an overriding incentive to work?

What is the tradeoff between fiscal relief and adequate benefits?

How rapidly should benefits be reduced as earnings rise? As the incentive to work increases, the program's cost and coverage rises rapidly.

Which recipients should be required to work?

Should public jobs be guaranteed? If so, to whom?

My recommendation to President Carter and to you is that trying to make incremental changes in the existing hodge-podge of income assistance programs is not the proper course to follow.

We must, instead, view the income assistance system as a whole and we must completely restructure that system so that it is comprehensive, fair and efficient. Given the inequities and administrative chaos caused by a welter of inconsistent and confusing programs, nothing less than a total effort at welfare reform will do. . . .

Source: Abridged from the *President's Statement on Principles of Welfare Reform—Hearings Before the Subcommittee on Public Assistance*, 95th Congress, 1st Session (Washington: U.S. Government Printing Office, May 5 and 12, 1977).

3 Collective Bargaining: Practices & Perspectives

"You have to learn to walk before you learn to run." This section is written with that old adage in mind. Collective bargaining can be analyzed only after the process is understood. One reviewer of this section said that parts of it read like a "how to do it" manual. Others commented that several parts made them feel like they were participating in the experience of bargaining. We try to inject that realism into the chapters. Description without explanation, however, is not enough. "Why's" and "wherefore's" either precede or follow the "how's."

The chapters build a factual basis for each topic. Then the variables involved in whatever aspect of collective bargaining is under examination are introduced, and the relationships between the pertinent variables are explained. The perspective is broader than economics. Collective bargaining lends itself less well than other topics to pure economic analysis. Much of the richness of bargaining would be lost from so narrow a view. The analysis includes a bit of history, law, psychology, sociology, and political science as well as economics.

Chapter 10 overviews the U.S. system of collective bargaining and industrial relations. It provides a comparison with the systems of other advanced market economies, the Soviet Union, and the developing nations. The U.S. system has evolved along a tortuous path of political and economic struggle. The labor movement past, present, and future is the subject of Chapter 11. Chapter 12 concerns the legal framework for bargaining in the public and private sectors. How contracts are negotiated and what goes into them occupy Chapters 13 and 14. Labor-management conflict is resolved through strikes, alternatives to the strike, and arbitration in Chapter 15. Chapter 16 is an issues and analysis chapter. The focus is on the union impact on wages, fringe benefits, and inflation. An examination of trade union political ties and union democracy and corruption complete the chapter.

The student who completes this section should be able to take a position on current collective bargaining issues. Newspaper reports of collective bargaining happenings can be critically assessed. And finally, since education involves an ability to ask the right questions at the right time, it is our hope that you not only ask the right question at the right time but that you pursue the answer in more advanced courses.

Chapter 10

Collective Bargaining and Industrial Relations

Collective bargaining and industrial relations—what are they? The term collective bargaining was coined by Beatrice Potter in 1891.[1] In a later book, she and her husband, Sidney Webb, define *collective bargaining* through an example:

> In unorganized trades, the individual workman, applying for a job, accepts or refuses the terms offered by the employer, without communication with his fellow-workmen, and without any other consideration than the exigencies of his own position. For the sale of his labor he makes, with the employer, a strictly individual bargain. But if a group of workmen concert together, and send representatives to conduct the bargaining on behalf of the whole body, the position is at once changed. Instead of the employer making a series of separate contracts with isolated individuals, he meets with a collective will, and settles, in a single agreement, the principles upon which, for the time being, all workmen of a particular group, or class, or grade, will be engaged.[2]

Collective bargaining, however, is only a part of an industrial relations system. Simply put, an *industrial relations system* refers to the way a country organizes its labor markets. Each country has evolved one or more unique ways to govern the exchange of labor for income. A more complete definition of an industrial relations system is presented by Harvard economist and former U.S. Secretary of Labor, John T. Dunlop:

> An industrial relations system is comprised of three groups of actors—workers and their organizations, managers and their organizations, and governmental agencies concerned with the work place and work community. These groups interact within a specified environment comprised of three interrelated contexts: the technology, the market or budgetary constraints and the power relations in the larger community, and the derived status of the actors. An industrial relations system creates an ideology or a commonly shared body of ideas and beliefs regarding the interaction and roles of the actors which helps to bind the system together.[3]

---

1. Beatrice Potter first used the term in her book, *The Cooperative Movement in Great Britain* (London, 1891), p. 217.
2. Sidney Webb and Beatrice Webb, *Industrial Democracy* (1920 ed.; London: Longmans, Green and Co., Ltd., 1926), pp. 173-4.
3. John T. Dunlop, *Industrial Relations Systems* (New York: Holt, 1958), p. 383.

There are innumerable exciting differences across industrial relations systems. Some countries, for example, allow the strike without reservation; others outlaw it entirely; and some, like the United States, condone its use by some employees but forbid its use by others. There are also a great many similarities across systems. In this chapter we explore the similarities and differences that exist in the world's collective bargaining and industrial relations systems. To provide a basis for comparison, the first section is an overview of our own system along the lines suggested by Dunlop's definition. This is followed by an international comparison of the United States with several other advanced market economies. Australia, Japan, West Germany, and Sweden were chosen because of the distinctive nature of their systems. Subsequent sections deal specifically with labor-management relations in the Soviet Union and the special situation faced by labor organizations in the developing economies. The chapter ends with a look into the future for the developing economies and a prediction for the future of American unions.

COLLECTIVE BARGAINING AND INDUSTRIAL RELATIONS IN THE UNITED STATES

This section provides an overview of our U.S. industrial relations system using aspects of John Dunlop's definition. The emphasis is on the actors and the commonly shared beliefs that have evolved. The technology, market constraints, and power relations of the environment are explored later in this chapter in the discussion of the postindustrial society and in later chapters on labor history, law, and issues.

The Extent of Collective Bargaining

Among the industrialized market economies, the United States has one of the lowest levels of union representation. One measure of this *extent of unionization* is the percentage of the nonagricultural labor force which holds membership in a labor *union* or employee *association*.[4] In the United States 26.8 percent[5] of the nonagricultural labor force belongs to a labor organization. The figure for the private sector is 26 percent.[6] The public sector is much more extensively unionized. Fifty-six percent of the federal government work force

---

4. Labor organizations are divided up into unions and associations. Associations are organizations which represent and collectively bargain on behalf of professional and public sector employees. Labor organizations which represent private sector employees are generally termed unions. However, unions also represent professional and public sector employees; so in terms of membership the distinction is not hard and fast. The name of the organization indicates whether or not it is an association or union, and since 1971 the Bureau of Labor Statistics classifies labor organizations as either unions or associations. The American Federation of Teachers is called a union. The National Education Association is an association. Both represent educators. See U.S. Department of Labor, Bureau of Labor Statistics, *Directory of National Unions and Employee Associations, 1971* (Washington, D.C.: U.S. Government Printing Office, 1972), p. 58. There are currently 174 unions and 34 associations. See footnote 5.

5. U.S. Department of Labor, Bureau of Labor Statistics, *Directory of National Unions and Employee Associations, 1979* (Washington, D.C.: U.S. Government Printing Office, 1980), p. 56.

6. Total manufacturing and nonmanufacturing membership was 18,116,000 in 1978. Private nonfarm employment was 70,827,000. The extent of private sector organization was about 26 percent.

is covered by a collective bargaining agreement.[7] Approximately 48 percent of the employees of state and local government are union or association members.[8]

The rest of the labor force is nonunion. However, it would be a mistake to think that they are unaffected by organized labor or to believe that the low extent of unionization figures imply a weak labor movement. The U.S. labor movement remains strong and has a significant impact on the economy and labor force beyond what the figures might suggest. For example, the United States has a system which requires a labor organization to be the *exclusive bargaining agent* for a well-defined group of employees called an *appropriate bargaining unit*. The exclusive bargaining agent must represent all employees in the unit whether or not they belong to the labor organization. Thus many nonunion employees are covered by bargaining agreements.

Wage bargains between union and employer also affect nonunion employees who are not covered by the contract. Through what are termed *spillover effects*, collective bargaining agreement settlements affect the wages paid to workers in nonunion establishments. Nonunion employers (those whose workers are not represented by a union) often pay the union scale to keep their work force from leaving to work for higher wage union employers and to diminish the desire of their workers to unionize. In addition to increased pay, nonunion employees share in the political gains made by unions for all workers. These gains include legislated standards such as those for minimum wages, education, safety, equal employment opportunity, and pensions.

But organized labor also costs nonunion workers. Some economists argue that unions force workers out of union markets into nonunion sectors. The increased labor supply lowers nonunion wages. The discussion in Chapter 3 about minimum wage laws suggested that this might be true. Some economists also believe unions may cause or contribute to inflation which, of course, affects all workers. Strikes affect both union and nonunion workers and consumers. It is obvious that union-nonunion linkages are many and complex.

Labor and Management

The building block of labor organizations is the *local* (unions) or *chapter* (associations). *National* or *international* labor organizations (internationals have foreign membership, usually Canadian) are composed of either locals or chapters. At the top of the organizational pyramid is the *federation* of nationals, the American Federation of Labor–Congress of Industrial Organizations (AFL-CIO). The International Association of Machinists and Aerospace Workers, for example, has a membership of 920,735 in 1832 union locals.[9] It is an AFL-CIO

7. Bureau of National Affairs, *Government Employee Relations Report* (April 7, 1980), p. 11.

8. U.S. Department of Labor, Labor-Management Services Administration, *Labor-Management Relations in State and Local Governments: 1979*, Special Studies No. 100 (Washington: U.S. Government Printing Office, 1980), p. 1.

9. *1979 Directory of National Unions*, p. 33.

affiliated union along with 108 of the 174 unions in the United States. The unaffiliated unions are called *independents*.[10]

There is a separation of functions between locals, nationals, and the federation. Most of the day-to-day labor-management contact is at the local level. The national provides supportive service to the local, coordinates the activities across locals, formulates policy on internal matters, and handles public relations and political activities. The role of the federation is to support and coordinate the efforts of the affiliated nationals. The AFL-CIO also acts as spokesperson to the general public and is organized labor's advocate before the government in national political matters.

Craft Unions. Labor organizations are generally classified as either *craft*, *industrial*, or *white-collar*. Craft unions are composed of skilled workers. They are also sometimes called trade unions. This refers to the fact that they were the earliest unions to be organized (1800s) and were organized by skill or trade. Even today, the term craft union is commonly used to refer to the 16 affiliates of the AFL-CIO Building and Construction Trades Department. Craft union locals, such as those of the United Brotherhood of Carpenters and Joiners of America (Carpenters), are organized on a geographic basis. They have jurisdiction over all union work in their trade performed by all unionized employers in that geographic area. Their collective bargaining agreements are generally only a few pages long and often are negotiated with an employers' association. The employers' association represents the unionized employers in the union's geographic jurisdiction.

Industrial Unions. Industrial unions were organized in the early 1900s. They are organized on an industry basis (hence "industrial" union) and not by skill or trade. Locals of industrial unions, such as those of the International Union, United Automobile, Aerospace, and Agricultural Implement Workers of America (the Autoworkers or UAW) are composed of workers at all levels of skill: unskilled, semiskilled, and skilled. They may bargain a *local agreement* which covers only the workers of an employer at one plant. Or, a *master contract* may be negotiated by the national with a large industry employer (General Motors, for example) to cover all the employer's plants. The master contract is then supplemented at each plant with a *local supplement*. Industrial union agreements tend to be very lengthy and detailed. The General Motors–UAW agreement is over 350 pages long, and that does not include additional agreements on fringe benefits such as the pension plan and health plan. In contrast to the geographic craft union jurisdictions, the local of an industrial union is associated with a particular plant or production site.

White-Collar Unions. White-collar locals are often composed of government and professional employees. They are usually more recently organized (since the 1960s) or, though they date back many years, have only recently

---

10. Ibid., p. 56.

begun to use collective bargaining as a means of gaining benefits. The agreements of white-collar labor organizations resemble those of industrial unions. They tend to be lengthy, detailed agreements. Whereas craft and industrial labor organizations are unions, white-collar employees are organized by unions and associations. Teachers, for example, may be represented by the National Education Association (association) or the American Federation of Teachers (a union).

Generalizations such as those above are risky and there are many exceptions to the rules. This is an overview, however, and the rest of the chapters will serve to help set the record straight.

Employers. Employers are classed into two major groups: private sector and public sector. Much about employer bargaining can be inferred from the discussion of labor organizations. Employers as the other party to labor-management agreements may bargain company-wide master agreements with plant or local supplement agreements, bargain a single local contract, or bargain as part of a multiemployer association. Private sector employers are very profit and cost conscious. Public sector employers share in the cost consciousness of labor-management relations, but they are not profit makers.

Unions and firms as organizations are alike in one respect and different in others. Managers of firms have a clear line of authority. Unions are political in nature. Union officers and representatives by federal law must be elected. There is less of a clear line of authority. Labor organizations are like businesses in the sense that both face budgetary constraints. Union organizational goals differ from those of businesses, however. Depending upon the labor organization, union goals may be almost entirely job related (improved wages, fringe benefits, and working conditions) or may also include very broad community-based goals (restoration of the central city, provision of low-income housing).

Collective Bargaining Structure

Collective bargaining structure is a term which is used to describe who bargains with whom. There are about 195,000 collective bargaining agreements in the United States.[11] The most common type of bargaining is that done between a local union and a single employer for a local producing unit. These are often local supplements to more extensive agreements. The number of agreements implies a more decentralized bargaining structure than really exists in practice. Roughly 250 agreements cover about 20 percent of all the workers subject to union contracts, and 10 unions are party to two-thirds of the agreements.[12] Bargaining proceeds at almost all levels. Some contracts are master agreements covering an entire firm (GM-UAW) or industry (coal, trucking). Others set an agreement pattern with one firm which is then copied by other firms in the industry (autos, agricultural implements).

In the United States a firm may negotiate contracts with several unions.

---

11. *1979 Directory of National Unions*, p. 74
12. Ibid.

For example, in the electrical equipment industry, General Electric has some plants represented by the International Brotherhood of Electrical Workers (IBEW) and others by the International Union of Electrical, Radio, and Machine Workers (IUE). In order to maintain a common front to the employer, the unions coordinate their bargaining efforts. Using the same philosophy, employers who are in industries characterized by a large number of firms bargaining with a single union will form multiemployer associations to bargain with the union (construction).

The Collective Bargaining Agreement

The collective bargaining agreement is the formal, mutual understanding governing the relationship between labor and management. What topics the agreement can include (called the *scope of agreement*) varies somewhat from law to law. A typical private sector agreement will include provisions on wages, hours of work, seniority, management and union rights, grievance procedure and arbitration, vacations, pensions, holidays, and many other topics. The contents of collective bargaining agreements are analyzed in detail in Chapter 14. To provide a basis for international comparison, we examine two aspects of the collective bargaining agreement: management rights and the grievance and arbitration procedure.

Employers in the United States have a strong *management rights* philosophy. These rights are decision-making rights. Management reserves the right (free from union interference) to make decisions regarding the efficient and orderly operation of the enterprise. Some decisions are long-run considerations: the type of product to produce (private sector), the mission of the government agency (public sector), how and where to produce, and investment in plant and equipment. Short-run decisions reserved by management include, among others, such things as personnel policy (grounds for discipline and discharge), scheduling, hiring, and promotion.

Such rights are not absolute. Government has modified them over time with laws on minimum pay, safety, and pensions, for example. Organized labor has restricted management rights as well, for obviously the whole agreement process limits management discretion. Rights not specifically given up in the collective bargaining contract belong exclusively to management.

During the life of an agreement, the *grievance and arbitration procedure* provides a check on management rights. It is a stimulus-response system. Management is free to exercise its decision-making right subject to challenge by the labor organization. The employees or union can file a grievance against management for its actions. Discussion of the grievance is often handled initially by a *union steward*. If after discussion between the steward and management no agreement is reached, the grievance moves through a series of steps in the grievance procedure. Each step involves higher levels of management and union leadership. If the two parties cannot resolve the problem to their mutual satisfaction, they submit it to a neutral third party known as an *arbitrator*. The arbitrator hears both sides and then issues a final and binding decision resolving the grievance. Because of the grievance-arbitration system, local union officers play a major role in policing the contract on a day-to-day basis. This enhances the locals' power relative to the national union.

Worker Participation

Because of the strong management rights philosophy and the stimulus-response nature of the strong grievance-arbitration system, unions in the United States have not achieved a great deal of *worker participation* in either long-run or short-run management decision making. Some contracts do provide for joint labor-management committees to deal with safety or productivity or job evaluation. In general, however, labor organizations have not been successful in placing members on corporate decision-making boards. There is dissension in the ranks of labor on the wisdom of doing so. There is a fear that by sharing in the management decision-making process, unions will not provide an effective challenge to actions which adversely affect workers.

There is a trend toward increased worker participation. In particular, firms and industries which face decline have been more receptive toward union and worker participation. In some cases, management and labor perceive a mutual threat to their existence and move to a cooperative, problem-solving relationship. Chrysler Corporation, for example, added UAW President Douglas Fraser to the Chrysler Board of Directors as part of a reform package to keep the company afloat.

The Role of Government

Most workers in the United States are covered by legislation which enables them to bargain collectively with their employer. Separate but similar laws cover the private sector, railway and airline employees, postal workers, federal government workers, state and local government employees. The legal system provides for fairly detailed regulation of the process of union organizing and collective bargaining, but with few exceptions it does not mandate the substance of the relationship. For example, labor and management must by law bargain in good faith, but the contents of the collective bargaining agreement, if one results from negotiation, is largely up to the parties themselves.

Other laws protect the individual rights of workers (as opposed to their collective rights discussed above). Laws exist which set minimum standards for wages, hours of work, Social Security, pensions, job safety, education, health care, and equal employment opportunity. These laws have a major impact on our industrial relations system including collective bargaining. Labor organizations have sought to achieve protection of individual and collective worker rights by working within the established political parties. The U.S. labor movement is unique among world labor movements in that there is no separate Labor Party.

Governmental Regulation of the Strike

When labor and management disagree, the results are many and varied. Some actions are noticeable and overt: sabotage, shootings, and work stoppages. Some are more subtle: high employee turnover, high absenteeism, low productivity, and low morale. All these are forms of *industrial conflict*. Every society has a policy concerning industrial conflict. In the United States, the violent forms of conflict are illegal. Government regulates work stoppages, but it does not regulate the more subtle and individual forms of dissent. In general, strikes which occur when a new labor-management agreement is being negotiated are legal in the private sector. They are, with few exceptions, illegal in the public sector. In both sectors, strikes are illegal during the life of an existing agreement. The agreement's grievance-arbitration procedure substitutes for the strike as a conflict resolution technique.

The thumbnail sketch of the U.S. system of collective bargaining and industrial relations serves as a basis for comparison with the systems of other countries. The next section is a cross-cultural comparison of the U.S. industrial relations system with those of other advanced market economies.

AN INTERNATIONAL COMPARISON OF INDUSTRIAL RELATIONS SYSTEMS

There is no single, universal industrial relations model. The U.S. system is very different in many ways from those of other countries. Four advanced industrialized market economies have been chosen for comparison with the United States: Australia, Japan, Sweden, and West Germany. They were chosen for their prominence among advanced economies and because they illustrate the very different ways in which economies organize their labor markets.

Common Denominators for Comparison

In keeping with Dunlop's definition, the same points that provided the basis for the discussion of the U.S. system are the common denominators of the cross-cultural comparison. These are shown along with some measures of each across the top of Table 10-1. The first variable is collective bargaining structure. Two rough measures of structure appear below that: the extent of unionization and the level of agreement. The role of government is indicated by the degree to which government becomes involved in the labor-management relationship. Worker participation is measured by extent and type. Extent refers to how widespread or common worker participation is. Type refers to worker participation in decisions affecting short-run personnel matters and/or the longer-run concerns of investment and the market.

Industrial conflict is measured by workdays lost per 1000 workers, 1971-1975. This statistic is calculated in several steps. First, for each year of the period 1971-1975, the number of people on strike is multiplied by the number of days they were on strike and summed for the whole country. This sum is then divided by the size of the labor force measured in thousands of workers. Finally, the figures for the years 1971 through 1975 are added and the sum divided by 5 to get the 1971-1975 average. The figure for the United States of

Table 10-1 Industrial Relations Systems

Country	Bargaining Structure				Industrial Conflict		
	Extent of Unionization[1] (%)	Level of Agreements	Government Involvement (Role)	Worker Participation (Type and Extent)	Work Days Lost Per 1000 Workers 1971-1975[2]	Work Stoppages	Distinctive Characteristic
Australia	55	Industry, plant	Detailed regulation and intervention	Little daily or long-run	1464	Illegal, criminal	Compulsory arbitration
Japan	35	Firm	Rule making	Extensive joint determination or consultation	328	Legal-private, illegal-public	Enterprise bargaining, consensus decision making
Sweden	82	Economy-wide	Rule making for bargaining, detailed for participation	Extensive national and workplace	62	Legal-private, legal-public	Centralized bargaining structure, industrial democracy
West Germany	40	Industry, region	Rule making for bargaining, detailed for participation	Extensive, codetermination	92	Legal-private illegal-public	Codetermination
United States	28	Plant, firm, industry	Detailed regulation for bargaining	Little daily or long-run	1173	Legal-private illegal-public	Decentralized bargaining structure

[1] Percentage of nonagricultural wage and salary labor force which is unionized, 1976. Reported in Benjamin Martin and Everett Kassalow (eds.), *Labor Relations in Advanced Industrial Societies* (New York: Carnegie Endowment for Industrial Peace, 1980), p. 47.
[2] Ibid., p. 111.

1173 means that on average in each year from 1971 to 1975 there were 1173 days lost due to strikes for each 1000 workers in the labor force. The legality of work stoppages variable really pertains to both the role of government and industrial conflict.

The last item for comparison suggests the diversity across industrial relations systems. Each system has one or more characteristics which contrast substantially with the U.S. system. These will be discussed as they apply to the common denominators comparison.

Bargaining Structure

Note that all the economies have collective bargaining as part of their industrial relations system. Just how much of each system involves bargaining is indicated by the extent of unionization. Remember that this statistic understates the importance of collective bargaining because many people who are not union members are covered by bargaining agreements. And, negotiated settlements often set the pattern for the nonunion sectors of the economy. The range of the extent of unionization is considerable. The United States is low at 28 percent and Sweden is high at 82 percent.

The level of agreements variable refers to the level at which bargaining takes place between labor and management as organizations. We characterize systems as being centralized or decentralized. As a polar approach, a completely centralized system of bargaining would have one collective bargaining agreement which would cover all employers and all unions. At the opposite end of the spectrum would be a completely decentralized system with thousands of agreements. Each plant or production site would have a contract between the local union and the local employer. While no system is completely centralized or decentralized, Sweden, Japan, and the United States illustrate the range of possibilities.

Sweden. Centralization is the key word describing the Swedish industrial relations system. The system approaches what may be called economy-wide bargaining.[13] There are essentially three agreements negotiated nationally between large union and employer confederations. The three agreements correspond to union and employer organization bargaining for manual (blue-collar), white-collar, and public workers.

The epitomy of centralized bargaining is that done by Sweden's manual workers. Over 90 percent organized, they are represented nationally by the Swedish Confederation of Trade Unions (LO). Employers are represented by the Swedish Employers' Confederation (SAF). The parties sign two types of agreements: long term and short term. The long-term agreements deal with noneconomic items or with specific items such as industrial safety. The short-

---

13. International Labour Office, *Collective Bargaining in Industrialized Market Economies* (Geneva: International Labour Office, 1974), p. 340. Unless otherwise stated, the country statistics quoted are from this source.

term (2-year) agreements deal with the economic terms and conditions of employment. The SAF-LO economy-wide bargain sets the basic limits for subsequent agreements reached by their constituent unions and employer associations. The affiliated labor and employer organizations at the industry and local level then negotiate agreements in line with the national accord. They also negotiate local issues not appropriate to a national bargain.

Japan. Rather than have separate agreements for blue-collar and white-collar employees, or for each plant or industry or region, or the nation as a whole, Japanese collective bargaining agreements are negotiated at the level of the firm. With few exceptions, all permanent workers of a firm (industrial, craft, and white-collar) are covered by one main agreement negotiated between the firm and the union. The main agreement is composed of two complementary subagreements. One is a permanent bargain over largely noneconomic items. The other agreement covers economic wages and benefits and is renegotiated yearly. In some companies local plant agreements supplement the main pact.

United States. With 195,000 agreements, the United States has the most decentralized structure. Recognizing that there are a substantial number of industry-wide master contracts and the practice of pattern setting, the U.S. system is not as decentralized as the number of agreements might suggest. But, it is not as centralized even with its lower extent of unionization as are Japan and Sweden. Agreements in the United States differ from those of Sweden and Japan, and many other countries, in that there is a single agreement between the parties, not two. In general, economic and noneconomic topics are covered in one contract and are subject to renegotiation (but may be left unchanged) each time the contract is reopened. Exceptions to this general rule include agreements in the construction trades which may have separate long-standing provisions regarding apprenticeship and some contracts that open after 1 or 2 years to renegotiate wages only (called a *wage reopener).*

Other Structural Contrasts. There is another interrelated aspect of structure which provides a contrast between the United States and other systems. The decentralized American bargaining system affects the role of the local union in the national scheme of industrial relations. There is more to this than just where contracts are negotiated. With over 60,000 local unions affiliated with national unions in the United States, the locals are where the day-to-day union business is conducted. They are organized around a specific work site (plant, office, school) in the case of industrial unions or for a small geographic area (county) in the case of craft unions. The steward system in the United States is strong. Union stewards police the contract on a daily basis and represent local union members in grievances with management. None of the other systems have the strong union steward role.

The unions in the other systems organize workers on an area-wide basis. Agreements are written to cover a region, entire industry, or an entire company. In contrast with the United States, where local agreements are detailed and are the focal point of union activity, local agreements in the other systems either do not exist or are not detailed and leave great discretion to management. Where an agreement is pitched at an aggregate level, be it company, industry, region, or economy, it must set minima. To set the economic bargain at a higher level than what marginal firms could pay would be to drive some firms out of business. As a result, workers at the more profitable plants bargain for add-ons.

The absence of strong local agreements and local unions has put much of the day-to-day labor relations concerns outside the control of organized labor. The trend in most countries is to strengthen the role of the local union and agreement (i.e., by introducing greater decentralization). In contrast, the opposite trend is seen in the United States. Bargaining structure is becoming more centralized. The problem for both systems is the same, however: writing an agreement which recognizes the economy-wide nature of many labor markets while simultaneously meeting the day-to-day needs of workers at the local level.

Government Involvement in Labor Relations

The U.S. industrial relations system is unique in one respect. In every other industrial relations system, labor unions are closely affiliated with what amounts to a labor political party—often called the Labor Party. The U.S. labor movement has no Labor Party, and it is not ideologically oriented toward establishing one. United States unions lobby for passage of legislation and support candidates favorable to organized labor but do not run candidates on a labor ticket.

This accounts, in part, for cross-cultural differences in the level of government involvement in the relationship between labor, management, and the economy. The least amount of government intervention would be to let labor and management find their own way without regulation, subject only to their relative power and the free play of economic forces. None of the countries has chosen that path. The next higher level of government involvement is termed *rule making*.[14] The government sets a minimum of very general rules regulating the system and lets the parties work out the details. Or, in contrast, the government might opt for *detailed regulation* of the processes of the system, but still allow the parties to bargain their own agreement. Beyond detailed regulation, the state may assume the role of *intervenor*. Here the state becomes involved in the substance of the agreement reached by the parties.

The governments of Japan, Sweden, and West Germany are rule makers with respect to collective bargaining, whereas the United States has detailed regulation and Australia has detailed regulation with intervention. On the other hand, Sweden and West Germany have detailed regulation for worker participation (extensive at the plant level), Japan has rule making (extensive at

---

14. Ibid., p. 138.

the corporate level), and the United States and Australia have very little worker participation and little or no legislation regarding it. For both collective bargaining and worker participation the general rule is that the degree of government regulation of their procedural aspects tends to increase as the level of activity moves closer to the work place.

From time to time proposals are made for revamping the role of government in U.S. labor-management relations. The 1977-1978 Labor Law Reform Act would have streamlined the U.S. union recognition process. This is discussed at length in Chapter 12. Occasionally it is suggested that the United States scrap its current system and adopt an interventionist system of labor courts. Australia has such a system, and we turn next to an examination of this approach to collective bargaining.

Australia has an industrial relations system characterized by detailed regulation and intervention through a system of *compulsory arbitration*. Arbitration tribunals exist at both the federal and state level which have the power to settle industrial disputes. The tribunals may be contacted by the parties to a dispute or intervene of their own accord. The tribunals usually do not become involved in negotiations until an impasse has been reached, i.e., labor and management have started negotiations and failed to reach agreement. The arbitration tribunal can mandate that the parties continue to negotiate. If there is still no settlement, the arbitration tribunal will issue an award which sets out in detail the minimum obligations of the parties. Strikes and lockouts are illegal, criminal activities and subject the perpetrators to fines and possible imprisonment.

Collective bargaining occurs along with the system of arbitration. It sometimes complements compulsory arbitration and sometimes substitutes for it. If labor and management do negotiate their own agreement, the tribunal usually makes it the arbitration award (called a consent agreement). The tribunal has the power to modify it if they see fit to do so, however. The parties may negotiate an agreement independent of the arbitration system and then submit it to the arbitration board for certification (certified agreement). Or, they may negotiate an agreement which exists completely outside the arbitration system (common law agreement). Only 1.4 percent of the agreements are common law. The negotiated agreements may be extensive ones covering all aspects of employment. More often, though, they are "over-award" agreements which sweeten the minimum terms set by comprehensive arbitration awards made by the boards.

The likelihood of such a system becoming law for the private sector in the United States is very slim. Its chief proponents argue that such a system would decrease private sector strikes. As we shall see later in this chapter, such has not been the case.

Finally, it should be noted that all governments intervene as the domestic or international situations make it necessary for them to do so. For example, strikes are generally illegal during a war effort or when they endanger national health or safety. In periods of high inflation, government may impose an *incomes policy* which limits the size of wage increases that can be negotiated in collective bargaining agreements.

Worker Participation

Two terms have been coined to describe levels of worker participation in the industrial relations system. *Industrial democracy* refers to the practice of giving workers a say in the planning (long-run) and operation (short-run) activities of a firm. Whereas industrial democracy involves a sharing of managerial authority, under *economic democracy* the worker shares in the ownership of the firm.

No advanced market economy has successfully implemented an extensive system of economic democracy, but Sweden has tried. Systems of industrial democracy are more common and the industrialized market economies show the vast range of approaches to worker participation. Sweden has proposed but not implemented economic democracy. West Germany has an industrial democracy system called codetermination. Japan has a system of worker participation at the firm level and at least one Japanese technique, the quality circle, is being adapted for U.S. use. These are examined in order followed by an overview of U.S. experiments with worker participation.

Sweden. Worker participation in Sweden is potentially extensive. At the national level unions have been of major importance in setting policy directly and also indirectly through their power within the Social Democratic Party. The decade of the 1970s saw passage of numerous laws extending worker participation. Unions have representation on the boards of directors of both private and public agencies by law. A worker participation act passed in 1977 makes both personnel and investment decisions subject to collective bargaining negotiation at the firm and plant level. However, through 1980 no such agreements had been negotiated. Other, more recent laws have dealt with the role of shop stewards and with work safety.

In 1976 the Swedish Confederation of Trade Unions proposed the Meidner Plan for gradual redistribution of Sweden's wealth. As a system of economic democracy, unions and workers would eventually become majority owners of Sweden's capital through a stock ownership plan called the Wage Earner's Investment Fund (WEIF). The Social Democrats lost the 1976 election largely due to their support of the WEIF issue. They had been in power continuously since 1932. As a result of this political setback, the WEIF plan was put on the back burner as a subject for revision and reconsideration in the early 1980s.[15]

West Germany. *Codetermination (Mitbestimmung* in German) dates back to the founding of the Weimar Republic in 1918.[16] It and collective bargaining operated side by side until the unions were dissolved by the Nazis in 1933.

---

15. Erik Asard, "Employee Participation in Sweden, 1971-79: The Issue of Economic Democracy," *Economic and Industrial Democracy,* Vol. 1, No. 3 (August, 1980), pp. 371-93.

16. Benjamin Martin and Everett Kasalow (eds.), *Labor Relations in Advanced Industrial Societies* (New York: Carnegie Endowment for Industrial Peace, 1980), pp. 139-60. *Mitbestimmung* is a system which gives the workers an important voice in the operation of the company through elected representatives on the company supervisory board.

Because of the substantial contribution unions made to the reconstruction of German industry after World War II, they demanded participation at the company level in the coal and steel industries. The practice extends beyond these industries, however. Worker participation at the shop level is regulated by the Works Constitution Law of 1972 and at the company or enterprise level by a law passed in 1976.

At the shop level, a group called the works council is elected by the work force. The size of the council depends upon the size of the establishment. Multiplant companies have a central works council as well. Works council members may or may not be union members, but in fact about 80 percent belong to the union.

> The works council has various codecision, consultation, and information rights, *vis à vis* the employer, ... to be exercised ... in a spirit of "mutual trust" with the employer; action is to be avoided that might disturb industrial peace at the shop floor; cooperation between unions and employers is required; and the procedure of collective bargaining agreements is to be observed. ... The most important general responsibility of the works council is to assure that all acts of parliament, regulations, safety rules, collective agreements and works agreements are adhered to for the benefit of the workers.[17]

The works council has an equal say with management on "social matters." These are items not covered by a bargaining agreement and, for the German system, include job evaluation and wage structures, labor hours and scheduling, layoff benefits, training and safety, employer-provided housing and rules of conduct. Disputes are settled by arbitration or the courts. The councils also have information and consultation rights on industrial environment changes and such "personnel matters" as hiring, firing, promotion, and layoff. They are pushing for actual codetermination in the personnel area as well.

At the company level workers also have representatives. German companies are controlled and operated by three groups: a shareholders assembly, the supervisory board, and the executive or management board. In the coal and steel industries, where codetermination is strongest, unions have gained parity representation with management on the supervisory and executive boards. The supervisory boards meet quarterly to make the major long-run decisions: financial planning, investments, and production changes. The executive board carries out the supervisory board decisions on a corporate day-to-day level.

Where true codetermination exists (coal and steel), the supervisory board consists of an odd number of people, say 11 members, selected by labor and management. Labor chooses 5: 2 from works councils, 2 from the industry union, and 1 nominated by but not from the labor union federation. Shareholders select 4 and nominate a nonshareholder fifth. The 10 select a neutral eleventh member. In addition to the 11 labor and management selected mem-

17. Ibid., pp. 146-7.

bers, 3 other members are added to represent the public interest. Outside of the coal and steel industries, codetermination is provided by law, but it is a weaker system from the union viewpoint. The law provides for fewer union-selected members on the boards and increases the likelihood of nonunion works council members being elected to the board.

The executive board has a labor director who is responsible for social and personnel matters. In the coal and steel industries the labor director is elected by the labor members of the supervisory board. Outside those industries the labor director is chosen by a majority of votes of all the supervisory board members and may not have a special relationship with labor and may even be chosen over labor's objection.

The potential for conflict between bargaining and codetermination should be evident. The emphasis, however, seems to be on accommodation, not competition.

> Collective bargaining, as the autonomous action of unions, establishes minimum standards in the field of employment, income, or working conditions. Participation at the shop and company level implements and adapts the rough indicators and criteria of collective agreements into the reality of a specific enterprise. Participation can provide the tools for the direction of industrial labor by developing manpower planning, new forms of work organization, work safety, training schemes, etc. Successful experiments at the shop level can be applied by management and by collective agreements to an entire region and may even eventually find expression in the law.[18]

Japan. Japan has an extensive system of worker participation based in a unique labor-management system. The relationship between labor and management is centered at the firm level. Japanese workers often spend their entire working lives with one company. The turnover rate is very low. Japanese management takes a holistic view of the labor-management relationship. That is, workers and employers view their relationship as a lifetime one in which employer concern extends to all aspects of employee life including housing, material goods, and even the employee's personal life. The employee is a part of the corporate "family."

The family relationship holds a number of implications for management decision making. Decision making is consensual.[19] All views (union, employee, and employer) are heard, and a decision is reached among the parties. Responsibility for the actions taken, and the results, is collective, not individual. Management control and direction are implicit and informal. Employees learn what to expect on the job through their long tenure with the work group. The evaluation and promotion of individual employees is a slow and lengthy process and there is no set career path. Promotions depend upon the capabilities of the person and the needs of the firm.

---

18. Ibid., p. 157.
19. William G. Ouchi and Alfred M. Jaeger, "Type Z Organization: Stability in the Heart of Mobility," *Academy of Management Review* (April, 1978), Vol. 3, No. 2, p. 311.

At the firm level, worker participation coexists with collective bargaining and supplements it. By collective agreement, joint councils are established which are composed of equal numbers of management and union representatives. They deal with both personnel matters and the longer-run production and investment decisions. In the most prevalent use of the joint council, both personnel and production decisions are discussed as a prelude to bargaining, but away from the emotionalism of wage bargaining. There is a strong emphasis on harmony and development of mutual interest or consensus. Where consensus is achieved, an agreement is written up.

At the shop floor level, there is widespread use of a technique called the quality circle. Because it is being adopted by companies in the United States, it will be discussed next as part of the American experience with worker participation.

United States. There is no law mandating worker participation in either the American or Australian industrial relations system. Both countries have a tradition of strong management rights which has tended to discourage any sharing of decision-making authority. Recently, however, the United States has begun to experiment with a number of labor-management techniques designed to improve worker productivity. The terms *quality of work life* (QWL) and *participative management* have been coined to refer to various new techniques. The Japanese quality circle is one method being adapted for use in the United States.[20]

The *quality circle* is a small group (5-10) of employees who meet with their supervisor 1 to 2 hours per week. Participation in the group is voluntary. The group meets to analyze work area problems, devise and implement solutions, and share in the results. The problems are confined to those which concern cost containment, improved productivity, and increased product quality. The supervisor is the leader of the quality circle. The role, however, is one of facilitator, not intervenor. The circle selects the problem to be solved, defines it, gathers data on it, agrees on possible solutions, presents the analysis to higher management, implements an agreed-upon strategy, and shares in the results of the group's activities. Success brings recognition and/or monetary reward.

In Japan in 1980 one in eight employees was in a quality circle.[21] In 1974, Lockheed was the first to use the quality circle in the United States.[22] By 1981, the newsletter *Productivity* found in a survey of 500 firms that one-half have quality circles or other worker participation programs.[23] Xerox, Polaroid, Bell Telephone, Honeywell, and General Motors are among these firms. Many such programs have been introduced in nonunion firms as a way to build a family atmosphere in an attempt to preempt the need for unionization.

---

20. Some analysts argue that the quality circle is neither a QWL method (it does not change the job) nor participative management (it involves little sharing of authority). We count it among both categories because it affects each to a degree.

21. Richard R. Redder, "What American and Japanese Managers are Learning from Each Other," *Business Horizons* (March-April, 1981), Vol. 24, No. 2, p. 66.

22. Ibid., p. 68

23. "Labor Letter," *The Wall Street Journal*, September 29, 1981, p. 1.

In organized firms, union leaders are not of one mind as to the wisdom of engaging in QWL and participative management programs. Quotes from two labor leaders indicate the variation of opinion.

> "I'm absolutely convinced that the future of collective bargaining is in quality-of-work-life. We can be cooperative on the plant floor and adversarial at the bargaining table." Irving Bluestone, retired United Auto Workers vice president[24]

> "We want participation from the bottom up. I don't want to sit on the board and be responsible for managing the business. I want to be free as a unionist to criticize the management." Glenn E. Watts, President, Communication Workers of America[25]

The decade of the 1980s promises to be one of continued experimentation with QWL and participative management schemes. The search is on for new labor-management techniques which will meet the needs of management for cost containment and improved productivity and product quality while simultaneously meeting employees' needs for improved pay and working conditions without threatening the viability of the labor movement.

Industrial Conflict

The range of industrial conflict among the five countries is remarkable. Australia at 1464 workdays lost has a work stoppage rate over 20 times higher than Sweden's at 62 workdays lost to strikes. The United States is very near to the Australian rate. West Germany is near Sweden for work stoppages, and Japan is about three times higher. What makes the figures ironic is the fact that in Australia strikes are illegal, criminal activities and in Sweden strikes are legal in both the private and public sectors.

A key difference between the low-conflict countries and those with high conflict lies in the attitudes held by labor and management toward decision making. There can be no doubt that there are other contributing variables: work force homogeneity, geographic size, extent of union organization, centralization of bargaining, the nature of the industrial base, and the existence of a labor party. However, the fact remains that industrial relations systems with joint decision making have lower conflict than those with a history of strong management rights.

Sweden and West Germany. In the Swedish and West German systems, worker participation is extensive. Unions and management make an effort to settle agreements rather than strike. In Sweden, for example, where union strikes and employer lockouts are legal for both the private and public sectors, both sides strive to avoid shutdowns. They extend negotiations and continue

---

24. "A New Way of Managing People," *Business Week*, May 11, 1981, p. 86.
25. Ibid.

to operate beyond contract expiration. They use a labor court or arbitration as an alternative to the shutdown. When strikes do occur, they are selective strikes against individual employers, not system-wide, major stoppages. Day-to-day conflict is handled or avoided by the stewards and worker councils.

Japan. Japan, with its somewhat higher level of conflict, also has extensive participative decision making. But, the strike serves an interesting function in the paternalistic Japanese system. Wages and other economic items are negotiated yearly on an individual firm basis. All firms negotiate at about the same time. Target figures for wage increases are announced by the unions at the start of what has come to be known as the "Spring Offensive." Before the union and management ever meet to negotiate a new agreement, the firm's employees take a strike vote. The majority controls.

> Even if the ballot is positive, it does not mean that a strike will be called immediately: the actual timing of a strike is decided by the union officers in the light of progress made in collective bargaining. A strike is called not when bargaining has broken down but when a breakdown appears imminent. Thus a strike ballot is held not so much for the purpose of consulting union members on the necessity for strike action as to impress upon the employer their determination to have their demands met. Consequently, if a strike proposal is voted down, the actual negotiations tend to lapse. Strike action is used not to break the deadlock in collective bargaining but to elicit a new counteroffer from the employer. In other words, no clear functional demarcation may be drawn between collective bargaining and strike action: they are both regarded as parts of the same process. . . . And by observing their strike schedule unions seek to bring home to the employers their sense of discipline and their determination to secure their demands.[26]

Thus strikes in Japan serve not as economic punishment to the employer, but as a signal or demonstration of union solidarity and resolve. As such, strikes are frequent, have full participation, and are short. Work days lost are few in number and represent widespread but brief conflict. This signaling effect is more often achieved short of a work stoppage. Many contracts have provisions for handling conflict during the life of the agreement, but the procedures are rarely used. Instead, grievances are settled short of a strike by a signal and show of discontent (wearing armbands) or may be referred to the Labour Relations Commission or be held until the next negotiations.

United States. We have seen that relative to the other economies, the United States has little participative management in the unionized sector. Bargaining is much more decentralized in the United States than in the Japanese and West European systems. The individual employer and union assume a more important role in the American system. With such a decentralized system, there are many more sites of industrial conflict. There also exists a

26. ILO, *Collective Bargaining*, pp. 304-5.

long history of union-management confrontation. Employers view the union as an intrusion into the employer-employee relationship and as a threat to managerial prerogative. Negotiations are often win-lose contests. During the life of an agreement, management exercises its exclusive right to make decisions subject to subsequent challenge by the union through the grievance procedure. The relationship is largely adversarial. Indeed, many union leaders are against participative management for fear that their independent role will be coopted in the process.

Australia. Australia is another decentralized system which has a very strong tradition of unilateral management decision making. Decisions about the day-to-day running of the firm and the longer-run decisions about methods of production, product, and company expansion are firmly in the hands of management. Industrial conflict is closely regulated in Australia. But, while strikes and lockouts are illegal, the statistics indicate clearly that they are common.

Strikes are often short protest strikes used to pressure employers to negotiate overaward bargains. Overaward bargains are contract concessions made by employers in excess of the terms and conditions of employment awarded by the arbitration tribunals. They are also used to protest worker grievances. Grievance procedures for handling day-to-day conflicts are few in number. In the absence of a grievance procedure and in the presence of powerful management rights, management makes a decision on the proper resolution of the dispute. If the union disagrees, it must resort to the use of a strike to force management to reconsider its position. The exercise of raw economic power is substituted in lieu of a system which provides for a conflict resolving dialog between the parties.

The next section presents the industrial relations system of the U.S.S.R. There are significant differences between the Russian centrally controlled system and the free-market systems.

THE SOVIET CENTRALLY CONTROLLED INDUSTRIAL RELATIONS SYSTEM[27]

The organization of this section parallels the discussion of the market economies. It proceeds from bargaining structure to the role of government, worker participation, and industrial conflict.

In order to understand the soviet industrial relations system, it is necessary to look at the larger environment in which it functions. The Communist Party plays the dominant role in an economy dedicated to rapid industrial growth through the use of extensive central planning. Five-year plans are worked out by the Gosplan (state planning committee) and are then adopted by the U.S.S.R. Council of Ministers and the Supreme Soviet (the elected legislative body). The plans determine the direction of industrial development

---

27. Emily Clark Brown, *Soviet Trade Unions and Labor Relations* (Cambridge, Mass.: Harvard University Press, 1966).

and the distribution of resources to obtain the development targets. They are carried out by the state agencies that manage the government-owned firms. The economic plans have the force of law for the firms. Trade unions and labor-management relations are structured to facilitate central control over planned growth.

Bargaining Structure

Democratic centralism is the basic organizational principle of unions. Their structure is governed by the production principle, meaning that each national union has control over all who work in an industry or related groups of industries. Authority flows from the top down, but at each level the leaders are elected by secret ballot. At the peak of the union authority structure resides the All-Union Central Council of Trade Unions (CCTU) elected by the All-Union Congress of Trade Unions. This body directs trade union activities. Below the CCTU, union members elect councils at the national union level, republic, and regional levels. In terms of daily implementation of policy, these regional committees (called *sovprofs*) are the most important. Their policies are carried out at the plant and shop level by elected union committees. The extent of organization is very high and includes nearly all people employed in industry, state farms, trade, education, medical service, and government organization. Union members receive better social insurance benefits and are given preferential treatment over nonmembers when it comes to recreation and educational benefits.

Role of Government

The government role is one of detailed regulation and intervention for labor-management relations. The scope of bargaining is narrow when compared with the market economies. Very many of the topics which are open for bargaining in market economies are established by law in the Soviet Union. Central laws, decrees, labor codes, and regulations established by the government cover the rights of union committees, managerial authority, job changes, transfers, promotion, discipline, discharge, labor disputes, wage and salary standards, premiums and incentives, hours, overtime, holidays, vacations; working conditions for women, youths, and invalids; safety, social security; and resources for plant changes workers want.

Worker Participation

Collective agreements are worked out yearly and their primary concern is mobilizing workers to improve production. The agreement really amounts to participative management decision making about what will be produced and how. It is not a wages and working conditions agreement; those topics are set by law. Collective decision making is a more accurate term than collective bargaining for describing the system.

The process of collective decision making is begun with a worker critique of the previous year's production contract. The workers make proposals for change. The proposals are collected and studied by the factory employee committee and the factory administration. Together they work out a draft agreement. This goes back to the shops for discussion and for suggested change. The revised draft is considered by the plant director at a general meeting of workers or their representatives. The final draft is drawn up and signed by the chairperson of the union committee and the plant director. Barring any dispute, the agreement is then registered.

In the Soviet Union, worker participation and collective bargaining amount to the same thing. Whether it is called bargaining or participation, the Soviet institutions produce an industrial relations system in which the activities of the employee and union are subordinate to the government's planned industrial advancement.

Industrial Conflict

Industrial conflict is difficult to discuss because little data exist on actual work stoppages. The process of collective decision making does not provide for work stoppages. If the workers and the plant director do not reach a consensus on the production agreement, the dispute is submitted to the sovprof for a final and binding decision. The agreement that results from the decision is then registered.

Conflict during the life of the agreement is handled by a grievance procedure. The worker with a grievance submits it to a joint commission on labor disputes. The joint commission is made up of an equal number of union and management people. The commission conducts a hearing and renders a decision. The worker can appeal the decision of the joint commission to a factory commission. Another hearing is convened to hear the contentions of both sides. The factory commission must render a decision. That decision can be appealed by the worker to the People's Court and may go from there to higher courts of appeal.

THE DEVELOPING ECONOMIES

The bulk of world population resides in the developing nations. Many of these countries have in just the last 10-20 years made the transition from colony to independent nation. One of the questions asked by analysts of industrial relations systems was, "What part of industrial relations systems in the industrialized countries can be used by the developing economies?" It became apparent early on that the industrializing nations of the 1960s, 1970s, and 1980s were not following the path blazed by the nations which industrialized a century earlier. The industrial relations systems of North America and Western Europe are not models for the new nations. The economic and social environments are far different.

There are some generalizations to be made about the developing economies beyond the basic truth that each system is unique, however. The economic setting is often the same. The nation is heavy in primary industries (coal, timber) and just developing the secondary industries (manufacturing). Much of the labor force is involved in agriculture, and this is often at the subsistence farming level. There is a burgeoning population. The unemployment and underemployment rates are high. There is a cadre of skilled workers at much higher wage levels than are commanded by the oversupplied, unskilled workers. In many cases, the unions were a major force involved in throwing off the yoke of colonialism. The new government's focus is on economic development and political stability. Central planning is the key economic policy.

The unions are heavily involved in politics. They have a strong ideological orientation which may be Marxist, socialist, or capitalist. Their source of power is in numbers and is political rather than economic. If there is much true collective bargaining, it is for the few skilled workers and/or in the more fully developed industries. Outside those industries, the strike is not an effective weapon because of the large number of unemployed eager for work. Strikes, even where economically feasible, may not be feasible politically. The union goal of higher wages is often labeled "counterproductive to national goals" because it siphons money away from capital investment into consumption. In the face of diversity, unions build a power base politically. They depend more on mass ideological support, less on economic power, and become a pressure group for the betterment of all people through legislation. Their goals are laws providing minimum wages, health care, and education—basic human capital growth. Union goals conform to those of the government either by choice or subjugation. Worker participation may at most be to seek a role in the central planning of the government.

A LOOK INTO THE FUTURE

There are many theories about the evolution of industrial relations systems. One book recently reviewed 18 of them.[28] Two theories are examined here. One provides a look into the future for the developing economies. The other makes a prediction for the fate of organized labor in the United States.

The Developing Economies: Pluralistic Industrialism

Struck by the uniqueness of the U.S. industrial relations system when compared with those of Western Europe, the communist block countries, and the developing economies, four eminent labor economists from the United States set out to "relate experiences from many industrial and industrializing nations in a common network of understanding." Their *Industrialism and Industrial Man*[29] set out the common network of understanding and was the culmination of a decade of research by a great many scholars. The theory was modified and refined by debate and research for another 10 years. The work

---

28. John Schmidman, *Unions in Postindustrial Society* (University Park, Penn.: The Pennsylvania State University Press, 1979).

29. Clark Kerr, John T. Dunlop, Frederick Harbison, Charles A. Myers, *Industrialism and Industrial Man* (New York: Oxford University Press, 1964).

was completed with the 1975 publication of *Industrialism and Industrial Man Reconsidered*[30] by Dunlop, Harbison, Kerr, and Myers (DHKM).

DHKM forecast a model of industrial relations for the developing economies which they call *pluralistic industrialism*. They believe that the developing economies will move toward a society headed either by leaders from the middle class (like the United States) or by communist leaders (as in the Soviet Union). In both situations labor, management, and government will share relatively equally in making the rules for the system. No one group will dictate the terms for the exchange of labor.

Government will be responsible for the macro concerns of growth, income distribution, individual security, political stability, and the provision of essential services. It will regulate the power struggles between labor and management, between producers and consumers, and between members and their organizations. The management of both public and private enterprises will remain powerful, and the distinctions between the two sectors will diminish. Management will be the source of much worker skill development. The work force will be trained to meet the education needs of industrialization. The other power center—labor organizations—will continue to grow in importance. Labor organizations will express workers' occupational and professional interests. The extensive web of rules that the interplay between the actors (labor, management, and government) generates will govern a power struggle less over the legitimacy of the industrial relations system itself and more over change within the existing system. Conflict will become institutionalized and will become less violent as the actors substitute problem-solving procedure for the use of power. Labor organizations will change to be structured primarily along the lines of occupation and profession as workers come to identify with their occupation rather than with their class. The individual will demand increased freedom bred of higher living standards, education, and leisure time.

In retrospect, DKHM suggest that the model outlined above will probably apply to roughly half the population in Third World Countries. Such nations as Taiwan, Argentina, Brazil, Mexico, Korea, India, and Hong Kong are industrializing. But a third of the economies may never industrialize for lack of size or natural resources. The rest of the world's economies, for example, Tanzania, appear to be developing dual (rich versus poor, rural versus urban) economies.[31]

Postindustrial Society and the Future of Unionism in the United States

John Schmidman in *Unions in Postindustrial Society*[32] develops a prognosis for the future of labor movements in the advanced industrial economies in

30. John T. Dunlop, et al., *Industrialism and Industrial Man Reconsidered* (Princeton, N.J.: The Inter-University Study of Human Resources in National Development, 1975).

31. Ibid., pp. 31-32.

32. Schmidman, *Postindustrial Society.*

general and for the United States in particular. These advanced economies have matured to the point where they have an extensive development of their tertiary or service sectors *(postindustrial society)*. A small proportion of their labor force remains in the primary industry of agriculture. Employment in the secondary manufacturing industries has peaked as a proportion of the labor force. The number of blue-collar workers is increasing, but their proportion of the labor force is declining. The tertiary service sector is expanding rapidly with large increases in the numbers of white-collar, professional, and technical workers. For example, in the 1980s in the United States, white-collar employees will make up half the labor force and blue-collar workers will comprise less than a third of it. The composition of the labor force will become proportionally more young, black, female, and highly educated.

Few would argue with this picture of the American economy in the 1980s. However, any set of facts is consistent with more than one explanation or theory of how they occurred. Theories of the consequences of these labor force changes for organized labor go in two directions. One group postulates the demise of unionism on the premise that the new worker, whom the unions have historically had difficulty organizing, will be even more unorganizable. The new worker is more affluent and less willing to accept authority than the older worker was. They are less responsive to the standard union-organizing appeals of increased income, job security, and grievance resolution. They will not accept union authority. Unions, according to this view, will be locked into the traditional blue-collar strongholds and decline with the decline of the manufacturing sectors.

Schmidman thinks otherwise. He believes that the new workers in the white-collar and the professional and technical occupations of government and the service industries will organize. The motivating factor, he argues, is the authority structure inherent in every enterprise. In order for an organization to produce, there must be manager and managed—a superior-subordinate relationship. Affluence will not overcome the worker's basic problem of lack of job control. At the lower end of the skill spectrum, the sales and clerical employees will unionize for defensive reasons, as did blue-collar employees before them, to protect themselves from arbitrary management decision making. The more highly trained and educated employees, on the other hand, will take the offense and organize unions to force changes in their jobs. The new labor organizations of highly trained and educated employees will mount an offensive to give professional and technical employees on-the-job autonomy and responsibility commensurate with their education and intelligence. The focus of the new unionism will, like the old, be on change at the work place. However, unions will come to have a more uniform occupational orientation than they do now. The unions of the future will be more like the craft unions of the past—organized by occupation—and less like the industrial union conglomerations of occupation and skill.

In addition to adapting to the needs of the new worker on the job, unions in the future will have to adapt internally to increase their organizational democracy. The worker who organizes to seek a greater say on the job will also want a say in the running of the labor organization. Unions will also adapt their external political stance to make more extensive use of their political power base. The unions of the future will function on two levels. The main union focus will remain representation on the job. However, in order to meet the needs of its constituency, the union of the future must represent the needs of blacks, women, and white-collar employees at the national level. With the modern problems of simultaneous inflation and unemployment, government will place a greater emphasis on economic planning. The role of labor organizations can no longer be limited to lobbying when this occurs. They must become a more active partner with the other interest groups in the planning of the economy.

> A welfare state, a younger and more highly educated labor force, a relative degree of affluence, and the evolution into a tertiary, service-oriented economy will not decrease the need for collective organization and action among employees. While there will be a similarity between some white collar unions and their blue collar predecessors, a new type of trade unionism will emerge along with the more highly educated and trained professional and technical employee. Even though this new type of organization will be more aggressive and less scarcity conscious than unions of employees with less degrees of training, it will be the result of the same universal phenomenon— the presence of an authority structure in all employing enterprises. This authority structure will be met with less blind acceptance and more hostility by the "new" worker. The prophets of doom who claim that organized labor has reached the pinnacle of its strength and extent of organization will prove to be as mistaken as those who choose to ignore employees' natural tendency to form collective organizations to achieve job-related goals which they cannot obtain as individuals.[33]

CONCLUDING REMARKS

The similarities across industrial relations systems are no less striking than the differences. To bring them all together under the umbrella of one theory is a monumental task. The idea of pluralistic industrialism provides a vantage point from which to view the day-to-day drama of the developing economies. The power plays between the Polish union Solidarity and the Polish government are a case in point. Perhaps an additional actor ought to be added as an exogenous influence on the development of Third World industrial relations systems. Russia and the United States certainly can have a very direct impact on the political and economic structure as recent events in El Salvador, Poland, Iran, and Afghanistan have shown.

CHAPTER SUMMARY

The purpose of this chapter is to introduce the concepts of collective bargaining and industrial relations with an interna-tional perspective. To provide a basis for comparison, the first section presented an overview of the U.S. system. The United

---

33. Ibid., p. 143.

States has a decentralized system organized according to the principle of exclusive representation for both the public and private sector. Unions and associations are structured along craft, industrial, and white-collar lines. Management may be a single-employer or a multiemployer association. The predominant agreement between labor and management is the local contract, but they often supplement master agreements which may or may not be pattern set. The role of government in the United States is one of detailed regulation of the process of bargaining, but with limited regulation of the substance of the labor-management relationship. United States agreements contain a strong management rights philosophy and resolve conflict during the life of the contract through an extensive grievance-arbitration system.

The international comparison provided cross-cultural contrasts with advanced market economies, the Soviet Union, and developing economies. The industrial relations systems varied from low to high as to the extent of unionization. The level of agreement between union and management is lower for the decentralized systems of the United States and Australia than for the more centralized systems of Japan, West Germany, and Sweden. The role of government is confined to rule making for the West European countries and Japan and interventionist for Australia. Worker participation is extensive and closely regulated in Japan, West Germany, and Sweden but minimal for the strong management rights countries of the United States and Australia. The United States is trying out some forms of participative management including the quality circle. Industrial conflict levels seemed to vary inversely with the level of worker participation for the economies surveyed. There are many other explanations for the great disparity of conflict across nations, but one factor does appear to be the traditional and legal stance of the systems toward worker participation.

The Russian industrial relations system provides for a reduced scope of collective bargaining. Bargaining in Russia is more like participative management in the other countries. Its emphasis is on output goals and the means of reaching them and not on economic benefits. The other economic and noneconomic terms of the labor-management relationship are set by law.

It is difficult to generalize about the developing economies. They are industrializing, but they lack the resource base to follow the pattern of the advanced market economies. The practice of collective bargaining is usually confined to a few developed industries which employ the nation's skilled workers. The role of unions is largely political in developing economies. They provide a power base from which to achieve legislative changes which provide basic human capital needs (health, education). Conflict in the form of strikes tends not to be effective or is not tolerated by the government.

What the future holds for the developing economies is the subject of an extensive study. The prognosis is for continued industrialization according to a form called pluralistic industrialism. There will be a relatively equal sharing of power among government, labor, and management. Government will provide the basic protections of health, safety, and education and will regulate the conflict between labor and management. Unions will be organized along occupational lines. They will be an active political participant and act as a countervailing power to management. Management will be the driving force toward industrialization. As part of that effort, it will be the primary source of training for the work force.

The industrialized market economies are becoming postindustrial states. They have a large service sector with a highly educated, young, white-collar labor force.

Some crystal ball gazers see a decline of the union movement as the blue-collar jobs decline and unions fail to organize the new affluent, professional worker. John Schmidman argues that one thing that has not changed is the basic authority relationship. The workers at the low end of the white-collar skill level will organize to protect themselves from management as employees have done for years, and the higher skilled employees will organize to wrest from management the job control and responsibility that is commensurate with their education and intelligence.

KEY TERMS

collective bargaining
industrial relations system
extent of unionization
union
association
exclusive bargaining agent
appropriate bargaining unit
spillover effects
local union
chapter
national (international) union
federation
independents
craft union
industrial union
white-collar union
local agreement
master contract
local supplement
collective bargaining structure
scope of agreement

management rights
grievance and arbitration
    procedure
union steward
arbitrator
worker participation
industrial conflict
wage reopener
rule making
detailed regulation
intervenor
compulsory arbitration
incomes policy
industrial democracy
economic democracy
codetermination
quality of work life
participative management
quality circle
pluralistic industrialism
postindustrial society

REVIEW QUESTIONS

1. Distinguish between collective bargaining and an industrial relations system. Is it possible to have an industrial relations system without collective bargaining?

2. Rank order the five market economies from most to least for the variables industrial conflict and worker participation. Do you think there is a relationship between overt conflict and the extent of worker participation?

3. What are the differences between the Soviet system of industrial relations and those of the advanced market economies?

4. What are the characteristics of the postindustrial society? What are the differences between those who believe unions will decline and Schmidman in his theory of future union growth? Which do you think history will bear out?

5. There is no right or wrong answer for this question. Given what you know about industrial relations systems, which one do you think works the best? Why?

ADDITIONAL REFERENCES

Dunlop, John T., et al. *Industrialism and Industrial Man Reconsidered.* Princeton, N.J.: The Inter-University Study of Human Resources in National Development, 1975.

International Labour Office. *Collective Bargaining in Industrialized Market Economies.* Geneva: International Labour Office, 1974.

Kerr, Clark, et al. *Industrialism and Industrial Man.* New York: Oxford University Press, 1964.

Martin, Benjamin, and Everett M. Kassalow (eds.). *Labor Relations in Advanced Industrial Societies: Issues and Problems.* New York: Carnegie Endowment for International Peace, 1980.

Schmidman, John. *Unions in Postindustrial Society.* University Park, Penn.: The Pennsylvania State University Press, 1979.

THE WORLD
OF WORK . . .

The United States and the United Nations' International Labor Organization

The United Nations' body for dealing with labor market policy is called the International Labor Organization (ILO). United States participation in the ILO has been a source of controversy in recent years. In this reading the controversy is reviewed in light of ILO activities.

The historical relationship of the United States with the ILO has been marked by periods of warm support followed by disillusionment.

Although Samuel Gompers chaired the committee that drafted the original ILO charter in 1919 (as part of the Treaty of Versailles), the United States did not join the organization until 1934. During World War II, when the League of Nations withered, the United States strongly supported the ILO's continued existence and hosted the historic 1944 conference that adopted the Declaration of Philadelphia, setting forth the organization's principles and purposes.

The 1970's, however, saw U.S. support for the ILO decay and eventually break over a number of serious issues.

Beginning in 1970, the U.S. Congress voted to withhold its contribution to the ILO budget (25 percent of the total), citing its concern with growing Soviet influence and the nonobservance of fundamental ILO principles and procedures. U.S. funds were restored in 1973, but the resumption of U.S. support was followed shortly by even sharper U.S. complaints about misdirected ILO activities.

In 1975, following a decision by the ILO conference to grant observer status to the Palestine Liberation Organization, Secretary of State Henry Kissinger formally notified the ILO's Director General that the United States would withdraw from the organization in 1977 unless progress was made on the following four issues of major U.S. concern:

1. *Erosion of tripartism.* U.S. concern was triggered by efforts of some ILO members to impose restrictions on the independence of worker and employer delegates to ILO meetings.

2. *Selective concern for human rights.* Although ILO machinery for investigating violations of ILO human rights standards worked well in most cases, one group of countries—principally the Communist states of Eastern Europe—successfully used political influence to gain relative immunity from the application of that machinery.

3. *Violation of due process.* The ILO's human rights machinery protects the rights of accused governments by requiring an objective investigation of the facts. But in some cases, this due process right was ignored by conference participants who adopted politically inspired condemnatory resolutions.

4. *Politicization of ILO meetings.* In far too many cases, delegates to ILO meetings introduced political issues which were totally extraneous to the work of the ILO and which detracted from the organization's legitimate responsibilities.

Because the ILO failed, in the U.S. view, to make satisfactory progress on these issues in the intervening 2 years, President Carter ordered U.S. withdrawal from the ILO in November 1977.

RECENT PROGRESS

Following U.S. withdrawal, a majority of ILO delegates—governments, workers, and employers—successfully joined together to promote a number of important reforms. The 1979 conference, for example, adopted a new procedure permitting voting by secret ballot to protect the independence of worker and employer delegates. In November 1978, the ILO Governing Body censured Czechoslovakia for violating ILO standards concerning discrimination in employment. More recently, the Governing Body has initiated investigations into alleged violations of trade union rights in the Soviet Union and Poland.

The principle of due process was strengthened by the decision of the 1978 Conference to reject a proposal to extend the life of a 1974 resolution criticizing Israel without benefit of any investigation. A special working party of the ILO is currently giving serious consideration to a new procedure to screen out future resolutions violating due process principles. Finally, the level of debate in ILO meetings on extraneous political issues has significantly diminished.

A special U.S. Cabinet-level committee on the ILO . . . carefully examined these and other developments during the summer of 1979. The committee concluded that although not all of the issues of concern to the United States had been fully resolved, the ILO had made significant progress. Moreover, the committee agreed that continued progress in reaching the fundamental goals of the ILO was now more likely if the United States resumed active membership.

As a result of this review, the committee unanimously recommended to the President that the United States rejoin the ILO. Acting on this recommendation, President Carter announced the U.S. return, effective February 18, 1980.

1980 CONFERENCE ISSUES

The significance of the U.S. return can be measured by, among other things, its potential contribution to ILO technical programs, starting with an active U.S. presence during the June 1980 conference. That conference will consider the issues that will underlie the major ILO programs during the 1980's.

The conference has four major technical issues on its agenda: older workers; equal opportunities and equal treatment for men and women workers; safety and health in the working environment; and promotion of collective bargaining.

Significantly, all four issues involve aspects of human rights. For older workers and women, job discrimination continues to represent a serious concern. Some observers also feel that certain early ILO conventions, designed initially to protect women workers, resulted instead in promoting a system of discriminatory labor standards, which actually limited the employment opportunities of women workers.

The question of occupational safety and health also involves serious moral and human rights aspects. The ILO constitution and other international accords recognize that workers must be protected on the job as a matter of right, not privilege. Moreover, an increasing number of governments and worker organizations are expressing concern that countries which refuse to adequately protect workers' health may be reaping—at workers' expense—an unwarranted competitive advantage over countries which provide adequate worker protection.

Collective bargaining remains an important and recognized human right, one which is all too frequently compromised in the name of economic development.

Other important issues will also be considered by the 1980 conference. The committee which supervises the application of ratified ILO labor standards, for example, will consider whether to modify or, as some governments have proposed, eliminate entirely the so-called "special list" and "special paragraphs." These devices allow the conference to highlight flagrant violations of workers' human rights. The majority of delegates will likely favor retention of these important tools.

A committee on structure will consider proposals to modify the organization of the ILO, including the size and composition of the Governing Body. Another committee will examine any resolutions submitted by conference delegates.

The results of this conference will provide important indications of the ability of the ILO to tackle those serious technical issues for which it has a unique competence. A successful conference could well mark the start, after the troubled 1970's, of a new decade of achievement for the ILO.

Source: Tadd Linsenmayer, "U.S. Rejoins ILO: The Agenda for 1980's Stresses Human Rights," *Monthly Labor Review* (May, 1980), pp. 50-51.

Chapter 11

The United States Labor Movement: Past, Present and Future

Why study history? Some say knowledge of history is a sign of being well-educated. Others find history interesting in and of itself. We include it for those reasons, and to see how the past has shaped the collective bargaining system of today. Collective bargaining did not occur overnight. The present system evolved along a tortuous path. Every part of the present system is there for a tried and true reason. By studying the history of our present system, it is possible to see why we have what we have today, what changes will be made difficult because they fly in the face of tradition, and what the response of the collective bargaining system might be in the future.

The chapter is divided according to topics into the past, the present, and the future. The segment on the past begins with John R. Commons' theory of the genesis of the American labor movement. Lessons learned historically by organized labor follow and lead to modern union history which we date from the passage of protective labor legislation in the 1930s. We proceed by topic to the present. The current status of collective bargaining includes a discussion of union structure and government and the success of public sector organization. Trends in union growth and union avoidance as an impediment to union expansion are examined in the last section on the future.

THE PAST

One of the more famous and frequently quoted theories of the beginning of the American labor movement was developed by John Rogers Commons. Commons was a famous institutional labor economist who had the dubious distinction of having once been dismissed from his academic position at Syracuse University for advocating the right of workers to play baseball on Sunday. His theory of the labor movement is called the *market theory* because Commons believed that employers, forced into product price competition by the market, cut costs by cutting or limiting wages. Market competition forced a wedge between employer interests and worker interests. Workers subsequently organized unions to protect their economic interests against their employers.

Before unions, work was performed through a guild system. For example, the shoemakers of Boston in 1648 formed such a guild. The product was "bespoke," or custom-ordered, work. The producer performed three roles: the master merchant who negotiated the quality of shoe and its price with the customer; the master employer who controlled the work place, tools, and orders to journeyworkers; and the master craftworker who combined skill and materials to actually produce the shoes.

In 1790 the shoe market still offered bespoke work. In order of increasing competition, there were also "shop work," shoes made without a prior order and sold retail at the shop; "market and wholesale order work," sold in a larger regional market; and lower quality work sold in the public market. Enter the split in interest. The wholesale market came to dominate shoe production. The employer who competed in the wholesale market incurred the additional costs of solicitation, transportation, inventory accumulation, and credit. No longer did the guild employer negotiate a monopoly price to cover all costs as was the case when all work was bespoke. Instead, price competition forced the wholesale employer to cut costs where possible. The master employer role assumed greater importance as the producer cut costs by holding the line on wages. Rather than looking out for the economic interests of employees by negotiating a price to cover their wage costs, the wholesale employer cut wages to cut costs. Employer and employee interests diverged.

> It was the widening out of these markets with their lower levels of competition and quality, but without any changes in the instruments of production, that destroyed the primitive identity of master and journeyman cordwainers and split their community of interest into modern alignment of employers' association and trade union.[1]

In response to these actions, shoemakers in 1794 formed the first union, The Federal Society of Journeymen Cordwainers. To raise their wages, the cordwainers (shoemakers) set the wage rates they would work for and engaged in a "turn out" (strike) to get them from employers. They refused to work with scabs (employees who would work for less) and sent committees around to make sure employers did not hire scab labor. Sound familiar? It should to students who work union construction in the summer. They must carry a union membership card to get work. A business agent travels to various construction projects to make sure all workers belong to the union and are paid union scale.

So begins the American labor movement with the formation of the first union local. Eventually local unions were grouped to form a national union.

1. John R. Commons and Eugene A. Gilmore, *Labor Conspiracy Cases 1806–1842*, Vol. III of *A Documentary History of American Industrial Society* (Cleveland, Ohio: The Arthur H. Clark Company, 1910), p. 31.

The Lessons from History Approach

Today's collective bargaining system evolved through trial and error. Labor and management used what worked to achieve their goals and discarded what did not work. Episodes in early labor history can be viewed as lessons learned by unions as they struggled to survive in a hostile environment. Some of the lessons remain true today. Others were learned and then discarded as the situation changed. And some were learned too well, were followed too rigidly, and were discarded only after union inflexibility exacted a considerable cost.

Lesson 1: Union Organization and Success Depend on the Business Cycle. The life of the first national union, the National Trades Union, illustrates the effect of the business cycle on trade unionism and collective bargaining in its first century. The 1820s were characterized by slow growth. Local unions were formed in the midst of this cyclical upswing. The first women's trade union was formed by tailoresses in New York City in 1825. Locals formed the first city-wide organization in the Mechanics Union of Trade Associations in 1827. This body was largely dedicated to political action and spawned workingmen's parties. Their goals included, among other things, equal citizenship, abolition both of debtors prisons and militia duty for the poor who could not buy out of it, the enactment of mechanics lien laws to protect the wages of workers employed by bankrupt firms, and free public education. Competition from the established political parties and internal dissension ended the unity of the workingmen's parties in the late 1820s.

The 1830s brought the wildcat era of rapid economic growth and a cyclical peak. Labor historian Selig Perlman describes the effect: ". . . the general business prosperity rendered demands for wages easily attainable. The outcome was a luxuriant growth of trade unionism."[2] Unions flourished. In 1830 the National Trades Union became the first national union. Composed of city-wide groups of locals, it eschewed political action and embraced the use of the strike to get higher wages and shorter hours. But the gains achieved were held only briefly.

As so often was to happen in the future, first the economic gains and then the unions themselves disappeared in recession and depression. The Panic of 1837 wiped the slate clean of unions. From 1837 through 1862, a prolonged depression with short recoveries befuddled the U.S. economy. Strikes in the midst of wholesale unemployment were folly. Workers could ill afford to join or support unions which could do nothing for them. The period was characterized by extensive social experimentation with ideas ranging from worker communes to co-ops.

---

2. Selig Perlman, *A History of Trade Unionism in the United States* (New York: The Macmillan Company, 1923), p. 19.

The episode illustrates lesson 1. Throughout much of the 1800s, the business cycle had a strong impact on union formation and ideology. Unions formed during economic recovery and used a mixture of political power and economic power as means to gain a better life. In prosperity unions relied almost exclusively on the strike to gain economic betterment on the job. When the economy faltered, so did the economic power base and union gains. In depression, unions died and workers turned back to politics or schemes for the revision of society. While the cycle is not hard and fast historically, it is true as a generalization. Today the business cycle still has a strong influence on collective bargaining, but it does not have as dramatic an impact as in the early 1800s.

Lesson 2: Why There Is No Labor Party in the United States. Why does the United States have no American Labor Party? Virtually every industrialized economy and a good many developing economies have a labor party. The United States is unique in not having one. The experience of the National Labor Union is one example of a philosophical confrontation between those who sought betterment on the job via economic power and those who emphasized political power.

The National Labor Union (NLU) was the first labor federation. It was comprised of the national unions and city trade assemblies which emerged in the 1860s and an odd lot group of reformist organizations including anarchists, socialists, and women suffragists. At their first convention in 1866, they embraced the economic philosophy of Ira Steward on the 8-hour day. Steward's homespun economic idea was that wages were set by the minimum standard of living a worker would accept. If the 10-hour day were cut to 8, the worker would have more leisure, would want more goods, and force the employer to pay higher wages. The employer would have to pay more because no worker would work for a lower standard of living (8 hours at the old rate of pay). "Whether you work by the piece or work by the day, decreasing the hours increases the pay,"[3] went the jingle. In 1869 the NLU admitted the first black unions and advocated the organization of black unions.

Long enamored of forming an independent political party, the reformist groups engineered a split of the NLU into industrial and political wings at the 1870 convention. They wanted to establish a new political party independent of the Democrats and Republicans. The trade unions and the black unions parted company with the NLU at this point. The black unions formed their own National Colored Labor Union and allied with the Republican Party.[4] The trade unions, concerned about the organization of their "cheap labor" competitors (blacks and women), split from the NLU to advocate "pure and simple unionism." That is, they intended to win higher wages and the 8-hour day on the job through the threat of the strike.

---

3. Foster Rhea Dulles, *Labor in America* (New York: Thomas Y. Crowell Company, 1949), p. 107.

4. Joseph G. Rayback, *A History of American Labor* (New York: The Free Press, 1959), p. 123.

Undeterred by the trade union disaffection, in 1872 the NLU launched the National Labor and Reform Party on a "Greenback" platform. The Greenbackers wanted civil war–issued U.S. dollars (greenbacks) to be converted on demand into government bonds at 3 percent interest. The effect would be to make them a source of cheap capital. Working persons could start their own businesses using capital borrowed at 3 percent rather than at the bank-controlled lending rate of 10-12 percent. The issue died in 1878 when greenbacks became convertible to gold. The NLU died long before then. They nominated Judge David Davis for President in 1872. Judge Davis (no friend of labor, said the unions) accepted the nomination until the Democrats nominated the popular Horace Greeley.[5] In the face of such stiff competition, Davis withdrew, leaving the NLU in disarray. The unions did not back the labor party.

The NLU is only one example of many situations throughout history where unions could have formed their own political party and did not. Why not? Some argue lack of class consciousness. In the early days of unionism (cordwainer era) workers sought property owner status and upward mobility. They did not see themselves as a permanent working class. The frontier, the West, was there for those who felt trapped into the working class. Later in the century, the great influx of immigrants made for such a heterogeneous work force that a class conscious party was impossible in the face of racial and ethnic diversity.

Others argue that the existing political parties either outfoxed or preempted the workingmen's parties. Issues which gained the widespread popular support of workers were taken over by the existing parties. A new party was not necessary. Still another thesis is that the propertied interests in the United States allied with the courts and frustrated the political power of unions. The economic power of labor was not so easily checked, and unions used what worked (collective bargaining) to gain betterment. By the time the labor movement had gained stability, the leadership was so distrustful of politics that it stayed with economic action. For whatever reasons, the political philosophy of American unions came to be fairly well established by the end of the 1800s. Unions would use economic action on the job and support the existing parties rather than form a labor party.

Lesson 3: Craft Unions Are Viable; Mixed Unions Are Not. The Panic of 1873 cut the number of national unions from 30 to 9 by 1877. With the return of prosperity in the late 1870s came the growth of two union federations based on two very different philosophies. The first, led by Terence V. Powderly, was named the Noble and Holy Order of the Knights of Labor. The Knights' executive board held that, "Strikes at best afford only temporary relief, and members should be educated to depend upon thorough education, coopera-

---

5. Perlman, *History of Unionism*, p. 57.

tion and political action, and through these the abolition of the wage system."[6] Employees were to circumvent the wage system by escaping into self-employment co-ops. "Cooperation of the Order, by the Order and for the Order,"[7] was their creed. The Knights organized everyone who would join regardless of skill level. Heavily populated by unskilled workers, some semi-skilled, and with a smattering of skilled employees, the Knights organized by geographic area and not by occupation. They had local assemblies, district assemblies, and a governing General Assembly—a structure of "One Big Union."[8] The rallying cry became, "An injury to one is an injury to all!"[9]

As a result of winning a series of rail strikes against the unpopular rail tycoon, Jay Gould, the Knights' membership ballooned almost overnight. Unskilled and semiskilled workers flocked to join the champion of the work-ingman. In 1886 the Knights had 700,000 members, seven times their mem-bership of 1885.[10]

At the same time, the skilled trades were forming another federation. They rallied about the Cigar Makers' International Union led by Adolph Strasser and Samuel Gompers. Strasser and Gompers were at one time social-ists, but they renounced socialist philosophy, believing it to be ineffective. Instead they undertook to develop strong unions to make gains at the work place through collective bargaining. To implement their new philosophy, they restructured the Cigar Makers to give the national complete authority over its locals. They built up a financially strong national from increased membership dues and set up a far-reaching benefit plan for the membership. Finally, they instilled a wage consciousness to union activities. The goal was betterment on the job, not reformation of society. In the immortal words of Samuel Gompers, workers wanted "more, more . . . now." In 1881, the trade unions formed the Federation of Organized Trades and Labor Unions of the United States and Canada. It was a weak organization initially formed more for political reasons (universal education, prohibition of child labor) than for economic reasons. It soon grew in importance as a result of the skilled trades competition with the Knights.

The occupations of some of the skilled trades were being eroded by the industrial revolution. Machines run by unskilled and semiskilled workers began to replace skilled workers. The Knights at the same time asked the embattled skilled trades to join forces to uplift the lesser skilled. The response was "no." Adding fuel to the fire was the rather promiscuous way in which the Knights chartered local assemblies—they chartered anyone regardless of skill or ideology. The trades believed in strict jurisdiction by craft. The battle lines were drawn and the major skirmish involved the Cigar Makers. In New York,

6. Dulles, *Labor in America*, p. 132.
7. Perlman, *History of Unionism*, p. 71.
8. Ibid., p. 114.
9. Dulles, *Labor in America*, p. 127.
10. Ibid., p. 141.

Gompers and Strasser had expelled a group of socialists from their union. The socialists went to the Knights and obtained a charter setting up a competing union called the Progressive Union. As an interesting aside, this is the origin of the union label. Gompers' Cigar Makers used a blue label, and the socialist Progressive Union a white one. The Progressives lost the fight.

Out of the competition, however, emerged the first stable federation. On December 8, 1886, the American Federation of Labor (AFL) was founded in Columbus, Ohio with Samuel Gompers at the helm. In 1886, they had 250,000 members to the Knights' 700,000. But the Knights quickly passed from view. Late in 1886 and in 1887, the Knights embarked on a series of strikes and either lost badly or ineptly capitulated just when victory was at hand.

Public opinion turned against the Knights as a result of the Haymarket Square Riot which was associated with a strike for the 8-hour day at the Chicago McCormick Reaper works. At a meeting called by anarchists to protest strike violence, a bomb was thrown which killed six policemen and wounded 200 other people. Recoiling from the hostile public reaction to the Riot and because the Knights provided few material benefits, what few skilled workers the Knights had fled to the ranks of the AFL. As the Knights faded, the AFL remained based upon the lessons learned from history. It was dedicated to the idea of *business unionism:* the exercise of economic power to gain better wages and working conditions on the job. The nationals were to retain power over their internal affairs. (This *principle of national sovereignty* exists in the AFL-CIO today.) Each national had an inviolable jurisdiction over one trade of skilled workers. There was to be no organization of unskilled and semiskilled workers. Skilled workers who organized themselves could apply to the AFL for a charter from the national union with that jurisdiction. There was to be no labor political party. The order of the day was to "reward your friends and punish your enemies" regardless of their party affiliation.

Lesson 4: Industrial Unionism Is Not Viable in the Late 1800s. A local union of unskilled, semiskilled, and skilled workers, all working at a plant, has come to be called an industrial union. In 1892 the Homestead Steel Plant of the Carnegie brothers had a collective bargaining agreement with the Amalgamated Association of Iron and Steel Workers. The Amalgamated was the largest and strongest union at that time. Composed of relatively skilled workers, had it been successful, the wave of industrial union organization might have occurred in the 1890s rather than the 1930s.

Henry Clay Frick rose in Horatio Alger fashion to head the management of the Homestead plant. When the collective bargaining agreement came up for renegotiation, Frick made two demands: that the workers take a wage cut, and that the union disband. Not too surprisingly, a strike ensued. Frick hired Pinkerton detectives to break the strike and attempted to land them from barges at the company docks. Having gotten wind of the Pinkerton plan, workers massed on the dock. Shooting broke out and a number of Pinkertons and strikers died in the daylong, pitched battle that followed. The strike spread to the nearby Pittsburgh mills. At Frick's request, the governor sent in 8000 militia to restore order. The mills opened with scab labor and the strike was broken. To make matters worse, a Russian-born anarchist, with no relationship to the striking workers, but who was infuriated by the use of Pinkertons, attacked Frick in his office with gun and knife. Frick survived the attack. As a result of the violence, public opinion tended to shift away from support of the labor movement. "The power of the union was henceforth broken and the labor movement learned the lesson that even its strongest organization was unable to withstand an onslaught by the modern corporation."[11] Industrial unionism would have to wait until unions gained a power base more equal to that of industry employers.

Lesson 5: The Government and the Courts Side with the Employer. A rail strike in 1894 proved costly to the entire labor movement. Eugene V. Debs had organized the American Railway Union in an industrial union model. Pullman Palace Car Company had cut wages by 25-40 percent during the slump of 1893 but did not cut the rent in its company houses. The Railway Union struck and made a plea for arbitration of their dispute. Pullman refused. The Railway Union then refused to handle Pullman cars on any rail lines. This brought the rail employers association, the General Managers Association (GMA), into the fray. Soon most of the rail traffic in the midwest was dead on its tracks. The GMA imported strikebreakers and had them attach U.S. mail cars to the Pullman cars. Cutting out the Pullman cars would later be construed to be interfering with the U.S. mail.

The GMA hired several thousand special deputies, and soon fighting broke out between the striking workers and the deputies. Fearing widespread violence, President Cleveland sent in troops over Illinois Governor Altgeld's protests. The strike spread amidst scattered violence. The GMA succeeded in getting a blanket injunction in federal district court prohibiting any person from interfering with the delivery of the mail or causing any other person to do so. Debs offered to call off the strike if the strikers would be reinstated, but the companies refused. Debs continued the stoppage in the face of the injunction. He was arrested and, after his appeal to the Supreme Court to end the use of the injunction was turned down, spent 6 months in jail. Selig Perlman writes,

> The labor organizations were taught two important lessons. First, that nothing can be gained through revolutionary striking, for the government was sufficiently strong to cope with it; and second, that the employers had obtained a formidable ally in the courts.[12]

Lesson 6: Revolutionary Unionism Does Not Fit the U.S. Model. "We must inscribe on our banner the revolutionary watchword, 'abolition of the

---

11. Perlman, *History of Unionism*, p. 135.
12. Ibid., p. 139.

wage system.' It is the historic mission of the working class to do away with capitalism."[13] That was the manifesto of the last significant revolutionary union, the Industrial Workers of the World (IWW or Wobblies). Formed in 1905, the core of the Wobblies was the aggressive Western Federation of Miners, joined by two socialist parties and a handful of unions. Their ideas provided an alternative to the conservative AFL. They aggressively organized the mining and lumber companies in the West, the Pacific Coast canneries, the steel industry in the Midwest, and textiles in the East into "One Big Union." Their organizers and leaders were rough and tumble, colorful people such as Big Bill Haywood and Mother Jones. Out of this era comes music and verse by and about Wobblies, for example, the songs "Hallelujah, I'm a Bum," and "Joe Hill." Wobblies organized where others dared not and for their efforts were horse whipped, tarred and feathered, lynched, and jailed at the hands of employers and anti-union citizenry in the West.

The IWW reached the height of its power in 1912 after a lengthy and well-disciplined strike by 20,000 textile workers against the American Woolen Mills in Lawrence, Massachusetts. National public opinion supported the strikers after two incidents were widely reported. In the first, journalists exposed an employer hoax to pin the planting of dynamite on the Wobblies. The second incident occurred when, short on food, the organizers attempted to move women and children by train to union homes in other cities. Police attacked and clubbed the departing women and children. In the face of IWW solidarity and the restraint shown by the strikers, the mills eventually acceded to all union demands.

The downfall of the Wobblies came during World War I. They took the position that the war was being fought "by" the workers, not "for" them, and that government was no more than a tool of the employers. The IWW engaged in several strikes for better working conditions. These hampered the war effort, and IWW leaders were convicted for espionage and sedition. The Wobblies were broken, and their supporters were siphoned off by the formation of the Communist Party in 1919. The last significant revolutionary union movement was dead.

Lesson 7: Propaganda and Scare Tactics Can Be Powerful Anti-union Weapons. From 1910 to 1917 unions expanded their membership. During World War I, in exchange for no-strike pledges, the government supported collective bargaining. Unions enjoyed the right to organize and bargain and made gains in achieving the 8-hour day and equal pay for women. Union membership grew significantly.

Post-World War I was a different story. By 1929 union membership had fallen to the old 1917 levels. The Bolshevik Revolution in Russia caused public hysteria in the United States. Red baiting was widely used as strikers and

---

13. Dulles, *Labor in America*, p. 209.

union leaders were denounced as Communists. Employers were able to use the red scare against unions.

The Steel Strike of 1919 illustrated the effectiveness of coupling anti-union with anti-Communist activities. William Z. Foster, who did have left-wing views and who was later to be a prominent communist leader, started organizing the steel industry in 1918. Steel workers averaged 69 hours working 6 days a week. Foster organized 100,000 steel workers easily and demanded that United States Steel Corporation bargain with the steel workers union for shorter hours and higher pay. United States Steel refused and soon a strike of 350,000 workers in nine states ensued. United States Steel used thousands of strike breakers, employed labor spies, smashed picket lines with the aid of local government authorities, and generally disregarded civil liberties. At the same time, a propaganda campaign characterized the steel strike as a Bolshevist plot against America. Upon investigation by a group of Protestant churches, the charges were found to have no merit. Nonetheless, Foster was unable to overcome the power and propaganda of United States Steel and was forced to call off the strike. Steel would remain nonunion for another decade. Strikes were broken in similar fashion in coal, meatpacking, and the railroads.

Lesson 8: Economic Prosperity Does Not Necessarily Mean Union Growth. The steel strike ushered in the "roaring twenties." From 1922 to 1929 the economy grew and prospered. But lesson 1 about the tandem relationship between economic growth and union membership did not hold true. "At the peak of 1929 prosperity, total union membership was 3,443,000—less than it had been in any year since 1917."[14] Part of the reason for the slide in membership was the pervasive feeling that poverty would vanish as all people shared in the fruits of a booming economy. The promise of job security and increased pay offered by unions rang hollow to workers who could have both without the pain and strife of organizing and collective bargaining.

At the same time employers mounted a carrot and stick campaign against unions. The stick was in the form of hundreds of anti-union groups which used the American Plan against unions. Union leaders were depicted as gangsters, extortionists, and Communists. The use of *yellow dog contracts* (which forbid union membership as a condition of hiring and employment), spies, black lists, discrimination, and private armies of company guards was commonplace. The carrot consisted of the scientific management ideas of Frederick W. Taylor. Management began widespread use of time and motion studies and piece rates. They formed their own employee groups to handle grievances. The *company union* (a union formed and dominated by the employer) became widely used. The term coined to identify the era's employer paternalism was welfare capitalism. When the economy crashed in 1929, so did welfare capitalism.

---

14. Ibid., p. 245.

A Change of Format

The first part of the sojourn through history was set in a lessons format. We depart from that format now. The modern labor history will proceed with a focus on significant events and legacies. The 1930s mark the transition from a legal environment hostile to union organizing and collective bargaining to one supportive of the legitimacy of both. Chapter 12 details the legal evolution. Here we concentrate on the institutional results of the changed legal climate.

Philosophical and Legislative Changes

In 1933, a quarter of the labor force was unemployed. The Depression was at its worst. As was noted in Chapter 9, society came to realize that even "rugged individuals" who wanted to work could not do so. Unemployment was no longer the province of the lazy who didn't want to work. The economic system could fail. Unemployment hit people who earnestly desired to work but couldn't find a job.

The role of government expanded to help businesses and workers help themselves. Union organization and collective bargaining were sanctioned by the government as a way of freeing workers from the vicissitudes of the market. Unions were valued as an expression of democracy and as a counter-vailing power to business in the division of income.

Unions were freed from the yellow dog contract and the labor injunction by the Norris La Guardia Act of 1932. Section 7 of the National Industrial Recovery Act (NIRA) of 1933 recognized the rights of employees to organize and bargain and protected those rights with a union recognition procedure, a set of prohibited employer unfair labor practices, a procedure for unfair labor practice prosecution, and a board to enforce the provisions. The Supreme Court declared the NIRA unconstitutional in 1935. Later that year, Congress passed the National Labor Relations Act (NLRA or Wagner Act) which embodied the NIRA provisions in a more workable form and established the National Labor Relations Board (NLRB) to oversee them. The Social Security Act was enacted in 1935 to provide unemployment insurance, old-age insurance, and assistance to the needy. In 1938, The Fair Labor Standards Act set the minimum wage at 25 cents per hour and required overtime for hours in excess of 44 per week.

Employers assumed that the same fate of unconstitutionality awaited the Wagner Act as had attended the NIRA before it. They ignored the NLRA and counterattacked with the "Mohawk Valley Formula" for union busting.

> This formula blueprinted a systematic campaign to denounce all union organizers as dangerous agitators, align the community in support of employers in the name of law and order, intimidate strikers by mobilizing the local public to break up meetings, instigate "back to work" movements by secretly organizing "loyal employees" and set up vigilante committees for protection in getting a struck plant again in operation.[15]

---

15. Ibid., p. 278.

The La Follette Civil Liberties Committee detailed industry spending of $9,440,000 between 1933 and 1936 on spies, strikebreakers, and munitions including machine guns, shotguns, revolvers, and gas guns.

The Supreme Court declared the NLRA to be constitutional in 1937. Organizing and collective bargaining were statutorily protected. A new era in U.S. labor-management relations had begun, but unions were not of one mind as to the significance of the change. The AFL had learned the lessons of history too well.

The CIO: Industrial Unionism

With the death of Samuel Gompers in 1924, the AFL leadership passed to another conservative unionist, William Green. The lessons of survival in a hostile environment remained: organize sparingly and on a skilled craft union basis; what the government gives, the government can take away; reward your friends and punish your enemies politically.

Within the AFL other leaders began to take advantage of the changed environment to organize industrial unions of unskilled and semiskilled workers in coal, textiles, steel, autos, and rubber. Chief among the new breed of unionists was coal miner John L. Lewis of the United Mine Workers of America (UMWA). Locals organized on an industrial union basis would be given a temporary "federal" charter by the AFL until such time as the new union could be split up or assigned to the exclusive jurisdictions of the old line crafts.

The question of granting industrial charters split the AFL. In favor of protecting the craft jurisdictions were Green, William Hutchison (Carpenters), and Daniel Tobin (Teamsters). Lewis, Charles Howard (Typographers), Phillip Murray (Mine Workers), Sidney Hillman (Clothing Workers), and David Dubinsky (Ladies Garment Workers) favored industrial charters. The two camps were also split over whether or not to be more active politically, with the Green group in opposition to and the Lewis group in favor of aggressive political action. The personalities and ambitions involved also played a part in the conflict. As feelings ran high during one AFL convention debate, Lewis punched Hutchison.

In the end the AFL rejected industrial unionism. Lewis formed the Committee for Industrial Organization and proceeded with organizing anyway. The AFL suspended the industrial unions in 1936. By 1937 the Committee had grown to encompass 32 unions with a membership of 3,700,000 as compared with the AFL's 3,400,000 members. In 1937 the AFL expelled the industrial unions, and in 1938 John L. Lewis became the first president of the new Congress of Industrial Organizations (CIO). The United States now had two competing federations.

Organizing Industrial Unions

One by one, the formerly unorganizable industries were unionized. In 1937 United States Steel, the union-busting giant of 1919, was caught in a market position which prohibited a strike. The company recognized the Steel Workers and bargained. After a Mohawk Valley–style fight, Little Steel was ordered by the NLRB to bargain in 1941. Unions used a new weapon to unionize the auto industry, rubber, textiles, and glass. Workers in those industries as well as bakers, clerks, opticians, dressmakers, and electrical workers acted out the lyrics of "When the boss won't talk, don't take a walk, sit down! Sit down!" Before it was outlawed, the *sitdown strike* was a major organizing tactic. General Motors bargained after workers occupied GM plants for over 44 days.

Some AFL members wasted little time before following the CIO example. Soon industrial unions were significant additions to the Teamsters, the Meat-cutters, and the Machinists unions—all AFL affiliates. Dual or competing CIO and AFL unions spent considerable effort and resources *raiding* each other. A raid occurs when another union vies with an already recognized union for employee allegiance.

World War II

The Depression of the 1930s gave way to the war production boom of the 1940s. The war effort could not long tolerate strikes disruptive of war production. The classic demand-pull inflation of too many dollars chasing too few goods threatened economic system stability. Resources could not be used to produce war armaments and consumer goods. It was a classic "guns versus butter" trade-off. Bidding by producers for scarce resources and by consumers for the few consumer goods available could cause a spiraling inflation. At the same time, workers who had fought so hard to gain union recognition joined or were drafted from their jobs to fight for Uncle Sam. The solutions to the three problems of production, inflation, and dislocation gave rise to four current day aspects of collective bargaining: maintenance of membership, arbitration, fringe benefits, and wage controls.

Maintenance of Membership. The problem of dislocation caused a problem of *union security* for organized labor which in turn caused a production problem. Union workers joined the armed forces and were replaced at work by women, minorities, and others who had not been party to the organizing battles. Union leaders felt employers might take advantage of the situation to weaken or dispose of the unions. To combat this, union leaders pushed for strong union security clauses in the agreements. The strongest clause was the *closed shop* which required employees to belong to the union in order to be hired. The second most secure union was that protected by a *union shop* clause under which employees were required to join the union shortly after being hired and to retain union membership as a condition of continued employment.

The problem came to a head in the coal industry. John L. Lewis wanted the union shop to be part of the agreement covering those coal mines which were owned by steel companies *(captive coal mines)*. The coal operators refused and wanted the open shop which provided no security at all. Lewis struck coal. The dispute was given to the tripartite National Defense Mediation Board (NDMB) to solve. The NDMB had no enforcement power and had to rely on voluntary compliance with its decisions. Lewis called off the strike to await the NDMB judgement. It refused to mandate the union shop. Lewis resumed the strike. Eventually, a three-person arbitration board awarded the union shop.[16]

The authority of the NDMB had been flaunted. No longer viable, it was replaced by the War Labor Board (WLB). The War Labor Board was created after labor and management met in conference and agreed to forego strikes and lockouts in favor of peaceful settlement of disputes for the duration of the war. The WLB had teeth—its decisions were final and binding on the parties. The WLB solved the union security issue by awarding the *maintenance of membership shop.* This was a compromise between the open shop and union shop. New hires who were not already union members had to decide whether or not to join the union. If they chose to do so, then or at any later date, they had to maintain that union membership as a condition of continued employment. If they didn't join, they still kept their job. The clause is still in labor agreements today and is sometimes used as a halfway point on the way to a union shop.

Arbitration. The WLB also wrestled with the production problem of solving conflict between labor and management during the life of a collective bargaining agreement. The War Labor Board wrote no-strike–no-lockout provisions into the collective bargaining agreements. Unions gave up the right to strike for the life of the agreement. As a *quid pro quo,* the WLB mandated a tandem provision—a grievance procedure capped with final and binding arbitration. Conflicts would be solved not by resorting to economic force, but through a procedure which provided for discussion of problems between labor and management. If no settlement occurred as a result of the discussion, the dispute was to be submitted to a neutral, third party—the arbitrator. The arbitrator issued a final and binding decision. Today this system is the heart of most bargaining agreements. Much of this type of arbitration is still done by the same arbitrators who started with the WLB in World War II.

Wage-Price Controls and Fringe Benefits. The inflation problem caused the government to invoke wage-price controls and labor and management to dodge them with fringe benefits. Wage-price controls were introduced during World War I. What is significant about the World War II experience is the linkage that developed between wages and prices and the fact that unions and management were both motivated to beat the government-imposed controls. The War Labor Board was given the power to control wages. They fashioned

---

16. Phillip Taft, *Organized Labor in American History* (New York: Harper & Row, Publishers, 1964), pp. 542-3.

the Little Steel Formula which tied wage increases to price increases (as measured by the forerunner of today's Consumer Price Index). The current day counterpart to the Little Steel Formula is the *cost-of-living adjustment* (COLA), or *escalator clause*. For example, one Aluminum Workers agreement in effect now reads, "a cost-of-living adjustment equal to 1¢ per hour for each full .3 of a point change in the Consumer Price Index shall be included in the Standard Hourly Rates. . . ."

Unions and management were both motivated to achieve wage increases above the control limits because both had something to gain by doing so. By paying higher wages, employers could keep their scarce labor supply from being bid away by competing employers. Unions, obviously, were not opposed to receiving higher wages. Only the contractual wage rates were controlled, not the pay for individual workers. Therefore, one way to get around the controls was to move individual workers to the top of their rate of pay ranges. If a further increase was necessary, the jobs were then reclassified into the next higher pay range and workers then moved up the pay scale for that range. The same methods for circumventing the controls in World War II were used during the Nixon controls of the 1970s and will doubtless be employed during any future use of controls.

Fringe benefits were initially a government-sanctioned dodge of the controls. At one point a wage ceiling was set. But, prices continued to rise, and this touched off a wave of strikes. President Roosevelt was compelled to stop the price increases. The War Labor Board also reacted by allowing unions and management to make up for lost ground by agreeing to indirect wage increases in the form of fringe benefits.[17] Soon agreements were expanded to include vacations, paid holidays, travel and lunch allowances, bonus and incentive pay, and health and pension plans. A recent study found that fringes amounted to 23 percent of the total compensation per hour paid to unionized private, nonfarm workers. Governmentally mandated fringes (e.g., Social Security) were 6.5 percent of compensation, and voluntary (negotiated) fringes made up the other 16.5 percent.[18]

Taft-Hartley Curbs Union Power

Strikes during the war (several crippling ones in coal led by John L. Lewis, in particular) and in the early postwar years led to public discontent with unions. Time lost due to strikes during World War II was about 0.2 percent of annual working time. In 1946 that figure jumped to an all-time historic high of 1.45 percent.[19] In 1947 the Labor-Management Relations Act (LMRA or Taft-

---

17. Ibid., pp. 559-60.

18. Richard B. Freeman, "The Effect of Unionism on Fringe Benefits," *Industrial and Labor Relations Review,* Vol. 34, No. 4 (July, 1981). The figures are calculated from Table 1, p. 496.

19. The Bureau of Labor Statistics estimates for the "Percentage of Private Nonfarm Working Time Lost Due to Strikes" are as follows for the war years: 1941, 0.32%; 1942, 0.05%; 1943, 0.15%; 1944, 0.09%; 1945, 0.47%.

Hartley Act) became law over President Truman's veto. The act moved the locus of power back toward management. The closed shop was outlawed, and states were given the right to outlaw other forms of union security; a set of prohibited union unfair labor practices was added; provisions were made for handling strikes endangering national health or safety; the NLRB was expanded to five members and restructured; and the Federal Mediation and Conciliation Service (FMCS) was created to mediate industrial conflict.

The AFL-CIO

John L. Lewis pulled the UMWA out of the CIO in 1942 after he was succeeded by Phillip Murray as president. In 1947, in part as a result of the Taft-Hartley Act, Murray and Green attempted reconciliation of the AFL and CIO. The attempt ended with Murray claiming the AFL did not want unity and Green calling the CIO a Communist organization. It was not until 8 years later that they united.

Green and Murray died within a few months of one another. Leadership animosities died with them. Plumber George Meany at the helm of the AFL and autoworker Walter Reuther as president of the CIO both made commitments to a merger. The Republicans won in 1952, and labor feared further antilabor legislation. The tremendous waste of resources squandered in union raiding was brought home by the fact that in 1951-1952 in 1245 cases of raiding involving 350,000 employees, only 8000 changed affiliation.[20] The CIO had long been criticized for its Communist membership. Reuther purged them from CIO ranks. The AFL, attacked for corruption, also put its house in order to the satisfaction of the CIO. After a series of meetings the AFL and CIO merged in 1955 to form the American Federation of Labor–Congress of Industrial Organizations. As part of the merger they encouraged competing unions to merge. To represent AFL-CIO political interests, they formed the Committee on Political Education (COPE), not to be "tied to the coat-tail of any political party." (Sound familiar?)

Shortly after the merger, the AFL-CIO set about to investigate corruption internal to the federation. They hoped to preempt government interference by cleaning their own house. To help overcome the long-held principle of national union sovereignty, the AFL-CIO asked Congress to give the federation leverage with its national union members by passing legislation which would require the nationals to register and report on union welfare and pension plans.

The Labor-Management Reporting and Disclosure Act

Congress had ideas of its own. On January 1, 1956, Senator John L. McClellan opened hearings to investigate charges of labor racketeering. They

---

20. Rayback, *History of Labor*, p. 424.

investigated the International Brotherhood of the Teamsters, the Bakers Union, and the United Textile Workers. The AFL-CIO simultaneously investigated on its own and added to the list the Allied Industrial Workers, Distillery Workers, and Laundry Workers. Subsequently, the AFL-CIO expelled the Teamsters, Bakers, Laundry Workers, and Textile Workers.

Congress pressed on with an investigation into the widespread abuses by Dave Beck and Jimmy Hoffa in the Teamsters. The investigation spread to several other unions as well. When the inquiries were finished, Congress enacted the Welfare and Pension Plan Disclosure Act in 1958 and the Labor Management Reporting and Disclosure Act (LMRDA, or as it has come to be called, the Landrum-Griffin Act). The latter act added more union unfair labor practices and regulated internal union matters by placing safeguards on union funds and property, establishing a union member "Bill of Rights" and regulating union elections.

THE PRESENT

Modern labor history obviously did not stop in 1959. There have been a number of noteworthy events since then. Chief among these has been the growth of public sector unionism, the passage of laws on safety and equal employment opportunity, extension of the Taft-Hartley Act to cover health care employees, and the failure to pass laws impinging more directly on bargaining. The legal additions are covered in Chapter 12. Here we look at selected aspects of modern unionism: union structure and government, independent unions, and public sector union growth.

Union Structure and Government

The union officials with whom students are most likely to come into contact are the union stewards or business agents on the job. Certain union presidents (say the Auto Workers' Douglas Fraser or the Teamsters' Roy Lee Williams) and AFL-CIO President Lane Kirkland should be familiar through the news media. These are the bottom and top levels of union structure. Let's examine these starting with the local union.

Local Unions. The key to understanding what happens in union local activities is to remember Ross' observation that "unions are political institutions operating in an economic environment."[21] The membership is the power in the local union. They elect the local union president, secretary-treasurer, and stewards, take strike votes, and ratify negotiated collective bargaining

---

21. Arthur M. Ross, *Trade Union Wage Policy* (Berkeley, Calif.: University of California Press, 1948).

agreements. The day-to-day conduct of union activities is carried out by the president and stewards. They handle member grievances, probably help negotiate the contract, conduct a strike if one occurs, and do the myriad of organizational chores such as dues and fees collection.

Craft unions are usually organized to have jurisdiction over all union craft workers and their employers in a specific geographic area, whereas industrial union locals will have a plant or firm basis. The craft union business agent inspects union construction sites to police the contract in the same way the union steward and president do in the plant for industrial unions. Almost 98 percent of the 65,000 locals are chartered by a national union. The national exerts substantial control over the locals. The locals pay per capita dues to the national, follow national collective bargaining policy, often must get national approval to strike, and receive national aid in grievance handling, arbitration, and contract negotiation. The "international rep" is the service liaison between the national and the local.

National Unions. The national unions (there are 174) have come to play increasingly important roles in union structure. Their chief function is collective bargaining. As product markets have widened beyond the jurisdiction of any one local union, the nationals have assumed the role of coordinating local negotiations. The nationals set the collective bargaining goals, often do or oversee the actual local level negotiations, and help police the contract once signed. The nationals are also democratic. Each has a governing constitution. A convention of representatives from the locals (weighted by local size) usually elects the officers and votes on policy. The day-to-day national functions are carried out by the elected executive board and the officers. In addition to servicing the locals' needs, some review local union government and finances, handle appeals, and settle jurisdictional problems that may crop up between locals.

Federation. Nationals which are affiliated with the AFL-CIO account for 77 percent of total union membership. The AFL-CIO is a federation. That is, the national unions join the AFL-CIO but are voluntary associates and retain control over their own internal affairs (the historically established principle of national sovereignty). Whereas the primary function of the nationals is collective bargaining, the chief function of the AFL-CIO is political. Its external political functions include lobbying, public relations (Committee on Political Education, or COPE), developing public policy, and dealing with the international trade union movements. Internally, the AFL-CIO resolves national jurisdictional disputes, coordinates collective bargaining, organizes, engages in trade union education and training activities, and does background research in support of AFL-CIO and national union economic and political activities.

All of this is overseen by the AFL-CIO Executive Council consisting of the president, the secretary-treasurer, and 33 vice presidents (usually national union presidents). Control over AFL-CIO policy and officers is vested in the biennial convention. Lane Kirkland succeeded George Meany as AFL-CIO president in November of 1979. Meany presided over the AFL from 1952 to 1955, and the AFL-CIO from 1955 to 1979. Kirkland set as AFL-CIO goals the reaffiliation of the large independent unions and increased representation of women and minorities on the Executive Council. Table 11-1 shows national unions and associations by size and AFL-CIO affiliation.

Table 11-1   National Union and Association Membership and Affiliation (in thousands)

Organization	Members	Organization	Members
Unions:		Unions (continued):	
Teamsters (Ind.)	1924	Government (NAGE) (Ind.)	200
Automobile Workers	1499	Railway Clerks	200
Steelworkers	1286	Rubber	200
State, County	1020	Retail, Wholesale	198
Electrical (IBEW)	1012	Painters	190
Machinists	921	Oil, Chemical	180
Carpenters	769	Fire Fighters	176
Retail Clerks	736	Transportation Union	176
Service Employees	625	Iron Workers	175
Laborers	610	Bakery, Confectionery,	
Communications	508	Tobacco	167
Workers		Electrical (UE) (Ind.)	166
Clothing and Textile	501	Sheet Metal	159
Workers		Transit Union	154
Meat Cutters	500	Boilermakers	146
Teachers	500	Transport Workers	130
Operating Engineers	412	Printing and Graphic	120
Hotel	404	Maintenance of Way	119
Ladies' Garment	348	Woodworkers	118
Plumbers	337	Office	105
Musicians	330	Associations:	
Mine Workers (Ind.)	308	National Education	1696
Paperworkers	284	Association	
Government (AFGE)	266	Nurses Association	187
Electrical (IUE)	255	Classified School	150
Postal Workers	246	Employees	
Letter Carriers	227	Police	140
		California	105

Note: Based on reports to the Bureau. All unions not identified as (Ind.) are affiliated with the AFL-CIO.

Source: U.S. Department of Labor, Bureau of Labor Statistics, *Directory of National Unions and Employee Associations, 1979,* Table 9 (Washington: U.S. Government Printing Office, 1980), p. 62.

The Independent Unions

There are 65 unions and associations not affiliated with the AFL-CIO, called "independent" unions. Most were at one time affiliates but either withdrew or were expelled. The largest union in the United States is independent. The International Brotherhood of Teamsters with 1,924,000 members, is independent. The next largest independent, the United Mine Workers of America (UMWA), is 308,000 strong.

The Teamsters were expelled from the AFL-CIO in 1957 for corruption. Since their 1957 expulsion, the Teamsters Union and its leaders have been the subject of almost continuous government investigation. Numerous investigations have centered on Teamster pension fund loans to underworld figures or Mafia-controlled businesses. Nonetheless, the Teamsters remain the largest and one of the most powerful unions in the United States. They commit large amounts of money to organizing activities and are involved in roughly 30 percent of all union elections held by the NLRB in the United States.[22] Discussions continue, but the Teamsters are unlikely to reaffiliate with the AFL-CIO in the near future.

The UMWA withdrew from the CIO in 1942 as a result of a dispute between John L. Lewis and CIO President Phillip Murray over an effort to reunite the AFL and CIO and over the UMWA's failure to sign a no-strike pledge in support of the war effort. The UMWA joined the AFL in 1943 and disaffiliated in 1947 over a question of filing the Taft-Hartley–mandated non-Communist affidavit. The UMWA has been independent since then. Current Mine Worker's President Sam Church is on friendly terms with the AFL-CIO, but no plans for reaffiliation appear to exist.

Between 1967 and 1981 the United Auto Workers (UAW) was the second largest independent union. In 1967, Walter Reuther withdrew the UAW from the AFL-CIO after a long-standing dispute with George Meany and the Federation. Reuther charged Meany and the AFL-CIO with having joined the establishment: hawkish on Vietnam; lackadaisical in organizing the poor, minorities, and the South; uncaring of the plight of U.S. cities and unrealistic in dealing with Communist unions in other countries. The UAW joined with the Teamsters to form a tenuous Alliance for Labor Action. The alliance crumbled in 1972. On July 1, 1981, the UAW, led by President Douglas Fraser, reaffiliated with the AFL-CIO. Reasons for the reaffiliation included organized labor's desire to provide a united political front against Republican budget cuts and regulatory rollbacks, to strengthen union ties with the Democratic Party, and to gain support for legislation to aid the depressed auto industry.

---

22. National Labor Relations Board, *Forty-Fourth Annual Report* (Washington: U.S. Government Printing Office, 1979), p. 296.

Public Sector

The third wave of union organizing is still in progress. Following the craft union growth of the late 1800s and industrial union expansion in the 1930s and 1940s, public sector unionism mushroomed in the 1960s and 1970s. In 1956 there were 915,000 government employees in unions. Few actually bargained. Most of these were in the federal postal service which was 86 percent organized by 1961.[23] Other federal workers (16 percent unionized) and state and local employees were minimally organized. Then, in 1962 President Kennedy issued Executive Order 10988 which provided recognition and bargaining rights for federal employees. EO 10988 stimulated bargaining at all levels of government: federal, state, and local.

By 1980, 56 percent of all federal employees were covered by collective bargaining agreements. The American Federation of Government Employees (AFGE) represents 697,000 employees and is the largest federal labor organization. The National Federation of Federal Employees follows, representing 136,129 workers.[24]

The figures for state and local government unionization tell a similar story. By 1980, 43 states had a labor relations law. Four states required collective negotiations, 10 provided for meet and confer discussions, and 29 states mandated both. *Collective negotiations* laws make management and employee representatives legal equals in the bargaining process. Decisions are reached through bilateral negotiations which end with the signing of a mutually binding agreement. *Meet and confer laws* allow the employer to meet with employee representatives to discuss conditions of employment. If a meeting of the minds results, it is put into a *memorandum of understanding*. But, the employer is not required to meet and confer nor to abide by the memorandum of understanding. Only seven states have no labor relations policy.

Nearly 5 million employees are organized at the state and local level. Table 11-2 shows the extent of unionization by function for state and local government. Full-time state government employees are nearly 40 percent organized, and local government employees are over 50 percent unionized. Fire fighters show the highest level of union membership at 70 percent, followed by teachers at about 65 percent.

---

23. All figures unless otherwise noted are from the U.S. Department of Labor, Bureau of Labor Statistics, *Directory of National Unions and Associations, 1979* (Washington: U.S. Government Printing Office, 1980).

24. Bureau of National Affairs, Inc., *Government Employee Relations Report* (April 7, 1981), p. 11. The actual membership of federal government employee unions is considerably below the number of employees they represent because, by federal law, those who are represented need not actually join the union.

Table 11-2   Percent of Organized Full-Time Employees,
by Level and Function of Government

Function	State and Local Governments	State Governments	Local Governments
Total	47.9	38.7	51.4
For Selected Functions:			
Education	55.2	29.0	61.1
Teachers	64.5	36.1	67.5
Other	38.2	25.4	44.9
Highways	43.6	50.7	37.0
Public Welfare	40.8	40.3	41.3
Hospitals	39.5	48.4	29.6
Police Protection	52.6	50.3	52.9
Local Fire Protection	70.5	–	70.5
Sanitation Other than Sewerage	43.8	–	43.8
All Other Functions	36.7	37.8	36.1

– Represents zero.

Source: U.S. Departments of Commerce and Labor, *Labor-Management Relations in State and Local Governments: 1979* (Washington: U.S. Government Printing Office), 1980, Table C, p. 2.

THE FUTURE

In Chapter 10 we set out John Schmidman's theory of unionism in the postindustrial state. Here we add perspective to the theory by examining the current trends in union organizing. In addition, we examine the widespread opposition to union organizing which seeks to maintain a union-free operation.

Trends in Union Organizing and Structure

The rapid growth of public sector unionization has not been mirrored by the rest of the labor movement. While the number of union and association members has been generally increasing, the percentage of the nonagricultural labor force which is organized has steadily declined. In 1978 (the most current data) there were 21,741,000 union and association members. But since the AFL-CIO merger in 1955 when 34 percent of the nonagricultural labor force was organized, the extent of organization has fallen to a 1978 low of 27 percent, including the public sector expansion. Organizing has been outpaced by the growth of the labor force.

Structurally the growth of the economy has been among persons and occupations not highly organized historically. Less heavily unionized white-collar jobs have grown more than blue-collar occupations. Nonmanufacturing industry has grown relative to manufacturing industry. The labor force is proportionally more young, female, and minority. Industry is shifting from the Northeast and Midwest to the Sunbelt.

Trends in union and association organizing follow but do not keep abreast of the pattern of structural change. Between 1976 and 1978, 58 unions increased membership, 78 declined, and 33 experienced little change. The rapid expansion of public sector unionism was detailed in the last section. Between 1960 and 1978, for example, the American Federation of Teachers, AFGE, and AFSCME all tripled in size. In the service sector, health care organizing expanded rapidly after the 1974 amendments to Taft-Hartley extended coverage to that industry. A discussion of current trends in union membership and structure must treat the recent changes affecting women and white-collar workers, the geographic shift of industry, and the wave of union mergers.

Women. The extent of union representation for women is summarized in Table 11-3. Between 1976 and 1978, women as a proportion of total union membership posted the largest increase in over 25 years from 22 percent to 24 percent. Adding in association membership, the figure jumps to 28 percent (6.9 million women). Still, the proportion of the female labor force which is union is 15 percent as opposed to 28 percent for men. Traditionally women made up most of the membership of a few unions (e.g., International Ladies Garment Workers) and associations (National Education Association). Today, women are joining unions and associations across the board, and their union membership is more dispersed. Their access to upper-level governing board and officer status in the labor movement is increasing, but it has lagged behind their growth in union ranks. Women held 7 percent of the positions on union governing boards in comparison with their union membership figure of 24 percent. For associations, the figures were 35 percent on governing boards out of an association membership of 60 percent.

White Collar. Discussion of white-collar organization is clouded by the imprecise definition of white-collar versus blue-collar jobs. To make matters worse, unions and associations do not keep detailed occupational records. Despite this difficulty, it appears that the latest figures show no growth between 1976 and 1978 in white-collar organization. If anything, there has been some decline over these 2 years. One estimate sets white-collar members as a proportion of total membership at 19 percent and for combined union and association memberships at 26 percent in 1978.

The changing industrial composition of the economy and its impact on union membership is shown dramatically by the figures for the decade of 1968-1978 in Table 11-4. The distribution of organized labor has shifted significantly away from manufacturing (–9 percent) toward nonmanufacturing (+1 percent) and especially toward government (+7 percent).

Geographic Changes. There will be changes in the concentration of organized labor by state. Six states (New York, California, Pennsylvania, Illinois,

Table 11-3   Organized Workers by Sex

Sex of Organized Worker	As a Proportion of	%
Female	Union Membership	24
Female	Association Membership	60
Female	Union and Association Membership	28
Female[1]	United States Female Labor Force	15
Male[1]	United States Male Labor Force	28
Female	Union Officers	7
Female	Association Officers	35

[1]This is read as female (male) organized workers as a proportion of the U.S. female (male) labor force.

Source: U.S. Department of Labor, Bureau of Labor Statistics, *Directory of National Unions and Employee Associations, 1979* (Washington: U.S. Government Printing Office, 1980).

Table 11-4   Union and Association Membership by Industry
(in thousands, except percent)

Year	Industry					
	Manufacturing		Nonmanufacturing		Government	
1968	9218	42%	8,940	41%	3857	18%
1978	8119	33	10,164	42	6094	25
Change	−1099	−9	+1,224	+1	+2237	+7

Source: U.S. Department of Labor, Bureau of Labor Statistics, *Directory of National Unions and Employee Associations, 1979* (Washington: U.S. Government Printing Office, 1980).

Ohio, and Michigan) account for 52 percent of all union members in the United States. Those six plus New Jersey and Texas account for 46 percent of all association membership. With the exception of Texas, these are states heavily dependent on oil and/or are the locus of struggling industries. The significance of this geographic shift is not lost on trade unionists. Alan Kistler, AFL-CIO Director of Organization and Field Services, took note of a *Business Week* article which reported that New York, New Jersey, Pennsylvania, Maryland, and Delaware totaled a drop in manufacturing employment of nearly 14 percent between 1960 and 1975. The Great Lakes states, including Illinois, Ohio, and Michigan, grew only 3.2 percent. At the same time, manufacturing in the Southeast grew 43 percent, and in the Southwest 67 percent.

So long as the tremendous gap in wages persists between Southeast and Southwest, on one hand, and the Northeast and the Great Lakes, on the other (between 15 and 40 percent, depending on the area), the trend will continue.

The main reason for this earnings gap is the relative scarcity of collective bargaining in the "Sunbelt" and the predominance of "Right-to-Work" laws.[25]

To meet the challenge, unions are pooling their resources and coordinating their efforts. The Industrial Union Department of the AFL-CIO has located two centers for organizing in South Carolina and Texas. Two recent victories are touted to be at the vanguard of organizing the South. At Newport News Shipbuilding in Newport News, Virginia, it took the Steel Workers 3 years to organize a unit of 18,000 employees. In 1980 an agreement was negotiated by the Steel Workers with Newport News Shipbuilding. Secondly, after 15 years of legal battles before the NLRB and the courts, some of J. P. Stevens' textile plants were organized and a collective bargaining agreement negotiated in 1980. If these two examples are any indication of the ease of future union organization, unions have their work cut out for them in organizing the Sunbelt.

Mergers. The decade of the 1970s was one of union merger. Since the AFL-CIO merger in 1955, 57 mergers have occurred and over a third of those in the 1970s. AFL-CIO policy in 1955 advocated merger to end "conflicting and duplicating organizations and jurisdictions." The reasons for increased merger activity in the 1970s and why this will continue as a trend through the 1980s are largely economic. As noted earlier, between 1976 and 1978, 58 unions and associations grew in membership, while 78 experienced a decline and 33 others were stable. Some unions are locked into industries which are declining. As industry employment falls, so do union revenues and with that the diminished capability to service union locals. Reviewing the reasons for mergers in the 1970s, Charles Janus notes:

> Large industrial unions are attractive because through them, workers have a stronger voice with today's industrial giants. Their greater size generates the resources to: provide extensive training in the collective bargaining and contract administration process; offer better strike benefits; lobby more effectively for legislation; and maintain a sufficient staff to combat unfair labor practices. With the growing prevalence of conglomerate and corporate mergers, small unions that do not represent key occupational groups are frequently unable to negotiate as an equal. As many smaller unions have found, however, a successful merger with a larger union can reduce the risks created by outside influences, such as downturns in the business cycle, technological changes, declines in industrial sectors, financial strains, unemployment and regional shifts in industrial development.[26]

And the process is expected to continue through the 1980s. Merger discussions are occurring between the United Auto Workers (UAW) and the United

25. Alan Kistler, "Trends in Union Growth," *Proceedings of the 1977 Annual Spring Meeting* (Madison, Wisc.: Industrial Relations Research Association, 1977), p. 544.

26. Charles J. Janus, "Union Mergers in the 1970's: A Look at the Reasons and Results," *Monthly Labor Review* (October, 1978), pp. 14-15.

Rubber Workers, the UAW and the Machinists, The Newspaper Guild and the International Typographical Union, and the Allied Industrial Workers and the Molders and Allied Workers. Merger negotiations are also underway in a host of other unions and associations from electrical workers to university professors.

Union Avoidance

Another trend begun in the 1970s and expected to continue through the 1980s is the *union avoidance* or "union-free" movement among employers. The percentage of union elections won by unions and the win margins have been declining. Part of this is due to the fact that unions are trying to organize groups of employees who have been historically more difficult to organize: white-collar, female, Sunbelt workers. The few workers who remain nonunion in the heavily organized industries have withstood several organizing efforts and are not easily organized. But, unions face an additional impediment to organizing in the guise of union avoidance.

"Any management that gets a union deserves it—and they get the kind they deserve."[27] That is the first sentence of the book *Making Unions Unnecessary,* and it sums up the union avoidance philosophy. The goal of union avoidance is to preempt organizing by providing a management-employee relationship which enables employees to obtain their occupational needs without having to resort to unionization. Simplicity, uniformity, consistency, and communication in the work place are the hallmarks of the program. Firms avoid unions by paying prevailing wages and fringes or more; simplifying the number of pay grades to avoid confusion and provide uniformity; simplifying the job structure to promote flexibility and employee responsibility; implementing a grievance-handling open door policy; and developing a sense of pride and community at the work place.

Union avoidance programs are often prepared, presented, and may be implemented by management consultants who frequently have an industrial psychology background. Management consultants who are hired to aid management opposition of union-organizing campaigns are required by law to register under the Landrum-Griffin Act. Records indicate about 200 such consultants. Some consultants specialize in defeating union-organizing drives once underway or in *decertification elections* to eliminate existing union representation. Their advice extends to the ins and outs of the NLRB election process.

The process is manipulated to employer advantage by using the legal delays and challenges built into the system. During the delays, a programmed plan of information to persuade employees to vote against the union is im-

---

27. Charles L. Hughes, *Making Unions Unnecessary* (New York: Executive Enterprises, Inc., 1976), p. 1.

plemented. This includes posters, handbills, notices, and letters to employees. While most of the consultants advocate legal means for defeating union-organizing drives, some use the age-old illegal means of unfair labor practices. For example, between 1975 and 1979, the number of NLRB discriminatory discharge cases for union activities rose from 13, 426 to 17,220, and bad faith bargaining cases went from 5633 to 8754. The NLRB required employers to reinstate 7405 employees and pay $11.3 million in back pay in 1975. Those figures grew to 14,627 and $16.5 million in 1979.

Union avoidance when measured in terms of election outcomes appears to be successful. The proportion of elections won by unions has steadily declined from 55 percent in 1970 to 50 percent in 1975 to 45 percent in 1979. Decertification elections challenging union representation status increased from 516 in 1975 to 777 in 1979, and unions won fewer of them (27 percent to 25 percent).[28]

The union response to union avoidance has been predictable:

> Today's workers "face the law of the jungle and the professional strikebreakers just as surely as their grandfathers did. Today's labor relations consultants carry briefcases instead of brass knuckles and they leave no visible marks on their victims. But their job is the same—frustrate human hopes and nullify human rights."[29]

To counter union avoidance, the AFL-CIO backed the Labor Reform Act of 1977 which would have streamlined the recognition process, awarded workers discharged for union activities double back pay, and forced bad faith bargainers to pay the area-negotiated settlement retroactively to the time they stonewalled negotiations. The Act, to be discussed in depth in the next chapter, died in a congressional filibuster in 1978.

CONCLUDING REMARKS

The goals of the labor movement of the 1980s are not so different from those of the cordwainers in 1794. The means used by craft unions today are virtually the same as those of the cordwainers. Present day business union philosophy, political philosophy, and the principle of national sovereignty date to Samuel Gompers and the founding of the AFL in 1886. Fierce organizational battles, be they in the steel industry in 1937 or the textile mills in the 1980s, breed distrust and animosities that affect the labor-management relationship for many years afterward. The labor-management institutions of arbitration and fringe benefits, found in virtually all agreements today, were the problem solvers of World War II. Our occasional resort to wage-price

---

28. Compiled from the 1975 and 1979 *Annual Report of the National Labor Relations Board* (Washington: U.S. Government Printing Office, 1975, 1980).

29. Phillis Payne, "The Consultants Who Coach the Violators," *AFL-CIO Federationist* (September, 1977) p. 22, quoting AFL-CIO President George Meany.

controls is fraught with the same compliance problems as the end-runs devised by labor and management in 1943. Wage escalator clauses and maintenance of membership union security clauses in agreements today date to World War II. Unionization of the public sector and the health care industry mushroomed with favorable legislation as did industrial unionization after passage of the Wagner Act.

The conflict over union organizing will shift toward the unionization of white-collar occupations, women, and the Sunbelt. Union avoidance seems to have a historical parallel in the "scientific management" of Taylor in the 1920s. Yet while the means of conflict have become more sophisticated over time, the nature of the conflict of interests between labor and management is timeless.

CHAPTER SUMMARY

The unifying theme of the chapter has been to follow organized labor from its past to the present and on into the future. From John R. Commons' market theory of the formation of the cordwainers in 1794 we moved to the lessons unions learned from history. The impact of the business cycle on union formation and strike effectiveness, the absence of a labor party in the United States, the viability of unions of skilled workers, the role of the courts and government, the failure of revolutionary unionism, and the extensive use of raw physical and economic power mark early labor history. With protective legislation came industrial unions and the formation of the CIO. World War II left the institutions of arbitration, maintenance of membership, wage-price adjustments and fringe benefits. The formation of the AFL-CIO was in part a response to legislative threats posed by the Taft-Hartley and Landrum-Griffin Acts.

Union structure and government were pursued at three levels: local, national, and federation. One goal of the AFL-CIO is to return the independent unions to the federation fold. The UAW has done so. As did industrial unions following the Wagner Act, unions of federal, state, and local employees and of health care workers have mushroomed following permissive legal changes.

Organizing in the future will increasingly include women and minorities, white-collar workers, and the labor force concentrated in the rapidly growing Sunbelt states. Unions concentrated in the occupations and geographic areas of employment decline will merge to remain viable.

Employers are resisting union-organizing efforts with a campaign of union avoidance. In the most common technique of maintaining a union free environment, employers preempt the union by meeting employee needs with a program of high pay, uniformity, and effective communication. The record on unfair labor practices indicates employers have also resorted to the timeless tactics of discriminatory discharge and refusing to bargain.

KEY TERMS

market theory
business unionism
principle of national sovereignty

company union
sitdown strike
raiding

union security
closed shop
union shop
captive coal mines
maintenance of membership shop
quid pro quo
cost of living clause

escalator clause
fringe benefits
collective negotiations
meet and confer laws
memorandum of understanding
union avoidance
decertification election

REVIEW QUESTIONS

1. Explain the market theory of trade unionism. Do you think that competition in the product market continues to drive a wedge between employer and employee interests?

2. It is argued that government as a monopoly has no competition for sale of its product. And yet public employees have rushed to unionize as soon as the law would allow them to do so. Does the market theory apply here?

3. "Any organization whose policy is based on historical precedent has difficulty adapting to environmental changes." Do you think this applies to the AFL in the 1930s? How about to the AFL-CIO in the 1980s?

4. "Once labor gets a foot in the door on a contract item it goes as far as it can with it." What historical support is there for this statement?

5. With whom does the power reside at the various levels of union structure? What happens to the sphere of concern and influence progressing from local to national to federation?

6. Contrast the employer view of union avoidance with that of organized labor. Unions paint union avoidance as being immoral and management embraces it as if it were a divine right. Is union avoidance moral?

ADDITIONAL REFERENCES

Commons, John R., and Eugene A. Gilmore. *Labor Conspiracy Cases 1806-1842*, Vol. III of *A Documentary History of American Industrial Society*. Cleveland, Ohio: The Arthur H. Clark Company, 1910.

District 1199, National Union of Hospital and Health Care Employees, *Images of Labor*. New York: The Pilgrim Press, 1981.

Dulles, Foster R. *Labor in America*. New York: Thomas Y. Crowell Company, 1949.

Estey, Marten. *The Unions: Structure, Development, and Management*, 3d ed. New York: Harcourt, Brace, Jovanovich, 1981.

Rayback, Joseph G. *A History of American Labor*. New York: The Free Press, 1966.

Taft, Phillip. *Organized Labor in American History*. New York: Harper & Row, Publishers, 1964.

THE WORLD
OF WORK . . .

Famous Quotations

The history of organized labor, filled with its triumphs and its tragedies, is the source of many famous quotations. We include a few of them here. The references in parentheses are to sources cited in the Additional References section at the end of this chapter. Other references are footnoted as usual.

"It is better that the law be known and certain, than that it be right." (Commons and Gilmore, p. 59)

Thomas Lloyd, the court reporter who took shorthand notes of the first labor union court case in United States history *(Commonwealth v Pullis)*, put this on the cover page of the court transcript in 1806.

"What distinguishes the present from every other struggle in which the human race has been engaged is, that the present is, evidently, openly and acknowledgedly, a war of class . . . it is the ridden people of the earth who are struggling to throw from their backs the 'booted and spurred' riders whose legitimate title to starve as well as work them to death will no longer pass current; it is labour rising up against idleness, industry against money; justice against law and against privilege." (Dulles, p. 42.)

Mrs. Frances Wright, one of the first female unionists, framed this philosophy in support of the Workingmen's Party in 1892. Her outspoken views earned her one newspaper's characterization as "the great Red Harlot of Infidelity."

"I regard my work-people just as I regard my machinery. So long as they can do my work for what I choose to pay them, I keep them, getting out of them all I can."

This is a quotation attributed to a textile mill manager in Holyoke, Massachusetts, circa 1840. Holyoke is the site of the first union with female members.

"An injury to one is an injury to all."

This was the motto of the Knights of Labor.

"More, more, . . . now!"

This is probably the most often quoted slogan attributed to Samuel Gompers. It epitomizes his philosophy of business trade unionism. "Reward your friends and punish your enemies" was Gomper's political philosophy. The more complete quotation is:

"Stand faithfully by our friends and elect them. Oppose our enemies and defeat them; whether they be candidates for President, for Congress, or other offices; whether Executive, Legislative, or Judicial."[30]

George E. Baer, president of the Reading Railroad and leader of the anthracite coal mine operators, wrote to a news photographer during a strike by the United Mine Workers in 1902:

"The rights and interests of laboring men will be protected and cared for—not by the labor agitators, but by the Christian men to whom God in his infinite wisdom has given control of the property interests of this country." (Rayback, p. 211.)

Baer was also quoted as saying, "They don't suffer; they can't even speak English." (*Images of Labor*, p. 48.)

It is difficult to settle on one quotation from

---

30. Samuel Gompers Centennial Committee, American Federation of Labor, *Samuel Gompers, A Brief History* (New York: American Federation of Labor, 1950).

the Wobbly era in labor history. One which captures the emotional commitment and often heard today is:

"Don't waste time mourning—organize!"

These are last words of the Wobbly organizer Joe Hill just before he was executed by firing squad for a crime some say he never committed.[31]

"There is no right to strike against the public safety by anybody, anywhere, anytime." (Dulles, p. 322.)

Calvin Coolidge, at the time Governor of Massachusetts, telegramed Samuel Gompers the answer above when asked to intervene in a Boston police strike in 1919.

"What more sacred property right is there in the world today than the right of a man to his job? The property right involves the right to support his family, feed his children and keep starvation from his door." (Dulles, p. 304.)

Homer S. Martin, first President of the United Auto Workers, had these words in defense of the use of the sitdown strike at General Motors Fisher Body Plant in Flint, Michigan in 1937.

The labor movement is about that problem we face tomorrow morning. Damn right! But to make that the sole purpose of the labor movement is to miss the main target. I mean, "What good is a dollar an hour more in wages if your neighborhood is burning down? What good is another week's vacation if the lake you used to go to is polluted and you can't swim in it and the kids can't play in it? What good is another $100 pension if the world goes up in atomic smoke?" (*Images of Labor,* p. 22.)

Walter Reuther was president of the CIO when it merged with the AFL. He became first vice president of the AFL-CIO and continued as president of the United Auto Workers.

"We still have those who believe in the archaic traditions of the 1880's and 1890's; those who believe that America is built from the top down, that if you keep the great corporations fat and wealthy, enough will trickle down to keep those at the lower level of our economic structure happy and contented." (*Images of Labor,* p. 28.)

George Meany, head of the AFL, became president of the merged AFL-CIO.

---

31. Phillip S. Foner, *The Letters of Joe Hill* (New York: Oak Publications, 1965), p. 84.

Chapter 12

Labor Law: Its Logic and Application

> The grand inquest . . . do present that . . . (the defendants) . . . being artificers, workmen and journeymen in the art and occupation of a cordwainer, and not being content to work, and labour in that art and occupation, at the usual prices and rates . . . (they and others) . . . were used and accustomed to work and labour; but contriving, and intending unjustly and oppressively, to increase and augment the prices and rates usually paid . . . and unjustly to exact and procure great sums of money, for their work . . . did combine, conspire, confederate, and unlawfully agree together, that they . . . would not, nor should work . . . but at certain large prices and rates for which they insisted on being paid . . . more than the . . . prices and rates, which had been . . . paid . . . to the damage, injury, and prejudice, of the masters employing them . . . and of the citizens of the commonwealth generally, and to the great danger and prejudice of other . . . cordwainer(s), to the evil example of others, and against the peace and dignity of the Commonwealth of Pennsylvania.[1]

The year is 1806; the place is the Mayor's Court in Philadelphia. It is an historic moment. For the first time in U.S. history a union is in court. The charge is one of three in a jury trial of eight cordwainers (shoemakers) for:

1. Insisting on wages above those currently paid
2. Preventing other journeymen cordwainers from working at wages below the demanded wage rate (scabbing)
3. Forming a combination to gain higher wages

The verdict: guilty!

> Sec. 7. Employees shall have the right to self-organization, to form, join, or assist labor organizations, to bargain collectively through representatives of their own choosing, and to engage in other concerted activities for the

---

1. John R. Commons and Eugene A. Gilmore, *Labor Conspiracy Cases, 1806-1842*, Vol. 3 of *A Documentary History of the American Industrial Society*, 10 vols. (Cleveland, Ohio: The Arthur H. Clark Company, 1910), pp. 62-64.

purpose of collective bargaining or other mutual aid or protection, and shall also have the right to refrain from any or all of such activities. . . .[2]

The time is now. The passage quoted above defines the current individual rights of employees covered by the Wagner Act as amended by the Taft-Hartley Act.

There are many differences between the legal situation of the labor movement in 1806 and the present. For example, a key question in 1806 was whether English Common Law governed the situation. The Common Law evolved from the decisions of judges in England over hundreds of years. The jury agreed that combinations of workingmen were so covered. Today's law is statutory; that is, it is enacted legislatively by Congress and the President. The role of the courts now is to interpret and apply the legislation. Joining together to form a union to raise wages in 1806 was judged to be an illegal *criminal conspiracy.* For most employees today the decision to join a union is a right protected by law. Now a part of public and civil law, labor relations questions at first were settled under criminal law.

This transition is the subject of the first section of the chapter. The second part explains how the law works now and details the controversial question of its reform. The last section examines federal, state, and local laws.

THE EVOLUTION OF U.S. LABOR LAW

Labor law evolved from 1806 to 1932 through several stages. Unions were prosecuted as criminal conspiracies. Then an ends-means test for the legality of union activities was constructed in the historic *Commonwealth v Hunt* case. The third stage begins with the widespread use of the court injunction against unions. The injunction is coupled in the final stage with antitrust laws applied against unions.

Criminal Conspiracy (1806-1842)

The decision against the Philadelphia shoemakers in 1806 set the pattern for numerous decisions thereafter. Commons and Gilmore[3] document 17 cases through 1842 involving criminal conspiracy charges. In nine of these, one or more individuals were found guilty and the usual penalty was to pay a fine and court costs. After 1830, a verdict of guilty became increasingly difficult to obtain because working persons and not just property owners began to serve on juries. The arguments remained the same, however: Combinations of journeymen united to achieve higher wages through refusing to work with nonunion workers were engaging in illegal acts against the employer, nonmember journeymen, and society.

Chapter 11 showed that this sympathetic relationship between the courts and the employers hindered union growth but did not prevent it. The state of industry and the economy had a greater effect on the formation and dissolution of unions in this period than did legal oppression. From 1830 to 1842, verdicts

---

2. The Wagner Act as amended by the Taft-Hartley Act.
3. Commons and Gilmore, *Labor Conspiracy Cases, 1806-1842*, Vols. 2-4.

of "not guilty" were rendered in three of five cases. In the fifth case Boston shoemakers were judged guilty of conspiracy, but they appealed to the Massachusetts Supreme Court and won. The 1842 decision in *Commonwealth v Hunt* set the standards for court involvement in labor-management relations for four decades, just as the cordwainers case had established the pattern for the nearly 40 years before.

Commonwealth v Hunt (1842-1880)

Unlike earlier charges of criminal conspiracy, the complaint in *Commonwealth v Hunt* was brought by a journeyman bootmaker, not an employer. The bootmaker had been thrown out for *scabbing*. The jury verdict in the lower court was guilty. Defense attorney Rantool appealed to the Massachusetts Supreme Court. The decision by Chief Justice Shaw has come to be a classic for all students of labor law, although the true legal impact of the case is open to controversy. Shaw set the standard by which unions were to be judged concerning criminal conspiracy. Several quotations are interesting. He defined criminal conspiracy to be a combination to commit a crime.

> But yet it is clear, that it is not every combination to do unlawful acts, to the prejudice of another by concerted action, which is punishable as conspiracy. Nor can we perceive that the objects of this association, whatever they may have been, were to be obtained by criminal means.[4]

And so long as the workers did not break employment contracts, they were:

> Free to work for whom they please, or not to work, if they so prefer . . . we cannot perceive that it is criminal for men to agree together to exercise their own acknowledged rights in such a manner as best to subserve their own interests.[5]

The standard developed was an ends-means test. If the combination set out to accomplish illegal ends, it was criminal. If it used illegal means, it was likewise criminal.

Between 1842 and 1862, there were only three labor cases involving criminal conspiracy. But between 1863 and 1880 there were 18, and most were successful prosecutions. The members of one coal union in Pennsylvania were fined for just presenting their demands to their employer.[6] The 1880s marked the end of prosecution for criminal conspiracy, however. A new, more effective tool for dealing with labor disputes developed—the injunction.

---

4. Walter Nelles, *"Commonwealth vs. Hunt," Columbia Law Review*, 1932, p. 1148.
5. Ibid., p. 1150.
6. Edwin E. Witte, "Early American Labor Cases," *Yale Law Journal*, 1926, p. 830.

The Injunction (1880-1932)

After a 10-year period of refinement, the next 40 years of legal history center about the use of the court *injunction* in labor disputes. One of the first uses of the injunction occurred in 1884 in Boone County, Iowa, where coal miners were enjoined from striking. However, it was not until after 1895, when the Supreme Court declared its use constitutional in the Pullman strike, that the labor injunction came to be widely used by employers.

By the 1890s, the AFL had formed and under Samuel Gompers' tutelage, business unionism had become the stable form of labor organization in the United States. The foundation of its stability lay in the successful use of economic power. Union recognition and gains in living standards depended upon the threat or use of pickets and strikes. The 1880s and 1890s became a legal transition period for dealing with the labor-management conflict. The legal arena for employer maneuvers moved from criminal court to "equity court." Employers no longer argued that they were the victims of a criminal conspiracy as a result of union activity. They argued instead that court intervention was necessary to prevent unions from inflicting irreparable damage to their property. The latter argument proved to become much more effective against unions.

The two courts are very different. Criminal court, a trial court complete with jury, is usually slow to grant relief and has the power to fashion remedies only after harm has been inflicted. Equity court is preventive; it has swift decisions by a judge, not a jury; and its remedies are designed to prevent harm from occurring. From the employer's standpoint, equity courts are slow to investigate the full facts of the case, but fast to grant relief. The following scenario typical of the times illustrates the point. An employer, faced with an actual or threatened strike, goes to a "sympathetic" judge and swears that he is about to suffer irreparable damage. The judge, without hearing the union side, issues a temporary restraining order (TRO) which prohibits the picketing or strike activity under penalty of fine or imprisonment for "contempt of court." Contempt of court is also decided by the judge who issues the TRO. The purpose of the judge's TRO is to maintain the status quo until the full facts of the case can be heard. The effect, however, is to help the employer and harm the union by preempting the union's threat or use of economic power. At a later date in a second hearing, union and management counsel appear before the judge to add to the facts, but no witnesses appear. The judge changes the TRO to a temporary injunction. Finally, at a later date, another hearing is held at which witnesses appear and cross examination is allowed. The temporary injunction may be dissolved as a result of the hearing, or it may be made a permanent injunction. Time is usually on the side of the employer, however, and even if the injunction is dissolved after a full hearing on the merits of the case, the effect is to weaken the union power position.

The courts' liberal granting of these *ex parte injunctions* (issued without the charged party being present to defend against the charges) was a major handicap to the labor movement. Crucial time, energy, and money which would have been committed to picketing and strike activity had to be diverted to court battles before unsympathetic judges. State and federal courts issued 1845 injunctions against unions from the late 1880s through 1831.[7] Although there were numerous attempts to gain state and federal legislative relief from the injunction, none was to be had until 1932. Three pieces of federal legislation and several court cases complete the story of the injunction era of labor law.

The Sherman and Clayton Antitrust Acts (1890, 1914)

In 1890, the Sherman Antitrust Act was passed to curtail the exercise of monopoly power in American industry. Congress forbade contracts, combinations, and conspiracy in restraint of trade. Federal courts soon began to apply the new statute to unions as well as to business firms. They used the act as a government behest to levy fines and issue injunctions in labor disputes. Unions were found to be combinations in restraint of trade. The U.S. Supreme Court did not rule on the law's applicability to unions, however, until the *Danbury Hatters*[8] case in 1908. The decision was severely detrimental to unions. The Court ruled that the United Hatters of North America was a combination in restraint of trade. This opened the door for full prosecution of unions under the law. In addition to fines, imprisonment, and injunctions against violators, the Sherman Act provided for suits to recover triple the amount of damages to the injured party. Employers began to sue unions for triple damages.

Faced with enforcement of the Sherman Act by a hostile judiciary, Gompers moderated his strict business unionism philosophy and entered the political arena. Gompers and the AFL exercised their "reward your friends and punish your enemies" political philosophy largely in support of the Democratic Party. As a result, a President and Congress sympathetic to organized labor enacted the Clayton Act in 1914. On the basis of Section 6, Gompers declared the Clayton Act to be labor's Magna Charta, believing that unions would no longer be subject to Sherman Act prosecutions.

> That the labor of a human being is not a commodity or article of commerce. Nothing contained in the antitrust laws shall be construed to forbid the existence and operation of laborers organizations . . . or forbid or restrain individual members . . . from carrying out the legitimate objects thereof; nor shall such organizations, or members thereof be held or construed to be illegal combinations or conspiracies in restraint of trade, under antitrust laws.

Gompers' belief, inaccurate, was short-lived. Two significant court setbacks occurred, however, before the Supreme Court clarified the Clayton Act.

---

7. Edwin E. Witte, *The Government in Labor Disputes* (New York: McGraw-Hill Book Co., 1932), p. 234.

8. Loewe v Lawler, 208 U.S. 274 (1908).

In 1917, the Supreme Court legitimized the use of the injunction to enforce *yellow dog contracts* to prevent union organizing. Workers at the Hitchman Mine in West Virginia had agreed, as a condition of continued employment, not to join the United Mine Workers of America (UMWA). The UMWA attempted to organize the mine site and was enjoined from doing so. The Supreme Court in *Hitchman* found the yellow dog contract to be a voluntary exercise of worker freedom of contract, and UMWA attempts to get workers to breach that contract were held to be an enjoinable action.[9]

In 1914, the Supreme Court dropped the other shoe held over from the *Danbury Hatters* case.[10] The Court ruled that not only was the union as an organization liable for triple damages, but so were its officers and its members as individuals responsible for damage awards.

Were unions exempt from these Sherman Act prosecutions as a result of the Clayton Act Amendments? The Supreme Court decided the issue in *Duplex Printing Press Company v Deering*[11] in 1921. The answer was "no." The International Association of Machinists (IAM) had organized all manufacturers of printing presses except Duplex. To organize Duplex, the IAM persuaded transporters, truckers, and customers of the firm to cease doing business with it. The Court found these actions to be a conspiracy in restraint of trade, unlawful under the Sherman Act and Clayton Act, and enjoined the activity. In addition, rather than reserving the use of the antitrust injunction for government use, the decision gave "to private parties a right to relief by injunction in any court in the United States."[12] The widespread use of the ex parte injunction in labor disputes was to continue for the next 10 years.

LEGAL SUPPORT FOR COLLECTIVE BARGAINING

Organized labor's outrage over the decision in *Duplex Printing* was fanned by several other significant anti-union court decisions strengthening the use of injunctions during the 1920s. The conservative manipulation of the law by the Supreme Court was criticized by politicians, legal scholars, and in dissenting opinions by members of the Supreme Court itself.

The throes of the Great Depression wrought legal change. The laissez-faire social and economic philosophies embodied in the court decisions of the 1920s succumbed to the realities of unemployment and poverty in the 1930s. Unemployment in 1933 stood at 25 percent. A new economic and social philosophy came to be embodied in law and manifest in court decisions.

---

9. Hitchman Coal Company v Mitchell, 245 U.S. 229 (1917).
10. Lawler v Loewe, 235 U.S. 522 (1915).
11. Duplex Printing Press Company v Deering, 254 U.S. 443 (1921).
12. Ibid.

The Logic Behind U.S. Labor Law

The construction of our contemporary labor law system governing collective bargaining was about to begin. The pieces of legislation can best be viewed from the vantage point of a unifying theory. Wellington provides one such theory in *Labor and the Legal Process*.[13] There are four basic *tenets* or beliefs which underlie current labor law, and the thinking goes as follows. Work is dehumanizing and uncreative when employees do not have a say in the work place. Unions provide employees with a participative voice in industrial government which employers must take seriously. This leads to the first tenet: Industrial democracy is desirable, and it is attainable through unions so long as unions are democratic.

Go beyond the work place and consider democracy in society at large. The essence of democracy is diffusion of power among interest groups. Without viable opposing interest groups, a concentration of power could destroy democracy. Thus we have the second belief: Interest groups are necessary to societal democracy, and unions should be one of these groups.

Conflict between economic and social classes is an inevitable part of industrialization. This conflict can best be resolved through the process of negotiation in collective bargaining rather than through the exercise of raw physical and economic power in class warfare. The third idea is: The establishment and practice of collective bargaining will reduce industrial strife.

Society values *freedom of contract* very highly. A voluntary agreement between two private parties is preferable to one mandated by government as a third party. But freedom of contract is a farce unless both parties have relatively equal power to agree. Without equal power, one party is in a position to mandate the agreement terms to the other. Individual workers are relatively powerless when dealing with an employer. The labor market does not adequately check the power of the employer who acts more like a monopsonist (single buyer) than a competitor. This leads to the final tenet: Unions are an equal, countervailing power to the employer and provide the employee freedom of contract.

In summary, the tenets are:

1. Industrial democracy is desirable and requires democratic unions.
2. Societal democracy demands unions as a viable interest group.
3. Collective bargaining is necessary to reduce industrial strife.
4. True freedom of contract between employer and employee can only be achieved with unions as a countervailing power to management.

---

13. Harry H. Wellington, *Labor and the Legal Process* (New Haven, Conn.: Yale University Press, 1968).

The Railway Labor Act (1926)

Ground was broken for the new system of legislation when the Railway Labor Act was passed in 1926. The Railway Labor Act provided for the parties to select representatives of their own choosing to bargain collectively. The choice was to be free from coercion. The rationale for the new law lay in the belief that collective bargaining would reduce industrial strife on the railroads. In 1930, the question of constitutionality found its way to the Supreme Court in a case involving employer refusal to bargain with a union free from company domination. The Supreme Court ruled the act constitutional. Freedom from flagrant abuse of the federal labor injunction soon followed.

The Norris–La Guardia Anti-Injunction Act (1932)

An influential and damning study of the injunction was published in 1930 by Nathan Greene and Harvard law professor Felix Frankfurter. The study chronicled the abusive and inequitable use of injunctions in labor-management disputes. It provided a substantiated, forceful statement of the need for a change of philosophy on the use of the injunction.

> The restraining order and the preliminary injunction invoked in labor disputes reveal the most crucial points of legal maladjustment. Temporary injunctive relief without notice, or, if upon notice, relying upon dubious affidavits, serves the important function of staying defendants conduct regardless of the ultimate justification of such restraint. The preliminary proceedings, in other words, make the issue of final relief a practical nullity. . . . The injunction cannot preserve the so-called status quo; the situation does not remain in equilibrium awaiting judgment upon full knowledge. . . .
>
> Emphasis upon procedural safeguards in the use of the injunction must therefore rank first. Whatever differences there may be as to the particular stages of the procedure at which changes are to be made, . . . there should be no reasonable basis for opposing such correctives, once the unique elements that enter into labor litigation are fully recognized.[14]

In 1932 the Norris–La Guardia Anti-Injunction Act was passed. Section One declares that:

> No court of the United States . . . shall have jurisdiction to issue any restraining order or temporary or permanent injunction in a case involving or growing out of a labor dispute, . . . nor shall any restraining order or temporary or permanent injunction be issued contrary to the public policy declared in this Act.

In 15 sections, the act changed the role of the U.S. courts in labor-management disputes from one of employer ally to neutral. In brief, the act did so by

---

14. Felix Frankfurter and Nathan Greene, *The Labor Injunction* (New York: The Macmillan Company, 1930) (reprinted Gloucester, Mass.: Peter Smith, 1963), pp. 200-3.

defining "labor disputes" in very broad terms, by allowing the use of the injunction in very restricted circumstances and then only after a full and speedy hearing, and by freeing the rank and file from liability as individuals for the actions of their union. The act ended court jurisdiction of labor disputes charging criminal conspiracy, and it enumerated a lengthy list of injunction-free union activities: peaceful assembly, organizing, picketing, and striking. It also outlawed yellow dog contracts. The new era of labor relations law was under way.

But it was off to a bumpy start. To aid industrial recovery, Congress enacted the National Industrial Recovery Act (NIRA) of 1933. The NIRA was designed to alleviate some of the pressures of competition. Section 7 of the NIRA gave employees the right to organize and to collectively bargain without employer interference. This provision was to be administered by a National Labor Board. Although it lasted only 2 years (the Supreme Court declared it unconstitutional in 1935), the NIRA was an excellent test model whose glaring inadequacies were remedied with the enactment of the Wagner Act of 1935. The National Labor Relations Act of 1935 is the foundation of current labor law. Because current labor law is treated in depth later on in this chapter, we concentrate here on the trend of events from 1935 to the present and not on the specific content of the laws.

The Wagner Act (1935)

The National Labor Relations Act of 1935, usually referred to as the Wagner Act, very clearly established the societal commitment to the new labor law philosophy. The law established the Section 7 rights for employees that were quoted at the beginning of this chapter. It created a National Labor Relations Board (NLRB) with powers to protect those rights. Substituting procedure for the use of economic power, the act established an election process to handle questions of union representation. A series of employer activities were outlawed as *unfair labor practices*. Another board procedure was set up to prosecute employers who commit unfair practices. Major amendments to the labor law system occurred in 12-year cycles after the Wagner Act: the Taft-Hartley Act in 1947 and the Landrum-Griffin Act in 1959.

The Taft-Hartley Act (1947)

The Labor Management Relations Act, often called the Taft-Hartley Act, was passed just after World War II. Bipartisan support for Taft-Hartley passed the bill by a 4 to 1 margin in the House and 3 to 1 in the Senate. President Truman's veto was easily overridden. The bill moved the locus of power back toward employers to "equalize countervailing power" and enhanced the rights of employees to "encourage industrial democracy." It was dubbed the "slave labor act" by organized labor. Management called it an act to free workers from "labor dictators."

The Taft-Hartley amendments to the Wagner Act were significant. Employee rights under the Wagner Act to form, join, and assist unions were amended to give employees the right "to refrain" from such activities. A whole new Section 8(b) added six union unfair labor practices parallel to the employer ones. In response to several critical wartime strikes and a high postwar strike volume, Congress added a section to deal with *national emergency disputes.* (See Chapter 15 for the details and experience with this amendment.) The emergency disputes procedure calls for an 80-day "cooling off" period for strikes which endanger national health or safety.

Several changes were made governing union security. The closed shop was outlawed. Congress also added the controversial *Section 14(b)* which gives states the power to enact more restrictive legislation concerning union security than does federal law, which only prohibits the closed shop. These more prohibitive state laws are known as *right-to-work laws.* Labor and management have been engaged in continuous state and national legislative battles on 14(b) and right-to-work laws since 1947.

The Landrum-Griffin Act (1959)

Based on the idea that industrial democracy requires union democracy and armed with substantial evidence that union democracy had eroded in several major unions, Congress enacted the Labor-Management Reporting and Disclosure Act (LMRDA) or Landrum-Griffin Act amendments to the Wagner Act in 1959. The evidence of union corrupt practices came from hearings held by the Senate's McClellan Antiracketeering Committee. The act that evolved from the hearings dealt primarily with internal union affairs in the areas of democracy and financial responsibility. The first title contains a *bill of rights* for union members including equal rights, free speech and assembly, secret balloting on dues and fees changes, the right to sue the union, and the right to have a full and fair hearing in union internal discipline cases.

Unions are required to file with the Secretary of Labor public information on their internal regulations (constitution and by-laws), current officers, and dues. Because some national unions, notably the Teamsters, had made extensive use of the *trusteeship* to raid local treasuries and displace elected officer dissidents, the third title deals exclusively with trusteeships. When a national places a local in trusteeship, it suspends the local's usual political process and assumes control over its assets and internal affairs. The Landrum-Griffin Act severely restricts the conditions under which trusteeships can be imposed on locals (for corruption, undemocratic procedures) and prohibits the national from expropriating the votes and treasury of the local.

The act also mandates that elections must be held for national officers at least every 5 years by secret ballot or by delegates chosen by secret ballot. Local elections open to all members and conducted by secret ballot must be held at least every 3 years. The last title of interest here deals with conflicts of interest of union officers, their financial responsibilities, loans and fines, and embezzlement of union funds. It also places restrictions on the holding of union office by members of the Communist Party (these restrictions have since been over-turned) and convicted felons. Concern was expressed at the time Landrum-Griffin was passed that rather than promote union democracy, it would cause union anarchy. Experience has proven these fears to be incorrect. Further discussion of Landrum-Griffin in this chapter is confined to those areas which have had an impact on both labor and management.

Recent Legislation

Since 1959 there have been several laws passed which affect collective bargaining. These are mentioned briefly here in summary form to bring the record up to date.

Equal Employment Opportunity. The heart of Title VII of the Civil Rights Act of 1964 begins

> It shall be unlawful employment practice for an employer . . . to refuse to hire or to discharge any individual, or otherwise discriminate against any individual with respect to his compensation, terms, conditions or privileges of employment, because of such individual's race, color, religion, sex, or nation-al origin. . . .

Since 1964, a whole host of laws and Presidential executive orders have fol-lowed extending coverage to almost every aspect of the employment contract for most people in the United States. As might be expected, the impact on bargaining has been substantial. Almost no part of the bargaining agreement has been immune to challenges on the grounds of discrimination. The key problem areas are the provisions which govern hiring and mobility in the bargaining unit. Employment, apprentice selection, job bidding, promotion, seniority, wages, and layoffs have been hotly litigated provisions.

Because the grievance procedure and arbitration have been the traditional mechanism for resolving contractual conflict, these too have come under scrutiny. As a result, the final and binding power of arbitrators has been limited in discrimination cases as the courts have placed a heavier emphasis on the law and less on the contract as a protector of individual rights. Almost 20 years after passage of the Civil Rights Act, there is a continuing impact on the bargaining process.

OSHA. The Occupational Safety and Health Act (OSHA) was passed in 1970. OSHA is administered under the Department of Labor and sets stand-ards in the work place to provide a reasonably safe and healthful place of employment. Compliance officers conduct on-site inspections to enforce OSHA provisions. The impact on collective bargaining has been to influence contract provisions dealing with safety and the handling of safety grievances. Employers charge that unions are going outside the contract to involve OSHA

inspectors in situations which could better be handled internally by the grievance procedure. The trend, however, has been toward increased cooperation
in the safety area through the formation of joint union-management safety
committees. Firms with joint safety committees are relieved from regular
OSHA inspections.

ERISA. Extensive congressional hearings were held on private pension
plans. The investigation followed charges of "severe age and service requirements before eligibility, . . . inadequate funding, . . . termination of plans
without funds to assure pensions to qualified employees, and . . . diversion of
pension funds for private use by employer and union."[15] The Employee
Retirement Income Security Act of 1974 (ERISA) which resulted from the
inquiry set standards and mechanisms for pension funding and administration. The direct impact has obviously been on the pension provisions of
bargaining agreements. However, the increased costs associated with meeting
ERISA's pension provisions have caused trade-offs with other cost items in the
contract.

Health Care Amendments. Also in 1974, the Taft-Hartley Act coverage
was extended to health care institutions. In doing so, Congress ratified what
the Board had been doing through asserting jurisdiction over hospitals and
nursing homes. The extension of bargaining rights to health care took into
account the unique problems of work disruption in the industry. A party
seeking to modify a collective bargaining agreement must notify the other
party 90 days and the Federal Mediation and Conciliation Service 60 days prior
to contract expiration. A 10-day notice and mandatory mediation are required
before a work stoppage or picketing action is legal.

CURRENT PRIVATE SECTOR LAW

Hardly a day goes by without a news story concerning collective bargaining. Usually the news item is a story about a strike or contract settlement or
union organizing. In this section, we present the particulars of labor law which
the student can use to gain perspective on current issues in collective
bargaining.[16] Table 12-1 presents a brief summary of the key labor cases and
laws reviewed previously.

The system of laws carves out areas of jurisdiction. The Railway Labor Act
covers railroads and airlines; federal sector employees are covered under the
Civil Service Reform Act; state and local government employees may or may

---

15. "Pension Reform, the Long Hard Road to Enactment," *Monthly Labor Review*, Vol. 97, No. 11
(November, 1974), p. 3.

16. There are a number of good supplements which provide the details of labor law. These are
listed at the end of the chapter.

Table 12-1:   Key Labor Cases and Laws

Commonwealth v Pullis, 1806: Cordwainer case
Commonwealth v Hunt, 1842: Ends-means test
Sherman Antitrust Act, 1890: Enforced against unions
Clayton Act, 1914: Antitrust also enforced against unions
Norris–La Guardia Anti-Injunction Act, 1932: Neutralized court use of the injunction
National Labor Relations Act (Wagner Act), 1935: NLRB, representation procedure, unfair employer practices
Labor Management Relations Act (Taft-Hartley Act), 1947: Unfair union practices, emergency disputes procedure, Section 14(b)
Labor Management Reporting and Disclosure Act (Landrum-Griffin Act), 1959: Bill of rights for union members, union democracy
Civil Rights Act, 1964: Discrimination in employment
Occupational Safety and Health Act (OSHA), 1970: Safety and health on the job
Employee Retirement Income Security Act (ERISA), 1974: Pension reform
Civil Service Reform Act, 1979: Federal bargaining law patterned after private sector law

not be covered by state laws; some employees are not covered at all; and a very large proportion of private sector workers is covered by the amended Taft-Hartley Act (hereafter, the act). We focus on law for the latter group of employees. The other laws are very similar to the act. This is because the philosophy and procedures of the act have worked well. Rather than reinvent the wheel each time conditions called for a bargaining law, legislators modified the reasonably successful act to fit the new situation.

The National Labor Relations Board

Overseeing the whole system is the five-member National Labor Relations Board headquartered in Washington, D.C. Members, with Senate approval, are appointed by the President to 5-year terms.

> On its statutory assignment, the NLRB has two principle functions: (1) to determine and implement, through secret-ballot elections, the free democratic choice by employees as to whether they wish to be represented by a union in dealing with their employers and, if so, by which union, and (2) to present and remedy unlawful acts, called unfair labor practices, by either employers or unions or both.[17]

National labor policy is shaped by Board decisions and is affected by the composition of the Board. Only the most important cases rise through the NLRB hierarchy to the Board level. Three members constitute a quorum and,

---

17. National Labor Relations Board, *Forty-Fifth Annual Report of the National Labor Relations Board, FY 1980* (Washington: U.S. Government Printing Office, 1981), p. 4.

to handle the case load, most cases are decided by three reserving only the most significant cases for deliberation by all five.

In fiscal year 1980, 57,381 cases entered the NLRB system.[18] Obviously, the full Board could not deal effectively with this many cases. An extensive network of NLRB organization implements the act at the grass roots level where labor-management conflict occurs. The United States is divided up into 33 regions, each with a regional office and possibly one or more subregional or resident offices. Here is where the action begins.

There is a rule of thumb that the law substitutes procedure for the exercise of raw power in labor-management relations. The Board administers two procedures directly and plays a role in two others. These last two, the emergency disputes procedure and grievance procedure, will be discussed in later chapters. Of primary importance now are the unfair labor practices procedure and the representation procedure.

Unfair Labor Practices

The unfair labor practices procedure accounted for 77 percent of the 1980 NLRB caseload. The Board does not act like a law officer searching out criminal activity. Employers and unions who violate employee rights can do so unless someone complains, for until a charge is filed, the NLRB does not become involved. The charge which triggers an NLRB investigation process may be filed by an employee, an employer, or a union at an NLRB office. They allege that one or more of the following unfair labor practices has occurred. The number refers to the section of the act.

What They Are. Briefly paraphrased, it is an unfair labor practice for an employer to:

8(a)(1)   Interfere with employees in exercise of their Section 7 rights.
8(a)(2)   Dominate or control any labor organization (company union).
8(a)(3)   Discriminate against an employee on the basis of union membership (union security clauses are an exception).
8(a)(4)   Take reprisals against employees who file charges or testify in procedures under the act.
8(a)(5)   Refuse to bargain in good faith with a labor organization.
8(e)   Make an agreement with the union not to handle or use the goods of another employer (enter into a *hot cargo clause*).

Taft-Hartley and amendments to it have established a similar series of prohibited union activities. Unions commit unfair labor practices if they:

8(b)(1)   Restrain or coerce employees exercising Section 7 rights; or an employer in the selection of its negotiation representative.

---

18. Ibid., p. 1. All NLRB figures are from the *Annual Report*.

8(b)(2)	Force an employer to commit an 8(a)(3) violation, i.e., discriminate against an employee on the basis of union membership.
8(b)(3)	Refuse to bargain in good faith with an employer.
8(b)(4)	Engage in a *secondary boycott* to force employers to recognize or bargain with a labor organization.
8(b)(5)	Charge excessive or discriminatory union dues or fees.
8(b)(6)	Force an employer to pay for work not done (featherbedding).
8(b)(7)	Picket an employer to force that employer to recognize or bargain with one union when it has lost a representation election or when another union is already recognized.
8(e)	Enter into a hot cargo agreement with an employer.
8(g)	Strike or picket a health care institution without giving 10 days prior notice to the Federal Mediation and Conciliation Service.

The Complaint Procedure. Figure 12-1 illustrates the unfair labor practice procedure once a charge has been filed. Cases which go through the unfair

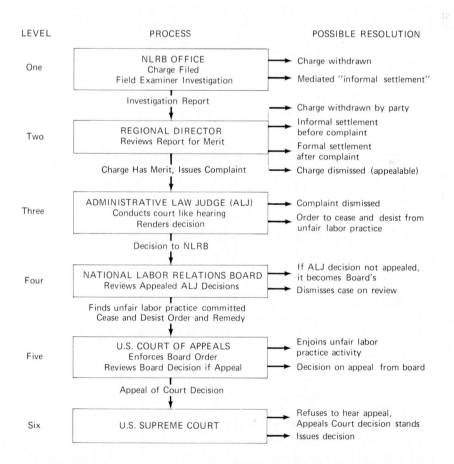

Figure 12-1   The NLRB Unfair Labor Practices Procedure

labor practice procedure are called *C* cases (for complaint). Cases which involve questions of union representation status are called *R* cases.

Important Points. It is as complicated as it looks. There are some basic points to be made besides the fact that it can be an involved process. First, the field examiner tries, if at all possible, to mediate an informal settlement between the complainant and the charged party. The system would break down if most of the thousands of *C* cases filed each year were not resolved at the lower steps. Second, if a complaint is issued by the regional director, the case is prosecuted for the charging party free of charge by attorneys from the General Counsel's Office of the NLRB. Third, the remedies for unfair labor practices that the Board has are called "make-whole" remedies and are not punitive damages or criminal prosecution. They are designed to restore the status quo ante, that is, return the parties to the situation that existed before the unfair practice occurred. For example, the Board can order that employers reinstate unfairly discharged employees with full back pay or that they bargain with the labor organization in good faith. The Board can issue a cease and desist order prohibiting the union or employer from continuing the unfair practice. Finally, the NLRB has no power to enforce its decisions. If the parties will not comply with its order, the NLRB must go to the U.S. Court of Appeals to get enforcement. Parties who then do not comply risk contempt of court penalties. Table 12-2 shows the level at which cases are resolved and the length of time each step takes.

Table 12-2   C Process: Resolution and Duration

	Cases Settled		Total Months[1]	
Step	Number	%	Level	Cumulative
(1) Field Examiner	35,543	84.5	——	——
(2) Regional Director	4,719	11.3	1.5	1.5
(3) ALJ	46	0.1	3.5-4.5	5.0- 6.0
(4) NLRB	1,199	2.8	4.0-6.0	9.0-12.0
(5) Court of Appeals	526	1.3	12.0	21.0-24.0
(6) U.S. Supreme Court	6	——	12.0	33.0-36.0
TOTAL	42,046	100	33.0-36.0	

1. Bruce Feldacker, *Labor Guide to Labor Law* (Reston, Va: Reston Publishing Co., Inc., 1980), p. 26. These are estimated minimum times.

Source: *Forty-Fifth Annual Report of the National Labor Relations Board, Fiscal Year 1980,* Table 8.

As is evident from Table 12-2 figures, few cases go the full distance to the Supreme Court and those which do take a considerable period of time. The purpose of the Board *C* procedure is to resolve conflict quickly. For the bulk of the cases, this goal is achieved. But it is possible to use the *C* process to achieve entirely legal delays as part of strategy in labor-management disputes. This will be revisited in the section on suggested reforms in national labor law (see "The Battle Over Labor Law Reform").

How Employees Unionize: Representation Cases

In the free-for-all environment that existed before the Wagner Act, employees who formed unions had to demand recognition of the union from the employer. When employers refused to recognize and bargain, the union was forced to strike to gain employer recognition. The production disruption caused by the recognition strike was a primary motivation to enact legislation which would take the question of union recognition out of the power arena. The system that largely replaced the "might makes right" approach has a cornerstone based in the principle of *exclusive representation.*

Exclusive representation means that a group of employees can be represented by only one labor organization. The group of employees who wishes to bargain is closely defined by the NLRB and is called an *appropriate bargaining unit.* The single labor organization representing the people in the appropriate bargaining unit is called the *exclusive bargaining representative,* or exclusive bargaining agent. Let's take a look at the process by which employees unionize.

The Organizing Phase. Before the NLRB becomes involved, there is an organizing phase. At some point in time a group of employees decides that the best way to change things on the job is to unionize. They may want to organize for one or more reasons: better pay and benefits, job security, better working conditions, to be heard on a grievance, or to be free from arbitrary management action and favoritism. The organization phase is usually done quietly and hopefully without the employer getting wind of it. Contact with a labor organization is made.

The union contacted may or may not be interested in organizing the group. Unions are not businesses, but they are like every other economic organization. They have organizational goals and a budget to achieve them with. Organizing is an expensive activity. Most unions do not have full-time organizers unless they target an industry or area for organizing and then launch a drive. Instead, their international field representatives, while servicing locals, keep an ear to the ground for organizing possibilities. If the union is interested, an organizer or field representative talks with the group which made the contact.

The initial contact is with the small group. The organizer cannot show up one day and organize employees who do not want to be organized. The firm's employees have to organize themselves with the aid of the organizer. In the initial meeting(s) the organizer identifies the leaders and the viable issues and helps plan a strategy.

Authorization Cards. Then comes the card-signing process. The leaders talk with other employees and ask them to sign *authorization cards.* The authorization card is just that—a 3 by 5 inch card on which is printed, "I hereby authorize the XYZ Union to represent me for the purpose of collective bargaining with my employer." It has a place for a date and signature below the statement. Employees are invited to off-the-job meetings for informational card signing.

It can generally be assumed that at some point in the card-signing process an employee will let the cat out of the bag. Often an employee with strong loyalty to the employer will inform the employer of the drive and the meetings. If a majority of the employees sign cards, the union may demand recognition from the employer. The leaders of the group will approach management, inform them that a majority of employees has signed cards, offer to let the employer count the cards in some fashion, and demand that the employer recognize the union and bargain. Some employers do. However, most, on advice by now of legal counsel, either refuse to see the group to begin with or throw them out of the office without looking at the cards. This puts the ball back in the labor organization's court. By not looking at the cards, the employer can claim a "good faith" doubt as to the legitimacy of the union's claim of majority support. In order to get employer recognition, the union must trigger the NLRB representation procedure. The union could have also gone directly to the NLRB without having demanded representation from the employer. In fiscal year 1980, the NLRB received 10,622 representation petition cases.[19]

The Representation Petition. The union proceeds to the nearest NLRB office. There it fills out a petition for representation and supports the petition with the cards. As part of the petition the union must state what group of employees it wishes to represent. That group is called the proposed appropriate bargaining unit. An NLRB field examiner checks to see if the NLRB has jurisdiction over the employer and then determines whether or not the union has a *showing of interest.* In order to achieve a showing of interest, the NLRB requires that a minimum of 30 percent of the proposed unit must be signed up. Many unions require something on the order of 70 percent before they will back an organizing effort because they assume some attrition once the employer's counterorganizing campaign has begun.

The Appropriate Unit. The field examiner tries to get the union and employer to agree on the appropriate bargaining unit and on an election date. But the employer may disagree with the union's proposed unit. It may argue, for example, that the unit contains employees privy to confidential material, or employees whose duties are supervisory in nature. Or, another union may claim the right to represent all or part of the proposed unit. If this issue cannot

---

19. Ibid., p. 14.

be resolved informally, the field examiner will conduct a hearing on the matter. The field examiner acts as a fact finder at the hearing and records the positions of the parties. This hearing record is submitted to the NLRB regional director who decides what the appropriate bargaining unit is.

The regional director bases the decision on several criteria:

1. The history of collective bargaining in the industry (the Board usually will not change an existing successful practice)
2. The community of interest shared by the employees (similar methods of pay and working conditions)
3. The interests of the employees (whom they want to be included)
4. The nature and interrelatedness of the occupations in the employer's operation
5. The extent to which the employees are already organized for bargaining (however, this is not to be the sole or controlling criterion)

Some common types of units are craft units, production and maintenance (P&M) units, and office and technical (O&T) units.

The Election Campaign. The regional director also sets a date on which the employees will vote on whether or not they want a union. During the campaign both sides compete for employee votes. The employer usually recounts the benefits employees have received in the past, points out that the employer does not have to agree to anything the union asks for, points to the union as a dues-hungry outsider interested only in the employees' money, publicizes any dirty dealings the union or its officers have been involved with (e.g., pension fraud), and highlights the cost of union membership, assessments, and strikes among other things.

The union hammers on the issues which caused the organizing drive to begin with. They promise better pay, benefits, and working conditions, the right and power to resolve employee grievances, an end to employer favoritism, arbitrary promotion and discipline; a democratic say in the affairs of the union; a say in local, state, and national issues backed by the political power of the union and the AFL-CIO; and they let people know how all of this is worth the few dollars a month for union dues.

The Election. On the appointed day, an NLRB election officer sets up a portable voting booth at the work place. The polls are open for a few hours on each shift. The employees pick up a ballot from the NLRB election officer, mark it in the booth, and place it in the ballot box. The union and employer have representatives (called election observers) at the election and can challenge individual employee ballots (by claiming a voter is not in the unit or is not an employee). The ballot itself is just a sheet of paper which states that it is an official NLRB ballot and which gives the voter two or more options. If only one union is seeking to represent the group of employees, the employee can vote yes or no on union representation. If two or more unions are involved, each is listed on the ballot along with a "no union" option.

At the end of the voting period, the NLRB election officer counts the ballots in front of the union and employer representatives and certifies the election results. In order to become the "certified exclusive bargaining representative," the union must poll 50 percent plus one vote of those who actually voted in the election. On a tie vote the no union option wins. Usually 90 to 100 percent of the eligible employees participate in the election. If there are three options and none polls a majority, there is a run-off of the top two vote getters. In 1980, the NLRB conducted 8198 elections in which 9 out of 10 eligible employees voted. Unions won 45.7 percent of the elections.[20]

There is an *election bar* which prohibits the holding of another election for 1 year from when the results are certified. If the union wins and negotiates an agreement, there is a *contract bar* for the life of the agreement (or 3 years, whichever comes first).

This is a streamlined version of the process. There are legal challenges and delays built into the system. These have become the subject of debate for labor law reform. That debate is the topic of the next section.

The Battle Over Labor Law Reform

The most recent attempt at anything approaching a major overhaul of the national private sector labor law occurred in 1977-1978. The amendments to the National Labor Relations Act were supported by organized labor and endorsed by President Carter. The National Labor Reform Act of 1977 would have included provisions to:

- Require the NLRB to establish general rules to determine the appropriate bargaining unit (rather than do so on a case-by-case basis).
- Conduct the secret ballot representation election within 15, 45, or, in unusual circumstances, 75 days from filing of the representation petition.
- Allow the union access to the employer premises to state the union case if the employer has required attendance at campaign speeches.
- Direct the NLRB to seek reinstatement by court injunction of an employee discharged for exercising a protected right during an organizing campaign.
- Award double back pay with no deductions for interim income to employees illegally discharged by employers.
- Award damages to employees when employers refuse to bargain in good faith (the damages would be equal to economic gains made in contracts with comparable enterprises).

---

20. Ibid., pp. 15-16.

- Expand the NLRB from five to seven members and extend their term of service from 5 to 7 years.
- Limit judicial review of NLRB orders to those appeals filed within 30 days.
- Allow a quorum of two NLRB members to affirm ALJ decisions.
- Bar willful violators of the NLRA from federal contracts.

The Union View. Proponents of the act argued that the current procedures of the NLRB are being used to delay justice, not speed it. The case for reform appears below.

The Board's "makewhole" remedies do not make whole. Repeated willful violators flaunt the Board's authority. In short, the laws are being used to subvert Section 7 rights, not protect them. The addition of two Board members and streamlining of procedures will make for a speedier, more effective law. The current median time for the NLRB to go to election is, at the least, 57 days for uncontested elections and 275 days for cases taken to the Board. The undue prolonging of the election clearly supports the employer. By using general rules, not the current ad hoc approach, NLRB elections could be speeded up. Currently, the employer can make captive audience speeches against the union, and the union cannot have equal access to the employees. Unions should have equal time to present their case so employees can make fully informed representation decisions.

For certain union unfair labor practices the Board must seek immediate court injunctions, but there are no similarly enjoined employer unfair practices. The Board should be directed to seek immediate reinstatement of employees by injunction when employers violate employee Section 7 rights by discharging them. Not to do so allows employers to chill organizing efforts. Right now the Board's makewhole remedies have no teeth. The Board should be allowed to take punitive measures against employer violators. Awarding back pay to an employee a year or more after that person was discharged for protected activities is hardly a penalty. This is particularly ludicrous when all employee earnings in the interim are subtracted from the back pay awarded.

Employers can unlawfully refuse to bargain with the union for an initial contract and stall the process for years. At most, the Board can mandate negotiations. A new remedy should be enacted whereby the Board can award damages to employees equal to the difference between what they finally negotiated and what the average increase was for settlements in similar firms since the firm first started stonewalling negotiations. Flagrant, willful violators should be barred from federal contracts.

The Employer View. Opponents of the bill such as the National Small Business Association, the Chamber of Commerce, and the National Right to Work Committee make the case against the new legislation. Employer arguments against reform follow.

Small business bears the brunt of union-organizing activities (98 percent of all elections involve fewer than 400 employees; 75 percent are in businesses with 50 or fewer employees). Quickie elections do not allow operators of small businesses time enough to obtain counsel and advice on their legal rights. They will not be able to present their views in opposition to the unions. The equal time provision will only cause confusion and intimidate small business management. Fear of union access and fear of NLRB punitive damages will keep proprietors from stating the case against unionism. There will be no fully informed reasoned choice by employees because they will not hear the employer side. Punitive damages awarded unfairly may force small businesses into bankruptcy.

Enlarging the Board and increasing the bureaucracy will be expensive to the taxpayer. The quickie election will railroad employees into unions and unduly encroach on the rights of employees to work in a union-free environment. The current law works very well for the 98 percent of law-abiding unions and firms. Why enact a law aimed at the few who break the current law and simultaneously punish the vast law-abiding majority?

The Outcome. The bill sailed through the House, but it died in the Senate in 1978 as the result of a successful Senate filibuster. The bill's provisions were a part of the AFL-CIO platform proposals made to the Republican and Democratic National Conventions in the 1980 Presidential race. Labor law reform is in limbo at the present time. Prior to the 1980 elections, the AFL-CIO announced plans to push the changes again in the early 1980s. With the election of a conservative Republican President and Republican control of the Senate, reopening the question of labor law reform would be a risky venture. It is not likely that any liberalization of national labor law will occur in the near future.

PUBLIC SECTOR BARGAINING LAWS

Federal and state laws concerning public sector labor relations closely parallel private sector law. Unfair labor practices and the procedure for their prosecution, the representation rules and procedures, and the administrative structure for public sector laws are largely borrowed from the private sector. The key difference lies in the fact that with few exceptions public employees cannot legally strike. We examine federal law first because it set the pattern for the state laws which followed.

Federal Bargaining

The federal sector operates under a different set of laws than do state and local government. Although the Lloyd–La Follette Act gave federal employees the right to join unions in 1912, they did not receive recognition and bargaining rights until 1962. Then, after extensive study of employee-management relations problems by a Presidential task force, John F. Kennedy conferred recognition and bargaining rights with Executive Order 10988. While the rights in the federal sector fell far short of those existing in the private sector, the order was the spark that set public sector bargaining afire. Executive Order 10988 was refined by President Nixon's Executive Order 11491 in 1970.

On January 11, 1979, after 16 years of living under executive orders, federal labor-management relations received the sanctity of statutory law. By then 60 percent of the federal civilian work force in 3500 units were under contracts. The Civil Service Reform Act (CSRA) carried through most of what had proven workable under the executive orders, but reorganized the administrative structure.

The law includes a representation procedure which provides for exclusive representation for an appropriate bargaining unit by secret ballot election. There is also a set of union and employer unfair labor practices and a procedure for their prosecution. The responsibility for overseeing the CSRA provisions was given to a new, independent, three-member Federal Labor Relations Authority (FLRA) whose members are appointed to 5-year terms by the President with approval of the Senate. Like private sector law an office of the General Counsel was created to independently prosecute unfair labor practices. Enforcement of FLRA orders and appeals to the orders go to the Appeals Court. Decisions of the Appeals Court can be appealed to the U.S. Supreme Court.

Negotiations in federal government differ from those in the private sector. The *scope of negotiations* (items about which they can legally bargain) is restricted to exclude wages and benefits. One exception to this is the postal service which under the Postal Reorganization Act of 1970 can bargain economic items. It is illegal to strike against the federal government. To deal with negotiation impasses there is a Federal Service Impasses Panel. The panel has at its disposal a variety of ways in which to deal with problem negotiations from mediation to directed settlement. The new law also mandated that all bargaining agreements must contain a grievance procedure. The procedure must be capped with final and binding arbitration.

State and Local Bargaining Laws

Laws permitting bargaining by state and local government employees were passed rapidly after EO 10988 in 1962. By 1980 only seven states had not granted or legislated some form of recognition and bargaining rights to employees. The right to organize and bargain has not been conferred so extensively at the county and municipal level, but it is growing rapidly. Because each state (and often municipal and county government unit) controls its own bargaining structure, there is substantial diversity in bargaining law. Several aspects of state and local law have been chosen to illustrate uniformities and diversities.

Forty-three states and 13,839 local governments have labor relations policies.[21] These have been established in a number of ways. Court decisions, attorney general decisions, executive orders, and legislative enactment have all been used to create bargaining laws.

Ten states have comprehensive laws which pertain to all public employees at all levels of government: Florida, Hawaii, Iowa, Maine, Massachusetts, Minnesota, New Jersey, New York, Oregon, and Pennsylvania. The other states with labor relations policies afford coverage for selected groups of employees such as teachers. Georgia, Idaho, Kentucky, North Carolina, South Carolina, Virginia, and Wyoming have no state level public sector laws. In every state, regardless of legal status, there is some form of negotiation ongoing. Table 12-3 summarizes this ongoing activity at the state and local levels.

Virtually all these laws provide for exclusive recognition of a labor organization for an appropriate bargaining unit. The secret ballot election determines the question of representation. The comprehensive law states have an NLRB-type board to administer the provisions of the acts. Where laws govern selected groups such as teachers, the administration of it is often entrusted to existing agencies such as the state department of education.

The scope of bargaining is often restricted. Civil service laws covering such subjects as pay, promotion, and grievance handling intrude into areas which would be bargainable in the private sector. Because government is so labor-intensive, wage settlements have a major impact on the cost of providing state and local public services. For this reason some laws require any wage settlement to be tentative until it receives legislative or executive branch approval.

Seven states have provisions which allow the strike for at least some public employees: Alaska, Hawaii, Minnesota, Montana, Oregon, Pennsylvania, and Vermont. The strike is permitted only after the exhaustion of extensive conflict resolution procedures and after suitable notice has been given. The other 43 states prohibit the strike under penalty of injunction, fines, and discharge. State and local governments have been the testing ground for alternatives to the use of the strike. They have proven to be reasonably successful. In fiscal year 1979, there were 553 work stoppages longer than one shift. Interestingly enough, only 80 were in the states which have legal work stoppages. Most of the stoppages were ended by further negotiation (37 percent) or mediation (29 percent). Fact finding and arbitration resolved 4 percent, court injunction resolved 11 percent, and the other 19 percent ended in other ways, such as discharge of striking employees or their voluntary return to work.[22] Alternatives to the strike will be discussed further in Chapter 15 on conflict resolution.

---

21. U.S. Departments of Commerce and Labor, *Labor-Management Relations in State and Local Governments: 1979* (Washington: U.S. Government Printing Office, 1980), p. 7.
22. Ibid., p. 4.

Table 12-3   State and Local Government Bargaining Activity

States	All State and Local Governments		
	Total	Governments Which Engage in CN and/or MC Discussions[1]	
		Number	Percent
United States, total	79,928	13,882	17.4
Alabama	953	29	3.0
Alaska	151	29	19.2
Arizona	420	103	24.5
Arkansas	1,347	57	4.2
California	3,807	1,453	38.2
Colorado	1,465	126	8.6
Connecticut	435	178	41.2
Delaware	211	20	9.5
District of Columbia	2	2	100.0
Florida	912	200	21.9
Georgia	1,267	15	1.2
Hawaii	20	5	25.0
Idaho	973	116	11.9
Illinois	6,619	853	12.9
Indiana	2,867	341	11.9
Iowa	1,851	484	26.2
Kansas	3,726	285	7.7
Kentucky	1,185	46	3.9
Louisiana	459	24	5.2
Maine	782	176	22.5
Maryland	427	38	8.9
Massachusetts	768	389	50.7
Michigan	2,627	897	34.2
Minnesota	3,439	638	18.6
Mississippi	836	11	1.3
Missouri	2,938	224	7.6
Montana	950	213	22.4
Nebraska	3,425	368	10.8
Nevada	183	37	20.2
New Hampshire	507	111	21.9
New Jersey	1,516	853	56.3
New Mexico	315	37	11.8
New York	3,307	1,110	33.6
North Carolina	875	—	—
North Dakota	2,706	192	7.1
Ohio	3,333	772	23.2
Oklahoma	1,695	182	10.7

Table 12-3   Continued

| States | Total | Governments Which Engage in CN and/or MC Discussions[1] | |
		Number	Percent
Oregon	1,449	387	26.7
Pennsylvania	5,239	1,146	21.9
Rhode Island	120	47	39.2
South Carolina	585	9	1.5
South Dakota	1,729	193	11.2
Tennessee	907	61	6.7
Texas	3,897	97	2.5
Utah	493	46	9.3
Vermont	648	154	23.8
Virginia	390	—	—
Washington	1,669	468	28.0
West Virginia	597	26	4.4
Wisconsin	2,519	587	23.3
Wyoming	387	47	12.2

1. CN, collective negotiations; MC, meet and confer.
Source: *Labor-Management Relations in State and Local Governments: 1979*, pp. 2-3.

CONCLUDING REMARKS

The current labor law system has been forged by almost 200 years of trial-and-error application. What is remarkable about our system is not its diversity but its uniformity. Private sector law, federal law, and state and local laws follow basically the same model. Their goals are the same: Substitute procedure for the exercise of power to accommodate the competing interests of labor and management. In federal law, the means are also the same: exclusive recognition, election procedures, unfair labor practices and prosecution procedures, administration by a labor relations board, and impasse resolution procedures.

The greatest variety in means occurs in the laws covering state and local employees. There simply is no single model of state and local bargaining law. However, over time the variation is diminishing as the governments discard unworkable legislation. Analysis of public sector experience will lead to a further refinement of the law. It is doubtful, however, that a single model will ever evolve because the needs of 50 states and 80,000 local governments are very different.

CHAPTER SUMMARY

Philadelphia shoemakers were found guilty of criminal conspiracy in 1806 in the first recorded legal case involving a union in U.S. history. In *Commonwealth v Hunt,* Justice Shaw relaxed the standard of judgment against unions by employing an ends-means test of union activity. This set the pattern for another 40 years. Employers found a more efficient method of union prosecution with the use of the court injunction. The courts also legitimized the use of the yellow dog contract so that to get and keep a job, an employee could not join or support a union.

It took the severity of the Depression to bring a new judicial attitude regarding unions in society. In 1932 the Norris–La Guardia Anti-Injunction Act effectively neutralized the role of the courts in labor-management disputes by placing significant restrictions on the granting of federal court injunctions. A new labor policy designed to encourage industrial democracy and reduce industrial conflict through unions and collective bargaining was embodied in the National Labor Relations Act of 1935. Key elements included the right of an employee to join a union, a representation procedure, a number of employer unfair labor practices along with a procedure for their prosecution and the National Labor Relations Board to oversee it all.

Twelve years later the locus of countervailing power shifted back toward the employer with the passage of the Taft-Hartley amendments. The amendments added a set of unfair union practices, allowed employees the right to refrain from union activity, outlawed the closed shop, set up an emergency disputes procedure, and allowed states to pass right-to-work laws restricting union security agreements. To restore union democracy, Congress passed the Labor-Management Reporting and Disclosure Act in 1959. It contained a union member bill of rights, required timely secret ballot election of local and national officers, and limited the use of trusteeships.

The unfair labor practices procedure and representation procedures substitute procedure for power in labor-management relations conflict. *C* cases start as a charge filed at the regional office and are investigated by a field examiner. Informal settlement at the lowest level possible is the goal of the process. The *R* cases begin with a representation petition, proceed to a Regional Director decision on the appropriate bargaining unit, and end with a secret ballot election. If the union wins, it becomes the exclusive bargaining representative and has 1 year to bargain a contract with the employer.

President Kennedy ushered in the era of public sector bargaining with the 1962 signing of EO 10988 covering federal employees. Federal bargaining was modified by Nixon's EO 11491 and then brought closely into line with the NLRA by the Civil Service Reform Act of 1978. Key differences lie in the restricted scope of bargaining and the prohibition against the strike in the federal system. The Federal Labor Relations Authority is the NLRB equivalent for enforcement and policy development. State and local bargaining exists under various legal structures in all but seven states. There is great diversity in structure and coverage. The principle of exclusive representation, the *R* process, unfair labor practices, and the *C* procedure are fairly uniform across states.

KEY TERMS

criminal conspiracy	hot cargo clause
scabbing	secondary boycott
court injunction	trusteeship
ex parte injunctions	exclusive representation
yellow dog contracts	appropriate bargaining unit
tenet	exclusive bargaining representa-
freedom of contract	tive
unfair labor practices	authorization card
national emergency disputes	showing of interest
Section 14(b)	election bar
right-to-work law	contract bar
bill of rights	scope of negotiations

REVIEW QUESTIONS

1. What is criminal conspiracy as applied to unions? What made them criminal? Contrast that doctrine with today's legal approach.

2. Why does the ex parte injunction favor management?

3. Most textbook chapters on labor law appear to be sympathetic to the union side in discussions of law from 1806 to 1932. Why? What is the employer side?

4. What common thread of thought can be used to make sense of the legislation passed from 1932 to the present?

5. Are you in favor of national labor reform or against it? Why?

6. The UAW filed a representation petition with 50 names on it backed by 50 cards. The appropriate bargaining unit the NLRB selected included 60 people. At the election, the voting went 29 for the UAW and 27 for no union. What will the NLRB certify to be the outcome of the election?
    a. What if the voting had gone UAW: 3, no union: 2?
    b. What if the results were UAW: 25, no union: 25?
    c. What if the results were UAW: 28, no union: 29?

7. Discuss the similarities and differences between collective bargaining in the public sector and collective bargaining in the private sector under the Taft-Hartley Act.

ADDITIONAL REFERENCES

Commons, John R., and Eugene A. Gilmore. *Labor Conspiracy Cases, 1806-1842, A Documentary History of the American Industrial Society,* Vols. III and IV. Cleveland, Ohio: The Arthur H. Clark Company, 1910. This has the original verbatim testimony in the court hearings.

Feldacker, Bruce. *Labor Guide to Labor Law.* Reston, Va.: Reston Publishing Company, 1980.

Frankfurter, Felix, and Nathan Greene. *The Labor Injunction.* New York: The Macmillan Company, 1930. Reprinted Gloucester, Mass.: Peter Smith, 1963.

Guide to Basic Law and Procedures Under the National Labor Relations Act. Washington: U.S. Government Printing Office, 1978.

Twomey, David P. *Labor Law and Legislation.* Cincinnati, Ohio: South-Western Publishing Co., Inc., 1980.

Wellington, Harry H. *Labor and the Legal Process,* New Haven, Conn.: Yale University Press, 1968.

THE WORLD
OF WORK . . .

The Impact of the Health Care Amendments of 1974

In 1974, amendments were made to the Taft-Hartley Act which promoted collective bargaining in the health care industry. Special care was taken to deal with the problems which can attend a work stoppage in this industry. This reading discusses the impact of the amendments.

PROVISIONS OF THE AMENDMENTS

The amended law provided for some special procedures designed to promote early bargaining and avoid strikes in the health care institutions. These procedures include: (1) advance notice to the FMCS of plans to modify or terminate a contract, (2) mandatory mediation, (3) a 10-day intent-to-strike notice to the institution and to the FMCS, and (4) a special factfinding or Board of Inquiry (BOI) procedure to be used in cases of threatened or actual strikes.

The BOI is designed to provide factfinding in an attempt to avoid strikes. Appointment of a BOI is at the discretion of the director of the FMCS if "a threatened or actual strike or lockout affecting a health care institution will, if permitted to occur or continue, substantially interrupt the delivery of health care in the locality concerned." The BOI is appointed for a 15-day term, during which the "findings of fact" and nonbinding recommendations are issued. Such appointment takes place no later than 30 days prior to expiration date of the contract, or within 30 days of receipt of the 60-day notice to the FMCS. In the case of initial contracts, the BOI, if convened, must be appointed within 10 days of receipt of the intent-to-strike notice.

IMPACT ON STRIKES

One of the most important concerns motivating the enactment of the 1974 amendments was the desire to eliminate strikes, particularly those involving recognition. A review of the 2½ years following the enactment of the legislation indicates that the strike rate in the health care industry is similar to that in the economy as a whole, with a stoppage occurring in about 4 or 5 percent of all bargaining situations. Of 2,585 health care bargaining situations between August 25, 1974 and December 31, 1976, 129 strikes occurred. Another similarity is the duration of strikes, about 27 days both in all bargaining and in health care situations, although there appear to be longer and more bitter strikes in nursing homes. In a number of nursing home strikes, no collective bargaining ever occurs nor is a contract signed, and the union walks away after gaining recognition.

Unlike the practice in other industries, picket lines are infrequently honored by other organized units, making strikes by small units less effective. This "nonsupportive activity" occurred prior to 1974 as well and before the required 10-day strike notice.

Despite the similarities between bargaining in health and other industries, there is an important and distinct difference. In the health care industry, about one-third of all bargaining involves initial contracts, a proportion substantially higher than in other industries. Viewed under this circumstance, it might be concluded that the strike rate is actually better than in the economy as a whole, because few, if any, other industries are undergoing the rapid rate of new bargaining.

Mediators found the 10-day strike notice useful in promoting negotiations, especially in initial contracts. Labor unions, in contrast, found the notice cumbersome and confusing, but most importantly also felt that it provided management time to hire replacements and prepare for a strike. While the number of 10-day strike notices issued is not known, in 65 percent of all Board situations, a strike notice had been given, but a strike occurred in only 13 percent.

INFLUENCE OF THE NATIONAL LABOR RELATIONS BOARD

Since the 1974 amendments were enacted, the National Labor Relations Board (NLRB) has decided a series of key issues which influenced collective bargaining in the health care industry. Two major decisions were the resolution of unit determination issues and denial of bargaining rights for interns and residents.

In extending bargaining rights to nonprofit hospital workers, Congress cautioned the NLRB to give "due consideration . . . to preventing proliferation of bargaining units in the health care industry." After much deliberation, the NLRB determined that five units would be appropriate in hospital settings: (1) all registered nurses "if they are sought and they so desire" to be represented, (2) all other professionals, (3) technical employees, excluding service and maintenance personnel, (4) clerical employees in business offices, and (5) service and maintenance personnel, including nonoffice clerical workers. A sixth unit was added in 1977 to include physicians, excluding interns and residents.

However, the clearly defined units have not solved election determination problems and have posed a threat to craft type unions which have represented health care workers.

Another group whose survival has been threatened is the American Nurses Association and its State affiliates which act as the bargaining representatives. Current developments, including the challenge of the organization's status as a bargaining representative because of alleged supervisor domination, may result in internal change within the organization, strong takeover challenges by other labor organizations, or the splintering of established nurses' groups into independent unions.

While the NLRB amended its five basic unit determination decisions to include physicians, it explicitly treated interns and residents as students and not as employees covered by the amended National Labor Relations Act. In March 1976, the NLRB reasoned that housestaff physicians were enrolled in a program designed as a prerequisite for licensing examinations and certification in medical specialties not for the purpose of earning a living. The question of whether interns and residents may engage in bargaining has generated considerable litigation and the introduction of bills to amend the 1974 amendments.

Source: Lucretia Dewey Tanner, Harriet Goldberg Weinstein, and Alice L. Ahmuty, "Collective Bargaining in the Health Care Industry," *Monthly Labor Review* (February, 1980), pp. 49-53.

Chapter 13

Basic Principles of the Negotiation Process and an Analysis of Outcomes

Chapter 12 showed how and why a group of employees becomes organized. Once recognized for purposes of collective bargaining, a labor organization has a 1-year period in which to negotiate a collective bargaining contract. How labor and management negotiate a collective bargaining agreement is the focus of this chapter. We first set the stage for contract negotiations by examining U.S. bargaining structure. This is followed by a discussion of a behavioral theory of negotiations from which to view the bargaining activities. The next sections are largely descriptive of the actual negotiation process. As was noted in the introduction to Part III, this detailed description is presented because we believe that the analysis of negotiation and collective bargaining should proceed only after the student has a thorough understanding of the realities of bargaining. To provide the necessary basics, we explain the selection of union and management teams, their preparation for bargaining, negotiation table skills, and postnegotiation wrap-up activities. Having considered the realities of negotiation, the attempts of scholars to model bargaining are examined. The last section provides an analysis of the outcomes of wage bargaining.

There is a great deal of respect and glamour that goes along with the labor-management negotiator position. It has been our experience as educators that many students would like to be negotiators one day. "The World of Work" section at the end of this chapter tells how one person became a negotiator early in his career.

COLLECTIVE BARGAINING STRUCTURE

The topic of *collective bargaining structure* has been discussed briefly in earlier chapters. Under the most restrictive definition the study of bargaining structure would be limited to an examination of who bargains with whom. But the subject matter extends beyond a cataloging of the parties to a bargaining agreement. The timing and sequence of who bargains with whom is also very important. In this section both aspects of the concept are explored.

Decentralized Plant Level Contracts

The most decentralized structure possible would be if each NLRB sanctioned appropriate bargaining unit had its own agreement. This would be a single plant contract between one union and one employer. For example, Union Carbide Corporation negotiates a contract with the International Chemical Workers Union which covers only its Sistersville, West Virginia plant. Most collective bargaining agreements are of this kind, that is, negotiated for a single plant. A recent study of collective bargaining by the Conference Board surveyed 668 companies and found that 64 percent of them conducted collective bargaining negotiations at the single-plant level and an additional 12 percent of the companies negotiated *local supplements* to a multiplant master contract.[1] But while most contracts are single-plant, there are some very important, very centralized negotiations.

Centralized Structure

At the single-plant level the *collective bargaining unit* is the appropriate bargaining unit. In more centralized bargaining structures, the collective bargaining unit is comprised of a group of appropriate units.

Multiplant or Master Agreements. One such situation is an agreement between a company and a union covering several plants—a multiplant agreement. Deere and Company (manufacturers of agricultural implements), for example, negotiates a multiplant or *master contract* with the United Auto, Agricultural Implement, and Aerospace Workers (UAW). The agreement covers eight plants in Illinois and Iowa which at first had their own individual contracts. In addition to the 12 percent that had a master-local supplement structure, the Conference Board study showed that another 18 percent of the firms also had a single, master agreement.[2]

Pattern Setting. Very often, single-plant and master agreement contracts are negotiated in what is called a *pattern-setting* structure. The union or association picks a target company in an industry and negotiates an agreement. That sets the pattern for negotiations with the remaining companies in the industry. The auto industry is probably the most famous pattern-setting structure. The UAW often patterns with General Motors and the rest fall in line. This pattern has been disrupted recently because of the industry's financial difficulties.

Multiemployer Agreements. Another form of structure is the *multiemployer agreement*. (These are often called industry, national, or master contracts.) Here, the employers band together to form an employers' association for purposes of bargaining. They bargain with one union often for an entire industry or geographic area. For example, the Bituminous Coal Operators Association (BCOA) negotiates a master agreement with the United Mine

---

1. Audrey Freedman, *Managing Labor Relations* (New York: The Conference Board, 1979), p. 4.
2. Ibid.

Workers of America (UMWA) for the soft coal industry in the East and Midwest. The BCOA is composed of approximately 150 mining companies.

Another example is drawn from the construction industry. The North Central West Virginia Construction Employers Association, representing over 50 construction companies, negotiates separate master agreements with a dozen craft unions for a 10-county region. Multiemployer master agreements are most often found in industries characterized by a large number of highly competitive companies. By negotiating one master agreement as a group, they provide a united front to the union. This takes wages out of competition and prevents the union from playing one company off against another (called *whipsawing*). The Conference Board study found that only 6 percent of the firms negotiated as part of a multiemployer collective bargaining unit.[3]

Coordinated Bargaining. Finally, there is a structure which comes close to a multi-union unit. This is the union parallel to the multiemployer agreement and is done for the same reasons. One company may negotiate separate contracts with more than one union in an industry. If a dispute arises over contract terms with one union, production can be shifted to plants which are represented by other unions or which are nonunion. The employer can also play one union off against the other. The negotiating union is clearly in a weaker position than if it bargained for all the company's plants.

To improve their bargaining position, the various unit unions engage in *coordinated bargaining*.[4] Representatives from the other units sit on the first union's negotiating committee. They attempt to get some common agreement terms and expiration dates to prevent the employer's whipsawing tactics. By way of example, the International Brotherhood of Electrical Workers (IBEW) and the International Union of Electrical Workers (IUE) coordinate their bargaining with General Electric and with Westinghouse for the electrical components industry. Much of the coordinated bargaining efforts are themselves coordinated through the Industrial Union Department (IUD) of the AFL-CIO.

The construction industry provides an example of a multi-union contract. The Carpenters Union had eight locals in an 18-county area. Rather than bargain on a local-by-local basis, the locals formed a Carpenter's District Council to bargain as a group with the Construction Employers Association for one agreement covering all eight locals. As one final example, the Operating Engineers have a local which covers the entire state of West Virginia. They negotiate one agreement for the whole state, and their employer counterpart consists of a group composed of five construction employers' associations.

One side effect of coordinated bargaining is an occasional merger of the coordinating unions. It may not be the only reason for merger, but it can be a

---

3. Ibid.

4. Following the customary distinction, coordinated bargaining means that the unions sign separate agreements with the employer. This is legal. Coalition bargaining is taken to mean the unions demand a single multi-union agreement. If the employer refuses and the unions strike, they commit an unfair labor practice. Coordinated bargaining is discussed here.

major one. In meatpacking, for example, after years of coordinated and pattern-setting bargaining, the United Packinghouse Workers merged with the Amalgamated Meat Cutters and Butcher Workmen of North America and took the name of the Amalgamated. (Since then the Amalgamated has merged with the Retail Clerks International Union to form the Food and Commercial Workers of America.)

The structure of bargaining for several major industries is shown in Table 13-1.

Table 13-1   Major Industry Bargaining Structures

Industry	Approximate Structure	Employer	Union(s)
Aerospace	Coordinated Bargaining Pattern Setting	Big Four	Machinists (IAM), Auto Workers (UAW)
Airline	Single Firm, Single Union by Craft	Numerous	Numerous
Bituminous Coal	Master Contract	Bituminous Coal Operators Association (BCOA)	Mine Workers (UMWA)
Electrical Machinery and Equipment	Coordinated Bargaining Pattern Setting	GE, Westinghouse	Electrical Workers (IBEW, IUE, UE, and 10 others)
Longshore, East and Gulf Coasts	Multiemployer Pattern Set by East Coast	CONASA (East Coast Employers' Association)	Longshoremen's Association (ILA)
Longshore, West Coast	Multiemployer Master Contract	Pacific Maritime Association	Longshoremen's and Warehousemen's Union (ILWU)
Meat Products	Pattern Setting	Numerous	Food and Commercial Workers (UFCU)
Motor Vehicle	Pattern Setting	Big Three	Auto Workers (UAW)
Railroad	Coordinated Bargaining Master Contract	National Railway Labor Conference	Numerous
Rubber	Pattern Setting	Big Four	Rubber Workers (URWA)
Steel	Pattern Setting	Set with U.S. Steel	Steelworkers (USA)
Telephone	Informal Coordination Nationwide Agreement	AT&T	Communication Workers (CWA), Electrical Workers (IBEW)

Sources: Various Bureau of Labor Statistics, *Collective Bargaining Industry Fact Sheets.*

A THEORY OF NEGOTIATIONS

There is an interesting analytical insight into the whole negotiation process provided by behavioral scientists Walton and McKersie.[5] They studied numerous negotiations and found that strategy and tactics in collective bargaining are part of four activities. Walton and McKersie provide valuable insight into the process that can be used by would-be successful negotiators and students of collective bargaining.

Distributive Bargaining

The first activity, *distributive bargaining,* is what most people think bargaining to be. One side's goals are in conflict with the goals of the other. What labor gains, management loses and vice versa. For example, the State Nurses' Association which represents all registered nurses at Bloomington Doctors' Hospital has demanded a $1000 increase in pay for the next year. The hospital counterproposed $750. Each side has set a goal to be reached somewhere in between the two figures. In the negotiations which follow, each side views its concessions to be losses which the other side gains. This is particularly true as the parties approach their negotiating targets. Management may be forced to exceed their planned increase, or the union may be forced to take less than they had originally planned.

The tactics used in distributive bargaining are the ones we normally associate with bargaining. Each side asks for more than they expect to get while concealing their true position. In the discussions that follow labor and management use word nuances, bluffs, and the threat of a strike to reveal their true positions without actually stating them. Here is where the art of negotiation comes in with the proper use of language skills at the table. Failure to listen to what the other side is really saying or failure to adroitly reveal what it takes to settle can lead to a work stoppage.

Integrative Bargaining

Integrative bargaining is a wholly different activity. The goals do not conflict. To a large extent they are mutual concerns for both labor and management: a common problem. It is a "win-win" situation. This type of bargaining calls for a reasonably open, problem-solving approach at the table. Better still, the integrative issue should be handled away from the haggling of the distributive bargaining going on at the table. Often these issues are studied by a negotiation subcommittee away from the table. The subcommittee then submits a recommended solution to be made part of the final settlement. Some

---

5. Richard E. Walton and Robert B. McKersie, *A Behavioral Theory of Negotiations* (New York: McGraw-Hill Book Co., 1965).

industries have standing joint committees to study an issue between contracts. They tender a joint proposal on the issue at the next negotiation.

As with all problem-solving situations, integrative issues require a sharing of ideas and information and a genuine desire on the part of the parties to settle the issue. Success requires a mature relationship in which each side respects the legitimacy of the other in bargaining. New bargaining relationships, particularly first contract negotiations, lack this maturity. Integrative issues go unrecognized and are seen as distributive ones in an "I win, you lose" negotiating battle.

The steel industry provides an example of integrative bargaining. Both the steel companies and the United Steelworkers of America (USA) recognized that their arbitration system was plagued with high costs and lengthy delays. A joint study committee was formed to study the problem and recommend a solution at a later negotiation. As a result, the parties agreed to an "expedited arbitration" system whereby cases are heard quickly, arbitrators are paid a flat fee per hearing day, and decisions are not precedent setting. Cases which are precedent setting go through the old system. Both parties gained from the agreement. Grievances are solved more rapidly and at a lower cost.

Intra-organizational Bargaining

Intra-organizational bargaining, the third activity, is literally bargaining that goes on internal to management and internal to the labor organization, not between them. Every organization has interest groups which conflict with one another. Intra-organizational bargaining refers to the process by which a side "gets its act together." A team which has not resolved its own internal conflict before going to the table may be picked apart by a skillful opposing negotiator.

Union Haggling. Intra-organizational bargaining is more characteristic of and more difficult for the union team. The team is often elected and the international representative (an outsider) may bargain the contract. Consider some of the groups whose interests may be in conflict: skilled and semiskilled workers, national union and local union, older and younger workers, men and women, whites and minorities, night-shift and day-shift workers. The differences must be resolved in order to decide which demands go to the table, the allowable compromises on these demands, and what constitutes an acceptable package to avert a strike.

Take age, for example. Younger workers, often single, are most interested in leisure time and money. They want cash money, up front, and the time to enjoy spending it. Their interests are money, as much and as soon as possible, holidays, the right shift, and a lax absenteeism policy. They are not particularly interested in health plans or pensions—they have little use for either. The younger worker makes the transition into the family-raising years. Money is still important, but health benefits are relatively more important; pensions are of less concern. After the family is gone and retirement is no longer that unforeseeable circumstance, pensions take on a greater importance.

Which demands are given the most weight at the table will depend upon the political clout of the group pushing them. Because union officials are elected, they may be reluctant to discipline the team or force agreement. The international representative is usually appointed, not elected, and may exert the pressure to bring the team into line to resolve their conflicting interests, but as an outsider there are limits to that power as well. More than one international representative chief negotiator has been booted out of negotiations for alienating the local team.

> Our committee, with the international representative, met with the company. We knew what the members wanted and we were going to get as much of it as we could. Our man from the international decided something else—he thought we could get some favorable changes in job rules. We didn't care if he tried to get them, but he got into a bad argument with a company man, and they called each other names. We saw right away that wasn't going to make our job any easier, so we asked for a recess. The union committee and the representative met and we told him to stay out from here on. He did, and we got the contract settled without hard feelings. He's a good man, but he and the company man have a long history of bad feelings.[6]

Management Conflicts. Management has its internal problems as well. Production managers want to maximize output. They do not want a strike, and they do want an end to restrictive work rules which inhibit their flexibility. The finance people want a low-cost contract and no strike which might interfere with potential stock or bond issues. The industrial relations people have goals of their own and may be willing to take a strike to obtain them. There is a difference between union and management intra-organizational bargaining. That difference is in authority. Someone on the management team has the authority to say undemocratically, "This is how it is . . . !"

Intra-organizational bargaining also occurs between layers in the organizational structure of management. The Conference Board study indicated that specialized labor relations staff at the plant level prepare their own proposals and the counterproposals to anticipated union demands. Then they must clear them with corporate management. The final decision on the economic package is made by the corporation's chief executive officer (CEO) in 80 percent of the firms. The noneconomic items are cleared with the CEO in one-third of the firms, and by the vice president for labor relations in the rest of the firms.[7]

Employer associations provide a fertile ground for political rifts. The firms

---

6. This statement, made by a local union officer, is reported in Robert Miller, Frederick A. Zeller, and Glenn W. Miller, *The Practice of Local Union Leadership* (Columbus, Ohio: Ohio State University Press, 1965), p. 28.

7. Freedman, *Managing Labor Relations*, p. 18.

involved may differ in size, extent of market, profitability, labor intensity, age of plant capital, ownership (single firm versus conglomerate), and corporate philosophy. Here, as with the union situation, the ability to be single-minded about issues on the table depends upon the political savvy of the association leadership.

Attitudinal Structuring

The fourth activity, *attitudinal structuring*, refers to the fact that all throughout the negotiations process each side's actions affect their mutal relationship. The relationship that exists at any point in time might be characterized as one of conflict, containment-aggression, accommodation, cooperation, or collusion. Bargaining relationships over a long period of time tend to progress from conflict to cooperation. Two important points emerge from this consideration. First, negotiation sets up emotional shock waves in the relationship that last far beyond the signing of the agreement. The tone of a negotiation helps set the tone for the continuing relationship of contract administration. Second, knowledge of this causes the parties to design bargaining strategy to use attitudinal structuring to their advantage. Before labor and management ever sit down at the table, they start attitudinal structuring tactics.

Handbooks for union stewards and for first-line supervisors emphasize the communications role they play between union and company. Both sides use this two-way interaction to "condition" the other side about the upcoming negotiations. Management will drop hints into the communications channel about maximum wage gains the union can expect in the upcoming negotiations (near to management's own target). The union will do the same concerning what economic and noneconomic items it will take to avoid a strike. In this fashion labor and management seek to condition the other side into a set of rational expectations about the final settlement. Both sides try to avoid unpleasant surprises at the negotiation table.

At the table, particularly at the first few negotiations, the labor committee members must restructure some of their own attitudes. When they are not negotiating, management and union representatives live in a day-to-day superior-subordinate or manager-managed relationship. At the table they are equal. Some members of the union team may have to be reminded of that equality by a "give 'em hell" pep talk from an old hand on the team or by the international representative.

After negotiation, the structuring of the attitudes continues. Hostile negotiations may beget a hostile relationship afterwards. The true success of a contract is measured by how well it works in practice. Companies and unions may actually negotiate only a month to reach an agreement. They have to live by it for its duration, usually 2 or 3 years. For that reason and because the economic cycle can shift power from a strong union at a cyclical peak to a strong employer at its trough, neither side kills the other at the table even when they can clearly do so. In the words of one management negotiator, "We try to do what's 'right' for the relationship, not what the market will bear." One last example of attitudinal structuring involves postnegotiation activities. To establish a healthy relationship after the agreement has been signed, some firms and unions hold joint meetings of first-line supervisors and union stewards. The management and union negotiators explain the changes made in the collective bargaining agreement to the group and field any questions concerning the new agreement. This facilitates a healthy day-to-day relationship because it cuts down on misinterpretations of the agreement.

Phases of the Negotiation Process

The actual negotiations process consists of four phases: the preparation of demands and counterproposals, the initial presentation of demands and counterproposals, the actual interaction of bargaining, and the culmination in a written agreement. Each phase will be examined in detail in the next sections.

PRENEGOTIATION ACTIVITIES

Let's pick up the action now. Either a union or association has just been recognized, or an existing collective bargaining agreement is about to expire. In the private sector, if an existing contract is to be renegotiated, the union or management should have given notice by registered letter to the other side that they wish to modify the agreement. By law the notice to the other party must come 60 days before the contract expiration date (90 days in the health care industry). The Federal Mediation and Conciliation Service and any state mediation boards must be notified 30 days (60 days in health care) before contract expiration.

Because so much of negotiation is done at the local level, we concentrate on bargaining at this level rather than on negotiation in a more centralized structure. For all bargaining structures, preparation for bargaining begins many months before the first face-to-face meeting. The success of negotiations is crucially related to the preparedness of the bargaining teams.

Selection of the Negotiating Team

Labor and management have the right to choose their own negotiating teams without interference from the other side. The qualities and skills that are required by the negotiators, particularly the chief negotiator, are the same for union and management. In fact, experienced negotiators could switch sides and be very nearly as effective at the negotiating table. The Federal Mediation and Conciliation Service (FMCS), which provides neutral mediators to help negotiators reach agreement, recruits its mediators from the ranks of both union- and management-experienced bargainers.

The chief spokesperson (negotiator) must have experience in and knowledge of labor relations and the operation covered by the agreement. This negotiator must also have influence with higher levels of authority in the organization. The personal characteristics of emotional stability, the capacity for quick thought, trustworthiness, and credibility are required of a negotiator. Negotiation is an art, not a science. The chief negotiator learns his or her skills at the table through on-the-job training. Some skills can be learned in the classroom, but most are the result of learning by doing.

The personal experience of one management chief negotiator is presented in the last section of the chapter. But experience is hardly enough. Successful negotiating requires emotional stability. Excitement and passions frequently run high during bargaining. The chief spokesperson must learn to maintain emotional control and to set the emotional pitch of negotiations to achieve team goals. Anger, humor, and sincerity are orchestrated to reach agreement. Because bargaining is face to face, direct and immediate, the chief negotiator must also be able to think on her or his feet as well as know when to get away from the table to think about the situation.

A key word used to describe those who negotiate is "credible." The chief spokesperson must be credible. This means the person must be believed and trusted to do what he or she says will be done. At a minimum, this includes the authority to bind (i.e., an agreement reached at the table by them will not be repudiated by someone else in the organization). It also means that the negotiator can say "no" and make it stick. In the final analysis a good chief negotiator must have the respect of the members of both teams at the table.

Both sides make use of experts who may or may not be on the actual bargaining teams. Because of the legal and economic complexities of such items as pension plans, health benefits, and contract language changes, both sides seek expert advice. Local management personnel and the local union leadership generally do not have the staff or resources to obtain such information. So, they obtain it from higher levels in their respective organizations or from those organizations which provide the benefits. (Insurance companies, for example, will itemize the costs of additional coverage.) For management, corporate may provide the services of a legal staff and compensation and benefits analysts. Local unions look to the international union staff, through the international representative, for negotiation support. When negotiations occur at the firm or industry level, the teams for both sides tend to be significantly larger. The experts, if not actually on the team, are immediately available to the negotiators.

The Management Team. Management teams often number three to five people. The chief spokesperson, chosen for the qualities mentioned above, is often a labor relations staff person, such as the director of industrial relations. The rest of the team is chosen for their special knowledge (labor relations staff or operations line people) or to serve a special function (note taker). Knowledge of one or more of the following may garner a place on the management team: the personnel function, day-to-day operations, union positions and politics, contract language drafting, cost of contract provisions, facility with language.

One person may be a corporate representative to oversee negotiations. At least one person is on the team primarily to take detailed notes of the contract talks. This position is not a trivial one. Note takers are invaluable aids to the chief negotiator. They must take down not only actual quotations from the opposing sides (picking up nuances in word meaning) but also the way in which it was said (emotional content). After the negotiations are over, these records are used for review purposes for the next negotiations and to provide support for arbitration cases.

The Union Team. Union teams are often larger than management teams. Members may be there for political reasons or for communication to the membership or to make sure the union constitution is followed. Not much information is available outside union and association circles about strategy in union team selection. Local union constitutions sometimes require that the executive board or top local officers be on the bargaining team. There may be a requirement that representatives from specific membership groups be on the team. These are selected by a secret ballot election among skilled workers, production workers, night-shift workers, etc. One or more stewards may be on the team because they have specific knowledge of how the old contract has worked and how workable any contract changes might be. Stewards are also there to serve as two-way conduits of information: back to the membership from the team and from the rank and file to the team.

The chief spokesperson could be the union's international representative. If not the chief spokesperson, the international representative is often present at the negotiations or in close contact with the team on strategy and tactics as a service to the local and for the national's own protection. This is increasingly true because the expansion of firms' markets and the current wave of firm mergers force national unions to closely coordinate the bargaining of their locals. They cannot afford to have a local set a negotiating precedent which will put other locals in a bad competitive position.

One strategy of team composition is to leave the local union president off the team. The local president is then free to handle community public relations, the day-to-day running of the union, and strike preparations. Plant managers on the management side may be left off the team for the same reasons: communications and daily plant operations.

Table 13-2 illustrates bargaining team composition for a Machinists negotiation with a printing company.

Preparing to Negotiate

Eighty percent of the time it takes to negotiate an agreement is spent in preparation. Thorough preparation can make up for inexperience at the table, but experience at the table cannot overcome poor preparation. Much of what

Table 13-2   Negotiating Teams

Union: International Association of Machinists	Management: Printing Machinery Company
IAM District Business Representative (Chief Negotiator)	Plant Industrial Relations Director (Chief Negotiator)
Local President	Corporate Vice President for
Vice President	Industrial Relations
Secretary/Treasurer	Plant Personnel or Industrial
Recording Secretary	Relations Representative
Grievance Committee Person	

the union does to prepare is also done by the company, but there are some basic differences.

Union Demands. Union demands come from the local rank and file up, and from the national union down. Local union meetings are held to gather and discuss demands. Polls are conducted. Suggestions are taken from individual members. Stewards are questioned by officers about problems with the current agreement. As a result of these activities, an extensive shopping list of local demands is made up. Some of these demands conflict with each other and some are not feasible, but a winnowing process of intra-organizational bargaining yields a set of local demands. The union team also tries to anticipate management demands and counterproposals in addition to determining its own demands.

Some demands originate from the national union or AFL-CIO. Every union has a national bargaining agenda. Agenda items are presented to the local membership to be included in the demands. They may be explained and sold to the local in a local union meeting by the international representative. Often they appear in the form of "model" contract language which the team must try to get into the agreement. The national may make the availability of negotiation assistance or strike funds contingent upon the local's putting the demands on the table and negotiating for them.

This is not to say that these demands are rammed down the local's throat. The national has a broader view, more expertise, and more research resources than does the local. Consequently, the national is in a better position to know what economic demands are realistic considering the firm and industry. It has the resources to do the research behind the complex and technical fringe benefit demands for changes in pensions and health insurance. And, its legal experts know what is legally or politically feasible given such laws as the Occupational Safety and Health Act (OSHA), the Employee Retirement Income Security Act (ERISA), and the myriad of equal opportunity legislation.

Management Demands and Counterproposals. Management formulates a few of its own demands, but it is basically concerned with the anticipation of labor demands and formulation of counterproposals to these. Some preparations for the next negotiations begin immediately after the last one. For example, as noted earlier, the note taker prepares an extensive record of the negotiations just concluded. The analysis of this yields a set of impressions of future union demands which may be made at the next negotiations.

Table 13-3 presents a checklist of items used by unions and management to prepare for bargaining. This is a short list which includes the basics of preparation. Note that with few exceptions union and management cover the same ground in preparing to bargain. One difference between the two is the extent to which management goes to cost out anticipated changes in the agreement. These figures are used by local management to bargain with higher levels of management for their authorized economic settlement figure. They are then used as a common denominator for bargaining with the union.

Table 13-3   Union (U) and Management (M) Negotiation Preparation Checklist

1. Review material on hand. (U and M)
   a. Minutes and notes from last negotiation.
   b. Grievance and arbitration record.
   c. Other contracts in the industry with the same and other firms and unions.
2. Notify other party, FMCS, state mediators (U and M).
3. Select negotiating committee (U and M).
4. Collect data.
   a. Pay and benefits in local labor markets, of competitors, at industry and national levels. (U and M)
   b. Firm work force distributions by job class, seniority, age, sex, minority (U and M).
   c. Cost of current agreement (M).
      1. Average straight time rate.
      2. Fringe benefits: holidays, pension, health, vacation, leaves.
5. Anticipate demands: economic and noneconomic (U and M).
   a. Review last negotiation's dropped and traded issues.
   b. Talk with first-line supervisors and stewards.
6. Develop strategy.
   a. Decide opening position, compromises, final positions that group will take a strike over (U and M).
   b. Prepare bargaining book with successive positions of acceptable language (U and M).
   c. Cost out each position and provide background support (M).
7. Get corporate approval (M) or national approval (U).
8. Prepare for possible work stoppage (U and M).
9. Meet with other side to plan negotiations arrangements: place, meeting times, agenda (U and M).

THE INITIAL MEETINGS

The opening meetings of negotiations are very important for a number of reasons. They provide a political platform for the labor organization. They set the tone for the rest of the negotiations. And for the first time each side gets a look at the demands and proposals of the other.

The first few sessions may be attended by more union members than are on the actual negotiating team. The extra members present act as observers and report back to the membership. The labor negotiators (union officers) may take this opportunity to show the rank and file that they, as officers, are truly representing membership interests. Without elaboration, the officers will issue a lengthy shopping list of demands as an ultimatum to management. The word then gets back that the negotiators really took it to management on rank-and-file demands.

That may be the first and last time some of the demands appear on the table. That is not to say that some labor demands are nonsense. Every demand that goes to the table is there for a reason. Some are there for internal political reasons and some are there as trade-bait or window dressing, but the majority of demands are there because the union wants all or a piece of them. The key to a successful negotiation is for each side to divine the true intent of the other. Providing there is room for compromise, they try their best to settle. There are few negotiations where either side wants a strike. It is safe to say that negotiators for both sides want to achieve their negotiation goals without a work stoppage.

After the labor organization presents its demands, the management team makes its own demands. There was a time when management made few demands of its own and confined its response to counterproposals to the union demands. That has changed. Management demands often deal with work rule changes as they relate to productivity. The Conference Board survey found:

> Management anticipating union demands in many areas, willing to trade on a limited number of subjects (chiefly on funded benefits), and seeking possible exchanges from the union in one subject area: flexibility in assignment of employees.[8]

The first sessions tend to set the tone for the later negotiations. One management negotiator who frequently negotiates with local unions takes two sets of management demands and counterproposals to the table with him. If he feels the local's demands are reasonable, he responds with his "reasonable" counterproposals. If he believes the local's shopping list to be "unreasonable," he responds with his "hard-nosed" counters.

SERIOUS BARGAINING

With few exceptions, it is not possible for management to respond to the initial union demands with immediate counterproposals. The union demands have to be fleshed out in order for management negotiators to know exactly

---

8. Freedman, *Managing Labor Relations*, p. 42.

what the labor organization is asking for. The content of some demands, like one for the union shop, is obvious on the face of it. A quick counter is possible. Most demands, however, require exploration before any actual bargaining takes place. Once the content of the demands is established, the parties begin the haggling of negotiations.

The Flow of Negotiations

Each negotiation is unique. However, in older, more established relationships, bargaining develops over the years into a ritual. The negotiators may have faced one another across the table many times. The flow of negotiations tends to take on a pattern even though the specific content is unique. There are some generalizations to be made about the flow of negotiations.

By starting with the easiest issues to settle first, the negotiators build momentum and a sense of problem solving as they move on to more difficult issues. In general, this order from easiest to more difficult issues is also simultaneously from noneconomic to economic items. Economic items such as wages and fringes are issues that have a calculable economic cost to the company. The common denominator of these is dollars and cents. The negotiation positions are costed out to the tenth of a cent. Some negotiators prefer to get all the noneconomic items off the table before proceeding to the economic ones. They refuse to talk money until the language issues have been settled.

Early in the negotiations, issues tend to be settled item by item. For example, the negotiators might agree to discuss five issues at a particular session, take them up and dispose of them in order, unrelated to one another. Later on in the bargaining the negotiators begin to *package* groups of issues. Obvious interrelationships among the demands emerge. For example, the union demand for an improved training program is linked to the demand for a change in the way vacancies are filled in the firm, and these are related to a management demand for a longer probationary status for new employees. The three will be settled as an integrated package since they all have a common denominator: access to vacancies.

Almost certainly the economic items will be packaged because they are all related to one another in terms of dollars and cents. Company-provided safety shoes, an additional paid holiday, shortening the workday, provision of a dental plan, and a 25-cent wage increase all have a cost. As was noted in the preparation for bargaining section earlier, the company negotiator is only authorized to spend a set amount. Each demand and counterproposal is viewed as part of this authorized total expenditure. It is the cost of the total package of wages and fringes that the management negotiator must try to keep in bounds of the authorized goal. An additional paid holiday, for example, may be the equivalent of a 2 cents per hour wage increase.

Time Outs

Negotiation is not necessarily nonstop, around-the-clock, everyone-glued-to-the-table work. Even when the negotiators are down to the last hour, they do not spend the entire time at the table. They are away from the table to *caucus* and for *sidebars*.

Caucuses. Negotiators caucus regularly. Along with the negotiation room there are usually one or two caucus rooms. When a chief negotiator at the table calls a caucus, the entire team gets up and exits en masse to the caucus room. Teams caucus away from the table to consider proposals from the other side and to formulate counterproposals. They caucus if the team becomes confused during the negotiations. They may caucus for strategy reasons—to give the other team a chance to think over their last proposal, or to eat up time to force a speedier pace of negotiations when they return to the table. Caucuses are a common, frequently used part of bargaining.

Sidebars. Somewhat less common and usually more secretive is the use of sidebars. Sidebars are meetings between the chief negotiators without the other team members being present. They may be clandestine or open meetings, but they are often kept secret. The purpose of the sidebar is to make more headway toward settlement then can be made with the full teams at the table. The chief negotiators may have negotiated with each other for years and know that to reach a settlement they need to talk away from their teams. At a time other than at a negotiation session they arrange to meet privately or talk by telephone. They may informally settle the contract terms in a one-on-one negotiation in the sidebar. Then the two chief negotiators must return to the table and skillfully maneuver their teams to the agreed upon settlement. The meetings are held clandestinely to avoid the accusation by the rest of the team that the management chief negotiator "sold out" to the union or that the union chief negotiator is "in bed with management."

Some sidebars are done openly while a negotiation session is in progress. During a caucus, for example, the union chief negotiator and a companion (to avoid the charge of selling out) may meet with the chief negotiator from the other team to "clarify" some proposals on the table. And sidebars can become part of the ritual. One management negotiator always expects a call from the union business agent the morning before the last negotiating session. They settle the economic issues by negotiating over the telephone.

Most negotiations go right down to the wire. They settle just before contract expiration. The last few minutes can be frantic. At some point, management submits its "last, best, and final" offer. The union must decide whether to accept it or hit the bricks. Some demands are dropped and others, where the parties were far apart, are suddenly settled. If they agree, the chief negotiators shake hands and the table play of negotiations is over. A tentative agreement has been reached.

WRAPPING UP THE AGREEMENT

There is yet much work to be done. The agreement must be put in final form. As the parties agree to language during negotiations, the wording is written on slips or sheets of paper and initialed by each side. These must be collected and put into agreement form. The new agreement is typed and signed by the parties, then run off in large quantities for management, union officials, and employees.

But the agreement may be tentative for another reason. It may have to be ratified. On the management side, higher corporate officers may have to give their blessings to it. Or, members of the employers' association may have to approve the contract. The labor organization side of things is more complex. A study of the prevalence of *contract ratification* requirements revealed the widespread use of ratification votes.[9] Of the 73 unions having 40,000 or more members (90 percent of union membership), 29 unions (40 percent of all union members) had a constitutional provision requiring some form of contract ratification vote by the membership. Many others have a tradition of ratification votes. Roughly one in ten contracts tentatively agreed to at the table is rejected when submitted to a vote by the rank and file. When this occurs the parties return to the table (possibly after a strike has resulted) to negotiate suitable changes in the initial agreement.

THEORIES OF COLLECTIVE BARGAINING

It should be evident from the last section that collective bargaining is a highly complex process of interaction between labor and management. The complexity of negotiations has not stopped scholars from attempting to model collective bargaining. Theories have been advanced about both the process and the outcome of bargaining. After a discussion of the nature of the various theories, we examine one theory about bargaining power.

An Early Model and a Controversy

The earliest economic model of collective bargaining was called *bilateral monopoly*. The model is aptly named because it pits the union as a single seller of labor (monopolist) bargaining against a single buyer of labor (monopsonist). The end result of this model is that there are any number of possible wage and employment settlements depending upon which side is the more skillful and powerful negotiator. The range of potential outcomes is called the contract zone. Because no single wage and employment levels could be determined from bilateral monopoly, it was called an *indeterminate model*. This unsatisfactory state of affairs led to a classic controversy over modeling collective bargaining. Some scholars, such as Arthur Ross, believed bargaining could not be reduced to an economic model. Others, including John T. Dunlop, took the position that the theory just needed to be refined.

---

9. Herbert J. Lahne, "Union Contract Ratification Procedure," *Monthly Labor Review,* Vol. 31, No. 2 (May, 1968), p. 9.

"We no longer have a satisfying theory of wages," according to Arthur Ross:

> ... the union is not a seller of labor and is not concerned with the quantity sold, and ... the upper and lower limits of bilateral monopoly theory have no more than a superficial correspondence with the union's initial demand and the employer's initial offer in collective bargaining. . . . Many of the most interesting questions concerning union behavior cannot be answered by any strictly economic analysis. . . .
>
> What is needed is to break down the walls between the separate disciplines of social sciences which have hitherto dealt with separate aspects of social behavior. . . . The central proposition, then, is that a trade union is a political agency operating in an economic environment.[10]

According to Ross, union wage demands are formulated according to the *standard of equitable comparison.* That is, the union rank-and-file membership always knows what other workers who are doing the same type of work are getting and demand that plus "more." Because of the political nature of unions, this pits union leaders against each other. The settlement agreed to by one union leader becomes the target to be beaten by other union leaders in subsequent negotiations. This leadership competition causes the formation of *orbits of coercive comparison* which set wage rates in the union sector.

John Dunlop countered straightforwardly:

> The price of labor services, like any price, is determined in economics by supply and demand. . . . It will be useful to regard buyers of labor services as confronted by a "business enterprise" (trade union) just as when raw materials or money capital is purchased. . . . The most suitable generalized model of the trade union for analytical purposes is probably that which depicts the maximization of the wage bill for the total membership.[11]

Subsequent to the Ross-Dunlop debate, theories of bargaining developed along two lines: the Ross-type, more behaviorally oriented models; and the economic models patterned after Dunlop's premise. One recent survey of the literature dealing with bargaining models reviewed 7 behavioral models (including Walton and McKersie), 18 economic models, and 3 mixed models.[12] The economic models illustrate the wide range of thought concerning modeling of the negotiation process. Included were (1) bilateral monopoly models, (2) game theory models, (3) strike duration models, (4) empirically based models, and (5) dynamic models. The survey authors, Peterson and Tracy, conclude:

---

10. Arthur M. Ross, *Trade Union Wage Policy* (Berkeley, Calif.: University of California Press, 1948), pp. 1, 4, 7, 12.

11. John T. Dunlop, *Wage Determination Under Trade Unions* (New York: Augustus M. Kelley, 1950), pp. 28, 32, 44.

12. Richard B. Peterson and Lane Tracy, *Models of the Bargaining Process: With Special References to Collective Bargaining,* Monograph Series (Seattle: University of Washington, 1977).

> The foregoing models represent the mainstream of economic thought on the bargaining problem. In recent years the stream appears to have been heading in the behavioral direction, attempting to account for the process of attitude change that seems to be at the heart of bargaining. . . . The details may differ, but all are looking to some process of attitude change as the key to bargaining.[13]

Many of the recent models involve economic and mathematical complexities beyond the scope of this text. But one model has elements of both economic and behavioral theory and does deal with bargaining attitudes. It is this model of bargaining attitude to which we turn next.

The Bargaining Power Theory of Negotiations

The bargaining power theory is a marriage of behavioral and economic concepts. In an early treatise on wage determination, Neil Chamberlain wrote, "Bargaining power can be defined as the capability to effect an agreement on one's own terms; operationally, one's bargaining power is another's inducement to agree."[14]

The theory is summarized nicely in a ratio suggested by Marshall, Cartter, and King.[15] One party's bargaining power in negotiations depends upon how the other party perceives the trade-off between the cost of disagreeing to a set of demands and the cost of agreeing to them. The two attitudes are summarized as shown:

$$\text{Employer's bargaining attitude} = \frac{\text{employer's perceived cost of disagreeing with the union}}{\text{employer's perceived cost of agreeing with the union}}$$

$$\text{Union's bargaining attitude} = \frac{\text{union's perceived cost of disagreeing with the employer}}{\text{union's perceived cost of agreeing with the employer}}$$

In order for there to be a settlement, one side must agree to the terms put on the table by the other. For example, the employer will agree to the union's terms whenever management thinks that the cost of disagreeing with the union exceeds (or equals) the cost of agreeing with the union. If we could

---

13. Ibid., p. 36.
14. Neil W. Chamberlain, *A General Theory of Economic Process* (New York: Harper and Brothers, 1955), p. 81.
15. F. Ray Marshall, Allen M. Cartter, and Allen G. King. *Labor Economics,* 3d ed. (Homewood, Ill.: Richard D. Irwin, Inc., 1976), p. 353.

quantify the ratios, the ratio would have to equal or exceed the value of one for a settlement to occur.

The value of the bargaining power idea is not in calculating whether or not a ratio is less than or greater than one. Its utility is twofold. First, from the economic side, it is possible to link bargaining power and outcomes to such microeconomic variables as the inelasticity of the demand for labor and firm profitability. The link between bargaining attitude and the macroeconomic variables of unemployment and inflation can also be explored. Second, the bargaining attitude model can also be used to analyze strategy and tactics during the process of negotiation.

Union and management negotiation strategy and tactics can be seen as ways to achieve settlement on one's own terms by affecting the other party's perception of the costs of disagreeing and agreeing. Table 13-4 suggests a few examples.

Table 13-4   Negotiation Tactics and Bargaining Attitudes

Union Tactics Designed to	
Increase Employer's Perceived Cost of Disagreeing	Decrease Employer's Perceived Cost of Agreeing
Threaten to strike	Grant a concession
Emphasize the imminence of contract expiration	Link employer concession to a union concession
Relate failure to concede to higher absenteeism or turnover	Show how both union and management gain from employer concession, e.g., improved morale and productivity

Employer Tactics Designed to	
Increase Union's Perceived Cost of Disagreeing	Decrease Union's Perceived Cost of Agreeing
Show willingness to take a strike	Grant a concession
Link failure to agree to future layoffs	Package demand with other items union wants
Emphasize loss of wages during a strike	Argue favorable comparisons between current position and other industry settlements

Union Strategy. Assume, for example, that the union demand for increased wages is $1 per hour over 2 years and management has countered with 40 cents. To increase the employer's perceived cost of disagreeing with the union, the chief union negotiator might rattle the sabers with, "We're miles apart on money. I have a strike vote in my pocket; we'll use it if you can't come closer than 40 cents." Or, more subtly, "The contract expires at midnight and we have a long way to go before then." Or, "Unless we get the dollar, we both know that there are a lot of guys who'll go to work across town at Acme. They settled for a buck last week."

To decrease the employer's cost of agreeing, the union might soften its demand to 90 cents. Or it could link an unaltered demand of $1 with a management demand on a work rules change. Or, they might argue that a wage increase in excess of 40 cents will improve employee morale and improve productivity so that both union and employer are better off.

Management Strategy. The same sorts of ploys are used by management. Suppose management has demanded that craft jurisdictions be softened to allow more flexible work assignments and the union has refused. "We don't like to hear the word strike, but we're prepared. We've got the raw material and supervisory people to run the place for months without you and you know it." And, "Unless we get more flexibility on work assignments and get that department out of the red, we're going to have to lay off. We can't stay competitive." And, "This is a minor concession on your part and only affects 12 people. Are you going to take 150 people out and lose $200 apiece a week over a minor change?"

To decrease the union's cost of agreeing with the work rules change, the management negotiator might soften the proposal somewhat by offering to combine only two current craft groups to form a new craft class instead of the three as originally proposed. The management negotiator might offer to increase the pay of the new craft class in line with the expected productivity gains from the combination. Or the unions in other industries may have already agreed to combine crafts, and this can be pointed out to the union. The union then is not setting a bad precedent.

There is no limit to the scenarios that can be imagined using the relationship between bargaining attitudes and table tactics. Every move at the table can be viewed as designed to affect the other side's bargaining attitude. But not every change in bargaining attitude is the result of the parties' control at the table. External changes affect bargaining attitudes as well. For example, unions who bargain with employers who face a slack product demand may have reduced bargaining power. The employer's perceived cost of disagreeing with the union will be lowered because a layoff may be imminent anyway. Similarly, a union's bargaining power is enhanced by a strong product market since the threat of a strike will inflict greater damage to an employer whose business is booming.

None of the models of bargaining predict the outcome of the negotiations very well. They all contribute to a better understanding of the process, however. A very simple model for predicting negotiation outcomes is tested in the last section of this chapter.

AN ANALYSIS OF NEGOTIATION COMPROMISES

Compromise is the essence of the give and take of collective bargaining. At least part of the process is distributive. The parties ask more than they expect to get. The union asks for a dollar and management offers a dime. Do they end up splitting the difference between the demands?

Do Negotiators Split the Difference?

Because of the confidential nature of negotiations, little information is available about this aspect of negotiation. However, two studies provide interesting but not definitive results. Bowlby and Shriver studied detailed management minutes made by the Tennessee Valley Authority (TVA) in wage negotiations with 16 craft unions. Unlike private sector craft unions, those with agreements with the TVA are precluded from striking legally. In the 16 years, 1960-1975, the 16 unions made 252 agreements. "The most important conclusion is that unions bluff more than management during collective bargaining. . . ."[16] On the average the union initially demanded 11 percent, the employer countered with 3 percent, and the settlement was 6 percent. Daniel Hamermesh made a similar study of 43 public sector bargains involving teachers, police, and firefighters. Although strikes were illegal, a number of them occurred anyway. On the average, the union demanded 23 percent initially, the employer offered 8 percent, and they settled for 12 percent.[17] One caveat to keep in mind is that in neither situation did the union have the right to strike. This may have caused them to increase their first demand to outweigh their relative lack of power compared with what could exist in a private sector situation where the right to strike would be theirs.

But Is the Settlement More Than Management Intended?

Although it appears that unions may bluff more, is the settlement what management intended? One way to judge the success or failure of negotiations is to put the final settlement alongside the prenegotiation goals. The Conference Board study (mentioned at the beginning of this chapter) asked management negotiators how close they came to their negotiation goals. It should be kept in mind that the answers by negotiators about their own accomplishments probably contain a measure of gratuity. Nonetheless, the results are interesting. "On wage and benefit targets, one quarter of the companies achieved their target. One quarter negotiated a package below the target price. The other half settled above their target."[18] For those who exceeded their target, 53 percent were over by less than 1 percent, and only 15 percent were 2.5 percent or more per year above. "With regard to nonwage goals of management, about 88 percent were attained."[19]

---

16. Roger Bowlby and William Shriver, "Bluffing and the 'Split-the-Difference' Theory of Wage Bargaining," *Industrial and Labor Relations Review* (January, 1978), p. 170.

17. Daniel S. Hamermesh, "Who 'Wins' in Wage Bargaining?," *Industrial and Labor Relations Review* (July, 1973), pp. 1146-9.

18. Freedman, *Managing Labor Relations*, p. 47.

19. Ibid.

Negotiators who exceeded their goals were firms with a higher degree of unionization, firms which were vulnerable to a strike (particularly in excess of 15 days), or firms which bargained on a multiplant basis as part of a master agreement. Negotiators are evaluated on their capability to avoid surprises at the table. Not strikes per se but unanticipated strikes are to be avoided. Only 20 percent of the firms, however, formally evaluate their labor relations professionals. The standard measures of performance are money measures. They include the effect of the new contract on labor cost and the size of the settlement when compared with the industry settlement. When it comes to contract losses, less is preferred to more.

CONCLUDING REMARKS

Over a 3-year period there are about 190,000 collective bargaining agreements negotiated in the United States. There are plant level agreements, master contracts, pattern-setting bargains. Blue-collar, white-collar and professional employees bargain in coal, steel, trucking, health care, education, and innumerable other industries. No less remarkable than the variety of situations where bargaining occurs is the fact that the process is essentially the same in each case. There are many variations on the negotiation theme, but there is a theme.

Getting that theme across has been the purpose of this chapter. We hewed to the center and discussed how bargaining proceeds in general. The exceptions and peculiarities by industry, by occupation, and per negotiator are subjects for further study.

Having negotiated an agreement, the next step is to see what is in it. The clauses in a contract, the rationale for their inclusion, and their performance in practice are the subject of Chapter 14.

CHAPTER SUMMARY

Collective bargaining structure refers to the parties who negotiate agreements and the sequence in which they are negotiated. Structures vary from decentralized plant level bargaining to the more centralized bargaining formats, including multiplant master contracts, pattern setting, multiemployer, and coordinated bargaining.

Prenegotiation activities include selection of the union and management teams and extensive preparation for bargaining. Management attempts to correctly antici-

pate union demands, formulates a range of counterproposals, and derives some demands of its own. Union team selection and demand formulation are more political in nature. Other negotiations, other contracts, and the grievance and arbitration record are fertile sources of demands and counterproposals. A behavioral analysis of the negotiation process suggests that there are really four activities going on: distributive bargaining, integrative bargaining, attitudinal structuring, and intra-organizational bargaining.

The initial meetings between union and management are important because of the politicking that occurs, because it is the first look both sides have at the range of demands, and because the tone for future meetings is set here. As bargaining proceeds, the trend is from less controversial items to more difficult ones, from noneconomic to economic terms, and from single items to packaging. Once a tentative pact has been bargained, there are postcontract wrap-up activities which may include ratification.

The early attempts at modeling collective bargaining resulted in the indeterminate model of bilateral monopoly. Arthur Ross and John Dunlop debated the usefulness of purely economic as opposed to more behavioral negotiation theories. Today there are many and varied economic models of bargaining. One of these, the bargaining power theory of negotiation, is useful both from the economic and the behavioral perspectives. The future of bargaining theory is in the formation of mixed economic-behavioral models.

Compromise is the essence of negotiation. Both sides put forth positions with the knowledge that they will move to some middle ground in some items. Some empirical results suggest that, at least for public sector or no-strike situations, the settlement is nearer to the initial management position. The performance of management negotiators is evaluated on the basis of how close the actual settlement is to the anticipated one and on the dollar cost of the agreement.

KEY TERMS

collective bargaining structure
local supplements
collective bargaining unit
master contract
pattern setting
multiemployer agreement
whipsawing
coordinated bargaining
distributive bargaining
integrative bargaining

intra-organizational bargaining
attitudinal structuring
package bargaining
caucus
sidebars
contract ratification
bilateral monopoly
indeterminate model
standard of equitable comparison
orbits of coercive comparison

REVIEW QUESTIONS

1. What is bargaining structure? What are the major forms? Give an example of each.

2. What are the differences and similarities in union and management preparation for bargaining? Why do they differ?

3. Could the same issue be distributive bargaining in one relationship and integrative in another? Give an example.

4. Why are economic items usually the last to be negotiated? Why as a package?

5. The rank and file fail to ratify the first tentative agreement two contracts in a row. What impact will that have on the next negotiation?

6. Does the fact that unions may move farther to reach a settlement mean that they are weaker than management? Why or why not?

ADDITIONAL REFERENCES

Balliet, Lee. *Survey of Labor Relations.* Washington: Bureau of National Affairs, 1981.

Davey, Harold W. *Contemporary Collective Bargaining,* 3d ed. Englewood Cliffs, N.J.: Prentice-Hall, Inc., 1972.

Freedman, Audrey. *Managing Labor Relations.* New York: The Conference Board, 1979.

Holley, William H., and Kenneth M. Jennings. *The Labor Relations Process.* Hinsdale, Ill.: The Dryden Press, 1980.

Kochan, Thomas A. *Collective Bargaining and Industrial Relations.* Homewood, Ill.: Richard D. Irwin, Inc., 1980.

Walton, Richard E., and Robert B. McKersie. *A Behavioral Theory of Negotiations.* New York: McGraw-Hill Book Co., 1965.

THE WORLD
OF WORK . . .

Negotiating As Seen By a Negotiator

Throughout the chapter we have examined the negotiation process as outsiders peering in. In this section, a seasoned management negotiator discusses bargaining, the route taken to become a chief spokesperson at the table, and the qualities of a successful negotiator.

The ultimate occupational thrill for an employee relations professional comes for many people when, for the first time, they can reach across a bargaining table, shake hands with a union leader and realize that they have successfully concluded their first labor negotiations. To many people, not knowledgeable in the process of collective bargaining, there is an inaccurate perception that the negotiations process is little more than loud voices and smoke filled rooms. There is also a belief that those of us who are fortunate enough to be able to negotiate labor agreements become skillful at our trade by some mystical process that is closely tied to witchcraft. In the current economic structure of the employee/employer relationship, nothing could be further from reality.

Negotiators become successful by the same method that anyone succeeds in any profession: a reasonable degree of innate talent, a solid education (academic or life experience), a healthy dose of hard work and long hours, and the desire to succeed. The exhilaration of the first negotiations when a person is in the principal negotiator's role does not arrive without having learned the basics of the process. The ways to become a successful negotiator are as varied as the number of people who pursue this occupation. In my personal situation, my interest in labor relations goes back to my youth when I was exposed to union-management relations as a result of my father's employment with a major manufacturing firm. That interest was translated into an academic career that prepared me for a career in industrial relations.

The initial exposure to the process of labor relations came very early in my career and that exposure took the unglorious form of taking notes at negotiation and participating in the laborious process of preparation. Many hours were spent developing an understanding of the collective bargaining process and the basic philosophical principles that form its foundation from this first "taste of honey." I then spent several years working as a day-to-day labor relations person handling grievances, arbitration and a host of other employee relations duties which in future years have proved to be extremely valuable experiences. During this fetal stage of the development of a negotiator, several other bargaining table encounters took place with each providing more understanding than the one before in terms of process. The grievance resolution area provided an opportunity to develop skills and techniques that are used extensively at the bargaining table. After having observed six negotiations in the first five years of professional employment, and having conducted several hundred grievance meetings, I was given an opportunity to sit "center chair" for the first time in a wage negotiation. By contrast, a wage negotiation is simplistic compared to a full and complete contract renegotiation which I would do the following year.

Before the start of my first negotiations, partly out of fear and partly out of inexperience, I spent hundreds of hours preparing myself for my first real labor relations test. I checked, rechecked and triple checked the economic costing data, reviewed minutes of other negotiations, practiced speeches and responses in front of a mirror, tried to anticipate any occurrences that could possibly happen and taxed my memory from other negotiations for style and techniques of others whose skill and ability I respected. This included not only company negotiators but union professionals.

Twelve joint sessions, twenty odd company committee meetings and nights of coaching by experienced negotiators came to conclusion one late May evening with the first "handshake." No other words I had heard professionally meant more than when a seasoned union negotiator said to me, "You've got a deal." From that first negotiation, many more have followed and my role changed from "center chair" to a teacher of others who sit in that seat.

Over the past years I have drawn some personal conclusions on what traits a person must possess to be among the very few of this profession to "make it" at the collective bargaining table.

The first conclusion I have drawn is that negotiation and success at the process is as much art and style as science. A second point that cannot be overstated is that the members of the union bargaining team are not the enemy. They have the same overall goal as a company negotiator—a fair and equitable settlement with the emphasis on the word settlement. Neither side of the labor-management relationship ever won on a strike and no one ever lost on a settlement if it was bargained in good faith.

The final observation on collective bargaining and the people who make it a vital part of our economic system is the universal traits for all talented negotiators no matter which side of the table they may sit on. Those traits, many of which are subjective in nature, are why I feel art and style are so critical to professional success. Those traits include *credibility*, first and foremost; *knowl-*

edgeability of the situation, the process, the interpersonal and political dynamics; *effective communication skills,* this extends to oral, written and nonverbal media of information and thought exchange; the ability to function under enormous pressure, both intellectually and physically; the ability to take risks without fear of failure; leadership capacity to your own group, all of whom participate in the process; *competitiveness,* the desire to do your best, accept nothing short of perfection but still being able to concede when the situation dictates concession; and finally, having a *gut feeling* for the right and wrong moves. If success at the collective bargaining table were to be tied to only one trait, however, it would be credibility—without being able to be believed, no relationship can be developed with those you are negotiating with and without mutual trust and respect for each other and your positions, all the tactics at your command will not produce a fair and equitable settlement and the thrill of those words, "you've got a deal."

Source: Personal conversation with William R. Hutchison, Director—Employee Relations, Coatings Materials Division and Specialty Chemicals & Plastics Division of Union Carbide Corporation.

Chapter 14

The Contents of a Collective Bargaining Agreement

Labor and management have negotiated a collective bargaining agreement. This chapter covers the contents of agreements. Types of contract clauses depend upon the nature of the industry and the nature of the occupations covered. We examine the major contract clauses, the rationale for their inclusion in an agreement, variations in clauses, and their prevalence.

HIGHLIGHTS OF A COLLECTIVE BARGAINING AGREEMENT—IS THE SKY THE LIMIT?

Are there any limits to what can go into an agreement? Is everything fair game for collective bargaining? Section 8(d) of the Taft-Hartley Act says the parties have a

> Mutual obligation . . . to meet at reasonable times and confer in good faith with respect to wages, hours, and other terms and conditions of employment . . . and [to execute] a written contract incorporating any agreement reached. . . .

The wages and hours part is not hard, but what constitutes "other terms and conditions of employment"? NLRB decisions have resulted in three categories of contract negotiation items: mandatory, voluntary, and illegal.

Mandatory bargaining subjects must be negotiated if either side requests it. If no agreement can be reached and an impasse is reached, a work stoppage is legal. If the parties agree, the accord must be put in writing. Wages, paid holidays, pension plans, health and welfare benefits, union security clauses, and seniority are a few of the several hundred mandatory items.

Voluntary bargaining subjects are nonmandatory but permissible to negotiate and reach agreement on. However, either side can also refuse to negotiate about them at all or refuse to continue negotiating about them once they are on the table. The distinction between nonmandatory and mandatory is that a work stoppage is illegal over a nonmandatory item. A party cannot negotiate to impasse on a voluntary item. A union, for example, could not strike over a company's participation in an employer strike insurance fund. Nor could they strike over a demand to put a union officer on the board of directors of a corporation. Management cannot insist to impasse that a union drop fines against members who crossed the picket line to work during a strike.

The last category consists of *illegal bargaining subjects.* Neither side can request that the other bargain over such an item. For example, a bargaining demand for a closed shop or for a hot cargo clause is bad faith bargaining because both are prohibited by national labor law.

THE TABLE OF CONTENTS FOR TWO TYPES OF AGREEMENT

Having set out the legal limits to contract contents, it remains to consider what commonly goes into an agreement. The abridged table of contents for two agreements are shown as Tables 14-1 and 14-2.

The first agreement (Table 14-1) is for a *P and M* (production and mainte-nance) unit between the United Auto Workers (UAW) and an agricultural implement manufacturer. It is a typical industrial union contract. This is just the agreement on the rules of the shop, and this portion alone is 192 pages long. There are eight appendices covering fringe benefits which are under separate cover. The second contract (Table 14-2) is a typical craft agreement. It is between a bricklayers' local and a construction employers' association. The full agreement is only 7 pages long.

Some of the differences between craft and industrial unions were dis-cussed in Chapter 10. The contracts are different because the nature of the employer-employee relationship differs between industrial and craft settings. Industrial union agreements are more lengthy and complex because of the long-term employer-employee relationship. The union and employer over time build a relationship which extends to the nuances of employment. The union quest for more has led to increased and finer coverage of employment on the job. In short, the union tries to control the supply of labor once it is *on* the job (after management has done the hiring). Craft union members, on the other hand, work for many employers over time. Their relationship with a single contractor may last until a construction project is over. Then they move on to another project and employer. The union, however, controls the supply of labor *to* the job. They do so, as best they can, by controlling entrance to the trade through an apprenticeship program and by encouraging employers to call the union hiring hall whenever they wish to put more workers on the job. Time is also more important on construction projects than for industrial pro-duction.

Because of the fluid and temporal nature of craft employment and because of union control over entrance into the trade, much of what is in the industrial agreement is handled elsewhere by union and management. Apprenticeship, for example, is often regulated under a separate, area-wide agreement. Move-

Table 14-1   Contents of an Industrial Union Contract

Table 14-2   Contents of a Craft Agreement

Table of Contents

Preamble

Article 1.	Jurisdictional Area
Article 2.	Union Recognition and Security
Article 3.	Management Recognition and Rights
Article 4.	Separability
Article 5.	Nondiscrimination
Article 6.	Bond
Article 7.	Wage Rate Schedule, Overtime, and Holidays
	Section 7.1—Overtime and Holidays
	Section 7.2—Wage Rate Schedule
	Section 7.3—Hours of Work
	Section 7.4—Shift Schedule
Article 8.	Pay Periods
Article 9.	Apprentices
Article 10.	Welfare and Pension Funds
Article 11.	Dues Checkoff
Article 12.	Hourly Savings Funds
Article 13.	Construction Advancement Program
Article 14.	Foremen
Article 15.	Conditions of Employment
Article 16.	Safety Conditions
Article 17.	Stewards
Article 18.	Working Code—Rules
Article 19.	Scaffolding
Article 20.	What Constitutes Masonry
	Section 20.1—Brick Masonry
	Section 20.2—Stonemasonry
	Section 20.3—Artificial Masonry
Article 21.	Settlement of Disputes
Article 22.	Union Cooperation
Article 23.	Termination

ment from job to job is controlled internal to the union and has no place in a labor-management contract. Some things are less complicated (grievance procedures) to save time on the job. Contractual differences are handled as soon as possible to avoid work delays. And, to a certain extent, craft employment is simpler to administer because the organization of the production process is less complex (fewer types of jobs with fewer attendant pay scales).

THE LOGIC AND COVERAGE OF SPECIFIC CLAUSES

The next sections expand on selected items in the agreements. The emphasis here is on what can be said generally about the logic behind each topic and the current trends in coverage. With over 150,000 agreements in the United States, there is a wide variety of clause types on each subject.

Agreement and Recognition Clauses

The first page of the contract opens with a *preamble* or *agreement* stating who the parties to the agreement are. The first article is often the *recognition clause* in which the employer states that it recognizes the union. This clause also establishes the collective bargaining unit covered by the contract. Production processes that occur at plant locations (industrial unions) are named specifically. The following example is taken from the contract between the Aluminum Workers and ALCOA:

> The provisions of this Agreement shall apply solely to those employees of the company at its plants located at Warrick, Indiana; Davenport, Iowa; Lafayette, Indiana; Lancaster, Pennsylvania; Massena, New York; and Lebanon, Pennsylvania, for whom the Union has been certified the exclusive bargaining agency by the National Labor Relations Board, or for whom the Company has recognized the Union as the exclusive bargaining agency.[1]

Craft agreements cover all union construction activity within the union's craft jurisdiction for a geographic area.

> The Employer hereby recognizes the Union who is signatory hereto as the sole and exclusive bargaining representative of all employees of the Employer over whom the Union has jurisdiction.
>
> The provisions of the Agreement shall govern the employment and conditions under which the Plumbers and Pipefitters shall work and the rates of pay they shall receive in the construction industry in the following bounded territory: Hamilton and Webster Counties.

Union Security

There are really three interests wrapped up in an agreement: those of management, the employees, and the union. The union represents employee interests, but in order to do so effectively, it has some institutional survival interests of its own. The labor organization can be voted out as exclusive bargaining agent. Therefore, in addition to clauses involving the direct interest of the employees, some contract clauses are included to protect the union as an institution. Union rights clauses include such things as union bulletin boards, access to the work facility, and the number of work-site union representatives. Another clause, prevalent in virtually every agreement, generates much controversy: the union security clause.

The Concept. A *union security clause* is an agreement between the company

---

1. *Agreement and Working Rules Between Aluminum Company of America and Aluminum Workers International Union—AFL-CIO* (June 1, 1980), p. 5.

and the labor organization wherein the company agrees to aid the union in getting employees to join the union and/or collect union dues and fees. Under the Taft-Hartley Act, the employer can legally make "an agreement with a labor organization . . . to require as a condition of employment membership therein on or after the thirtieth day following employment. . . . " The employer must discharge the employee if the employee fails to pay the periodic dues and initiation fees uniformly required for acquiring or retaining membership. Therefore membership in the labor organization can be made a condition of "employment" beyond the thirtieth day only to the extent of paying dues and fees. Membership in craft unions, due to the transient nature of the work, can be required after the seventh day. If an employee is expelled from the union for any reason other than refusing to pay dues, or if a person is denied admission on the basis of discrimination, the employee can keep the job.

The Clauses. There are numerous levels of union security. The least secure labor organization is one which has just the recognition clause. This is the *open shop* where the union must approach workers individually to join and must collect the dues and fees by itself. A BLS study showed 244 of 1536 major agreements had only a recognition clause for union security.[2] In the next most secure situation the labor organization has an open shop coupled with a checkoff provision. Once in the union, the employee signs a *checkoff* or dues authorization form which allows the company to automatically deduct the membership dues and fees from the pay check. This is remitted by the company to the financial officer of the labor organization. The checkoff can be coupled with all forms of union security and is widely used (BNA 86 percent of all contracts, BLS 83 percent).

Maintenance of membership clauses state that employees who are already union members must maintain that membership for the duration of the contract as must new employees who elect to join the organization. There are no membership obligations for current nonmembers or for new hires who decide not to join. As noted earlier, this was widespread during World War II. It has since declined because of the prevalence of the union shop. It is sometimes used as a stepping-stone compromise position in moving from the open shop to the union shop (BNA 4 percent, BLS 3 percent).

---

2. Throughout the rest of the chapter references are made to two surveys of the contents of collective bargaining agreements. One was compiled by the U.S. Bureau of Labor Statistics from 1536 "major agreements," each of which covered 1000 members or more on January 1, 1978. The figures are calculated as a percentage of the 1536 major agreements. References to the study will be preceded by the initials "BLS." See U.S. Department of Labor Statistics, *Characteristics of Major Collective Bargaining Agreements, January 1, 1978* (Washington: U.S. Government Printing Office, 1980).

The second survey was conducted by the Bureau of National Affairs from a statistically selected sample of 400 agreements out of a file of 5000 current contracts. References to this survey will be preceded by "BNA." Bureau of National Affairs, *Basic Patterns in Union Contracts*, 9th ed. (Washington: The Bureau of National Affairs, 1979).

The *agency shop* requires persons who are not members of the labor organization to pay a service fee to the union equal to union dues and fees. This is to eliminate so-called *free riders* who otherwise would receive the benefits of union representation for nothing. (Recall that by law the union must represent everyone in the unit, union member or not.) A recent Supreme Court decision has ruled that in the public sector the service fee must be reduced below regular union dues by that proportion of the dues which is used by the labor organization for political purposes (i.e., not for union representation at the work place).[3] The agency shop is used moderately (BNA 6 percent, BLS 7 percent).

The *union shop* is the most widely used form of union security (BNA 62 percent, BLS 29 percent). It is, as the survey figures show, less prevalent among major agreements (BLS 29 percent) than among contracts in general (BNA 62 percent). A typical union shop clause might read:

> It shall be a condition of employment that all employees of the Company covered by this Agreement who are members of the Union in good dues standing on the execution date of this Agreement, shall remain members in good dues standing and those who are not members shall, on the thirty-first (31st) day following execution of this Agreement, become and remain members in good dues standing in the Union. All employees covered by this Agreement and hired on or after its execution date shall, on the thirty-first (31st) day following the beginning of such employment become and remain members in good dues standing in the Union.

In some contracts (BNA 12 percent, BLS 6 percent) the *modified union shop* is used. It exempts some employees (usually those who would have rather quit than have joined the union when the firm was first organized). All new hires must join the union. By attrition, a full union shop is formed. The modified union shop may be used as a negotiation stepping-stone to the full union shop.

Outlawed by Taft-Hartley in 1947, the *closed shop* makes labor organization membership compulsory as a condition of hire. In order to be hired, the employee must already be a union member. Note the distinction between the union shop and the closed shop. The closed shop makes a union membership a condition of hire; the union shop makes union membership a condition of continued employment.

One other practice, which is not a form of union security in the strictly legal sense, does make a union more secure practically. The practice of union referral through a *hiring hall* is widely used in construction. The employer calls the local hiring hall which sends out the number of employees the employer wants. Referral to the job cannot be on the basis of union membership, but it can be done according to length of time in the occupation, industry, or bargaining unit. This is technically not a form of union security because referral does

---

3. D. Louis Abood et al. v Detroit Board of Education, 431 U.S. 209 (1977).

not and cannot require the person to be a union member. The BNA found that 21 percent of the agreements used hiring halls. Seventy-five percent of these were union run, and 25 percent were operated jointly by the union and the employer. They are prevalent in the construction, maritime, retail, printing, and service industries.

The Right-to-Work Controversy

Few topics in collective bargaining raise the ire of people more than the issue of union security. Congress started a running battle between labor and management when it enacted Section 14(b) of the Taft-Hartley Act:

> Nothing in this Act shall be construed as authorizing the execution or application of agreements requiring membership in a labor organization as a condition of employment in any State or Territory in which such execution or application is prohibited by State or Territorial law.

In other words, states and territories can enact laws forbidding the execution of union security agreements. Federal law only forbids the closed shop. The state laws are called *right-to-work laws*, and 20 rural and/or Southern states have them. For example, all but two of the Sunbelt states have right-to-work laws. Right-to-work states include Alabama, Arizona, Arkansas, Florida, Georgia, Iowa, Kansas, Louisiana, Mississippi, Nebraska, Nevada, North Carolina, North Dakota, South Carolina, South Dakota, Tennessee, Texas, Utah, Virginia, and Wyoming. Indiana passed and then later repealed such a law, and Missouri came very close to passing one in 1978.

The controversy over union security and right-to-work laws is hard fought, often bitter, and always emotional. Organized labor has tried since the enactment of Section 14(b) to gain its repeal. The Labor Law Reform Act of 1977 originally contained a clause in it which would have repealed Section 14(b). That clause was dropped for fear that the whole bill would be defeated on that clause alone.

The battle against union security and for right-to-work laws is carried on by employer groups including the National Association of Manufacturers, the Chamber of Commerce, and the National Right to Work Committee (NRTWC), which was formed in 1955 as a political action lobby. In 1958 the NRTWC added a legal defense and education arm which is involved in considerable litigation against union security. Just as unions have pushed to repeal Section 14(b), the employer groups have pushed to extend right-to-work prohibitions as part of national law. The battle over union security and right-to-work laws has been fought so many times, the arguments pro and con are like a litany.

The Case For Right-to-Work Laws. Those who are pro–right-to-work law and anti-union security make the following arguments. Compulsory unionism (their catch phrase for union security) violates the constitutional and democratic right of free association. Union security does not exist in the leading, often socialistic economies of Western Europe. Why should it be allowed in the leading free world economy, the United States of America? It forces employees to pay tribute to earn a living. Union security forces employees to pay money to unions which can advocate political, social, and economic causes the employees oppose.

Union security clauses (the checkoff) frees up time for union officers who do not have to collect dues. They use this excess time to harass management. Union officers who do not have to meet union members face to face to collect dues grow complacent, careless, and unresponsive to the membership. If unions as interest groups are good for U.S. democracy, then interest groups (nonunion employees) are good for unions too. Not everyone should be forced to join. If unions are as good as they claim to be, employees will join of their own free choice. As a result of outlawing union security clauses, strikes will decline because one more item of potential conflict is removed from the table. Right-to-work states show greater economic growth as a result of their increased attractiveness to firms.

The Case Against Right-To-Work Laws. The AFL-CIO and others argue the pro-union security, anti–right-to-work law case. A union security clause, realistically speaking, cannot be negotiated into an agreement unless a majority of the unit wants one. Before it was repealed by the Taft-Humphrey Act, a ballot of union members had to okay the right of a local union to bargain for a union security clause. The votes were invariably and overwhelmingly in favor of security clauses (80-90 percent of the votes cast). Union security clauses are as democratic, then, as the U.S. system of government itself. The minority is bound by the acts of a majority of Congress no matter how small the majority vote is. Negotiated union security clauses favored by a very large majority of members are no less democratic. Legally, the employees can file a deauthorization petition and have a secret vote on whether to retain a union security clause. Management is at best hypocritical when it comes to union security. They are unresponsive to their employees' rights and needs. As a result, the employees unionize, and then the employer becomes concerned about the employees' individual rights. "Right-to-work" is misleading. No one has the right to work. If they did, there would be no unemployment. Belonging to a union is just another condition of employment. It is no different from the conditions an employee must meet for the employee to keep a job.

The truth of the matter is that employers oppose union security clauses to weaken the union in numbers and finances. Union security clauses actually help the employer because they free up time for the union officers to deal with on-the-job problems. They give the union the authority to maintain order within their own ranks. They decrease the likelihood that an employer will suffer as two unions battle out a raiding attempt. By the legal principle of exclusive representation, unions must represent all employees in a unit whether or not they belong to the union. The nonunion people are free riders.

They get all the benefits of union representation and pay no costs. Finally, the right-to-work law states are among the lowest in per capita worker income in the United States.

Controversy Continues. So where is the truth in all this? There is no easy answer. Much depends on the values of the individuals involved. The choice is yours. There are at least two truisms, however, one legal and the other institutional. The courts have ruled that both union security clauses and right-to-work laws do not violate the constitutional rights of an individual. It is also true that labor organizations with union security clauses are stronger financially and in numbers, whether or not this strength is used to stabilize or destabilize the labor-management relationship.

Management Rights

A clause parallel to that of union security relates to management security. Called a *management rights* clause, in theory it reserves certain activities exclusively for management. A partial listing of these include the right to introduce new technology, close or relocate the plant, formulate plant rules, control production, manage the business, and direct the work force. In short, management rights are decision-making rights.

Realistically management makes no decisions without constraints. Budget constraints, higher levels of management, government, and stockholders serve to constrain management decision making. What management seeks to achieve in a management rights clause is the freedom to make decisions unfettered by the labor organization and the agreement. Before the work force was organized, management had those rights. The first collective bargaining agreement was a single page of wage rates nailed on a shop door. Considering that it is not unusual today for a contract to run to 200 or more pages, exclusive of lengthy pension and health supplements, the erosion of management rights over time is plain to see. On the other hand, as was pointed out in Chapter 10, the United States is nowhere near the codetermination of Western Europe.

Management philosophy on management rights is very clear. Almost universally, management believes that any rights not explicitly given up in the contract are reserved exclusively for management. Management embodies that philosophy in a contract in one of three different ways. One way is to make an extensive list of management rights. Some lists run two or three pages. Others put a short paragraph in the agreement called a *savings clause:*

> The Company retains the exclusive right to manage the business and to direct the working forces, except as specifically limited by the terms of this agreement. All rights not specifically surrendered or curtailed by the express provisions of this Agreement are reserved to Management.

A general or specific management rights clause was found in 69 percent of the agreement samples by the BNA. The third way to establish management rights (BNA 31 percent) is to not include a management rights clause. Managements with this philosophy believe that it is then understood that all rights not specifically given away in the contract are the residual rights of management. They do not want to put a clause in the agreement for fear that they may leave something out. Also, such a clause could become something for the union to soften in negotiations.

Seniority

A typical seniority clause might read:

> The parties recognize that promotional opportunity and job security in event of promotion, decrease of forces, and recalls after layoffs should increase in proportion to seniority. Seniority shall be considered as the length of continuous service calculated from the date of first employment with the Company.

One measure of the importance of *seniority* to organized labor is the simple fact that seniority provisions occur in 88 percent of BNA's sample. It is the foundation stone of industrial unions. Earlier it was stated that industrial unions control the supply of labor *on* the job and craft unions control the supply of labor *to* the job. For industrial unions almost all occupational movement is tied in some fashion to the length of service an employee has with the employer.

For craft unions, construction jobs terminate once the project is built and the craftsperson moves on to other jobs and possibly other employers. Length of continuous service with a specific employer (seniority) does not control craft movement, and so seniority clauses do not exist in craft contracts. What does count, as we saw in the discussion of hiring halls used extensively in construction, is the length of time in the occupation. And that type of record keeping is done by the union which is the constant in the employment situation of craftspersons, not the individual employer.

Layoff and Recall. Seniority often provides the basis for decisions regarding *layoff* and *recall provisions*, promotion, pay progression, vacation length, and other fringes. The layoff and recall process is a good example. A firm, faced with economic exigency, must reduce its work force. Layoff starts with the least senior person and proceeds to the next senior. But what if only one department must lay off? Can those employees to be laid off who have higher seniority replace (bump) employees with lower seniority in other departments? That depends upon the contract. Seniority may be by occupation, department, plant, and even firm. Unions in general prefer wider seniority units (plant-wide) to provide maximum job security, and employers prefer smaller units (departmental) to minimize the disruption of a layoff.

Can any junior employee be bumped? Again, that depends upon the contract, but it is common for layoff and recall clauses to limit bumping to minimize disruption. Envision, for example, a department of 20 people. As a result of a layoff in another department, a worker with more seniority than 15 of the employees in the first department wants to bump in. If that employee were allowed to bump the fifteenth most senior person, chain bumping would result as each person bumped the next one below in seniority. Finally, the least senior worker would be bumped out. To avoid chain bumping a more senior employee may be allowed to bump the most junior employee, not just anyone with less seniority.

Similarly, the contract may require that the employee either be capable of performing the job he or she is bumping into or be able to learn it in a short period of time. Recall to work from layoff is done in reverse order of layoff and is often subject to the same limitations placed on layoff.

Posting and Bidding. *Posting and bidding* provisions in agreements (BNA 52 percent) control internal promotion. This gives rise to the "internal labor market" discussed in Chapter 3. The philosophy is that job openings should be offered to inside people before the employer goes outside to hire. Typically, any vacancy (new job or turnover vacancy) must be posted on the bulletin board for a specified number of days. All interested employees can bid during that time to fill the vacancy.

Seniority plays a role in determining the successful bidder. If the union has a very strong posting and bidding clause, the most senior of the bidders gets the job on the basis of seniority only. If management has the upper hand, seniority will play no role, and the successful bidder will be picked on ability alone as judged by management. (In the strongest management situation, management would not be required to hire from within at all.) There are variations on a theme in between these two. Management may narrow the number of bidders to the people who are able, for example, and then select from these the most senior person for the job. Only if a vacancy remains after meeting the posting and bidding requirements can the employer go outside for applicants.

Pros and Cons. Labor organizations favor seniority because it takes the arbitrariness out of management decision making. Seniority or time in the craft is quantifiable and fairly certain. It is a common denominator for all employees. They argue that it provides job security for older employees who are more skilled than younger employees. After working for years for the same firm, the employee builds equity in the job. Controlling movement by seniority is more equitable. Disemploying older workers because they are not as strong or as fast works a severe hardship on them, for they are less employable. Younger, more mobile workers can better bear the brunt of unemployment.

Management sees these things differently. They argue that the seniority system causes higher costs and inefficiency. Both increase when decisions must be based on seniority and not on skill and ability. Seniority discourages incentive for younger, more capable workers. It also hinders employer achievement of equal employment opportunity goals. And it disrupts orderly layoff and recall when people bump into departments other than their own.

Grievance Procedures and Arbitration

These clauses will be explored at length in the next chapter. They are a way to handle conflict during the life of an agreement. Written into agreements extensively during World War II, they are found in nearly all contracts (BNA 99 percent, BLS 99 percent).

Wages

Few employees outside of the union stewards and officers may read the whole contract, but everyone reads the wage articles. There are innumerable ways to pay wages, but two major categories predominate: time and incentive pay. Of the 1536 agreements surveyed by BLS, 97 percent paid wages on a time basis and 28 percent used incentive pay.

Time Payment. Time payment plans are either *single-rate* or *rate-range* systems. Single rate systems date back to the first cordwainers' agreement. They are, very simply, a two-column list, as shown in Table 14-3. The left column is a list of jobs or job classes; the right column is a list of wage rates attached to each.

Table 14-3   A Single-Rate System

Job Grade	Standard Hourly Rate
1 and 2	$9.68
3	9.57
4	9.47
5	9.36
. . .	. . .

Rate ranges provide more flexibility but are also more difficult to administer. Attached to each job grade is a range of pay. Employees start at the range minimum and progress to the maximum on the basis of length of time on the job and/or merit. Variations on the movement from minimum to maximum include progression automatically by length of service only, length of service if the employee has the ability to do the work, automatic progression to the midpoint followed by merit to the range maximum, and merit only.

Table 14-4   A Rate-Range System: Automatic Progression and Merit Rating Table

Labor Grade	Automatic Progression from Minimum to Midpoint				Merit Rating: Midpoint to Maximum		
	Min.	After 3 mos.	After 6 mos.	After 9 mos.	Score 81-85	86-90	91-100
1	$9.04	$9.17	$9.28	$9.41	$9.54	$9.66	$9.79
2	8.74	8.86	8.99	9.12	9.24	9.36	9.49
. . .	. . .	. . .	. . .	. . .	. . .	. . .	. . .

Table 14-4 illustrates a typical rate-range system which combines automatic progression to the midpoint with merit to the maximum rate. (Another example of the rate-range system was presented in Chapter 3, Table 3-1.) All employees at or above the midpoint in Table 14-4 are merit rated at 6-month intervals. Merit is rated according to six factors:

Quality of output	(30)	Dependability	(10)
Quantity of output	(20)	Cooperation	(10)
Job knowledge	(20)	Adaptability	(10)

Each factor has a weight or total point value attached to it which is shown in parentheses. For example, quality of output is worth 30 total points or 30 percent of the total merit rating.

Each factor has five levels of accomplishment, and each level has a specified point value. For quality of output, level 5 gets 18 points, 4 receives 21, and so on to level 1 which receives 30 points. Employees are rated by level for each factor, and the total points are summed over all factors to give a merit rating score. In Table 14-4, an employee in labor grade 2 who was rated at 87 points would be paid $9.36 per hour.

Note the potential problems and labor-management rifts over understanding the system, management judgment of scores, the definition of merit. Only 26 percent of all agreements use some form of merit rating.

Incentive Pay. Under incentive plans, wages are tied directly to performance based, usually, on some measure of output. There is a minimum or base or "occupation" rate paid to those who start incentive jobs. Associated with the occupational rate is a normal nonincentive performance level. The normal nonincentive performance expected of average employees in their assigned tasks is 100 percent performance. Performance beyond 100 percent is compensated for on a one-for-one principle, and potential earnings on incentive work time are expected to average 30 percent above the occupation rate.

For example, Brenda Smith worked an 8-hour shift running a drill press. The occupation rate for the job is $8.00 for up to 100 pieces drilled per hour. Production in excess of 100 pieces per hour is paid proportionally more. Brenda produced 1000 pieces on her 8-hour shift. Because she produced 25 percent above the 100 percent level of performance, she is paid as calculated below:

$$(8 \text{ hours}) \times (\$8.00 \text{ per hour}) \times (1.25) = \$80.00$$

Incentive pay is limited almost exclusively to manufacturing where it is found in half of the contracts. Incentive systems can be difficult to devise and administer. Consider, for example, the controversy which could arise over what constitutes 100 percent performance. In addition to performance rating, incentive systems have to deal with personal time, fatigue, operator waiting time, downtime, and job delay. Just calculating the proper amount of pay is a problem over which many grievances are filed.

Wage Increases

The most prevalent way of handling wage raises is to negotiate wage increases to take effect in the future. These deferred increases exist in 95 percent of the agreements sampled by BNA. Deferred wage increases are negotiated as so much money *across the board,* as percentage increases, or as increments to an occupation or job class.

Types of Increases. Newspapers often report across-the-board wage settlements as so much money over the life of the agreement; for example, "The Teamsters negotiated $1.50 over 3 years." The distribution of the deferred increase is important. The $1.50 might be paid $0.75 now, $0.50 at the beginning of the second year, and $0.25 for the third year. Most agreements use *front end loading* with the largest increase up front. There is a big income difference to a worker (and cost to the firm) if that $1.50 is paid up front at $0.75, $0.50, $0.25 rather than $0.25, $0.50, $0.75 over a 3-year contract. Table 14-5 illustrates the difference in the increase in employee income over the life of the contract under the two pay schemes.

It is evident from Table 14-5 that a front end loaded contract will pay a wage increase of $7000 and the rear end loaded agreement will increase income by only $5000 over the life of the contract. The difference between the two pay schemes is $2000 in cash to the worker.[4]

A problem with cents across-the-board wage increases is that they cause compression of skill differentials. Suppose, at the bottom, that labor grade 10 is

---

4. These calculations do not take into account the fact that dollars paid 2 years from now are valued less highly (especially during periods of high inflation) than dollars paid now, i.e., the figures are not discounted to present value.

Table 14-5   The Significance of Front End Loading

	Basic Data		Front End Loaded			Rear End Loaded		
Year	Hours Worked	Hourly Pay Raise	Total Hourly Pay Raise	Income Increase	Hourly Pay Raise	Total Hourly Pay Raise	Income Increase
One	2000	$0.75	$0.75	$1500	$0.25	$0.25	$ 500
Two	2000	0.50	1.25	2500	0.50	0.75	1500
Three	2000	0.25	1.50	3000	0.75	1.50	3000
Total	6000	$1.50		$7000	$1.50		$5000

paid $5.00 and the top grade, labor grade 1, receives $10.00. The grade 1/grade 10 ratio is 2:1. Labor and management agree to a wage raise of $1 across the board. The new pay ratio is $11.00/$6.00, which is less than 2:1. Labor grade 10 received a 20 percent increase, but labor grade 1 managed only a 10 percent raise. By paying wage increases in percentage terms rather than in dollar terms, the differentials stay the same and there is less chance that skilled workers will be alienated.

After a series of cents across-the-boards, the wage increases may include occupational increases. That is, wage increases will differ for each occupation to restore the skill differentials. The following language illustrates all three types of increases: cents across the board, occupational increases, and percentage raises.

> With the effective date of this Agreement the Standard Hour Rates shall increase by twenty-five (25) cents. One year from the effective date, the Standard Hourly Rate shall be increased twenty (20) cents and the increment between Job Grades shall be increased one (1) cent. On the second anniversary of the effective date of the agreement, the Standard Hourly Rate shall be increased fifteen (15) cents and the increment between Job Grades shall be increased five-tenths (0.5) cent.
>
> Incentive Rates shall be increased by six (6) percent with the effective date of the agreement, three (3) percent on the first anniversary of the agreement and two (2) percent on the second anniversary.

COLA. How wage increases are negotiated and the duration of the bargaining agreement are tied closely to the rate of inflation in the economy. In periods of price stability, agreements have a longer duration. When the uncertainty of inflation looms ahead, the union tends to push for shorter agreements. They do so to avoid getting locked into a long agreement with wage increases that lag inflation. One way to hedge against inflation uncertainty has been to tie wage rates to the consumer price index with a *cost-of-living adjustment* (COLA), or *escalator clause*. Another way is to reopen the agreement before it expires to negotiate wages only.

COLAs were found in 48 percent of the BNA sample and were in 46 percent of the major agreements examined by the BLS. The number of workers they cover has increased rapidly throughout the inflationary 1970s, illustrating that the rationale for their inclusion is to maintain wage parity. If inflation increases over 1 year's time by 10 percent and wages remain constant, the real value of those wages will have declined by 10 percent. In order to have the same buying power, wages must increase by 10 percent. COLAs, or escalator clauses, tie wages to a measure of the cost of living [82 percent of COLAs use the BLS Consumer Price Index (CPI)]. Labor organizations push hard for COLAs. Companies resist becoming tied into the unforeseen cost increases mandated by COLAs and prefer instead to negotiate known, fixed amount, deferred increases in anticipation of inflation.

The logic of COLAs should cause them to be written in percentage terms. If the CPI increases 5 percent, so should wages. But only 14 percent of COLAs are percentage adjustments. Instead, the rest use a formula such as 1 cent increase per four-tenths of a point change in the CPI. (Almost half of the COLA contracts used adjust at the rate of 1 cent per 0.3 change in the CPI.) Typical COLA language might read:

> Effective on each quarterly Adjustment Date for the duration of the Agreement, a Cost-of-Living Adjustment equal to 1¢ per hour for each full 0.3 of a point change in the Consumer Price Index shall be included in the Standard Hourly Rates.

Use of a formula like the one mentioned above causes a number of side effects:

1. Paid as cents across the board, COLAs compress skill levels.
2. The same rate of inflation further from the CPI base year gives a larger adjustment than one nearer the base year. See Table 14-6 which illustrates this.
3. It can be shown using the data from Table 14-6 that more highly paid employees do not keep up with inflation; yet lower pay grades gain real income. A 34 cent COLA adjustment paid across the board for a 10 percent inflation means workers earning $3.40 per hour maintain real income; those under $3.40 gain, and those over $3.40 lose real earnings.

Table 14-6   COLA Pay Adjustments

	Year	CPI	Inflation Rate	CPI Point Change	Pay Adjustment
Example 1	Base	100			
	+1 Year	110	10%	10	25¢
Example 2	+8 Years	170			
	+9 Years	187	10%	17	34¢

Formula: 1¢/0.4 CPI Increase

Fringe Benefits

Fringe benefit seed was sown on fertile ground during the wage control era of World War II. The average value of fringes as a percentage of the total cost of compensation per hour has since gone from almost zero to 23 percent.[5] Governmentally mandated fringes including Social Security, unemployment insurance, and workers' compensation amount to 6.5 percent of total compensation. Voluntarily negotiated fringes add up to another 16.5 percent of total per hour compensation.[6] The major, voluntarily negotiated fringes are discussed below.

Supplementary Pay. Most agreements require time and a half for work over 8 hours a day, over 40 hours per week (required by the Fair Labor Standards Act), and for work on Saturday (sixth day). Sunday (seventh day) work pays double overtime. If the employee reports for work (reports in) or is called back to work (call back), he or she is usually entitled to a minimum of 4 hours of pay. Employees who work the second (afternoon) or third (night, red-eye, graveyard) shift are paid a per hour shift differential in the amount on average of $0.15 (second) or $0.25 (third). The trend is toward double overtime and larger shift differentials.

Time Off With Pay. The median number of paid holidays is 10, but the range is from 3 to 15. The trend is toward more holidays, especially floating (employee choice) holidays. Vacations appear in 98 percent of agreements outside construction. Most make the length of the vacation a function of continuous service. The trend is toward longer vacations. Sixteen percent of the agreements have a maximum of 6 weeks off. Leaves of absence include personal, union business, maternity, funeral, illness, and military. The trend is toward more days off and more leave types. Demands for extended maternity and paternity leaves are increasing.

Insurance and Health Care Coverage. Over 90 percent of all agreements now provide life, hospitalization, and surgical insurance. Over half have maternity, major medical, and accidental death and dismemberment insurance. Trends are toward better coverage. The newer areas include psychiatric care, drug costs, dental and optical plans, and legal aid.

Pensions. Virtually all agreements have pension plans. Over 90 percent are noncontributory (financed solely by the employer). Most have provisions for early retirement and the *vesting* of benefits. Under plans which have vesting provisions, employees who leave the firm before retirement are entitled to a percentage of their earned pension benefits when they retire. There is usually a

---

5. Richard B. Freeman, "The Effect of Unionism on Fringe Benefits," *Industrial and Labor Relations Review*, Vol. 34, No. 4 (July, 1981). The figures are calculated from Table 1, p. 496.
6. Ibid.

minimum service requirement before a partial vesting occurs. The greater the tenure of the employee with the firm, the larger is the proportion of the pension which is vested. After a stated number of years (oftentimes 20 years), the pension becomes fully vested.

The normal retirement age for most plans is age 65. Employees may retire before 65 under disability or early retirement provisions. Most plans provide a percentage of the earned retirement benefit if total or permanent disability occurs after an employee has 10 to 15 years service with the employer. Nearly all plans provide for voluntary early retirement. In order to qualify for early retirement, the employee must meet an age plus years of service requirement. The earliest retirement age is usually set at 55.

Income Maintenance. Almost half of all agreements provide for income continuity in the event of economic layoffs. A few guarantee a minimum pay level or number of hours of work. About 16 percent of the major collective bargaining agreements surveyed by the BLS provide for a Suppiemental Un-employment Benefit (SUB) Plan. SUB plans are employer financed and are used to make up a portion of the difference between state unemployment compensation and the worker's usual pay. For example, under the UAW agreement, the combination of SUB payments and state unemployment ben-efits is designed to pay laid-off workers 95 percent of their regular take-home wages. Work-related expenses, such as lunches and transportation, and other outside earnings may be deducted from the SUB payments. In the case of permanent layoffs, almost all agreements provide *severance pay* upon job ter-mination. The amount of severance pay is usually based on years of service.

CONCLUDING REMARKS

Collective bargaining agreements have come a long way since a one-page list of wage rates was tacked to a master cordwainer's door. Agreements now run from a few pages for crafts to several hundred pages in industrial settings, exclusive of fringe benefit addenda. It is doubtful that shorter agreements will be negotiated in the foreseeable future. The trend toward "more, more . . . now!" will continue to expand existing benefits and extend into areas as yet untouched. Voluntary items will slide into the mandatory category through frequency of negotiation. If the elimination of inflexible work rules remains the focus of management intransigence at the table, future labor gains are likely to be on the wage and fringe benefit side of the agreement. In financially troubled industries such as the auto industry, wage concessions will be coupled with job security provisions for union workers.

CHAPTER SUMMARY

The purpose of the chapter was to get into the meat of a collective bargaining agreement to see just what labor organiza-tions have attained over time. Each clause is there for a reason. The clauses selected for discussion are at the heart of the agree-ments.

Most agreements open with a recognition clause in which management recognizes the labor organization as the exclusive bargaining agent. It delineates the appropriate bargaining unit. Two clauses pertain to the union and management as institutions. The union security clause has variations of security from the open shop to the union shop with a checkoff provision. The whole topic of union security has been hotly debated at the state and national level. The management correlate to union security is the management rights clause. A management rights clause may be no clause at all, a short statement, or a lengthy, detailed provision. The philosophies vary on the best strategy to protect management rights.

The seniority provisions are the heart of the industrial agreement. These control the supply of labor on the job. Layoff, recall, posting and bidding language governs movement into, out of, and within the plant. The arguments pro and con have generally been resolved in favor of seniority as a controlling factor in the allocation of labor.

Wages are generally paid based on time worked or as incentive pay according to some measure of worker output. Hourly pay schemes include single-rate and rate-range systems. Rate-range systems are more complex and often employ a combination of time on the job and merit for progression through the rate range. Incentive pay requires some way to measure output.

Several methods for paying wage increases were illustrated along with the pros and cons of their use. Cost-of-living adjustments, or escalator clauses, have several implications for wage parity and wage compression.

Unions and management have shown great ingenuity in the negotiation of fringe benefits. Supplementary pay includes such items as shift differentials and overtime. Time off with pay includes holidays as well as leaves for reasons which vary from union business to maternity/paternity leave. This category also encompasses holidays. Recently, extensive gains have been made in health and insurance benefits. Pension plans have become almost entirely noncontributory, and have provisions for vesting, early retirement, and disability retirement. A few contracts provide for income maintenance through supplemental unemployment benefit plans and severance pay.

KEY TERMS

mandatory bargaining subjects
voluntary bargaining subjects
illegal bargaining subjects
P and M unit
preamble
agreement clause
recognition clause
union security clause
open shop
checkoff
maintenance of membership
agency shop
free riders
union shop

modified union shop
closed shop
hiring hall
right-to-work laws
management rights
savings clause
seniority
layoff
recall
posting and bidding
single rate
rate range
incentive pay
across the board

front end loading
cost-of-living adjustment
escalator clause

vesting
severance pay

REVIEW QUESTIONS

1. Are any topics not subject to bargaining? Give examples.

2. What is the difference between an industrial union recognition clause and a craft contract recognition clause?

3. Which set of arguments on the right-to-work controversy do you find persuasive? Why? Discuss the agency shop as a compromise between the two polar positions.

4. Have management rights increased or decreased over time? Would it be incorrect to call a management rights clause a management security clause?

5. Why do craft contracts not have seniority provisions? Explain how industrial unions control the supply of labor *on* the job.

6. What are the advantages and disadvantages of time versus incentive payment methods? Methods for paying increases in wages have pros and cons as well. Discuss the pros and cons associated with each.

7. Using the COLA formula of 1¢/0.4 CPI change, what would be the wage adjustment for a quarterly change in the CPI from 227.6 to 234.0?

8. Is it cheaper for a firm to increase wages by $0.03 per hour or to give an extra holiday to a $6 per hour employee? Show how you would go about answering the question.

9. Using Table 14-4 as a reference, by how much would the worker's income increase over the life of the agreement if the wage increase were paid $0.50, $0.50, $0.50?

10. If Brenda Smith had produced 1100 drilled pieces per her shift, how much would she have been paid? What if she produced only 750?

ADDITIONAL REFERENCES

Any readily available collective bargaining agreement.

Bureau of National Affairs. *Basic Patterns in Union Contracts.* 9th ed. Washington: The Bureau of National Affairs, 1979.

Heisel, W. D., and Gordon S. Skinner. *Costing Union Demands.* Chicago: Chicago International Personnel Management Association, 1976.

U.S. Department of Labor, Bureau of Labor Statistics. *Characteristics of Major Collective Bargaining Agreements, January 1, 1978.* Washington: U.S. Government Printing Office, April, 1980.

THE WORLD
OF WORK . . .

Contents of Recent Settlements

To underscore the variety and commonality in the contents of labor-management agreements, some recent settlements are presented. The illustrations are from both the public and private sectors. Note that some settlements contain labor compromise as well as the more expected "more, more . . . now."

Postal Settlement

Bargainers for 3 of the 4 major postal workers unions settled with the U.S. Postal Service in late July, averting the possibility of a strike that would have hampered delivery of the 360 million pieces of mail that move through the system each day. The 3-year accord with the two largest unions, the American Postal Workers Union (APWU) and the National Association of Letter Carriers (NALC) actually came 16 hours after the termination date of the prior contract, but the leaders of the two unions had held off calling a walkout because of increasing progress in the talks, which had seemed to be at an impasse just 2 days earlier. The Postal Reorganization Act of 1970 prohibits strikes.

The National Rural Letter Carriers' Association accepted essentially the same terms for the 60,000 workers it represents. The fourth organization involved in the bargaining, the Mail Handlers division of the Laborers' International Union, elected to resolve its economic differences with the Postal Service under the factfinding and arbitration procedures of the Postal Reorganization Act. The Mail Handlers represents 40,000 workers. Unlike 1978, when all four unions bargained jointly with the Postal Service, friction between the two larger and the two smaller unions led to separate negotiations.

The AWPU-NALC settlement provided for a $300 increase in annual salaries in July of each of the three years. In addition, the 500,000 workers involved were to receive a $150 one-time "contract signing bonus" if they ratified the terms within 45 days after the settlement date. They also will receive annual cash payments of $350 plus possible payments under a new productivity plan.

Employees will continue to receive semi-annual cost-of-living adjustments in annual pay of $20.80 for each 0.4-point increase in the BLS Consumer Price Index for Urban Wage Earners and Clerical Workers (1967=100). The $3,619 in cost-of-living increases accrued under the prior contract will be incorporated into basic pay rates in October 1984, 3 months after the termination date of the new agreements. However, employees who are now eligible for retirement or who will become eligible prior to July 21, 1987, will have the option of having the $3,619 incorporated into basic pay in November 1981. This would increase their entitlement under the pension plan, but it also means that their contributions to the plan will be increased by $253 a year (7 percent of $3,619).

Source: *Monthly Labor Review* (September, 1981), p. 49.

Woodworkers' Local Accepts Pay Cut

A shutdown of International Paper Co.'s Longview, Wash., cabinet operations was averted when the 235 employees accepted the 20-percent pay cut that Long-Bell Cabinets had set as a condition for purchasing the plant. Long-Bell is a subsidiary of Thor Industries, Inc., a diversified holding company.

Duane Wend, president of Local 536 of the Woodworkers Union, called the 3-year contract "lousy," saying that "what it came down to was that people took a look and decided at least they had jobs to go to." According to a company official, International Paper had spent $6 million since 1975 to improve productivity at the plant, but its rejuvenation efforts were hurt when the housing industry slumped.

Shipyard Workers Negotiate 'Gain-Sharing' Plan

A settlement between Bethlehem Steel Corp.'s Shipbuilding Department and the Marine and Shipbuilding Workers featured provisions for experimental "gain sharing" and "employee involvement" programs. The bargainers said the gain-sharing plan "endorses the concept that employees should share in the benefits of their contributions to increase productivity and efficiency." A target date of April 1, 1982, was set for gain sharing to be implemented at one or more of the four shipyards covered by the 3-year contract.

The intent of the employee involvement program is to set up union-management groups throughout each yard to improve morale and working conditions by discussing and resolving problems. Although details of the program remain to be worked out, the overall approach is similar to the negotiated "labor management participation teams" in the steel industry and to the "quality of worklife" plan at General Motors Corp.

Other contract provisions included set wage increases of 40 cents an hour in August 1981 and 30 cents in August of 1982 and 1983. The automatic cost-of-living adjustment clause was continued, with each of the 12 quarterly adjustments not to exceed 11 cents an hour or a combined total of $1.26.

Benefit changes included a 13th annual holiday and a $2 increase in pension rates, bringing the formula to $14 a month for each of the first 15 years of service, $15 for each of the next 15 years of service, and $16 a month for each year of service in excess of 30.

Guild Members Agree to Moratorium on Raises

Members of the Newspaper Guild employed by the *St. Louis Globe-Democrat* followed the lead of 11 unions at the *St. Louis Post-Dispatch* and accepted a 42-month contract that deferred the initial 7-percent wage increase until March 1, 1983. The 218 Newspaper Guild members also will receive a 7-percent increase on March 1, 1984, and a 2-percent increase on September 1, 1984, plus automatic cost-of-living adjustments and improvements in benefits.

The contracts for the *Post-Dispatch* employees were negotiated with the parent Pulitzer Publishing Co., which prints both newspapers. Both newspapers indicated that the 18-month moratorium on pay increases was necessary to help counter operating losses.

Source: *Monthly Labor Review* (November, 1981), p. 54, 51, 54.

Chapter 15

Labor-Management Conflict

Strike! The word is another of those labor-management terms cloaked in popular misconceptions. Each strike when viewed individually (coal, steel, baseball) seems negative and irrational. Yet, the strike occupies a very positive and rational place in the industrial relations scheme not only in the United States but also in the rest of the world. The potential for labor-management conflict exists in all stages of the relationship, not just when contracts are negotiated. Organizing drives, contract negotiations, and day-to-day agreement administration all breed conflict situations. It is inevitable. Labor and management have some (not all) interests which clash. The goal of policy concerning this disagreement is not to eliminate the conflict but rather to deal with it to minimize the negative effects of the conflict. Private and public sector labor laws represent society's attempts to maximize the positive effects of conflict and minimize its negative effects.

The logic is to substitute procedure for the exercise of physical and economic power. Private and public sector laws substitute the recognition balloting procedure for the strike. How the government and the parties to collective bargaining resolve conflict in the negotiation and contract administration of the agreement is the subject of this chapter. First we deal with conflict during contract negotiation, and then with conflict during the life of the agreement.

THE STRIKE

Why are strikes beneficial? To whom are they beneficial? Why and how do they occur? How do labor and management prepare for them? How much do they cost? Why are strikes legal in the private sector but not in the public sector? Are there any alternatives? Why are they not used? These important questions are addressed in this chapter.

Why Strikes Are Allowed to Happen

Strikes over contract terms are a part of the American system of free collective bargaining in the private sector. Procedure is substituted for power only to a certain extent. When one party intends to modify the existing agreement, it must notify the other party and the Federal Mediation and Conciliation Service (FMCS). The FMCS can aid the parties during their negotiations by trying to mediate a settlement. But the FMCS cannot force a settlement on the parties.

As a society we favor a voluntary free choice settlement between labor and management over one mandated by a third party. What would a third party mandate? What would be the correct settlement? Who is to say what the settlement would, could, or should be in the absence of agreement by the parties themselves? As a last resort, if the parties cannot agree at the table, a test of economic strength and will decides the issues. One or both sides modify their expected settlement goals and agreement is reached. Or, as sometimes happens, the business may close or the labor organization may be broken. The cost of the strike to society at large and to the parties is the price we have elected to pay for free collective bargaining.

What is that price tag? Not as much as publicity on newsworthy strikes might suggest. The cost of strikes is treated at length later, but measures of prevalence are in order here. FMCS records show that out of 20,414 agreements negotiated in 1979, only 14.2 percent involved strikes.[1] On average, about 25 percent of strikes last less than a week, and 50 percent last less than 2 weeks. In 1981, the monthly average of total working time lost due to strikes was 0.11 percent.[2] That is roughly the same as 2 hours and 12 minutes per worker over a year's time. For a 40-hour week it amounts to under 3 minutes, 20 seconds. None of these measures by itself is a good one, but taken as a group they provide perspective.

If you ask labor and management (when they are not engaged in one) who benefits from a strike, as likely as not they will both say no one does. They certainly do not engage in a work stoppage to preserve free collective bargaining for society. Altruistic motives rarely make for a strike. Why then do they occur?

Avoiding Strikes

There are no statistics on such things, but few negotiators go to the table with a desire to have a work stoppage. They want to settle without a strike or at least without an unanticipated strike (see Chapter 13). Work stoppages are usually strikes, not employer *lockouts*.[3] It is usually to the employer's benefit to keep producing, and so it is up to the union to walk off the job. On the other

---

1. Federal Mediation and Conciliation Service, *Thirty-Second Annual Report—Fiscal Year 1979* (Washington: U.S. Government Printing Office, 1981), p. 15.
2. U.S. Department of Labor, Bureau of Labor Statistics, *Monthly Labor Review* (March, 1982), p. 95.
3. In a lockout, an employer refuses to allow employees to work. Historically, employers literally locked employees out of the work place.

hand, while it is the union that walks, both labor and management are party to a strike. It takes two to disagree.

Contract Extensions. Often the parties will take steps to avoid an unnecessary strike. They may agree as part of the bargaining ground rules to extend the contract expiration date if they are near agreement. Some agreements have automatic extensions written into them. The extension is in effect for a set time or until either side decides to terminate it. Usually, the extension contains the proviso that the terms of the new agreement are made retroactive to the expiration date of the old agreement. Sometimes negotiators stop the clock at 1 minute before the time the contract is to expire if they are close to a settlement.

However, some unions, such as the United Mine Workers (UMWA), have a flat "no contract, no work" policy. In the 1981 coal talks, UMWA President Sam Church tried to set an artificial expiration deadline 10 days before the actual expiration of the nationwide UMWA-BCOA coal agreement. The 10-day buffer was to allow for the constitutionally mandated ratification vote on the new agreement. The artificial deadline passed, but the parties reached a tentative agreement 5 days before the expiration of the contract. Nonetheless, as part of this long-standing policy of "no contract, no work," the miners left the pits when the agreement expired in the middle of the ratification process. They voted not to accept the proposed agreement. This suggests the reason for the "no contract, no work" policy. Without it, the miners would have worked and the employers produced coal under an unacceptable agreement.

Mediation. Mediators may request or be requested by the parties to attend the bargaining sessions to help them reach agreement. The mediator's services are provided free to the parties by the Federal Mediation and Conciliation Service. The FMCS was created by the Taft-Hartley Act as an independent agency "to prevent or minimize interruptions of the free flow of commerce growing out of labor disputes, to assist parties to labor disputes . . . to settle such disputes through conciliation and mediation." The FMCS mediators may have either labor or management backgrounds, and they must have extensive negotiation experience. They cannot force a settlement on the negotiators. Mediation, like negotiation, is an art. Mediators can call the parties for single or joint sessions with the mediator, be a scapegoat, suggest alternatives, cajole concessions, and do whatever labor and management will go along with to reach a settlement. Occasionally, the parties will tell a mediator to leave the negotiations. Considering that mediators cannot force the parties to settle, mediators are successful by virtue of their considerable persuasive skill and ability. But strikes still occur.

Reasons Why Strikes Happen

As part of their preparation for bargaining, union negotiators arrive at a list of demands. Initial and fallback positions are determined. At some point in the deliberations they arrive at a set of positions that will have to be met or a strike will be called. It is the minimum acceptable package that must be met to avoid a walkout.

Management attempts to anticipate labor's demands and formulate initial and compromise positions. As we saw in Chapter 13, there is a maximum authorization on the economic and noneconomic package, that is, the maximum acceptable settlement package. If an agreement cannot be reached with that package, the firm will take a strike.

If a strike occurs, it must be in one of two situations. In the first, management's maximum acceptable settlement package does not match or exceed the union's minimum acceptable requirements. In the second situation, a strike occurs even though a settlement is possible (the packages overlap).

Nonoverlapping Positions. Think back for a moment to the discussion of bargaining theories in Chapter 13. If a settlement is to be reached, one party's bargaining attitude must reach the point during negotiations where their perceived cost of disagreeing exceeds their perceived cost of agreeing to the terms on the table. When the bargaining goals do not overlap, no amount of skill on the part of the negotiators can forge an agreement. In order to reach a settlement, the bargaining goals must be reassessed. Or, in terms of our bargaining theory, some form of learning must occur to reshape the range of perceptions to include an acceptable settlement.

The lack of overlapping goals can be caused by any number of reasons. On the management side, perhaps the firm cannot afford to settle any higher. The economic situation of the firm will not allow it to go the distance to meet union minimum demands. Or, although the firm can go higher, it may have elected not to and is willing to take a strike to force the union to reorder its goals. Or the management negotiator may have assessed the situation incorrectly due to inexperience.

On the union side, the leadership may be in a political bind. Parallel to the idea that a firm's economic situation may not allow a settlement, the union's political situation may not allow one. Union officers may have to "win big" at the table to stay in office in the face of strong political opposition in upcoming elections. The union might push for an industry package pattern when the firm expected a lower area package of demands. The union negotiator may be new and, due to inexperience, have an unrealistic set of bargaining goals. Or, a seasoned union negotiator may reach a tentative agreement but be forced to return to the table because the rank and file rejected the package. For whatever reasons, labor and/or management are forced by a work stoppage to reassess their unrealistic expectations in order to reach agreement.

Negotiator Problems. In the second situation, the bargaining goals are attainable. Skillful negotiating can result in a party assessing the situation such that the cost of agreeing is less than the cost of disagreeing. Failure to reach a settlement must be due to a problem with reaching the goals. One or more of the following might pertain. Much of negotiating involves learning to listen to what the other side is really saying. Learning to read nuances in words, facial expressions, and body language is a skill. Inexperienced negotiators may not pick up the necessary signals of concession.

It is not always easy to make a concession without appearing to be weak. If the other side perceives that a concession has been made from weakness, they will believe that the cost of disagreeing has decreased along with the cost of agreeing due to the concession. These work against each other. Negotiators' egos can get in the way of settlement. Concession on a pet demand may be difficult without loss of face. (Enter the mediator as scapegoat.[4])

Firm and union politics can get in the way. Intraorganizational bargaining may not have been completed before the start of negotiations. The corporate representative and the plant employee relations manager may be at odds. The union president may be caught between the skilled and semiskilled worker demands.

Labor and/or management may be unprepared to negotiate. They may be unable to deal with and respond to demands or counterproposals without undue deliberations which eat up time. The timing of the strategy may be off. A negotiator may not have the authority to bind and be constantly on the phone to the person with that authority. There are any number of reasons why parties who could settle do not settle. Even experienced, prepared negotiators sometimes cannot agree.

Strike Issues

What issues are the negotiators most likely to go to strike over? Economic ones. Data on work stoppage issues for 1978, for example, indicate that general wage changes, supplementary benefits, and wage adjustments were the primary issues in 70 percent of work stoppages.[5] The primary issues in a majority of the rest of the stoppages included conflict over union security, seniority and job security, and plant administration (discipline and discharge). The figures indicate that most strike issues are economic in nature. It is more difficult for a union to stay out over noneconomic issues. Language controversies are more difficult to explain to members and harder to relate to (unless they have a direct economic effect) than is money.

This is not to say that strikes are single-issue contests of will. Usually there is more than one issue on the table. The strike is over a package which is largely economic in content but which may include one or more of the stickier noneconomic issues as well. In some cases, the strike may be superficially over money,

---

4. The mediator in this situation can take the blame for the compromise on the pet demand. The negotiator can concede in the spirit of compromise as suggested by the mediator. The negotiator can later say the idea to compromise was the mediator's.

5. Department of Labor, Bureau of Labor Statistics, *Handbook of Labor Statistics* (Washington: U.S. Government Printing Office, 1980), p. 427.

but in actual fact it may be a conflict over a less clearly economic item. For example, the union may have demanded that the employer stop the subcontracting of work. Later on in the negotiations, the union may drop the demand with the idea that failure to put an end to subcontracting can be compensated for with a larger wage gain. If management does not come across with the expected larger wage increase, the resultant strike appears to be over wages, when the root of the discontent is really subcontracting.

Preparation for Strikes

Both labor and management prepare for a strike whether they expect one or not. It is too late to prepare at contract expiration. Neither side wants to be caught unprepared at impasse.

Management often has a "strike manual" to deal with a strike should one occur. It will provide for the orderly shutdown or operation of the struck facility. The exact contents of this manual will depend upon the type of goods or service produced by the firm. While some elements may be common to both, a manual for a hospital will differ from a manual for a chemical plant. Table 15-1 shows the table of contents for a strike manual for an oil refinery. The entire manual is a detailed 140 pages long.

Table 15-1   Strike Manual for an Oil Refinery

Table of Contents

Article	Paragraph	
I.		Objectives of the Emergency Operating Plan
II.		Personnel, Authority Structure, and Duties
III.		Operating Plan
	A.	Manpower Requirements to Operate
	B.	Selection, Training, and Call-out of Manpower
IV.		Take-Over Plan (with Prestrike Notification or Wildcat)
V.		Supply Flow
	A.	Raw Materials
	B.	Utilities (Power, Gas, Water)
	C.	Transportation (Rail, Truck, Water)
VI.		Communications (Phone, Two-Way Radio)
VII.		Disaster and Safety Planning (Training, Fire, Medical)
VIII.		Plant Protection
IX.		Operating Personnel and Their Family Needs
	A.	Family Problems (Day-to-Cay, Crises, Protection)
	B.	Access to Plant
	C.	Living Accommodations (Beds, Laundry, Food, Clothing, Recreation, Medical Care)
X.		Legal Action (Legal Counsel, Video Taping, Photos, Witnesses, Law Enforcement Agencies)
XI.		Public Relations (Authority for and Items in Press Releases, Radio Stations, Newspapers)
XII.		Departure Plan

Beyond the immediate plans to operate or shut down the facility, there are other preparations. Firms may increase their prestrike production, ship inventory to warehouses or stockpile it, urge customers to buy early and stockpile, or join with other employers in some form of strike insurance plan.

Unions are no less prepared for strikes. Members save more, postpone large expenses such as appliances and autos, and look for short-run alternative employment. The labor organization sets up strike funds, looks for possible loans and aid from other unions, and aids the membership in applying for food stamps or other public assistance. Of course, any increased prestrike production by the firm also increases the income of employees through overtime pay. But the costs of striking are not borne by the parties alone. The public bears a burden as well.

Measuring the Cost of Strikes

There are no very good measures of the cost of strikes either to the parties involved or to society. Strike statistics collected by the Bureau of Labor Statistics relate to the frequency or duration of strikes. A cost can be inferred from these, but no strike statistics are regularly measured in dollars.

A Current Measure. A statistic commonly used to indicate the impact of strikes on the economy is the "percentage of estimated total working time lost due to work stoppage." The measure is calculated by dividing the estimated work time lost by those involved in a work stoppage by the total work time available from all people in the work force whether union or nonunion. The measure has the effect of spreading strike losses over the entire labor force.

Table 15-2   Recent Work Stoppages

Year	Percentage of Estimated Working Time Lost Due to Work Stoppages	Year—Month	Percentage of Estimated Working Time Lost Due to Work Stoppages
1970	.37	1981 January	.05
1971	.26	February	.04
1972	.15	March	.08
1973	.14	April	.24
1974	.24	May	.28
1975	.16	June	.17
1976	.19	July	.12
1977	.17	August	.09
1978	.17	September	.08
1979	.15	October	.06
1980	.14	November	.02
1981	.11	December	.01

Source: *Monthly Labor Review* (March, 1982), p. 95.

Table 15-2 indicates work stoppage figures for the most recent data available. The average percentage of working time lost due to strikes during the 1970s was 0.20 percent (one-fifth of 1 percent). On a 40-hour week basis, that is about 4 minutes and 50 seconds per week for each employed worker in the labor force. As was discussed in Chapters 11 and 12, the highest amount of time lost due to strikes ever recorded occurred in 1946 when the statistic stood at 1.43 percent. That was due in part to the reconversion from a war to peacetime economy. Union members sought to make up for wartime relative wage losses in the face of employer intransigence. The high strike volume precipitated the Taft-Hartley Act of 1947.

The monthly figures for 1981 clearly illustrate that there is a seasonal pattern to strikes. The usual seasonal pattern shows lower strike activity in the first and fourth quarters and relatively higher activity in the second and third. The reasons advanced are numerous. First- and fourth-quarter strikes are fewer and shorter due to inclement weather (cold picket line, poor vacation time), higher utility bills, pre-Christmas buying demands, and post-Christmas bills and scarcity of alternative employment for strikers. The rationale for more and longer second- and third-quarter strikes follows from the above: good weather (easier picket duty, good vacation time), lower utility bills, and the availability of seasonal alternative employment.

These statistics are relative rather than absolute measures of strike impact. The percentage of time lost figures only include the figures for workers on strike. They do not include strike-related losses to nonstrikers in the form of shorter workweeks and layoffs. And, again, there is no dollar value measure of strike losses. What would be a good measure and why is there not one?

Why Is There Not a Better Measure? If the goal were to measure the impact strikes have on the economy, one measure would be the output lost to the total economy due to strikes. Those who complain about the barbarism of a contest of economic power to settle differences at the bargaining table usually are concerned about the external effects strikes have on other parties. If only the labor and management directly involved in the disagreement were the ones hurt, there would be much less disapproval of the strike. But that is not the case in general. The economy has become so interrelated and bargaining in key industries so concentrated (autos, steel, coal, trucking, longshoring, rubber, and electrical equipment to name a few) that the impact of major strikes reaches far beyond the primary parties.

A complete measure would have to measure losses both forward and backward in the production chain. For example, a steel industry shutdown has an impact back down the production chain to suppliers of the steel industry such as the coal, iron ore, utilities, rail, and trucking industries. It affects users of steel products up the production chain such as the auto, appliance, and construction industries. Then there are the industries affected by the loss of sales to striking and laid-off workers. Retail sales of restaurants, bars, barber shops, auto dealers, furniture stores, and even grocery stores which are in areas dependent upon the struck or related industry drop off severely. Universities and schools are hurt due to reduced tax revenues. An accurate measure of economic loss would have to avoid double counting. (The true economic loss is measured only by the lost final product.) But there can be no doubt that strikes in key industries have significant ripple effects on people throughout the economy.

It is easy to overstate the losses associated with strikes. Much of it is more of an inconvenience than a permanent loss. Purchases of autos and appliances may be postponed, not foregone. Producers of substitutes for the struck goods expand output to meet the increased demand. Producers of the same product who are not on strike fill the void left by the strike. Foreign and nonunion producers enlarge their share of the market. Consumers of final goods are inconvenienced but not truly harmed by the strikes. Collecting and analyzing these figures would be a monumental task. To date the federal government has not seen fit to expend the money to do so. The value of collecting more detailed statistics is open to question. The dollar impact of strikes would be interesting, but current statistics provide adequate information on relative strike incidence.

Recall that the logic of private sector labor law is that the cost of strikes to society is the price paid for free collective bargaining. Does society ever say the price of a strike is too high? The next section answers the question.

EMERGENCY DISPUTES

Both the Railway Labor Act and the Taft-Hartley Act have emergency dispute settlement procedures. Under Taft-Hartley a lengthy procedure of checks and balances may be invoked, "Whenever in the opinion of the President of the United States, a threatened or actual strike or lock-out . . . will, if permitted to occur or to continue, imperil the national health or safety. . . ."

The Procedure

The emergency disputes procedure is initiated by the President of the United States with the appointment of a fact-finding board of inquiry. The board reports to the President who can then direct the U.S. Attorney General to petition the district court for an injunction. If the court concurs with the Presidential prognosis, it can enjoin the work stoppage. Once enjoined from striking, labor and management are to bargain with mediators present for 60 days. At the end of the 60 days, if no settlement has been reached, the reconvened board of inquiry must report to the President the results of the negotiations including the employer's last offer of settlement. In the next 15 days, the NLRB must conduct a secret ballot of the striking employees on the acceptability of the employer's last offer. Five days later the results must be certified to the Attorney General who must then petition the court to lift the strike ban. The strike or lockout can then continue. The President must report to Congress on the events and make recommendations for settlement. Because the whole process involves an 80-day injunction of the work stoppage, it has been dubbed the *80-day cooling-off period.*

On 31 occasions U.S. Presidents have convened boards of inquiry to begin the procedure. In 26 of these cases injunctions were issued.[6] Since its inception, the procedure has been a source of considerable controversy. Much of the discussion centers about the criteria which should be used to judge when a strike endangers national health or safety. The law specifies none. It leaves it up to the judgment of the President checked and balanced by that of the courts. Proponents of the procedure say it fulfills its role as a useful safeguard against damaging strikes. Critics argue that it favors the employer, is inconsistent (the strike can be continued after the 80-day hiatus), and that the measure of national emergency is subjectively political, not objective, in nature.

Its Political Nature

Its most recent use during the 109-day coal strike in 1977-1978 lends substance to the critics. The strike began with the expiration of the contract on December 6, 1977. Few observers of the coal industry doubted there would be a strike. Coal users had stockpiled coal well in advance. The United Mine Workers of America (UMWA) was fraught with internal political discord. Two months into the strike a tentative agreement was reached and then rejected by the UMWA bargaining council under pressure by the rank and file. With the rejection of the pact, the White House intervened to pressure the negotiators to settle. Pressure to use the emergency procedure came amidst various predictions made by special interest groups of the impending dire consequences of the strike. Governors of the coal states and members of Congress joined in the call for use of Taft-Hartley. John Ackermann, in an analysis of the impact of the coal strike, pointed out that at the same time the Secretary of Labor was emphasizing the urgency of the problem of dwindling coal supplies, the Deputy Secretary of Energy was going on record that the coal problem was not critical.[7]

A second settlement was reached before the President was to announce the use of Taft-Hartley. On March 5 the agreement was rejected by the rank and file and on March 6 President Carter started the emergency disputes procedure. A temporary restraining order (the first step in the injunction process) was issued by the court on March 9. Negotiations began again March 10 and on the 14th an agreement was reached. The President was unable to substantiate his claim of a national emergency to the satisfaction of the court, and the restraining order was lifted on March 17. The agreement was ratified on March 24, 1978.

---

6. Federal Mediation and Conciliation Service, *Synopsis of Presidential Boards of Inquiry Created Under National Emergency Provisions of the Labor-Management Relations Act, 1947* (Washington: U.S. Government Printing Office, 1973).

7. John Ackermann, "The Impact of the Coal Strike of 1977-78," *Industrial and Labor Relations Review,* Vol. 32, No. 2 (January, 1979), pp. 175-88.

The work loss statistics are interesting. At the peak of the strike impact (before Taft-Hartley was used) the five states hardest hit by the strike suffered a layoff loss of only 0.44 percent of the total manufacturing work force. Including strike-reduced labor hours, the loss rose to 2.1 percent. Ackermann concludes:

> President Carter's invocation of Taft-Hartley in the coal strike of 1977-78 reflects the fact that popular perceptions of the impact of prolonged strikes in major industries may well create virtually irresistible political pressure toward settlement, pressures that will ultimately lead to federal intervention in the name of national health and safety.[8]

The decision as to whether or not a strike is truly a potential or actual national emergency is a political one. There are no hard and fast criteria by which to judge when a dispute actually or potentially endangers national health or safety. Economists and collective bargaining authorities have suggested some measures, but it appears they are not necessarily used by those who make the political decisions.[9] Without any clear consensus on a measure of national emergency, the best that can be done is to advocate reasoned decisions in a system of checks and balances.

Few strikes are major, of the "national emergency" nature, or even lengthy. In 1978, for example, 28 percent of strikes lasted less than a week and 47 percent lasted less than 2 weeks. Only 9 percent lasted 90 days or longer.[10] But are there ways to cut down on the number and duration of strikes? Are there alternatives to the strike?

ALTERNATIVES TO THE STRIKE

The search for viable alternatives to the strike has been carried out in both the private and the public sectors. The situations differ between the two sectors. In the private sector the strike is legal. In the public sector it generally is not. Therefore, most of the experimentation with alternatives has been carried out in the public sector. Thus far the private sector has not adopted the methods found to be effective in the public sector.

Private Sector Alternatives to the Strike

Two approaches have been taken to reduce strikes. One is to improve the current system of negotiation to minimize the resort to power. The second is to

---

8. Ibid., p. 188.

9. Irving Bernstein, for example, suggests six tests which must be met for a strike to constitute a national emergency. See Irving Bernstein, "The Economic Impact of Strikes in Key Industries," in Irving Bernstein, Harold Enarson, and R. W. Fleming (eds.), *Emergency Disputes and National Policy* (New York: Harper and Brothers, 1955).

10. *Handbook of Labor Statistics* (1980), p. 417.

provide an alternative to the strike. Measured in terms of individual cases, both methods have been successful at decreasing strikes. However, the aggregate statistics do not show a downward trend. Over the past decade the percentage of FMCS mediation cases which involves strikes varies from a low of 11.4 percent in 1973 to a high of 15.5 percent in 1970. The figure stood at 14.2 percent in 1979.[11] There is no discernible pattern over the decade.

Technical Assistance. The Federal Mediation and Conciliation Service has been at the forefront of the effort to reduce labor-management conflict through its Technical Assistance (TA) efforts. The FMCS helps form and assist labor-management committees and councils. These committees deal with collective bargaining problems away from the heat of the negotiating table. In 1979 the effort included 375 such committees. They also were involved in 1591 Relationships by Objectives (RBO) programs.[12] The RBO focus is on firms with poor labor-management relationships. Key union and management people in the firm meet with mediators to identify and analyze their problems. The parties are urged to approach their problems from an integrative bargaining (win-win) perspective, as opposed to their current distributive bargaining (win-lose) perspective. With FMCS help they set objectives for improving their relationship and a timetable for achieving them. The use of the TA program has grown steadily in recent years, but federal budget cuts threaten the continued availability of federally supported efforts to reduce industrial conflict.

There have been few private sector experiments with alternatives to the strike. There seems to be little desire on the part of labor and management to seek an alternative in the absence of a mutual threat. Two examples of alternatives support this contention.

ENA. The steel industry experimented with a strike alternative from 1973 to 1980. The reason behind the experiment began years earlier. In 1959 there was a 116-day steel strike which ended in a Taft-Hartley injunction. There were no strikes in the succeeding negotiations, but labor, management, and steel customers geared up for one each time. Therein lay the problem. Prior to the contract expiration date, the steel companies would work overtime to stockpile steel. Then, when no strike occurred, there would be large-scale layoffs until the stockpiles were worked down. To make matters worse, steel customers, uncertain of their domestic supply, turned to foreign steel in anticipation of strike disruptions. Foreign steel began to erode the domestic steel market, threatening the security of both the companies and the union.

Cognizant of their mutual problems, the United Steelworkers of America (USA) and the Steel Coordinating Committee, representing the employers, negotiated the *Experimental Negotiating Agreement* (ENA) in 1973 to take effect with the 1974 negotiations. Under ENA, the negotiations were to proceed as

---

11. FMCS, *Thirty-Second Annual Report*, p. 15.
12. Ibid, p. 28.

usual up to a predetermined date well before contract expiration. At the predetermined date, if the parties had not settled, the issues were to be submitted to a panel of impartial arbitrators for a final and binding settlement. The Steelworkers agreed not to strike over national issues. In order to make the ENA palatable to the Steelworkers, the ENA provided for a guaranteed minimum wage increase of 3 percent per year, an unlimited cost-of-living escalator clause, and a $150 bonus premised on the profitability of avoiding a national steel strike. Locals were allowed to strike over local issues only after a favorable local strike vote and only then with permission from USA President I. W. Abel.

The ENA continued through the 1977 and 1980 negotiations. It became a political issue in the elections following Abel's retirement in 1977. Right-to-strikers rallied behind Ed Sadlowski against pro-ENA candidate Lloyd McBride. McBride won the election by a 3:2 margin, but lack of support for the continuation of the ENA was clearly evident.[13] During the 1980 negotiations no agreement was reached to extend the ENA beyond 1980. In the corporate view, ENA is too expensive. In the face of a declining U.S. steel market, with the need for massive capital outlays to become competitive once again, and with the continuing high rate of inflation, the ENA with its guaranteed 3 percent per year plus unlimited COLA makes for a very high, nonnegotiable wage package. Under the 1977-1980 agreement, hourly wage increases were 88 cents, and COLA increases came to $1.86 over the 3 years.[14]

No strikes occurred under ENA, and its voluntary arbitration provisions were never used. It was welcomed as a major breakthrough in private sector labor relations when it was first signed. Students of collective bargaining were hopeful that ENA would spread to other industries as a viable alternative to the strike. It has not.

Most recently there has been some discussion of the suitability of an ENA for coal. The proportion of union mined coal has dropped from about 70 percent in the early 1970s to 44 percent in 1981.[15] The coal export market is jeopardized by lengthy U.S. strikes. Domestic coal consumers are in the stockpile mode of behavior, exploring the use of nonunion Western coal or seeking noncoal backups. United States dependence on foreign oil is increased by uncertain domestic coal production.

The chances for a coal ENA seem slim at best. An ENA is a subject for integrative bargaining. It would require a mature bargaining relationship between the UMWA and the BCOA. Both groups are fraught with internal political problems, and all bargaining issues are win-lose items. The perceived threat is not great enough and the relationship is not mature enough to support a coal ENA at the present time.

---

13. *U.S. News and World Report* (May 26, 1980), p. 86.

14. Ibid., p. 85.

15. William Miernyk, "The 1971 Coal Strike: A View from the Outside," *Labor Law Journal*, Vol. 32, No. 8 (August, 1981), pp. 566-67.

Construction. A case study from the construction industry provides one other example of a move to reduce strike uncertainty. One way to reduce the incidence of strikes at negotiation time is to negotiate less frequently, that is, negotiate agreements with longer duration. This was attempted in the auto industry during the economic stability of the early 1960s. Economic stability is important because contract duration is particularly affected by the rate of inflation. Unions do not want to be trapped in long agreements with fixed wage increases during high inflation. The uncertainty of high inflation makes for shorter agreements, and this consideration often overrides that of industrial peace.

For the local construction industry in one area the threat of nonunion construction proved to be a greater fear. Historically contracts were negotiated yearly. Union firms faced the possibility of strike delays and penalties for late completion. They were uncertain what wage costs would be over the length of a construction project. Because of these problems, union contractors were placed at a disadvantage relative to the nonunion ones in competitive bidding. The success of nonunion firms was perceived as a mutual threat to their jobs, so construction firms and unions agreed to negotiate 3-year contracts. They hedged against inflation by including a provision which would reopen the agreement to negotiate on wages only if the Consumer Price Index exceeded a specified value by the end of the second year of the agreement (a form of wage reopener). The result has been fewer strikes, more certain and easily estimable costs for bidding, and more union job security.

The structure of bargaining in construction is also changing to reduce the number of agreements. Two routes are being used. The wide-area agreement was discussed earlier. In this method local unions of the same craft combine to negotiate one contract with an employers' association. The second approach, wherein locals of different crafts bargain as a group with one or more contractors' associations, is used less frequently. This multicraft approach is more difficult to create and less stable than the single-craft wide-area structure.[16]

Public Sector Strikes

Should the police be allowed to strike? The U.S. Army? Fire fighters? School teachers? Garbage collectors? Professors? Transit workers? Nurses and doctors in VA hospitals? The right to strike in the public sector ranks alongside union security when it comes to controversy. The arguments pro and con have been made so many times at the federal, state, and local government level that a cataloging is fairly easy. The positions pro and con are sketched below.

---

16. Paul T. Hartman and Walter H. Franks, "The Changing Bargaining Structure in Construction: Wide-Area and Multicraft Bargaining," *Industrial and Labor Relations Review*, Vol. 33, No. 2 (January, 1980), pp. 170-84.

The Case Against the Strike. The private sector rationale for the strike as an economic test of power to settle economic issues has no parallel in the public sector. The public employer is not a profit maker. The demand for government goods and services is political, not economic. The revenues are from taxes, not sale of product. Many services are essential with no close substitutes (e.g., national defense, police, and fire fighters). This inelastic demand coupled with the very labor-intensive nature of government production and with almost no increased productivity offsets causes wage increases to be forced on the public in the form of higher taxes.

Taxes are raised by the legislative body, and contracts are negotiated by the administrative arm of government. The negotiators do not have the power to bind the legislature to agreements, and so strikes against the administration are misdirected. Two bad situations result from this. Negotiations may drag on interminably because the administrator may not have the power to bind or the politician may commit to an agreement too quickly to save his or her political hide and then pass the cost problem on to the legislature.[17] Finally, strikes against the public are really against the sovereign power of the government and cannot be tolerated.

The Case in Favor of the Strike. The problem for the employee is the same in the private and public sectors: income and job security. Public sector employees are not second class citizens and must have the right to strike in order to be taken seriously by their employers. There may not be competitive, profit-based pressures on government prices, but there is a continuous drive to contain government costs. These pressures cause government employers to hold the line on wages and cut out jobs. Considering the political unpopularity of tax increases, public sector employees are hostage to the political ambitions of elected officials.

The lack of substitutes for government services is not always true. Not all, actually very few, services are essential. In fact, quite a number which are provided by the public sector in some locales (garbage collection) are performed by the private sector in others. Nurses and doctors in VA and state or municipally run hospitals cannot strike, but they can in profit and nonprofit private sector hospitals. What is the difference and why is one essential, the other not? With proper safeguards almost no government functions are essential.

The sovereignty argument is false as well. Government buys other resources such as electricity, gas, oil, raw materials and bargains for them or is forced to pay for them. How is labor different? Government can even be sued by citizens and firms. And finally, the strike may be outlawed, but not effec-

---

17. One of the strongest cases made against collective bargaining and the use of the strike in the public sector is made by Harry Wellington and Ralph Winter in *The Unions and the Cities* (Washington: The Brookings Institution, 1971).

tively. The large increase in illegal public sector strikes proves first that existing bargaining structures are not meeting the needs of parties and, second, that fines and jail sentences meted out to strikers are not effective deterrents. The public sector strike, given proper safeguards, is essential to public sector collective bargaining.

The winner of the strike debate is almost invariably the antistrike side. Only eight states (Alaska, Hawaii, Minnesota, Montana, Oregon, Pennsylvania, Rhode Island, and Vermont) allow public employees to strike, and these allow it only after a lengthy procedure of conflict resolution techniques has been exhausted.[18] The next section provides an overview of the contract resolution techniques used to avoid or substitute for the strike.

The Search for Strike Alternatives

Almost all of the innovation and testing of alternatives to the strike have come from the public sector. Many strike substitutes have evolved, but as yet none has emerged as the single best way to handle disagreements over the terms and conditions of employment. Each alternative to the strike involves the intrusion of a third party into the labor-management relationship. The approaches can be ordered by the amount of power given to the third party.

The Alternatives. All public sector laws mandate mediation during the negotiations. Mediators have power, depending upon their skill and ability, to keep the parties talking and moving toward settlement. Mediation is often coupled with several of the other dispute resolution tactics.

If the parties reach impasse, the next step could be a form of *fact-finding.* The fact-finding may be done by one person (neutral) or by a tripartite panel (one labor, one management, one neutral). Fact finders hold hearings to determine what has happened in negotiations to that time, what the initial and concession positions of the parties have been, and what the current positions of the parties are. The fact finder's report may go to an administrative agency or to an executive branch official charged with responsibility for dispute settlement. The fact finders may or may not be allowed to make recommendations for settlement. The fact finder's report with or without recommendations may or may not be made public. The publication of the report is usually delayed to allow the parties to negotiate their own settlement before public pressure is brought to bear on them. Regardless of the variation on the fact-finding theme, it is important to note that fact finder decisions are not binding on the parties.

Advisory arbitration is little more than fact-finding with recommendations. The individual arbitrator or panel hears the parties' contentions and then

---

18. David Lewin, "Public Sector Collective Bargaining and the Right to Strike," in David Lewin, Peter Feuille, and Thomas Kochan (eds.), *Public Sector Labor Relations: Analysis and Readings* (Glen Ridge, N. J.: Thomas Horton and Daughters, 1977), p. 236.

issues a nonbinding recommended settlement. The settlement may be publicized.

Med-arb involves more third-party power. Med-arb has been called mediation with a club. The mediator is also an arbitrator. He or she first tries to mediate a settlement. If the parties cannot agree, the mediator puts on the arbitration hat and issues a final and binding decision. At this stage of intervention, a question arises as to whether or not an arbitrator should have the power to bind a public employer (hence legislature and the people) to a settlement.

Voluntary arbitration allows the parties to choose to arbitrate their dispute. If they so choose, the decision of the arbitrator or panel of arbitrators is final and binding. Under *compulsory arbitration*, the disputants have no choice. They must arbitrate negotiation impasses and abide by the arbitrator's decision. This type of arbitration is also called *interest arbitration.* The controversy is over the terms and conditions which will be included in the arbitrated agreement.

There are three systems of compulsory or interest arbitration currently in use. In *conventional interest arbitration,* the arbitrator has the authority to render whatever decision he or she judges to be appropriate. If using the *item selection* variation, the arbitrator obtains the terms of the employer's last offer and the terms of the union's last set of demands. The arbitrator is then required to make an award item by item but must choose either the last position of the employer or the last position of the union on each issue. There is no allowable middle ground. The other system in use gives the arbitrator even less authority to fashion a decision. In *final offer selection* the arbitrator's decision is confined to either selecting all of the final position of management or selecting all of the union's final demands as the settlement.

Problems and Possibilities. Why all of these tortuous twists and turns of procedure? It is very difficult to simulate a strike threat. The goal is to design a procedure which will give the impetus to settle that a strike has without actually having one. It is the ultimate problem of substituting procedure for power. The key to it is to design a procedure which will facilitate the negotiation process, not interfere with or chill it. The dilemma is epitomized by the chief argument against compulsory arbitration. Dubbed the *weaker party argument,* the position is that so long as one side has more to gain by the impasse resolution procedure than by negotiating, they will go to impasse rather than negotiate a settlement. The argument is expressed in labor-management behavior in the form of two effects.

The first effect is called the *chilling effect* of dispute resolution procedures. If the weaker party believes it can get a better settlement from an arbitrator, they will make no concession during negotiations for fear their concessions will be used against them at arbitration. Conventional arbitration is the method most prone to this type of behavior because the arbitrator is free to fashion any agreement. The parties may fear the arbitrator will "split the difference" between the last positions taken by labor and management. Final offer and item selection arbitration are designed precisely with the weaker party problem in mind. By forcing the arbitrator to choose all of one party's final position, or item by item one or the other, the procedure suggests to the parties that extreme positions will not be chosen. The most reasonable one(s) will. This encourages the parties to come down to their last, best, and final positions; concessions will not count against them.

The second effect has been dubbed the *narcotic effect* of impasse procedures. As the parties become familiar with the dispute resolution procedure, they come to rely on it more frequently and use it as a substitute for an agreement reached on their own. This is likely to occur most frequently where negotiations are complex politically both for the union and management.

One strategy to avoid weaker party problems is to create uncertainty in the mind of the weaker party about the settlement likely to result from going to impasse. The *choice of procedures,* or "bag of tricks," places an array of impasse procedures in the hands of whoever is charged with responsibility for disputes (a secretary of labor or public employee relations board). Something similar to this is used by the Federal Services Impasses Panel which can mandate anything from mediation to a directed settlement. Hypothetically, the array might include mediation, fact-finding with or without recommendations, and compulsory arbitration. It would be at the discretion of the secretary of labor to choose a procedure at impasse (pull a trick out of the bag). The weaker party, not knowing what might be used against an impasse, is encouraged to bargain rather than chance getting a worse deal from the holder of the bag of tricks.

Evidence on the Viability of Alternatives to the Strike

The question of what is a viable alternative to the strike is an empirical one. Does the weaker party logic hold only on paper and not in practice? Hundreds of books and articles have been written on the effectiveness of public sector alternatives to the strike. One recent survey of the literature summarizes some of the conclusions regarding the effectiveness of public sector fact-finding and arbitration.[19] These conclusions include:

1. Proportionally more cases go to impasse under conventional and final offer arbitration than under fact-finding, and over time the use of all types of impasse procedure is increasing.
2. There is no significant difference in the number of cases which go to impasse under final offer and conventional arbitration, but more cases are settled before an award is issued in final offer systems.

19. Thomas A. Kochan, "Dynamics of Dispute Resolution in the Public Sector," in Benjamin Aaron, Joseph R. Grodin, and James L. Stern (eds.), *Public Sector Bargaining* (Madison, Wisc.: Industrial Relations Research Association, 1979), pp. 150-90.

3. Arbitration deters strikes more effectively than does fact-finding or the absence of an impasse procedure (the evidence here is primarily with police and fire fighter laws).[20]

4. There appears to be a narcotic effect in operation in both fact-finding and arbitration; and this is particularly true in large jurisdictions (e.g., city units like San Francisco).[21]

5. There is a chilling effect, and that effect has become more serious as the parties have become more experienced with negotiating under dispute resolution procedures.[22]

The analysis of the relative effectiveness of impasse procedures has led a number of states to change their public sector bargaining laws to substitute arbitration for fact-finding. Currently 20 states have some form of compulsory arbitration for some groups of public employees.[23] There has been no similar movement toward revamping public sector laws to allow public sector employees to strike. No ultimate, clearly superior alternative to the use of the strike in the public sector has emerged.

It seems apparent that different situations require different impasse resolution systems. In the absence of any movement to increase the number of statutes allowing the right to strike, or to rescind laws allowing bargaining, the alternatives appear to meet the most basic test: workability. One final note: None of the public sector strike alternatives has inspired private sector practitioners to make a substitution for the use of the strike in the private sector.

GRIEVANCE ARBITRATION

This section deals with conflict during the life of the contract. It shows how grievance arbitration has come to be an effective alternative to the strike once an agreement has been signed. The topics discussed include grievance handling, grievance procedures, arbitration hearings, arbitrators, and costs and delays in arbitration.

---

20. Ibid., pp. 162-63.

21. Ibid., p. 177. The narcotic effect for police and fire fighter negotiations in New York was discussed in a recent exchange of articles in the *Industrial and Labor Relations Review.* There is little doubt that such effect does exist. The question under debate is more one of how to properly measure the effect and what causes it. See Thomas A. Kochan and Jean Baderschneider, "Dependence on Impasse Procedures: Police and Firefighters in New York State," *Industrial and Labor Relations Review,* Vol. 31, No. 4 (July, 1978), pp. 431-39; Richard J. Butler and Ronald G. Ehrenberg, "Estimating the Narcotic Effect of Public Sector Impasse Procedures," *Industrial and Labor Relations Review,* Vol. 35, No. 1 (October, 1981), pp. 3-20; and Thomas A. Kochan and Jean Baderschneider, "Estimating the Narcotic Effect: Choosing Techniques that Fit the Problem," *Industrial and Labor Relations Review,* Vol. 35, No. 1 (October, 1981), pp. 21-28.

22. Kochan, "Dynamics of Dispute Resolution in the Public Sector," p. 177.

23. Peter Feuille, "Selected Benefits and Costs of Compulsory Arbitration," *Industrial and Labor Relations Review,* Vol. 33, No. 1 (October, 1979), p. 64.

A Distinction

The arbitration discussed earlier in this chapter is called interest arbitration because it involves the settlement of the parties' economic interests when the terms of a new agreement are set. The decision of the arbitrator *is* the agreement between the parties. The subject of the remainder of the chapter is *grievance arbitration,* or *rights arbitration.* This occurs whenever labor and management have an existing agreement and during its life they have a dispute over what it means or how it is applied. In short, they go to an arbitrator to obtain a decision as to what their rights are *under* their existing agreement.

Why There Is Conflict

You would think that if labor and management spent months negotiating an agreement, they would know what it meant once they started living by it, would you not? That is not always the case. Whether it is a 10-page craft agreement or a 200-page industrial one, the administration of the agreement causes conflict. Labor and management may believe the same contract language to mean two different things. This can occur for a number of reasons. The language may have been drafted too hastily at the table—the parties thought they were together on the meaning of it but actually were not. The parties may have known they had differing interpretations of the language when it was drafted at the table, but they agreed to it to get a settlement, planning to deal with the ambiguity later.

A situation may arise during the life of the agreement which could not be foreseen when the bargainers agreed to the language. The people (both union and management) charged with the day-to-day implementation of the agreement may never have been educated as to the meaning of the contract or changes in it. Management may feel they gave too much away at the table and try to get it back in daily operations. The labor organization may feel that not enough was gained at the negotiating table, challenge the daily administration of the agreement, and hope management will cave in or that an arbitrator will rule in labor's favor. No matter how carefully the negotiators construct the agreement, the day-to-day administration of the contract will cause conflict. Forewarned is forearmed, and the parties once again substitute procedure for power. How the contract is designed to handle conflict follows.

Bargaining Agreement Logic and Conflict

Prior to the 1940s unions commonly struck to force employers to act upon their grievances during a contract. During World War II, when the war effort could not tolerate work stoppages, the War Labor Board (WLB) wrote grievance-arbitration procedures and no-strike–no-lockout clauses into agreements. The logic behind writing these procedures into an agreement is straightforward. Disputes over interests and the content of the agreement are to be settled with or without a strike when the agreement is negotiated. Once the agreement has been signed, the focus of labor-management conflict must shift to question the rights of the parties under the existing agreement. Conflict raises a question concerning the interpretation and application of the agreement. The grievance procedure provides the mechanism to channel the disagreement into constructive discussion. If the parties cannot agree, they are to arbitrate their differences rather than resort to force. The trade-off for giving up the right to strike is a decision by a neutral, disinterested party. The logic has withstood the ravages of time, the scrutiny of the courts, and the NLRB, and meets the needs of the parties.

Labor and management agree with the logic by and large. Ninety-four percent of major contracts have no-strike–no-lockout provisions, and 96 percent have grievance-arbitration provisions.[24] The grievance-arbitration and no-strike–no-lockout provisions do not stand alone. They are potentially related to every clause in the contract because every clause can be changed in interpretation and application by a labor-management practice or arbitration decision.

However, there is a very direct relationship between management rights and the grievance-arbitration clause. The duty of good faith bargaining extends not only to contract negotiations but also to grievance negotiation. Management tries to limit having to negotiate new items not in the contract during the life of the agreement by including a "zipper clause" in the agreement:

> This Agreement and its supplements represent the complete agreement between the parties for the term hereof, it being understood and agreed that neither party shall have any right to change or make any additions or deletions to this Agreement, or any of its provisions unless otherwise mutually agreed in writing. The parties hereby expressly waive the right, during the term of this Agreement, to bargain on any subject unless such right to bargain is herein expressly and specifically provided for.

The clause does not imply that management can refuse to negotiate on grievances about what the contract means when challenged by the union. Management must provide the union with information germane to specific grievances. Herein lies the relationship between management rights and grievance arbitration. Under the system of bargaining followed in the United States, the tradition is for management to exercise its management rights to administer the contract subject to challenge by the union via the grievance procedure.

Management rights may be gained or lost at the negotiation table, or they

---

24. Bureau of National Affairs, *Basic Patterns in Union Contracts* (Washington: Bureau of National Affairs, Inc., 1979), pp. 15, 78.

may also be changed through the grievance-arbitration mechanism. Where the contract says one thing and management does another, management may set a precedent which will be upheld by an arbitrator. The effect of the language will have been modified but not the language. The true agreement between the parties, zipper clause notwithstanding, extends beyond the contract to include the way the parties actually co-exist—their past practices. *Past practice* refers to the way in which the union and management have historically been living under the agreement. If the agreement is hazy or ambiguous on an issue that is grieved by the union and subsequently taken to arbitration, the arbitrator will rely on the past practice of the parties to determine a proper interpretation of the language.

The above discussion should not be taken to mean that there is a continuous free-for-all as labor and management try to expand upon the agreement. The next section examines what constitutes a legitimate grievance and how a grievance procedure works.

The Grievance Procedure

A typical grievance procedure contains the definition of what constitutes a grievance, the negotiation steps, and provisions for arbitration if the negotiations fail.

Definition of a Grievance. The definition of a grievance can be very inclusive or very narrow. The national coal agreement illustrates the broad language:

> Should differences arise between the Mine Workers and the Employer as to meaning and application of the provisions of this Agreement, or should differences arise about matters not specifically mentioned in this Agreement, or should any local trouble of any kind arise at the mine, an earnest effort shall be made to settle such differences at the earliest practicable time.[25]

Contrast that with this language which very narrowly defines a grievance:

> "Grievance" as used in this Agreement is limited to a complaint of an employee which involves the interpretation or application of, or compliance with, the provisions of this Agreement.

Whatever the definition, the purpose of the grievance procedure is to deal with conflict and to relieve the tension between labor and management as quickly as possible. Mainline arbitrator Harold W. Davey proposes that "all

---

25. United Mine Workers of America–Bituminous Coal Operators of America, *Contract*, 1981, Art. XXIII, Sec. (c).

employers and unions should endorse the psychological proposition that *a grievance exists whenever an employee feels aggrieved,* whether or not the source of his grievance is contractual."[26] Some contracts differentiate between "complaints" and "grievances." Complaints need not have a contractual basis; their resolution is not precedent setting and they are not arbitrable. In other agreements a problem may be termed a "complaint" in the early steps of the grievance procedure and become a grievance only at the higher steps.

Craft and Industrial Procedures. Craft union and industrial union agreements have somewhat different procedures because of the nature of employment.

Craft. Here is a typical craft grievance procedure two paragraphs in length.

> There shall be no suspension of work on account of differences as to the meaning of the Agreement, but an earnest effort shall be made to settle such differences immediately.
>
> 1. Between the aggrieved parties and the job foreman.
> 2. Through the job superintendent and the business agents.
> 3. By a Board consisting of four (4) members, two (2) of whom shall be designated by the Union and two (2) by the Employer.
>
> Should the board fail to agree, the matter shall be referred to an umpire selected by said Board, or if they can't agree, the umpire shall be selected by the president of the Employer and the president of the Union. The decision of the umpire shall be final. The umpire's salary and expenses shall be paid equally by the Union and the Employer.

The craft procedure is relatively short because the employment relationship is more fluid. Craftspeople change employers more frequently. They are more independent of the individual employer. Time is of the essence in construction and emphasis is placed on informal, speedy settlement of grievances.

Industrial. An industrial union procedure is flowcharted in Figure 15-1. The full procedure is 10 pages long.

Note that the grievance must be started within 48 hours of when it occurred and that each step is timed. There is a progression up the authority ladder at each step. The first step is oral, and the following ones are written. Putting the grievance into writing at step 2 usually means that a standard grievance form must be filled out including the time, date, place of the incident, a description of the alleged contract violation, the specific articles of the agreement which were violated, the relief sought, and the signature of the

---

26. Harold W. Davey, *Contemporary Collective Bargaining*, 3d ed. (Englewood Cliffs, N.J.: Prentice Hall, 1972), p. 144. The italics are in the original.

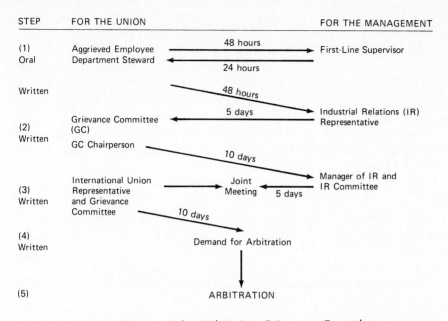

Figure 15-1: Industrial Union Grievance Procedure

grievant and/or union steward. The procedure ends in arbitration. There is no set time limit between the demand for arbitration and arbitration because that varies with the availability of an arbitrator.

There may actually be several grievance procedures in an agreement. Each is designed for a specific type of grievance. For example, there may be a formal, general purpose procedure which is precedent setting. To avoid lengthy delays on some grievances, there may be an expedited, non-precedent-setting procedure. (This is the case in steel, for example.) Safety grievances often have a short, fast procedure. Discharge grievances often have an expedited procedure. Some grievances may use the regular general procedure but start at a higher step. A grievance involving an entire shift, for example, should not logically start with a first-line supervisor.

The grievances which are most difficult to settle and are most likely candidates for arbitration are discussed in the next section.

Arbitrated Issues

The FMCS keeps records of arbitrations. The FMCS serves as both a referral and a tracking system for arbitration. The arbitrators are hired by the parties involved and are only referred by FMCS, but FMCS also monitors the cases. Table 15-3 shows the distribution of recent cases by major arbitration issue with some subclasses shown below the major issue.

Table 15-3   Issues Taken to Arbitration

Issue	Number	Number	Percent
General		1959	24
Seniority	721		
Work Assignment	387		
Economic: Wages and Pay		1120	14
Fringe Benefit Issues		250	3
Discipline or Discharge		3322	40
Technical (Job Evaluation, Bidding)		421	5
Scope of Agreement		234	3
Subcontracting	136		
Arbitrability of Grievance		692	8
Procedural	354		
Substantive	168		
Not Classified		272	3
TOTAL		8270	100

Source: FMCS, *Thirty-Second Annual Report*, pp. 38-39.

Discipline or discharge grievances top the list. Economic issues loom large as do seniority grievances. The arbitrability of a grievance is called into question procedurally when, for example, the time requirements of the procedure are violated. A substantive question arises when management believes its management rights preclude the filing of a grievance.

Arbitrators lump grievances together to form two groups. Discipline or discharge arbitrations form one group. All others are combined into a group called language interpretation cases. The way in which the arbitration hearing is run and the standards for decision making are different for each. Once the demand for arbitration has been made, the next step is to choose an arbitrator.

Selecting the Arbitrator

The craft grievance procedure has a very informal, unstructured way of selecting a single arbitrator. Occasionally, the contract will call for a panel of three arbitrators: one union, one management, and one neutral. But three-quarters of rights arbitration procedures call for a single arbitrator. Arbitrators are either *ad hoc* or *permanent*. The vast majority of arbitrators is chosen on a case-by-case (ad hoc) basis. Only 12 percent of contracts have a permanent arbitrator or panel of arbitrators who serve for the life of the agreement.

The arbitrators may be selected from people the parties know and trust, or in a high proportion of cases, they use an impartial referral service. The FMCS and American Arbitration Association (AAA) both provide a panel of arbitrators upon request. The panel is an odd number of names of available arbitrators. Along with the list comes a biography on each arbitrator. On the basis of this information (and whatever other research each side may do on the individual arbitrators) labor and management proceed alternately to strike a name from the list. For example, for a five-member panel, after labor and management have each struck twice, there would be one name left. That is the selected arbitrator. The parties contact the arbitrator to set up a hearing date.

In permanent arbitrator systems the parties select one arbitrator to hear all their cases. The permanent arbitrator serves for the life of the agreement or until labor or management decides that the arbitrator is no longer acceptable (i.e., their side just lost once too often).

The Hearing

Good industrial relations practice requires the parties to a grievance to adopt a problem-solving (win-win approach) attitude during the grievance procedure. Such is not usually the approach in taking a case to arbitration. The goal in arbitration is to win the case by getting a favorable ruling from the arbitrator (win-lose).

A hearing date is arranged with the arbitrator. The place may be on neutral ground (a motel), or, if a grievance requires a tour of the premises, the hearing might be held in the firm's conference room. The arbitrator serves at the will of the parties (they hire the arbitrator), but he or she runs the hearing. The room is set up in a conference format. The person presenting for the union side (often an international representative) heads up one side of the table flanked by union witnesses. Management's chief advocate is opposite the union advocate and is flanked by management witnesses. Advocates may or may not be lawyers. The arbitrator sits at the head of the table with a witness chair to the arbitrator's side.

View the proceeding from the arbitrator's perspective. In ad hoc cases especially, the arbitrator may know only who the parties are, the time, the date and place of the hearing, and whether it is a language or discipline case. During the hearing the arbitrator must learn enough about the case to make a decision.

The hearing is designed and run to gather that information. It proceeds roughly in three phases. The hearing is convened, and witnesses are sworn in if the parties so desire. Then each side makes an opening statement which states what the grievance is about (a statement of the issue) and what they intend to show. This tells the arbitrator the nature of the grievance and what to expect in the next phase.

Phase 2 consists of the presentation of evidence through testimony by witnesses. The hearing is run roughly according to the rules of evidence used in court. First one side presents its evidence and witnesses. The witnesses are questioned in order by their own advocate (direct testimony) and then by the advocate for the other side (cross-examination). When one side finishes, the other proceeds with its witnesses and evidence. The arbitrator may ask questions of the witnesses as well.

In the final phase, each side gives its closing arguments and the hearing is over. A transcript of the hearing is taken by a court reporter in about a quarter of the cases, and in two-thirds the parties file prehearing and/or posthearing briefs.

The arbitrator, after closing the hearing, leaves. After the transcript and/or briefs come in to complete the hearing record, the arbitrator studies the case and writes a decision and award.

The Decision and Award

The decision and award consist of several parts. The decision first states the issue. The issue is phrased as a question which requires a yes or no answer. For example, in a language case: Under article X of the agreement, is Mildred Atkins entitled to overtime pay for work performed on May 25? In a discharge case it would be phrased: Was Frank Delgado discharged for just cause? The arbitrator then develops the case as seen first by one party, then the other. This is followed by the arbitrator's reasoning given what the arbitrator found to be credible and persuasive. Finally, the last page is the arbitrator's award. In the Frank Delgado case, for example, if the union won it might read: "Grievance is hereby sustained. Frank Delgado shall be reinstated with full back pay and all contractual benefits dating from the time of his discharge."

The arbitrator is not free to make any decision he or she pleases. The courts, parties, and the system of industrial jurisprudence (common law of arbitration cases) limit the decision. The Supreme Court in the Steelworkers trilogy cases used language which has since been written into many agreements limiting the powers of the arbitrator. The agreement might say: "The arbitrator is confined to the interpretation and application of the collective bargaining agreement. The arbitrator shall not add to, subtract from, delete, change, nor modify the provisions of the agreement."

The goal of the arbitrator in language interpretation cases is to "determine the mutual intent of the parties when they drafted the language." In language cases, convention has it that the labor organization must present its case first at the hearing and bears the burden of proof. In these cases the arbitrator looks to see if the language is "clear and unambiguous" (has only one meaning). If not, the language is "ambiguous." The arbitrator then falls back on numerous possible standards for deciding what the "true meaning" of the language is. For example, the arbitrator may use the parties' past practice to determine contract intent. Arbitrators also construe the agreement as a logical whole, meaning that a word used in one fashion in one part of the agreement will be taken to mean the same thing elsewhere in the contract.

The situation is reversed in discipline and discharge cases. Management must present its case first and bear the burden of proof. Usually management must show that the action they took was for *just cause*. The standards for proof of just cause are well established. Management must show the grievant knew of the work rule violated, that the rule was reasonable, that they conducted a fair investigation, that the evidence is substantial, that their discipline is uniformly applied, and that the punishment fits the crime.

Perspectives on the Arbitration Process

There are not very many full-time arbitrators in the United States. About 300 do most of the rights arbitration in the nation. Many of these people began their work back when the War Labor Board started the process for conflict resolution. The limiting factor is not education, although most arbitrators are either lawyers or university professors. The limit to the number of arbitrators is acceptability. Labor and management want arbitrators with an established track record. A would-be arbitrator without a track record cannot make one. The result of the vicious circle is that as age takes its toll of Labor Board arbitrators, the supply dwindles at the same time the demand for arbitration is increasing.

The result should be classic economics. Reduced supply and increased demand mean higher arbitration costs in time and money. Requests for arbitration panels jumped from 10,055 in 1970 to 27,189 in 1979. However, over the same time period, the elapsed time between filing of a grievance to arbitration award dropped from 246 to 231 days, and the time from hearing date to award fell from 49 to 35 days.[27] Costs, however, proved to be more predictable as shown in Table 15-4.

Table 15-4	Arbitration Costs	
	Dollar Amounts	
Costs	1970	1979
Per Diem Rate	$156.00	$256.95
Total Charged	539.88	911.83
Fee	457.97	804.51
Expenses	81.91	107.31

Source: FMCS, *Thirty-Second Annual Report*, p. 35.

Those figures are nominal, not real; corrected for inflation, the differences would not be nearly as large. The expense above is for the arbitrator only. It does not include the cost of each party's preparation, legal fees, paid time for witnesses, transcript cost, or the amount of the award. Arbitration is expensive, and there is a move toward expedited arbitration for that reason.

So far, however, no one has devised a better system. On balance, the

---

27. FMCS, *Thirty-Second Annual Report*, p. 34.

system works well as a method of resolving conflict during the life of the agreement. It is not likely to be shelved by the parties in the near future.

CONCLUDING REMARKS

Industrial conflict is inevitable. Its expression in work stoppages is not necessarily inevitable. Our system for reducing work stoppages at contract negotiation time has worked less well than our system for reducing strikes during the life of an agreement. United States work loss figures are much higher than those of other economically advanced nations with the exception of Australia. There is a similarity between the two industrial relations systems which may explain this in part. Both systems have strong management rights attitudes. Their bargaining is more distributive in nature than that of Western European economies where government plays such a substantial role in income distribution. Given this orientation toward win-lose bargaining, our substitution of procedure for power works well. Experience has shown that when labor and management perceive accommodation to be in their interest rather than confrontation (steel, construction), strife is reduced. That has been particularly true of our grievance-arbitration system. As relationships mature and major industries face decline, work stoppages will decrease. This will be counterbalanced by an increase in work stoppages as employers in the South are unionized and begin to find their way through new labor-management relationships.

CHAPTER SUMMARY

The function of the strike in the U.S. industrial relations system is to force the parties to reach their own settlement, which is preferred to a mandated settlement by an outsider. In the vast majority of negotiations, the parties earnestly seek to reach agreement. In roughly 15 percent of negotiations they do not agree without a strike. Strike issues, largely economic, were presented. How the parties prepare for strikes was explored. The cost of strikes was discussed along with the emergency disputes procedure which is used when a political decision has been made that the cost is too high.

There are alternatives to the strike. A few have been tried in the private sector with mixed results. There has been con-

siderable discussion of the obsolescence of strikes but little movement toward a private sector alternative. The real experimentation with strike substitutes has occurred in the public sector where a wide array of approaches is in effect. While public sector strikes have not been eliminated using these procedures, there is no move toward abandoning them.

Rights or grievance arbitration is used extensively in the United States to resolve labor-management disagreements during the life of an agreement. Grievances proceed through a series of steps where they are discussed and usually resolved at the lowest level possible. The procedures vary by industry but the principle behind each is the same; 95 percent of contracts provide for final and binding arbitration as the last step in the grievance procedure. An arbitrator is selected to hear cases on an ad hoc or permanent basis. The hearing is conducted with the purpose of establishing a record with which the arbitrator can make a decision. The standards for the decision vary for language and discharge or discipline cases but are well established. The system appears to be working well, and there is no suitable alternative to it at present.

KEY TERMS

lockout
80-day cooling-off period
Experimental Negotiating
    Agreement
fact finding
advisory arbitration
med-arb
voluntary arbitration
compulsory arbitration
interest arbitration
conventional interest arbitration
item selection arbitration

final offer arbitration
weaker party argument
narcotic effect
choice of procedures
grievance arbitration
rights arbitration
past practice
discipline or discharge grievance
language interpretation grievance
ad hoc arbitration
permanent arbitrator
just cause

REVIEW QUESTIONS

1. What is the rationale for the use of the strike in the U.S. industrial relations system?

2. What is the logic of grievance arbitration in a collective bargaining agreement? What clauses are related to the grievance arbitration clause in an agreement?

3. Assume there is a lengthy work stoppage in the auto industry. Trace the forward and backward linkages to see the impact on the economy.

4. What issues are the greatest source of industrial conflict as indicated by their prevalence in strikes? What issues are most prominent among arbitration cases?

5. Trace the system of checks and balances in the emergency disputes procedure.

6. Should strikes be legalized in the public sector? Why or why not?

7. Distinguish between interest and rights arbitration.

ADDITIONAL REFERENCES

Aaron, Benjamin, Joseph R. Grodin, and James L. Stern. *Public Sector Bargaining.* Madison, Wisc.: Industrial Relations Research Association, 1979.

Coulson, Robert. *Labor Arbitration—What You Need to Know,* 2d ed. New York: American Arbitration Association, 1978.

Cullen, Donald. *National Emergency Strikes*. Ithaca, N.Y.: New York School of Industrial and Labor Relations, Cornell University, 1968.

Davey, Harold W. *Contemporary Collective Bargaining*, 3d ed. Englewood Cliffs, N.J.: Prentice-Hall, 1972.

Elkin, Randyl D., and Thomas L. Hewitt. *Successful Arbitration*. Reston, Vir.: Reston Publishing Company, Inc., 1980.

Elkouri, Frank, and Edna Asper Elkouri. *How Arbitration Works*, 3d ed. Washington: The Bureau of National Affairs, 1979.

Somers, Gerald G. (ed.) *Collective Bargaining: Contemporary American Experience*. Madison, Wisc.: Industrial Relations Research Association, 1980.

THE WORLD
OF WORK . . .

Conflict Resolution Through Mediation

Mediation is the most extensively used method for conflict resolution of labor-management disputes. This reading discusses differences in approach between state-appointed mediators and Federal Mediation and Conciliation Service mediators.

The differing roles mediators play, "deal maker" or "orchestrator," reflect respective common sense theories about how disputes between the parties get resolved. Mediators from a State agency, who generally want to make a deal, believe that such a deal, if achieved, results from their knowledge of the components of a reasonable settlement (and, by implication, the parties' ignorance of such components), combined with their ability to persuade the parties to accept such a "reasonable" settlement. Federal mediators, however, prefer a settlement to be achieved by the parties themselves. By orchestrating a full exploration of their differences with some assistance and "injections of reality," Federal mediators believe that parties generally will be able to resolve their own differences.

These theories held by mediators about how disputes get resolved emerge from the roles the mediators attribute to the other parties in the process. The State mediators believe that they need to put together a deal because the other actors in the process—the union and management committees—lack the expertise to do it themselves. The inexperience of the bargaining committees is readily apparent to the mediator. Committees, particularly those on the union side, come to mediation with long lists of demands—demands which are often unrealistic in the estimation of the mediator. Inexperienced committees get "wedded" to their positions and are therefore exceedingly reluctant to lower their sights or to delegate the authority to the negotiators they hire (who have the expertise to negotiate more effectively). Committees on the management side, often made up of politically elected representatives, are likewise described as inexperienced. They adopt exceedingly conservative positions and adhere to these positions tenaciously.

Federal mediators, interestingly, describe the union negotiating committees they encounter in the private sector in much the same way as do the State mediators. These committees are inexperienced: they come unprepared to mediation with too many demands, many of which are unrealistic and, because of their inexperience, only make changes reluctantly. The management committees the Federal mediators work with are often as inexperienced as the union committees, but the inexperience is manifested differently. Management committees tend to overprepare, and to adopt bottom line positions early in the negotiations that leaves little room for exploring options. However, as opposed to the union committees which have a democratic structure and require a majority (if not a consensus) to make a move, the management committees have a hierarchical decisionmaking structure. The process of generating movement, therefore, differs between the two types of committees.

In most of the cases studied, negotiating committees on both sides had chief spokesmen, most of whom were professional negotiators. These professionals, because of their experience and frequent encounters with mediators, are called "pros." For the most part, pros are either labor relations attorneys or business agents from the union. Both State and Federal mediators had pros on their cases with approximately the same frequency, but the expectations about how these pros would act in their relationships with their committees, with the mediator, and with each other differed.

The State mediators looked to the pros to help them make a deal, a deal the committees, because of their inexperience, presumably would be unable to reach themselves. When working with two pros, the State mediators expected that most of the mediation would be conducted in off-the-record meetings. As a team, the pros and the mediator, both knowledgeable in the prerequisites of a reasonable settlement, could come gradually to an agreement. During the case, the mediator would then, in concert with the pros, "sell" the agreed upon package to the respective committees. With just one pro on the scene, the mediator had assistance on one side in the form of insights into the committee's behavior and the pro's assessment of "what it would take" to get a settlement—the bottom line. But the pros did not always function in this way. The problem from the State mediator's viewpoint is that the committees, because they are inexperienced, control their spokesmen in such a way that their ability to make an off-the-record deal may be severely circumscribed. When this occurs, the pro isn't acting like a pro. According to one State mediator, "There are pros, but it's not just his experience. Only if they have the authority to bargain, are they true pros. And for a true pro, if he doesn't have the authority, he'll grab it, he'll demand it as a condition of his continued employment."

State mediators often found that their expectations about what the pros would do went unfulfilled. Many pros, according to the State mediators, acted unprolike during a case. And the mediators' explanation for this behavior rested with the inexperienced committees. They were so inexperienced that they controlled the pro too tightly, and thus the effect of having a pro at all was negated. This inexperience of the committees (manifested in their tight control and the presence of pros who often did not act like pros) reaffirmed the mediator's sense of his role. He needed to "educate" the parties about the realities of mediation, which he did by demonstrating the elements of a reasonable settlement (his deal).

To the Federal mediator, the pro is an experienced, knowledgeable, and effective negotiator who is as well acquainted with the elements of a reasonable package and often better informed about the local character of the issues in dispute than the mediator. Though the pros and the mediator would be capable of reaching a reasonable settlement, the acceptance of such a settlement rests with the committees. Thus it is the pros, each working with his respective committee, who, through the ever narrowing exchange of proposals, move a committee toward a settlement. With the hierarchical management committee, the pro's advice was more likely to be heeded. But with the inexperienced union committee, the process was likely to be long and arduous, often requiring more assistance from the mediator.

For the Federal mediator, the mark of the true pro is not that he grabs authority but that he acts like a "closer." A closer is a pro who, based on his experience and knowledge, uses that expertise to move his committee by suggesting alternative options for a settlement when negotiations have reached a stalemate. The Federal mediators see their role as lending credibility and assistance to the pros as they work with their respective committees to "close" the deal. The dose of reality the Federal mediators say they inject in a caucus is often no more than reiterating what the pro has been saying all along. The only difference is that when the mediator says it, it's from a "neutral mouth." By adopting the role of orchestrator, the mediator provides the forum for the committees, guided by their pros, to directly negotiate their agreement.

Source: Deborah M. Kolb, "Two Approaches to the Mediator's Role," *Monthly Labor Review* (June, 1980), pp. 38-40.

Chapter 16

The Impact of Unions
on the Economy and Society

This concluding chapter is written in a question-answer format. It could be retitled, "Answers to some commonly asked questions about unions." It has been our experience that certain questions about the impact of unions on the firm, economy, and society are always asked during the first course in labor economics. Do unions raise wages? Do unions not reduce productivity and business efficiency? Do unions cause inflation? Are not unions corrupt and autocratic? There may not be a labor party in the United States, but do not unions usually support Democrats?

PRODUCING ANSWERS

It would be pleasing if the answers to those questions were simply yes or no. They are not. This is true for several reasons. The accepted analytical approach (methodology) to answering weighty questions may provide no answer or more than one answer. The *methodology* is supposed to work as shown in Table 16-1.

Table 16-1   A Methodology

Step 1:   *The Question.* State the question.
Step 2:   *The Theory.* Develop or use an existing theory to generate a hypothesis about the economic (social) system which if proven will answer the question.
Step 3:   *Empirical Testing.* Using the data that exists, test the hypothesis to see if the data support or disprove it.
Step 4:   *The Answer.* On the basis of whether or not the results support or disprove the hypothesis, answer the question.
Step 5:   *Policy.* Using the results from step 4, formulate a policy to make changes in the system to move toward a "more desirable" state of affairs.

The five steps in Table 16-1 are a rendition of the methodology of *positive analysis* which was discussed briefly in Chapter 1.[1] More than one answer can result from its use. In step 1, the question may be phrased in several ways. There are often several competing step 2 theories. (This is particularly true when it comes to inflation.) Or, there may be no well-developed theory at all. Step 3 problems are myriad. There are numerous sources of data. The data vary in quality. Data sets may not be comparable because they are measured in different ways. The econometric techniques for testing the hypotheses are plagued with problems. Because of the problems in the earlier steps, step 4 becomes a judgment call. Judgment calls are not always value-free; so analysts may read into the results what they wish to see. Step 5 always involves values and is called *normative analysis*. The key words are "more desirable." Desirability depends upon what the analyst values and believes to be a better situation.

All of this is to say that these are difficult questions. There are no easy answers. The answers that are given may not be a clear-cut yes or no. An effort will be made to make the answers definitive and value-free, but that is in fact an impossibility. In the final analysis it is as it should be: On the basis of the research presented and the arguments made, you must answer the questions to your own satisfaction.

DO UNIONS RAISE WAGES?

In general the answer is yes. The controversy here surrounds the amount, and for whom. There are several analytical problems concerning, for example, what is meant by wages: wage rate, and fringes, or total earnings? And, similarly, what is the meaning of raise? There are a number of possible standards. One might be a raise relative to the wage rate if no unions existed. Another standard that could be used is the wage rate of nonunion workers.

Why not just ask unions and management the question: Do unions raise wages? Of course the union will say yes. And so will management. In order to determine the truth, call on the economist who hopefully does not have a vested interest in the answer. The economist models the question and searches empirically for the answer.

The Approach

First, discard the notion that anyone can compare what union wages are today with what they would have been if there were no unions. There is no way to determine what wages would be without unions. They exist and have existed for almost two centuries. Concentrate on the question of union wages

---

1. The methodology is not just confined to economic analysis. It is a general methodology which can be applied for any issue which has an associated theory and data. However, the topics of union political affiliation and union corruption will not be analyzed using the methodology. Instead, perspectives on these issues are presented as a normative analysis.

versus nonunion wages. The model is completely general in the sense that it can be used to see what impact unions have on wages at the individual, firm, industry, regional, or national level. This is explained using Figure 16-1.

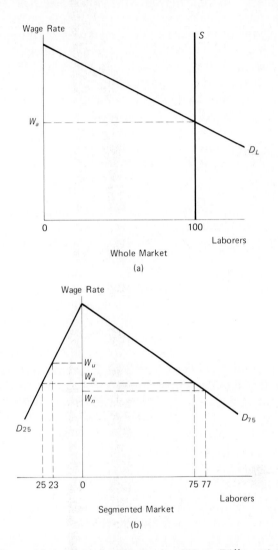

Figure 16-1   Union-Nonunion Wage Differentials

Assume a labor market for homogeneous laborers in graph (a). There is a market demand for labor, D_L. There is a market supply of labor, S, which we will assume to be fixed at 100 laborers. The market clearing wage rate is W_a. Now split the market into two segments arbitrarily so that one-quarter of the laborers (25) is in one market and three-quarters (75) are in the other. Demand is also split additively with one-quarter of the demand in one segment (D_{25})

and three-quarters in the other (D_{75}). Part (b) of Figure 16-1 depicts the situation. The vertical axis is the wage rate. The horizontal axis is the number of laborers measured out from the origin in both directions. Workers can freely shift from one market to the other since the split is artificial. Only the diagram has changed; so the equilibrium wage rate is the same for all workers as it was in (a): W_a. Employment in the 25 percent market is 25 laborers, and in the 75 percent market it is 75. One hundred laborers are still employed at W_a. Now unionize the one-quarter segment. The union in the 25 percent segment negotiates a wage, W_u, and enforces it in the union market only. Employers in the union market can hire all the laborers they want but must pay the going union rate, W_u. At W_u in the union market employers only want to hire 23 workers now, and 2 laborers are forced out of the newly unionized market. They go over and seek employment in the nonunion market, expanding the supply of labor over there to 77. They compete with the other nonunion labor and reduce nonunion wages to W_n.[2] (These changes have been exaggerated in Figure 16-1 for clarity.)

Now we can discuss the impact of the union on wages. If the union does have an impact, it will be to raise union wages and lower nonunion wages (if labor is mobile). In fact, we can break the union-nonunion wage differential into two components. Unions raise their wages relative to that of all labor ($W_u - W_a > 0$) and lower the wages of nonunion labor ($W_n - W_a < 0$).[3] Note that the resulting wage changes are not equal. Even if the demand for labor is of the same elasticity in both markets, the reduction of two laborers in the union market is an 8 percent change (2/25), and in the nonunion market the addition of two persons is a 2.67 percent (2/75) change in employment. The percentage wage increase in the union market will exceed the nonunion wage reduction. For example, if the elasticity were 1 for both markets, a union wage raise of 8 percent would cut employment by 8 percent. The laborers shifting over to the nonunion market would raise employment by 2.67 percent and cut wages by 2.67 percent. The total difference between union and nonunion wages would be 10.67 percent (8 percent + 2.67 percent).

The Classic Study

No discussion of union impact on relative wages would be complete without presenting the results of the study of unions and relative wages in the United States done by H. Gregg Lewis. Table 16-2 summarizes the Lewis results for selected time periods from 1923 to 1958.

Several significant patterns emerge from the data. The range of the aver-

---

2. The "crowding out" of two workers here in the union-nonunion setting is analogous to the crowding-out phenomenon discussed in Chapter 8 relative to minority and women workers.

3. H. Gregg Lewis, *Unionism and Relative Wages in the United States* (Chicago: The University of Chicago Press, 1963).

Table 16-2   Union Relative Wage Effects in Selected Periods

Time Period	Extent of Unionism in Economy (%)	Average Relative Wage Effect of Unionism (%)		
		Union Labor Relative to Nonunion Labor	Union Labor Relative to All Labor	Nonunion Labor Relative to All Labor
1923-1929	7-8	15-20	14-18	−1
1931-1933	7-8	>25	>23	<−1
1939-1941	18-20	10-20	8-16	−4 to −2
1945-1949	24-27	0-5	0-4	−1 to 0
1957-1958	27	10-15	7-11	−4 to −3

Source: H. Gregg Lewis, *Unionism and Relative Wages in the United States*, abstracted from Table 50, p. 193.

age effect is a union-nonunion differential from zero to 25 percent. Many studies have been done on particular industries, and the figure shown is an average of these. The differential varies per union and time period. For example, unions of skilled workers in construction in 1939 enjoyed a wage differential of 25 percent over nonunion skilled labor, while unionized unskilled workers earned only 5 percent more than their nonunion counterparts. The union with the most variation in impact is the United Mine Workers. Their wages effect went from 130 percent in 1922 to zero percent in 1945.[4] Overall, very few unions have achieved a 25 percent difference and then have done so only for short periods of time. (We will examine more recent studies shortly.)

The historical fluctuation is intriguing. How could unions have an impact of over 25 percent during the Depression, and none in the period 1945-1949? The standard explanation is that union wages are more rigid than nonunion wages. Unions get locked into contracts that fix wages. Nonunion wages are more sensitive to supply and demand changes. Hence, in the Depression union wages held or were raised while nonunion wages fell. A large differential was induced. But rigid wages are not always a boon. Recall that the 1945-1949 period was one of postwar inflation. Unanticipated postwar inflation found unions locked into contracts while nonunion workers enjoyed larger wage raises. The differential disappeared.

4. Ibid., pp. 184-6.

There are two opinions about biases in the wage differential estimates. The first is called the *threat effect*. A good case can be made that nonunion employers view union wage increases as a threat to retaining their nonunion status. In response nonunion employers match union wages. As a result, the wages of both union and nonunion employees rise together, and the union-nonunion wage differential *understates* the true impact of unions: The estimated effect is too small or biased downward. On the other hand, other critics point out the estimates are really too large. Their argument is twofold. First, union employers paying higher wages attract better, more productive workers; second, they tend to substitute capital for labor, raising labor productivity. Because better skilled and equipped workers earn more, the differential includes a quality component. The measured union-nonunion differential is too large by the quality component. No one has yet unraveled the question of which bias outweighs the other.

More Recent Results

Recent research in the area has continued the earlier industry focus (particularly new public sector unionism) and added research on individuals. The studies try to remove the quality biases spoken of above.

Results from some of the recent studies are shown in Table 16-3. At first glance, it looks like a confusing array of figures. They say quite a bit actually. First, the new figures are not much different from Lewis' earlier study. However, the evidence does point to a higher effect in the mid-1970s than the mid-1950s. Daniel J. B. Mitchell, for example, believes the mid-1970s differential to be more on the order of 20 to 30 percent compared with Lewis' figures of 10 to 15 percent. (Figures for Great Britain are also about 25 percent.) Second, there is not that much variation in the figures. No one shows huge values, for example. They vary, depending upon type of industry or occupation, but no one argues for average values of 50 or 100 percent. Finally, the studies on individuals have better data than the industry studies do and can do a better job of working out biases. These more refined data show a reduced union differential in a range from 5 to 17 percent for all individuals. The Mitchell data show how varied the results are by race and sex when all the individual figures are disaggregated.[5]

---

5. These results are abstracted from Lawrence M. Kahn, "Union Impact: A Reduced Form Approach," *The Review of Economics and Statistics,* Vol. 59, No. 4 (November, 1977), pp. 503-7; Daniel Hammermesh, "White Collar Unions, Blue-Collar Unions, and Wages in Manufacturing," *Industrial and Labor Relations Review* (June, 1971), pp. 159-71; Farrell Block and Mark Kuskin, "Wage Determination in Union and Nonunion Sectors," *Industrial and Labor Relations Review,* Vol. 31, No. 2 (January, 1978), pp. 183-92; Orley Ashenfelter, "Union Relative Wage Effects: New Evidence and a Survey of Their Implications for Wage Inflation," in Richard Stone and William Peterson (eds.), *Econometric Contributions to Public Policy* (New York: St. Martin's Press, 1978); Daniel J. B. Mitchell, *Unions, Wages, and Inflation* (Washington: The Brookings Institution, 1980), pp. 99-100.

Table 16-3   Results from Recent Studies

Author	Data Source	Period	Estimated Effect of Unionism (%)
Kahn	Industry	1960	22-38[1]
Hammermesh	Manufacturing	1960-1967	
	Blue Collar		20
	White Collar		5
Block and Kuskin	Individuals		
	All Occupations	1973	16
	Manufacturing	1973	5
Ashenfelter	Individuals	1967	12
		1973	15
		1975	17
Mitchell	Industry	1975	20-30
	Individuals[2]	1976	
	White Males		13-22
	White Females		16-31
	Black Males		22-54
	Black Females		20-41

[1]Assumes an industry experiences a 40 percent increase in unionization.
[2]Range of results from these data sources is Mitchell's Table 3-11.

Source: These results are abstracted from studies mentioned in footnote 5.

There are numerous studies on the effect of public sector unions. So many studies have been done (a dozen on teachers, for example), and with such varied results, that we do not pursue them at length here. The estimates for the public sector do appear to be lower than for the private sector. One study using 1971 data on individuals is representative. David Shapiro concluded, "There is no evidence of a positive union wage effect within the public sector on the earnings of either white or black men in white collar jobs." For blue-collar workers in the public sector Shapiro found a positive union effect in excess of 20 percent for white men and 10 percent for black men.[6]

The previous discussion has concentrated on the union effect on wages as opposed to the union impact on fringe benefits. Two recent studies indicate that unions have a very substantial impact on voluntary fringe benefits (fringe benefits in excess of those mandated by state and federal law). The Mitchell

6. David Shapiro, "Relative Wage Effects of Unions in the Public and Private Sectors," *Industrial and Labor Relations Review*, Vol. 31, No. 2 (January, 1978), p. 202.

study cited earlier found a rough estimate of union impact on voluntary fringes that ranged from 127 to 164 percent of nonunion fringe benefits.[7] Richard Freeman analyzed establishment data for the period 1967-1972 to determine the impact of unions on voluntary fringe benefits. Using a variety of econometric models, he found the positive effect of collective bargaining to be in a range from 10 to 18 percent for all private production workers and from 8 to 15 percent for manufacturing production employees.[8] Collective bargaining resulted in a significant increase in pensions, insurance, and vacation benefits. Interestingly enough it also decreased some benefits relative to those had by nonunion workers for overtime, sick leave, and bonuses. This leads to the conclusion that studies of union wage effects which exclude fringes understate the impact of unions by one estimate of 17-25 percent.[9] The empirical evidence varies, but it definitely supports the conclusion that unions have a positive effect on the wages and fringes of union workers when compared with those of nonunion workers.

DON'T UNIONS HURT BUSINESS EFFICIENCY?

Usually the student who asks this question has either done construction work during the summer or has a relative who is in a managerial position in a firm. There are several economic questions wrapped up in this one. Do unions affect productivity? Do unions cause unemployment? (Presumably the people who ask this mean, "Don't unions price themselves out of the market?") The logic chain usually goes something like this. Unions organize a firm and negotiate a contract with restrictive work rules and higher wages. Labor productivity declines even though wages rise, and so per unit labor cost increases. This increases total cost, which results in an increase in the price of the product. Either the firm hires cheaper nonunion labor if possible, substitutes machinery for labor, or is driven out of business by more competitive nonunion firms.

Arguments Pro and Con

Is the scenario mentioned above true in general? No, say the economists. Union labor is not less efficient than nonunion; it is more efficient. But that is not the whole story as we have seen in the logic chain above. First we examine the common ways unionism is said to affect business efficiency. Table 16-4 summarizes the common arguments on unions and efficiency or productivity or labor costs.

---

7. Mitchell, *Unions, Wages, and Inflation*, p. 95.
8. Richard B. Freeman, "The Effect of Unionism on Fringe Benefits," *Industrial and Labor Relations Review*, Vol. 34, No. 4 (July, 1981), pp. 500-1.
9. Ibid., p. 502-3, and 504.

Table 16-4:   Arguments Concerning Unionism and Efficiency

Unions inhibit productivity by:

1. Obstructing the use of new technology
2. Negotiating restrictive work rules such as
   a. Limiting piecework or subcontracting
   b. Restricting output (e.g., limiting the number of bricks laid per day)
   c. Forbidding management to do union work
   d. Requiring more workers than necessary (e.g., crew size)
   e. Protecting the jurisdiction of unions (e.g., carpenters versus masons over who cleans wooden cement forms)
   f. Requiring unnecessary work (e.g., knock down and rebuild prefab units)
   g. Featherbedding in other innumerable ways
3. Harrassment of management with grievances
4. Stifling worker motivation and reducing morale by forcing management to reward for seniority, not merit
5. Turning the employee-manager relationship into an adversarial one

Unions improve productivity by:

1. Encouraging use of the latest technology (craft apprenticeship training)
2. Forcing management to become more efficient
3. Encouraging firms to invest in on-the-job training
4. Reducing the quit rate and lowering turnover costs
5. Improving employee morale and motivation by providing job security and freedom from arbitrary management decision making (seniority, grievance procedure)
6. Providing a cooperative voice

Results From Recent Studies

On balance, who wins the argument? Recent studies pretty consistently show that unions can have a positive impact on productivity. But first a negative note. Albert Rees used Lewis' results on the impact of unionism on relative wages to estimate the combined losses to the economy due to union wage and employment distortion and also featherbedding. The figure for 1957 was 0.4 percent of GNP.[10] The more recent studies estimate the union-nonunion productivity differential by industry and for individuals.

Construction. Residential construction is an industry perenially under discussion when it comes to productivity. Who has not heard the story about the bulldozer operator, who, while driving his machine across the building site, got off it to move a 2 by 4 out of the way and then was fined $50 for not calling the supervisor to call a laborer to move the wood instead? Certainly the

---

10. The estimates are interindustry 0.14 percent, interindustry plus intraindustry less than 0.3 percent, and add 0.1 percent for featherbedding. See Albert Rees, "The Effects of Unions on Resource Allocation," *The Journal of Law and Economics*, Vol. 6 (October, 1963), pp. 69–78.

momentum of "merit shop" (open shop) nonunion construction which has eroded union markets should give pause to anyone arguing that unions do not impede efficient production in construction. Two somewhat dated studies address the issue.

Haber and Levinson examined the impact of nine restrictive work rules used by building trades unions in 1952. Union, management, and public representatives were surveyed in 16 major sites across 10 states. They found that the overall effect was to increase labor costs by at most 17-18 percent, at the very least 5-6 percent, and on average 10-12 percent. Figuring all other costs of constructing a home (materials, etc.), elimination of the union cost effect would translate into a reduced market price for an average house of 2.5 to 7 percent.[11]

Allen Mandelstamm compared the cost of union-constructed residences in Ann Arbor, Michigan with nonunion-built homes in Bay City, Michigan in 1957. It took fewer hours for union labor to build a house than it did nonunion labor. The higher wage rates paid to union labor offset this efficiency however:

> The estimated (total) labor costs for all trades combined were virtually identical in the two cities: thus, the greater efficiency in Ann Arbor counterbalanced the higher wage rates in this instance. . . . Nevertheless, the results of the study give some cause for believing that unionization may bring an increase in efficiency and a much smaller rise in costs than had heretofore been expected.[12]

That research is 25 years old. More recently, Steven Allen used the 1972 Census of Construction to compare union and nonunion productivity. The study extends to all aspects of construction using a nationwide sample. He concludes: "Output per employer is at least 29 percent greater in unionized establishments in construction. If the extra productivity is entirely attributed to labor, then union members are at least 38 percent more productive than other workers in construction."[13] Allen controlled for differences across firms in the amount of capital per worker, the age of capital, firm size, labor quality (worker age, schooling, and occupation), geographic region, and type of construction. He attributes the results to superior union training and to the use of the hiring hall which cuts employer recruitment, screening, and training costs.

The erosion of the union market in construction suggests that these results may not tell the whole story. There is a current trend toward extended construction bargaining agreements and for union-management cooperation

---

11. William Haber and Harold M. Levinson, *Labor Relations and Productivity in the Building Trades* (Ann Arbor, Mich.: Bureau of Industrial Relations, 1956), pp. 193-7.
12. Allen B. Mandelstamm, "The Effects of Unionism on Efficiency in the Residential Construction Industry: A Case Study," *Industrial and Labor Relations Review* (July, 1965), p. 521.
13. Steven G. Allen, *Unionized Construction Workers Are More Productive* (Washington: Center to Protect Worker Rights, 1979), p. ii.

programs in construction. These are designed to stabilize wage costs, reduce restrictive work rules, and decrease work stoppages. The result should be to improve productivity and lower unit labor costs to make union construction more competitive. Wage increases need not be sacrificed so long as they can be counterbalanced by productivity increases.

Manufacturing. Brown and Medoff studied 20 manufacturing industries in 1972 to research union productivity effects. They controlled for quality of labor differences across industries to isolate union effects. They found that without controlling for labor quality differences, union establishments were 24 percent more productive than nonunion ones. "Even when the characteristics of workers most frequently associated with productivity differentials are held constant, union establishments are about 22 percent more productive than those which are not." Their results also confirm what has been indicated earlier, that union-nonunion wage differentials are of about the same size as the productivity differentials. They conclude: "Union and nonunion establishments (in United States manufacturing) can compete in the same product market despite the fact that the former pay their workers more because unionized workers (establishments) are more productive by a roughly offsetting amount."[14]

The Shock Effect. One argument advanced about unionism and efficiency is that unions have a *shock effect* on management. That is, when a company becomes unionized, it forces management to become more efficient and take managing more seriously. There is support for this hypothesis from several studies, but one case study in particular highlights the shock effect. Kim Clark studied six cement industry firms that went from nonunion to union status over the years 1953-1976. The study revealed wage effects of 12-18 percent. Also, "the evidence suggests that unionization led to an increase in productivity, with the magnitude of the effect likely to fall in the range of 6-10 percent." Management styles changed toward formal control. Goals, objectives, and the strategies for their attainment were developed and were accompanied by more extensive evaluation procedures. Not only did management practices change, so did management personnel. Plant managers were replaced at all six plants, and in most of them new middle management and first-line supervisors accompanied the change from nonunion to union status. "Our tentative conclusion, therefore, is that an improvement in plant management is one of the key adjustments to unionization. These results may be interpreted as evidence of a modern union 'shock effect.' "[15]

---

14. Charles Brown and James Medoff, "Trade Unions in the Production Process," *Journal of Political Economy,* Vol. 86, No. 3 (June, 1978), pp. 367-8 and 377.

15. Kim B. Clark, "The Impact of Unionization on Productivity: A Case Study," *Industrial and Labor Relations Review,* Vol. 33, No. 4 (July, 1980) pp. 460 and 467.

The Quit Rate. One of the efficiencies attributed to unions is a reduced quit rate. It is argued that union workers making higher wages, certain of upward mobility according to seniority in the internal labor market, protected from arbitrary discharge, and cushioned by layoff provisions are less likely to jump firms than are nonunion workers. Further, the argument continues, employers benefit from this reduced turnover as well. Search costs decline, and employer expenditures for on-the-job training pay off longer. Morale and motivation are higher. And if, as some economists claim, wages accrue to the job and not to the employee who fills it, the more productive the employee the lower the labor cost.

Richard Block compared manufacturing industry quit rates against the strength of negotiated seniority provisions. He used industry data for the period 1961-1972. Block's observations included:

> These results also suggest that a greater area of discretion for management with respect to employee movement within the internal market, and a correspondingly smaller role for seniority, is associated with more quitting. This implies that production and related workers do not have a great deal of confidence in management's ability to differentiate among them based on a criterion other than seniority (such as skill, ability, qualifications, or experience). . . . Thus, these results suggest that the strength of union-negotiated seniority provisions, especially of those provisions relating to promotion and transfer, does have a substantial impact on quits. . . . On balance, employers clearly appear to benefit from seniority provisions.[16]

A similar relationship between quits and unionization has been found for individuals as well as industries. Richard Freeman analyzed data collected on individuals between 1973 and 1975. He found "that coverage by a collective bargaining agreement brings about a substantial and statistically significant reduction in the probability of quitting (controlling for many other factors, including wages and fringe benefits)." Quantitatively, this means "unionized workers job tenure is more than 25 percent greater than that of comparable workers who are not unionized."[17]

Conclusions. Now if, as these studies seem to indicate, union workers and firms are more efficient than their nonunion counterparts, why has management not embraced unions with open arms in the interest of increased profits? There would seem to be a number of possible responses. The studies could be wrong. They could be measuring something other than true union productivity effects for any number of reasons: inadequate control for labor quality,

---

16. Richard N. Block, "The Impact of Seniority Provisions on the Manufacturing Quit Rate," *Industrial and Labor Relations Review*, Vol. 31, No. 4 (July, 1978), pp. 481, 486, 487.

17. Richard Freeman, "The Exit-Voice Tradeoff in the Labor Market: Unionism, Job Tenure, Quits and Separations." Mimeograph. Cambridge, Mass.: Harvard University, 1977. Results reported in Brown and Medoff, "Trade Unions in the Production Process," p. 357.

capital stock, or statistical anomalies. It has been shown several times that union wage effects offset the productivity gains so that labor costs are roughly the same for both types of firms. The shock effect of the unionization of a firm requires more and better work from management. Managerial authority is eroded and challenged. We have seen also that through the use of union avoidance, management attempts to provide the benefits of unionization to workers to avoid incurring the cost of actually having to deal with one. It is simply easier for management to manage without having to cope with a union.

Restrictive Work Rules

There are obvious situations where work rules have become a problem affecting industry economic viability. Railroads, longshoring, meatpacking, and construction are good examples. However, management did not have to negotiate those work rules into the agreement. At some point when the work rules were originally negotiated, management made a decision that agreeing to them was less costly than taking a strike. Management may have been short-sighted. The decision may have been made looking at a contract length time frame of 2 or 3 years. Longer-run considerations are often difficult to predict. Once in the agreement however, work rules are not easily changed. The union sees any work rules change as a major concession on its part, and unions do not go to the table to give things up.

The current state of the industry has an impact on management attitudes toward work rules. Work rules negotiated in an expanding, profitable industry are just another cost of doing business and may be written off. When that industry contracts, the rules are seen in a different light. What management saw before as a "livable cost of doing business" suddenly becomes an "onerous, efficiency-robbing burden" put upon them by a "union insensitive to the economic exigencies faced by management."

The emphasis here is not to point the finger of blame at either unions or management. It takes two to negotiate and times change. Slichter, Healy, and Livernash did what has become a classic study on the impact of collective bargaining on management. Their observation on work rules is probably correct: "Make-work rules do not usually begin as attempts by unions to force employers to hire an excessive number of workers."[18] At the time the work rules are negotiated, they make economic sense. Over time economic and technological changes occur. Diesels replace coal-fired locomotives, and firemen are no longer necessary. Semi-truck size cargo containers replace smaller parcels, and fewer longshore workers are necessary. Sides of beef are knocked down at the meat packing houses; individual cuts, not hanging beef, are shipped to grocery stores; and fewer grocery store butchers are necessary.

---

18. Sumner H. Slichter, James J. Healy, and E. Robert Livernash, *The Impact of Collective Bargaining on Management* (Washington: The Brookings Institution, 1960), p. 317.

Spray guns and rollers replace paint brushes, and fewer painters are needed. Who is willing to give up a job in the name of technological progress? Who would not like to share in the increased profits of technological advance? When an industry is faced with economic decline, who will voluntarily give up a job for the good of fellow workers, the industry, and the economy? Remember, unions are political institutions operating in an economic environment.

Solutions. How do unions and management cope with situations which require work rules changes? The answer depends upon how the problem is perceived by the parties to the agreement. If the situation is viewed by the union as a "management problem," management will probably have to buy a work rule change. That is, any work rule change requires a monetary buy-out. The Conference Board study mentioned in Chapter 13 lends support for this. A summary statement concerning company objectives for bargaining on non-wage items makes the point: "The non-trading territory is more associated with incalculable (but potentially major) costs; with productivity-altering outcomes; with institutionalizing the union as a participant in work force discretion. The trading territory, on the other hand, is simply 'money.' "[19]

If the problem is viewed as a mutual one, the tendency is to form a joint union-management committee to explore it, suggest solutions, and negotiate changes to deal with it. This approach often calls for a long-range solution whereby wage increases become more directly dependent upon productivity changes, labor redundancy is solved by attrition, and labor needs are met by retraining. Examples of these efforts can be found in the auto, steel, construction, retail, food, printing and publishing, meatpacking, railroads, and long-shoring industries.[20]

Future Trends. Two other approaches bear watching for signs of trend value. Douglas Fraser, president of the United Auto Workers (UAW), negotiated for a position on the Chrysler board of directors as a quid pro quo for contract concessions to the ailing car manufacturer. Subsequent negotiations with Ford and GM however did not result in a UAW representative being placed on the corporate board. The Teamsters have a member on Pan American World Airways' board of directors as part of a contract in which wages were cut 10 percent and frozen through 1982 in return for an employee stock ownership plan.[21]

Second, some firms have negotiated provisions transferring ownership to the employees. Rath Packing Company in Waterloo, Iowa became an em-

---

19. Audrey Freedman, *Managing Labor Relations* (New York: The Conference Board, 1979), p. 42.

20. For an excellent summary of these efforts, see Joseph P. Goldberg's "Bargaining and Productivity in the Private Sector," chap. 2 in *Collective Bargaining and Productivity* (Madison, Wisc.: Industrial Relations Research Association, 1975), pp. 15-44.

21. "Teamsters Propose Candidate for Seat on Pan Am's Board," *Wall Street Journal*, October 20, 1981, p. 10.

ployee owned and controlled firm in 1980. Its plant was outdated, the company was losing money, and banks would not lend Rath money to make changes. Rath and the Food and Commercial Workers negotiated an employee stock ownership plan (ESOP) which transferred ownership to the employees through stock purchases by payroll deduction. The union selected 10 members to add to a 6-person board of directors and obtained control of the company. A $4.6-million federal loan was obtained to modernize the plant. A new company president was selected. It remains to be seen how the experiment will fare. The question labor-management observers asked is voiced by Rath consultant Warner Woodward, "How can workers be union members, owners and stockholders?"[22]

As a postscript to the questions surrounding unions and productivity, there is the argument made by some analysts that the inquiry is misdirected. Economic efficiency is seen as an inadequate measure of social efficiency. Even if one assumes that unions decrease economic efficiency and misallocate resources, that is a small price to pay for a less easily measurable but greater benefit: industrial democracy. (Recall the basic tenets of our labor law system discussed in Chapter 12.) Freedom of contract and the job security of our system of industrial jurisprudence are provided by unions. If unions also misallocate resources to some extent, that is on balance not a bad trade in terms of societal welfare.

DO UNIONS CAUSE INFLATION?

The answer is yes or no. Economists divide on the issue according to two camps. The prevailing schools of thought on the causes and cures for inflation were presented in depth in Chapters 4 and 6. This section is a short synopsis of the role unions play according to each school. The post-Keynesians believe unions either cause inflation or contribute to it. The neoclassical, monetarist-accelerationist set believes unions do not cause inflation. We will review each camp's theory in brief. The argument is similar to the old story about the half-filled glass which the pessimist saw to be half-empty and which the optimist saw to be half-full. The neoclassical theorists see the economy as basically a competitive one. The post-Keynesians see it as one characterized by noncompetitive, administered pricing.

The Neoclassical View

In the neoclassical theory markets are competitive and deviate from full employment only randomly. There is a natural rate of unemployment, and it is all voluntary unemployment. Deviations from the equilibrium rate of unem-

---

22. "When Employees Take Over," *Newsweek* (June 1, 1981), p. 75.

ployment occur because firms and people with rational expectations sometimes err in those expectations. However, they soon learn from their mistakes
and correct for them, returning the economy to full employment. There is little
need for stabilization policy here. A problem arises if government does not
acknowledge that the natural unemployment rate is voluntary and attempts to
use fiscal or monetary policy to lower the unemployment rate below its natural
rate. There will be a short-run expansion, and the unemployment rate will fall
as firms and workers mistake money price and wage increases for real ones;
then they will see that they have succumbed to money illusion as inflation sets
real prices and wages back to where they started. The result is inflation and
increased unemployment (a return to the natural rate). Unions in this model
are along for the ride. They negotiate wage settlements that would exist largely
whether there were unions or not. The cause of inflation is an unforeseen
change in the money supply or an attempt to lower unemployment using fiscal
or monetary policy.

The Post-Keynesian View

The post-Keynesians see the world in a quite different light. The product
and labor markets are largely oligopolistic. Powerful firms and unions set
prices and wages for long periods of time. These prices and wages set the
pattern for most markets and may fluctuate up, but they are never adjusted
downward. Prices do not fluctuate to clear product and labor markets. Instead
sales and employment fluctuate. Employers sell all they can at the administered price; inventories fluctuate; the derived demand for labor fluctuates; and
at fixed, negotiated wage rates, unemployment increases and decreases. But
here unemployment is involuntary. Further, the economy is not self-adjusting
and without appropriate minimum adjustments using monetary policy and
fiscal policy, it will remain below full employment. The cause of inflation is the
exercise of market power by unions and firms. Employers agree to pay wage
increases in excess of productivity, driving up unit labor costs. Firms pass this
increased cost on to the public, but only after adding on a markup to maintain
or increase profits. The cost-push inflation which results is comprised of both
wage-push and profit-push inflation. Because the increased income does not
generate enough consumer demand to clear the market, unemployment and
inflation occur simultaneously. Yes, unions do cause inflation (management
also contributes to it), and if anything else (say an oil price rise) increases
inflation, unions will help perpetuate a wage-price spiral.

The post-Keynesian view is supported by the study by Daniel J. B. Mitchell
cited earlier. Mitchell found that the union-nonunion wage differential increased over time from Lewis' estimate of 10-15 percent in the 1950s to about
20-30 percent in the 1970s. Inherent in such a differential is the market power to
raise wages to keep up with or catch up with inflation. This is coupled with
some empirical support for Ross' orbits of coercive comparison concept (see
Chapter 13). Key union-management agreements do cause wage imitation

effects that spill over to wages and prices which are well beyond those of the key agreements. Escalator clauses are a component of the spillover mechanism. The system which results is one in which labor unions may or may not initiate wage-push inflation, but whatever is the cause of inflation, unions help perpetuate it:

> If the initiating causes of American inflation are mainly monetary and fiscal policies and occasional exogenous price shocks, wages might appear to play little part in the process. . . . But it (wage determination) is an important element in explaining the perpetuation of inflation. The wage-price spiral is not a figment of some editorial writer's imagination; it is very real and flourishing in the modern American economy.[23]

Where does the truth lie? As a methodological rule of thumb, theoretical questions are supposed to be settled empirically. Once the debate is settled empirically, the appropriate policy for dealing with the problem should follow directly and be implemented. But the debate has been carried on in one form or another for years. It has accelerated recently because of our experience with stagflation in the 1970s and early 1980s and the change from a Democratic to a Republican administration. Both sides count prestigious economists in their ranks and master convincing and opposing econometric support for their positions. Policy does not have time to wait for academic debate. The economist with the government's ear employs the policy consistent with his or her school of thought.

Which brings us to unions and politics. Some argue that whether or not unions have a direct effect on inflation, they do have an indirect effect in their exercise of political clout in favor of inflation-causing fiscal policy. Since the United States has no labor party, how do unions get prolabor legislation passed?

THERE MAY BE NO LABOR PARTY, BUT DON'T UNIONS ALWAYS SUPPORT THE DEMOCRATS?

Up until the 1970s that statement was basically true. Since the 1968 Presidential election, organized labor's political activities have been in a state of flux. After a brief historical sketch, we will concentrate on the 1970s and the 1980 Presidential election.

It was not until the unofficial AFL endorsement of Democrat William Jennings Bryan over Republican William Howard Taft in the Presidential race of 1908 that organized labor entered the political arena. Samuel Gompers' "Reward your friends and punish your enemies" philosophy was embodied in Section 8, Article IV of the AFL Constitution: "Party politics, whether they be

---

23. Daniel J. B. Mitchell, *Unions, Wages and Inflation*, p. 219. Also, see especially pp. 208-29.

Democratic, Republican, Socialistic, populistic, prohibition or any other, should have no place in the convention of the American Federation of Labor."[24]

The political activities of organized labor are now extensive. They complement but rarely substitute for organized labor's primary business unionism focus: betterment on the job. Labor organizations unite to form city central bodies, county labor councils, and state labor federations which exist primarily for political activity. They lobby their representative legislative bodies. They endorse, support, and occasionally run candidates for office. At the national level organized labor lobbies extensively, endorses and supports candidates for office, and has an indirect effect on its on-the-job successes by influencing the appointment of NLRB members. It is at the federal level that the AFL-CIO once earned the reputation of being the right arm of the Democratic Party.

Presidential Politics

Links between the Democrats and labor grew stronger following World War II. The passage of the Taft-Hartley Act over Truman's veto contributed to their close association. Democratic Presidential candidates received significant support in 1956, 1960, 1964, and 1968 from the AFL-CIO's Committee on Political Education (COPE). The first Republican Senate candidate to receive COPE support was Pennsylvanian Richard Schweicker in 1974. Very few Republican House candidates have ever received AFL-CIO support.

The strong Democrat-labor alliance was broken in 1972 when the Democrats nominated George McGovern for President. The split between the two was an expression of the issues which split society at large and which had caused the UAW to withdraw from the AFL-CIO in 1967. The AFL-CIO with George Meany at the helm was opposed to the liberal concerns not only of the reformed Democratic Party but also of some of the constituent unions. They parted ways on the issues of housing, welfare for the poorest segments of the United States (ghetto dwellers and migrant labor), and the war in Vietnam. Internal to the Democratic Party, the McGovern Commission recommended and subsequently the party adopted a more participative (less machine controlled) delegate selection for the national convention. In George Meany's eyes that "reduces the power of labor and increases that of middle class radicals."[25]

The AFL-CIO explored the possibility of ties with the Republican Party, but rejected that strategy largely because of President Nixon's general economic policies (in particular, the unpopular wage-price controls). No party was palatable to organized labor in 1972. The AFL-CIO Executive Council voted 27

---

24. Jong Oh Ra, *Labor at the Polls* (Amherst, Mass.: University of Massachusetts Press, 1978), p. 16.
25. Graham K. Wilson, *Unions in American National Politics* (New York: St. Martin's Press, 1979), p. 43.

to 3 to remain neutral in the 1972 elections. George McGovern went on to suffer the worst defeat of any Presidential candidate in U.S. history.

The McGovern defeat and the subsequent Richard Nixon impeachment machinations were a sobering experience for labor and the Democrats. Fearing another neutral stance in the 1976 elections, six AFL-CIO affiliates and three major independents formed the Labor Coalition Clearinghouse to coordinate labor's efforts in support of the Democratic candidate for President. To avoid a split in labor ranks, Meany and COPE endorsed and unenthusiastically supported the candidacy of Jimmy Carter.

Labor's candidate for Democratic nominee in the 1980 elections was Massachusetts Senator Edward Kennedy. Although Kennedy enjoyed strong labor backing, he was not successful in his bid to unseat Jimmy Carter as the party's nominee. Following his loss to Carter, Kennedy's support for the Carter Presidential campaign was lukewarm. Organized labor's attitude was very nearly the same. When the voting was over, Ronald Reagan won the election and garnered over 40 percent of the union vote.

Congressional Lobbying

A strategy voiced by Lane Kirkland, president of the AFL-CIO, highlights a second major political activity of labor: lobbying.

> In the best of circumstances it is extremely difficult to push major programs without the support of the executive branch. Hence, it is obvious that most of our efforts will be trying to preserve the gains of the past and attempting to assure fairness and equity for American workers in the programs the Reagan Administration will be pushing.[26]

Every international union has at least one Washington lobbyist. The AFL-CIO maintains seven full-time lobbyists on Capital Hill. The quote from Lane Kirkland emphasizes their primary purpose: to defeat legislation inimical to labor's interests. On offense they work to secure legislation favorable to their interests. These interests go well beyond collective bargaining and industrial relations. They extend to legislation regarding unemployment benefits, social security, national health insurance, housing programs, funding for education, import restrictions, and environmental protection. One goal targeted for the early 1980s is tax reform to provide business tax incentives for industries hit by the recession to help them rebuild.[27]

NLRB Appointments

The National Labor Relations Board is organized labor's regulatory commission. Its decisions materially affect the success of union activities from

26. "Labor's 1981 Game Plan: Defense!," *Nation's Business* (January, 1981), p. 29.
27. Ibid.

organizing to bargaining. Theoretically it is an independent agency devoid of political philosophy, but realistically it is subject to some political pressure and philosophy. The Board's five members are appointed to staggered 5-year terms by the President with the advice and consent of the U.S. Senate. These appointments allow a President to shape labor policy. It has been generally true that each President has maintained at least a 3 to 2 majority on the Board.

A study done by Carter Secretary of Labor, F. Ray Marshall, indicates the significance of Board appointments to labor's goals. Marshall noted four ways in which the NLRB board appointed by Democratic Presidents Kennedy and Johnson aided unions in their attempts to unionize the South. Unfair labor practice cases of workers discriminatorily discharged for protected union activities were speeded up to minimize worker discouragement and turnover. The NLRB tended to define bargaining units such that unions were more likely to win recognition. The Board adopted a more strict standard against employer anti-union statements than did the Eisenhower Board. Finally, the Board was more permissive in its attitude toward union recognition picketing while organizing a plant.[28]

There is no labor party. Organized labor does characteristically support the Democratic candidates for office but does not run its own. This labor–Democratic party relationship has ebbed and flowed over the last decade. It appears to be on the mend at present as Democrats and organized labor are both on the defense in the face of Republican political successes. The record of union voting (e.g., Reagan's 40 percent) makes it apparent that organized labor cannot "deliver" a vote to any party, but rather that union voters are as much issue oriented as party oriented.

AREN'T UNIONS CORRUPT AND AUTOCRATIC?

This issue is one internal to unions and less of a topic concerning their impact on society. But it is a commonly asked question, and so it is taken up here. Corruption and union democracy should be treated as two separate questions and because they are intertwined treated also as a single question. On union corruption, the answer is that the leaders of a very few unions show strong evidence of corruption, but most unions are not corrupt. As a value judgment, most of us agree that union corruption is bad. Democracy within unions is more difficult to deal with. And depending upon how one defines democracy, there is less unanimity on the part of the experts as to the value of union democracy. If union autocracy is defined to be rule by powerful leaders who exert their will over and against that of the rank and file membership, very few are autocratic. If instead we define autocracy as a union leadership largely unchallenged by the membership but which meets mem-

---

28. F. Ray Marshall, *Labor in the South* (Cambridge, Mass.: Wertheim Publications in Industrial Relations, 1967), p. 332.

bership needs, most unions are autocratic. This last sentence could just as easily have been written: If instead we define "democracy" as a union leadership largely unchallenged by the membership but which meets membership needs, most unions are "democratic." We first consider union corruption and then proceed to the topic of union democracy.

A Perspective on Union Corruption

A Gallup Poll in 1979 found that only 55 percent of the U.S. population approves of unions—the weakest endorsement of organized labor in more than 40 years of polling by Gallup.[29] In the polls, the public has ranked the status of the occupation of labor leader near the bottom in comparison with other vocations. The reasons for these rankings are somewhat unclear, but certainly labor's popular image has been hurt by numerous incidents in recent years. These include illegal public sector strikes in general, illegal police and fire fighter strikes (accompanied occasionally by arson) in particular, the gangster-style disappearance of the Teamsters' Jimmy Hoffa, continuing Department of Labor–Teamsters legal wrangling over Teamster pension funds, the FBI sting operation in 1980 involving union pension fraud, the conviction of UMWA President Tony Boyle for ordering the murder of Mine Workers' dissident Jock Yablonsky, his wife, and daughter, and the nearly unanimous 1981 election of Roy Lee Williams to the Teamsters' presidency 1 week after his indictment by a federal grand jury on charges he attempted to bribe a congressman. National television reporting shows "20/20" and "60 Minutes" have detailed corruption in some construction, longshoring, and maritime unions.

There is a tendency to reason from the particular incidents cited above to the general conclusion that unions (all or most) are corrupt. To do so is to indulge in the fallacy of composition. The *fallacy of composition* is the incorrect thinking that what is myopically true of an individual part is also true of the whole. Students of union structure and government generally believe that corruption in labor organizations is no more pervasive than corruption in corporations or in society at large. There are approximately 175 national unions and 68,000 locals in the United States. At its height during the Senate hearings in 1957-1959, investigation into union corruption was limited to a half dozen unions. Most of the abuses were found in the Teamsters union. With few exceptions the same argument can be made about the more recent widely publicized incidents. They are either confined to a few unions or are the acts of individuals not representative of the leadership as a whole or the union membership.

One generalization can be offered. Union autocracy is a necessary but not sufficient condition for union corruption. That is, corrupt unions are undemo-

---

29. "How Unions Try to Clean Up Their Image," *U.S. News and World Report* (October 22, 1979), p. 70.

cratic, but a measure of autocracy in a union does not mean the leaders are corrupt. So saying we turn to consider democracy in unions.

The Legal Framework for Democracy

Union democracy was one of those tenets discussed earlier which is said to underlie our labor law system. Unions, it is understood, give workers a say in the work place and are an interest group required in a democracy. But both of the above require that unions be governed democratically. The Labor-Management Reporting and Disclosure Act (Landrum-Griffin) reiterated that point in 1959. Landrum-Griffin dealt almost exclusively with union democracy and financial propriety.

Labor law and union constitutions establish the legal framework within which democracy does or does not occur. Landrum-Griffin gave union members a "Bill of Rights" safeguarding their right to equal participation in union elections, freedom of speech and assembly, a secret ballot on dues and fees increases, the right to sue the union, and the right to due process in any union disciplinary action. The Act also set the frequency and procedures for conduct of union elections. Union constitutions govern such matters for the membership. Constitutional provisions can provide more stringent safeguards for democracy than Landrum-Griffin but cannot be less protective of democracy. No constitution mandates autocracy, yet it sometimes occurs.

A Perspective on Democracy

Almost a century ago, Sidney and Beatrice Webb observed, "In the Anglo-Saxon world of today we find trade unions are democracies: that is to say, their internal constitutions are all based on the principal of 'government by the people and for the people.'"[30] Today researchers seek to investigate the hypothesis known as Michel's *iron law of oligarchy*. According to this line of thought, a union is an "organization which gives birth to the dominion of the elected over the electors, of the mandataries over the mandators, of the delegates over the delegators. Who says organization says oligarchy."[31] Which is true?

The inquiry is complicated by the fact that there is no measure of what democracy is. The Webbs suggest the union constitution to be a measure (a legal approach). The iron law of oligarchy points toward a behavioral measure. The earlier conclusion that unions are by and large democratic was based on a definition of democracy which required officer responsiveness to rank-and-file needs. The issue becomes more complicated when the variety of governmental forms of locals and nationals is considered. There are few generalizations to be made. We examine one aspect of union democracy, membership participation.

---

30. Sidney and Beatrice Webb, *Industrial Democracy* (London: Longmans and Green, 1897).
31. Robert Michels, *Political Parties* (Glencoe, Ill.: The Free Press, 1949), p. 401.

Membership Participation. With the exception of a few unions, notably the International Typographical Union, unions are not characterized by a two-party system. Participatory democracy flows from rank-and-file activity at the local and national level. At a minimum it requires an active subgroup (referred to as the *middlemass*) which is interested and active in union affairs and represents the interests of the inactive membership at large.

Studies of industrial union democracy, such as Sayles and Strauss' *The Local Union*,[32] almost invariably indicate that there is very low participation in most union activities by the rank and file at the local level. Attendance at union meetings varies in direct proportion to the agenda's relationship to the immediate and recognizable interests of the membership. For example, contract ratification meetings (pay and benefits) are well attended, while meetings on the more remote concerns of rules changes and elections are poorly attended. On balance then, and with rare exception, unions are not democracies in the two-party sense. Unless the leadership alienates a majority of the membership or an active and influential middlemass, the union is generally theirs to run as they see fit. Individual union members have the right to participate, but many choose not to do so.

Union Politics. As markets and competition have broadened, the locus of bargaining and its control have ascended from the local to the national level. Agreements have become more complex. For example, funding and operating pension plans are highly complex activities. The result of this was summarized by Emanuel Stein as early as 1963:

> It is utterly unrealistic to expect that the membership will be able to pass informed judgment upon the mass of economic, actuarial and technological considerations underlying a collective bargaining agreement. Hence, the membership is obliged to rely upon the recommendations of the leaders; . . .[33]

This quote points up the importance of examining national union politics as part of any study of union democracy. National union conventions are probably no less stage managed than are corporate stockholders' meetings or political party conventions.

There are determined oppositions and issue fights in union politics, however. All is not peace and tranquility at union conventions. Edward Sadlowski, for example, mounted a credible but unsuccessful challenge against Lloyd McBride for the presidency of the Steelworkers. The primary issue was the restoration of the right to strike under the Experimental Negotiating Agreement. Within the Teamsters, there is a group called the Teamsters for a Democratic Union (TDU). The TDU is active and successful at the local level.

---

32. Leonard Sayle and George Strauss, *The Local Union*, Rev. ed. (New York: Harcourt, Brace and World, 1967).

33. Emanuel Stein, "The Dilemma of Union Democracy," *The Annals of the American Academy of Political and Social Science* (November, 1963), pp. 48-49.

However, TDU's presidential candidate won few votes during the 1981 election of Roy Lee Williams to the Teamsters presidency.

Democracy or Anarchy?

Some argue that union democracy is not always good. There is a fine line between union democracy and anarchy. The United Mineworkers of America is a case in point. John L. Lewis ran the UMWA with an iron hand: " . . . Autonomy has no relation to higher wages, to shorter hours, to improved conditions, to pensions, to medical aid, to all the things of value to the mine worker and his family."[34] Tony Boyle continued that practice. But the outcomes of autocracy were quite different. Lewis has come to be revered as a strong-willed, but canny and benevolent dictator. Tony Boyle has been used as an example of what the excesses of union power can lead to.

In reaction to Boyle's autocracy, part of the membership formed the Miners for Democracy, wrested power from the Boyle supporters, elected Arnold Miller to the presidency, and gave the rank and file the right to a ratification vote on the UMWA-BCOA national coal agreement. In a three-way race for president in 1976, Miller won in a contested election with only 40 percent of the vote. Under Miller, the industry experienced very high rates of wildcat work stoppages during the life of the 1974-1977 agreement. Wildcats, because they are not sanctioned by the national, are a sign of weak union leadership and control. The wildcats continued against Miller's demands that the miners return to work.

At the same time, political intrigue and turmoil created dissension and turnover in the national union staff. Consequently Miller went into the 1977 UMWA-BCOA negotiations without experience, inadequately prepared, and at the head of a union splintered into numerous political interest groups. William Miernyk, in an analysis of coal bargaining, summed up the situation:

> By the Fall of 1977, the reform movement that had toppled Boyle—and which had introduced such innovations in the UMWA as the bargaining council and the rank-and-file contract referendum—was in almost complete disarray.[35]

Subsequently the union was party to the longest coal strike in history (109 days) involving two contract rejections (once by the bargaining council and once by the rank and file). In 1979 Miller declined to run for the presidency and his vice president, Sam Church, was elected. The wildcats decreased during the 1978 agreement, and the union stabilized at the national staff level. The 1981 coal negotiations ended in a strike which lasted 78 days. Once again the

---

34. John L. Lewis, Address before the 43rd (1960) Consecutive Constitutional Convention of the United Mine Workers of America, *United Mine Workers Journal* (November, 1960).

35. William H. Miernyk, "Coal," in Gerald G. Somers (ed.), *Collective Bargaining: Contemporary American Experience* (Madison, Wisc.: The Industrial Relations Research Association, 1980), p. 45.

rank and file rejected the first agreement after the bargaining council voted 2 to 1 for it.

After reviewing the UMWA experience through 1977, Miernyk asked the question, "Does this mean that the attempt to introduce democracy into the UMWA had failed after more than a half century of autocratic rule?" He concludes, "There is, unfortunately, no objective answer to the question. It is impossible to separate the experiment in union reform from the men who led the union when the reforms were introduced."[36]

In the final analysis union democracy is what the membership makes of it. Most unions are democratic so long as not too strong a definition of democracy is introduced. Lack of democratic participation in the absence of a two-party system is not necessarily damning. By way of comparison, even in the multi-party 1980 U.S. Presidential race only 53.9 percent[37] of those eligible to vote actually did.

CONCLUDING REMARKS

The chapter began with a discussion of the methodology for pursuing commonly asked questions about unions and bargaining impact. As the chapter progressed, the empirical support for the answers given declined. The results from studies on wages and productivity show remarkable consistency. That consensus disappeared when the issue of inflation was raised. Any set of facts is consistent with more than one story as to how they happened. Each of the competing theories of inflation derives some empirical support. A decision on unions must either await further analysis or must be based on what seems to be the most persuasive argument.

In the political arena, general measures have been suggested for the ties between organized labor and the Democrats. Concerning the issue of union corruption, few studies have been done. Those that exist are generally descriptive in nature. No good measures of the extent of wrongdoing exist. It is doubtful that labor organizations are any more corrupt than firms or society in general. Numerous studies of union democracy have been conducted. Unfortunately, the definitions of union democracy are also numerous. The conclusion that unions are democratic is based on a definition of democracy as union responsiveness to rank-and-file interests. That opinion may be the result of a desire to say something more than "some are democratic, some are not" in the absence of a definitive empirical answer.

This part of the book has provided a basic analysis of collective bargaining. The sojourn has proceeded through the topic of comparative industrial relations systems, labor history, labor law, contract negotiations, contract con-

---

36. Ibid.
37. Martin Plessner and Warren Mitofsky, "What If They Held An Election and Nobody Came," *Public Opinion* (February-March, 1981), p. 50.

tents, conflict resolution, and the impact of collective bargaining on the economy and society. The concentration has been on basic concepts and factual background. With that as a base, you are prepared for more advanced analyses of the concepts and issues. It is our hope that your appetite has been whetted enough to pursue the answers to your questions in additional course work or reading in the labor economics area.

CHAPTER SUMMARY

This chapter provided answers to commonly asked questions about unions and bargaining. There is a problem-solving methodology which is generally used to answer these questions. Data problems, estimation problems, and value judgments interfere with accomplishing the ideal.

Unions do raise wages of union workers and decrease the wages of nonunion workers. The union-nonunion differential is in the range of 15-25 percent, although there is substantial variation across unions. Over time, the differential tends to decline in inflationary periods and increase in recessions. Unions also have a significant impact on fringe benefits.

Studies of union effects on productivity indicate that, in general, union workers are more productive but that this productivity edge is offset by higher union wages. Firms newly organized undergo a shock effect. The old management is often replaced with a new one shocked into becoming more productive in the face of a union which challenges management decision making. The quit rate is also reduced. Over time negotiated work rules can become an efficiency burden as technology and the market evolve. When this occurs, changes may be made by a management buy-out of the situation or labor and management may work to solve the problem in the face of what they perceive to be a mutual threat.

There is no definitive answer to whether or not unions affect inflation. The post-Keynesian school of thought believes the economy to be largely noncompetitive. Unions are a source of economic power, and they exert that power to gain raises in excess of productivity. The neoclassical school of thought views the market as a competitive one. Inflation is the result of monetary policy which causes short-run changes in inflationary expectations. Unions and corporations establish prices which would have existed in their absence anyway.

Unions are politically active today, well beyond what Samuel Gompers envisioned when he said, "Reward your friends and punish your enemies." Unions support friendly candidates for office with money and manpower, but they also lobby extensively and attempt to influence the composition of the NLRB. Historically labor support for the Democrats has waxed and waned. After lukewarm support of Democrats in the 1970s, organized labor appears to be strengthening its ties with Democrats in the presence of a Republican administration.

The position taken on union democracy and corruption has the least empirical support. Corruption in unions is believed to be no more widespread than in corporations and society at large. Union democracy is workable, but not as a two-party democracy. Participative democracy appears to be successful in that union officers are responsive either to a concerned middlemass of interested workers or to the majority of the rank and file.

KEY TERMS

methodology
positive analysis
normative analysis
threat effect

shock effect
fallacy of composition
iron law of oligarchy
middlemass

REVIEW QUESTIONS

1. Distinguish between normative analysis and positive analysis. Which of the sentences below is positive and which is normative? Why?
   a. On the average unions raise wages when compared with nonunion wages by about 20 percent.
   b. At the very least union benefits ought to exceed the cost of joining the union.
   c. Because unions distort the allocation of economic resources, it would be better for all concerned if the labor market were deregulated.
   d. Because they provide dignity and democracy in the work place, unions should be supported with protective legislation.

2. Do unions raise wages? Are unions the cause of inflation?

3. How does the quality of union labor relate to the results reported for the impact of unions on wages? How about for unions and efficiency?

4. Someone once quipped, "If you laid all of the economists end to end they couldn't reach a conclusion." Do you agree or disagree with the statement? Why?

5. How would you define union democracy? Is it enough that the union leadership be responsive to the desires of the rank and file? What other measures of union democracy would you suggest?

ADDITIONAL REFERENCES

Freedman, Audrey. *Managing Labor Relations.* New York: The Conference Board, 1979.

Industrial Relations Research Association. *Collective Bargaining and Productivity.* Madison, Wisc.: Industrial Relations Research Association, 1975.

Lewis, H. Gregg. *Unionism and Relative Wages in the United States.* Chicago: University of Chicago Press, 1963.

Mitchell, Daniel J. B. *Unions, Wages and Inflation.* Washington: The Brookings Institution, 1980.

Rees, Albert. *The Economics of Trade Unions.* Chicago, Ill.: The University of Chicago Press, 1962.

Rosow, Jerome M. (ed.) *Productivity: Prospects for Growth.* New York: D. Van Nostrand Company, 1981.

Slichter, Summer, et al. *The Impact of Collective Bargaining on Management.* Washington: The Brookings Institution, 1960.

Strauss, George. "Union Government in the United States: Research Past and Future." *Industrial Relations,* Vol. 16, No. 2 (May, 1977), pp. 215-42.

Wilson, Graham K. *Unions in American National Politics.* New York: St. Martin's Press, 1979.

THE WORLD
OF WORK . . .

COLAs and Wage Parity

Whether or not unions cause inflation, they do negotiate wage escalator clauses. Do these COLAs keep wages even with the rate of inflation? This reading suggests the initial prognosis is that they do not.

. . . A basic question raised by the foregoing discussion is the degree to which escalator clauses afford protection against inflation. The 1948 GM-UAW escalator provided wage increases of 1 cent for each 1.14-index-point rise in the CPI. At then existing levels of wages and the CPI, this formula yielded pay adjustments proportionate to price changes. In 1959, Joseph Garbarino concluded that most of the COLA provisions of contracts then in effect "fully compensate for price changes."

One could not reach this conclusion today. In the 10-year period 1968-77, the average annual escalator increase—for workers in major bargaining units where clauses resulted in pay increases—ranged from 1.6 percent in 1968 and 1969 to 5.8 percent in 1974. In no year did the increase match the CPI rise. The closest correspondence was in 1971, when escalator increases were 91 percent of price changes; the lowest, 26 percent in 1969. A simple average of the annual escalator yields for the period is 57 percent. . . .

Several factors contribute to the average COLA's less-than-full compensation for inflation:

1. *Formulas are insufficient to produce full compensation.* The most common formula—1 cent increase for each 0.3-point CPI rise—is relatively liberal. (Among covered employees are those in the auto, steel, trucking, and railroad industries.) At the April 1978 level of the revised CPI for urban wage earners and clerical workers (191.4), such a formula would produce full compensation with a wage rate of $6.38 or less. However, in each of the 10 largest bargaining units with this formula, average straight-time earnings were greater, averaging $8.44. (Together, the 10 units covered 1,538,000 workers, about half of all workers covered under the 1-cent for 0.3-point formula.)

2. *Limits may be placed on the maximum COLA increase.* At the beginning of 1978, one-fourth of the workers in major bargaining units with escalation were affected by "caps" or ceilings on escalator increases. Average annual caps on wage increases over the contract term ranged from less than 1 percent to 6.1 percent, averaging 2.7 percent. The largest concentration of caps was in the railroad industry, affecting 469,000 workers. Somewhat related are "corridor" provisions of General Electric and Westinghouse contracts precluding adjustments for annual CPI rises between 7 and 9 percent.

3. *Escalator adjustments lag behind price changes.* The significance of a lag, of course, is related to the pace of inflation. In the 1968-77 period, escalator yields were more than 60 percent only in the 4 years with diminished rates of price increase. While the lag effect on wage rates may be important in an individual year, the long-run impact is on aggregate purchasing power. The degree of lag depends largely on frequency of escalator review. As of January 1, 1978, 43 percent of covered workers had annual reviews (including those in trucking, communications, and electrical equipment); 39 percent had quarterly reviews (mainly metalworking); 15 percent had semi-annual; and the balance had monthly, CPI triggered, or other periodicity. Of all workers covered, 51 percent were *not* covered by a review in the first contract year; only 1 percent were not covered in the second and 2 percent in the third. Primarily in Auto Workers contracts, a minor lag is introduced by using a 3-month average CPI rather than a single reference month.

4. *Escalator yields may be diverted.* Often, escalator yields are withheld, either permanently or temporarily, to finance supplementary ben-

efits. About 1 million workers are so affected, most covered under Auto Workers' contracts.

5. *Escalators may not operate until a significant CPI rise occurs.* For example, contracts covering 100,000 Clothing and Textile Workers yield gains only for CPI advances of more than 7.5 percent in the second contract year and 6 percent in the third.

In addition, overall costs of escalator clauses are commonly curbed by not immediately including such payments in base rates, thereby possibly isolating benefit obligations from current COLA impacts. Conversely, periodically incorporating all or part of the COLA float into base rates curbs the downward flexibility of escalators, for wage reductions commonly are limited to the size of the float.

One conclusion is inescapable: COLA provisions vary considerably, as the degree of protection afforded by a particular clause depends on the outcome of collective bargaining. Liberality of escalation is part of a settlement package—including other wage and benefit items—that reflects attitudes, skills, and power of the negotiators.

Anticipated and past price changes usually are considered in negotiating immediate and deferred wage adjustments. Hence, total wage-rate changes over the contract term could be the same with or without escalation. Remembering that escalator reviews are less frequent in the first contract year, it is notable that 1977 major settlements for longer than 30 months, with and without COLA, showed little difference in first-year negotiated adjustments, but second- and third-year gains were substantially larger without escalator clauses.

Other things being equal, bargained changes that anticipate price increases produce greater take-home pay; catch-up increases have the opposite effect, due to the lag involved. To compensate for wages eroded by inflation, negotiators frequently front-load settlements, which provide greater increases in the first contract year. The larger deferred increases in contracts without COLA's are more typical of the anticipation of *future* rises in the cost of living. However, negotiators may be conservative in estimating future price changes; between 1972 and 1977, major settlements of units without escalation coverage showed greater year-to-year variability in average first-year than in deferred increases.

The key issue, of course, is how overall wage gains compare, in timing and amount, between units with and units without COLA's. In major units concluding bargaining in 1977, prior negotiated wage adjustments averaged 5.9 percent annually over the contract term in units with COLA provisions in the expiring and renewed agreements and 8.3 percent in units without COLA in either contract. Adding COLA yields subsequently received, the total gain in the former group averaged 10.1 percent a year under the expiring contract.

One might have expected the unions without COLA coverage to seek to compensate in 1977 bargaining for this shortfall. However, the new average negotiated adjustments—4.9 percent annually in units with COLA's and 7.0 percent in units without—were in almost the same proportion as in the prior bargaining. Whether this result testifies to the wage impact of COLA clauses, is a reflection of conditions peculiar to the period studied, or stems from differing environments in the two sectors—which could in fact determine the incidence of escalation—is still an open question. Findings of existing studies do not appear conclusive.

Source: Abridged from Victor J. Sheifer, "Cost-of-Living Adjustment: Keeping Up With Inflation?," *Monthly Labor Review* (June, 1979), pp. 14-17.

A Collective Bargaining
Simulation Exercise

GAME DESCRIPTION AND OBJECTIVES

This game is designed to give students a first-hand look (via simulation) at the dynamics of the union-management relationship during contract negotiations in which the collective bargaining process is realistically illustrated. The game creates in the classroom the atmosphere of actual negotiation sessions by confronting union and management teams with current real world issues. Learning theory and experience suggest that student interest and learning are enhanced when textbook information and concepts are related to practical, real world situations, and this enhancement is the purpose of the simulation game.

As a player, you will be assigned (or given by choice) a role on either a union or management team. The goal of each team will be to negotiate a favorable settlement on the demands which it believes to be the most important in the situation presented. To effectively achieve its goals, each team must examine both the union and management positions, anticipate the opposing team's important demands, react to them, and devise a strategy to achieve its goals.

The intent of this game is to familiarize you with the process of collective bargaining and the materials, tools, skills, and perspectives of a person participating in contract negotiations. To this end, individual role profiles with the personal perspectives of an actual member of a negotiations team have been provided. This should also assist the group by allowing some specialization in the necessary research, materials collection, and strategy formulation. The game provides students with the opportunity to apply textbook material, to participate in a particular role in group decision making, and to feel the conflicts, trade-offs, and constraints of actual contract negotiations. It is not intended to teach you how to bargain, but rather to allow you to experience the dynamic political and economic forces at work in collective bargaining.

BASIC RULES

1. No consultation with any other team is permitted.

2. Demands must be based on problems presented.

3. A strike deadline will be set at the termination date of the existing contract. No extensions are permissible.

4. Outside research may be necessary, but it should be to supplement, not change, the game.

5.   Initial proposals, while not binding, should be realistic.

6.   The chairperson of each team (the president of Local 905 or the Industrial Relations Director) will coordinate all sessions, work assignments, and negotiations. All members of each team should play an active role in preparing for negotiations and in actual negotiation sessions.

7.   Each team will prepare and present not more than eight nor less than five demands (or contract changes).

THE INDUSTRY

The switchgear and switchboard industry would be classified by economists as monopolistic competition. There are approximately 600 companies engaged in this line of activity at the present time. The most successful firms are those that are quality conscious and have the ability to achieve high levels of product specialization. Among the typical performers in the industry are those firms producing fairly homogeneous products, such as low-voltage (115 volts) power connectors, switches, circuit breakers, and sockets. Since there is only a slight degree of product differentiation, manufacturers have a limited degree of price discretion. In other words, a firm's pricing policy must be in line with other competitors in the industry.

Clients in this industry are very demanding, and are primarily concerned with product quality, reliability, and durability. For instance, a high-quality switch is one which has a low amount of load resistance, thus preventing a heat buildup that leads to equipment failure. In the case of reliability, clients look for maximum overload specs or the ability of a component to function effectively under variations in line voltage. The final consideration is durability, which refers to the mechanical life of, for example, a switch or relay that may be mounted on a rotating cam. Thus, it is a combination of these requisites upon which a company's reputation is built. A company that cannot fulfill these demands tends to be pushed out of the market by competitive forces.

Firms that engage in such specialized production have certain strict demands to which they must conform. They must be innovative. They must have the ability to change product and design specifications quickly. Of utmost importance, these firms must meet deadlines, as clients have their own production schedules. If a supplier delays a client's schedule, the supplier can count on loss of future business. In this portion of the market the chief clients are utilities, large industrial manufacturers, and the federal government.

The number of production workers varies frequently in this industry. One of the higher levels of employment was in the early 1970s, when an increase in construction occurred wherein homes and buildings were adapted to electric heat (51 percent of new homes and buildings installed electric heat). Industry forecasts indicate that with the continuing shortages of petroleum and rapid escalation of petroleum costs, more consumers will change to gas heat, decreasing overall demand for electrical parts and equipment.

At times the labor force has been severely cut back. For instance, as a part of President Reagan's attempt to cut back the federal budget, the budget for the space program was cut significantly. Within the switch industry, many firms thrive on these programs which provide them with guaranteed business. When the space budget was cut, layoffs occurred in many firms.

The majority of the jobs can be classified as semiskilled. Most of the work ranges from simple assembly operations to difficult assemblies that must be performed in a dustless environment. Due to recurrent price increases in rubber and plastic sheets, many firms which maintain their own fabrication departments have been considering subcontracting. It is believed that economies can be achieved through this alternative. Specifically, subcontractors could mold the plastic switch housings and insulators that are needed for each firm.

THE COMPANY

Elmo Incorporated was founded in Somerset County, New Jersey, in 1952. The company originally directed its efforts toward a specific market (common home electrical switches and accessories), and it soon began to prosper. In the late 1950s and early 1960s Elmo Incorporated grew rapidly, and the company began to diversify its operations into other related fields, primarily industrial electrical component needs. By 1965 the company employed over 500 employees and a hierarchical job structure had developed. In 1969 a second plant and research facilities were opened in Scranton, Pennsylvania. About this time, Elmo entered the lucrative field of government contracting. The years 1967-1972 were the golden years for Elmo, as employment expanded to over 2400 employees in the two plants by 1972.

Elmo Incorporated is one of the leading manufacturers of switchgear and switchboard apparatus in the East. The company maintains two major lines of production, broadly defined as specialized and nonspecialized. Elmo's technology can be found at work in radar, satellite communications, missiles, and remote and fine control devices (e.g., traffic lights). In addition, the company's custom switchboard metering panels and power switching equipment have been widely recognized and praised by buyers as quality equipment. In short, quality and innovation have been the key to success for Elmo in this line.

Elmo's nonspecialized line of production consists of common home 110- and 220-volt items; circuit breakers, fuses, light switches, light dimmers, sockets, plugs, and other such conventionally used items. These products have given the company full access to consumer markets through hardware, department stores, and home improvement stores. This wide range of products and a wide geographic market help protect the company against a major loss of sales resulting from a downturn of business conditions for any one product or in any one section of the country.

By 1976 the economy's general downturn severely affected Elmo. Government contracts became scarce, and the firm's profitability margin decreased. The demand for Elmo's industrial goods dropped sharply. At first the company cut its workweek back to 32 hours and then it was forced to go to a 24-hour workweek. With its future outlook dimmed, Elmo finally decided to lay off 30 percent of its workers. Disputes over who was to be laid off arose, and a union organizational drive was started by the International Electrical Equipment Workers (IEEW). The drive was successful, Local 905 of the IEEW was recognized, and the first contract was quickly ratified. Since then, three successive agreements have been negotiated between Elmo and Local 905.

THE UNION

The 1248 workers in Elmo's Somerset plant chose the International Electrical Equipment Workers to represent them when they decided to organize. Employee relations had been good until the mid-1970s. Employees received wages and benefits at least comparable to those of most other companies during this period. Since then, however, Elmo's once progressive employee treatment has become somewhat outdated. Employee benefits now lag behind those of many other companies.

The 1976 business downturn and the resulting 30 percent employee layoff was the catalyst in the Somerset plant's union formation. At this time, a consistent bump and layoff system was not used. Supervisors were allowed to lay off those employees they felt were the least productive. Charges of discrimination came from every section of the plant. People who had been with Elmo since the late 1950s were laid off. A group of laid-off employees contacted the closest office of the IEEW, and an international representative was sent to help organize the drive.

Within 5 weeks, the majority of workers had signed cards requesting IEEW representation. The union was elected as bargaining agent by a 2 to 1 margin, and Local 905 was established. Elmo and the union quickly reached agreement on a basic contract, and the employees approved it with little discussion.

The subsequent agreements, including the current contract which is about to expire, have not involved major changes in language or benefits. Management has consistently argued that adverse economic conditions did not permit the acceptance of many of the union's demands, while the union was hesitant to push any particular issue to a strike for fear of alienating its new members. The employees were not happy with the final terms of the current union contract, but ratified it by a slim majority.

The dissension and factionalism brought out in the last contract negotiations have built up since then. Many employees felt the union should have gained more and were very upset when they learned that the Scranton plant, which unionized under similar circumstances with the International Union of Television and Electronics Workers, had gained higher wages and benefits in their last contract. As a result, a quiet organizational drive within the rank and file to switch unions was started, and many insiders feel that only a successful contract will stave off this movement. The local union officials are up for election 2 months after the present contract negotiations are scheduled to end.

CURRENT LABOR RELATIONS

Recently a rash of grievance complaints have been coming from the plant's young black workers over the alleged discrimination to which they felt they were subjected. The focus of their complaints has been the departmental seniority system the company uses (instead of a plant-wide seniority system). The young black workers feel that they have been pushed to departments with little or no hope for advancement and with higher average hour cuts and layoffs than other units. The affected workers feel that the plant should use a plant-wide seniority system as well as have higher minority representation in the other departments. Workers in other departments feel threatened by the proposed change to plant seniority because they might incur hour cuts or layoffs which they otherwise would avoid. Management is concerned about a possible discrimination suit and the loss of government contracting, and the union is becoming increasingly sensitive to the seniority issue as its black membership increases.

To ensure product completion as scheduled, Elmo has a policy of mandatory overtime to which the employees strongly object. Standard procedure is for the supervisor to assign overtime to employees on a rotating basis by giving them 1 or 2 days' notice. The union, vehemently objecting to this policy, filed a grievance against this practice which ended in arbitration. The arbitrator ruled that, since the contract did not forbid the company from doing so, the management rights clause in the contract allowed management this option. The workers reacted to the arbitrator's ruling by engaging in an effective slowdown while following all work rules to the letter. Because it had no grounds upon which to discipline the workers, the company's only recourse was to avoid overtime whenever possible.

Absenteeism is a serious problem at Elmo's Somerset plant. On several occasions, especially during the warmer months, Monday and Friday absenteeism almost forced the closing of some departments. Management's attempts to deal with this problem have not been successful, and the contract is silent on the issue. Management has indicated that it wants serious discussion of this problem at the bargaining table, with the possibility of strong contract language.

Elmo employees, hearing rumors of the company's upcoming machine modernization program, are quite concerned with the possible impact of future automation upon their jobs. Some members of the union's negotiation planning committee have proposed that the next contract require labor-management consultation prior to the introduction of any automated change. Other committee members have proposed special job and wage provisions for down-graded workers to offset any income losses suffered by such workers.

BASICS OF THE CURRENT CONTRACT

Some of the key elements in the current contract include the following:

Wages and Benefits

The company's average wage is about 5 percent lower than the wages paid by other surrounding electrical equipment firms. The union obviously will want to push wages up to where they are at least equal to the wage level in surrounding firms and to the average wage level at the Elmo Scranton plant. However, the union is aware of the fact that Elmo faces a monopolistically competitive market, and it does not want to incur massive layoffs because of high labor cost increases.

In the past, management has adamantly opposed any cost-of-living adjustment provisions. The union is expected to push strongly for a cost-of-living provision for this contract because of the workers' strong concern about the erosion of their paychecks by the rising price level. The union is expected to stress the existence of this provision in the contracts of other area firms and industries.

The current contract calls for the workers to receive five basic fringe benefits which remained basically unchanged in the last contract. These are:

1. Eight paid holidays: New Year's Day, Memorial Day, July 4th, Labor Day, Thanksgiving Day, Good Friday, Christmas Day, and each employee's birthday

2. From 2 to 4 weeks paid vacation, depending on an employee's length of service with the company

3. A pension plan: 100 percent contributed by the company; vested after 10 years of service; mandatory retirement at age 70

4.   A group health insurance plan: 75 percent contributed by the company

5.   Paid 15-minute morning and afternoon coffee breaks plus a 45-minute unpaid lunch period

The union feels that most of the benefits are outdated and need to be increased. Specific groups within the union are pushing for differing benefits. For example, the younger workers are concerned with increased vacation time and a greater say on when it occurs (management presently assigns vacation periods at the beginning of each year). The older employees are more concerned with increased pension and health benefits. Grades 9 and 10 employees feel that the greater skills required for their job classifications merit a greater wage differential between grades 8 and 9. Black employees are concerned with a more effective grievance procedure and a change in the seniority provision. Of growing symbolic importance to them is having Martin Luther King's birthday as a holiday. Generally, employees are also concerned with gaining some form of dental insurance plan and a guarantee of a half day's pay for work stoppages beyond the worker's control, such as machine failure.

Union officials are sensitive to the possible conflict between the young, the old, the skilled, and the minority workers' wants, and they are anxious to satisfy each group as much as possible since elections for union officials occur shortly after the present contract expires.

Union Security

The existing contract contains an agency shop provision. The union has previously demanded a union shop, but management has adamantly refused. At present there is heavy pressure from the international union to get a union shop provision included in the next contract. The growing dissension and dissatisfaction within the union ranks has prompted some members to discuss the possibility of affiliating with another union. Union officials both in the local and the international feel that a union shop is a "must" to ensure the Somerset employees' continued affiliation with the IEEW.

The current contract does not contain a checkoff provision. As a result, union officials must put a great deal of effort into dues collection. Presently, the shop stewards are assigned the task of collection, and they are doing so mainly during working hours. Management has insisted that dues collection not be done on company time, but it has no adequate means of controlling this practice. Management opposition to a checkoff provision is based mainly on philosophical grounds.

Seniority

Seniority is a delicate issue because it was the underlying issue of the Elmo Somerset plant's original unionization. The contract established seniority on a departmental basis as the means of determining the sequence of promotion and layoffs in the Somerset plant. Recently this has prompted a marked increase in the number of grievances filed. Both the union and management feel that the present provisions are too vague, leaving many questions unanswered.

The issue of "super-seniority," which was heatedly debated during the last negotiations, is expected to be a hot issue again. The union maintains that preferred status in the event of layoffs should be given to all union officers, including stewards, regardless of their length of service. Management feels that there should be no exceptions to the seniority concept because exceptions are difficult to administer.

Management Rights

In past contracts, management has maintained a hard line against including any provision which would interfere with its ability to operate the business efficiently. In other years only a very small amount of assembly work had been subcontracted out. However, in the past year subcontracting has increased. At one point the workers threatened to walk out. To appease the workers, management agreed not to use subcontracting until this issue could be resolved in the upcoming negotiations. Rumor has it that the union wants veto power over all subcontracting work and will demand that the company be required to prove that time, expense, or plant restrictions prevent the company from allowing union employees to do the work. Management is concerned with the possibility of future walkouts and wants to add a more adequate penalty system to the existing no-strike clause.

Contract Administration

Management is concerned with the rise in the number of cases going to arbitration, because the company now pays 75 percent of arbitration costs. Management believes that since the union is relatively unconcerned with the costs involved, it will push a grievance to arbitration, hoping to get a more favorable settlement. Both the union and management feel that the definitions and time limitations at each stage of the grievance procedure are too vague, and as a result both sides are expected to push for improvements in the language of the grievance procedure.

Current Contract Between
Elmo Incorporated
And The
International Electrical Equipment Workers

Article 1: Agreement

Agreement effective October 16, 198-, by and between Elmo Incorporated, for its Somerset, New Jersey plant hereinafter referred to as the "Company" and Local 905 of the International Electrical Equipment Workers, hereinafter referred to as the "Union."

Article 2: Purpose and Intent

It is the purpose of the parties hereto to give recognition to the mutual desire for industrial and economic harmony through the orderly and expeditious adjudication of all matters pertaining to wages, hours of work, pensions, insurance, working conditions, and other conditions of employment.

Article 3: Recognition

Section A: In accordance with the certification of the National Labor Relations Board, dated October 13, 1977, the Company recognizes the Union as the exclusive bargaining representative for all hourly production and maintenance employees at the Company's plant in Somerset, New Jersey, excluding office, professional, supervisory, and guard personnel as defined in the National Labor Relations Act.

Section B: The Union agrees that its members employed by the Company will work for the Company under the provisions set forth in this agreement. The Company and Union agree that all employees employed since October 1, 1977 will have the right voluntarily to acquire, not acquire, maintain, or cease membership in the Union. The Company agrees that all employees will be required as a condition of employment to remit to the Union one of the following: (1) the regular monthly dues of the Union, or (2) a monthly service charge equal to the monthly dues if not a member. The Union, however, will be solely responsible for collecting such dues or service charges.

Article 4: Hours

Section A: The regular workweek shall consist of forty (40) hours, eight (8) hours each day, 7:45 a.m. to 4:30 p.m. inclusive. A forty-five (45) minute lunch period, without pay, will fall in the middle of the regular workday. Each member of the bargaining unit will receive a paid fifteen (15) minute coffee break each morning and each afternoon.

Section B: All work performed in excess of the normal eight-hour day at the request of management will be considered overtime and subject to a 50 percent premium based on the hourly wage rate. All work performed in excess of the 40-hour workweek at the request of management will be considered overtime and subject to a 50 percent premium based on the hourly wage rate.

Section C: All work performed on the following holidays will be subject to a 100 percent premium based on the hourly wage rate: New Year's Day, Memorial Day, Independence Day, Labor Day, Thanksgiving, Good Friday, Christmas Day, and the employee's birthday.

Section D: Each employee shall receive pay for each of the above holidays not worked provided: (1) he/she has worked not less than 30 days, (2) he/she worked his/her last scheduled day prior to the holiday and his/her scheduled day following the holiday, and (3) he/she shall not have been on disciplinary suspension at time of holiday. The rate of pay for such holiday shall be the average straight time hourly wage for eight hours as appropriate for each employee.

Article 5: Wages

Section A: Wages shall be paid each Friday for the work performed the previous week, except when such payday falls on a holiday when checks will be available the day immediately prior.

Section B: The wage classification and conditions in effect in the plant at the signing of this agreement shall continue in effect during the life of this agreement and shall not be subject to arbitration.

Section C: The wage schedule in effect prior to contract settlement shall be immediately increased thirty-five (35) cents per hour for every worker. Another thirty-five (35) cents per hour shall be added on the first and second anniversaries of this contract.

Section D: The Company shall have the right to establish wage rates for new work or a change in process of manufacture. The Union may within 5 days object to such wage rates through the established grievance procedure.

Article 6: Vacations

Section A: Employees shall be eligible for vacations with pay based upon the following schedule:

Continuous Service with Company	Vacation with Pay
1 year but less than 7 years	2 weeks
7 years but less than 15 years	3 weeks
15 years or more	4 weeks

Section B: Vacation pay for hourly workers shall be computed upon his or her average weekly pay for the month prior to said vacation. Payments will be made on the payday immediately prior to the beginning of the vacation period.

Article 7: Other Benefits

Section A: Group Health Insurance. The Company agrees to provide, paying 75 percent of the total expense, health insurance for its employees on the active payroll and for the dependents of such employed in accordance with the plan and schedule of benefits submitted to the union as of the effective date of this agreement.

Section B: Pension. The company agrees to provide, paying 100 percent of the total expense, a pension plan for its employees on the active payroll and for the dependents of such employees in accordance with the plan and schedule of benefits submitted to the Union as of the effective date of this agreement.

Article 8: Grievances

Section A: (1) Grievances shall first be taken up by the department grievance person (shop steward) in an informal manner with the department first line supervisor.

(2) If not settled, the complaint shall be put in writing and shall then constitute a formal grievance. The grievance shall then be submitted to the plant superintendent within one (1) week. If not settled with the superintendent, the grievance shall be submitted within two (2) weeks to a grievance committee composed of the General Manager, the Union President, and one additional person designated by each of them. This committee shall have authority to settle the grievance or refer the matter to arbitration.

Article 9: Arbitration

Section A: Disputes and grievances unsettled through the grievance procedure may be submitted to arbitration as provided. The cost of such arbitration shall be borne 75 percent by the Company and 25 percent by the Union.

Section B: The Company and Union shall within one (1) week from the receipt of an arbitration request contact the Director of the Federal Mediation and Conciliation Service for a list of six arbitrators from which the Company and Union shall choose one. If the Company and Union fail to choose an arbitrator within 1 week, the Director of the Federal Mediation and Conciliation Service shall be notified to appoint an arbitrator. Any decision by the arbitrator shall be final and binding.

Article 10: Seniority

Section A: Probationary employees shall consist of those employees employed by the Company for a period less than sixty (60) days.

Section B: Layoffs shall be made in the order of seniority beginning with the least continuous service with the Company. Recalls shall be made in the order of seniority beginning with the greatest continuous service with the Company.

Section C: An employee whose services are terminated either voluntarily or involuntarily shall lose all seniority rights.

Section D: Seniority shall consist of departmental seniority for actions within the department, between departments, or on a Company-wide basis.

Article 11: Strikes and Layoffs

Section A: The Union agrees that there shall be no strikes, slowdowns, or work stoppages for any reason whatsoever, during the life of this agreement. The Company agrees that there shall be no lockout for any reason whatsoever. The Union agrees in lieu thereof and without assuming any obligation for damages, that it will attempt to induce any employee engaged in a strike, slowdown, or work stoppage to return to work.

Section B: The Union will not impose any restrictions or limitations on the production of an individual employee or group of employees, but try to eliminate any restrictions or limitations on production being exercised by any Union member.

Section C: It is agreed that any strike, slowdown, or work stoppage on the part of the Union or a lockout on the part of the Company shall be a violation of this agreement, and that under no circumstances will there be discussion of disputes or grievances while such work interruption is in effect.

Article 12: General Provisions

Section A: The general and overall management of the business and property; the direction of the work force including the right to hire, promote, demote, transfer, lay off, suspend, or discharge for proper cause; and the right to establish rules pertaining to the operation of the plant is vested in the Company provided that this is not done in a manner which is contrary to any provision in this contract.

Section B: The Company shall provide the Union with bulletin boards upon which notices of meetings and other matters of proper Union business shall be posted. Bulletins shall not contain anything that is of a controversial or objectionable nature.

Section C: In case of sickness, leave of absence shall be granted without pay or penalty for a period of six (6) months upon presentation of a Doctor's certificate of illness.

The failure of an employee to return to work at the end of a leave of absence shall be considered to be a voluntary termination of employment unless a request for a further leave of absence is received and approved.

Article 13: Duration of Agreement

This agreement shall continue in full force and effect for three (3) years at which time either party may announce its intention to terminate this agreement within a period of not less than 60 days prior to expiration of this agreement.

GLOSSARY

absolute approach to defining poverty This is an approach defining poverty as a state wherein some predetermined minimum amount of essential goods and services cannot be afforded.

across the board Wage increases are often paid as so many cents or a percentage increase for everyone.

added worker hypothesis This theory suggests that as unemployment increases and normal family breadwinners lose their jobs, additional family members enter the labor market in an attempt to maintain family income.

ad hoc arbitration This is a form of grievance arbitration in which an arbitrator is selected for each separate arbitration case.

advisory arbitration As a strike substitute in the public sector, advisory arbitration is a form of fact-finding. After a hearing the advisory arbitrator recommends a nonbinding settlement.

affirmative action compliance programs These are programs, including statistical work force analysis and goals and timetables to increase employment of underutilized groups, which are required of government contractors and subcontractors under Executive Order 11246.

agency shop This form of union security requires that nonunion employees pay a service fee to the union for sharing in the benefits of unionization as a condition of employment.

aggregate demand This is the relationship between various levels of employment in the economy and the expected revenues from consumption, investment, and government expenditures.

aggregate supply This is the relationship between various employment levels in the economy and the aggregate revenues required to justify that employment.

agreement clause The contract may start with this clause which states who the parties to the agreement are.

allocative efficiency This refers to the allocation of resources which produces the greatest total amount of desired production for the society.

appropriate bargaining unit This is the group of employees that a labor organization represents for purposes of collective bargaining and who are covered by the agreement.

arbitrator The arbitrator is a neutral who renders a final and binding decision settling a labor-management dispute.

association An association is a labor organization composed of professional and public employees.

attitudinal structuring In the process of negotiation, labor and management each develop a set of expectations about the future behavior of the other party.

authorization card This is literally a card, often about 3×5 inches, on which is printed a statement giving the named labor organization the right to represent the employee for purposes of recognition, negotiation, and grievance handling. Signed by the employee, it becomes evidence in support of a demand for bargaining when submitted to the employer and a showing of interest when submitted to the NLRB.

average labor cost This is the labor cost per worker incurred in production (with homogeneous labor, equivalent to the wage rate).

average product of labor This is the average output of each worker.

***Bakke v the California Board of Regents* (1978)** In this U.S. Supreme Court case, the Court ruled that strict preferential quotas in college admissions, in the absence of past discriminatory patterns, are unconstitutional.

bilateral monopoly This model of collective bargaining portrays the union as a single seller and the firm as a single buyer of labor services. It is indeterminate in the sense that no single wage-employment settlement results from the model.

bill of rights   This Landrum-Griffin article gives union members the right to free speech, assembly, to sue, and to vote on dues and officers in union affairs.

business unionism   This philosophy of unionism emphasizes the achievement of better wages and working conditions on the job as opposed to improvement through societal revision.

capital   Capital is the durable, but reproducible, input in the production process.

captive coal mines   These coal mines are owned by steel companies.

caucus   These are negotiation team meetings called to recess negotiations for a time. They are used to restore team composure, and formulate counterproposals, and are a part of strategy and timing.

CETA prime sponsors   These are state and local officials or political jurisdictions granted planning and operational authority for CETA administration.

chapter   The local level of an association is called a chapter.

checkoff   Under this form of union security, union members sign an authorization form which allows the employer to deduct union dues and fees from the worker's pay and remit them to the union.

chilling effect   The presence of an impasse procedure may inhibit negotiations (chill them) if the weaker party feels that they may have more to gain through use of the procedure than by compromise bargaining.

choice of procedures   This strike alternative, also called the bag-of-tricks approach, gives the authority charged with dealing with disputes an array of weapons to deal with impasses.

civilian labor force   This is the number of civilian, noninstitutionalized people 16 years of age and older who are either (1) working full- or part-time for pay or profit or (2) unemployed and actively seeking work.

Civil Rights Act (1964)   This federal act prohibits a wide range of types of employment discrimination based upon race, color, religion, sex, or national origin.

closed shop   This is the strongest form of union security. Illegal under the Taft-Hartley Act, a closed shop requires union membership as a condition of hire.

codetermination   This is a form of worker participation in which employees or their representatives serve on corporate supervisory boards or boards of directors.

collective bargaining   This refers to the process wherein labor and management negotiate over wages, hours, and conditions of employment.

collective bargaining structure   This refers to the level at which a contract is negotiated. It varies from decentralized single-plant agreements between a local union and plant management to concentrated industry-wide master contracts between an international and an employer association.

collective bargaining unit   This is the group of employees who are covered by an agreement.

collective negotiations   As a form of collective bargaining, unions and management are legal equals at the bargaining table. Negotiations culminate with a legally binding, written agreement.

company union   This union is organized, financed, and run by an employer for its employees.

Comprehensive Employment and Training Act (1973)   This is that act coordinating all governmental employment and training programs in a decentralized and decategorized framework.

compulsory arbitration   As a strike alternative, negotiators who reach impasse must submit their dispute to a neutral who makes a final and binding decision.

conflict theory   Conflict theory is a theory of society which suggests that power conflicts among social strata are the natural state of society.

consumption   Consumption is the process of using goods and services to achieve the satisfaction of human wants.

continuous longitudinal manpower survey   These are governmental surveys to track the employment and earnings experience of a sample of CETA participants over 3 years.

contract bar   The representative status of a

labor organization cannot be challenged for the duration of a negotiated agreement or 3 years, whichever is shorter.

contract ratification   Some unions require, according to their constitution or as a matter of practice, that negotiated agreements be submitted to the rank and file for approval.

conventional interest arbitration   The neutral in this type of final and binding settlement has the authority to include in the decision whatever is judged to be appropriate to the situation.

coordinated bargaining   When two or more unions bargain separately with a common employer, they may avoid being played one against the other through close cooperation. They obtain simultaneous contract expiration dates and put forth the same demands, but sign separate agreements.

cost-efficiency criterion   This is an evaluation standard which suggests that effective poverty policies should achieve their goals at minimum cost.

cost-of-living clause   This contract clause links wage increases to changes in the Consumer Price Index.

cost-push theory of inflation   This is a theory which asserts that inflation occurs when firms pass on excessive wage or profit costs in the form of higher prices, independent of demand forces.

court injunction   A court injunction is an order by a judge that prohibits a party from threatening or continuing an act against another (e.g., union picketing or strike activity). Violation of an injunction garners contempt of court penalties including fine and/or imprisonment. The full injunctive process is: temporary restraining order (TRO), temporary injunction, permanent injunction.

craft union   This form of union is organized on the basis of the trade of the individual, for example, carpenters.

credentialism   This is the hypothesis that educational credentials (certificates, diplomas, degrees) are used by employers as proxies for desirable employee characteristics.

criminal conspiracy   This is a combination of persons judged to be illegal by virtue of merely existing (per se violation) or because the ends sought and/or means used are illegal.

cyclical unemployment   This type of unemployment arises from cyclical downturns in economic activity where insufficient aggregate demand exists.

decertification election   When the status of a union as the representative of a group of employees is challenged, the NLRB conducts a secret ballot to determine by majority vote the will of the employees. If a majority votes against the union, it is decertified and can no longer bargain for the employees.

demand-pull theory of inflation   This theory asserts that inflation is caused by excessive aggregate demand when the productive capacity of the economy cannot meet the demand for goods and services at existing prices.

detailed regulation   Under this system of government regulation for labor and management, government provides specific rules for the behavior of the parties, but not for the substance of their relationship.

discipline or discharge grievance   This type of controversy is one of two types of disputes taken to arbitration. The arbitrator looks to see if management has met the standards of just cause for the discharge or discipline action.

discouraged worker hypothesis   This theory suggests that as unemployment increases, displaced workers will become discouraged in looking for work and will drop out of the labor force.

distributive bargaining   Items which the parties view as "I win, you lose" issues involve this type of bargaining. The parties conceal their true positions and reveal them through the give and take of negotiation.

dual labor market theory   This theory proposes that there are two distinct types of labor markets (primary and secondary) with little mobility of workers between the two.

economic democracy   In a system providing for economic democracy, government redistributes wealth (ownership of industry) among the workers.

economic exploitation   This term describes the situation when labor's wage is less than its marginal productivity.

economic inputs   This refers to all resources used by an economic system to produce goods and services which satisfy human wants.

economics   Economics is the study of the problem of scarcity and the various ways in which scarce goods and resources are allocated in a society to satisfy human wants.

80-day cooling-off period   The Taft-Hartley emergency disputes procedure provides for an 80-day injunction against any strike which threatens national health or safety.

elasticity of demand for labor   This is the percentage responsiveness of employment to a percentage change in the wage rate.

election bar   After the results of a recognition election have been certified, there is a 1-year moratorium before another can be held.

The Employment Act (1946)   This act commits the federal government to use all practicable means to promote maximum employment while fostering free enterprise and maximum purchasing power.

employment discrimination   This refers to the use of different hiring, firing, and promotion standards not related to worker productivity.

Equal Opportunity Act of 1964   This act was the first major federal antipoverty initiative which included employment and training programs such as the Job Corps and the Neighborhood Youth Corps.

Equal Pay Act (1963)   This is a federal act which prohibits sex discrimination in wages where equivalent jobs, skill, effort, responsibility, and working conditions are involved.

escalator clause   This contract clause links wage increases to changes in the Consumer Price Index.

exchange theory   This social theory argues that people compare costs and rewards in determining courses of action.

exclusive bargaining agent   This is the labor organization which represents all of the employees in the appropriate bargaining unit and which signs the collective bargaining agreement with management.

exclusive bargaining representative   This is the organization recognized by the NLRB for purposes of representing the employees in the appropriate bargaining unit in the negotiation and administration of the collective bargaining agreement.

exclusive representation   Employees can be represented for purposes of collective bargaining by only one labor organization.

ex parte injunction   This is an injunction granted after a judge hears only one side of the issue without notifying the other side of the charge and without allowing a hearing on the charge.

Experimental Negotiating Agreement (ENA)   Between 1973 and 1980 in the steel industry negotiators agreed that if they failed to reach agreement on contract terms by a specified date, they would submit the unresolved issues to binding arbitration.

extent of unionization   This is a measure of how much of a labor force is organized. One commonly used measure is the percentage of the nonagricultural labor force which is unionized.

external labor market   The external labor market is characterized by interjob movement between different firms.

fact-finding   As a strike alternative, hearings are held by a neutral person or panel to determine the progress toward settlement and the current positions of the parties. A settlement may or may not be recommended.

factors of production   These are all resources used by an economic system to produce goods and services which satisfy human wants.

fallacy of composition   As an error in logic, the fallacy of composition is committed when one reasons incorrectly that what is true of an individual part is true of the whole. For example, it is true that if one person stands up at a football game, that individual can see better. It is not true that if everyone stands up, they all have a better view.

federation At the top of American labor union structure is the federation which is composed of national unions.

final offer arbitration In this form of interest arbitration the neutral party is constrained to choose either all of the union's last negotiating position or the last position taken by management. The term is used more generally to include item selection arbitration as well.

fiscal policy This refers to the governmental taxation and expenditures policies utilized in an attempt to stabilize the economy.

fiscal substitution effect This is the use by state and local governments of Public Service Employment funds to pay employees whom they already employ or whom they would have employed without the Public Service Employment funds.

flexitime Flexitime refers to schemes which provide for some employee choice in work scheduling, subject to weekly or monthly total hours worked and daily core hours requirements.

free rider A free rider is an employee who enjoys the benefits of union representation but who does not join the union.

freedom of contract This is the idea that labor and management can make a fair deal on conditions of employment only if they have relatively equal power.

frictional unemployment This is unemployment resulting from short-term fluctuations in labor supply and demand, and from imperfect information and labor immobility.

fringe benefits Fringe benefits are indirect pay. They include such additions to money wages as overtime, health plans, vacations, and pensions.

front end loading Multiyear agreements which put the largest wage increases in the first years are called front end loaded contracts.

full employment (Beveridge definition) This refers to an excess of job vacancies as compared to unemployed persons.

full employment (current consensus definition) This definition refers to the maximum employment level consistent with a nonaccelerating rate of inflation.

functionalism Functionalism is an anthropological and sociological theory which argues that individual and social behavior can be viewed as an attempt to develop and preserve interrelated subsystems, such as the family, in order to maintain a stable society.

the general level of money wages This is the economy-wide average of all firms' wage decisions, unadjusted for changes in the price level.

the general level of real wages This is the economy-wide average of all firms' wage decisions, adjusted for changes in the price level.

general training This training is equally useful in all firms and industries.

GNP gap The GNP gap is the difference between the actual amount of goods and services produced annually (actual GNP) and the amount that would have been produced if all the economy's resources were fully employed (potential GNP).

grievance and arbitration procedure During the life of an agreement, labor and management try to settle their differences through the stepwise procedure. If they have not agreed by the last step, a neutral arbitrator issues a final and binding decision.

grievance arbitration During the life of an agreement the parties submit questions concerning the interpretation and application of the contract to a neutral party for a final and binding decision.

hiring hall This is an agreement between union and employer wherein the employer agrees to contact the union for new hire referrals.

hot cargo clause This is an agreement between union and management in which they agree not to handle the goods of another employer with whom the union has a dispute.

human capital theory This theoretical framework is concerned with activities intended to enhance the resources in people, where such enhancement affects future earnings streams.

human resource development policy This refers to all endeavors designed to improve the quality of the labor supply and more efficiently use its potential.

Humphrey-Hawkins Act (1978) This is the act establishing goals, although neither funding nor specific programs, for the reduction of unemployment to 4 percent and inflation to 3 percent by 1983.

illegal bargaining subjects It is unlawful to demand to bargain about these topics, e.g., the closed shop.

implicit contracts theory This is a theory proposed by Arthur Okun which contends that our economy is now characterized by a long-run cost-oriented price and equity-oriented wage system intended to preserve buyer-seller and employer-employee relationships over time.

incentive pay This is a method of wages payment based upon the level of worker output.

income effect The income effect is the desire for more leisure, and hence fewer work hours, when wage increases provide workers with more income.

income-maintenance criterion This evaluation standard suggests that effective poverty policies should guarantee a minimally adequate income for all.

incomes policies This variety of policies involves direct governmental influence on wages, prices, and real incomes.

independent An independent is a national union which is not affiliated with the AFL-CIO.

indeterminate model Economic models which have no single solution are indeterminate. See *bilateral monopoly.*

industrial conflict When labor and management disagree, the result is conflict. Overt conflict means a work stoppage. Conflict might also be expressed in high absenteeism, low morale, high turnover, or in other ways short of a work stoppage.

industrial democracy Labor participates with management in making decisions regard-

ing the short- and long-term operation of a firm.

industrial relations system Labor, management, and government interact subject to economic and technological constraints to form a web of rules which determine wages and employment.

industrial union Industrial unions are labor organizations composed of unskilled, semi-skilled, and skilled workers organized by industry.

input markets These are markets where households sell economic inputs which they control to firms.

integrative bargaining Items which labor and management believe can be settled to their mutual gain involve this type of negotiating. The parties take a more open, problem-solving approach on the issues.

interest arbitration As an alternative to the strike, the unresolved issues in a contract negotiation are submitted to a neutral panel or person for a decision.

internal labor market This is a labor market characterized by interjob movement within a single firm.

intervenor When a government intrudes into the substance of the labor-management relationship rather than letting the parties decide for themselves, it acts as an intervenor.

intra-organizational bargaining Before either team can go to the table and be effective at negotiating, they must resolve their own internal differences. There is intrateam negotiation between interest groups within both the labor and management teams.

iron law of oligarchy This is a rule used to characterize union politics. The power which is supposed to reside with the rank and file is usurped by a few elected officials.

item selection arbitration As a form of final offer interest arbitration the neutral party is confined to select issue by issue either management's last position on that issue or the union's last position on that issue.

the job competition model This is a theory of labor market operation which argues that (1) the number of job slots are technologically determined; (2) wages are determined by social custom or institutional forces; (3) employers use various screening devices to hire from the existing labor supply, or queue; and (4) worker skill is not closely related to the number of jobs filled.

job evaluation system This system categorizes all labor grades within the firm and defines the relative worth of each grade through a formal wage schedule.

Job Service Job Service is the current name for the federally funded state-operated services to match the unemployed with available jobs.

job sharing This refers to the situation where a given job is divided between two people.

just cause Management bears the burden of proof that their decision to discharge or discipline an employee was for just cause. There is a set of standards they must meet to have their decision upheld by an arbitrator.

labor Labor is the factor of production that represents the human element in the production process.

labor economics This is the study of the various principles and institutions which govern the operation of labor markets.

labor force participation rate This refers to the percentage of persons in a given population who are classified as in the labor force.

labor market discrimination Differential labor market treatment based upon something other than worker productivity is called labor market discrimination.

labor productivity This is the output produced by 1 labor hour of work.

land Land is the factor of production that represents resources that are fixed or nonrenewable.

language interpretation grievance This type of dispute is one of two major categories of grievances taken to arbitration. The arbitrator has a set of standards with which to interpret and apply the language of a bargaining agreement.

law of diminishing returns This is the hypothesis that as more and more of a variable input (labor) is combined with a fixed input (capital) in the production process, beyond some point the added units of the variable input will yield diminishing additional returns (output).

layoff Workers who are part of a reduction in the work force are laid off.

local agreement This type of contract is between a local union or association and the employer for a single plant or production site.

local supplement This is an agreement between labor and management at a local production site which covers local working conditions in addition to what is covered by the master contract.

local union The local union is the lowest level of trade union structure. The local conducts the day-to-day union-management relationship under a contract.

lockout As the employer equivalent to the strike, the employer does not allow employees to work. The place of work is closed, and employees are literally locked out.

maintenance of membership This form of union security requires workers to make a decision about joining the union after 30 days of employment. If they join the union, they must maintain that membership as a condition of employment. If they elect not to join the union, they continue to work as nonunion employees.

management rights Management holds that some decisions regarding the operation of the firm are theirs to be made without bargaining with or consulting the union. This contract provision reserves certain decisions to management discretion.

mandatory bargaining subjects These items must be bargained if a demand to do so is made at the table. Either side can insist to impasse on a mandatory topic.

Manpower Development and Training Act (1962) This is the first comprehensive federal human resource program providing institutional and on-the-job training, experimental projects, and support services for the unemployed and disadvantaged.

marginal labor cost This cost is the additional

labor cost to the firm of hiring one more worker, or group of workers.

marginal product of labor The additional output forthcoming to the firm from hiring the last increment of labor is called the marginal product of labor.

marginal productivity theory This is a theory which explains the distribution of income. Each factor of production is paid according to its contribution, or its marginal productivity.

marginal revenue product This refers to the additional revenue forthcoming to the firm from selling the output of the last increment of labor hired.

market The market is an interface between buyers and sellers where the exchange of commodities takes place.

market theory John Rogers Commons theorizes that labor movements evolve as a result of a divergence of interest between labor and management caused by price competition which sets producer against producer in the market.

master contract This agreement is made between the union and management to cover an entire firm or industry.

med-arb This is an acronym for mediation arbitration which is an impasse resolution technique. The neutral acts as a mediator, but if the parties still cannot reach agreement, the neutral party makes a final and binding decision.

meet and confer As a form of public sector labor-management relations law, meet and confer laws allow employers to meet with employee representatives to discuss working conditions. If an agreement results, it is set down in a memorandum of understanding. The employer, however, is not required to meet and confer, nor is the employer required to abide by the memorandum.

memorandum of understanding If labor and management agree on working conditions as a result of negotiations under a meet and confer law, the agreement is set down as a memorandum of understanding which is not binding on the parties.

methodology This is a system for problem solving. A methodology is an approach for answering questions. It progresses through the stages of statement of the problem, selection of an applicable theory and hypothesis, collection of data, estimation of empirical results, proof or disproof of the hypothesis, and formulation of policy.

middlemass This is an active group of union members who challenge the union leadership to be responsive to their needs. They usually have a base of support in the larger rank and file.

modified union shop Under this form of union security, those employees who choose not to join the union when the firm is first organized can keep their jobs, but all newly hired workers must join the union at the end of 30 days of employment and maintain that membership as a condition of employment.

monetary policy (monetarism) This refers to the Federal Reserve Board control of the growth of the money supply in an attempt to stabilize the economy.

monetary rule This is the rigid control of money supply growth in accordance with the long-run growth in real aggregate output.

monopsony labor market A monopsony labor market contains only one buyer, or employer, of labor.

moonlighting The holding of more than one job is called moonlighting.

multiemployer agreement This contract is negotiated between more than one employer and one union.

narcotic effect In some labor-management relationships, the parties come to rely on the impasse resolution technique as a substitute for negotiating to reach a settlement.

national emergency dispute This is a strike which is found to endanger national health or safety.

national longitudinal surveys These are a series of federally supported studies which trace a broad array of labor market experiences of various age cohort panels over time.

national union (international union)   This form of union structure is composed of local unions. The national coordinates the efforts of the locals.

natural rate of unemployment   This refers to the long-run rate of unemployment below which, according to accelerationist economists, the economy cannot be pushed by fiscal and monetary policy without accelerating inflation.

need-based poverty programs   These are programs which determine benefits on the basis of recipient need (minimum wages, AFDC, SSI, food stamps, Medicaid, housing assistance).

negative income tax   This is a tax system allowing families automatically to qualify for cash allowances if their income falls below an established level. This system is composed of a guaranteed basic allowance and a marginal tax rate on earned income.

normative analysis   This term is used to describe the type of analysis wherein the analyst's values are allowed to enter into the process. Normative analysis is concerned with "what ought to be" and is embodied in policy.

occupational discrimination   This is the segregation of certain groups into certain kinds of jobs which does not reflect productivity differences among the groups.

Occupational Safety and Health Act of 1970   This act is a federal statute providing federal authority for establishing health and safety standards for the work place, and work site compliance monitoring.

open shop   As a contract clause this provides the least union security. Union membership is not a condition of hire or employment.

orbits of coercive comparison   The term was coined by Arthur Ross to describe the competition between national union leaders to get the best national union settlement.

P and M unit   Appropriate bargaining units composed of production and maintenance workers are called P and M units.

package bargaining   As negotiations progress, unresolved issues tend to become grouped together around a common denominator. Economic items are usually so grouped because they all have a common base: money.

participative management   As a style of labor-management relationship, workers and supervisors work together to set and obtain production goals.

past practice   The parties to an agreement develop a way of life under the agreement. The day-to-day behavior of labor and management is the past practice of the parties. Arbitrators use it to help interpret and apply ambiguous language in a language arbitration.

pattern setting   This bargaining structure exists in industries where the union picks one firm and reaches agreement on a contract. The other firms then agree to essentially the same contract in subsequent bargaining.

permanent arbitrator   This person is retained for the duration of the agreement (or until dismissed) to decide all issues submitted by the parties for arbitration.

the Phillips Curve   The Phillips Curve is an empirically derived, inverse graphical relationship between changes in money wages and changes in unemployment rates.

pluralistic industrialism   As a model of the evolution of industrial relations systems in developing economies, it involves a sharing of power between labor, management, and the government which leads to a web of rules governing the employment relationship.

the political business cycle   This refers to the political manipulation of stabilization policies to achieve favorable economic conditions just prior to Congressional or Presidential elections.

positive analysis   This type of analysis is supposed to be value free. It concentrates on the application of theory to factual data and is concerned with "what is."

postindustrial society   At this stage in the evolution of an economy, the society's labor force is primarily involved in the service sector including extensive government employment.

posting and bidding   This contract clause requires that job openings be filled internal to the firm if possible. The vacancy is posted on a bulletin board, and current employees bid on it. The vacancy is filled on the basis of seniority and ability.

present value of future earnings   This is the amount derived by discounting the future earnings stream by an appropriate discount rate such as the market rate of interest.

primary labor markets   Stable jobs with high wages, good working conditions, ample training opportunities, and good promotion possibilities are found in primary labor markets.

principle of national sovereignty   The national unions in the AFL-CIO control matters internal to their own union.

private rate of return to human capital investment   This is the rate of interest at which the present value of individual earnings attributable to the investment is equal to the private cost of the investment.

product markets   Product markets are markets where firms sell goods and services to consuming households.

production   This is the process of making goods and services to satisfy human wants.

public service employment   This refers to direct job creation by the federal government, primarily through the Comprehensive Employment and Training Act (CETA).

quality circle   In this form of management, a small group of employees works with its supervisor to define, analyze, and solve production problems concerning productivity and product quality.

quality of work life   This term refers to a number of labor-management strategies for restructuring jobs to improve the nature and environment of work.

quid pro quo   This is a trade-off or exchange which links one item with another.

raiding   One union challenges the representation status of another union which already has NLRB recognition for a group of employees.

rate range   One method of time payment of wages sets a range of wage rates for each job class. Movement from the bottom to the top of the range is made on the basis of seniority and merit.

real wage insurance   This term refers to a proposal whereby tax refunds would be paid to workers who adhere to a wage guideline if the annual inflation rate exceeds that guideline.

recall provision   When business picks up after a slump, workers who were laid off are rehired (recalled) most senior person first.

recognition clause   The first article of an agreement states that management recognizes the union as the exclusive bargaining agent for a defined appropriate bargaining unit.

relative approach to defining poverty   This is an approach defining poverty as a state wherein income is significantly below the average income.

reservation wage   This is the wage rate below which a worker will choose not to work.

right-to-work law   These are state laws enacted under Section 14(b) of the Taft Hartley Act. They outlaw any form of union security beyond dues checkoff.

rights arbitration   During the life of an agreement the parties submit questions concerning the interpretation and application of the contract to a neutral third party for a final and binding decision.

rule making   As a form of regulation of labor and management, government sets the boundaries for union-management relationships but lets the parties determine the specifics.

savings clause   This contract provision reserves all rights not expressly given up in the agreement to management.

scabbing   People who work for less than the union rate or who work while the union is on strike are scabbing.

scope of agreement   The specifics of the labor-management relationship which are legal to bargain about and are legal to put in an agreement determine the scope of the agreement.

scope of negotiations   This refers to the range

of topics over which labor and management can legally bargain.

secondary boycott   Union *X* has a labor dispute with its primary employer *A*. Employer *A* does business with secondary employer *B*. The union pickets or strikes secondary employer *B* with whom it has no dispute to force employer *B* to refuse to do business with employer *A*. The action against secondary employer *B* is a secondary boycott. Hot cargo clauses are a form of secondary boycott.

secondary labor markets   Unstable jobs with low pay, few skill requirements, and little chance for training and promotion are found in secondary labor markets.

seniority   The length of employment since the date of hire is used as a basis for determining layoff, recall, promotion, and other benefits under the agreement.

severance pay   A worker whose employment has been terminated receives this pay for length of service with the firm.

shock effect   When a business is first unionized, management is forced to become more efficient. Often a new management replaces the old one, and the new management methods are more formal and efficient.

showing of interest   The NLRB requires a labor organization to prove that it represents a minimum of 30 percent of the employees in a proposed bargaining unit before it will go further with the representation procedure.

sidebar   Confronted by lack of progress at the table, the chief negotiators of the two teams may meet quietly to discuss the negotiations. Often they reach an understanding on a possible settlement to be negotiated by the full teams at the table.

single rate   As a method of time payment there is a single pay level for each job classification.

sitdown strike   Rather than strike by walking out of the place of employment and risk the use of strikebreakers, striking employees occupy the work place but do not work.

social discrimination   This is differential treatment based on something other than individual merit.

social rate of return to human capital investment   This refers to the rate of return from education and training calculated from society's total costs and expected benefits.

specific training   This is training that is useful only to the firm that provides the training.

spillover effects   The terms of union bargaining agreements sometimes affect (spill over to) nonunion workers.

standard of equitable comparison   Arthur Ross used this term to refer to the process by which local union wage demands are formed. The individual rank-and-file members know what other employees doing similar work are getting and they demand that as the standard plus "more."

statistical discrimination   This term refers to an employer's reliance on perceptions of the average characteristics of a group, rather than the individual's characteristics, where employee information is insufficient.

structural unemployment   This is unemployment characterized by a long-term, persistent mismatch between labor supply and demand due to the changing composition of demand, technological change, and geographic shifts in economic activity.

substitution effect   This refers to the substitution of work hours for leisure hours as the wage rate increases, due to the increased "price" of leisure in terms of the wage given up.

supply-side economics   This term refers to the theories associated with economist Arthur Laffer and Reagan administration policy makers, which identify governmental taxation, expenditures, and regulation policies as major sources of inflation and unemployment.

taste for discrimination   This is a willingness to "pay" something to be associated with some persons instead of others; taken from Becker's economic theory of discrimination.

tax-based incomes policies   This system of special tax penalties and/or rebates provides incentives to business and labor for compliance with wage and price guidelines.

tenet   A tenet is a belief, a value, or principle held by a school of thought.

threat effect   Unions which negotiate improved wages, benefits, and working conditions jeopardize the nonunion status of competitive firms. In order to stay nonunion, the management matches union gains. Measured union-nonunion wage differentials then understate the true effect of unions on wages.

total product of labor   This is total output where labor is the variable input.

transfer payments   These are government expenditures for which no goods or services are received by the government in return. These may take the form of money transfers, or nonmonetary in-kind transfers such as food stamps.

trusteeship   A national can suspend the local union's political and administrative powers and assume control over its finances and internal affairs when it places a local in trusteeship.

underemployment   This is the situation where employed individuals are less productive then their skills and abilities would dictate.

unemployment   Unemployment is the difference between the amount of labor supplied at existing wages and the amount of labor hired at those wages.

unemployment (BLS definition)   By this definition we mean the estimated total of all individuals who did not have a job during the survey week, and who were either actively seeking work or waiting to be called back to a job from which they were laid off.

unfair labor practice   This term refers to those employer and union activities prohibited by law.

union   The term union is used specifically to refer to labor organizations which are not associations. It is used more generally to refer to both unions and associations.

union avoidance   This is a modern management technique for maintaining a union-free work place by meeting employee desires for pay, consistency, and communication before they resort to a union to gain them.

union security clause   This clause in a contract requires union membership, payment of dues or a service fee, or otherwise encourages workers to join the union as a condition of employment.

union shop   After 30 days of employment, a worker must elect to join the union and maintain membership to the extent of paying union dues and fees as a condition of continued employment. Failure to join will result in discharge.

union steward   Most of the day-to-day policing of a labor-management contract is done by this individual who represents the immediate work-area interests of workers and the union.

unit labor costs   The unit labor costs are the average labor costs to the firm associated with a single unit of production.

***United Steelworkers v Weber et al.* (1979)**   This is a U.S. Supreme Court case where the court ruled that a preferential training program which was private, voluntary, temporary, and designed to eliminate racial imbalances against blacks was not in violation of the Civil Rights Act.

vesting   This term applies to pensions. After a period of employment with an employer, the earned pension benefits must be paid to the employee upon retirement even though the employee no longer works for the employer. The proportion of the pension vested generally increases with the tenure of the employee at the time of termination.

vocational education   This is education directly related to preparation for specific jobs.

voluntary arbitration   Parties who reach an impasse on contract terms may decide of their own free will to submit the dispute to an arbitrator for a final and binding decision.

voluntary bargaining subject   If both labor and management agree, these topics are bargainable. Neither side can insist to impasse on a voluntary topic.

voucher plan   This is a method of financing education proposed by Milton Friedman and others, under which a voucher equal to the average cost of public education would be provided for each child to be used at any educational institution.

wage discrimination   This is defined as the payment of different wages to different individuals based upon some standard other than productivity.

wage price spiral   This process, by which increases in money, wages and prices feed upon each other, results in intensified inflation.

wage reopener   As part of an existing collective bargaining contract, the parties may agree to open the contract for negotiation of wages only.

the wage structure   This term refers to the economy-wide array of wages for all occupations and individuals.

wage subsidies   Wage subsidies are the governmental payment of partial wages, or the provision of tax credits, to private employers who expand their employment.

weaker party argument   If one party to a negotiation is at a disadvantage to the other, they may choose to go to impasse rather than negotiate on the belief that they can get a better settlement from the strike alternative. Negotiations are chilled. This is a common argument against such strike alternatives as compulsory arbitration. The habit of continuously relying on strike alternatives is called the narcotic effect.

whipsawing   This can be done by the union against two or more employers, or by an employer against two or more unions. Very simply, one side plays two parties against each other to get a better deal than that party can get from each individually.

white-collar union   Unions composed of professional, office, and technical employees are called white-collar unions. There is no very clear-cut distinction between these unions and their blue-collar (manual labor) counterparts in industrial and craft unions.

work experience–based poverty programs   These are programs which determine benefits on the basis of prior work experience (OASDHI, Medicare, Workers' Compensation, Unemployment Compensation).

work-incentive criterion   This is an evaluation standard which suggests that effective poverty policies should preserve incentives to work.

work sharing   Work sharing refers to the efforts to spread the available work among more workers by shortening the workday or workweek.

worker participation   This general term refers to direct involvement by the employees in areas which might otherwise be considered management rights. These include decisions regarding personnel policy, investment, and plant operation.

yellow dog contract   This is an agreement between an employer and employee signed as a condition of hire and employment. The worker agrees not to join or support a union upon penalty of automatic employment termination.

INDEX